THE LETTERS OF ELLEN TUCKER EMERSON
Volume Two

VOLUME TWO

The Letters
of
ELLEN TUCKER
EMERSON

Edited by Edith E. W. Gregg
Foreword by Gay Wilson Allen

THE KENT STATE UNIVERSITY PRESS

Frontispiece: Ellen Tucker Emerson in London, 1872.

Copyright © 1982 by the Ralph Waldo Emerson Memorial Association
All rights reserved
Library of Congress Catalog Card Number 82-10069
ISBN 0-87338-274-9 (2-volume set)
ISBN 0-87338-276-5 (Volume II)
Manufactured in the United States of America

Library of Congress Cataloging in Publication Data

Emerson, Ellen Tucker.
   The letters of Ellen Tucker Emerson.

   Includes index.
   1. Emerson, Ellen Tucker. 2. Emerson, Ralph Waldo, 1803-1882—Correspondence. 3. Emerson family. 4. Forbes family. 5. Concord (Mass.)—Social life and customs. 6. Daughters—United States—Correspondence. I. Gregg, Edith Emerson Webster. II. Title.
PS1631.A4   1982   814'.3 [B]   82-10069
ISBN 0-87338-274-9

Contents - Volume Two

LIST OF ILLUSTRATIONS	vii
CHRONOLOGY	ix

October 1872 — May 1873   3
RWE and ETE on trip to Europe and Egypt, October 1872-May 1873. Voyage on the Wyoming; *Edward meets them. Chester, London, and Canterbury. Paris. Journey to Rome and stay there. Egypt and voyage up the Nile. Alexandria and Naples. Social life in Rome and Florence. Return to Paris and London; visits in England.*

May 1873 — December 1874   88
Return to Boston and welcome by the town of Concord. Long visit at Naushon. Edward Forbes born. Forbes children visit Concord. 1874. Concord and Milton. Naushon. Trip to Providence and New York. Edward Waldo Emerson's marriage.

January 1875 — November 1876   158
Visit in Boston. Trip with RWE to Philadelphia. Centennial Celebration of April 19, 1775, in Concord. Lecture trip with RWE to New Hampton, New Hampshire and the White Mountains. 1876. Visit to the Cabots in Brookline. Trip to New York, Philadelphia, and Centennial Exhibition with RWE. Oration at University of Virginia; trip to Charlottesville. Visit to Washington, D.C. Charles Emerson born. Emma Lazarus visits.

January 1877 — December 1878   236
Concord activities. Stay at Naushon. Aunt Lizzy visits. Sickness in Concord. Annie sent to Milton. 1878. John Emerson born. Visit to the Wards in New York. Aunt Lizzy dies. Work on RWE's lectures with James Elliot Cabot. Trip to Niagara with RWE; Saratoga Convention. Dean Stanley's visit.

January 1879 — December 1880   331
Waldo Forbes born. John Emerson dies. July 4th Celebration in Concord. Grove meeting at Lake Winnepesaukee. Trip to Concord, New Hampshire with RWE. 1880. Visitors. Circuit meeting in Concord. Ellen Emerson born, and Charles dies.

January 1881 — December 1882   406
Sickness in Milton. Forbes family visits California. Work on Emerson-Carlyle correspondence. Cooking school in Concord. Visits to Manchester, Naushon, Canton, and Providence. Search for a minis-

Contents

ter. 1882. Spring in Concord. RWE sick. Death of RWE. Alexander Forbes born. Mr. Bulkeley ordained minister. Conference at Saratoga. Florence Emerson born.

January 1883 — November 1885   487
Quiet winter. Mr. Cabot works on RWE's writings. William James lectures. Picnics and social life. Fires at Walden. 1884. Matthew Arnold visits. Trip to Plymouth, Milton visit. 1885. Social life and parties in Concord. Circuit meeting and visiting ministers. Family visit to Plymouth.

February 1886 — December 1889   561
Raymond Emerson born. Temperance conference. Talks, picnics, and meetings in Concord. Visits to Milton and Naushon. 1888. Forbes family travels in Europe. John Forbes dies. Visit in Milton. 1889. Quiet year at home. Short visits to Naushon and Lenox.

January 1890 — December 1892   614
1890–91. Short visits. Lidian Emerson losing strength. 1892. Quiet year. Ellen and household take care of LE, who has her 90th birthday in September. LE dies in November.

    EPILOGUE   660
    APPENDIX   663
    INDEX   679

LIST OF ILLUSTRATIONS

Frontispiece: Ellen Tucker Emerson, 1872	ii
Page of a letter, June 29, 1876	211
ETE and her donkey Graciosa	219
RWE, Edward, and Charles Emerson	239
The Emerson house, late 1870s	267
Bust of RWE	346
Lidian Emerson in 1879	354
RWE's study, the Emerson house	361
Family group, Thanksgiving, 1879	369
Annie Keyes Emerson and Ellen Emerson	402
ETE at age 40	412
Edith Emerson Forbes and her children	490
ETE in 1888	586

Chronology

1872	RWE and ETE travel in Europe and Egypt
1873	Ulysses S. Grant reelected president
	RWE and ETE return to Concord, are welcomed by the town; Edward W. Forbes born
1874	Edward Emerson marries Annie Keyes
1875	Centennial Exposition in Philadelphia; RWE publishes *Parnassus*
	RWE speaks at New Hampton, New Hampshire and visits the White Mountains
1876	RWE publishes *Letters and Social Aims*
	RWE gives oration at the University of Virginia, and visits Washington, D.C. and Philadelphia; Charles Emerson born
1877	Rutherford B. Hayes becomes president
1878	James Elliot Cabot works with RWE on collecting and editing lectures; RWE and ETE go to Niagara Falls; John Emerson born
1879	Waldo Forbes born; RWE travels to Concord, New Hampshire; John Emerson dies
1880	Ellen Emerson born, and Charles Emerson dies
1881	James A. Garfield becomes president; Chester A. Arthur becomes president on Garfield's assassination
1882	Ralph Waldo Emerson dies; Franklin B. Sanborn publishes *Henry D. Thoreau*
	Alexander Forbes born; Florence Emerson born
1885	Grover Cleveland becomes president
1886	John M. Forbes, Jr. dies; Raymond Emerson born
1887	James Elliot Cabot publishes *A Memoir of Ralph Waldo Emerson*
1888	A. Bronson Alcott dies; Louisa May Alcott dies

Chronology

1889 Benjamin Harrison becomes president; Edward Waldo Emerson publishes *Emerson in Concord*
1892 Lidian Jackson Emerson dies
1909 Ellen Tucker Emerson dies

THE LETTERS OF ELLEN TUCKER EMERSON
Volume Two

October 1872 - May 1873

RWE and ETE on trip to Europe and Egypt, October 1872-May 1873. Voyage on the Wyoming; *Edward meets them. Chester, London, and Canterbury. Paris. Journey to Rome and stay there. Egypt and voyage up the Nile. Alexandria and Naples. Social life in Rome and Florence. Return to Paris and London; visits in England.*

Str. Wyoming, 11.40 a.m.
Octr. 23rd 1872

Dear Mother,

We received with rapture your, Annie's and Edward's letters this morning; also the hat and book; and beloved Will came soon after to help finish my packing. Then Father and carriage; and Haven rode down with us. Tom too to see us off. Now we are passing Staten Island and it is a calm warm gray day, very pleasant indeed. Two missionaries on board, Rev. T. Thomas and Rev. H. Parker bound for India, singing hymns "We're out on the ocean sailing" and "My native country thee." Several very young children. The Helvetia is right behind us sailing for London. Will brought me any quantity of grapes and flowers. I sit in Edith's chair. Father just approached and said "I shall want for the first time in my life the fur collar Mr. Forbes gave me." I told him it was down in his berth. He laughed amazed and amused, and said he thought he had at last been able to think of something we had forgotten. I wish we had thought to bring a chair for him, but probably I shan't be much on deck, and he will have mine. He hates to have me sit and write, so I will send my will all unfinished and Edith must make what she can of it. But she isn't likely to use it I suppose. Father and I are now made happy in an extremity by the use of the invisible Mrs. Richardson made me, and Father exclaims "Pins too?" and holds out his hand. "I'll thank you for a purse of doubloons if you please." The missionary's wife picks up her little girl and says "If we only had dear brother now we should be happy!" "*Why* didn't you bring him," asks Baby. "Oh! Poor little brother must stay and go to school." She now says to her friend "I was 20 when I went out eleven years ago." Will told

1872

me not to spend much time writing, and Father wants me to look round, so no more. Goodbye! We are as happy as clams.

> E. T. E. who never thinks to say she is really a most affectionate daughter.

October 1872

Addressed to Mother and Edith, particularly, also to all my friends. Oh Annie! Monday I expect to see that boy. I keep dreaming of it.

Wednesday. Quite calm and mild all the afternoon. While we waited for dinner I saw Father reading Edward's letter and quite scarlet with laughing. We stayed on deck till supper-time 7.30; so did most people. Saw Fire Island light and thought of Mme. Ossoli; met a steamer which showed us a Bengal light and we returned the compliment. Right after supper I went to bed. I made the acquaintance of Mrs. Rodgers.

Thursday. Windy, rainy, very cold. Seasickness prevailed; Father didn't suffer. At half-past 12 the chart was exhibited. We had sailed 245 miles. Father visited me in the afternoon and said "About dinner-time the cries of nature resounded in every direction." I asked him if he could eat. He said "We ate with gladness of heart and thankfulness that we were not as our brethren." There were four young ladies and a few gentlemen at the table. In the state-room next me were a very sick missionary and wife, Mr. and Mrs. Brown, and a fearfully lively child Lily. My chum a German woman scorned the name of seasickness, and finally relieved the sufferers of their four-year-old and took her up for a walk on deck, as it had stopped raining. Father came and read me Edward's letter, and we laughed for an hour over it.

Friday. Heavenly weather, warm and blue and still. We crawled on deck for a sunning. Father arranged my chair. A handsome gray-haired lady, Mrs. Wood of Utica, approached and we made acquaintance, and held sweet communion on the subject of feeing servants. Father reappeared; she went. He stood by me a long time wrapping here and tucking there as well as the poor man could, then withdrew. Miss Harriet Buchanan (I didn't learn her name for a day or two later) next passed, taking a walk. She has a beautiful face, handsome enough and remarkably sweet and sensible. She said she could move my chair so my head would be in the shade, and did, stopped and talked a while, and then went on. At noon we had sailed 265 miles more and had got to Cape Sable I believe. Then I believe I went to dinner. Opposite us sits a

— 1872 —

German business-man who has great experience in crossing the sea. He said they were hoisting the sail and we presently did hear the singing. We said yes but said no more. He was quenched, and for five days never spoke again. An untidily stuffed head of reddish hair adorned Father's next neighbour, a woman. Her name was Mrs. Needham. After this day she came no more to the table, and she never spoke. Beyond her was Mr. Fleischmann, an Austrian officer, who in consequence became Father's left-hand man. He speaks English well, and once in four or five meals he and Father succeed in discovering a subject that may last five minutes. On my right sits a rather handsome youth, Mr. Christie, young and quiet. Between him and me is a great gulf fixed that amuses me very much. His eye has never turned in my direction; never has he uttered a word except with his face towards his right hand neighbour. Whatever is before him he passes to the right; what is passed to him from the right he helps himself to and passes back again. Not being aggressive myself, I keep an equal silence, though I look out for chances to pass things to him. Next to my German vis-à-vis sit Miss Pultz and Miss Blackmar when not too sick to appear, and I imagine neither of those two ever in their lives spoke to anyone; certainly they don't to each other though they are chums. They are not of the upper ten. Behold then the great desert of silence in which we sit, and I whisper to Father all dinner-time, to relieve it a little. For beyond Miss P. & Miss B. sits a Quaker preacher & her silent husband, who never open their lips unless I shout to them. This afternoon I told Father to find a place for my chair in the most populous part of the quarter-deck. I now make acquaintance with Mrs Buchanan, Mr Wood, a white-haired gentleman, husband of my friend of the morning. They were going abroad with two daughters. I seized the excellent opportunity to hear who was who. Eight missionaries for India, a Methodist party from Pennsylvania, a very humble, very innocent people—one wonders how they will go at it. Then Dr Warren, a Presbyterian missionary, with a long white beard. After twenty years in India he came home twenty years ago, and now lately married again to a giantess, whose size is his daily joke, he sets forth once more. Then Dr James, the editor of the Congregationalist who is taking Mr Christie abroad to visit Egypt, Sinai, the Holy Land, Greece, take Paul's voyage & then pay special attention to Germany. Mr & Mrs Alexander are cultivated people from Mass. Mr A. has been settled over a Presbyterian church in Wisconsin, and now goes under the auspices of the Congregationalist Board of Foreign Missions to establish Protestantism in Italy. Rev. Mr

— 1872 —

Buchanan, brother of our former president, with his wife & two delightful daughters. Father's chum is a Mr Laughey, an Irishman from Belfast, a democrat, a violent sympathizer with the South, having relations in Charleston. He devotes himself to the young ladies. Mr Moore, with white canvass shoes, and Mr Fleischmann are the other two beaux, and always wherever the girls are. Mrs Needham, Father's original neighbor at table is a young Mormon woman from Utah, going home to England for a visit. Did you ever hear so many religions? Oh I forgot that some of the Methodist party are Baptists.

Saturday. Again a lovely day. I was on deck a good deal; so were the whole company. I made acquaintance with Mr. James. He told me a good deal about ships and this ship. At noon we had sailed 270 miles. This afternoon I heard someone sing Happy Land behind me. Then a few minutes afterward a tune I never heard. I rolled over in my chair and asked who sang. It was Mrs. Brown. And what was that last tune? That was one of the native tunes, she said, and came to me with her Hindoo hymn-book. "They call hymns Budgeons," she said, "and I was singing a few to Miss Blackmar to show her." Then she related that Hindoos like their own tunes much better than ours, so the missionaries wrote Christian Budgeons to native tunes. I set her to singing to me, and had a delightful concert, but I liked best the one I heard first with its perpetual refrain of Koi Kani nahin, which she says means "There is no other way." At dinner-time I found my acquaintance with Mr James valuable. I have put two stars where he & Dr Warren sit at the table for they are the lights of that end, and now Mr James imported Father & me into the conversation a little bit, and it was cheering.

Sunday Oct. 27th. It rained, so no one went on deck but it was pretty still. We were told there would be a service at half-past ten. And there was. Whole company, plenty from the steerage too. Mr Buchanan and his daughters led the choir. They sang some of the anthems but read the Te Deum. I sat afterwards with Mrs Rodgers, the Quaker & had a little talk, then Miss Bessy Wood asked about May Alcott whom she is very fond of, and I had a long talk with her & Miss Houghton till dinner-time approached. We had a magnificent dinner in honour of the day, and the chart announced 280 miles. After dinner the English passenger whom I haven't mentioned, Mr. Stevenson, was rallying the Mormon on her faith, and Mrs. Brown, Mrs. Cherington and Miss Blackmar were a delighted audience. But when I asked for some Budgeons, Miss Blackmar got the book and Mrs. Brown sang half a dozen. Then Mr. Brown came up stairs, and she told him she had promised me he should sing them to me. Then ensued a dialogue in Hindostanee between them, but at last he took the book and sang. There is a peculiarity about all the native tunes of stopping abruptly. I spoke of it, and Mr. Brown said "Yes, when I first heard them I used to suppose they stopped there because they had forgotten the rest," a speech which pleased me, for I had thought the same thing. Then Dr. Warren came up and listened with interest, and presently Father passed, and I ordered him to attend, and he was not sorry to hear. Now I had more talk with Mrs. Rodgers the Quaker. I find she is a missionary too, going out quite independently because "It is impressed on her mind that in the South of France there is a great opening for the Gospel, since the war." It is a perfect astonishment to Father and me such an enterprise, for I have the greatest doubt whether she can speak anything but English. After tea came the second service, not Episcopal, and I found it delightful. First we sang Coronation; then Dr. Warren read a chapter from the Epistles that seemed to be just the thing; then Mr. Brown made the prayer; then "Nearer my God to Thee" was sung; and then Dr. Warren preached a sermon which I liked. Poetry always is a wonderful "discloser of the thoughts of the heart," and I now discovered that a service is. The Dr. Warren, Mr. Brown, and Dr. Buchanan we had hitherto seen had opened and showed us as in a long acquaintance what manner of men they were. Never till just these circumstances made it manifest had I imagined what a revealing power there was in acts of worship. The differences of theology also appeared and I got the first chance I ever had of well comparing ours with others, and I felt sure that we are nearer the truth in our whole swing than they are, though they may touch it nearer in some one point. Then Dr. Warren's manner, which I said was facetious because it was slow and exact in his table-talk, was still just as slow and exact but just right, very serious, and I couldn't help noticing and comparing the two styles; yet don't know now how he makes one so funny, the other so earnest—there seems to be so little difference. What I immensely enjoyed in the sermon was that he took it for granted that all his hearers were Christians. It didn't begin at the beginning to instruct them, but talked as if we all knew our relation to the Lord, while almost all Unitarian preaching is an address to the unconverted: "Sin is sinful, be good and you will be happy," and I am always planning to say to ministers, do go a step farther.

 Monday. This morning we had a rough sea; indeed we began to

— 1872 —

roll in the night. Great dismay prevailed, except with Father and the young ladies and beaux who came to the table and walked on deck while everyone else pined in their berths, and we were mercilessly rolled all day and all that night. At noon we were told for our consolation that we had gone 284 miles. Father brought me pears, and I gave him some grapes from Will's basket which caused him to make many laudatory speeches. Poor Mrs. Brown and Mrs. Barnet, my chum, had some too. Mrs. Barnet was one of the undaunted who stayed on deck all day.

Tuesday.   Still rough below but fine above, so Father put my chair on deck, and there came Mr. James to talk with me. I told him we were going to Egypt and he said he was, and we had a good deal of conversation on the subject. We saw the officers take the observation, and soon after were told we had made only 268 miles. I came to dinner and began to feel quite conscience-stricken about our opposite neighbour, and after dinner asked Father why he never spoke to him. He said he supposed he didn't speak English, but I knew that he did. In the afternoon, being again in my chair on deck, just over the galley, I had another visit from Mr. James, who brought his guidebook and showed me maps. I forgot to say that Father said one evening before that he had got acquainted with him and "talked quite cosily with him, never suspecting he was the editor of a paper." He recorded a vow to look out for him in future. While Mr. James and I talked learnedly about Carnak, Luxor, &c. and looked at the map, a squall came. It rained quite hard but I couldn't bear to go below and stuck it out in my new English waterproof, Mr. James gallantly standing by sheltering the maps under his coat and intending to proceed when the weather permitted. I was sitting with my chair against a boat, and the boat now began to drip too hard on me, so Mr. James compassionately moved me out, but alas! At the next lurch of the vessel I tipped over, chair and all. Great was his consternation. The deck was so wet I couldn't think of standing on it, so as soon as my chair was straight again I mounted it and Mr. James went to call Father to bring my rubbers. When they came I subsided to the berth. Mr. Alexander today told me he desired to get some good out of Father's being on board, not only for himself, but also for the other passengers, for most of whom it was the single opportunity of a lifetime to hear him. I said he never did anything extempore but no doubt he would like to read. Wednesday, Oct. 30th.   I told Father that this was Waldo's birthday and astonished him by telling him how old he would be. This was a pleasant day. I was early on deck (about 9 a.m.).

— 1872 —

The motion was pretty violent. Dr Warren was promenading his giantess about, rather against her will, for she was afraid of falling & dragging him to common ruin. She says she is far from agile. As they struggled past me Dr Warren casting a funny glance at me solemnly pronounced a text from the Psalm concerning voyages. "They reel to & fro, and stagger like a drunken man. And are at their wits' end." It was perfectly enchanting. I shouted with joy, and seized an early opportunity of repeating the text to Father who fully relished it. The inimitable Bible! Father & I have quoted many texts on this voyage; among others "Their soul desired the first-ripe fruit." After her walk Mrs Warren came to rest by me and we had a very pleasant talk. The gentlemen were playing shuffle-board, and Mr Alexander for the second time came to ask me to join. Dr W. wanted his wife in the game also, and we did play. I liked it exceedingly. At noon we had sailed 290 miles and went down to dinner quite happy. Let me record with joy that we broke ice in all directions at dinner. I talked with Mr Fleischmann. Mr Christie not only passed me things but spoke & smiled. When I spoke to Mr James about the probable length of the passage, the quenched vis-a-vis showed immediate signs of life, and I eagerly encouraging, broke forth into speech and gave us volumes of information. He said we shouldn't land before Monday. Mrs Rodgers called across the table to us. Miss Blackmer appeared & smiled & even spoke. We began to feel lively & happy even in the region of absolute silence. I heard Dr Warren order goose. Soon after I heard the waiter saying "I'm afraid it's tough, sir," and Dr Warren cheerfully replying "Oh! it's all right, just what we expect in a goose." It turned out however quite uneatable, and one of his neighbors presently said "You don't seem to be making a dinner, Doctor." "Well," he said "he that eateth not, to the Lord he eateth not, and giveth God thanks," and he said it with the extreme of comic gravity. Father was delighted and exclaimed "Such a man of the world as that must be a great card for a missionary." What did happen in the afternoon? I don't seem to remember. I had a walk on deck with Father and found it very interesting to climb the impromptu hills and be precipitated to the bottom. We talked long with the Captain, who said steamers were far safer from waves, lightning, or fire, than sailing vessels, and promised to be in Queenstown in 70 hours. In the evening Father, under Mr. Alexander's auspices, gave a reading from his black "Anthology," which was as successful as could be expected. I really fear the Alexanders are the only people *quite* up to poetry, though the

— 1872 —

Woods and Buchanans are pretty near it and Mr. Langtree may be. He certainly took careful notes all the evening. Some pieces, as Kilmeny, pleased all.

Thursday, October 31st. A detestable, cold, rainy day. Down in saloon all day. It was also rough. I sent Father for pears—he keeps the basket—and when I questioned him as to their general condition he showed ignorance. I scolded him. "But it is no easy work," said the poor man, "All the trunks are volatile, and the basket itself recalcitrant, and if I lay the pears on the floor they run eagerly into all corners." Also he said of dressing, "I run a muck at the window, and then am thrown to the other side of the room when I didn't expect to go there!" This evening Mr. Alexander made Father read his own poems. Not so successful as yesterday, but pretty well. Mr. Alexander liked it, and thoroughly enjoyed "The Titmouse."

Friday Nov 1st Dear Will's birthday.

Saturday. Off Queenstown. Happy P.M. Beautiful coast. They call for letters. I've written none but this. My love to all. Each possession proved useful. Each passenger holds up his & her hands in envy & admiration of my outfit. Edith's book is copied by thankful ladies, & pleased husbands proclaim the wisdom of the maxims. Also promise their wives that next voyage they shall have a chair, ten blankets, & hot water bottles like Miss Emerson. The friendless say "We couldn't have got along without her delicacies", that means judicious doses of Cousin Elizabeth's soft molasses gingerbread & Will's grapes & John's pears. I can't enumerate all now with Father calling for letter but nothing seems to lie idle. Farewell.

E. T. E.

Chester Nov 4th 1872
I am sitting this evening in a happy domestic parlour with my papa & brother, the tea-table standing round as Edith says I love to have it at home, and Father & Edward are writing too.

Dear Mother,

I hated to be cut off in writing to you of our voyage and never shall finish that story for now we must talk about Edward. We all three

— 1872 —

laugh ourselves weak every few minutes, he is so funny and so delightful. He & Father have just been out calling on the Bishop of Chester, and we are to breakfast with him tomorrow. Our rooms here are handsome & pleasant, the hotel is a beauty, and in the courtyard is a sort of prim pretty garden. I have had a hot bath, and Father's is ordered for half-past nine. My presents to Edward have been delivered, and I hear the crack of the pea-nut, the crunch of the gingercake, the rattle of the letter. Let me not omit to say that Uncle George's opera-glass was in our hand all day Saturday & Sunday and we were so thankful to have it, that I want him told. I shall never doubt again that they essentially assist the sight. The whole coast is remarkably beautiful & interesting and when it was in sight we were happy. But oh! how cross we were tossing across the rough Irish sea in a bitter cold wind all Sunday forenoon. The wind & sea made us really hate the Episcopalian service, as Father said "What a heathen service it was." I heartily seconded the sentiment, but I knew we were chilled to the bone & wretched. The evening Congregational service I enjoyed immensely.
[Unsigned]

Chester Nov 6th 1872

Dear Mother,

This morning we went straight to the Bishop's to breakfast. I was surprised that the tall good-looking well-dressed young gentleman who opened the door was a footman. I am surprised that the respectable middle-aged man who to my unpractised eye looks one of the solid men of Boston should here at the hotel set the table for us, and wait upon it. It seems really frightful. We were shown into an empty parlour, and presently Mrs Jacobson came in, very healthy & lovely-looking with gray curls. She sat down & talked with us a minute, told us the river was the Dee and was giving us some information about the walls when the gong rang, and she instantly rose & invited us in to breakfast. One of the canons of the Cathedral lived in Devonshire, and had just come to Chester yesterday and brought them a present of Devonshire cream so here it was on the table, looking like the butter & sugar all whipped for cake. They gave it to us with raspberry jam and it was exceeding good. After breakfast we saw the library, and the Bishop told us what to go and see in Chester. Then we came away and Edward and I went to Chester Rows and did the shopping Edith advised me to do in Liverpool. I found stockings cost exactly the same that they do in Boston. I looked at some & concluded it wouldn't pay to buy. Next we went to a tailor's & Edward bought a pair of trowsers. Next to an apothecary's where I found sponges a little cheaper than at Mr Friend's. When we came home the sun was shining, it was warm and pleasant. Father said the man had just told him they hadn't had such a warm day for three weeks and he was impatient to go out. So he & Edward went to the Cathedral and I ascended the sofa, for my ankle, which was quiet on the steamer, began to cry the moment I stepped on shore, and I am just as lame as ever, must buy a crutch tomorrow.

At breakfast at Bishop Jacobson's Father wore Edith's velvet cap. Edward saw him in a cowl for the first time, and praised him very much. He thinks it becoming and romantic. At noon Father carried it but forgot to put it on. When they went at night to the Archaeological Society he wore it again, and Edward said the occasion was stupid, though on some humanitarian grounds interesting; but to him it was an hour of great joy and glory, for not only was Father made much of and lauded to the skies, but in the end of the proceedings when a vote was offered thanking the Bishop for presiding, a voice from the multitude said, "Will Mr. Emerson be so kind as to second this motion that we may have the opportunity of just hearing his voice?" and Father rose and spoke beautifully. Edward said not only was it delightful to hear Father speaking in public once more when he hadn't heard him for more than a year, but he spoke so well, and showed such power that he (Edward) threw off the anxiety which my letters had taught him to feel. This was very good news. We were to have started for London at nine this morning but they decided to wait till one, and Father has sat quite still in a chair all the forenoon, declaring that idlesse is the business of age, and he loves above all things "to do noshing," and that he never before had discovered this privilege of seventy years, and that he finds there is a convenience in having a name—it serves one as well as a good coat—also bragging that Edward was a lion over at the Cathedral yesterday, knew dates and facts like an antiquary, and saying he was glad to have him go to dinners with him, "so that when I am fumbling for the name of my wife he can remember it for me."

London Friday Nov. 8th. We came from Chester on Wed. noon, rode in the cars all the afternoon, and Edward & I talked over his list of presents & what we would buy together in our days in London, while Father was most of the time looking out of the window at the cultivated desert—all fields and no houses, or almost none, wondering where the inhabitants lived. That is the only thing that I was wholly unprepared for, the solitary land. On reaching London we came straight to rooms where Aunt Lizzy had spent Sunday, and on the table was a lovely note from her to welcome us. We arrived at half-past seven, dined at 8.15— my hair stood on end—and then Edward went off to St. Thomas's [Hospital]. The next morning with breathless fear, and assumed courage, I sent for a cab & started alone, ordered my bonnet at Elkins's, my clothes at Christian Adams's, according to book, but my mind misgives me they are very dear places, for the things cost all & more than I should expect to pay at home. Also I did one or two errands, painfully calculated my fare, counted my money, and got back alive, without offending my driver. Edward soon came, directed Father how to get to Mr Carlyle, and wrote out a plan for our shopping campaign, while I had Bath buns for lunch. We did much shopping together, spent much money very well. Then I went to St. Thomas's & saw his pleasant room. Your most beautiful letter came, you must write as much as you can, you write uncommon letters, I think, & I rejoice you are well. Father is. He is every day surprised at his appetite & yesterday had a truly delightful day with Mr Carlyle. Today he & Edward have gone to Kensington Museum. Goodbye.

E. T. E.

November 9th, 1872.
(A letter begun at St. Thomas's, left there, hunted for, tumbled, found, brought home, continued at intervals, and finished Nov. 9th, Grandma's birthday).
My own dear beloved neglected Edith,

Sprained ankles are great wasters of time. It takes twice as long to do each thing, so that dressing occupies all the morning hours. Oh dear! I mourn for my fellow-passengers. I had become so settled among them, and I had really begun to make friends with Netz Buchanan, and more still with Mr. Alexander, who was from the beginning the only man who understood what a treasure they had on board in Father, and who most quietly watched and befriended us, never daring, for he is a modest person, to come and talk to Father except when he had a reading to propose, and then using his chance; early discovering that I was the true access to Father, and coming first to consult me about everything. Then by natural degrees he became my assistant when Father was out of sight, and sometimes took me to walk, and twice invited me to play shuffleboard. One day I told him what they had said was his errand and asked him what it really was, and he said there was a rising Protestant element in Italy the moment that freedom came, and there were already four or five thousand people who had left Catholicism, and were establishing themselves in churches, but ministers were very scarce, and they wanted a Divinity School, and he and three other ministers had been called to help start it, and teach in it; not to be missionaries, and preach to the people, but to help train their young ministers. Edward isn't really strong at all, and he is imprudent. He sits up very late. His conscience worries him so much that he never feels as if he had given Father enough time, and then he has his own business to attend to when he has left us at bed-time. I am going to lecture him to-day, and extort confessions from him. Father admires his practical powers, as the ignorant new-comer must admire the wisdom of his guide, and moreover stares at his historical knowledge. It is curious to see how much Father enjoys the *rest*. I didn't know that he wanted it so much. He feels that he has nothing to do, and it is a pure delight to him every day. He goes to bed by ten, and comes down at nine in the morning, singing songs like the following, "A warm bed is the best medicine. It cures all the little ails. I get up very late. I like to lie in the morning. And one gets such good sleep in this country—good strong sleep." At the table he says, "The land of England desires much food in its inhabitants." He actually enjoys sitting quite unoccupied, and when I observe his leisure and cast about for some amusement or business, he says that "Old age loves leisure." Yesterday he and Edward went to Kensington Museum and lunched in the Morris room. But what seems to have chiefly impressed Father was the Albert Memorial Monument which they passed on the way. He greatly rejoices that modern men could do so well. Edward went out again to call on Mr [Thomas] Hughes who came back with him to call on us. We read in the paper the other day an article saying his constituents quarreled with him, and that he had resigned, blaming him for so doing as Liberal Members were so important that he ought to have held on fast to his place. So Father repeated it to him and asked him not to be too hasty. He said his leading constituents had written to him that they couldn't carry him again, and though he believed he had a right to snub them and say, no matter he would try it, he didn't wish to do that, and had said "If you have no need of me, I have no need of you." But Father still said "No, no", and Mr H. said "Oh yes! the world would go on without him" and quoted a charming verse of Mr Lowell's that none of us knew, to the effect that while going wrong all the way, the world always succeeded in coming into port as the next generation bears witness. Then he told us that tomorrow is Lord Mayor's Day "and you must come and see the Lord Mayor's Show." Father & Edward accepted Mr Hughes's invitation to come to his office at Lincoln's Inn Fields, and go to the "Benchers" lunch (for Mr H. is a Bencher, whatever that is) and see as much of the Show as they care for. Mr Conway came last night and was most kind in every offer of help but Father would take nothing, and I couldn't but feel that he "swiftly shrank away", and pitied him, but Edward thought Mr. C. had been prepared for Father's wanting to do nothing, he thought he wasn't hurt. Mr McCormac came and stayed ten minutes. After him Mr Carlyle who struck me as young & sound-looking after the photographs and he hadn't been here two minutes when Mr Hughes & Father came in. Then a knock & reenter Mr McCormac and he told Father he would like to make him Hon. Member of the Jr. Athenaeum Club on this street. Just what Father had been desiring this morning! Mr Carlyle stayed a short time, I couldn't understand him, but he kept Father & Mr H. laughing. Mr Hughes brought us tickets to the Temple Church, and laid out our time for tomorrow with us. I was thankful indeed to get your letter so soon, and I wish I could see my preciouses. I think John sober is handsomer than C. sober, but Cameron takes the premium on a smile. Tell me when Violet is in earnest, and when Ralph is good. Much love to everyone at both houses, & Sophy's, and M. Watson.

E. T. E.

Canterbury Nov 14th 1872

Dear Edith,

We left London yesterday and Father says I dragged him away; and wishes himself back by turns, and between whiles says "we will live in Canterbury & send for Mamma". I don't know whether he is really sorry to leave London or not. He was invited to a great dinner last night at the Inner Temple, and Dean Stanley & Lady Augusta came to see us the moment Edward had left us and asked Father to dine today "with the most learned men in England and the Queen of Holland at a small round table" where there would be no room for me—they didn't know when they came that he had any encumbrances—and me to come in the evening. He didn't want to go to either place when he found I wasn't invited and refused on the score that he was going away. Saturday

— 1872 —

night, dear Mr Hughes who always makes me happy by his entrance brought us tickets to Temple Church. Sunday morning we all went, beheld the Templars lying there with their crossed legs, their helmets and shields with such a solemn air. It felt exactly as if you saw the man himself, with the real armour he had worn going to that far crusade, through its battles, his coming home, and through this long sleep of death. I wanted to sit with them all the afternoon. Every fresco and device in all the church was interesting. After the steamer I didn't incline to hear the service, and wasn't so glad to get to church as usual. Presently I was separated from Father & Edward by some official & led to the very altar and allowed to sit down on the step. I had no book, the service was chanted both by priests and people, I didn't understand a word, but I had a saint beside me who really loved the service, and faithfully & affectionately took care of me from beginning to end. The length of the service was immense and it was 1.15 when church was done. Then away they rushed to meet Mr MacC. at St. Th.'s leaving me to explore till the doorkeeper requested us to go out.

Monday P.M. Miss Norton came with her nieces. It was my first acquaintance with her. I like her. Miss Aitken too, a pretty little girl! And dear Mr. Hughes once more, and I had a chance to show gratitude for the Temple tickets though I was surly the night before, having hoped to find a Unitarian church. Then Edward and I to see Una [Hawthorne]. He will tell you about that. Monday, after he had gone, Dean Stanley, who talked with Father, and Lady Augusta with me. She was delightful, and when we asked her about Egypt as Bishop Jacobson advised us to do, she and the Dean were encouraging, and presently her narration of journeys led her to say they always went 2nd Class and had no sitting room, that they might have the luxury of a travelling servant. I asked her advice on that subject, and she recommended hers very earnestly. She said he was now in London, and I might write if we wanted him. Then to the Nortons to dine; how good, how homelike and how gay they were. Mr. Norton told at dinner many stories of Mr. Carlyle. One was that he said to him when Frederick the Great had come out and Father had written acknowledging his copy, "I have a letter from Emerson, after a long silence, and though there were few words in it that did not give me pain, it says the only thing about my book that has been said that was worth saying" (I think he said the only truth about the book), "and therefore when I had read it through I wrapped it up in a piece of paper and put it inside the book, and there it will stay till I am dead, and it will fall into other hands than mine." As Edward had charged me I asked Mr. Norton every question I could think of, and he planned our journey as if it was his own. It was a great comfort to me. The next morning we went to Stanfords with passports, & Father got money. Also bought 2 campstools as Edward bade. I came home & Mr & Miss G. Norton came & then Father, and Mr Norton took Father to Mr B[urne] Jones's studio & lunch & left him at 2.30 at Mr Carlyle's, while Miss Norton took me to drive in a Hansom & showed me the Thames embankment & St Pauls, and then some of the handsome houses, insisted on taking me to do my last errand & asked me home to lunch. After lunch Miss Grace said she would like to go with me and do my packing, had intended it all along, if I was willing. It was such a godsend! She packed my trunk and Father's entirely without my stirring. Mrs Clough called meanwhile but Father hadn't come home, and she stayed but a minute. No sooner had my dear kind friend gone, after looking at the cards on the table and telling me that I must write notes to acknowledge the calls of those who didn't know we were going away, than Father came in. He sat down to write notes with me. The moment these were posted Una came and spent the night. It was a cheerful visit. Mother's letter came that night, and Una was hungry to hear all Concord news. She went early the next morning and I counted out the business not yet done and found it alarmingly much. Father also said he must find Mr Stillman for he owed him money & went for his hat. While Father was upstairs Mr Channing, who had come twice before in vain, came in. How good & kind & lovely he was, and hearing Father's destination he went with him. Now I thought, there is time for accounts & for letters, for I was quite too lame & had too bad a cold to stir to help do the errands, and I was just sitting down when Mr C. K. Newcomb came in, and half an hour later again enter Mr Channing. He and Mr N. talked delightfully till Father came and was overjoyed at sight of Mr N. Then Mr C. came to me. "You have a cold. What are you doing?" "Nothing." He meditated. "Have you any French gold?" I said Father had bought it this morning. Father confessed he had forgotten it. Mr Channing said "I'll do all these errands, and get you whatever you want for your cold", recommending several; and Mr N. then took upon himself every remaining odd and end. Mr Channing's plaster & medicines relieved me, and his talk & his kindness were too delightful. I see that angels come for our help in every need, and my courage grows. It will be Thanksgiving when you get this.

— 1872 —

I suppose the Keyeses will have Edward, but you'll be thankful he's at home [EWE sailed for home November 12 on the *Batavia*], and indeed we all have more than ever to be thankful for. I am daily thankful for my sister, and never go without her book. Father doesn't like writing and won't.

E. T. E.

Lord Warden Hotel, Dover
Nov. 14th 1872

Dear Will,

I am anxious about the money and wish to confess to you that at the end of 9 days after our landing we had spent for food & lodging etc. £89, 11S, 2d, that is 198 dollars, over 20 dollars a day. Edward is counted in but Edward wasn't with us at all our meals. I hoped London was more expensive than other places but I found Canterbury more expensive than London, and tonight the Ld. W. Hotel is more expensive than Canterbury. We travel 2nd Class, I ask for single bed-rooms, up high, the cheapest they have, & no sitting-room, but at C. they said it was a rule of the house no meals to be had in bed-rooms, and ladies didn't come into coffee-room. I stuck it out as far as possible, and asked if I had come alone must I have a parlour to take my supper in, and pay as much for it as two rooms? "Yes, ladies do." Another time, if it happens again, I'll say I *will* go into the coffee-room. In spite of this fear that we shall go quite beyond our card, I have sent to Lady Stanley to engage her servant [Curnex], who she says is a servant, and doesn't insist on first-class cars & parlours but does what he is bid, is good-natured, willing & skillful, wages 10£ a month and his fare, for all advise it earnestly. Father at first resisted, but on hearing that he knew the way about, would do errands & pay bills, did want him & is glad though he fears the expense. I haven't told Father how much we have spent, it seemed needless to trouble him, as I keep the accounts & do the deciding. Tell Edith my foot is a little better. Canterbury Cathedral today seems not to have hurt it. Father doesn't take to sight-seeing, he would rather sit quite still in the parlour. He is just saying "It would be ungrateful to my friends to go stingily along; we must be frank & fearless. This is their room—not mine." I say yes, and never tell him how fearless we have been. He was talking to himself about going to the theatre in Paris when he said it.

E. T. E.

— 1872 —

Paris. Hotel de Lorraine
7 Rue de Beaurn
Saturday morning, 16th Nov. 1872

Dear Mother,

Father is so thankful to have got through the journey from London, and to have reached a place where he "can stay today, and tomorrow, and the next day, and longer" that he sings praises all the time. And that is not all. He has come to Mr John Holmes and Mr & Mrs Lowell, people who make each meal a festivity, and can answer all the awkward questions that arise hour by hour, and now Mr Lowell has gone with him to the banker's to help him on all errands and show him the way. Our only grief is that we can't stay all winter. I hate Egypt. It won't let us stop anywhere. Our journey yesterday from Dover to Paris was a tale with three heads, like Cerberus. I mean it was eventful, though not to Father, and proved three things: first, that a travelling servant is an absolute necessity; second that I can speak French easily and have little difficulty in understanding, none in making myself understood. The thorough drilling in grammar that I have had I now find is most valuable. I should be willing to go ahead without a servant if Father was well. My courage after yesterday's experience is doubled. When I came to the Hotel Mr Lowell was out. I had to do all unassisted, and was never at a loss for a word. Our rooms please us and are warmer than the London rooms, and our fare is better. The price is just half. The third thing proved is that fellow-travelers are likely to be a great comfort and assistance. I made friends on the boat from Dover to Calais with a young American girl who gave me much information that I wish I had had before—exactly what the guide-book ought to tell you but doesn't. Next came a lady saying "Surely I am not mistaken. You are Miss Emerson!" And it was Mrs Frederick Dabney. She had a French servant with her and once or twice he helped me by her orders. When we came to our car I couldn't get in because my hands were too full. A very lovely lady in the car reached out and took my bags. I thought her American and began to talk with her, but when she answered and I heard the beautiful English voice I was frightened and became very modest. Presently got in a gentleman. As soon as he had struggled to the seat by me he turned round and held out his hand. "Why Miss E. I never imagined I should find you here!" Captain Whineray. I was very glad to see him. At last Father, who was getting my hot-water bottle filled, came and was in turn surprised and pleased to find the Captain there. And what a comfort and entertainment he was all day! He had never

— 1872 —

learned a word of the language, and was very gay about it, very eager to see the country and compare it with England, full of play and vigour, and waited on me, handed my bag, arranged my possessions and saved Father from lifting his finger. At the Paris station my lady helped me constantly and we came easily to our hotel.

Lyons depot. Nov. 22nd.   Love to my beloved Edith on her birthday, and alas! no present ready. We have Curnex, and kindest letters of advice from Lady Augusta. Still fellow passengers are as it were my nurses to take care of Father and me and keep me straight. Still we are cared for like babes, especially in Paris by Mr Lowell.

[Unsigned]

Florence, Nov. 26th, 1872

Dear Edith,

Well, I must tell you of our doings. In Paris from Friday Nov. 15th till the following Thursday we had a warm snug home, a capital table d'hote, where one side of the table was our friends and selves, and the other all French. "It is a legitimist hotel, and very respectable people come here," said Mr. Lowell. Two or three members of the Chamber of Deputies, among them the Marquis de Gramont, grandson, tell Mother, of that beloved sister Rosalie of our friend Madame de Montagu, Madame Lafayette's sister. How I longed for French ears and tongue to ask him about all his ancestors, relatives, and family! They talked politics daily. 'Twas as good as a play to see, and Mr. Lowell highly enjoyed the privilege of hearing. No one else could. Imagine my alarm when on the fourth day one of the deputies took to looking at me on ending his remarks, and as I strove to mind the rule of manners the Storers discovered and to put on an intelligent expression, he wasn't slow in going a step farther and addressing various remarks to Mademoiselle. There was no help for it. I struggled hard, understood, composed my reply in the expectant silence of the whole table, and brought it out, whereupon there was the same kind of applause on the French side of the table as there is at home when John Murray performs a trick or says "Dane" or "Papa." Monsieur was encouraged and talked to me more, and next spoke to Father, who finds it harder to understand than I do; and there is no subject ancient or modern that we didn't hobble painfully through. One was delightful—the language of America. They all supposed it of course was the American Indian speech, and that the higher classes learned a little English. Mr. Lowell especially enjoyed the chance of enlightening them on this head. I have in Paris had the great pleasure of seeing much of Charles and Therchi, who were utterly satisfactory. Charles seemed to feel real joy and relief in seeing us, and Therchi strikes me as a lady, and is pretty decidedly, has a most beautiful mouth, and takes very kindly to me, as I to her. On Sunday we went to church. For a whole month Father never missed going to church on Sunday!—to the Chapelle Evangelique de l'Etoile; Monsieur le Pasteur Bersier, a handsome man whose speaking charmed Father and whose sermon on the life of Baruch was a revelation to me of a Bible history I hadn't understood before, and it was a place that seemed homelike and churchlike. Mrs. Lowell took us, and rejoiced in her success. She of course was my authority and refuge in the house and we had a delightful time together when there was a chance, and Mr. Lowell seemed to me the spirit of strength and counsel. I never stirred till I had talked with him. He devoted himself to Father very much and was his guide about the city. Harry James came several times, and once took Father to the Louvre, and Father came home enchanted. I was lame in Paris all the time, but Mr. Lowell gave me a piece of magic paper for my ankle which seemed to do it real good. Today I have walked half an hour. On Wednesday we dined with the Laugels, and that was a most happy occasion. We all enjoyed it. The Lowells went too. On returning we found Curnex, our servant, and the kindest letters from Lady Augusta Stanley, full of advice, had come before, so I knew what to say and how to deal with him. Then in our room was the budget from home, yours about the hunt—oh Edith! Wasn't I glad about that large cheerful party of young men, and of Selma Bowditch's coming! 'Twas so good too that you had pleasant weather. Father took pride and pleasure in Will's killing the bucks, and the luncheon on the warm day he liked to hear of. We left Paris Thursday at 3 o'clock for an endless journey to Marseilles. We of course passed a mis'able night, but at four I did make a bed that rested me and slept till we reached Lyons at six. Poor Father is determined to be uncomfortable and resisted any plans of alleviation, so he suffered much more than I. One hour at Lyons to wash, braid, and breakfast and we ascended once more to our dungeon, expecting a hateful day, but oh! *la belle France* is not a mere figure of speech. The Cornice road isn't more beautiful and interesting than every moment from Lyons to Marseilles. Father, tired as he was, was in ecstasies and said, "If you want to do the greatest kindness possible to anyone, send him from Lyons to Marseilles." We saw Avignon beautifully. Then

— 1872 —

darkness fell, and there was nothing but weariness and hunger till we at last saw the beautiful lights of Marseilles. We went to the Hotel de Noailles, where of course I was happy in the name, Madame de Montagu's maiden name, and rested till one the next day, when we took the cars for Nice. Ah! this surpassed the day before and everything since. The kind of mountains, the enchanting bays and curly rocks and villages on the Mediterranean. Again all was joy till dark when we came to up-grades and the engine couldn't pull us up. Funny times we had starting and stopping and going at a foot-pace till we reached down-grade again. This made us two hours late at Nice, but it was Saturday night and Father was happy in the prospect of a halt. Nice is perfectly beautiful. Of course I couldn't go out except to church, which was 20 steps off. I am sorry for Father that I am lame. He never goes anywhere, while if I was about he would do everything for my sake. This day at Nice was a happy exception. While I was at the Scotch church Curnex took him to the public garden, the English promenade, and various places, and he came back praising all, and very much edified by the sight of palms, oranges, pepper-trees, roses and all the Southern vegetation. Sunday ended with a reading of our last letters from home. Curnex called us at 5:30 to see a moon shining in the first cloudless sky we had seen for a month certainly. So we left the Hotel Paradis, and the obliging Curnex made the omnibus drive the longest way to the steamer that "Mees" might see the dates growing and other sights he had showed Father the day before. The port is a romantic place. The sun shone warm; a nun on the quay was superintending the embarkation of a young lady, and I got a good look at all her attire. We were got on board at last and I sat on the quarter-deck in the sun. Suddenly there stood before me a very tall slim girl, light and pale, dressed in black and looking elegant and lady-like, holding out her hand and saying "Aren't you Miss Emerson?" "Yes" I exclaimed, giving her mine and all agog to know who this fellow-traveler could be. She said she was Alice Bartlett, and I was delighted. In a few minutes she had offered her services. In a few hours we talked so fast that Father was really worried lest I should lose scenery. By afternoon we sat together on a chest and became great friends. By sunset Father was begging her to change her plans and stay with us. And this morning we parted with first names, and by severe control just managed not to swear eternal friendship. She was going straight to Rome to meet Mrs Sumner, and we to Florence to find Aunt Lizzy if we could. So having come together to Genoa, we took the Leghorn boat there, sailed at 9 or 10 o'clock, and waked in Leghorn in

— 1872 —

the morning. Alice told us to take the 9 A.M. train to Pisa, see the wonders there, leave there at 1:30, and that would bring us to Florence at 5 o'clock. I took out Uncle George's memoranda of hotels. She knew them all, agreed with his remarks on them, but said she could recommend one even more to our purpose, the Hotel du Nord. Next she looked at his Roman houses, and said the German one he recommended was just the right one for us. Also she wrote me a letter of introduction to Madame Tellenbach, who keeps it. She got the book of R. Roads on the steamer, and looked out trains and prices, and finally gave me full directions about seeing Pisa, so I entered Italy as bold as if I had been here twenty times, knowing exactly where and when I was going, and what I had to do. In all this pleasure there was one drawback: her voice is so low that Father, much as he liked her and wished to hear her talk, had to lose all that she didn't address to him, for he doesn't feel equal to the continual effort of close listening. We had beautiful effects of haze & clouds & clear sky all day. The water was like glass most of the time, and of a heavenly light blue. The mountains looked to me a little bald & barren. It wasn't quite as beautiful as our Friday's and Saturday's marches had been. Father didn't seem carried away either, as he had been hitherto, except once in a great while. Coming into Genoa was more beautiful than one could imagine beforehand. It was dusk and the lights, not few and far between, but set very close, twinkling in and out all up and down high hills, gave the effect the infant imagination forms on reading the word "bejewelled," which never appears in precious stones but does in entering the harbour of Genoa. We saw a little of Leghorn as we drove through, and here let me say that from the moment we left Lyons things began to look Fayalese, and Nice and all Italy is Fayal over again, except the superior architecture, which is by no means without a certain smack of Fayal too, so that I feel quite at home here. I see the Nespra [loquat] trees in blossom with particular pleasure. The Campo Santo I saw with indifference, except that I received a little instruction from Andrea Orcagna, for which I owe him gratitude, and I saw a picture of the newborn twins Esau and Jacob which electrified me. The echo in the Baptistry was all Alice had promised, but the leaning tower utterly failed to interest me. The interior of the Cathedral truly delighted me, but my foot complained and I only glanced at it and left it. The guide, whom he could not understand, worried Father, and I fancied he would say about the same that I do of all these things.

Then away to Florence, and we are happily installed in Hotel du

— 1872 —

Nord and find Mrs. Sumner here, perfectly beautiful to look at and a bright next-neighbour to Father at table. The little Belle and I take frequent peeps at each other across our parents but have not yet got so far as to smile.

November 26th.
Thanksgiving Day.

We have found Aunt Lizzy and had a long delightful call from her and Cary last night. It was dusk, so I can't tell how she looks. Today we three, Aunt L., C., and I are going to church together to keep the day, and we suppose either with you or the Keyeses there is joy over Edward. Alas dear Bush. I mourn for its emptiness today. We are hoping for news of Boston fires and E.'s return; also to hear Dolly's state.

E. T. E.

Rome. Dec. 3rd 1872

Dear Edith,

We arrived in Rome Saturday night and Monday morning Father went to the bankers and got your two letters. We were most thankful for the whole budget. In Florence Father fell in with some gentlemen (whom he calls missionaries—at least he is sure they either are going to a convention or have attended one, or are connected with a Sunday-school. and this seems to him sufficient ground for so calling them) who are about starting for Egypt; and he has offered them his heart and hand, and they are to mature their plans, then come to Rome and send him word, and on them our plans depend. Father is well. I am sure at last that my ankle begins to improve, but it is always meeting with unexpected and necessary claims, so that I never dare plan any exercise for it, lest it should prove too tired for the next emergency. Now for the questions about the house. I prefer having the k. walls painted, and always liked the straw-colour & brown-yellow of my dear Bridget's day, but if you & Mother have other ideas I don't care. I go in strong for the varnish in pantry & in den, and as to floor in pantry I should say have it like kitchen-floor, and a piece of cocoa-matting such as you use. I agree with Mother on the white paint everywhere and I sent my views on the nursery-question by Edward. I am glad Mother is well & with you. And blessed Edith, don't try to write to me *twice* a week, your health is so important you must not do too much. And give up Bush. Your own work is enough for you. Leave mine for me. Tonight we dine with Miss Sarah Clarke, whom I love, and on Saturday or Monday we go to make a

— 1872 —

week's visit to Lily [Ward] von Hoffmann, who has won Father's stony heart, and her husband hardly less.

E. T. E.

Rome Dec. 4th 1872.

Dear Mother,

Because so much is now planned for us that I foresee little writing-time, I shall give a wickedly short account of our late pleasures. Seeing my dear Aunt Lizzy was the greatest event of Florence. She took me to the Cathedral and the church of Santa Croce, also to drive in the Cascine and it was delightful. The American Consul, a young Mr Graham, showered attentions on us, took us to drive in a lordly chariot, sent us flowers, called several times, and invited us to dinner, but that fell through. I had one or two good times with Cary Hoar. Then let me not omit to say that Mrs Sumner's great beauty was my daily feast. How much Father and I both enjoyed it!

Do you remember a "Resolution of the City Government of Florence" about building an edifice that should be a work worthy of so great a people, that Father likes and has read in one of his lectures? Well, that resolution was for the Cathedral, and truly the outside is all they could have planned, just one of those pieces of fine work (that one can look at with a microscope, so to speak, close to, and of pattern large enough to be enjoyed a great way off) that one can't convey any idea of. I had no suspicion that it was going to be so handsome—even Mark Twain and I could discern its beauty unassisted—and I thought how crazy the people who built it must have been at their success. But dear me! Go inside and you can't believe that this is all it turns out to be. The outside seems so enormous and is one great Florentine Mosaic, and polished, and the inside is plain gray freestone, dark and unsatisfactory, and struck me as small. After I had been in the choir and seen the chapels I felt better, and I don't know but it may be wise to have the outside, which all see perpetually, handsomer than the inside, which the few see occasionally; yet our ideas are the other way. When we came home and Father heard that I had been not only at the Cathedral but at St. Croce, where are tombs of Galileo, M. Angelo, and Alfiere, and Macchiavelli, I was amused to see that he felt as much elated as if I had met these four in person. He seemed to respect me as if I had been in exalted society. Aunt Lizzy helped me pack my trunk too, and came again in the evening to bid us goodbye. The journey from Florence to

— 1872 —

Rome, 10 hours in the cars, was so beautiful and interesting a ride that we positively enjoyed the whole. On this ride we scraped up all our Italian to compose a sentence asking the name of a town we were passing—which work of art when finished I was ashamed to exhibit but Father wasn't—and attracting the attention of the Signor in the other corner, he recited it aloud and clearly. It worked beautifully. The signor gave us the information with effusion, and encouraged by this linguistic firework to believe we understood Italian, sprang joyfully to his feet, and standing between us opened a conversation. Alas! I hated to see his efforts increase and his words grow fewer as he saw how it was. At last he simply pointed to my window, exclaiming "Lago!" as we say to John, "See the beautiful Moo-cow!" I looked but no water was to be seen. I stared at him. "Lago!" he cried once more. Still as there was no lake, I was puzzled, and thought the plain might appear big to him, so like Alice in Wonderland I said, "Did you say 'lago' or 'largo?'" Now he was puzzled, but at last Lake Thrasymene hove in sight, and he was justified. We brought out the guide-book, which informed us that "Here Hannibal defeated Fabius, which casts a gloom over the lovely landscape." You ought to have seen our intercourse with our Italian friend the rest of the day. Dictionaries guidebook, fingers, French, English and Italian had to help. We were established at 7 o'clock at Madame Tellenbach's, Piazza d'Espagna, and found Mr. B. S. Lyman's sister among our fellow-boarders. On Sunday morning I went to church, and in the afternoon Father and I drove to St. Peter's. It was magnificent enough—certainly didn't disappoint me in anything—till I remembered Harry James's letter about it, and I found he had described it much bigger than it seemed to me. But it was quite big enough, and very handsome, and all the angels on the bridge as we came towards it interested me very much. On Monday morning I sent Curnex to ask Alice Bartlett when I should come to her. She said three, so we took a cab and went to the Coliseum and sat and walked a while inside; then drove round it and up to Villa Celimontana. Lily [von Hoffmann] came down as pretty as a picture and was her very old self, her husband with her as gentle and affectionate to us both as a man could be. They made us stay to lunch, and by serious persistence and every imaginable wile, persuaded Father to come and stay with them, while we are here, some time. We came away with a handful of violets, and Father really delighted exclaimed, "That is the prettiest little visit that ever I made!" I left him at home and went to see Alice; carried my sewing, and had such a good time as kept me awake way into the night. When I got home, Father had been having a visit from Mr. von Hoffmann, and had liked him. He was very much pleased with his coming instantly down to make a call after our morning's visit. We were surprised before breakfast next morning by a basket of flowers that looked as if they came from Fredonia or Bagatelle, and a note from Lily, with another note for Father from Mr. von Hoffmann giving him Miss Sarah Clarke's address, and full of pretty polite sentences, and Father was again charmed. Our visit to Miss Clarke was the first adventure after breakfast, and was eminently happy and interesting to us all three. It seemed like a continuation of the pleasant times we had together when she was in Concord last June. She said when she heard that the house burned down she thought she had been one of its last guests. She asked us to dine at 6 o'clock. Then away we drove (always in a single barouche with top back and Curnex on the box with the driver, pointing out to us with an artless good-natured delight every palace, fountain, or antiquity that we pass in a language meant for English but curiously compounded of three others) to the Temple of Vesta, which I regarded with the same toleration that I do its various copies in bronze all over the world; but Father seems to respect and even to like it, and next to the Capitol. The afternoon we spent chiefly in the house, though Father made one sally to see the Eng. Library, and another to learn if those "missionaries" he means to go to Egypt with had come. At six we went to Miss Clarke's. She has a Miss Foley and a Miss Hadwin for family so we were five at table, and besides the solids were feasted on wine (at least Father) from Sicily, never brought off the island before, and unknown to fame, but wonderfully good on crema montata, and pistachio nuts, which again came from Sicily, for Miss Foley spent last May there and made friends who send her these things. In the evening came Mr Howitt and Meggy, and Meggy is charming and speaks with a strong brogue. Mr Tweedy also came and a Mr & Miss Cram. We had a very pleasant evening. Today Alice was to take us to see some places and pictures. She began by taking us to see Guido's Aurora. I have heard so much against it that I was consoled to find I liked it as much as I should wish. Then we went to the Borghese Gallery, met Lily Cleveland & Miss Booth, and had a very good time with them, but I found I cared nothing for galleries so vast & dark. I want time & light to see in. Father was enchanted with the richness that discouraged me. I must stop here for today. Are you happy in getting Edw. back? And how are all the Forbes descendants? Write to me all the time, as you did in Fayal, you are such a capital hand at it!

Your affectionate daughter
E. T. E.

Rome. Friday, Dec. 6th, 1872.

Dear Edith,

    I must begin with the remarks I wanted to put into my yesterday's letter. Lily and Mr v. H. seem never to forget us for a moment. The Baron comes daily either to call or leave flowers. Father is very amusing to me in his easy conformity to the customs of the Turkeys, as Will says. I haven't seen a pickle offered to him, but if it were I think he would unhesitatingly eat it. He invariably puts grated cheese in his soup, helps himself repeatedly to fried potatoes at breakfast, eats cabbage, though at this last he is apt to murmur, ask me what it is, say it seems to have no taste in particular, and wonder why it was added to the dinner. Your letters have just come. He was so very much disappointed that "there wasn't a *line* for him" that I beg someone will address the letter to him each week. These letters bring the welcome news that ours from England had begun to arrive. I have a pride and pleasure in the fact that we are invariably taken for English. Of course foreigners would naturally suppose so from the language, but that all English and Americans too should testify surprise when we reveal our nationality pleases me. I think from my happy experience that it gives us an advantage—we are so delightfully received everywhere by the English travelers. My ankle, I think, is perfectly and permanently well, I have not spared it for two days. I have accustomed myself & Father to expect almost nothing from it. I never get a chance to praise thee & thy works, Edith dear, in my letters, but I am always telling Father that you provided me with exactly the right attire for each occasion that turns up, that I haven't one thing too many or too few, and that I live in that peace of mind which Miss Fanny Forbes said religion did not bestow. I *know* I'm all right, a new sensation to me. This goes without telling of the numberless dinners & teas & excursions, and how Curnex meets us when we come in in great glee, sheaves of cards in his hand. "The American Minister has been here, and the French Minister, and the Baron, and a great many ladees." Also we have seen the Campagna. My dear Alice I see only once in a week at leisure, but Father likes to have her show us round better than anybody else. She lives with Mrs

— 1872 —

Sumner, appreciates her beauty, and says it seems absurd to go round for statues & pictures when she has both combined at home. Tomorrow we go to the Villa Celimontana, and I expect great pleasures. Today we have seen Egypt people, and shall go, I hope, next week. And now my love to dear Mamma and thanks for her letter. Tell her she put in a tale worth millions. Father delights to laugh over it with me. And thank Annie for every enchanting word. Happy New Year to all!
E. T. E.

Villa Celimontana, Rome
Saturday Dec. 14th 1872

Dear Edward,
Our plan for Egypt lay in fragments on Tuesday noon. The "missionaries" (who are tourists) sent word they couldn't think of missing Christmas in Rome, and we couldn't think of waiting. I felt rather adrift all of a sudden, but have learned at last that when everything goes it is because something is coming, so rather waited with curiosity than lamented. Father too. We hadn't many hours to wait. Mr & Mrs Whitwell, May & Bessy, the Scotch lady Miss Farquahr, and Father & I seem today to be the party that sails for Egypt from Naples on the 21st. So funny, or as Mother would rather I would say, so interesting is the shifting of scenes & characters around us that I am as it were in a theatre expecting to be amused, and to see the play turn out right in spite of the untoward passages. Think of Miss Farquahr's being able to go! I had a chance to go with her and Miss Lyman to see the catacombs, and on the long drive I told her we were going to Egypt. She said she had had some thoughts of it but had given it up. I implored her to go with us. Today I have a letter from her asking many questions and reading very much as if she had decided to go. If she does, she will go with Father and me to Naples on Wed. 18th and we shall have a day or two of Naples before sailing. Father & I live in great glory here with Lily and her husband whom we like very much. Father says he is the politest man he ever saw, and remarkably exact in his information. Every morning a man comes and prepares Father's clothes for putting on, brings hot water, makes a fire, and Felice does the same for me. When I am dressed I open my window on a landscape with every imaginable accessory, and I unwillingly record it is more beautiful than America can be. Then I go to breakfast with Father in his study and after breakfast comes the Baron to arrange the pleasures of the day.

Then Ferdy may come in, pretty creature! Then I see Lily a minute or two, then away with the Baron in a carriage to see churches, gardens or galleries. Come home to lunch with Lily, who is lovely, and then at 2:30 away we go again. Company to dine finishes the day. No time for a word of all we see.

E. T. E.

Christmas Day 1872
Abbat's Hotel, Alexandria Egypt

Dear Mother,

Since we went from Rome there has been no chance to write. The hospitality of Villa Celimontana "ran fine to the last." Father said to the Baron in parting from him "You are one of the knights of King Arthur's Round Table," and since has praised him as "truly noble, chivalrous, and affectionate." You see it is the longest visit Father ever made, and he never took so kindly to visiting before. They understood making him happy very well. He enjoyed Lily and often said, "That is a lovely little girl." He delighted in the sight of Ferdy when he was led through the entry in the morning to visit his mamma. Lily was on her bed most of the time, thinking, thinking what she could do for us. Whatever questions I had in manners, management of Curnex, laying out of our travels and preparation therefor, shopping, everything, dressing for the various parties, she elicited from me every day, and the next time I saw her she had capital answers ready. I had much comfort in that, and to know in going out that I had been finished by such hands made me quite secure. Last Wednesday 17th, the Whitwells, Miss Farquahr and we came to Naples, placed in the car by the Baron himself, with a basket of luncheon & wine and a garden of roses, and came to the Hotel de Russie, had our late dinner and went to bed. While we were breakfasting the next morning the door opened and Cary Hoar walked in, followed by Aunt Lizzy and Miss Pierce and Helen V. V. Great was the clamour of joy on all sides. So that morning we visited the Museum together, that night we had a very happy dinner together. The next day we went to Pompeii and Aunt E. didn't. We met at night, compared notes, and showed each other everything we had bought. The next morning, Saturday, Baron Osten Sacken came one day too late. He told me in Rome it would delight him to go to Pompeii with Father. Father introduced him to Aunt E. and then & there we all parted, and our party took the steamer Nil, Messagerie Imperiale de Marseille à Alexandria at 12 o'clock.

— 1873 —

All Saturday and all Sunday 'twas smooth and sometimes sunny. The Bay of Naples was more than fancy painted it. But I remembered the only two voyages in the Mediterranean that I knew much about—St. Paul's and Sir Pavon's—and expected adversity. It came on Monday morning, and we had a forty-eight hours of rolling that wore us all out. Our berths were built across the boat insead of along the sides, and wow! but it is fatiguing to be darted against the headboard of your bed, and the next moment to begin a process of slipping the other way which lasts till you are all in a heap by the footboard, ready to be projected again headboardwards! It's a kind of exercise amusing for a few hours, but it gets tedious at last and I got out my Bible and read of St. Paul's atrocious voyage in a ship of Alexandria sailing into Italy with deep sympathy, when I had had a *tisane* and felt better.

Mrs. Whitwell eagerly followed my example and said she read with new eyes. You see this was very nearly the same route. We passed Crete and Malta. Landing in Africa was the most amusing adventure I ever have had. The foreignness of every creature and thing surpassed expectation. 'Twould have been misery but for Curnex. The natives attack you like a pack of wolves, but Curnex buffeted and scolded like any ten Americans, and Father, Miss F. and I were passive. Along the streets Euphorbias grow ablaze with scarlet leaves; loaded camels are led; donkeys abound; the tailor sews on his window-seat; the merchants of all kinds, likewise crosslegged, in gorgeous costumes, sit at the doors of the dark square little dens full of goods. I fixed my eye on a bandana which I hope to get. I understand at last how a turban is made, but the whole costume isn't quite clear to me. Goodbye, and say to Mrs Forbes and the girls that I will write my notes to them next week if I don't write a letter home. I am so ashamed. Your affectionate daughter
                                                                Ellen T. Emerson

    Cairo
    Wednesday to Saturday Jan. 1st, 2nd, 4th, 1873

Dear Edward,

It pleases and amuses me daily to hear the commendations Father showers on Tangerinas at dessert. He is sure to say as much as, "This seems superior to all the fruits they offer us—even goes ahead of pears, I'm afraid." And very often he breaks out into further praises, as last night he said, "They are the ideal orange! They charm by their tractability—yes their tractability—their lovely anticipation to your wishes. One might call it 'Christianity in apples,' an Arabian revenge

1873

on the Fall of Man." The Tangerine here is built quite differently outside from its Portugese and Italian brethren, has quite a coarse skin with a hump at the stem.

Oh Edward, how shall I express my joy in Africa? I sit on my donkey and turn my head from side to side and every second I see a new sight, greater fun, more beauty. First of all I must tell the best. There is a creature common in the streets of Cairo more like an angel from heaven than anything left below. Their passing gives me a real rapture, and I feel like singing their praises all the time. I am not quite sure that it is an angel that they remind me of. Perhaps it is a fairy on the stage; perhaps it is ideas called up by Miss Powell's "leaping," but they remind me of something and they are the perfection of beauty. As an introduction I will confess that I have lost my prejudice against colour. Why! Brown is far handsomer than white! far handsomer! There are different species of this creature, differing greatly in glory, but I promised to introduce the best first, and here he comes, running so beautifully that Father bursts into exclamations of admiration—so silently, freely and gaily that it is evident that he is at his ease, and yet when he roars out "Shammelak" or "Ocah," or "Waddy" you are taken by surprise that his lungs are in such good order, utterly unaffected by his running. He carries a wand straight and steady right before him, and it is another wonder to see that. He is all in white, except the black or green Zouave jacket without sleeves, embroidered with gold, and the long scarf wound five or six times round his waist below it. He has Greek trousers that come just below his knees and his sleeves are tied behind his shoulder-blades together by a little white string, and balloon out grandly like great white wings behind him as he runs, while a little crest of them flutters on his shoulders without falling over, so that I am puzzled. It looks so utterly unconfined but behaves quite against nature. He is called a "sais." He comes usually from Nubia or Abyssinia. Gen. Stone, whom Charley wrote a letter about to Father in New Orleans days, has settled here, is "Chief of Staff of the Egyptian Army," and calls himself a Turkish officer, when he talks of himself. Father likes him very much, and now Mr. Bancroft is gone finds great comfort in him. He says his *sais* will run fifteen miles a day, four or five miles at a stretch, and think it easy, always arriving ahead of the horses, not blown, and ready to take the horses out and rub them down. I haven't said I see that everyone who has a carriage has a "sais" running before it to herald its coming and clear a passage for it in the narrow streets,

— 1873 —

and the wand is brandished and plied there, but in the broad streets it goes straight. Noble people have two. The reigning family have two in front and two or four behind. In the night those in front carry torches. All rich people have their "sais" as handsome as the Viceroy's; humble people have him without the wings or jacket. The first that won my heart had neither. Only a boy of fourteen or fifteen he was, in white with a red scarf round his waist and a red fez on his head, but he was as beautiful as he could be, and his running was killing. I don't mean he had a good face. I have never had time to see the face of one. I am making a careful study of the dress of the "sais," that I may have R[alph]. and Cameron so attired some day.

Father is always ready to admire the walking of all the native people—he says he has never seen anything like it before—and when I look at the little boys everywhere in the streets I see that their chests decidedly round out, which I believe I have heard is the right thing, instead of being straight across like our children's in civilized countries. I see so many kinds of dresses every day that I can't guess which is the prevalent kind, but a plain white nightgown is very common, and very striking and handsome too, only it takes a beautiful brown man to wear it. They look better in any dress than a white man, however. Oh such dignified red turbans as you see here, and amusing old old men, large and tall, with solemn faces and white beards, riding on donkeys the size of a rocking-horse, who just lift their feet off the ground. The children almost without exception have one eye only, or bad eyes covered with flies. They are also all dirty. The women are all fellah-women, which means Arab peasant women, I am told, and all dressed in indigo dyed cotton with a veil just like it that covers them from head to foot. Some have their faces out; some covered with a hideous black silk stocking-leg or something that looks like it. They are never a very pleasant sight, for their attire is ugly and they are dirty.

We have met a few ladies with veils either black or white and dresses either of blue, pink, or pea-green silk unlined over brown calico, or dark figured cashmere trousers, and they had an effect less pleasant even than the poor indigo coloured women. A baby usually rides astride of its mother's left shoulder holding on by her head. Plenty of babies less than a year old go so without the least attention of the mother, even in a crowded street. Often too she holds on to one of its feet. I am going to teach John to ride so on my shoulder. The foreignness and delightfulness of the Turkish bazaar and the Tunis bazaar no words can

— 1873 —

tell, but here again it is principally because the people are black and Mahommedan and altogether no concern of mine that it is pleasant. The moment you look at them as human creatures, it is dreadful to think how far they are from any hope of what we should call happy and comfortable life, though General Stone says there is no doubt they are now started towards it by a wise and good ruler. I have here drawn out all the dark side there is to us. We feel all day long amused and interested to the last degree and the streets are as cheerful as they are extraordinary. Unluckily everything costs gold instead of silver. I see at every turn brilliant little things for you all, but alas! when I ask the price I am astonished at it, for it is four times as much as it ought to be, and I turn away. (The Hotel is four dollars a day in the first place and the Nile boat will cost twice as much). We have at last engaged our dragoman,—Mahmoud Bedowy is his name—and our boat, which is called a dahabeah, is named Aurora. We are likely to start on the sixth of January and get back to Cairo by the middle of February. Father sometimes makes homesick speeches now, and if he could follow his inclination would doubtless make a bee-line for home, but he says he shall cheerfully spend a fortnight with Mr. Lowell in Paris, and in England he desires to find Tennyson, Ruskin and Browning. Then he shall be ready to go home. He never speaks of the beauty of views here, I am sorry to notice, but he often does mention certain trees that he likes to see. There is a banyan under his window that interests him very much—it is very handsome—and the pepper he likes very well. He has been cheerful ever since we came to Cairo, and Mr. Bancroft's being here was a great blessing. They spent most of those days together. Mr. Charles G. Leland is here in the Hotel, and Mr. Hare and his wife and one of the daughters have just gone. Mr. Leland's talk interests Father, so his calls are pleasant, and Mr. Hare often amused him. One day he told us that half the reason why things cost so much in Egypt was that "all the shoddy Americans rushed over here to get the baptism of respectability in the waters of the Nile, and spent right and left till foreigners were regarded as made of money." And Father laughed afterwards and said he usually had some malice in his talk but he was bright about it too. Yesterday was New Year's Day, and at six o'clock we went over to General Stone's to dine. There was a very attractive daughter who can already talk Arabic like English. The only other guest was Colonel Ward, also American. We had a very pleasant evening. I am glad I have been there and heard about the sickness and the doctors, for

— 1873 —

Father is quite sick today and now I know which way to turn. I am going to take Curnex and go over there and ask about the doctor and have C. find his house, so that if Father wakes up no better I can send for him. I have been so unlucky as to leave my Aconite, Bryonia and Nux Vomica on the steamboat, and have no medicines but Brandy and Jamaica Ginger, which do not seem the thing for fever, and this seems to be fever as far as it is anything. Probably it is only a day's disorder. But I started with the intention of telling you how greenly Father looked at Egypt when we first landed. He was full of dismally witty speeches against it all the way from Alexandria to Cairo. They were all to the effect that it was a hopeless marsh, and could anything argue wilder insanity than our leaving a country like America and coming all this way to see the bareness of mud, not even an inhabitant. At last he called me, pointed, and said, "There is some water! And see, there is a crowd of people. They have collected with the purpose of drowning themselves." I thought we saw beautiful sky and charming sunset lights, and I keep thinking so, but Father never acknowledges it. You ought to have seen the clear yellow & then rose of a cloudless sky this morning between halfpast six and seven, with the banyan trees against it. You ought to see how pretty a minaret is, and what a capital figure in a landscape a pyramid can be. There's a great deal of haze almost every day, and the weather is cold. We had hoped for 80° but we find 58°, and they say here as in Boston, "when the days begin to lengthen, the cold begins to strengthen." If Father is well enough, our party will visit the pyramids tomorrow. A detachment of six yesterday visited the palace & palace gardens. Father said the gardens were magnificent. Your shipwreck letter has come. Ten thousand thanks for writing & drawing it all out for us. It was a pity you couldn't see Father hearing it. Thank Annie for her enchanting letter about your return, it was perfect bliss to Father & me, and every scrap of Concord news was so precious. Edward, I haven't told thee the half of what I long to, and yet I can't.
Ellen T. Emerson.

Cairo. 3rd January 1873

Dearest, faithfullest Edith,

On New Year's morning as I opened the door I saw Father coming along the passage. He caught me with Happy New Year! and held me out a letter. It was from Alice Bartlett. She had given it to him to give to me on that occasion, and he said he had suffered agonies of responsibil-

— 1873 —

ity with it. The morning was full of shopping and visits from Miss Farquahr, and the Whitwells. On Monday before leaving Rome we dined at Mr Marsh's, the American Minister's. Mrs M. was very kind & thoughtful in all she did for us, and on this occasion told me beforehand all the foreign convives who would come, so that I expected no English speakers at all. No sooner did I arrive than I was introduced to Mme Gianotti, but Mrs M kindly added "who was Miss Kinney" so I began in peace with English. Then Mrs Marsh said "I know you don't like trying languages so Dr Wister will take you in to dinner & Signor Minghetti on your other side can talk English." That was a great pleasure, for Dr W. is one of the most delightful of men. Father had as good a time as I. To come back to yesterday which I suddenly disgressed from, I wrote to Edward and began to think it was time for New Year's breakfast. Father came in about five o'clock. I called to him that he might hear Alice's letter, and he came running and having heard it exclaimed that it was the sincere speech of a good girl. Then I spread the feast, reminded him what was going on at home, and presented him with a poem and a purse, and he was charmed. Then did I open my present from Will, oh! what riches! And then I opened yours, what oriental magnificence! I put on the gorgeous broad scarf and swelled about in it for some time. I send my thanks. Yes we had a very cheerful New Years. And now I have just got the mail after abstinence of 18 days, and it was a fat & satisfying bundle. I called Father, who is well again today and we began with Edward's steamer letter and Father was almost slain both with terror & with laughter from beginning to end. The lunch-bell rang, and he wouldn't stir to go down till the letter was finished. Immediately after lunch he went with the Whitwells to see the whirling dervishes. This is their Sabbath.

I must put in a synopsis of the past. Landed in Alexandria Christmas day. I stayed in exhausted; the rest waded through mud and saw Cleopatra's Needle and Pompey's pillar. Thursday morning we divided. Mrs. W., May and Bessy stayed behind; Mr. W., Father, Miss Farquhar and I with Curnex came to Cairo.

Friday Miss Farquhar and I on donkeys, Father and Mr. W. on foot, visited bankers, post offices, consulates, all the forenoon. We found Mr. Bancroft at same Hotel but off on an excursion. He came home at night, received us joyfully and affectionately, and we dined with him and spent the evening in his rooms, General Stone being also his guest. Saturday all day Miss F. and I did shopping with Abdel, a dragoman in green. Father and Mr. Bancroft went to the Museum. The dragomen besieged Mr. Whitwell for the honour and profit of taking the party up the Nile. Sunday Mr. B. and Father breakfasted with the Khedive, the ruler of the country, and Miss F. and I went to church. The Whitwell family came from Alexandria, and we changed Hotel. It is curious when every shepherd is an abomination to the Egyptians that the best Hotel is Shepherd's Hotel. We are now dwelling there. Monday Mr. Bancroft went to Brindisi (Italy) and Mr. and Mrs. Hare wanted us to look at a steamer that was going up the Nile. We looked and refused, saw the dahabeah and liked it. In the afternoon to the Tunis bazaar with Abdel, a beautiful expedition. Tuesday Miss Farquhar & I spent in my room reading Conybeare & Hansen's Life of St Paul & doing our mending. Wednesday was New Years Day and I have described it. Thursday Father was sick. He slept all the afternoon, woke feeling brighter, liked a cup of hot tea, read a little afterward, then went to bed and was well in the morning. They went to the Howling Dervishes in the afternoon and Father came home simply wearied and disgusted with the sight, which interested no one. This morning, Saturday, they have all gone off to the pyramids & I discovered Father had gone without his overcoat, so I have given it to Curnex, now, about three in the afternoon, and told him to saddle an ass and ride out into the desert and meet the party before sundown. I hope to get Father home safe by that means, and consider that Curnex earns his wages for the whole month by this single service. I am also daily thankful when I go to walk and Father doesn't that I needn't go unattended, for it strikes me as more risky here than in Rome and Paris, where you hear it is risky though it doesn't seem so. Thursday morning I sent for my clean clothes (promised on Tuesday) for the fourth time, and Curnex returned in consternation. "The laundry was burned down last night and the secretary sends his compliments, and is sorry but your clothes is all burned up." By good luck I hadn't put in Father's flannels, so his set is still entire. But all my new clothes I grudged to the flames. I sent by Miss Farquhar, who had also lost hers and went to buy new, and she brought me enough to take the voyage comfortably, for 36 francs. If you see Pauline, tell her my pride in my dressing-case is ever new. I find it delightful, and if she could only be by to hear Father go on about the corkscrew that is in it she would be amused. He says the man who invented that is equal to Columbus, and asks who gave it to me, where it was made, whether anyone ever had one before, and romances over it as he does about the Tangerinas. He takes the same pleasure in the writing-case Miss Forbes gave him, says a great deal about it, uses it every day, and keeps raising monuments to the memory of her wisdom in choosing it. When he was sick the mosquito-net bothered him and he looped it up. When I came in he said, "See my net. I have displayed great talent in arranging it. The spiders envied me when they saw me do it." Well he has come home from the Pyramids delighted. Curnex caught him with the coat, but he was warm enough riding a donkey and wouldn't put it on. Good-night.

E. T. E.

Saturday. January 4th

Dear Edith,

When the letters came yesterday the same old scene was renewed, Father thinking every one was for him and always disappointed. At last Mr Forbes's appeared, and seemed to satisfy him. Later Will's separated itself from one it had stuck to. It was to him and he felt much better. Up to this moment I have been practically the miserable invalid, though pretty well, and Father feels quite discouraged and astonished. He says to everyone "She used to be a great hardy girl. I don't know where she learned all these whims." But now my foot is strong. Unluckily I am to be confined to a small boat for five weeks, and I am afraid I shall lose rather than gain. It looks to me as if I should get very little chance to write in the Nile weeks. We must have readings aloud to get the party acquainted, and some of the time I shall sit with Father. Of course writing will be my joy, but I shall sacrifice it to the general well-being of the party and success of the trip. Father feels as I knew he would, unwilling now to put a hair's breadth between him & home. I fear you'll see him by 1 May. He won't hear of going to Athens, says he has decided to give up Venice, not to stay in Rome, nor make one stop between there & Paris. I trust that pleasant weather, my being well, and the pleasure he takes in staying still, will operate a relaxing of these grim resolves when we get back to Rome. The visit to Mr Hodgson was abandoned, as Mr Tennyson couldn't come. Tell Mother I don't speak to her today but only because I'm preparing the next letter for her. And now beloved a good kiss & farewell!

E. T. E.

— 1873 —

Cairo Jan 4th 1873

Dear Will,

You always give me enchanting things, and you have again, and I am proud & thankful. Also two days after them came a letter from you, an immense gratification to your sister of Africa. I love to be written to & comforted & told that I'm not in the path to ruin though it is suspiciously broad & easy to travel. I was very glad to hear of the journey to Washington. I find that our expenses, which are now paid up to the 10th of February, are 360£ since we left England. That will be three months exactly, and I fear when we get home we shall find it has cost four thousand dollars. Father however has thought and talked about it since we left Dover and says he is willing it should turn out so much. Our man is a comfort, and when Father sees him fighting at depots, he exclaims that he is worth a hundred dollars an hour at such times. He & I were most thankful for your letter to him, and your Father's.

E. T. E.

Syoot Egypt. Jan 12th 1873

Dear Mother,

You asked how Father felt about the newspaper slips. If it is a slip about the college, he is pleased. If it is about Mr Greely or Dickens he is displeased. Judge Hoar's letter and that about Mr Tyndall's lecture, and both the Mark Twain letters have been his perfect delight. The Mrs Cheney lecture and Mr Phillips's he at first received with disdain (because there was so much less writing in your letter than its weight promised) and wouldn't look at them. A week later he read them with interest, when he had no letters in his eye. Today we have been a week on the Nile, and I cannot yet tell whether Father likes it or not. I think he is lonely without any companion—without me too to all intents & purposes, because there is no place where I can go and sit alone with him. But it is doubtless very good for him to sit on deck all day long as he does, and I hope when we come to seeing the wonders up the river he will be really interested & happy. Everyone else enjoys the voyage, we have been shaking down and getting acquainted. We have a general reading on Egypt two hours a day, and every other day Miss F. & I read C. & Hansen's Life of Paul. They elected me mistress, for that isn't Miss Farquhar's nature, and Mrs Whitwell has come to avoid every atom of responsibility, so won't even pour out coffee—and I rule with a more undivided sway than at Monadnoc even. No one will even vote usually, and I say now read, now stop, now go ashore, this you must do yourselves and that you must let the servant do, you may have butter at this meal and at that you mustn't ask for it, you must dress for dinner, and so on. The loyalty and obedience of the party is beautiful—couldn't be surpassed. It is a great responsibility at first to establish manners and customs that shall please everybody and wear well, and of course I feel every jar and discontent as others do not, but the progress towards success and happiness in one week is all that could have been hoped for and table talk at last begins to flourish, the last best flower of all. I was afraid, I told Edith, that I shouldn't prosper in health on the water, but I found that almost every day I could have an hour on shore and we all rejoice greatly in the privilege of walking to and fro in all the land of Egypt, sometimes in fields of onions and cucumbers (Num. XI 5), sometimes through mud cities, or palm-groves which are really beautiful and romantic and utterly unlike New England, once in the mountains of the desert and the dens and caves that abound in them more than I had imagined. That especially was perfect bliss. It felt like Monadnoc, and being the first scramble since Naushon, my ankle was wild with joy, and I couldn't have enough climbing and jumping. Father is just saying to Mrs. Whitwell that it says in the Bible that "The strength of the Egyptians is to sit still," and he thinks the Yankee learns that strength for the first time when he comes to Egypt. The Nile is very muddy and winds so much that we seem to be all the time in a large muddy pond, and only once in a while do we get lights on it that make the water beautiful. Every day is pleasant, nothing less than heavenly (if it were only 10° warmer! It hovers round 60° and we are comfortable in the sun on the deck and in the cabin, but oh! if it were 70° we could get up early and have the delight of dawn and sunrise. Now it is too cold). The moon was three days old when we started. Our deck is the most cosy parlour you ever saw, without walls or ceilings, and we are apt to sit on our sofas wrapped in blankets and talk through the beautiful brilliant moonlight evenings. The palms disappointed me in Cairo, and I see a date-palm is different from the beauties in pictures, but take great groves of them here on the banks of the Nile and they are handsome. The desert on the East side shows us the boundary-line, and though not more than three miles off, is apt to have opal-colouring all day; clouds near the horizon are sometimes rose-coloured even at noon.

— 1873 —

The camels, donkeys, buffaloes and natives on the shore are every moment entertaining. The crew! words fail me! Happily May Whitwell sketches, and you will see pictures. Our dragoman is named Bedowi Mahmoud. Our waiters are Mazouk and Hassan. They delight in teaching us Arabic, and I can understand and answer several questions and greetings. Bessy is already quite glib with it. She is pretty, and is our picture when we are downstairs. No more to-day.
      Your affectionate daughter
        Ellen T. Emerson

      Thebes—in other words Luxor Jan 21st 1873
Dear Edith,
 You & Mother are waiting for some account of our life here. I find poor Father is in the frame that he styles Dr. Crump, and finds the sky a copal black, so that I am often in doubt whether I did well to come, but looking back always makes me sure I decided right at the time every time, and it is evident that he prospers in health, and when he gets home he may look back on it as all pleasure. Now imagine, we have at last come to a place where the therm. is at 70. All day long that man is out in the broadest sweetest sunshine that the heart of man can conceive of, and he has a ten hours' night every night. It is true that he has nothing to amuse or interest him, for he has read out his small library except Martial, which he works at for hours daily, and he doesn't particularly enjoy seeing the scenery or the ruins because he is Dr. Crump, and never has had the luck since Cairo of meeting anyone who enlivened him, but perhaps this utter emptiness of life is rest and will prove good for him. Today he is actually in treaty with Bedowy to prolong the voyage to Phylœ—that is 10 days—and it shows he is willing to have more rather than less of it after all. I must now begin my own song of glory about this enchanting place. It is incredibly beautiful, and the days are all of them like our first-class days. Imagine standing in a doorway of a light yellow stone and looking up. What acres of light and sky you see! Such blue sky, like over Gay Head. Imagine seeing through vistas of columns a patch of greenest green grass, then smooth water, then mountains of fabulous pink and violet and every colour that belongs only in pictures, then this sky. Then again get up on the roof of a temple and look out in each direction—plains wide enough to content the most greedy eye, covered with this amazing verdure, plenty of palm-trees now of the regulation shape, quite outdoing the pictures,

— 1873 —

the Nile smooth enough to take the sky and be blue shining water, mountains whose colours I have named but not their shapes, which make me keep looking again to see if it wasn't a mistake, if they were really so interesting and lovely, ruins to set off all the rest, yea and Memnon and his brother (whom the Arabs call Shamy and Damy—oh my happy ears! Shamy! & Damy!) sitting there in the green expanse looking on—and this sun all round you comforting and warming you to the heart's core, and this endless blue sky, so that you feel distinctly that you are breathing the sun and sky and all in it. Then you come down and mount the world's proudest throne, a donkey, and ride through the green and up to a mountain which is so polite as to have a door, and you walk in expecting a deathly chill. No indeed, that mountain is as warm inside as out, so you are happy, and a candle being lighted, the mountain shows you the manners and customs of the ancient inhabitants. You come home to your boat tired in a most comfortable way and it seems homelike and clean and quiet, and washing feels so good and Nile water is so acceptable to drink (when filtered) that you are ready to say it is the best you ever had (but it isn't up to Fairyland spring). Then comes such a sunset with all the accessories, except that it is apt (though not sure) to be cloudless, and up peeps the evening star and makes a path of light on the water, and it is warm on deck all the evening under the constellations. You see I am happy. Give my love to Mother. Beseech her to write. I'm sitting up late. Good-night.
            E. T. E.

                  Luxor Jan 24th 1873
Dear Edward,

  I hear of one more chance for a letter and I must have a minutes talk with you. We arrived three days ago, first day to Medinet Abou, great temple with monster columns & monster intaglio pictures on the walls and every part of wall & pillar hieroglyphic'd over, painted too, and something of the paint left everywhere. A ruin offers as good climbing as a mountain, and I at once started for the roof, encountering much botheration from the beggars & donkey boys who scampered before & on all sides, like a cloud of horseflies round Dolly's head, and showed me the way which I wouldn't take and I mounted in hot altercation with them all. Once on the roof I could run about at will, but when I saw a tower & made for that the wretched guide seemed to go mad with terror, and to implore & threaten. I threatened him if he dared interfere or help and got up to an enchanting window. Then came Mr Whitwell and we found the garret stairs, beauties, in perfect preservation, and by degrees the party all came up and enjoyed trying them as partridges are said to love to walk in a little path. In the afternoon we went to Gourneh & saw a statue of the most beautiful granite (black & bright red) I ever saw, twice as big as Shamy & Damy, polished too, knocked all to pieces, & we felt dreadfully. Then into tomb 35, where we found Dr Ebers of Leipsic, a charming man who showed us what everything meant. Next day to Karnak, big as promised, but utterly perplexing. We enjoyed saying "Here is the hawk-, dog-, ibis-headed deity," almost as much as if we knew what we meant, but not quite. In the afternoon we met a Philadelphia party who imparted to us a valuable secret, viz. that buildings are embellished with the seals of the kings, and since then Mr W. & I have one real interest & delight hunting, copying & verifying these seals. I soon saw my way to the roof and was climbing with delight when a troublesome man saw me and with exclamations of alarm gave chase. I barked at him till he desisted, and had gone some stages in peace when I heard him again. I turned. He had gone and brought Curnex. I told him to leave me alone, and soared on. When I had reached a commanding height I saw his next expedient and couldn't but laugh. He had got Mr. Whitwell and was guiding him up. I stood and enjoyed the wonderful view till their heads came in sight, when he called, as if he was sure he had done what I wanted, "Mees! Mees! Gentleman!" and a broad grin of complacency accompanied his words. We trotted about the roof awhile, and when they started down, both were afflicted that I wouldn't come by the easier way. Wednesday we went to the tombs of the kings. If I don't see Sahara, I have had at least that long ride in a world consisting entirely of sun and sky and sand and stones. It put us all in higher spirits than any entertainment we have yet had. We rode along laughing at nothing. Suddenly when we had seen nothing in particular, the guide stopped the donkeys. "Tomb 17, sir." So we looked round and saw a door in the hillside, lighted our candles, and entered. Truly a very interesting palace, and very elaborately frescoed and stuccoed. When we had seen one story, we went down and saw another. The snake was all over the walls. I wondered at him. After several descents we burned a magnesium wire in the grandest hall which was very handsome. Mummy found here has gone to London. Coming into next hall was a long staircase leading down. Guide said it went nowhere. Father asked him to take the candle

— 1873 —

down. I went too. It lasted forever. I wondered whether they could still see us from above. At last I heard cries of "Where are you going to?" and knew we must be disappearing. Still no sign of an end. Down we went. The guide got ahead. I saw the walls narrow a little & that the stair turned to the right. Down again till my fears began to rise, and at last there was so low a passage we should have to crawl. Here I turned back & found Father not far above with another guide. That poor man had been scared at seeing me disappear in the bowels of the earth, and had gone down 70 steps after me & had to climb them again. I am very sorry, but he didn't say a word. We penetrated other tombs—9 and 11—but none so fine as this, though interesting in other ways. Coming back we met Dr Eber, happy in having just discovered a brand new one, till that morning unknown to Europeans. Father & Mr W. have made a new contract with Bedowy and we sail tomorrow for Assouan and Phyloe. We hear the Wards & Clover [Hooper Adams] are anchored at Phyloe. Now we may not get back to Rome by 1 March. You won't hear again for 3 weeks. I'm keeping Father up, and will only say that he is feeling happy today, and proposed settling here & never going home. Edward, I'm so thankful thy shoulder has healed!

Ellen T. Emerson.

Have lilac hedge cut down. Have new fence built. Cut down greening at parlour S. window.

Nile between Edfou and Assouan
Monday January 27th 1873

My dear daughter [Edith Davidson],

We are having a most beautiful sail in true heaven-weather, every day the enchanting cloudless blue & reviving sun, every night the stars in full glory and an evening warm enough to allow us to lie on deck and watch them. Yea, I even go to bed with both windows of my berth wide open, so that as I lie I can see the stars, and that is a pleasure I have often coveted and have never enjoyed except at Monadnoc. Towards morning it grows cold & I shut one. You would enjoy learning to manage a latteen sail. We have two, a big one at the bow & a little one at the stern. I can only have the pleasure of looking at them. They have a blue striped edge, very pretty, and are always in a pretty position. The shadows on them by moonlight are beautiful. Our sailors are a constantly changing picture. Understand once for all that a brown man is handsomer than a white, and I won't keep repeating it. Whenever I

— 1873 —

speak of Captain, sailor, dragoman, donkey-boy, little girl, beggar, baby, always picture to yourself an absolutely handsome person with a superb gait, beautiful teeth, a brilliant smile, and most picturesque array—for the Egyptians are a very handsome race and their brownness greatly enhances their beauty. You may imagine the first personages quite clean too, the rest more dirty than anything you ever saw, their faces covered with flies and their eyes quite surrounded with them. Now I want to tell you what happened this morning. Our Captain is the most *respectable* (in the French sense) man we have seen in Egypt. He has a fine face, a white beard, immense dignity. He is very skillful, vigilant & silent. He wears a crimson turban, a long blue robe, & a brown cloak faced with crimson, with a hood. This morning arose a great shouting when we were all sitting on deck in the sun. "What is it?" we asked our dragoman. He pointed to a moored boat on the bank & said "The Captain's son is on that boat." As we approached, a small boat with a big latteen sail left the other boat, crossed our course with four men in her, but one so beautifully conspicuous that no one doubted that he was the son. As he passed over our bow a rope was thrown him. He jumped on board, a stately fellow, and kissed his hand as he alighted. Then with such a smile! that hand went to his father's shoulder while he kissed him first on one cheek then on the other twice over, then stepped back, laid his hand on his heart, and gave it to his father. One shake, and again on his heart and another shake. I never saw anything as pretty as this, though every meeting of relatives or dear friends is lovely here. His following seemed to have friends in our crew. There was much beautiful salutation on all sides, some with smiles of delight, some with a gravity that went equally to one's heart. We have a sailor named Hassaine who is a born ladies' man. He began to attract our attention the moment we came on board. He loves to go with us as guide and teach the girls Arabic. He points at the sun and tells us it is *Shems*, or at the stars and tells us they are *Nagoum*, and the moon is *Gamma*, besides making a great deal of conversation that we cannot understand. There never was so good a chance for astronomy, and we are learning some constellations as we sit on deck in the evenings. The Whitwells know a great many.

Phylœ, or rather Assouan. Jan 29th. We arrived last night at Assouan and tomorrow shall begin our voyage home. Here the weather is so perfect that I'm afraid we shall be dissatisfied with it in France & England. I wish you could see the Abyssinians on the shore close under

— 1873 —

me who are trying to make me look at their swords & shields & javelins & buy some of them. Their hair is rather woolly & very black, and they are black themselves, but their robes are wound and looped round them as they are in pictures & statues round saints & ancient men, just in the way that I have always believed was impossible in reality because it must be so hard to arrange, and when arranged surely wouldn't stay. However it does stay quite well, and with the hair which lies on their shoulders, or rather flies out behind, they look like black Hamlets to me. I feel like bestowing on you some good advice. Be prepared before you come abroad by some knowledge of the history & people of each country you are going to. Knowing absolutely nothing I miss so much. Every interest I have ever had comes in beautifully, but then they are so few. My Tacitus was worth everything to me in Rome. My Viri Romae I had not properly entered into. One must know mythology perfectly. My education in that was uncommonly thorough, probably better than any other girl of my generation got, yet in the last twenty years much has leaked away and I was in despair because I didn't know mythology. Again Mrs Wister asked me how it happened that no Boston girl was versed in the Acta Sanctorum and all the legendary History of the Church. "They are at such disadvantage when they see pictures" she said. In France the books that helped me most of all were Cinq Mars and Mme. de Montagu. They had made me acquainted not only with people & with much history, but with different parts of France, & made me interested from end to end of the country. England I haven't yet seen. Rome & Egypt are the only places I have seen much of—a little of Florence. And how much do I know of Florentine history? Two things: the vote to build the Cathedral, Father has read me, and the misty impressions that I retain from reading Dante of his relations to the city. So my advice is, read & understand & care for many things before you come abroad. One more piece of experience: travelling abroad is nothing like so pleasant as staying at home. I always supposed it was delightful, and was very much surprised & disappointed when first Cousin Elizabeth & then Edith showed in their letters that they were glad their journeyings were soon to end. Aunt Lizzy said, "Yes, one enjoys seeing things but one doesn't enjoy one's *self* as one does at home." Don't understand that I am not having as good a time as any one ever had—everything perfect—and I at last strong enough to use my advantages, only to cheer you up now and to moderate your ecstasy when the time comes for you to go to Europe, I tell you that for real

— 1873 —

happiness, home and work go utterly beyond anything in the world. I am thankful to have seen the beauty of this land of Egypt, and I find an unexpected pleasure in seeing Bible country. I supposed I shouldn't care much about it, but it is a great amusement to see how the Bible words describe things, and how little words & expressions are really accurate. I have not yet received any letter from you since the one of December 1st, but I suppose at Cairo I shall find one. If not I shall forgive thee because of all thy cares & labours, and my own sins. Goodbye my beloved bairn.

Ellen T. Emerson.

Assouan, Egypt. Jan 29th 1873.

Dear Mother,

Behold I am at the goal of our pilgrimage, and tomorrow we start on our way back. One month more of Egypt, a week or ten days of Italy, a fortnight of Paris, and we shall be in England, where I hope Father will stay seven weeks, though it is more likely to be six. We came to Assouan at the first cataract of the Nile yesterday. If you look in the Bible you will find the tower of Syene mentioned several times. That and Phylœ are just above the first cataract, and Father has gone there, at least to Phylœ. I am not sure that Syene, whose tower is gone, is in the programme. Alas! a great blow awaited him here. To see Mr Ward has been his great desire, never out of his mind a moment. We found on arriving that the quarantine was removed and the Wards and Adamses had sailed on Saturday for the second cataract, so we shall come to Concord without seeing them. Just before this news I went into Father's room and saw Curnex bring in his best coat and a collar washed and ironed in civilization. He had ordered out his gorgeous raiment. Now it might return to his trunk. He also called Bedowy, "I shan't want the donkey now." He had charged him to have a donkey called the moment we arrived that he might lose no time in riding to Phylœ. I don't like to have my Papa disappointed. I went down early to dress for dinner, and soon May came to say that Bessy and I must hurry up for some Englishmen had come to call and were on deck. When I came up there were three, one beside Father. I sat near Father and had the pleasure of hearing Mr. Owen talk as well as Willy or Harry James would. Unexpected joy! There was a companion for Father while he stayed. In a few moments a new pleasure. Mr. Whitwell invited them all to stay and dine, and Mr. Owen and Mr. Elliot accepted. Father went

— 1873 —

to his room and donned the gorgeous raiment after all, and I, being invited to place the guests, set Mr. Owen and Father together. A very gay dinner we had, though all the time of soup and chicken Mr. Owen was quite turned away from Father, and Father sat silent and solitary. I was very sorry, but about the middle of the next course I found a conversation was springing up between them, and it was not dropped again. After dinner May told me that Mr. O. said to her in the second or third course, "Can you tell me, is this Mr. Emerson related to the writer?" "It is he himself," she told him. "And have I been talking so to *him* without knowing it?" he said. "Henceforth my silence shall be golden!" He then proceeded to tell her how Father had been his idol and his guide from his earliest youth. Soon afterwards he began to talk with Father again. After dinner the gentlemen invited us to tea with them. They said their boat lay next to ours, that they had no other party—were her only passengers—if we would come over they would like to show it and their birds to us, and to-morrow morning they started for Cairo. We went over and Mr. Owen heaped incense and offerings on Father's shrine—not only then, but came over this morning before sailing, bringing over "the book he most valued in the world, his Shakespeare," and asked Father to write his name in it, also a Religio Medici with an inscription as a present to Father. So Father wrote name and date and place in the Shakespeare, and I am happy to record that he wrote it very well, and after once refusing, accepted the R. M. for the sake of the inscription. Then they bade farewell, returned to their dahabeya, and with the salutes of firearms on both sides they started homeward. They told May and Bessy that till last Saturday there were 17 boats lying here, all full of English and Americans who did everything together—picnics, parties, and dinners and constant calls had made them all acquainted—and they had had a delightful time, but last Saturday seven went up, and five had gone down since. They had never seen the Wards before, but knew them now quite well. Such stories fired Father's heart and those of the girls with envy and despair.

I cannot tell certainly whether there is any change in Father's spirits, but I feel sure it is for the better rather than for the worse since I wrote last. For me, I am getting very much attached to my quarters here. I wish you could see my little white and yellow room with its two windows. It seemed too small to squeeze into at all when I first entered it, but now if I was told I should never own a larger, I shouldn't repine for a moment. I have learned to use it and keep it in order with comfort and ease. The joys of the world and the weather cannot be overstated. Every moment of each twenty-four hours is perfect in every respect. Miss Farquhar has abandoned any idea of other occupation than taking it all in. She wonders at the rest of us that we can sew, read and stay down below and lose the moments from gazing. Poor May can sketch, devotes herself to it most of the time, and is in constant despair at the unapproachable beauty of nature and man in Egypt.

Luxor. February 1st

We have come as far as Thebes on our way down, and find our Englishmen again here. The Whitwells dine with them to-night. There are many boats here—four American—and Bessy knows some of the people. We do not. I often promise myself I will tell you little particulars, and then forget them when I am writing. Did I say that Mustapha Agar, the English Consul, sent his Arabian horse with regular circus trappings, blue velvet and gold, and tassels and ornamental bridle and head-stall for Father to ride to Karnak on, and two donkeys in gorgeous red and blue robes for Mrs. and Mr. Whitwell? And did I say that Ali Fendi Murrad, the American consul, hearing of these civilities, hastened to outdo them and invited us all to come and spend a month at his house? They are enemies and alternated their visits, explaining what guided their conduct. It was rather uncomfortable, I thought, but the gentlemen didn't mind the English consul's visits, as he spoke English, and seemed a worthy man. He gave us a letter to a friend at Assouan, who immediately made a call and sent us his donkeys in the morning for Phylœ. This morning we took a walk at Herment and met Mr. Owen and Mr. Elliot there. We were admitted to a garden for a walk, and saw oranges, bananas and lemons growing—also pears half ripe. I was puzzled to know when they blossomed. They looked doubtful and uncomfortable, as if they had been taken in. I am writing to Edward of the delights of yesterday, and so won't mention them here; but I will put in that I have given Father summer-clothes for the last two weeks, and his surtout lies neglected. It is real summer weather. The summer overcoat is very useful in the evenings. His outfit as well as mine is very perfect. When we go on excursions Curnex carries his chocolate bag with the Murray, the opera-glass, and the little tumbler, and ought to carry the coat, but that Father doesn't allow. I wear my white silk waist that Edith gave me, and when cold put on my scarlet over it. When I sit down in cellar-like ruins for lunch I am most thankful for the small eider down black waist you made me bring, and I have been very glad of it all the winter—sometimes I have felt like extolling it as you do, as the greatest possible convenience. It is Saturday night and we hear there is a Coptic Church in Luxor so we go there tomorrow. The Copts are the Egyptians who have retained the Xn religion once prevalent in Egypt, but most of the population has adopted the religion of their Arab conquerors. And now it's too dark to write and the last moment has come. So goodnight from a most affectionate daughter.

Ellen T. Emerson

On the way to Luxor. Jan 31st 1873.

Dear Edward,

You know I never did want to see anything without you, and yesterday in the delight of seeing Edfou I missed you more than ever. Hitherto the temples we have seen have been enough in ruins to baffle the most faithful endeavors to imagine what they were meant for, and we are as ignorant of how they once looked as of their purposes. But by blessed fortune one of them was early and almost completely buried and lately dug out by the government. The thoughtful & industrious Persian had been there and carefully picked away the bas-relief of every god & goddess on the walls, even up to the third tier, only, as Father called us to notice, he had spared their petticoats. Except for this, the temple was in perfect preservation. I have never till then been really pleased with the temples we have seen, but now I was. It made me want to be an artist that I might keep and carry home for you the effects of the different courts of the temples. Feb. 10th. Now, I'm sorry I am so long separated from them that what I write must be reminiscence rather than record. I wish I knew more Arabic. Every word I acquired was a precious treasure. When I came back to Cairo I found I understood something of all that went on around me, so much pleasanter than the helplessness of knowing nothing. Mem: When you go to Edfou, walk all round the outside & on the West side see what a beautiful piece of flower & fruit work there is. My genius doesn't run in that direction so it must have been remarkably interesting even to attract my eye. There was no time to sit down and draw it for you. And scarcely a particle of reading could I find time for. It was as it is at home. I had to absorb information; couldn't go to work to acquire it, so I was nearly unprepared for the intelligent study of the temples. I said in an early letter that we read Egypt aloud two or three hours every day. That lasted while I had command. In ten or fifteen days we got accustomed and felt enough at home to do without a government, and thenceforth all reading aloud ceased, so my only channel of communication with books was closed. I should say Edfou was my southernmost temple. We were there one morning, and the afternoon before we came to Edfou, we passed Silsileh. Imagine. A smooth face of rock rising out of the river cut with finished doorways all hieroglyphic'd leading right into the rock; through some you saw inner doorways. One part was cut into a piazza-like place and the neatly picked-out scars of ancient gods who sat in it of old time still remained. As we went up the river I looked at this place with special interest, hoping to get at it some time. When we came down, Bedowy indulgently put a plank from deck to shore and I was across it in an instant. No one else seemed to wish to go. I could only reach the piazza place, but liked it and planned camping there with you and Annie and Lizzy. Presently Bessy and her Mother came. We sat there and our feet hung over the Nile. The old gods heard a few Sunday school tunes. Presently we were recalled. Here all drifted beautifully smooth lay yellow fine sand wherever there was a passage from the West for it to blow through. I believe it was from Sahara—Sahara that I have so longed to see—and shall not see. I took a great handful. When I reached the boat it was a little one. But Mr. Whitwell was as much struck with it as I, and Bedowy at his suggestion sent a sailor with the pudding-dish and he brought it home full. A bottle of it has gone home in my pea-green chest. I loves it. Next came Edfou, then Esneh that I didn't see, then Thebes again. We went to the Rameseum and with the aid of Murray's plan and memory of Edfou understood it very well. For once Murray mentioned particular pictures and told what they meant. With glee I beheld Rameses with Amun-Re, Khonso, the goddess Maut, and Phthah, and saw him burn incense—actually found out that that curious spoon was a censer—saw him receive the sacred Tau, saw him smite his enemies hip and thigh. The dear mighty graven image that lies at the door of this temple awakened the indignation of the party against those who smashed it with such malicious thoroughness. It was so big it would have satisfied that desire of the eyes to behold vastness, which is so seldom satisfied, and it had been as minutely and smoothly worked as if it were marble and not coarsest granite. If they had let it alone 'twould have been as handsome to-day, and almost as shiny, as when first set up; that according to one book was 3000, by the other 3400 years ago. Then away we coursed to Medinet Abou. We approached in a different direction from what we did before,

— 1873 —

and I not recognizing it, though it was Dair which I knew Mr. Whitwell meant to omit. We were a 10 m. ride ahead. I commanded a halt, jumped down and felt uncommon joy at having by good luck a sight of such enchanting ruins that I might have wholly lost. When you go there, see if that palace doesn't take your fancy. I dared not wait a moment lest the donkey-train should sweep past, so rushed alone into the ruins and found a way into the tower of the Queens of Rameses, and looked up at my favourite view of Thebes through its windows, then compassionate of the anxiety of Papa at losing me, came down just in time, for he had discovered my absence, and he said the guide said this was Medinet Abou. The whole party arrived & swore to the same effect. Here Murray was quite full, and I had a little satisfaction out of it. We meant to go to Karnak once more the next morning, but it blew such a dust that we stayed on board most of the day. The next place was Denderah. By this time we were in company with the Clifts & Roosevelts of N.Y., the Clarks of Philadelphia, the four classmates, Nat Thayer, Merriam, Godey & Jay, also our friends Mr Owen & Mr Elliot. So the party to Dendera was large. My donkey's name was Masour. I want to record all my donkey's names. Sagów took me to Bibu el Melouk, and Sabruka to Karnak. This day Father's was named Abou Keefir, "very clevery donkey drink birra, drink Hasheesh." At Ballyana mine was named Assali ("You are like honey"), Father's Bulbul. At Beni Hassan Father's was Aktar (red) but I can't remember mine. Dendera was perfect & curious, not ancient, full of chambers, had staircases, & on the roof a small temple & more chambers; had sphinxes' heads on the capitals of the columns; had what they call a zodiac on the ceiling. I thought it rather a stretch of imagination. You can imagine no smell more suffocating and detestable than that of every part of an Egyptian temple that has a roof and four sides to it. Here as the temple was so perfect, there was a great deal to endure, and when I went into the subterranean passages and crawled into holes so small I could hardly get my hat through, it was intensified. I suppose no change of air ever got in there. But the sculpture in there had been spared by the Persian and Coptic Christians and was very perfect. In this temple there is said to be a portrait of Cleopatra, but the room is filled solid with sand which the Government chooses to keep there, so no one can see it. The next place was Abydos, ancient This. Here we rode over seven miles of what fully corresponds with an expression common in books, "rich plains," so green, the vegetation so rank and tall, the air so sweet with blossoms, the Egyptian animals, black sheep and goats, darling donkeys, big buffaloes, camels, grazing in great crowds, and many horses (we had scarcely seen any before). It was absolutely flat; the mountains on two sides stood up bare, abrupt and tall from its floor. Seven miles of width on this side (W.) the Nile overflows it. We came to this ancient temple, far older than Rameses II. He was 18th or 19th dynasty; this was built by Scthos I—he was of the 11th. This was 4000 years old. Here by happy chance we met Mr. Brugsch, Egyptologist. He told us what the chapels were for, who were the personages on the walls, what the pictures meant. Here we saw the famous tablet of Abydos, showing the succession of kings. Here Father had a talk with Mr. Rogers which he enjoyed. No more temples. After that tombs at Sioot, beauties, wide airy caves high in the mountains with broad doors looking out over beauteous, beauteous Egypt. A visit to the consul in the town and much shopping in the bazaar. Then tombs of private persons at Beni Hassan—very old—some beautifully cut with lotus pillars, some with painting on the walls, most interesting to those who can understand it, not to me.

Thy devoted sister,
E. T. E.

The end of our sight-seeing.

Luxor Feb. 3rd 1873

Dear Edith,

Your letter of 26 Dec. came to me unexpectedly yesterday, for I thought I shouldn't get it till I came to Keneb. You tell me much news for so short a letter, & much about Mother is good, but I'm disappointed that she should keep having colds. Every festivity that you & she go to is a piece of good fortune for me here in foreign lands. We are now great friends with four dahabeyas here at Thebes. We had a dinner-party last night, and beauteous was our boat as we crossed the Nile coming home from our day's excursion. Bedowy had strung the rigging with coloured lanterns. You should have seen the dinner. Bedowy is fond of show, and indulged his taste. When the fish was coming in I saw him in the passage (he is near-sighted) scrutinizing it and I looked with curiosity when it was put on the table. It was amusingly covered in a blanket of yellow sauce laid out in patterns with long thin string beans and slices of cucumber, the whole surrounded with a luxuriant wreath of sliced egg. The turkey had on gold paper ruffled pantalettes,

— 1873 —

and the chickens stretched their every wing and drumstick for aid from a pond of drawn butter with a fringed signal of distress apiece. After dinner our illuminated deck had a contest with the evening-star, the moon and the Nile, and we thought the latter could well afford the premium for one night to the circumscribed but powerful attractions of the brilliant and sociable out-door parlour. All the inhabitants of the neighbouring dahabeyas turned out and called on us. It was a great company, but I was too tired with twelve hours of going and two of dinner to feel like sitting up, and wasn't needed, so I went to bed. In the morning Miss Farquhar and I went to the Coptic Church. We were told on the way there were a thousand Coptic Christians here, and expected an immense congregation. This was what we found: a large church with a little cage on one side, one man and many shoes outside and twenty men and boys and one old woman inside, standing or sitting on the floor. Within a chancel and altar and a priest swinging a censer over the altar. The service was conducted in Coptic, a language none but the Bishop understands, but the little boys who formed full half of the congregation sang all the hymns—often started them—and helped the priest all through. They walked about inside their cage—at some points shook hands all round. The Bishop came late, intoned from Mark in Coptic, while a boy of ten received an Arabic book and followed in silence. The moment he ceased intoning, the little boy began to read aloud. I was told he was reading the same passage in the vernacular. The priest soon took it from him and read the rest himself. Then the priest consecrated the elements I was told—it was humming in a strange way, lifting cloth after cloth on the altar, using the censer, and sometimes giving it to the boys, who reaching up their little hands to the utmost were holding the candles all round him. Then a tall man with something in his shawl came round; a man reached a plate from a shelf and out of the shawl came three cakes which were brought on the plate to Miss F. and me and the consul, and then the man went into the men's place and gave one to each man and boy. I looked to see what they did. I think they put them into their garment answering to our pocket. Then he passed behind us. I turned round for the first time. There was a large cage of mud bricks within which I saw a woman or so—there may have been more—and the doorway swarmed with girls between three and twelve all holding their hands for cakes and receiving them—the babes with much clamour. Next bells were brought. Every one sang, the bells rang for some time, the priest seemed to dip the bread with care holding his other hand underneath lest a drop should fall, put it into the mouths of four little bits of boys, with the same care drank the wine, rinsed the tumbler and plate four times, drinking the rinsing. Gave the fifth rinsing to one boy, and the ceremony ended. No one else received. The Bishop then stood up & all the men approached and were blessed and dispersed. We were asked in to see the books and the altar, and showed the font in the women's cage, then asked up stairs to take coffee with the Bishop, but refused. I came away very much puzzled—of course disagreeably impressed by a part of it—but delighted with the prominent share of the children in the service and knowing very well that I had been in church—that was good—and most of all curious to know something about it all. I forgot to say that birds wild and tame assisted on the rafters, and three sheep came late and were turned out. Father is well. There has been talk of waiting till steamer of 27th February. I was sorry. To-day Father assures me that if he has to leave the boat and take cars from Rhoda to Cairo (100 miles) he means to catch the boat of 17th. That suits me much better. Let our house alone. There's no hurry about our moving in. Cousin E. will take us. Father and I are both very well. I haven't been so fat for many years. Father has real comfort in Mr. Owen. He has been calling on the consuls and I tell him that he shan't any more, he brings home so much spoil—stone monuments, wooden statues, yards of mummy cloth they give him. 'Twill take another trunk. Much love to Mother, Will and the Forbeses and Mary W. and Miss Roxy. Her name is one star of your letter.

E. T. E.

Steamer Egitto.
Harbour of Alexandria. Feb. 19th 1873.

Dear Mother,

I last sent letters from Luxor, since then we have been coming as fast as letters could come so I have sent none. Now I'll relate the history. Mr. Owen became a great comfort to Father and on several occasions took a long donkey-ride by his side, or sought his company at a picnic, and gave the poor man the single chance of congenial society that he had between Cairo and Cairo again. We fell in at Luxor with four boats, and they had among them sixteen or more passengers. We swelled the company to something like 25, and one night the Dongola invited all to a dance and supper. Father went, and came home pleased with young

— 1873 —

Nat Thayer, but charmed with the behaviour of Frank Merriam, who had sung college songs, played for the dancing with a whistled accompaniment, then danced himself, all so well, so easily and unconsciously that Father was proud to have the English see what accomplishments and good manners our country could give. He really enjoyed that evening. Also he liked donkeys nearly as much as I, though with less enthusiasm. It must have been good for him—all this donkestrian exercise—and he usually seemed very gay while mounted, though sometimes he had a slow donkey and he had apparently an ambition to be at the head of the caravan. The driver keeps the donkey agoing sometimes with a stick or goad, but oftener by applying his nails or teeth to the root of the creature's tail. This always amused Father. He called it "a graceful method," and said he observed whenever "the pinch was removed the donkey paused for reflection," and he and Mr. Whitwell keenly felt their inability to start their beasts for themselves. The last excursions I carried my camp-stool and Father joyfully brandished the stick all the way in his hand as if it gave him increase of control. He liked the names of the donkeys and laughed very much over Bulbul. Another thing I have valued for him, and he for himself: this winter in an orange country. Of course he has never tasted such oranges before, and he for a long time expressed new surprise and pleasure every day, they were so good. He also sometimes has said that he felt they did him real good, and thought it must be good for everyone to have them so steadily. Dear Mamma, I know you are planning as you read to have more boxes of oranges than ever. But remember, those are a very different thing. He is getting spoiled for those. He says, "I think at home that an orange is a very different fruit, but these are very good." We are, to be sure, in the native land of the date rather than the orange, but the effect of the date on Father is quite different. He tries them once in a fortnight perhaps and exclaims, "This is a very poor food! Can't you give me a pine chip?" And I see with wonder how very dry is the every-day date of the Arab. Sticky ones like ours are to be had, but they are not what the people expect to live upon. These are to ours as a wine-biscuit is to soft molasses gingerbread. May Whitwell and I like them better than ours; the others not. On one dahabeah were the Roosevelts of N.Y., friends of Mr. G. C. Ward. Father and Mother, one daughter of 20, and three children under 13—Elly, a boy who is a born naturalist and always carries his gun, Theodore, and Corinne. Enchanting children—healthy, natural, well-brought-up, and with beautiful

— 1873 —

manners. By degrees we came to like this family very much, and as we returned from the tombs at Beni Hassan, Mrs. R. asked Father and me to come and lunch with them. We agreed, but first went to our boat to get brushed. Almost before we were ready, the pretty little light boat the Roosevelt children used was waiting alongside, and we were rowed over to the Abou Erdan by Theodore, whose round red cheeks, honest blue eyes, and perfectly brilliant teeth make him a handsome boy, though plain. He rowed with a pair of sculls, and a sailor behind him with another, talking to us as I hope Ralph will talk when he is three years older and as big as Theodore. Oh how much I enjoyed that visit! I approved all I saw, I felt the comfort of a family, I had the delight of seeing children again, and we agreed together and could talk endlessly. It came to an end all too soon, and we saw them no more. We reached Mimih that afternoon, Wednesday the 12th, rowed on in the night to Kolosna, and in the morning (Thursday) Father, Miss Farquhar and I took the train for Cairo, we were so desperately afraid we might miss this boat which was to sail Monday 17th. An Englishman whom we all liked was our sole companion in the car. We got well acquainted in the course of the day, but though he also was at Shepheard's Hotel we didn't meet him there, except Father did once for a minute. We felt the luxury of large rooms and beds, and Father said "he felt very gay for he had accomplished a good day's journey towards Concord," and he was so thankful to feel the solitude of a hotel. We immediately received the cards and letters of introduction of several Englishmen, whose calls were pleasant to Father, and one told him that Prof. Richard Owen was there. Father was delighted, and called on him but he was out. Friday at Cairo was a busy day from 9 in the morning till 12 at night. The calls on Gen. Stone, Mr Beardsley (Consul), and Prof. Owen, the shopping which is an endless business in slow Oriental countries, the packing of the box to be shipped to Roosevelt and Son in N.Y., the making out of the invoice and writing the directions, then the packing of our own trunks, and last & best, though not last in time, the going to Tod & Rathbone's, settling our account, and RECEIVING OUR LETTERS filled the day over full. But truly I wish you could have seen how pleased Father was to receive so many letters. I kept finding him retired to his room reading them, which I told him was base conduct, and at last he desisted, chiefly because I took them away and locked them up; he, innocent man, not discovering the fraud because I left him two. He said the next morning that he had fancied that he had more, and I took them

— 1873 —

out and we read your letters. How good they were! One I put away to solace the voyage to Naples. The others I divided into a large share & a small—gave him the large, and they lasted half the 130 miles from C. to Alexandria. The small were our occasional consolation during the days we spent there. For on Sunday a great storm set in, and the boat sent word it could not go out. Again on Tuesday the storm was worse and it sent word it couldn't sail. This morning, Wednesday, the sun is out, the wind going down. We have come aboard, but the pilot says 'tis so rough outside he couldn't get back in his small boat, so we don't sail, and the nightmare of the Mediterranean voyage still hangs over us, while the days saved for Rome are ebbing away at Alexandria. It proves a comfortable enough boat, happily, and we each have a room to ourselves—only eight other passengers, and all Americans. The passage is 180 francs and takes five days. We reached Alexandria Saturday noon, took our luncheon, and made inquiries about the Rubattino boat & office. We called on our consul Mr Babbitt, who is very pleasant & kind, and lent us newspapers which amused Father's evening. On Sunday morning we went to church, Miss F. & I, and in the afternoon we inspected this boat, secured the best staterooms. Found the harbour very rough, but little suspected how long a storm was beginning. Mr Babbitt called on us Tuesday night, and said this was the worst storm of the winter. Well, we were glad to be on shore. Monday & Tuesday were spent chiefly in writing letters, though we walked out to see the high waves, & I did some mending while Miss F. read the Life of St Paul. Father & I had the treat of another letter from home. Now I have given you our history. Your homily on exercise amused Father. He wondered if you thought he never heard them things before. He was pleased to think how many useless letters he has escaped, when you told him of the autograph requests etc. He absolutely can't write. He has some business remarks to make to Will, and is writing a note to him. I'm afraid it's the only word he'll ever write. He is well but never feels like writing, and is more discouraged every time he tries. I think he has never regretted going to Egypt, but I believe the place he has enjoyed most so far, and will enjoy most in future is Paris. Few social duties, Mr Lowell for his daily comfort, a snug warm parlour. I mean to stay there a fortnight, 17 days if I can. I think London will be too populous a place for him, but I shall plan to stay there a month, and we can journey off when he is tired. I am most thankful that you are having a happy winter. February 24th Dear Mother, It's my birthday, so I must write and

58

say (though I'm passing Mt. Etna and Father wants me to stay on deck) that the Mediterranean voyage has been prosperous and is nearly over. We land to-morrow in Naples, and to-day (of course, since it is my birthday) is the loveliest imaginable. Calabria on one side and Sicily on the other are just in their early spring, the fields and hillsides beginning to be green and the apple trees to bud. It is very pretty and touching to see spring after Egypt. The day is still warm and blue, reviving to our seasick souls. And now I'm just going to open my birthday present from my dear sister. But shall write no more to-day, except to say that I only learn every year that I'm the happiest girl in the world, and whether I look at past, present or future can only exclaim, how broad how bright how full my life is! And I think you will think of it too to-day.

Naples. Feb 25th. We have landed and find letters from Alice waiting for us to say Rome is full with people to see the Carnival so we must wait here at Hotel de Russie for two days. I mustn't send this off without a word about our voyage. We saw Crete, which principally interested Father because Jupiter was born there, but its wonderful beauty of course held him longer. There Minos lived, there was the labyrinth & the Minotaur, but I thought Mamma would remember with the strongest interest that there Ariadne grew up and thence she eloped with Theseus. The high mountains were white and like the top of Pico covered with snow—tell Miss Roxy. Father is quite right: "I find all Europe only a little Fayal." Then we thought of the Cretan war a few years ago. Curnex came to remind me that 'twas along this side of the island that St. Paul sailed. I tried to remember the names of the mountains. I thought Ida must be one & so did Father. We asked the Captain the name of the tallest & most beautiful peak. "Monte Ida." "Verily it takes us!" we exclaimed. There was a little cloud on Etna's peak when we reached Sicily but the Captain said it was always smoking. Vesuvius today is clouded. Stromboli we passed very early. I didn't feel strong enough to land at Messina, nor Father. The others did and were pleased. I wish I had been able. Our eight Americans, all of Pennsylvania, were very pleasant. We had a very sick but most affectionate six days together, all of us. They all knew how to make the most of Father, and we had readings and much talk. Sunday night I produced my dear hymn-book. There was a piano in the cabin, and they took to singing, and I am thankful to say couldn't leave off. Our concert lasted an hour or two. We also introduced Sir Pavon. Goodbye. There's never any end to what I have to say, the paper cuts me short, or the time. Your affectionate daughter,

       E. T. E.

             Rome. Mar. 1st 1873.
Dear Edith,
 I find Alice out, and while I wait I can speak of the photographs. Before I came to tear the envelope I came to know what they were and to scream for joy. They are lovely, but alas! it almost makes me cry to think I have nephews that I do not know—that Cameron doesn't look quite natural, and that my John is an utter stranger. Where is one of Ralph, and of Violet? I trust there were some taken. And oh beloved! the stories you tell of them all are such nuts to us both! I see how fast Ralph and Violet are growing up, and see it with pleasure & with pride, though it is losing Ralph. I expect Violet to stay by me till I die, but not the boys.
 Mar. 7. We go to Flor. Mon. Not 1 min. all these 10 days either to write, or to visit galleries etc. Steady succ^n. of lunches, dinners & calls, no time to put away my things, chamber one heap, strength nevertheless slowly increasing, slept last night. Best thing, a ride on the Campagna. Galloped as I never believed before that horses could. With Alice & Mrs Wister, I on Alice's horse, she on Mrs Sumner's for Mrs S. sick. She & Mrs S. still our sole delight & home in the city. Speeches that have pleased me most since I came back. Alice loq. "You both look so well, and so brown, and so fat, it is beautiful."
 Miss S. Clarke loq. "Your father is wonderfully improved, he seems himself again. Well, he is always himself, but when he was here before there seemed some cloud over him, I don't know what, and now that has passed away. Egypt seems to have been the right thing for him." Father has had so good a time here that he put off going away, but is ready now. Harry James is a true comfort to him. Aunt Lizzy came yesterday, very tired but rejoiced to hear our letters & to see the babies' pictures.

Second page of letter is missing.

         R.R. between Florence & Macon
Dear Edith,
 I mean to talk with you on business. I have ordered your candle-

shades at Bazzanti's, and finding that he seemed a gentleman and spoke & understood English as well as I, I paid for them, on his assurance that 'twas the simplest thing in the world to ship his wares to Boston. You said I might get anything else I thought you would like. Now he had a sort of globe for a hanging lamp, which I supposed was a bowl or vase for flowers, and I liked it so much that I took it for you. I found country linen unbleached was to be had in Florence and I bought enough for two pair of sheets and a dozen towels. We didn't go near Sorrento so I couldn't buy you a Sorrento sash, but I bought one or two plain Roman ones, and a woollen Florentine one instead. Oh such a good time as I have had in Florence! The first two days we were nearly unknown and unsuspected, and the freedom and delight of walking about the city, seeing what there was and buying what I chose, and of going to galleries all alone with Father, was a new sensation. You know when I was in Europe before I was lame, and this time so far it has been one rush of company, often quite the wrong kind though sometimes the best. When I go to galleries with people who know about pictures, it discourages me to find that I never like the good ones and those I do like are bad. That has happened always hitherto but now when I went with Father and no one else I found it amusing to range about and see the things and like what I chose, and once or twice Father also liked what I did. We went to the Uffizi and found the dying Alexander, and Father was delighted with it and with a bust of Seneca, and a Juno, and I liked them too. We went to the Pitti Palace and saw it nearly through. So Florence was a success.

Shopping is more delightful to me than Art, and Annie's commission was a great and protracted pleasure. For an hour or two a day Father and I stood round on the Lung Arno examining the shop windows, and this being in my favourite line of jewelry, I was in ecstasies every minute. I had consulted with Alice and Mrs. Sumner on the subject and they had made me understand a little what to look out for. But this letter was to be business. We give up Milan and Venice, I don't see how we could do otherwise, and I can't do your Venice errands. I am sorry. You wrote I must get several things that I think I shan't need, for instance, a blue evening silk. Now that would cost a hundred dollars & lie heavy on my hands for years after I got home. I think what with the muslin and the various sashes I can get along for 5 weeks of London. Lily Ward advises me to buy a big lace arrangement for my neck to give the appearance of square or open necked dress over my high necked waist, and seeing that she & Alice looked very gorgeous in such things I think I will. Aunt Lizzy & Miss Farquhar have so praised my travelling bonnet that my mind is at ease about it. I supposed it was a great fright.

[Unsigned]

Florence. March 11th 1873

Dear Mother,

To think that there should have been no time to record the events and pleasures of Rome! We dined with Mrs Sumner & Alice; with the Storys; with the von Hoffmans; with the Tiltons; and one night Father with Lady Ashburton and I with my two dear friends. We went also to an evening party at Miss Clarke's, to lunch with the Storys, the other guests being Mrs Wister, the Duke of Sermoneta, and the Princess Tiani; alone to lunch with Lily & her husband, I twice indeed, and Father to an evening party at the Story's when I was too tired. All the time that we were not making calls, people were calling upon us, so that I had to say, "Now I must be excused, for we are going out etc." My ride so kindly planned & arranged for me by Mrs Sumner and Alice I assure you was by far the grandest I ever arrived at. The horse was a constant wonder to me. So were the other horses. There seemed to be no limit to their powers of galloping. They seemed to think, "The longer and harder the better," so away we went over the daisies creating such a gale by our speed that I was surprised. My hat was tied on with every possible precaution or it would have flown. It was a beaver. I saw Alice ride and considered it worth while to see her, as Harry James said. The horse that I rode was hers, minded the slightest movement of the hand (so the great torment of riding was removed) and had learned to trot at one sign and canter at another, so it was all pure pleasure to ride. At a party at Miss Clarke's I saw Mrs Howitt, and she was so motherly and interested and kind and knew how to be consolatory. She talked about Egypt, and tried to dispel many of the detestable theories that the books had tired me with. One's mind is always more or less homesick while travelling no matter how smoothly things go, and Mrs Howitt went to the right place. On Tuesday what a delightful time I had with Lily and her husband! She gave me a ring with many prayers for my conversion I know, poor child. But I hope I shan't be a Catholic though I desire all the rest may be answered. We could often talk together quite freely in spite of the bugbear, but it would go to my heart to see her tremble and her hands grow cold when she talked to me, and

— 1873 —

I meanwhile sitting motionless under my shield in an attitude that seemed heartless, though I suppose I couldn't have done otherwise. Mr von Hoffmann is more skillful in compliments than anyone I ever saw. He can twist round whatever you say to him into a chance to compliment you. Father & I made a mistake & came to dine at 6:35 when we had been invited at 7, and thinking we were a little behind the hour, for we were aiming at 6:30, Father said, "I'm afraid we are late." "You are always late when you come here," said Mr. v. H. My conscience acknowledged it, and I said, "I believe we always have been." "Yes, and always must be," he went on, "for here you are always so much desired that no matter how early you come, to us it seems late. I believe, however, that to-night you will have to wait a little, for dinner is at seven." He was always so. He was truly fond of us both and made us feel it every minute. The day we came away from Rome in the half past eight morning train, imagine how early our friends got up in a late-rising city. Aunt Lizzy came at half past seven. Happily Curnex and the trunks were just going, and I had my things on and had done my breakfast. Father too. So we sat down by the fire in the parlour and talked at greater leisure than has been possible at any time we have seen each other before. Father told her what we thought she knew already, but she didn't, about the 10000 and Judge Hoar, and both cried, and many more stories did we tell each other, and enjoyed every minute. At quarter past eight came Mr. Tilton, an artist who loves Father, in his own carriage to take us to the train. When we stopped at the station, Baron von Hoffmann opened the door to let us out. Then, having placed us in the train, they stayed to talk with us. Father had discovered with disgust and consternation that a certain princess who had been very devoted was not unconnected with the press, and told these gentlemen his affliction, and asked counsel. The dear Baron's words on this occasion were lovely and wise. And when Father said, "To Americans the word Princess is dazzling. We suppose it to imply high society and high manners," I wish you could have seen Mr. von Hoffmann's face. He looked so delighted with Father's innocence, so contemptuous of the class spoken of. "Well," he said, "I must give you one word of advice: Mefiez-vous des Princes——et des Princesses."

Paris March 17th.   Now that we are in Paris I want to tell you of the present, but more must be said of Rome. First you want to know something of Aunt Lizzy. She has had a rest in Palermo, and felt all the time she was there that it was the right place. She suffered in leaving, but

— 1873 —

now has made up her mind to go home in June. I told her all my disgusts with "the world" which I have "seen" for the first time since I came to Rome this time, and she heartily sympathized. "Indeed, Aunt Lizzy," I said, "the advantage of living in Concord seems to me so very great that I think there is no place to be compared with it." "Yes, Ellen," cried Aunt Lizzy from the bottom of her heart, "that is what I think. I only think so more and more wherever I go. When Canon Burbage dined with Edward & Lizzy something was said about Concord and I exclaimed, 'Oh Concord! Why Concord is the Kingdom of Heaven!' and Canon Burbage laughed and asked, 'Where is this happy place?' "

I desire to record that as Miss Clarke and Mrs. Sumner and Alice were our comfort among women, Harry James was our comfort among men. (I leave out our dear Lily and her husband because we only saw them in their own mountain fastness. They were not a part of every day.) What a difference his being there made to us! With what joy and alacrity Father welcomed every proposal I made relating to him! It was with Harry as it was with Mrs. Sumner. Father couldn't feel as if he had had or could have enough of his society, and though unluckily calls several times prevented his going to bring Harry to dinner, or getting him for a walk or a visit to a gallery just when he was starting out with ardour to find him, he did succeed several times and when I had an afternoon of my own business and Father would have sat still by himself, Harry came in and I asked him to take charge of Father and they had a delightful visit to the Capitol together. Father's only grief at night was that I couldn't have had the same pleasures. When I asked Harry, he said, "Why yes, he was just about to timidly propose to Father that he should make use of him in some way." He was a comfort because he was a friend both in himself and by inheritance—the best kind of a friend, Mrs. Hemenway says, so that he could be to Father a sort of son, and much more because he had a real mind and was sincere and good, so that when he spoke it cheered you instead of tiring you to listen. We saw Lady Ashburton several times and I liked her very much. One night at dinner at Mr. Tilton's I learned that Mrs. Howitt wrote "Will you walk into my parlour said the Spider to the Fly," but I can't quite believe it till my Mamma confirms it. Did she? I thought it was older. Next came up the question, who wrote "Twinkle, twinkle little star?" No one knew, neither could its antiquity be settled. Father said it wasn't more than fifty years old. When we asked the American Minister, Mr. Marsh, a very learned man, he was only surprised that the question had now for the first time only occurred to us. He said he had never heard anyone profess to know anything of its origin. On Thursday night after my ride we dined with Mrs. Sumner, and Father read "In State" and she recognized it. "Oh yes, she knew that and liked it." Alice and Mrs. Tilton heard it for the first time, and were properly impressed. They wanted more reading, and Father read Timrod and William Strode. Then I proposed he should read Punch on the Death of Abraham Lincoln. He refused. Later in the evening Alice said to me, "Do make him read Punch about President Lincoln. I like that better than anything. I always carry it about with me, and I want to hear him read it." And he did read it beautifully. Then Mrs. Tilton gave thanks publicly, for she had never heard it before, and desired a copy, which Alice promised her. Now for our days at Florence. I have told Edith in my business letter the joys of the first two days. Father heard Hermann Grimm was there and inquired right and left when people began to call upon us, and sent Curnex to the German booksellers. At last came a note saying that the bookseller heard that H. G. was at Genoa. If he came back to Florence he would let us know. On Wednesday 13th I had a beautiful letter from Mr Lowell which I mean to enclose, and we decided to come straight to Paris. People began to call upon us. Mr Graham the American consul sent me a mountain of spring flowers, hyacinths, pansies, violets & lilies of the valley, set off with camellias of all colours. Father had a most delightful room with interesting old-fashioned furniture. And he paid 3 francs a day for that beautiful room. The sun shone in and the great piles of flowers made it a small Paradise. We were returning to the Hotel at night when Mr. Bigelow, former minister to France, called to us and came to meet us. He had visited us in the morning. "Who do you think I met an hour ago?" he said. "Hermann Grimm! I told him you were inquiring for him, and where you were." When we came in we found his card. Father started straight for his hotel. He was out. Father left word he would visit him next morning. And that evening we called on Mr. and Mrs. Graham. Mr. & Mrs Bayard Taylor were there. The three gentlemen smoked in one parlour, while we three ladies had a really pleasant evening in another. In the middle of it came an earthquake. I have never felt one before—always wished to—and Miss Sally Cary's description is so exactly the same as experiencing one that I felt like an old hand, and enjoyed the whole from beginning to end, while the other ladies were a

— 1873 —

little slow in believing, and looked for some cause for the motion of the door-handle and the shaking of the room—then exclaimed with some terror, "An earthquake!" I waited for the second shock but none came. At least I have had one good strong shake. Thursday morning at 10 Father asked me to go with him to see Hermann and Gisela, but I couldn't so early. It was time to consult Bradshaw and plan our Paris journey. I told him to go alone and if he couldn't understand them to come back and get me. He didn't return for hours—and then full of joy. Hermann Grimm could speak English perfectly, there had been no trouble, only pleasure, —"and his wife seems a most sensible, cheerful & agreeable woman, nothing whimsical about her." Oh how thankful I was to hear that. I had trembled. They were coming to dine with us at six. We then went and it poured hard, we & Curnex, doing all the errands, settling all the business of Florence in order to leave the next morning. They came late—we were already at dinner. I asked Mr Grimm to ask Madame to come upstairs and take off her things. He said "No, you must speak in German to my wife." So that was gone through with, and we sat down at the end of the long table d'hote. When we were seated Gisela turned round and looked me over. "Oh!" she said, "you are beautiful and sensible and good. You look wonderfully like your brother." Then she took hold of my hand. "Your hand is thin. You look so healthy. Why should your hand be thin?" Then came the dinner, and the wine to be asked about, and next she began asking me where I had been and what I had done, and I to ask her, and we went regularly to work to get acquainted. It was exceedingly easy. Later she said "I want you to get acquainted with my husband. Forget me a while; just listen to him and your Father." By and bye she came back and wanted to hear of Edward and of William James and of Edith. In fact we had a really beautiful time. At dessert she said "You talk German very well. You know a great many words, and a great deal of what you say is quite right. If you should stay in Berlin a fortnight I think you would talk perfectly easily." I thought of Ida and the immense pains she had taken to make me understand grammar and construction and the reason why. I was enchanted that all her faithful labour had stayed put through these fifteen years of disuse. We went up into Father's room after dinner, and they admired the flowers. We lighted your candles so the room looked quite bright, and Father and Hermann sat down at a table, and Gisela on the funny couch, and talked just as hard as we could for another hour. She asked if we were Unitarians, wanted to hear something about that denomination and about Concord. You can imagine my tongue was untied by such questions. She said a German couldn't perfectly understand how it would feel to live in such an order of things. She talked about Father a little—how much she loved him and why—and said the sight of him was such an agreeable surprise. "He was so much handsomer than his pictures. Such fresh cheeks!" Presently Hermann Grimm rose to go, but they didn't go for some time, only he and Father came and stood by the sofa and Mr Grimm exclaimed, "There! I can't say it in English," and finished what he was saying in German for me to translate. Father had been telling him about Princess Wittgenstein and I told him of Father's speech to Mr von Hoffmann. I wanted to see the effect on them. It was just what it had been on him. It appears German princes are a miserable set. Hermann now began telling me of his pleasure in beholding Father, and said every photograph did him cruel injustice. "They all represent a feeble old man of seventy. He looks a strong man of fifty. *They* look as if he were made of iron—of copper. *He* looks as if he were made of steel. He has a fine sharp manly face; and such bright colouring which is all lost, of course, in the photographs." And when we came to Paris Mrs Lowell said very much the same thing. And when I had waited in vain for Mr Lowell to speak on the subject I asked him if he had no compliments to offer Father's hair. He said, "Yes, indeed! I didn't like to say anything but I was delighted to see that it had returned. I don't know when I have had such a pang as when I saw him the first time without any, though I got used to it and came to like him very well so. But it is wonderful how well it has come back, and I am glad, he looks so much better with it." Well, to return to Hermann and Gisela, they remembered that we were to make an early start the next morning, and that it was time for them to go to the opera, and we parted great friends. The dreaded interview had been a perfect success. Father had enjoyed every minute, and only wanted to see more of Hermann, and Gisela had been plain, comfortable & lovely. I wasn't afraid of her. Father has often since that evening rejoiced that we did see them. We started from Florence very early Friday morning, and never stopped till we reached the Hotel de Lorraine on Sunday morning, March 16th at 5 o'clock, waked the garçon who soon let us in, and we went straight to bed and were called by Curnex at 9. I'll send off this letter at this

— 1873 —

point, and as soon as possible will write another. Your affectionate daughter

E. T. E.

Paris March 18th 1873

Dear Edith,

It is high time your letters should be answered and everybody's else for that matter. Now this day I mean to sit & write by the hour and see how much I can do. You all ask about Curnex. His time expires on Thursday and I am truly sorry to let him go, for on the whole he is an immense convenience and when I go shopping next week I would far rather have him than Mme. Conneau. I mean to try to do without her, but sometimes I must take her I suppose. He is a sort of valet-de-chambre to Father in the morning, and Father seems to dread dressing without him, and when we make calls he always goes to find the way and to carry up the cards and make sure the people are at home so that we don't have to mount the stairs for nothing. Also he does all the small errands and gets the cabs and pays them, brings us hot water at dressing-time, and like a good nursery girl sees to it that we aren't late to dinner, and comes to fetch us home from parties at the proper hour. In all this he is a comfort, but being utterly without brains, he is of less use in emergencies and in travelling than you picture to yourselves, and he always gives enormous fees to servants wherever we go. I don't think he has often saved us anything, and I rejoice that the drain on our exchequer for him is to be stopped. Your representations of the woes of house-cleaning and furnishing have been working in Father's mind ever since he read them in Rome, and have damped his ardour for going straight home. My present idea is to sail the 10th of May, but it has no solid foundation. Don't be too glorious over the good accounts I give of Father. They come from the mouths of many witnesses, so I believe them a little, but I see no great improvement myself, indeed I see none whatsoever. His hands are as cold & as numb as ever, he remembers no better, he feels the same inability to write the smallest note. But in Florence one day he sat in his room for some hours, and when I came in he said he had been looking over the green book of poems, and to some purpose. He had struck out several poems entire, and corrected many lines. That is the first work he has done, and it cheered me very much—him too, no doubt. As to me, I am as well as I am at home, no better, but then I am fatter and came back brown from

— 1873 —

Egypt's blessed sun, so everyone notices my healthy look. I am taking great pains to be well, and have at last decided to try Dr Miller's pills and see if they will give me a start. I suppose the voyage from Alexandria to Naples which took all my strength is hardly yet recovered from. Perhaps in a week or two I can speak more cheerfully. I seldom slept a night all winter. But in Florence I began, and have slept every night since. Not sleeping has made no difference as I have had nothing to do or think of in the daytime, and I have taken great pleasure, and had profit in my nights. It was only annoying as showing that something was wrong.

March 19th. Your reports about papers, carpets etc, for Bush are very interesting. I hope the dining-room carpet will be of many colours and a bewildering figure that won't show spots & crumbs like a carpet of quiet, sober, good taste. You beg us not to come home too soon, and yet you must see that if we don't, someone has got to do my work for me, either you, or Mother, or Annie. So be consoled if we do come too soon for your plans, beloved. Though I don't seriously threaten it yet. We gave up all Italy & Venice & Milan because we are not young, energetic curious travellers, but old & lazy. Now to return to letters; all that is said about Mother pleases us very much. I think she is going to be well and young again. You ought to hear Father's daily discourses on John Murray F. junior. He addresses him often & says he looks at life with philosophy, that the fact doesn't entirely please him as it is, and he brings some endurance to meet it. I remind Father that at the moment the picture was taken he was not occupied in large contemplation but was witnessing some trick of Mr Whipple's. This sudden comedown makes Father laugh. Again he approaches the mantel-piece, views the baby and says "Very different from the others. He looks wise, yet with a perfect innocency." I don't remember the half that he says to and about that picture. Father and Mr Lowell had been out together yesterday and Father said when he came home that he had just seen a very pretty thing—a monocle—he thought he must buy one. I told him that was de vely sing that you had ordained for his New Years Present. He was edified, and said his wishes were forestalled. Charles came yesterday and spent an hour. He is going back to St Aubin the first of April. I think it a great pity C. has property, he is able to live as he likes without earning, and so I fear he will never work. Except on his farm, he really does work there, works hard. Thy affectionate sister

E. T. E.

— 1873 —

Paris. March 21st. 1873.

Now, dear Mamma, to finish our history and answer your letters. We had eaten our breakfast and established ourselves in our quarters before we saw a soul on Sunday morning, but about twelve the doorbell rang and Mr. and Mrs. Lowell were outside in the entry when I opened the door. And they came in and sat an hour with us, and we were as happy together as we used to be last November. It was so pleasant to be welcomed back and to feel at home, and we liked our rooms, and they were glad we did because they chose them for us.

I remembered how much I had liked M. le pasteur Bersier, and proposed to Mrs. Lowell to go and hear him again. She said, "Oh yes she always went," and we put on our things and started forth in a coupé—had exactly the same seats we had in November—and I again felt at home. How much more as the service proceeded! for my ears are more open to languages now. I can follow without hearing the words one by one, just as in English—not yet at the table, but when I am spoken to—and much more in preaching where all is said slowly and amid perfect silence. I like the man. Most of his views are like ours. He is quite as broad as a Unitarian, always prays for and speaks of the great Church universal embracing all sects, is a Christian, has really studied and thought, believes with all his heart. Mr. Lowell says he is eloquent and has a beautiful manner. The church is free, like Mr. Winkley's; is crowded like his. Everybody sings. There is a Bible-class for girls on Tuesday afternoon and Exposition of the Prophets on Wednesday. I hope to go to both while I am here. Oh! if I could only talk French, with what eagerness should I go to the Bible-class, if it is conducted on the same principle as ours, so as to ask him where he got certain views and why he should understand this and that as he does, for he gives a turn entirely new to me to various things. There was a beautiful sunset going on as we drove home, and I thought of Egypt and saw and confessed that there is a difference in the colouring of different countries. I never did believe it, but now I do. I find I mourn for Egypt, and there is reason to be thankful that we did not go with the Wards, for if it had been perfect heaven below, I should have had to wait a long time to recover from longing for it. Now every evening we go into Mr. Lowell's parlour and sit there. I am sorry to say the gentlemen smoke. Otherwise it would be perfect bliss. At dinner time the first day Father found a bottle at his place and asked about it. No one knew till Mr. Holmes came down. He confessed that he had ordered it to celebrate our return. Then Mr. Lowell said he had a desire to join in such festivities, and ordered a bottle of champagne. The next day Mr. Holmes again had a celebration, an oyster and champagne breakfast. When Count Savinsky, a Pole, who was here with us before, came to the table, he ordered a bottle of Burgundy and said to Mr. Lowell, "Will you present me to Monsieur and we will drink together." And it was done with all the clinking of glasses, and bows and polite remarks proper on such occasions. We have an author M. Léozone Le Duc, two Poles, a young man, very pleasant! and my old delight the Marquis de Grammont (so dear to me for the sake of his great-aunt and great-grandmother and grandmother—he looks worthy of them all) at the table every day, and I know what they talk about, which is more than I used to, but not exactly what they do say, and when I am deeply interested it is exasperating. Last night we and Mr. and Mrs. Lowell went to the theatre together, Theatre Français, to see Moliere's Malade Imaginaire, another little drama intended to be very moral, called L'Ouvrier, and Maitre Pathelin, a famous old farce. We enjoyed it all. The acting was better than any I ever saw before except in private theatricals. Of course it couldn't vie with plays where Anna Agassiz and such people act. It was delightful to see people mourn and confess, etc., without that braying sound always used on the American stage, and the heroines were pretty and ladylike. The funny things were very funny. Father was delighted. A little girl acted Louison in the Malade Imaginaire. It was very pretty. Every day Mr. Lowell takes Father somewhere or Charley does. Curnex has gone. I don't believe Father will ever answer a letter. He always says, "We must," and even makes good resolutions every morning; especially when it is proposed that he should do something he has the answer ready that he hasn't written any letters for some time and means to today. I am no longer taken in by such words. So I have read him your remarks on Tyndall and Uncle Charles and he pays attention and is glad to hear it. About Father and me you make a remark that surprises me, that we both abound in moral combativeness. I didn't know it. So the other day a professor of palmistry examined our hands, and said the leading feature in both our characters was ambition. That I can hardly believe. Do you call Father ambitious except to do his work perfectly? He further said I was of a most jealous nature, realistic, reflective, destitute of imagination, and appealed to me to know whether it wasn't true. And when I set out to consider the matter, I couldn't tell in the least, but I rather thought not. I was dreadfully

— 1873 —

disappointed. What I hoped to hear was whether in studied science those lines commonly called Life and Marriage were recognized as such, but I got no interesting information at all.

April 8th London. Your letters of Mar. 9th came yesterday. They gave details of the new house furnishing, and most of it pleases me very much. I am sorry to hear of a Brussels carpet for the dining-room, and I had set my heart on having the front entry exactly what it was before, a marbled paper varnished. Father is in the full tide of dinners and calls, busy every moment, and likes it better than usual, but he is homesick nevertheless, and often proposes "to take the Fitchburg train." He is planning to sail on the

The bottom of the page is worn away, and the writing is illegible.

Paris. March 28th 1873

Dear Edward,

There I wanted to write you a good letter after neglecting you so long, but I couldn't get a moment. I have been in the shops or at their windows early & late, and in the evening always dining out or having company. So a few lines in pencil while waiting for breakfast to come. I have been hard at work shopping, and have now allotted 3 days to see the city. March 29th. Father took me this morning to the Louvre, & I found that I liked pictures, not famous ones, pretty well after all. I saw with delight the angels in the kitchen that Edith celebrated, and Aunt E.'s Ghirlandaio that you sent me. Now we are starting for the Jardin des Plantes. Charles took Father there the other day and was pleased with his pleasure, and Father has gone alone several times since. One day Charles took Therchi and me in an open carriage round to see the ancient churches of St. Germain de Près, St. Sulpice, and Notre Dame and Etienne du Mont (Here were the tombs of Pascal, and Racine, and Boillau), which last two he thinks the most beautiful things in Paris. Also we went through a flower-market and the great market and Pere-la-Chaise. Nine funerals arrived in the half hour we were there. This surprised Therchi and me very much.

We are going to England next week. Mr. Lowell and Mrs. Lowell as ever most kind. Father has had the pleasure of dining with M. Taine and Yvan Toughenoff, if that is the way to spell it, and has had conversation with Ernest Renan, Elie de Beaumont. We have also gone twice to the Theatre with great joy. Now I must leave without another word.

E. T. E.

— 1873 —

Note in RWE's handwriting on the last page of this letter:

Dear Edward, No one can be so grieved as I that I do not write my thanks to you—first to Mamma—& to Will & Edith, & all my dear friends & benefactors in the doing & writing way, for letters & services which I fully appreciate—not less that I do thus ill acknowledge them,——but I suppose that I shall presently perhaps tonight or tomorrow begin the reform—Your loving Papa
R W E

Paris April 1st 1873

Dear Edith,

It's a shame to write so little. Paris hours are bad, we don't get our breakfast till quarter-past ten, so that it is early to get out at eleven, and before breakfast I can't go out. This makes my days short, and though I was faithfully at it from 11 to 6 I didn't get all the work done last week, and now Father wishes me to turn my attention to sightseeing. We are both very happy in Paris, for this is the only place where we have found company in the house, except the three happy days with Mrs Sumner in Florence, and the two days at Naples with Aunt Lizzy where Father has had any one to speak to at dinner-time. Then there is plenty to see. I have made myself acquainted with the general form and aspect of the Hôtels in which ancient French nobility lived. Yesterday there was a Comte or something here at dinner whose château had been used by the Prussians and he told us all about it. He said when he heard they were near, he sent away his gardener and all his servants except his own man and the cook, so as not to seem too well off. He became so excited in relating how they came upon him that I lost it, till he exclaimed "Ah! ce triste quart-d'heure!" and sighed. "How many were quartered on you?" asked Mr Lowell. "Eighty-two soldiers, 25 officers & 26 horses," he said, and every morning, he told us, they began calling to him at 6 o'clock in the morning "Monsieur! Thé! Monsieur! Chocolat! Monsieur! Café au lait!" and he and his cook had to supply them as fast as they could. The officers would come in calling "Monsieur! Omelettes!" and what was hardest of all, they took all his horses, he said that now when he looked at his stable the tears came into his eyes. He said they drank all his wine, and rather carelessly he thought, otherwise he had nothing against them, the officers had all behaved like gentlemen. "And oh! their discipline! One night at one o'clock two officers came and brought orders that all were to move at 8 o'clock in

— 1873 —

the morning. "Et á huit heures ils sont tous partis, sans bruit, c'etait comme le marcher d'un seul homme. Chaque homme est allé tranquillement a l'ecurie et á monté. Pas un coup de sifflet, pas un coup de trompette. Avec nous lorsqu'il est 'A cheval!' on crie, on court ça et la, on chante, des sifflets, des trompettes, tant de bruit! Ici rien de la sorte. On n'entendit rien, et á huit heures tout le monde fut là, et ils partirent." I may have made some mistakes in the French but this is as I remember. The other night at Mrs Langel's I had a very pleasant time with Lili Forbes. She struck me when she came into the room as very delightful-looking, partly probably because she was American. I also liked her dress. Then I was introduced to her Mother, and had a little comfortable talk with her. They asked us to dine but Father refused. She called on us two days after and today we return the call. I am just going to dress now, so perhaps I can't write till I get to England for we have lodgings now & go Saturday.

16 Down St. Apr. 7th. I won't miss this mail to finish the sheet. We arrived Saturday night, and Sunday while I was at church Mr Froude & Max Müller came; Lord and Lady Amberley a little later. Before we went to bed we were invited to dine Sunday with Mr Grenville, Monday Lady Stanley of Alderly, Tuesday Mr Edw. Dicey, Wednesday Mr Froude, Thursday Lady Amberley. Mr Hughes and Mr Newcomb and Mr Conway have also called—small hope for letters and sight-seeing. Father, bold as a lion (for him) about all this going out, is said to be much improved. Precious letters from you and Cam; enchanting picture of J. Many more letters yet unopened have come in. I must go.

        Thy affectionate sister
            E. T. E.

                              London 14 April 1873
Dear Edith,

Your letters from Magnolia telling of the lovely weather, the company, Will's leisure and the babies were very delightful to us. Now about your things. I think Marshall & Snelgrove have nothing to please you in the way of Himalayas. I haven't yet tried E. & Grahams but they are in Ludgate Hill near Strahan of whom I am to buy some books so they'll be on my road. I have ordered boots of Daniel Neal according to your memo. and shall take immense pleasure in executing the crockery order & the soap order, also the lamp and monocle order, provided I

— 1873 —

have any money. I hope Will will send the 100£. Father says that when he said to Mr Russell Sturgis that he thought he was near the end of his account, Mr S. said "Oh no! plenty of money left! Shall you want some now?" Father saw he personally knew nothing about his particular account and explained that he knew he was near the end. Mr S. said, no matter, he would honour all his drafts. Now I'll talk about my birthday present from you & Will. I have three things in my eye, but shan't decide till I get out again. When the Countess of Airlie called on us the other day she wore a velvet cloak trimmed with fur, but a woollen dress. So the next day I called on the Norton's in my street dress, and asked Miss Jane if that would do to call on Lady Stanley in. She said she shouldn't think of dressing better to call on a Duchess. She said they often wore woollen now, and Americans were always allowed to do as they pleased. I have only worn my dark silk once or twice to Table d'Hote and have been mortified to find myself more gorgeously got up than any lady present. I did piously wear my silk to make our first calls on Mrs Conway & Mr W. H. Channing. When we dined at Lady Stanley's I wore my pearl-coloured silk and found everyone in dark silks & quasi highnecks. When I dined with Mr & Miss Froude, Mr Carlyle & Mr Stevens I wore my dark silk and found Miss Froude in white. Nevertheless I am content, can't expect always to hit exactly right. Dear Lady Augusta Stanley pets me like a baby. I wish I could get really acquainted with her.

(Rather this than nothing)

April 16th. 1873

Dear Mother,

Father is very amusing. He is still apt to pitch upon the wrong word (as he called the dressing-gown last summer "the red chandelier") and it is always a daily delight to hear what word he will pitch upon. When we went to Westminster the other day, he expected to go to Charing Cross and then turn, whereas the driver took us across the top of Green Park, turning south where Father thought he should turn north. I quieted his alarm, but he took it out in talking, painting the most dismal pictures of our arriving dinnerless, no one knew where on the Brompton Road. When I pointed out the towers of the Abbey before us, he said, "Well, the case was urgent and required a miracle, and the Abbey has pirouetted and settled in the other end of London. Happily the fairies are our friends and see to it that at all costs *we* come out

— 1873 —

right." Everyone says here that he looks another man from what he was in November, and yet that terrible feeling that he had in Rome last December came back—came again & again for a day or two. I consulted Mr Norton. He advised Dr Quinn. I told Father. Meanwhile the feeling had stopped coming, and it hasn't returned, so he said he wouldn't see any doctor and forbade my taking any steps. I have disobeyed, for this feeling is very alarming to him when it comes. He says he never felt anything like it, can't describe it. It comes suddenly in a carriage, in company, at the table, in his bed-chamber, walking in the street, without cause and without consequence. When it is over—it lasts a minute or two—he feels perfectly well. He said he remembered Grandma's sometimes saying, "The water comes into my mouth", and looking very doleful when she said it, and he thought perhaps she felt this feeling. I wrote yesterday and asked Dr Quinn to come. Our future is thus arranged. Till Apr 27th in London, 30 to May 2 Oxford at Mr Müller's, 2 to 8 Stratford on A., Warwick, Coventry, Durham & journey to Edinburgh. Edinburgh till 11th. Then Manchester & 13th Liverpool. I am disturbed about my prospects of staying at home. I'm half afraid I shall have to go to Edith to be near the Doctor. It is a long time since I have dared to stand while dressing because it wasted the little strength that had to last through the day. But I am trying exceeding prudence, and maybe 'twill bear good fruits, for I am very healthy, everyone remarks on that, and I still sleep sound, have ever since Florence, and that ought to help.

April 18th. The doctor came and said he thought it was indigestion, Father was indignant at me for sending for him and at the Doctor for accusing him of that he never had. I am daily interested to see how Father's mind goes back to Mr. Owen on the Nile. He seems to think of him in his degree as I do in mine of Alice Bartlett, as one delightful companion and real, sober friend among a host of transient acquaintances. In Paris too he found an Englishman, Mr. Morison, a Comtist, who after two dinners came and spent a long evening with him in his room which did his very heart good, and he mentions him often with Mr. Owen. He has all the invitations he can manage here, and often worries a little over the difficulty of having time for any real conversation, but with Mr. Leckie and Mr. George Howard he has been fortunate enough to get on rather far. Yesterday, too, when we went to call on dear Lady Augusta, the Dean was at home and Father had a most beautiful time with him. He had begun to feel disappointed in him (if

1873

one can say that when he hadn't expected much) and yesterday set it all right. He has exulted several times since and said, "That is a visit I am very glad to have made." Mr. Howard has quite won his heart, and he likes the Duke of Argyle. Today when we called on Mr. Froude, I saw they seemed to be really interested in talking, he and Mr. F. stayed so long. But he hasn't told me about it yet. I spent this p.m. with Una. She is quite well and more cheerful.

Unsigned. Sent along with preceding letter to Edith.

London. April. 1873

Dear Mother,

This is the catalogue of our doings. I told you who called on Sunday April 6th before I came from church, and Lord and Lady Amberley in the afternoon. Father dined at Mrs. Grenfell's with Prof. Müller and Dowager Lady Stanley of Alderley. Mr. Conway called here meanwhile. After that dinner Father went with the gentlemen to the Cosmopolitan Club, where he met Mr. Hughes and Mr. Dicey.

Monday April 7th. We went out and found on coming in a note from Dowager Lady Stanley asking us to dine, and cards of Mr. and Mrs. Edward Dicey, and a note asking us for Tuesday. We called on Mrs. Conway. Both out. But on turning back to London, we met Mr. Conway—went back with him—made a visit very agreeable all round. He explained about Hotten, etc. He told us of an invitation through him from Mrs. Robert Crawshay of Cyfartha Castle, Myrthyr Tydvil in Wales to make her a visit. We came home and dressed for Lady Stanley's. There were no guests beside ourselves and her eldest daughter, the Countess of Airlie with her husband and daughter Clementina. The family at home was only Lady S. and her daughter Miss Maude Stanley. We had a lively and domestic time. The Airlie family were charming, and Lady Stanley cockered me well, had me sit right before the fire, and give me a little bottle of camphorated ammonia for my cold. They busied themselves thinking that they could do for us, and Miss S. is to take us to Windsor, also to the National Gallery.

Tuesday April 8th. After breakfast I went to see about some new white cravats for Father, and soon after I came back appeared Mr. Newcomb. He stayed while we had lunch. Then we called on Mr. W. H. Channing, as lovely and as affectionate as before. Mrs. Edwin Arnold was there. She had just come from Constantinople. When we returned we found we had missed Mr. Hughes. Mr. Conway came in and stayed while I dined. Then Father went to dine at Mr. Dicey's and met Mr. Stevens.

Wednesday. April 9th. When I came in from shopping I found Mrs. Paulet, Miss Newton and Miss Jewsbury calling on Father. We promised to lunch there on Sunday. Then Father went out, lunched with Mrs. Grenfell, called on Sir Henry Holland, Sir. Fk. Pollock, and Mr. Hughes, found all out but the first. When he came back we went to the Nortons, lunched with them, and Mrs. Baird Smith, De Quincy's daughter, went to Barings', took our passage. Then called at the Deanery—found them just starting to call on us (Lady A. in a woollen dress, Edith). They brought us home in their carriage and invited us to come to the Deanery and go with them to the service in the Abbey on Good Friday afternoon and Easter Sunday. Mr. Hughes came just after we came in. He was lovely as always, and before he went came Mr. Allingham. At seven we dined at Mr. Froude's. Mr. Stevens and Mr. Carlyle were the other guests; Miss Froude and I were the only ladies, and went up stairs and got acquainted after dinner in a tête à tête over the fire, both being cold. She was as healthy a child as you could find in the world, and she seldom goes to bed before one, and gets up at seven. I was amazed. We had a very pleasant time. I like Mr. and Miss Froude. The Countess of Airlie and her little son Lyulph, 11 years old, called. She invited us to dine, regretted that we shouldn't stay in Europe till people left London for she wanted us to see English country life. "Now all the great houses are shut up." She said all her children were furious aristocrats, and when she said something unkind about the Prince of Wales she had three of them at once in tears of anger that she should "judge" royalty.

Thursday April 10th. Miss Norton called on me, and Lady Stanley and Miss Stanley. Mr. Carlyle also came. Father was out, but he stayed and made a little call. That evening we dined at Lady Amberley's. She was dressed in a beautiful crimson velvet, and like many ladies—even Miss Froude had a miniature one on—wore a muslin cap on the top of her head. The other guests were Mr. J. S. Mill, his step-daughter Miss Taylor, and Prof. Frazer. The talk was chiefly on Goethe. I went home early but Father stayed and was introduced to a Mr. Leckie whom he liked particularly. Lord Amberley asked us to go with them and lunch at his Father's the next day. I refused. Father accepted.

Friday April 11th. Good Friday. Mrs. Bennett sent us over a plate

— 1873 —

of hot-cross-buns for breakfast and they have made an excellent luncheon ever since. At twelve Father went off with the Amberleys. I at three to the Deanery. Lady Augusta had invited crowds of people and it was very interesting to see her manage a most difficult and complicated business with such skill. Receiving people all the time while marshalling companies of those already there and sending them in charge of a niece or other habitué to their places, discovering that one had had no lunch and providing for her, introducing those she must leave together in the parlour, and still receiving. I saw many a young beauty. One of her nieces was very handsome. I was introduced to the Duke and Duchess of Argyle, also to a daughter of Chev. Bunsen who sat by me in the Abbey and was very lovely and comfortable. Before the sermon they had much of the Oratorio of the Messiah. Coming out I fell in with Lady S. of Alderley who took me by the hand (metaphorically) and pursued that petting process which all the elderly ladies are accustoming me to, and which I greatly enjoy. Then I went up to the Deanery parlour once more, where Lady Augusta and the beauties were giving everyone a cup of tea. I went with Miss Grace Norton into the dining room and saw her two nieces taking tea with Lady Augusta's & her nephew, little pretty polite Bruce children. The baby snarled once, and the nurse said "Oh no, no, no! All Augustas are good, you know, and so you must be good." I came home and waited dinner long for Father, then sat down without him, but he came by seven, very happy, and said, "This is a memorable day." Lord & Lady Amberley and he & Prof. Frazer had gone out in the carriage and had had real conversation by the way. Lord Amberley had talked freely & well. They had found Earl Russell, but Lady R. was upstairs sick. She sent Father a lovely note inviting us to stay with them "as many days as we can spare", but Father refused. He had excellent talk with Earl Russell, who knew everything, remembered everything, and talked with the liveliest interest. It was a cold & drizzling day, but they showed him Richmond Park and it was beautiful. They took him to call on Sir Henry Taylor who wrote "Philip von Artevelde", but he was out. Father liked Mrs Taylor. We had a very gay evening recounting our adventures to each other.

 Saturday. April 12th. I laid out our future according to the enclosed slip. We read notes from Lord Houghton inviting us to visit him in Yorkshire, and from Prof. Max Müller inviting us to make him a visit in Oxford. This Father accepted with joy. Lord Houghton's was for a time when we couldn't go, and we were both extremely sorry. Then

— 1873 —

Father went to the Barings' and did errands, I wrote on this, and finally we went to the Conway's to dine. The company was Mr W. B. Scott, Mr Hixon, Mr Ellis, and Mr Allingham. I sat by Mr Allingham. he was very good company. The next day in quite another company I heard the praises of a beauty, a Southern woman sent out by Jefferson Davis during our war to use her influence in gaining England's favour for his cause. In telling Father how beautiful she was, the lady said, "The ship went down and she was drowned on her voyage home. We were all so sorry! And Prof. Owen almost shed tears to think that so beautiful a specimen of a woman was lost in such a way."

Sunday (Easter) April 13th. After breakfast as I recounted our invitations, and among them Lady Augusta's to go to church with her, at the Abbey, Father suddenly resolved on going. He wished to see the Abbey and to hear the Dean. So he went. Our waiter said service began at 11 everywhere, but "when we reached the Deanery door" we learned that in the Abbey it began at 10. However he took us through the house, through ancient cubbies, etc., most delightful to me, and opened a door into the nave. Thence we crossed to the North transept. He brought us chairs, and we heard, or tried to, almost half the service and one hymn. But the sermon we could hear. Curious indeed is the effect of the Church of England on the minds of its clergy. I know it by heart now—I have seen it so long in so many places—but cannot in the least express it or even define it to myself. I pity them, is the upshot of it. Happily there was some history in the sermon, and that interested Father so much that he was glad he went. After church we called on Mr Carlyle. I have seen no house yet that seemed to me quite so interesting and pleasant. He was in a more amiable and cheerful humour than he had been a few days before when Father walked with him, and Father has been very happy in the remembrance of this call. He said things about W. S. Landor that relieved Papa's mind moreover, giving him a hope that the sins of his hero were not so great as he has supposed. From there we went to Mrs. Paulet's to lunch, and oh! wasn't I petted by the three ladies! Partly because I belonged to Father and quite as much I think from the natural delight in anything younger than one's self, and they are an elderly household. I picked up many facts new to me and very interesting. The last Druid of an unbroken line from the beginning had just died. He always said his being a Druid didn't prevent his being a Christian. But he could not communicate the Druidical lore to anyone who hadn't taken the Druid's vows, and the man was not

— 1873 —

found to take them, and all has perished with this last representative. Mr Allingham came & took Father to Mr W. B. Scott's, & I came home. I think we had no calls that day.

Monday. April 14th.   Father went after receiving a note from Prof. Müller inviting him to read a couple of lectures at Oxford (he has refused) and an invitation from Mr. Hughes to the opening of the Workingmen's College, of which he is a new-elected principal succeeding F. D. Maurice. He is to give the address. We accepted. I remained alone to write. Miss Stanley called, Lady Amberley's sister. She is exceedingly kind and thinks always what she can do for us, and in this enlightened manner, that she always aims for something that no one else is likely able to do. For instance, the wife of the Queen's private secretary is her friend and lives in Windsor Castle, and she is going to take us out to see Windsor Park and then to this friend's to lunch and she is going to show us the Castle and the Queen's private garden and dairy. I am delighted with this. She stayed a long time and I enjoyed every minute, and was sorry to see her rise. She has also obtained seats at St. Paul's for us on Sunday to hear Dr. Liddon. She meant to have taken us to Eton, but it is vacation. Then came Mrs. Scott and wanted to see a picture of you, and we talked of children and housekeeping. When Father came home Mr. Conway came and stayed till we went out to dine at the Deanery. Dean Liddell of Christ Church, Oxford, was there and Mr & Mrs Leckie, and Dean Church of St Paul's with his wife, and the Duke & Duchess of Argyll. Alas! my main desire, which was to see Lady Augusta, wasn't entirely answered, though after dinner in a rather general conversation among the ladies I had the pleasure of seeing her pretty ways and hearing her talk ecclesiastical talk with Mrs Church. But I had a most delightful time nevertheless. At dinner I sat between Deans Stanley & Liddell & much delectable conversation between them passed over me. They talked of Egypt. Why and how has Egypt such a hold upon me? No other subject seems to interest me to the same degree, and the memory of it is so lovely. They talked of committees; there again they touched what I like best. They talked of the portraits of former Deans on the wall, and of the Abbey, of fires, and of London. It was enchanting. I suddenly realized that I wasn't likely to see Lady Augusta again, she is going to Paris.

Tuesday Apr 15th.   Many callers. Very early Mr Smalley & Philip a beautiful boy seven years old. Then Mr Norton & Baron MacKaye. Then Sir Frederick Pollock & Dr Garth Wilkinson. All these calls truly

— 1873 —

delightful. Then came Mrs Smalley, very handsome, though delicate, and took me to drive in Hyde Park. She had Philip, Eleanor & Evelyn with her. She gave me good advice about shops, and wished to do a thousand things for me. Mr S. had undertaken Father's small jobs in the morning. I came in and found Father very sorry to have missed all these calls, he had been out since Mr Smalley's. We dined at home. Had a beautiful time. Dr Hinton came to see him, author of Man & his Dwelling Place. At ten he went, & Father went to Lady Amberley's where he met Mr Browning and was well pleased. They disagreed about poetry. Mr Browning praised Shelley.

Wednesday Apr 16. Today breakfast at Argyll Lodge, and a beautiful time. Saw Ladies Elizabeth, Mary & Constance Campbell, and the youngest son. Then went with Mr Geo. Howard to his house, perfectly beautiful. You can't imagine the interest of portraits in these houses. I've omitted the very interesting call of Mrs Conway & Miss Biggs

Letter ends abruptly.

R.R. May 1 1873

Dear Family,

My last account ended just a fortnight ago I think, on April 16th. The next day we dined at the Nortons', had a beautiful time. Mr Lewes who wrote the Life of Goethe & married Miss Evans was there, and was skillful in telling stories. I spent the P.M. with Una. On April 18th we went to breakfast with Mrs Smalley. The company was Mrs Jones, Mr Cyrus W. Field, Mr Boughton the painter of my "Pilgrims going to Church", Mr Hill the editor of the Daily News, I think no one else. My chief occupation on the occasion was seeking names of good children's books, and the dear pretty children brought me all their books and discoursed on their merits. Another pleasure was being shown over the house. The furniture renewed my old longing to carry home a quantity for Edith & us & Edward. Friday afternoon I called on Lady Stanley. She always sits from four to six in her parlour with the tea things on a table close by, and a nice broad cricket before her with the newspaper on it, and twice I have found her alone, twice with daughters. That evening we dined with the Howards. Mr Howard is a young gentleman who loves Father as all the Stanley family seem to, and whom Father always enjoys. His wife is Rosalind, Lady Stanley's youngest child, who is handsome and very sweet. The dear Lady Augusta and Dean Stanley came for us and took us to the dinner in their carriage. It was one of the

1873

glories of the evening—such a comfort to have another lady to go with too. The other guests were Sir Arthur Helps, Mr Browning, Mr Froude, the Duke & Duchess of Argyle. Saturday morning we called on the William B. Scotts but they were out, on Mr Carlyle, also out, and dined at Kensington Museum and looked it over with Mr Allingham host, & Mr Browning. We had very good talk & I saw Raphael's Cartoons, & a baby-house of Queen Anne's time. Sunday to church. Then to lunch with Dr Carpenter, then to St. Paul's to hear Dr. Liddon, then for a moment called to consult with Miss Stanley & say Father would dine there, & I would stay at home. He did accordingly with Mr Dasent and others. Monday I went to Seven Oaks to see Knole Park, and Father the House of Commons; the Duke of Bedford & Mr Playfair seemed to be the people who talked with him most. I came home, we dined together, and he went with Mr Hughes to the Workingmen's College. Tuesday we breakfasted with dear Sir Henry Holland—perfect bliss. Then at eleven o'clock went to Eton and Windsor with Miss Stanley & Mr Howard, lunched with Mrs Ponsonby in the Castle, and saw all my soul desired, the family rooms, the family miniatures, as well as the state apartments and the Home Park. Came home and dined with the Hugheses and W. E. Forsters. Wednesday, breakfasted at Mr Cyrus W. Field's with Mr Gladstone, the Duke of Argyle, Mr Hughes, Mr Norton, Mr Smalley. Another most important conversation. At one we lunched with Mr Tyndall, Mr Huxley and Mr Hurst being the other guests. Mr Allingham took us at three to see Guild Hall and the other antiquities of the city. At eight we dined with Lady Airlie. The company was the Duke and Duchess of Cleveland, Duke and Duchess of Argyle, Mr Campbell, Mr Howard, Lady Stanley, Mr Browning and Mr Cowper, who was once in Concord. Lady Clementine Ogilvy was the only child of the house at dinner. Thursday Father breakfasted with Mr Gladstone at 10, having received a call at 9 from Mr Dasent, and Mrs Conway & I went and did the crockery and shawl buying. I wound up with a farewell call on Lady Stanley, and Father, after breakfast with Mr Gladstone, spent the forenoon with Mr Carlyle with real comfort, bade him goodbye, and then went to the Howards' and lunched with Mrs Lewes. We dined at Sir Frederick Pollock's with Sir William Boxhall and Tyndall Oliphant, and had very good talk at dinner. Friday, calls all day, lunch at Mrs E. Arnold's with Mr W. H. Channing. Dined at the Conways' with Mr Sterling, son of Father's love, Mr Francis Wm. Newman, Mr Colvin and two others. Saturday packed and went Sunday to Tintern Abbey and Ravenscroft, stayed with the Amberleys, liked

— 1873 —

them very much. Rachel a beauty and sweet. Monday to Cyfarthfa and luxury and the kindest hostess. Mr Conway also for two days. Then to Oxford.

E. T. E.

Stratford on Avon May 3rd 1873

My dear Childy [Edith Davidson],

Your letters are just what I like, and I am so thankful for them every time they come that I hate not to answer them. It was a happy day for me when you took to writing to me before you went to bed. We have just come from Oxford. I thought of Tom Brown and Mary and of Norman and Meta when we walked in Christ-Church meadows, and I was allowed to see many things—Hall, for instance, where the students dine, with the tables all set for dinner; the buttery where they go for luncheon; the rooms where they hear lectures; the chapels with service going on; and best of all, I thought, the kitchen of Christ-Church with its ancient fire-places just as you read in books—really all the way across the room three of them—and spits twelve feet long covered with legs of mutton turning by the jack before the fire, open coal fire. The quadrangles and gardens were as beautiful as you can imagine. The students, all in caps which look well and gowns which are absurdly short and ugly, came to the two lectures which I went to, Mr. Max Müller's and Mr. Ruskin's, and behaved like any other audience. I didn't see them enjoying cloisters, quadrangles or gardens, but was told it was because I came in hours when they were working or dining. If I had time darling, wouldn't I tell thee long yarns! Of Prince Leopold's coming to lunch with us and our going to tea with him and his showing me the pictures of his family. You know my sentiments on the subject of the Royal Family and can imagine how pleased I was. Of Mr. Ruskin whom I fell in love with—the seriousness of his talk, the sweetness of his ways, the interest of his rooms and things he showed us. Of dear Mr. Max Müller and his delightful family, especially the little girls, and all little English sisters. Of a hundred things that come and go all unrecorded. It is too bad. Goodbye, in thirteen days after this I shall get home and hope to see thee at once. E. T. E.

Stratford-on-Avon.
Monday. May 5th. 1873.

Dear Edith,

I lost the mail I meant to send this by, so I'll write all I can. First I'll

— 1873 —

tell you about our visit here and then backward if there's time. We left Oxford and the dear kind Max Müllers early Saturday morning and came to Warwick where Mr. Flower met us to take us to the Castle and Father went over it, but alas! my dissipation in London and the daily overwork ever since had told so far that I couldn't. I sat in the carriage meanwhile and saw its glories from outside, and Mr. F. also drove me over the town; then we came home by Charlcote and Hampton Lucy and saw the beautiful park with old elms, and finally came to the house at The Hill about noon, tired to death and frozen, and you can imagine how kindly Mrs. Flower received me. I begged off from seeing anything and she promised I shouldn't and asked Father to stay another day on my account, so now for three days I have done nothing, been in bed, or warm and still before the fire, and petted besides, till this afternoon I am quite able to hold up my head and begin to feel well again. It has been also such a comfortable opportunity to mend the clothes which required a few stitches in order to look as respectable as they really are and to write the six notes which manners absolutely demanded. So that now I am more at ease morally as well as physically. That class which Father calls "very young persons" have discovered that he is in England and he has letters asking him to arrange an interview anywhere, anyhow, only not to refuse. Some he answers and often he has to let them go. When Mr. Flower brought us to the door he began to call to Mrs. Flower that we had arrived, so that she came out and met us in the entry, and Miss Graves with her. Lunch was waiting, so I said we wouldn't go up stairs first, and they took us into the dining room and let me sit by the fire, with those charming stuffed foxes on each side—do you remember them?—and began proposing brandy, port, sherry, claret, Chablis, ale and beer—a game which they amused themselves with repeating all the visit through—and Mrs. Flower gave me wine jelly because there was no rule against eating wine. What a delightful room I had over the dining-room with a bay window to the South and a couch in it, where the sun shone, and a large light table that rolled close up or pushed away easily. Mrs. Flower said, "Now I know you long to be in bed and by yourself, so stay up stairs as much as you like." And what comfort I did have resting in the sun! Never had so much luxury before in my life. They went to church to Shakespeare's church for our sake, and Father went too. At the door the clerk met us and told Mrs. Flower that Mrs. Walters was sitting in the chancel and we might sit there too by Shakespeare's tomb, so we did. They had the grand choral service which seems to be always used in England now, and which English people seem to prefer, but I can't like it. Mrs. Flower and Miss Graves said all I could desire against it. After church we went to see both the married sons. What beautiful, beautiful houses! And the eight children under twelve, all together, all with curly hair, all fresh dressed for Sunday were a sight after my own heart. If you could only have seen the triumphal entry of Oswald, aged two, both arms out and shouting with delight! It was magnificent. He came, as Lotty said of Augustus, as if he had been shot from a cannon. Meanwhile Father went back to the church to take a better look at the tomb and see how Miss Bacon probably would have planned to disturb those mysterious bones. We met Mr. Flower coming down "the Hill," and Father got out, and they walked up together. Then dinner, and Polly came to the table and would do nothing except say "Polly" in a most agreeable English voice till she was banished to the conservatory, when she whistled several tunes and Father was edified. They walked out in the afternoon and Mrs. Flower made me write my mental photograph next to yours, then Father's for him in the evening. I'll mail this this minute. No, Father won't let me. Father read aloud in the evening and Mr. Flower made Mrs. Flower recite Tennyson's "Daisy."

[Unsigned]

Edinburgh May 9th 1873

Dear Edith,

The amount of writing I daily accomplish is really respectable, for instance I have sent six notes today, but then none of it is to America so I don't count it at all, and I really feel dreadfully to think how I neglect you all, though Annie has been much worse treated than any one else, so that my remorse centres on her. I want to answer your last note and see no chance but now, while I am eating my dinner (at Kennedy's Hotel, which I exceedingly like), alone, for Father is dining with Dr Smith who was good to you and Will. That letter enclosed my dear Ralph's & Violet's pictures. You don't know what a start it gave me to see them so big and old. I looked for infants and behold! a big boy, and a big girl. Ralph has his own dear mouth, but the rest of his face looks as if his character were under a cloud. The little Violet is very well taken, the likeness is very true, but not lucky. Photographers have a trick of insulting my niece, they always did. I see the resemblance to Mother, it interests me as much as you knew it would. She is the only one of the children that I think of with pleasure and security that she will take any

— 1873 —

comfort with me, the other three seem like delights out of their aunt's reach. My daughter has written me a capital description of them all. I have bought me from you and Will two presents that are a pleasure all the time, a gold watch-key from you, and an alarm clock from Will. I've been buying 6 Scotch sheets for Bush & some flannel for petticoats, your magic-lantern, & I bought the monocle in London, but in Stratford Mr Flower insisted on giving Father his, which is bigger. I'm looking out of the window on those white-jacketed Highlanders you admired.

Goodbye, beloved, for only one week.

E. T. E.

May 1873 - December 1874

Return to Boston and welcome by the town of Concord. Long visit at Naushon. Edward Forbes born. Forbes children visit Concord. 1874. Concord and Milton. Naushon. Trip to Providence and New York. Edward Waldo Emerson's marriage.

Boston. May 27th. 1873.

Dear Miss Clara,

Four years ago last night Mary Watson and I sailed up Boston Harbour on the Fredonia, and landed the next morning, and again last night I sailed up on the Cunard just too late to land, and came ashore this morning, exactly keeping the anniversary. Wasn't it curious? It was beautiful yesterday afternoon. We had had bitter cold weather at sea, and when we came in sight of land it began to be warm. Everything was in fresh spring green and looked most lovely, and Boston seen from the sea was quite as beautiful and imposing a sight as I had hoped; then the sunset was magnificent, the best I have seen since we were in Egypt. On the Fredonia we were too late to see anything for she came in slowly against the wind, but yesterday we reached the dock at seven. We had good singers among the passengers—on Sunday we had a general hymn singing that was truly delightful—and they sang all the patriotic songs they could think of as we approached home. I am spending the day in the depot as they haven't got the house in order at home yet and hoped we shouldn't arrive till afternoon, and Father is going about to attend to business and see friends in the city, and I am pleased to have the chance to finish my accounts etc. The first piece of news that meets me on landing is that Sylvia Watson is engaged to our distant cousin Ralph Emerson. I hope it is a pleasure to Mary.

Concord. June 7th 1873.   Ah! it is well I began before I came home. There has been no chance for writing since, and I'm afraid the Fredonia sails on Monday. Thank you for your letter, very interesting to me, with its stories of you all. I won't have you call going to Europe more interesting to me than going to Fayal without protesting. For whatever reason, Fayal was a greater experience, very much. It seems as if this going abroad would always occupy a smaller place in my memory. And yet I have travelled far and wide, and have seen so many people that I feel as if I had seen all there are. Mr Ruskin was the man that interested

— 1873 —

me most, and his sadness went to my heart, but Father was displeased with it. Everywhere the want of sincerity troubled and tired me, and when I found a person who said what he meant, I valued him immensely—and Mr Ruskin did. But Father said he was wilfully gloomy. Every time we went out to dine the first fortnight in London, we met Dean Stanley and Lady Augusta, and at last the Dean said, "I'm sure you must be tired of meeting the same people. It will get to seem to you like a family-party." Of course it did, and that made it all the pleasanter. He is very cold in his ways and it took some time to get used to him, but I did at last, and sitting by him at the last two dinners before he went to Paris was absolutely delightful. At his house I sat between him and Dean Liddell, who is a great friend of his apparently, and they talked together across me. That was lovely, especially when they talked about Egypt, now a favourite subject with me. One night at Mrs. Howard's he and Mr. Froude and Sir Arthur Helps were talking, and he said he never liked so well to address an audience that agreed with him as one that didn't, and that started a most interesting conversation. Then he was led to speak of Rugby and Dr. Arnold, and I heard that with still greater pleasure. Lady Augusta was my good angel in London as she had been all winter. I took great comfort in her. Did I tell you Dr. Wister said she was the most attractive woman in England? I must tell you now of our coming home, it was so wonderful. Father and Will and Edward came to the depot where I was writing to you, and we got off in the two o'clock train. Edward sat with me and we had a great chatter all the way. But when we rolled into Concord depot, and I began to collect my eight small pieces, I wasn't allowed to take one—not the lightest—which seemed to me unreasonable when my brothers were so loaded down, and I was disposed to bicker, and insist on knowing why. Edward said, "You'll want your hands to give to your friends." So I thought some of them would be there. My dear Irish saint stood before me as I jumped out. I thought she must be going to take the train, and asked her. She struggled hard not to cry and said she had come to meet me. Well certainly, I had one friend to shake hands with, but I didn't see any more, except those who were getting out of the cars. However, it was well to have my hands for them, so I was more submitted to Edward's wilfulness. As I came through the depot to look for Dolly & the carry-all, I beheld Uncle George Bradford outside. Now I had understood from late letters that he had just sailed for England, and was surprised and glad to find he hadn't, so I ran out to him, and, speaking with him,

— 1873 —

saw nothing but him for an instant. Then I looked up, and oh! what a sight! what a sight! My whole dear town all assembled. Just as they always did in the war to see the Company off or receive it back, just as they do on Decoration Day, or any great town occasion, a sight always festal, and that makes each individual proud anew of Concord every time it occurs and fills us all with joy that we belong together and that we are so fond of each other. And *this* was all for us! Just at this moment Father came out of the depot. Sam Hoar ran to his side and cried out, "Now three cheers for Mr. Emerson!" and the town shouted. The train moved, and all its windows were opened and another cheer from the people in the cars, as they went on. There was a grand barouche for us, and when we were in I had a capital position for a survey of the whole. There were all the schools, marshalled under their own teacher. That was for me I knew. Even the outer districts were there—schools three and four miles off. There was the band, our new pride—we have only had one four years—all of our own boys, and it is growing to be a first-rate one. There were crowds on foot, and almost every wagon and carryall in town, full. One drove up beside us, full of babies. Ralph and Cameron and John Murray Forbes Jr., and two Edith Forbeses and Edith Davidson helping to hold the little boys. Father was so delighted when I showed him this carriage, and the proud Edith held first one and then another out of the window, but we couldn't get at them really, only admire them very much. Then other carriages drove up to speak, and presently the band began to play, and the carriages formed in line, the schools started off on each side-walk, and everyone followed, and so we had a triple procession down the street, and at all the windows of the houses were the aged and lame and feeble people who couldn't come out, waving their handkerchiefs; and by differences in pace every part of the sidewalk processions passed and repassed us so that on the way home we saw every one, how much each child had grown, and how each person was looking, and had perpetual bows and shouted conversation. By degrees all the walkers got ahead of us and when we came to the fork of our own road, just at the corner of our yard we found a great arch with "Welcome" on it, covered with vines, and with mounds of pots of flowers all round its feet—the schools in two lines four double, reaching just to its foot, singing Home Sweet Home, and the town in its order round about, just as at the depot. No one came into the yard. We came in peacefully by ourselves, and found Mother at the East Door, and then we went through the shining new magnificence of

— 1873 —

the house to the Front Door, and stood to see all the people. It at once reminded me of the many descriptions I had heard of the day of the fire. Ten months ago they had all been there to help us save what they could, and had stood and cried to see the house burn. And now they had all come once more to see us into the house again. Father went out to the gate to thank them, and then they all went away, and we began to hear the history of it—how the Judge—Judge Hoar—had thought of it and there had been meetings and consultations and arrangements—how the night before the bells were rung to let everyone know the steamer was in, and early in the morning the bell tolled the hour at which we should arrive, so that every one might know, and the telegram Edward sent at noon, to follow up the first which gave the probable hour, didn't arrive, so there was still a little doubt and Concord telegraphed to the President of the road to let the engine give notice whether we were on board when it approached, so, sure enough, no sooner did the train emerge from the woods than it began to whistle and that engine just bawled all the rest of the way! "No one ever heard such a noise before!" said my informant. Then we were led all over the house, which in most particulars is exactly the same—the new curtains are like the old, the new carpets are the same colours, and so are the new papers. The old furniture and knick-knacks and pictures are for the most part in their old places. But everything is new and fresh and handsome, and a shade grander than before in some places. Our children were all delightful. Ralph seemed simply improved. Little Edith was shy but she got acquainted at last. Cameron & John were pretty strangers, but I made some progress with them before they went. Goodbye, and give my love to Mrs Dabney and Alice, and your present daughter Francy, and Mrs Oliver.   Ellen T. Emerson.

Milton June 14th 1873

Dear Mother,

I went first in to see Mrs Forbes before I presented myself in Paradise. I found her in the library with company, Mrs Jack Hale and Mrs Machin, and Alice behold! had just returned from Burlington! and she was there. Also Jenny Perkins and Nelson were on the floor. Presently Sarah came down. They made my visit utterly delightful, and Alice & Sarah accompanied me across the lawn towards Edith's. I went right to her room and found her sitting up on her couch, sewing, dressed in her dressing-gown, and Florence reading to her. Presently Cameron strayed in with a cart and came up and kissed his aunt with great piety, and John passed the door, and when earnestly pressed to come in replied prettily "I won't", and began backing downstairs to his supper, but he didn't object to being caught and made much of. When Will came, he invited me to see the new house, and we walked over, saw the great cellar nearly stoned, and the beams lying sorted on the grass, with the holes, or mortises, or something, all cut in them, and behind, a vast spreading wilderness of dirt, reminding one of the Mokattan scenery of Egypt, enlivened by the presence of a brown boy, a gray girl, and a yellow dog, to wit my darlings & Nip, who revelled in the small Sahara, and Nip seemed to be a true playmate to understand and join all the plays entirely and add very much to the fun. I thought them a most enchanting sight. Presently Jane came in search of them and Will had to exercise all his authority to bring the four human feet bedward in the strait paths of virtue, but Nip followed voluntarily. They disappeared, we had tea, Edith didn't come down. This morning Edith is dressed and seems pretty well. She has a cook at last, a capital one.

E. T. E.

Friday June 20 1873

Dear Edith,

I was thankful to hear from Sophy that you got off yesterday. I hope we shall have a note announcing your state and the looks of your Naushon house to you very soon. I ought to tell you of the lovely wedding (Ned Bartlett & Sally F.) and all the pleasures I there enjoyed, but no time. Uncle C., Aunt S. and Lidian are going to stay till Sat. & keep Uncle C.'s birthday here. Louie & John are here, the preparations for our reception press today for yesterday I did little more than get rooms ready. With both my new handmaids I find the old Maxim startlingly true, "If you want a thing *done*" Our strawberry crop fails from drought. My love to my darling Ralph & Violet, and the precious little scamps, and oh! my Alexander* & his mamma! Kate Hoar said you had the four most beautiful children that ever were seen.

Ellen T. Emerson

June 22nd 1873

Dear Edith,

Our reception was more pleasant than my anxious mind has be-

---

*Ellen was so anxious to have a nephew named Alexander that she began to call each new baby by that name.

— 1873 —

lieved possible, as pleasant as Annie said it would be. The joys began on Friday with the lemon-squeezing bee, which was an assemblage of that most delightful class, the old and frolicsome. Louisa Alcott, Annie & Lizzy Bartlett, C. Cheney, E. Storer & Mrs Sanborn who brought Tommy. He was an invalid & lay on the sofa and his mother reports that he enjoyed it exceedingly. We laughed till we almost died all the time, and Mother was there arranging flowers, and we felt all so busy & sociable, it was blissful. Dear Lizzy Bartlett & Louisa took the lead. Lizzy managed & Louisa had the tasting, till at last Lizzy called out "Here! I want someone with less extravagant tastes than Louisa. She likes pure lemon-juice & sugar. We should have to send for a box of lemons to satisfy her." So with much mutual abuse on Lizzy's & Louisa's part, Cary C. succeeded to the tasting. They staid till seven & Louisa & Lizzy promised to come early the next day & be hostesses. We actually had the house perfect from top to bottom in good season. Lizzy Bartlett came at 3, just as I had gone up to dress, and brought "my friend Mrs Bartlett" who stayed with me & assisted & sympathized through the various mischances of putting on a new dress for the first time—my blue muslin—and Lizzy put on a long dark calico apron over her white flounces and went down to mix & ice the lemonade. When I descended I tried to produce symmetry on the table. It seemed to me much like the "A man had a goose, a fox and a bag of corn, etc." and I puzzled in vain. Presently I called Louisa to my aid. She squinted learnedly at the problem for a minute, suggested the simplest possible change, and that being made brought all right. "That is what I call applying MIND to Matter!" cried she triumphantly. All was scurry and that is my only excuse for the awful fact that our own two dozen lemonade glasses, bought on purpose, our three dozen plates and dozen tumblers, stood idly in the closet, and we used and broke only our Neighbours' china! Did you ever hear so disgraceful a story? Well, our dear Annie presently came & took hold & then Elise Holmes and Cary Wood arrived. Next came Miss Clara Garfield, and Emma her niece. Then people began to come in floods. I had a beautiful time, though often afflicted by the memory of one family or another that I thought would come & didn't and it made me fear they hadn't heard of it. But so many came, and the party was so cheerful that I was surprised and happy. When it was nearly over, came the little Lidian to take leave, for at noon had come a most alarming telegram saying Uncle Charles had had a paralytic shock. At first Mother was in despair, afterward remembering those times which he has often had, she became more hopeful. Since then Father has seen him, and we have better news. He can speak. This is far more serious than previous attacks.

Friday morning.   Aunt Susan wrote yesterday, more anxiously. She thinks him worse. Mother may go down today to see him. I am at the Manse with Nina & Annie all visiting Cousin E. together. Yesterday at the Museum was so good. I long to tell you all about it, also Father's Commencement, but no time now.

E. T. E.

Concord June 23rd 1873

Dear Edith,

Thy letter from Naushon has come and we are most thankful for its surpassing good news of yourself and the pretty stories of the babies' entrance on their new domain. Mother who knows them best said they were most characteristic. Tues. eve. Now, from disability, and all my time yesterday and today being taken up with examining schools for promotion, I have let Annie go off without the black serge & forgot the soap which was all ready. I'll try to get them to Miss Leavitt. Tomorrow I go to the Dentist, Thursday to the meet at Mr Agassiz's museum, come home to meet Nina and spend the night at the Manse. Next Tuesday Mr Gurney & Ellen are coming. Ida has invited me to Beverley. You know you are to send me the note beforehand, and telegraph to Alicia. Mother asked me yesterday if I wasn't going when the Baby came. I said you were to send when you were ready for me.

E. T. E.

Beverly July 9th 1873

Dear Mother,

I came down in the cars with all Concord, so to speak. Everyone I knew seemed to be there, and we had a gay excursion to Boston. Then I went round doing errands till eleven when I came to Beverly. Ida was sitting on the platform waiting for me. Having exchanged greetings I told Ida I had three notes to write, and she said now was the best time, so I rushed into the parlour and wrote three, carried them to the office and finding there was yet time before the mail went, I came home & wrote another, and then felt free to enjoy myself. In the afternoon Ida and I drove over to Amy Cabot's new house, which is beautiful. It has a cool and spacious look, just right for a summer house. We found the family on the beach, and sat with them there in the sun for some time.

— 1873 —

The babies look pretty & healthy, but a little small, Amy quite feeble. Yesterday we had a call from Saidie Cabot, one from Mrs Geo. Russell, both perfectly delightful. All calls here are, people know each other so well. Robert Peabody came down and spent the day. We had many questions to ask him, and spent a very talkative hour. Then I went up to Mrs Cabot's, saw Charley, Richard and the twins, and had a beautiful time with Mrs Cabot, to say nothing of having overtaken Mrs Parkman on the way, and walked up the Ave. with her. We took tea with Col. Pierson, a bachelor who has been building and furnishing a little summer-palace here, and he showed us from garret to cellar, kitchen & closets and all. It was most perfect. The company were Miss Amelia Russell, Annie Agassiz, Ida and I. Having studied the house and had a grand tea, and admired the china, and cloth, waiter, napkins, and doileys, & the markings, also the candle-sticks and hot-water-pot, we next saw the interior of the side-board, and turned over the table-cloths which were the finest fine, and of beautiful figures. Then we had a fire, for it was cold, in the parlour, and looked at war photographs and talked over war-times, a most exciting subject. Wednesday we went to Nahant to see Pauline. Before we went we read the Advertiser's account of the opening of Mr Agassiz's new school at Penikese, and were very much amused. At Nahant Mrs Agassiz's letter, you know she has a talent for letter-writing, filled out the picture. The day at Nahant was very happy, if I only had time to tell you all about it. All the five Shaws & little Cecile together, all such good pretty interesting children, Mr Shaw at home, and funny and charming with all the children, also he had been in Egypt, and we talked together about it, Pauline herself always lovely, and easy to talk with. Then I made acquaintance with the junior Feltons, Lisa, Conway and Tom, and was glad of that. I wished you could have heard Mr Shaw on Woman's Rights. We came home & had Mr Elliot Cabot, Dr Hooper with Clover's letters, Mrs Parkman and Fanny Morse to tea. High festival. I shall come home Sat. at 3.15.
E. T. E.

Naushon July 17th 1873
Dear Mother,
Haven't I got my new blessed creaking darling under my left hand this minute, patting him with all my might for fear the creaking should become crying. His whole family is perfectly delighted with him. Miss Leavitt says she is the only one who is indignant because he is not a girl.

— 1873 —

A minute ago he was awake and good and Mrs R. carried him in to show him to Edith who hadn't seen him since he was first dressed yesterday. I went in too. Edith looks well and was quite pleased with the sight, hideous though it was, of his big red face, little half-open eyes, for they were swollen, and plentiful brown hair. Will & I say he looks like Ralph, though Ralph didn't have those broad fat cheeks and round plump hands, he was thin when he was born, but this one weighed 12 lbs! They telegraphed for me and the Doctor early yesterday but the baby had no thought of waiting & Mrs Rounsavelle & Will only were with Edith when he was born at five minutes past eight in the morning. His grandmother Forbes was in the entry and had him to hold. The children were not allowed to see him till afternoon. My own story had better begin here. Henry Cook came to row me over and with many smiles told me that the baby was born in the morning and was a son. (I had heard the news from Mac at the office before coming down.) When I reached the wharf no carriage, no one. It was just about sunset, and I was anxious to see Alexander before dark, so I walked up fast, came in softly, and was half-way upstairs when I saw Ralph, and he ran to me on tiptoe with broad smiles saying in a loud whisper "Aunt Ellen! Did you know we've got a little new baby?" Mrs Rounsavelle came and said I might go in and see Edith and come right out again. Mrs R. said the object was ready for exhibition, and we went to the window of the yellow room, the blanket was turned back and the round dark red countenance was revealed. He is patient & sweet in disposition.

[Unsigned]

July 18th 1873 Naushon

Dear Mother,

With little baby right beside me, for Mrs Rounsavelle lets me have the basket in my room by day, I sit down to finish my tale (my letter yesterday was snatched from me in the midst by the departing boatman). Will came up and invited me down to tea, the baby was whisked back into twilight regions, pretty Violet went to bed, and Ralph descended with me. After supper I caught Mrs R. just long enough to hear that they telegraphed to Milton for Dr Holmes, and sent to New Bedford & to Falmouth for doctors. The Falmouth doctor came first and found Edith all comfortably resting and the baby washed & dressed and then came Dr Abbe. Before they had gone came Dr Holmes, who spent

— 1873 —

the night. Our children are all crazy about the baby, none of them ever showed so much pleasure before. This morning Ralph ran & brought Cameron very softly for a peep & a kiss, then John Murray was brought, in a willing not enthusiastic mood, and sat in my lap resting his folded arms on the edge of the basket, gravely contemplating the wonder inside. R. & V. stayed & admired him undisturbed for an hour. Miss Leavitt & I went over to the Mansion House to tea, and I spent the night there, because Mrs Forbes was left alone in the house, the family are away. She came home with me this morning; we came upstairs and found the lamb wide awake. We brought it & its basket into my room & Mrs F. sat down & held it and presently Miss Leavitt brought Ralph up and Jane collected the rest of the family. The loveliest sight! I wish you could have seen. All four gazing with such pretty smiles, and the three eldest never tire, never get through enjoying him. Jane is inclined to think he will outshine W. C. & J. M. Please send word how you do, and if my conduct was wicked. I enclose a list of things that I want in my trunk. My love to Father & Aunt Lizzy.

E. T. E.

Sunday July 20th 1873 Naushon

Dear Mother,

Father's letter came last night and afforded us all great satisfaction, though what he said about you tended to increase my fear that it is naughty to leave you. Send for me when you think you are not so well without me. Yesterday afternoon Sarah Forbes came home from Newport and New Bedford and appeared among her nephews & niece like a summer St. Nicholas with two great bags containing bundles, and these bundles proved to be magnificent presents for the children. Sarah is one of the best aunts I ever saw, and the children are very fond of her, and Edith very grateful. Annie Anthony came too, and both were interested in the new baby. But he is most hideous.

Monday 21st. This morning Edith is better, really had a good night. Yesterday Alice & Sarah visited me in the afternoon and we sat in the nursery with the little boys. Alice makes them so polite to her, I wish everyone did, they must always look at her when she speaks, and perform all the ceremonies. The little baby has ceased to be a great curiosity, and no longer occupies the children's whole thoughts, but they like very much to see him and give him a kiss, and Ralph likes to

— 1873 —

hear schemes of what four brothers can do. I am prevented from writing by the care of Cameron.

E. T. E.

Naushon July 21st 1873

Dear Mother,

The baby is fading from his original glorious scarlet into a common brown colour I am sorry to say. He is remarkably good & cries very little, but when he does cry it is a very loud and ugly noise. Violet has been here with him and plays very prettily with the kitchen her Aunt Sarah gave her, stirring up a pudding of wild-rose leaves & stamens and cooking it on the stove, then dishing it in a plate & carrying it out to her doll.

Tuesday July 22nd   My trunks have come and I am delighted with the profusion of letters within. Annie's was a pleasant surprise, and tell her I was most thankful for the news of you, and for her care in sending me all the things I wanted. I shall send back on Friday some that I have done with with my dirty clothes. When Father comes he must bring me what is on the enclosed list of things. Mr Forbes says Father must come down with him from the club next Saturday. Mr Agassiz is coming. Edith has set her heart on his appearing then, and taking possession of his study, and abiding with her till the fall of the leaf. She sends her love to you and thanks for your pleasure in the baby, and is also much obliged for the present of me for a month. Cameron went into water yesterday and behaved pretty well. So did Violet. Alice took us (Miss Leavitt, the bairns & me) a long ride yesterday afternoon and I saw the island in glory, the sun through flat beech boughs, the beautiful smooth valleys of dried leaves, and blue seas with plenty of schooners.

Your affectionate daughter
Ellen T. Emerson

Dolly is wanted here. Oh Mamma, meaning to wind up with it, I omitted to thank you for your delightful letter, all balm to my soul. It is so good to get one from you.

Naushon Monday July 27th 1873

Dear Mother,

Today John is 23 mos. old and Edward Waldo Forbes is 11 days old. His papa wrote a letter last night to his Uncle Edward to tell him he had a namesake, and Violet has her wish, and so has everyone at the

— 1873 —

other house. Will named him and kissed him for his name, and there is complete satisfaction everywhere, and I'm sure that there will be at Bush, and that even at the Massachusetts General Hospital there will be pleasure, and as for Annie!——John behaved like a hero in the water yesterday, didn't much enjoy it, but not a whimper escaped him. Cameron who had cried wildly till he came in was encouraged by his example and behaved better. Ralph & Edith didn't go in at all. Ralph has been so good and sensible and has obeyed so cheerfully lately that life is another thing. For the first week the only feeling I had after a meal was "It is over at last, and we are none of us dead". But now for days we have enjoyed our meals. Will says he has a written power of attorney from Uncle Charles. My trunk brought all I want. I'm much obliged.

Tuesday July 28th. We have just returned from a most delightful bath on the North Shore in Weepecket Bay, a new place. Will had one of the Northwest Gutter bathing-houses moved down there, and proposed trying it this morning. Only he and I and Jane & John went in. The day is as warm as toast and we rode down in the lovely sunny wind, walked down to the water over hot stones & smooth white sand. Will said he must view & correct my swimming today. To my surprise & joy he said "Why you get ahead beautifully. Why yes! you swim perfectly well." So I came out very proud and happy. Will was in high spirits, charmed with the place. If Edith was only well, we thought, what days of bliss we might have out there! to go blackberrying after breakfast, take our bath when the day was warm, dine under a tree and go deer-stalking in the afternoon. Edith is thriving as well as usual, and the baby who hasn't been quite free from indigestion for a day or two has seized the opportunity of showing his beautiful moral character, his courage, hope & patience. Yesterday I dined at the other house with Mr Agassiz, Annie & George, their last day there. You would have been interested in the dinner-conversation on spiritualism, only you couldn't have borne Mr A's arrant unbelief. I am now busy when in Edith's room with choosing & making letters for all the new linen, and we have very pleasant quiet hours together. Will I seldom see except at the table because we relieve each other in sitting with Edith, when he isn't with her, I am. Sometimes I have good plays with Ralph & Violet but oftener with the little boys because R. & V. are able to go off alone, and do, very much. Their delight now is berrying and their teeth are always blue. I hope you really eat your meals. Ask Father if he hears of anyone's coming to send my watch. When does he mean to come himself?

Your affectionate daughter
E. T. E.

Naushon July 31st 1873

Dear Mother,

Your letter of Tuesday arrived before breakfast, and we enjoyed hearing how you were pleased with the name. A letter from Annie came at the same time and delighted us. Yesterday afternoon Violet invited Cameron to go blackberrying with her, and they started out hand in hand and had a beautiful time, we could see the two hats among the bushes close together, and at last they came home, Cameron with the basket. I didn't see how many there were in it. I am glad you have found a way out about your curtain-tassels. Did your bonnet strings ever come? It is most gratifying to hear of a dinner-party. What you say of Father is an especial solace to Edith and me both. I shall send home the milk-bills tomorrow and ask Alicia if she will with John's & Rose's aid finish them. All four children went into water yesterday. Even Cameron liked it, and Ralph swam a little way alone. I have great hopes of his learning entirely.

August 1st. Edith has a hard headache today, and I feel very sorry to hear it. I'm afraid we did it by being too gay in her room yesterday. Will & I both sat there for an hour or two. He read aloud part of the time, but we talked and played every now and then. In the evening Mr Emmons & I were invited to join the picnic from the other house to the Weepeckets. We started about six and went in the long white boat named the King Fish, rowed by four pair of oars, Frank Watson, Jim Perkins, Mr Emmons & Nat Stone being the crew. It was warm & still & no fog. I never had visited the Weepeckets before. You ought to have seen the crowd of gulls who objected to the invasion and filled the whole sky as long as we stayed, all screaming at once, so that Frank Watson exclaimed "Is all this music furnished free of expense?" A very gay supper we had, and after it singing. There was a beautiful sunset, the boys built a bonfire on the beach at dusk, and we started for home by its light, and were rowed to the tunes of all the new college songs. I longed for Papa to hear. After I went to bed our bonfire still shone on the big Weepecket. Cameron has been very cunning. He is always sharp set for his meals. Invariably is the first to obey the bell, and we are pretty sure to find him in his chair ready for action when we come in. I hope I'm not too late for today's mail.

E. T. E.

Naushon Aug 2nd 1873

Dear Father,

Will received your letter about Aunt Susan last night and is thinking of it, he speaks as if he were not a very good person except that he should do it for nothing, and others would charge, but on the other hand he not being a lawyer would have to employ counsel and that might amount to the same thing. We have letters from Edward warning W. & E. against his name, but on the whole adopting the baby. That dear little boy has just been out taking a walk in the woods with his aunt and Cameron, he was awake all the time and looked about him with open eyes.

Alice Forbes said the other day "Do you know Sarah is getting steeped from the crown of her head to the sole of her foot in your father's writings?" "And the best yet is 'Behaviour' " said Sarah. "We read 'Behaviour' out in the woods" said Alice, "the other day when Annie Agassiz was here." "Oh, I had read it three times before that," said Sarah. Last night we took a ride, Will, Jane, Miss Leavitt, and I, with the four children. Miss Leavitt, Ralph, Violet & I were dropped near the trotting-course, and stole softly into it hoping to find deer. And we did. There was a beautiful yellow buck with branching horns. We sat in the bushes an hour but no more came. It grew dusk and we heard Will calling so started to meet the wagon. Ralph pointed. "What's that?" 'Twas a firefly. They never had seen one before. There were many about, and it was a great pleasure to the lambs. Edith's headache has gone today, but she doesn't feel as well as she did before she had it. Will is going to Boston on Tuesday. I enclose a note for one cent stamps. Would you rather I would write only four times a week? Remember I want some stamps, have only 9, and owe Will 19. I think it will be pleasanter for you to come down later, as now you couldn't see Edith. The table except at tea-time is a scene of nursery discipline merely. But I wish you could have this bathing now while it is so warm.

Your affectionate daughter
Ellen T. Emerson.

— 1873 —

Naushon Aug 6th 1873

Dear Mother,

Cameron is now my constant and almost sole companion, Ralph & Violet are big enough to be off by themselves, and when anyone is with them it is better that it should be Miss Leavitt because they have to mind her. Baby John is usually with Mrs Kelly and Jane, but Cameron is just the age to like an aunt, and sits where I sit and goes where I go. He went yesterday huckleberrying with Miss Leavitt and me. His innocence and enjoyment were refreshing every minute of the time. When he had what seemed to him a great many in his pail, that is about twenty, poor ignorant, he tripped and fell and the berries flew. Falling down is to his mind a natural part of walking, four or five falls an hour regularly through the day, and the berries weren't all lost. At breakfast-time they were divided among the children and Cameron was radiant. After the berrying I went to ride on horseback with Will, and oh! such a scene as the horse Billy went through with just as we were coming up to mount. For some unknown cause he was frightened to death, and desperately determined to get away. He was struggling & plunging, and throwing himself, it was a dreadful sight to see, and Will couldn't go near he was so wild. So Will stood as close as was safe, and commanded him, and made sympathizing inquiries till he at last quieted down and allowed Will to approach, though he kept threatening to begin again. Will said it was lucky he was tied with a strong new rope. As we rode Will talked with me about the guardianship of Aunt Susan. I do hope he'll undertake it, but he can't decide till after he goes to Boston. I shall send my blk. bag up on Friday A.M. Please send express for it to O.C. Depot, and he can bring it out by 2.30 train, so there'll be time to wash my things.

E. T. E.

Naushon August 11th 1873

Dear Mother,

Your letter about our new misfortune in the kitchen was a heavy blow. I hope it will soon appear which we must lose, though it would be better still if the priest could settle matters between them. Thank Father for his note with the postage stamps. The news has just come that Cora Lyman, the Theodore Lymans' only child, has died. I am so sorry. And Mrs Lyman had a little boy in Italy, in the winter, and he only lived a few days. On Saturday morning Miss Roxa [Dabney] came to the

— 1873 —

Mansion House. That was a great pleasure. I was interrupted by the mail going a little earlier than I thought, just as I was going to tell you about our little boys, both cantering over hill and dale as independently as Ralph could, on their hobbies. At last Jane came for them and I asked Cameron where his hobby slept. "In de shordet (closet)" he replied. Yesterday they were arrayed in blue ribbons, and their best hats, which they hadn't seen for six weeks and went over to the Mansion House. Their hats occupied their thoughts like Anne's & Martha's. "Isn't mine pretty, and isn't {Tam's / Baby's} pretty?" they asked some six times each, then Cameron raising his eyes to my best hat said "Oh! and isn't yours pretty too!" Baby following with exactly the same words, and so with cheerful mutual admiration we pursued our dusty way to the great house, where some fifteen of the family of twenty were pleased to see and take turns in holding the small bears. Ralph meanwhile appeared. He wrote you his letter of his own accord—probably being fresh from his mamma's room & her prompting—and liked to do it. He said "I wonder if she'll write an answer to it?" Edith is doing very well, free from all pains. I shall need ten dollars to pay my dentist.

Your affectionate daughter
E. T. E.

Naushon Aug 12th 1873

Dear Mother,

Today I am to spend the day at the Mansion House. I am expecting a beautiful time, but unluckily 'twill leave poor dear Edith all alone, for it is a capital sailing-day and Will is going out on the Azalea. I proposed changing the day, but Edith says "Oh no! do have it over." She is really better, and today Mrs R. lets her sit up in the rocking-chair for the first time. Ralph asks every now and then "Has Grandmamma got my letter yet?" He feels as Dr Holmes describes authors, he has sent out into the world a great production, and is awaiting its effect with the most impatient hope that it will be unparallelled. The other night we acted the Three Bears most beautifully, and Violet made a most perfect Silverhair, so that as she jumped out of the window with the three bears behind her Ellen Russell exclaimed "Don't she look just like the picture!" She & Ralph paint every day with Miss Leavitt, and she can now paint her picture with great exactness, seldom goes over the line. I must have some money before I go, $10.00 for the dentist & 5 more for

myself I think, also a Concord ticket, for I have none to return with, I cannot yet tell by which train I shall come. Tell Annie I was most grateful for her letter, and hope to get acquainted with her once more myself, it does seem to me a long time since we dwelt together too.
Your affectionate daughter
E. T. E.

Naushon Aug 13th 1873

Dear Mother,

 Edith proved not strong enough to try sitting up yesterday, but Mrs R. thinks she may today. I or rather Miss L. had a letter from Mrs Sanborn full of such good news of my class last night that I went to bed very happy. I also had a pleasant day at the Mansion House. Alice and Miss Roxy and I went to Imogen's Cradle in the morning and carried our work, and President Eliot's speech to read, but our attempts to read were vain, we had too much to say, we talked fast all the time. It was a great pleasure to see my two friends so long and peacefully, and the beauty of the day and place which we were meant to look at, utterly disappeared. I never saw it after the first glance. Then in the afternoon Miss Roxy read us her letters from home, and in the evening she took her guitar and sang the songs Mrs Oliver sang two years ago. I was especially pleased to hear the "O my soul" again. When she comes to Concord Aunt Lizzy will hear. The baby is four weeks old. He was weighed and is now 13½ lbs. I shall hate to leave him, and all. Your letter of Monday has come. I am sorry you have been sick, but pleased with your news of home, and your sympathizing with your grandchildren which does not surprise me. Poor Aunt Susan, I hope she will take a guardian. Thursday Aug. 14th. I have to announce that Edith did sit up yesterday for half an hour successfully, so I suppose she will again today. It rains this morning for the first time since April on the island, that is there have been two or three hours of rain, hard rain, they have had one or two showers of an hour's length in the course of the summer. My bag has never come, if it is at the O.C. depot I'll look for it when I come home. I shall come up at 2.20 I suppose, and I mean to get Anne to help me unpack. I shall rejoice to get back to my parents and my place, if I do hate to leave Edith.

E. T. E.

— 1873 —

Concord Monday Aug 18th 1873

Dear Edith,

We reached Boston at quarter of three, I mailed the letters, and then went straight to our depot and ate my dinner & wrote to Miss Clara till it was time to come home. Edward Bartlett saw to my disembarking, and John was there with Christopher & the wagon. He asked for you & the baby, said when those boys were grown up Will would have a rigiment of his own. He inquired eagerly for Dolly, and I for the cows, and then we plunged into the state of the farm in general. When we came home, Anne immediately appeared, always as good as a play, amusing me with accounts of Mother's expectation & promises of her immediate descent then an introduction as Mother came to the door. I didn't think she looked well at all. We ascended to my own domain, the house looking so handsome all the way, you don't know how impressive it was! and there I found Lily K[eyes]. had adorned the room with clematis & dishes of lilies & ferns & nasturtiums, and Mother had had my own bedstead brought down from the garret, and the best counterpane done up afresh for it, and Annie Keyes had worked me a new cover for my camp-stool, and altogether everything looked too palatial and my dear sofa seemed very inviting. At this moment Lotty Brown came & made a call. As I was going down to see her Annie Keyes came in. When I had been 5 m. in the parlour I heard Father come home, and call me, & go up stairs. Presently he came down and sent away my dear pretty child, and took me into the study and showed me a copy of Titian's Columbus by Raf. Mengs. The Chamberlaines, Lizzy Bartlett's relations, have come home and brought it, and puzzled Father well about their intentions. Sometimes they make it seem as if they brought it for him, sometimes as if they only asked his advice what to do with it. He said he had proposed that they should hang it for one year in the Town Library, and then present it to Harvard College. However last night came Mr C. & said he really desired to give it to the Town of Concord, a town whence all his light had sprung. Next we went up stairs and I went to call Anne to unpack my trunks. Having thanked Annie for my stool & collected a little work, I proposed that we should occupy the parlour, and thither came Father with his chocolate bag—unprincipled man!—full of Bloodgoods for me, and sat down with us and inquired into the virtues & beauties of that minute Titan I left in his basket on the dressing-room bed. I gave him a most discouraging

— 1873 —

account. Then Father asked for Dolly. I told him I hadn't seen her but repeated Will's tale that as he passed the stable he heard a horse murmuring "By the rude bridge that arched the flood", and knew thereby that Dolly had arrived. We were at tea, and Father had just lifted his cup to his lips. Never did a man come nearer to choking, and escape it, than Father. He was completely upset and laughed so much that he had to put down his cup, while Annie nearly died on the other side, and Mother was perfectly delighted. I collected at once all Will's follies that I could think of. At four o'clock yesterday the Sunday walk was performed, a very short one. It seemed very pathetic that Dolly should tread her pasture no more, and Father related her departure, tied to Ben Brown's market wagon she walked off to Boston one evening. We are to dine at Judge Hoar's today with the William Prichards. I am sorry to say Mother won't go. We had a beautiful Sunday-school yesterday. Farewell my love.

    E. T. E.   No remarks yet from our kitchen.

                   Concord Aug 21st

Dear Edith,

Mother sends her love to you and says she thirsts to know something about you and the babes, and will you ask Miss Leavitt with her love to write her a note once a week till you can write again. I wanted to tell you about dining at Judge Hoar's on Monday—we had a beautiful time, and had so much fun, the ladies, after dinner, that we laughed till we cried, while in the library Judge Hoar read a pathetic case to the gentlemen which made them cry in earnest. The next day Mother went to Boston, and I took the wagon right after dinner and rode till night doing errands. I got Miss Leavitt & Tommy & Francis to bear me company and it changed it from an occasion of terror & fatigue (for I am afraid of Christopher all the time I'm in the wagon and I mind getting out very much when I'm alone for it takes so long to tie & untie him & he gets so nervous when he's tied, and is so sure to start when I get in) to a very agreeable afternoon. We made delightful calls at the Manse & the Alcotts'. Mrs A. is well again. Wednesday, having lain awake an hour in the night, I devised a party & concluded it must come at once, arose soon after six & presented myself at the Keyeses' at seven for I thought I couldn't do it without telling someone. I received from Annie & from Mrs Keyes the sympathy & encouragement & advice I needed, and scoured the town & invited all the people whose husbands go in the ex.

— 1873 —

train. Then I told them in the kitchen & told Father, and his remarks and the frolic that ensued I meant to record if there had been a minute. Mother suspected nothing till about 5 o'clock I ran out to get a pokeweed to put with gladiolus. Now Mother had herself said she wished she had one in a certain vase, and if she did unluckily chance to be driving out a fly from her south window when I went to the pokebush she ought to have seen in that little act nothing but attention to her wishes. But no! up flew the window and the fatal question laid me senseless under the Juxtaporter "Ellen, do you expect company tonight?" But after all it was 5 o'clock, and she didn't get worried about anything. Rose & Mary vied with each other in sweetness & ardour. Anne spread a protecting wing over the whole business, Annie came along at 6, and we had out the Paris china & Liverpool pitchers & tumblers & a pretty good tea. Every soul I invited came, 27 I think, except Mrs Keyes, who was sick, and I was very sorry not to have her. I haven't had my ears cuffed for it at all. And I'm quite happy about it. Tom Ward's baby came Aug 7th, a little girl. Mrs Wm Pritchard says Haven & Susy's is to come this autumn, Oct. she thinks!!! Cousin Abraham has sent Aunt Susan a quitclaim deed. Uncle Charles is worse, screams a great deal & is moved to the excited ward. But he walks out daily still. Cousin Gore & Cousin F. are again at the Manse.

E. T. E.

Concord Aug 25 1873

Dear Edith,

We were perfectly delighted to get a letter from you, and the account of Dolly was just what we wished. If it has rained the whole week at Naushon as it has here, you must be recovering greenness a little. The verdure here is amazing, looks like the first of May, and in yesterday's and today's brilliant N.W. weather it is a glorious sight. As to plans. I'll see Annie today & find out if there are any yet made. You had best fix a day for Father for his present line of conduct is always to mean to do, but never take a step towards doing anything expected of him but not binding. He has asked Mr Whittier to come on Thursday and make him a visit, and go to the Saturday club with him. Then on Tuesday he expects his young friend Mr Wm. B. Wright to spend a day and night. He has gone today to consult W. R. Emerson as to his & Sylvia's visit to us. On Friday came my children, Jenny Barrett & Lotty first, then Alicia & Emma Smith, and Martha Gray & Mary Dakin arrived. Then came

— 1873 —

Ida Hobson & Fanny Hayden & Mabel Dennis, all overjoyed to get back again, and behold themselves as in days past. They had brought their work, and they gradually settled about the room and I ascended my throne. And behold us launched for the afternoon. Clara Hoar, blessed child! came in just a minute after this, and the circle was complete, for Annie Witherbee and Emma Goodwin were out of town. The conversation of the next 3 hours would fill ten octavo volumes. We all talked a great deal faster than Phillips Brooks can speak the whole time, and the avidity with which my bairns looked at all I had to show made me feel as if I had brought home an immense collection of interesting things, whereas I have always hitherto thought I had nothing or next to nothing. We had really a hubbub of delight from the first. On Saturday afternoon I perceived Mother had a deep-seated woe. I asked her to confide it to me. It was this. The skylight & nursery closets ought to be cleared up. Of course we did it with ease and Mother offered me an ovation, and generally showered applause & thanksgiving and gratulation at supper-time, and Father said he was equally blest & puffed up, for had he not piously finished and successfully wound up this afternoon a weighty job, long on his conscience, to wit, the collecting, conveying & presenting a pile of books to the Concord Library. So we took hold of hands & danced round a tigerlily in the garden, and sang "How pleasant is Saturday night". On Sunday morning we had a preacher who took us all by surprise. I believe I never heard anything equal to the fervour of his services. At first I was puzzled, but inclined to think it was real. Next an idea dawned on me. This must be William Everett, and every word I ever heard about him came back and I was still surprised and interested. I saw the youth of Concord drinking in the sermon with gratitude. Everyone wished to speak of it afterward. Most that I saw rejoiced in it, some said nay. My blessed children and I were happy for a brief half-hour after church. Have I said that Miss Dabney has been in Concord, came Thursday night and stayed with me till Friday noon, then went to Mrs LeBrun's? Such a good time as that was. Mother & I enjoyed every moment of her visit. I have just visited Annie but she is gone to Gloucester for the day.

E. T. E.

Tuesday Concord 1873 Sept 2

Dear Edith,

I left you suddenly on Thursday. Mr Whittier didn't come. I spent Thursday afternoon with Martha Gray, had the pleasure of taking tea

— 1873 —

in the kitchen for the second time in my life, and of seeing the lovely skillful way she managed everything, she made her fire, made her muffins & baked them with an apron on over her clean gorgeousness, and as far as I saw she didn't tumble her apron, much less get a speck on her white dress. In the evening Mr Gray was showing me his curiosities & photographs, he has been a sailor, when Edward whom I didn't expect, came for me. His vacation had begun! Suddenly, all in a moment. He & Annie have been so good, giving most of their time to the family. Friday we spent at Easterbrook, a beautiful warm day, and Father read aloud "The Trust", after picnic dinner. Saturday we mounted my Egyptian & other photographs. Fanny Brown went at noon. Sunday was to me principally marked by S.S. of course and a happy time we had. The class is learning Herbert's "Providence", and is slowly with better acquaintance waking to a full enjoyment of it, which pleases me extremely. In the afternoon we had a good Sunday afternoon walk, Cousin Sarah went too. She is delightful. To the Cove, of course. In the evening a sing; Annie was pianist. Cousins Gore & Elizabeth came later and we had a cheerful evening. Mr Channing was here. Monday I wrote as much as I could on this letter, it was only a little. Opening the schools took the morning, trying work sometimes, when teachers are swamped in the uproar of the school! And when I was settled at my letter there came clouds so black I couldn't see, then when it cleared, errands. I have been thinking you might like our Mary Dakin for laundress & chambermaid. She leaves us next Thursday, and I am to have Mary Lina, a little girl of 15. No one can tell how that will prove. Father will come with Edward & Annie on Friday. Today came Mr William B. Wright, Father's new poet. He did Mother good. His unexpected advent just at noon seemed the drop too much, but he was a doctor and he & she & Edward had such a lively time at dinner that it made her feel ten years younger. How do you do? I hate to be away from you, beloved. And all my precious babes. I hope you will be well, and peace will reign in the kitchen, that the weather will be fair and the bairns in an uncommon streak of goodness so that you can enjoy your united family. The news from Uncle Charles doesn't vary. Thank Mrs Rounsavelle for keeping my nephew reminded of his affectionate aunt.
E. T. E.

Concord Sept 8th

Dear Edith,
    I forgot after all to put in Cousin Mary's letter, for Jim Putnam ar-

rived. I had a very pleasant visit from Jim. We talked fast all the afternoon. I carried him to Easterbrook to get those cardinals that "made the dark water with their beauty gay" (from Emerson) when we were there the other day. He took in the delights of the place at once and promised that when he was engaged he would bring his fiancée up to see it. Tomorrow comes a great Temperance Convention. Today Mrs Sanborn is to spend the day with me and help prepare for next Sunday's lesson. Sunday, yesterday, we had the comfort of our own pastor again, and Miss Bartlett came to sit in our pew and we arranged that she should always henceforth sit with me. Last night the utter bliss of Teachers' Meeting, and promise of another next Sunday. Mr Channing came to tea. Now for business. I think you had better spur Father up, and write to Mr Hunt, so that he'll give a sitting on his way home. Tell Mr Hunt, I should suggest, Papa's bad trick of consciousness. How would it be to let him read something he liked? Poss[ibly] Mr H. knows something of his looks déjà. Dear Edith I am puzzled by your remarks about the children. Of course, you didn't suppose that I considered them so bad as to prevent your enjoying life, and of course when they are naughty you can't help feeling it, and when they are good they make you happy. What do you mean?
E. T. E.

Concord Sept 17th 1873

Dear Edith,

Father says you would like to have me come to Milton, and I should like to come quite as much, to see such dear people & the little mite of a creature, but as I am lame I could be of no use, and it may be safer for me to stay at home. We don't absolutely give up the hope of seeing you here. Your room is furbished. Your letter was a great pleasure, I wonder if anyone else's ever make me so glad. I was & Mother too charmed with every picture of Don [little John M. Forbes]. I have several notes to write so can give you no details of life at Bush. Father's story of the hair-show was very interesting, and his remarks about the children are just what I should expect. This time John is just the right age, so of course he is the most promising, indeed he is absolutely perfect. Edward came up for an hour and his remarks also were interesting but they both were only superficial observers. Both were pleased with Miss Leavitt's rule over her bears. Both of course had had a good time. Anne was pleased with your message.
E. T. E.

— 1873 —

Concord Sept 22 to 29th 1873

Dear Edith,

I'll begin with birthday. Mother had a very sick day which neutralized her pleasure very much, yet she enjoyed it. I came to her about 11.30 and found her quite sick and forlorn, but happily the letters we came across (in reading the pile of old papers which we have lately attacked again) were delightful, and did her good. One was from her about me when I was about 3 mos. old, and dwelt with remarkable frankness on her sentiments and hopes, and Father's about the first daughter, so we were deeply interested in it. Then out into the garden she did condescend to go, and found the morning-glories still in bloom, and a Japan lily which she had thought wouldn't blossom this year, and I picked marigolds for me, and ladies' delights for you, and sweet alyssum—because Mother has a particular attachment to it—for Father & mignonette for Edward; and Father was also in the garden with us. I left them and arranged the four sorts of flowers in four of my glass bowls round Mother's plate, and in their shadow I placed your pin properly cushioned in its box, upon my book bare in its green covers, and Edward's yardstick openly displayed beside them. Mother came in, arranged a bowl with her lily & various flowers and put them on the table. We had a very amusing time with her and her presents, and she never before was half so innocent. Her raptures over her pin were great, and she delights to wear it. She looked at the device and thought it was a great many things, and handed it to Father who said it was a cherub tooting for the Queen's birthday. Then she took it back and said "Yes, and this other cherub seems to be" I've forgotten what she thought, but Father said "That one I supposed to be waiting for the next millenium which comes in May, when I shall be we will not say how old, and he means to toot for me." So it was agreed. Father's conversation is as usual delightful. Having a bad cold he came down one morning saying "Your mother was anxious I should wear my purple escritoire this morning, and took it out for me, but I have escaped without it." I suppose you see he meant the gaberlunzie. Isn't that equal to the red chandelier? Well to return to Mother's birthday. In the afternoon I went out in the wagon. When I went into the kitchen on my return Anne said to Rose "I'm afraid Miss Ellen won't be pleased with the new arrivals." What is it? "Two beautiful little cats." Sure enough Mrs Burke had brought a basket of kittens & Mother had picked out two maltese thin little objects. Their names are September & Twenty. Those creatures are now the axis of the domestic economy, the theme of Anne's conversation, and her chiefest care. It is as good as a seat at the theatre to live in the house with them and their friends. Anne, what on earth have those kittens got round their necks? "It's just a piece of red braid that was in the box. Now they should, it's but fair to say, they should have a nice piece of blue ribbon." What did you put it on for? "Just to keep them up, ma'am." I didn't investigate further, but I suppose she meant not to let their spirits go down. "Good morning Miss Ellen. Now those two cats is splendidly this morning, they've just had their breakfast. Rose got up at five o'clock and gave them some milk." We all wish from Father (who also is interested) down that our children could see their play. My time is gone. I hope this beautiful weather is also beautiful at Naushon. Annie & Edward have been at Monadnoc in it. Mother & I have read "Love in XIX Cent."

E. T. E.

Concord Sept. 26th 1873

Beloved Will & Edith, list to the prayers of a household, the dumb cries of a town.

On Wednesday Oct 1st at 3.30 P.M. the new Library is to be presented to the town. Father is to make a speech (30 min.), so is Judge Hoar, besides smaller ceremonies. Everything is to be done to make it a gala day, as grand as we know how. Could you be present? You both know and don't know how much we desire it, and Edith has a little heart that is naturally patriotic, so I think she will feel it is natural for the dear old town to love to gather its sons and daughters on its occasions. Oh Edith I have too much to say to you ever to get it on paper and can't get at my writing-table with such ease as formerly, to economize minutes.

Father will be happy to sit to Mr Hunt at his studio. Oughtn't it to be started? Wouldn't it be well to publish Parnassus this autumn? It makes me frantic to have had you so near again and not to have seen you. Did you bring little Baby? I have had Mrs Clark for your jelly $11.34. Rose is sick and is going away. I have a young temporary girl.

E. T. E.

Oct 2d '73

Dear Edith,

Thy note saying thee would like to come was a pleasure to all thy family. We mourned not to have either of you. The day was perfect, the Hall crowded, the speeches first-rate. If you had been there you would

— 1873 —

have enjoyed the Judge's Scripture quotations. In speaking of Mr Munroe he skillfully brought in "he is worthy, for he loveth our nation and he hath built us a synagogue", and several others, but that chiefly amused me. I was proud of Father's voice, proud of his skill, and more thankful for it than can be told, for I had read the address in part and was dismayed at its fragmentary nature. But when he came to deliver it he neatly connected it extempore in a manner no one would suspect. I sewed it together that there might be no hitch. But he brought it to me at 3.25 (the celebration began at 3.30) and I hadn't time to go through it. When he came to the end, the end was either left at home or shuffled. Wasn't it a pity? But again he happily covered it up. No one knew but he & I.

E. T. E.

Thy wedding tomorrow. I wish I were there.

Uncle C. another stroke. Has recognized John with great delight but thought Aunt S. was his daughter.

Concord. October 10th. 1873.

Dear Edith,

Edward and Annie came home yesterday afternoon, made a fire in the study, walked out with me to stake out John's house, for which Edward had made a plan that suits Mr. Staples and John and me, with some alterations, well enough to use. I'll send you a picture of it. So I shall not have to trouble you to make another and wear out your industrious brain which has already too much to do. You ask about Mr. Staples's position in the matter. He is the friend to whom I applied for counsel in making the plan a reality. I asked him how much it would cost, and to whom I should go to have it built. He said immediately, "I'll see to it for you. You get the plan to suit you, and I'll see it through." He has engaged mason and carpenter, staked the ground with John and me (and Edward and I altered it a little last night), and he tells me he said to the carpenter, "All the Emersons are likely to get cheated, so I couldn't help looking out that they shouldn't be, and I'm going to follow you up building this house." Now he knows a great deal about everything, and has ideas about looks and convenience as settled as your own, and I am not of the stuff that can combat them under the circumstances. All I can do is to arrange and twist them till something is devised that he and I both like. Then Edward & Annie went to the train for Father & Mother, and we had tea in great peace & sat around

— 1873 —

the evening fire, and poor Edward said domestic life was more beautiful than he could remember when he was away from it. I read him your letter & he laughed well over it. Then he went off to the train. Today Mother is very sick, it casts some doubt on my coming, but I hope she will mend fast.

E. T. E.

Concord Oct. 20th 1873

Dear Edie [Davidson],

I was very much consoled to get a message from you through Helen Slocum at the wedding. [Sarah Coffin Jones to J. Malcolm Forbes] The wedding was every bit as pleasant as Will & Edith's, a most brilliant one, you know the day was perfect, and the sun shone in on my back & kept me warm & well in spite of low neck and a little cold so that I was absolutely at liberty to enjoy the dresses and the people. Mac & Sarah were charming, such smiles! The service was beautiful. Ralph, darling boy! so solemn and interested, he felt the romance & the importance of the occasion more deeply than anyone there I believe. We came up on Saturday, all the children are highly delightful to their aunt. The new house is far behindhand. They won't move in till February. Shan't we enjoy it? Haven & Susy have a little boy named William. Isn't that good? Have I lost a letter from you or don't you feel like writing? Mr Phillips Brooks preached in Lincoln last Sunday night and Alicia went. He gave out for hymn "Jerusalem the Golden" and Lily said she was thankful she had learned it the Sunday before, for few people knew it and she was able to lend strong support to the singing because she did know it. Beth Hoar went to my dear Manchester Convention very unwillingly and came home enough pleased to satisfy me. I lost it. I am very much interested in Emily Russell's engagement. Luckily I saw Col. Pierson this summer when I was at Beverly.

E. T. E.

Tuesday P.M.

Dear Edith,

Mother heard a shout at 3.30 and said "Isn't that the children?" I ran out and Violet all brilliant & jumping with excitement was on the East stairs, Ralph below her in the entry. He walked soberly up to me and handed me his purse, then emptied his pocket and gave me his check

— 1873 —

and his key, and repeated his message "So if you want to buy anything for us." How did you come? we asked them a dozen times before we could quite understand their statement. Finally it appeared that leaving Bridget at the depot they had walked down all alone and had felt neither scared nor elated, which was the best of it. O joy! a kitten made its appearance. Anne promised to capture them both & bring them into Mother's room. When the cats made their entry they fled under the bed, and our children piously consented to sit still and wait for their voluntary appearance. They hadn't quite patience enough however and having given our way a trial, next tried their own, of throwing horse-chestnuts, and soon all four were racing hither and thither in a state of wild excitement.

Wed. Oct. 22nd. The trunk was found safe at the depot when I went for it last night and I have unpacked it and think I understand the directions. The morning was so cool I couldn't help putting Violet into her Tweed, but the day is turning out warm. The kittens gave great pleasure to the children till tea-time. The children were good, went to bed as they ought, and waked and dressed as they ought. It hasn't yet occurred to either to be homesick. I meant not to command or restrain if it could be helped, but they are sure to plan exactly what they mustn't do, e.g. to keep the kittens in the wood-box to make sure they shan't escape, to put them to sleep on beds, to eat chestnuts all the time, to stray round picking up chestnuts when all the school-children are hungrily peeping through the fence, so that I am a worse bugbear and marplot than I had any idea of being, and have to be watching & correcting every minute. I believe that is always the first day's experience till they have learned the ropes. Ralph recited "Toll for the brave" to Father this morning, and Father having heard of your trial said "Why Ralph, you don't speak like yourself. You used to have a beautiful voice of your own, but now it sounds as if you had taken somebody else's." "Ezra taught me to drawl," said Ralph with pride in the accomplishment. He informed me that he didn't have a bath every day. I told him he did in Concord. Violet didn't distinguish herself in bathing; she cried. At dinner Ralph refused to eat beef-steak, so he had only squash and potato. He wants to spend his day in his "house-shoes" & rubbers. I think I shall make a rule that boots must go on before dinner. Edie is quite willing to be out of doors. Mother is better, she sat at the table yesterday.

E. T. E.

— 1873 —

Concord Oct 24th 1873

Dear Edith,

Ralph was frightfully indifferent and slow this morning and finding commands and appeals were vain I washed him, and subdued him thereby, he finished like a saint, and was pretty good till dinner-time when he whistled and lost his pudding. Since then he's angelic. Violet very good. I couldn't without force take them on my necy errands this morn as they wanted to stay at home, so I can't answer for recess, but the rest of the day they've seen no one but E. Heywood & T. Sanborn. They're now at Aunt Annie's and I met her taking them to the Battleground to hear the history. R.'s expression was rapt.

E. T. E.

They're absolutely well.

Concord Oct 27th

Dear Edward,

I have here a "young friend" who I hope some time can be a sort of a son to Father, and as he has a real mind if he proves sincere and good I think his conversation will cheer instead of fatiguing; and as you guessed, his rather absorbing presence is the reason why I haven't written. Mother is getting well and gave up that medicine before I came home. She walks up in town now. I have Alice and Miss Roxy here and am very happy with them. The children are always a picture and often too amusing even in their sinfulness to be looked at without laughing, especially this morning when they sat at their breakfast each with two tears on both their red cheeks, Ralph because Edith had kicked him, at least "I felt something *just like* a boot coming against my leg", and Edith because she said she hadn't kicked him, and was indignant at the false accusation. Violet is infinitely innocent and looks so lovely! We have a new bossy and the children are delighted. Tomorrow is Violet's birthday. Certainly you should go to see Aunt Susan.

E. T. E.

Dear Edith,

Oh how I miss my darling blessed sweets! Mournfulness over their departure, mortification at losing the right train for them mingle in my mind. Edith I beg pardon for that. Mrs Lowell told me that her son Charles's motto was "never take anything for granted", and she further impressed upon me that it was the only safeguard of life. I constantly am brought to reflect upon the truth of her remarks, and I mean to act on them, but failure still shows me every day that I have taken something for granted. Today three times. First that John as usual would be here. He *was* at the Swamp. Second when I sent Mary for him in haste to his house I took it for granted that she would ask him to come right down. Alas! I found too late that she had said I wanted him for the noon train which he of course thought was 1.30. Father came in joyfully to say the R.R. carriage had passed down the road, and he would stop it as it came back, so I thought all was right. He came in again and said it was taking the Alcotts to the other depot but promised to come back in season to take the children. As it became 12.30 & 12.35 I ran to Father my mind for the first time misgiving me that I had taken for granted here again that he knew which train I wanted it for. So it was. He had never heard of a 12.44 train, and had told the R.R. carriage 1.30. He walked straight to the Telegraph office but it appeared he was too late to save Will's coming down from the Office to meet them at 1.30. Mrs Quincy Brown took charge of them going down. I'll send Ralph's sponge & Edith's tooth-brush by the first chance. Give my love to the darlings and tell them I miss them very much and couldn't bear to find no little Violet in my bed at night. Oh I had such a good visit from Alice & Miss Roxa, and it was so delightful of you & Will and baby to come too.

E. T. E.

Concord Jan 3rd 1874

Dear Edie [Davidson],

Our New Years was perfectly beautiful and every present was so exactly what was wanted and we had such a good time that the scarcity of poems made less difference than one would have thought. We had only one very funny poem, and that was Will's to me with a pair of sealskin gloves. My presents were magnificent and ran in that line, a muff, a fur cloak, and these gloves. From blessed R. & V., watch-key & buttoners. Also I had a set of ruffles, a pair of brown gloves, a bashlik, and a picture, and a promise from my daughter. Your poems were beauties. You ought to have seen our children. John was so quiet & bashful and so soon dazed by his presents. He enjoyed the first one or two, but after that seemed incapable of taking in anything. Cameron on the contrary stamped and shouted with delight all the time and was all ready with his pleasure every time his papers were removed. His

— 1874 —

mobility of feature increases with his age and the grimaces he unconsciously makes electrify me. You would have said it was some elf, not a mortal baby, testifying joy. Violet, poor little conscious child, could not bear the excitement nor the eyes of her relations. Her behaviour was pathetic, not disagreeable however, and made us love the dear little creature. Ralph by my side heartily entered into everything and behaved like a gentleman. The foolish baby sat in Edith's lap like a rose with just intelligence enough to take hold of his presents and put them in his mouth, amid the jeers of the company. We visited the new house in the afternoon, and went to the other house to tea, and Father & Mother & my Miss Dabney met and Miss Dabney pleased them both as much as I could wish. She is staying there taking care of Alice Dabney who is still sick. You left your cracker here. I found it when I came home, also a letter from you thankyou dear. I'm glad you liked your portfolio.
E. T. E.

Concord Jan 6th 1874

Dear Edward,

I am coming to Boston on Friday instead of on Thursday, and maybe I shan't come to see you unless you wish it for any reason. Father is reading his Advertiser and September has been rubbing round and round his ancles. "Strange!" he says, "this courting of the cat! Here she is winding about my feet. Perhaps she wants me to open the door!" I told him no, she loved human kind and it was only for her own gratification that she was expressing it. Presently she sat down at his feet and threw back her head and gazed and purred at him in an ecstasy of devotion. "Look now at her worshipping attitude," said I, for the paper hid it. He looked "Oh!" he exclaimed, quite touched. "Poor creature! I wish I was worthy of it!" We have all been made happy by your letter to Mother. I went yesterday to bring her home and found Edith in bed suffering much from rheumatism. She hasn't been able to brush her hair for three days. Anne K. has gone to take care of her. I saw the 5 bears there who seemed hale & hearty, even the newly vaccinated, who has given up jumping and smiling and sleeping, but never cries only remains awake and still. Mother is safe at home.
E. T. E.

— 1874 —

Concord Jan 15th 1874

Dear Edith,

High times at Bush. Edward at home, Much laughing at meal-times and all day semi-sociable work, Annie and I drawing Edward's diagrams, and he sometimes superintending. His labours end tonight and we hope he will sleep 24 hours without turning over. Father spent Tuesday night at Ellen Gurney's. Mr Thayer also was there and he had a good time, enjoyed the company. Jan. 16th. Edward is now free and very gay. Annie is staying here and we are as happy all together as you can imagine. A. meant E. should sleep this P.M. but he won't. We are admiring this brilliant day. Oh Edith, January! blessed dear January is here and lengthening days and streams of warmer & warmer sunshine, and deep snow & clear blue! how good it is! I hope to hear good news from you. I don't deserve it, I have been so silent, but I've been working for Edw. Tonight a parish party, and I shudder to think that none of us can go. I promised you a story of your parents. Mother the other night was arranging her flowers, and turning an observant eye upon her I discerned her with the pruning-scissors trimming a calla—not the stem—no indeed!—the corolla. I could not restrain the gibes that this brought to my tongue's end. "Certainly," said Mother indignantly, "it makes it as fresh and handsome as ever all the time it lasts." I pursued my avocations and forgot it. Presently Mother came to me, all innocent delight at her success. "See! I'm sure you can't mock at that. The edge is as even as Nature made it, and that beautiful pistil! I think it's *very* pretty." The other day Father couldn't find his INDEX by which he finds places in his mss. He as usual devised various extraordinary explanations for its disappearance. I hunted for it in vain. Meanwhile Mother sent for me "Tell your Mother", said Father, as I left the study "if she has dared to touch my INDEX"—he stammered—then with great energy he burst out "*Aramantha!*" So I hastened to deliver the message exactly. She was puzzled, had it repeated once or twice, then said "Tell him I return his Araminta and he may do with her as she deserves," then she tried in vain for the right word. At dinner-time she exclaimed "He meant Anathema Maranatha!" and Father was relieved at getting it right. The other morning (she always is arranging plots to make him take a bath you know) I had orders from her to draw a bath for him and then call him. I obeyed, and he took it, as she knew he would, rather than waste the warm water. At breakfast-time he said "I

— 1874 —

got into that awkward bath, but I didn't see how I was going to use it. At last I saw a sponge hanging there, my own sponge. That solved the problem at once. Indeed one hardly sees how a bath could be taken without a sponge. The Divine Providence seems to have anticipated our needs—" I caught his idea and exclaimed "Why Yes! He made sponges so that we could enjoy our baths!" "Yes, it looks like that", he said. "Here is the poor man quite helpless in the water, wondering how he shall make it available and suddenly he sees the sponge before him, created on purpose! I had forgotten there ever had been such a thing in the world. I should never have thought of it if it hadn't presented itself."

Your affectionate sister
E. T. E.

Copied from EEF edition.

Concord. January 16th. 1874.

My dear Sally [Emerson],

Father is at work in the study, Edward and Annie must be left to themselves in the dining-room—the only room we can be warm in in such cold weather—and I came up stairs to read to Mother and behold! Mother has done an unheard of thing. She has sat down by her fire and opened a novel. Of course that is the last of her, as it would be of anybody, but she never was seen to take the first step in that downward path before, and I am amazed. Also I am pleased. It seems as if she felt well like other people.

Indeed this winter we are so happy and well and live in such a pretty house that we might think it heaven below if we hadn't the usual thorn in the kitchen. Father's health which he gained in blessed Egypt stays by him. He is as well as he ever was, and, as you will be next year, twice as happy in being at home as he was before he had tried leaving it. His enthusiasm about the beauty of the house and the comfort of his own study is ever new. It is just like a novel, the burning and restoration of the house, and we always feel it so, and survey every day our rooms and our possessions with a feeling of romantic interest.

Edward is always in the Mass. General Hospital working so hard that when he is at home for an hour, as he used to be occasionally in the autumn, he seems tired; but very deeply interested in his profession and his patients and thankful for the opportunities he has in his present position—opportunities for learning, observing and practising—and especially he says it is good for him (his head he says doesn't act quickly in emergencies) to live where every moment is an emergency. But it is quite sad to think how little he and Annie see of each other, and lovely to see how anxious they are not to be selfish . . .

I love Paris and remember it all with delight as the good Bostonian is supposed to, and I hope you will too. I hope you like your hosts and servants as entirely as we did ours in Paris, and that you will make surprising progress in French and in painting . . .

Cameron is the best one to give anything to of the whole five—he is so pleased and shows it so prettily . . .

Copied from EEF edition.

Concord. January 16th. 1874.

Dear Haven,

[. . .] At New Years all (the children) behaved so well that Father, who is a very critical ancestor and feels the children's sins more than anyone else, was very proud of them all—and as to the rest of us, we said they couldn't have behaved better if they had been angels . . .

The mighty mansion—Edith never allows any such words in Will's presence, he is ashamed of its bigness—is nearly done . . .

Think of our loss in Cambridge: Mr. Agassiz and Annie Agassiz. I think hers was the saddest funeral I ever went to. I don't remember whether you knew her. She was one of my friends, a wonderful creature, and a poem about her that I saw had very true lines. "Those lips that knew no speech but of courage or kindness" was one of the truest. Then dear Mrs. Lowell. Never was anyone more beautiful in her coffin than she was. She used to be beautiful when she was well, and all her beauty returned. Annie's funeral was just a fortnight before, and Mrs. Lowell and I sat together, and afterwards we had a minute's talk. I thought it a blessing then; now I am still more thankful, for she didn't die without my seeing her. If the people who owed everything to her had all come, the house couldn't have held them [. . .]

Milton Jan 27th 1874

Dear Mother,

I am safe in Milton with Don's head right against my paper as he stands on tiptoe to behold the new doll which arrived in my trunk at

— 1874 —

the same time with me. Ralph informed me, Edie joining in, that her name would be Hester Cunningham Forbes. So the box was opened, and blanket, cap, gown & pillow were admired by each in turn. When I began this note all four were seeing "Baby Hester" rocked in her own cradle. While she took her next nap Ralph induced Violet to play engine and away they went shooshooing with feet and voice. Violet rushed for Cameron, and with a preparatory ding-dong the shooshooing began and the train swept back into the parlor & at the corner the poor passenger car got such a sloo he could hardly keep his legs, and when Will called from above to stop that pounding the train moved noiselessly all the rest of the time. They played beautifully, no fighting, and perpetual pleasure. Now for business. On Wed. & Thursday I want the washstand dishes washed, the coffee-pot, brass water-pitcher, blaze & d.r. candlesticks cleaned, the slide-closet scoured, also the dish-tub. On Friday I want the garret swept and the stairs washed, all the upstairs house thoroughly dusted, and the nursery-stove blacked. No sweeping is needed—instead let Mary wash & wash again the dining-r. mantel-piece & jambs & get the soot off. Of course clean the up-stairs brasses. Let Sarah make her pies & hard molasses gingerbread on Friday, it is bad for cleaning to let them wait till Saturday. Please give her some orange-peel to put in the dried apple sauce and tell her to pick over her apple carefully and boil it very long in a great deal of water. Remind her of her tins on Thursday & specify butter-box, farina boiler, dredger & rinser.

[Unsigned]

Copied from EEF edition.

Concord. Mass. February 3rd. 1874.

Dear Sally,

[. . .] Every Tuesday I go to Edith and stay till Friday or Saturday to help her move from her cot to her palace. The palace I think I shall approve and admire. It is very large, has plenty of windows and is to be furnished in the style of cheap pretty contrivance which is Edith's forte. I like that even better than magnificence, and I have great pleasure in magnificence . . .

But the three babies are all real babies still and I'm afraid the three together are not so intelligent as Ralph. But Tammy (as Cameron is usually called) is such a faithful practical little creature that he is worth a great deal. Don's beauty makes up for his mental sluggishness, and the other is still a toothless idiot; we don't know what he may turn out. He is very strong and rosy and cheerful [. . .]

Milton Feb 5th 1874

Dear Mother,

I find I must spend Sunday here, so probably I shan't come home till the 13th. If Father comes to Boston please ask him to leave a bundle for me at the office for Will to bring out, and let it contain stockings, nightgown & drawers. I shall send home my wash on Saturday. Edith is a little better. Baby is well. He has had one cheek frozen and it is always blue. Ralph and Violet are delighted with the deep snow and come home wet through. They play cars as before and I never get tired of the spectacle. Edward shows a strong inclination to creep, it amuses me to see his impotent attempts. Will you please send this note over to the school-house as early as possible. If you are able to come to Boston and want any shoes, it is so favourable a time for buying them, as Moseley and Tuttle are selling their shopworn things off. Also there are many kinds of silk selling off, see the advertisements. I hope all are doing well. I hate to leave you for so long though I am glad to be with Edith.

E. T. E.

Concord Feb 11th 1874

Dear Edie [Davidson],

I came home on Monday night because Mr Forbes and Mr Agassiz were coming to dine on Tuesday, and I meant to return to Milton to make a visit to Mary Russell, but I received a telegram from her husband saying that Jim & Ellen have the scarletina. Mr Forbes & Mr Agassiz rode up yesterday on horseback and dined, and rode away again at about half-past three. It was a delightful occasion. They talked of mountains and I learned a little geography thereby. It is very pleasant to know facts in geography. They expressed themselves on the subject of women's voting in a manner greatly to please Mother. They then talked about the Boston School-Committee. Mr Forbes said he hoped it would prove that by our Constitution women could not hold that position, for then we should certainly have to change our Constitution. Then Mr Agassiz gave his experience on the School Committee and his views on the subject of schools. That was all very interesting, and espe-

— 1874 —

cially to me. On Monday those theatricals came off. Father & Mother went. They say they were perfect. I wish I had been there. Tonight we have the M^n Quintette Club. Tomorrow Bible Class. Also I mean to have all the Bartletts to tea tonight. See how full of dissipation Concord is! I congratulate you on your invitation to visit Lilla. I'm hoping for a letter about last Sunday and your class and the Hospital. I'm glad to hear of a recruit. Here is the ticket. Lily says she expects you Fri. as early as poss.

E. T. E.

Fri.

Dear Edith,

We came safely home at one yesterday. I had to introduce the no Sir & no Ma'am subject at dinner, and foresee a long fight. The boys both said "Thankyou Sir" at breakfast very prettily, and I hope by slow degrees we shall succeed. This morning they both came down quite lovely & smiling and played very peacefully and prettily though Father couldn't help saying that the little bear seemed to be always oppressed. He was so content with his subjection however that we didn't interfere and finally they went upstairs with Mrs Kelly. I then proposed they should play out of doors but they had no blouses or playing clothes, so Mrs Kelly took them to walk. If there should be lovely spring days wouldn't it be well for them to have some old coats and play out in the E. yard & woodpile as R. & E. used to? When they came in I saw Cameron was otherwise minded to everything, and at dinner-time he was lying in Mrs Kelly's arms with a grieved lip & a hot head. When she proposed he should go to bed the invalid replied that he wanted to go down. So he did & ate his dinner & laughed as he ate. So that I conclude that costiveness and a little homesickness are all the trouble.

Saturday morning. Cameron has slept like a top from 7 till 6 and is well this morning. I hope the homesickness will wear off today. It has showed itself in great unwillingness to come outside the nursery and lose sight of Mrs Kelly, and the frequent request "I want to go home to Milton". But they will be soon wonted.

Monday morning. Cameron was mending all day yesterday, but his eyes were still heavy. Sat ni. he waked at supper time and thought he wanted to sit up & eat it, but as it came to the point preferred to be held, and ate little. But yesterday morning he exclaimed "It is good!" the moment he began his breakfast. He was sweet & good all day. Don on the contrary was very contr'y. But John is waiting for this note. I haven't seen the creatures this morn. E. T. E.

Copied from EEF edition.

Concord. March 9th. 1874.

My dear Haven,
   [. . .] No light yet breaks on the kitchen difficulty. Edith expected to get through with the need of me in February,—far from it—she will not let me off till the end of next week. The house has lingered like other houses. When I came home the other day and brought Cameron and John to have them out of her way, the old house was pretty thoroughly dismantled and the chambers of the new had been abandoned by painters and paperers, and carpet-women were at work . . .
   Edward's last exploit was writing for the Boylston prize. He did not get it, but it was worth while in several ways. He has been trying to introduce in the Hospital the practice of taking the patient's temperature, as he saw it in Germany, and I believe he has succeeded. His Essay was on this subject. There were six competitors. The judges said four essays were so excellent that they had been puzzled what to do. They decided to give two first prizes, to make honourable mention of the other two essays, and to propose an extra meeting to hear them read. This meeting was voted and Edward's essay was one of the good ones. It was read on Friday. This gives him a chance to make clear the reasons and advantages of this practice to all the members of the Society, and makes it possible that E. W. E., and not Dr. Bigelow, will get the credit of having introduced it [. . .]

Concord Sat. Mar. 14th 1874

Dear Edith,
   We have hoped every mail for a letter saying we might keep the children a little longer, they are such a delight since their homesickness diminished. We hoped you would like a smaller family on first moving in, so that you would have time for all the little endless jobs that I'm sure will present themselves. Cameron this morning has showed the first symptom of positive drawing. I wish I could keep him and supervise his practising. I never proposed he should draw, it came to him. The weather has been very bad so they have hardly been out this week, but this forenoon they have played in the yard. Oh Edith! my soul

— 1874 —

within me fails. My advertisements are out & on Tuesday & Wednesday I shall go and see girls at Aunt Susan's. How to decide among them, oh how? Poor Cameron whines at the thought of the new house, he wants to "do home" to Milton, but Don looks forward with cheerfulness to the change. You don't know how sad Father is about Mr Sumner, he cannot read the paper aloud. And the first day he lost his voice the moment he came to Judge Hoar's holding his hand, and when the message came he had to stop. We spent Thursday night at the Jameses in bliss, and saw Hatty P. & Mrs Agassiz the next day, yesterday.

E. T. E.

Monday

Dear Edith,

How are Cameron & Don? They were a little melancholy the last forenoon, and at the depot I was afraid J. M.'s eyes were heavy. I hope nothing was coming on. Please return Mrs Jenning's letter, and write me about that, and about Glasgow.* Father carried the letters to Mr Norton and to Judge Hoar for their opinion. Father would like to accept, stand, and be defeated, and he thinks he may but I don't think he has yet leaned practically to either side. Please write fully. Judge Hoar came to see Father yesterday and while he told his story both wept much. In vain at dinner Father tried to tell us—a second and a third time he gave it up—but by degrees he did repeat the best the judge had told him—of the coming home and the concourse that watched the train all the way, whole cities coming to meet it—and in a solitary place one black family drawn up to see it pass and take off their hats. He said he had told the delegates, "If they would like to hear a funeral service for Charles Sumner he would invite them to go to any church in the State of Massachusetts to-morrow, and they would hear it." Ours was so beautiful—Bible, prayer, hymns, text, sermon and all, ending with the Governor's message and God save the Commonwealth of Massachusetts. I think everyone is surprised to find how much they cry about it.

E. T. E.

*RWE had been nominated by one of the student parties at Glasgow for the rectorship of the University, in opposition to Disraeli. See Rusk, *Life*, p. 490.

— 1874 —

F.R.R. Wed P.M.

Dear Edith,

By all means advertise whenever you want anything. Seldom has my amusement been more delightful, and I have had very good offers. I cannot say that I have chosen rightly, but I have hopes that the two girls I have taken will be good, both look strong and wiry, and have recommendations. Oh! may Anne like them! Your letter filled me with joy. First the boys returned safe. Then the moving-in and the success of the house, everything you said pleased the ancestral hearts. That you & Will and Mr Forbes felt as I feel about Glasgow was also a satisfaction and settling to my mind, and afforded Father equal gratification I thought. He gave the letters to Judge Hoar on Sunday. On Monday as they met just before the funeral the Judge told him he had hardly read them but would make it his business to do it before he went back to W^n. I do not know his answer. On Monday Father went at ten and was made pallbearer, mate to Mr. Whittier—they gave them badges and gloves, and Father said to Mr. Whittier, "Where does one put the crape?" Mr. W. smiled and said, "I have put mine in my hat." Father believed, followed his example. He said the funeral was beautiful, the whole day's experience was beautiful, and the concourse greater than had ever been known,—the streets lined all the way from King's Chapel to Cambridge. We expected him home by ex. train, then by 7 o'clock. In vain. At quarter of eight we went to Bible Class, Mother quite anxious about him, but I remembered my constant experience of what it is to Father to be what he calls "old," in other words, so well-known and beloved. I suppose no one else has seen as I have seen how he is watched over by all eyes, how every service is done for him, every door opened to him, every attention shown him, how he is everywhere sure of at least one member of his body-guard which seems to me to be a million strong. Knowing Judge Hoar to be a prominent member of this body-guard, we stopped at the house and asked if he knew why Father was not at home. The answer was, "He is coming on the 8:15 train on the other road, and my carriage will be there to meet him." When we came home and found him we asked him if he found his tea comfortable. "Oh no," he said, "I took tea in Boston at the Depot Saloon, and the proprietor came and talked with me while I was taking it, and when it was over he wouldn't be paid—wouldn't hear of such a thing." "There," said I to myself, "That's always the way."

— 1874 —

Thursday morning. Judge Hoar agrees with us all. Father has written to accept and will telegraph today.
E. T. E.

Concord April 24th 1874

Dear Edith [Davidson],

I have spent all my time this month on English letters, and that is why you are so neglected. I have led a varied life of spring-cleaning, high-life in Boston, Bible Society, School work, and tea-party. This last was so big that we were obliged to use the Thanksgiving table-cloth which I don't remember ever using before. It was for May Alcott, and in a less degree for Sam & Kate [Hoar], & Ned & Sally [Bartlett], & Florence & Mr Walcott. Mr & Mrs Storey came out for the occasion, and we had a very good time. We played Twenty Questions and Where are you Jacob? & Consequences. Kate had never seen Jacob, and was perfectly delighted. We have been hatching a plan for constant game-parties, and I think we shall now have them. Yesterday at Bible Society I had such pleasure—the getting acquainted with people whom I don't constantly meet and who lead utterly different lives from mine. And besides the young & gay came of their own accord and sat around me and talked to me about the dancing-school and I am more flattered by such behaviour than anything else. Alice Wheildon has begun her lessons beautifully, she seems to have uncommon talent for teaching. Father and I stayed one night at Mrs Tappan's last week, and Dr Holmes dined there with us. It was the first time I ever heard him talk, it was worth while. William James was there too. I can imagine how he made you feel. The intellectual always make me feel so. But at Mrs Tappan's he didn't soar, was only very pleasant. Miss Putnam was there, Georgy Putnam, but I only saw her a very little, and Bessy Lee came in in the evening, but I had only a bow from her, my real companion after dinner was Mrs Ben Crowninshield, a new acquaintance but we got on quite far. Did you mean to take a little handkerchief you left here? It looks as though Mother had given it to you for Charley. You were very good to write me twice unanswered.
E. T. E.

Concord April 24th 74

Dear Edith,

Mother's tulips are coming up gaily but no crocuses or other things show themselves, so we conclude the rats ate something else and left tulips and Mother is very happy that these are alive. I am expecting Eugenia & Lidian next week and after they go I propose to have Mr & Mrs Forbes invited. I am having a beautiful time now with housekeeping and enjoy my cook very much. Mother and I had a visit from Alicia yesterday, and we immediately with one accord took up again "What Katy did" of which she had read us five chapters the last time she came, and we were delighted with it. Afternoon. Lily came back this morning, and we have got far on, indeed to the last chapter, and have constantly exclaimed at the naturalness of it. What do you think of my going to New York? I may as well as not, one way that I look at it, and again I don't see how I can possibly. Has thy inkstand dried up? We haven't heard for a long time from you either on W.'s views about Court St. or about our precious children. I imagine the blooming E. W. shaking his old head, and my dancing smiling Tammy and beautiful Don, and little blessed Violet flat on the floor with her beads, and stout Ralph beholding the spring with delight. Father went to Mr Hunt today, I suppose Edward has told you. Mother sends her love and begs for visits from all or any.

E. T. E.

Tuesday morn. Your blessed letter came last night and gave us immense amusement. I'm glad your various businesses prosper. Mine do pretty well. Edward has got his office furnished, and is pleased with it. I have asked Mr & Mrs Forbes for Thursday & Friday. Back me up & come with them.

Providence May 6th 1874

Dear Mother,

Tell Edward I have gloriously proved him a false prophet; he said my catching the 2 o'clock train was not doubtful, was impossible. Oh no! I reached the Providence depot at 6 m. of 2 and piously checked my trunk, bought my ticket and chose my seat before the train started. I was in Providence at half past three. I always think Providence is a beautiful place. I thought so again yesterday. And I found Emma and Mr Diman as cordial and hospitable as ever. We began at once to talk as fast as if we shouldn't have half time enough to say all we want to. I always praise Emma's wisdom in bringing up her children, and she goes on as she began. May is prettier than she used to be, is tall, strong

— 1874 —

and red-cheeked, when she promised neither. Johnny was out with the boys yesterday so I have only seen him this morning reciting his Latin to Emma before he went to school—Concord children ought to see how well his exercise looked—but Emma tells beautiful stories of him. She made one rule in their infancy and has always kept to it, that she would never read stories to them, and she says she is surprised to find how easy it has been to keep the rule, and how much solid reading there is that is delightful to young children. She is now reading Plutarch's Lives to them and they are ecstatic about them. They read stories to themselves when they like but the family reading, a regular institution, has always been solid. The Channing Conference is going on here. Oh bliss! We are to have an hour there today. Dear Mrs Stimson is well, we took tea there last night with Conference birds, the Norton minister Mr Beach and his wife, and had a beautiful time. Farewell! Your affectionate daughter
                                        E. T. E.

                            81 Madison Avenue New York
                                Wednesday May 18th 1874
Dear Mother,

I had the pleasure of seeing Will last night for an hour and hearing of our babies and their mamma, and that Court St. was prospering apparently. This morning I had a letter from Edith enclosing the superb & imposing photograph of our youngest. I think no one will believe me when I tell them how essentially homely he is after they have seen that. I am going to carry it to show Aunt Lizzy today, and tomorrow Sally shall see it. I am having so many interesting interviews and so little time to write that I can't give you any idea of all that is going on. Cousin Charlotte is doing beautifully. She looks well too. Cousin Samuel & his wife & Mary came over to call upon me, and I was surprised & complimented. I loves my Cousin Samuel, and as usual was exceedingly happy with him. Glasgow is a staple subject with relations. I read them the letters, and explain it, and they are deeply interested. They want to know if you will be Lady Rectoress, and it is a foregone conclusion with everyone that Father will be elected, and that I shall go to Glasgow with him. Blessed Tom [Ward] dined here on Saturday, he looks in poor condition, and Sophy was gratified that I thought so. The next day Aunt Lizzy and Hetty Everts spent the day with us, and Tom came in in the afternoon. He said he was getting wild to go to Concord, and explained in so Tommish a manner his state of mind that we could all have danced with delight. I invited him to bring his family for a visit in June. I went yesterday to see Sophy and the baby, whose name is Elizabeth Howard. I spent the day on Monday at the Gibbonses, had a good time and oh! seeing Julia! It was the first time for fifteen years that I had had any talk with her and she is as delightful now as she was in Lenox. She & Sally and I had an afternoon of great comfort. In the evening they walked home with me, I sit every morning with Susy while she washes the baby and curls Ruth's hair, and have really a good chance to talk with her and get acquainted with them. Willy has the happiest disposition ever seen. He is always smiling, he smiles when he comes into the room always and that is gratifying, he smiles when you take him, when you kiss him, when anyone speaks to him. He often smiles at his own thoughts. If you play with him he is in ecstasies. I love to see Susy with him, and Ruth is a most faithfully brought up little girl. It does my heart good to see how she is made to mind. She is always a pretty picture, her eyes & russet face, blue eyes, bright smile, and extraordinary spread of romantic ringlets look so healthy and so lovely, and she is so exactly like my dear Aunt Susan that I am always looking at that in her. I called on Miss Mackey and Amy on Monday, they were charmed to hear that Edward had taken you in hand & was making you well. Everyone asks about Edward's wedding and about Cousin Gore & Cousin Elizabeth.

Your affectionate daughter
Ellen T. Emerson

Concord May 20th 1874

My dear Miss Dabney,

I don't know where you are, but I hope you are near and that we can arrange a visit to Concord from you. I want it to include the 10th of June, for on that day comes the Arlington meeting of our County Conference, which you know is a favourite institution of mine, and I can't help thinking you would like it too. Aren't you delighted with the return of Spring? I hope you are. I supposed that I shouldn't care much about it, except for the convenience of long days and freedom to go all over the house instead of staying in warm rooms. But I had forgotten that spring was so beautiful, and every day I am surprised again and think if this one day was the whole, it would be good enough, and then the next day is just as good. Even rainy days are pleasant and the garden looks just as pretty as it does on pleasant days. I have been in New York for a fortnight, New York and Providence, and coming home was a great pleasure. The single thorn in my lot has always been the kitchen, and for six weeks I have had a respite there, so home is positively happy. We have only one woman in the kitchen, who does the work of two for the wages of two, and is cheerful and friendly. This blissful arrangement is drawing to a close; but at least I have had a month or two of comfort, and to have seen the spring. I wonder whether you are in Milton. I don't know when I can come and see you even if you are there, but a time may suddenly present itself, and if it does, I shall take advantage of it.

Ellen T. Emerson.

Concord June 12th 1874

Dear Edith,

Did you leave your veil and gloves? They shall be sent. We mourned for you and Will, and Mrs Storey said she missed you and the children very much. My Carnival is over and has been very pleasant. On Tuesday after you went we sat on the doorstep and sewed most of the afternoon. I visited Mrs Beal, and Mrs Gregory for eggs. Then we dressed and went to the Keyeses. A remarkably beautiful sky to admire all the way. Arrived there, what bliss burst upon my view! A great big tea-party! Everybody I loves and never sees assembled in one place where they could hardly escape me. I plunged in with ecstasy, it was utterly delightful. At tea we sat at a round table in a corner, Mr & Mrs S[torey], Mr & Mrs Sam [Hoar], and Cary H. and I. With Harriet Eaton and Susy Hubbard I had much sweet converse after tea, on schools, music and housework, and their sisters. With Miss Bartlett and Lizzy and Mrs Kettell I planned out Mother's strawberry festivity, and we laughed much over it. I think now that I shall have it June 24th, and have the Bee the same afternoon. Wednesday morning early start. Screams and embraces at the depot, accompanied by much laughing, dancing for joy, and crazy marchings up and down the platform, because we were such a multitude, and going to a Conference and it was a heavenly day. I don't believe any other thing throws people into such a state of wild delight, it surpasses starting for Class-Day when you're young, this going to a Conference when you're old. Mrs Cheney & Mrs Folsom just as happy as the rest, though Mrs C. hadn't been able to close an eye all night. Away we frolicked to Arlington, desirous to extend the right hand of

— 1874 —

fellowship to every mortal that got into the cars as doubtless they were going too. We instantly pervaded the whole vestry and found the Arlington ladies in as high spirits as ourselves, all cutting bread and buttering it, and parading about in swarms, with hams and table-cloths and baskets and cans, all in clean calicoes and broad smiles and making such a noise of talk and play. The organ drew us right into church, and we began to sing before we could find the place in the hymnbook, church already full and everyone too happy to live. Oh didn't we get the last crowner to our satisfaction when, some committee being called on to report, Mr Reynolds appeared with the report! We were afraid we had left him at home. Then I enjoyed the address that opened the subject, aside from its real interest, because all my grandfathers figured there, the sorrows and success of Peter Bulkeley, and even much was made of my own grandfather and his work in the First Church. Then dear Mr Sears spoke and much of what he said was interesting and may lead to better work for the Conference. Then two others both just right. Then the Collation, where I made several new acquaintances, felt the immense advantage of belonging to the Government, for it brought me much more serious and real conversation than could otherwise have been addressed to a strange young woman, and had such a good frisky time with my Concord friends and the Arlington girls who waited on us. Then a Government discourse in the church with a fellow-member; then began the afternoon session. Frank Peabody was in the same pew with Sarahs R. & Perry & me, and Mr Barber in the next, Mr Reynolds & Mr Sears close by. I watched the faces of all during the speeches. It was worthwhile. Dear Mr Green of Chelsea was one of the best of the afternoon speakers. And Mr Westcott of Lexington. I had much pleasure with him and with Sarah Reade, his wife and with two new acquaintances from Newton and Arlington after all was over. Mr Reynolds & Sarah R. and I rode together coming home, and acting on the light we received at the Conference, consulted, talked, and made plans together all the way. Father has received a letter this morning from Mr Herkless of Glasgow which pleases me saying that he learns late in the day that he ought to have officially acknowledged Father's letter, as well as Dr Stirling, and he writes a very pretty apology and acknowledgement. Mother sends her thanks for the seeds and Will's note. She wishes to know how the Plymouth wood-lots stand, if Will knows. Whether anyone has them in charge, who it is, and whether he has ever reported or moved in the matter. Father says he will see Mr

— 1874 —

Gardner. One kitten is backing round the floor with Mother's scissors in her mouth, and the other prancing after them trying to catch them. Mother is enchanted. Goodbye. It is very pleasant to have you all here, and melancholy to have you go.

E. T. E.

Copied from EEF edition.

Concord June 12th 1874

Dear Haven,

[. . .] Edward did begin his partnership with Dr. Bartlett on the first of June, and though everyone is well he does seem to be employed a little. He and Annie and indeed all of us are mourning the changes Cousin Gore is making at the Manse. Building a bay-window! It seems incredible. He himself grows stronger steadily but it is evident that Cousin Elizabeth and his wife feel no security about him. They never leave the house at the same time. Next week, or rather on the 24th, the Memorial Hall at Cambridge is to be dedicated and we are all expecting to enjoy the ceremonies very much. After that I have some idea of giving Mother a great stand-up party, but I haven't quite decided [. . .]

Concord June 13th 1874

Dear Miss Dabney,

You didn't come to the Conference alas! You would have liked it, I am sure. I am so glad you are in a pleasant place, I don't know where it is, but evidently it is a country part of Dorchester, and all of Dorchester that I know is delightful. I spent one spring there. I have been having five or six people of my age & Edward's here this last ten days, that used to come when we were all young, and we have had a very good time and have stayed out of doors as much as the weather would let us. Now they have gone and today I have had my Sunday School class, trying to make them see the good of Coventry Patmore. They begin to take a more real hold of the books I am always showing them, but Coventry Patmore is a new field, and I can see they don't begin to catch his whole meaning. Do you mean to go on the 24th to the Dedication of the Memorial Hall at Cambridge? You ought to arrange to do so if possible. It is the last great War Commemoration. They have been glorious hitherto, and we trust this will be. We all mean to go. I don't know yet how tickets are obtained, but shall begin on Monday to inquire, and you ought to too. You know hitherto each soldier-graduate has had three so you would be

— 1874 —

entitled to Mr Charles Dabney's if the same plan is followed this time. My love to Edith and you.

Ellen T. Emerson.

Concord. June 17th. 1874.

Dear Edith,

Sarah Richardson said to me yesterday, "I see in the paper that you are going to entertain all Boston to-morrow." I hadn't heard of it. She explained that the Christian Union was to come up and have a picnic at the Monument, an address by Mr. Keyes, and then "visit R. W. E. in his home." Ah! also that the paragraph ended with apparently a cordial invitation to the public. "Come one, come all! Only one dollar for the round trip and lunch!" Father came home at night in semi-dismay, having read articles on the subject in both Advertiser and Transcript. On Sunday a young gentleman visited him to tell him of the picnic and ask if some of them might come into our grounds, perhaps fifteen. Now the day has come and proves rainy. I suppose no one will come.

Friday.   They did, however, to the number of 72. I wasn't here, but at the E. Q. school. On my way home as Bell Wright and I approached the Alcotts' we thought we heard a band. It proved to be the Christian Union singing a serenade for Mrs. Alcott, who had proposed it on the spur of the moment. It sounded beautifully. Going in, after they had filed away, I found the family in battle array and heard the whole story, which they made very interesting—and the young man had told them that they hadn't expected more than to pass through Mr. Emerson's yard, but "Mr. E. had come to the door himself and invited—yes insisted—upon their coming into the house! with all this mud!!" and they had all come in and he had made them a beautiful speech. As I heard this and looked at the mud all over the Alcotts' carpet where, as May cheerfully said, "you could plant potatoes," my heart sank, imagining the looks of our front carpet. I was frightened in vain. Our marble walks and stout mat inside the door and broad doorsteps made such a difference. The Alcotts' muddy walk was only separated by 18 inches of doorstep covered by a rope mat from their carpet. The Union had conscientiously wiped their feet at our house and had no chance there. Father said when I returned that it had been very pleasant; the youths had been affectionate. I enclose some letters. Shall we meet on Tuesday? If you & Will will come up last of next week we'll go out on Walden or river. Your affectionate sister.

— 1874 —

Concord Monday July 6th 1874

Dear Edith,

Alas! I cannot come today, nor at all before you go, I hoped ardently that I could till last night, but 'tis of no use. Your visit was full of pleasures for your family, they each felt the comfort of it. Last night as Edward and Annie and I picked strawberries for tea Edward said "I hope that in another world birds will be taught to control their feelings—to govern their temper—not to give way", and followed it up by many remarks and anecdotes about the needless worrying and unmeasured lamentations of birds. "How many times do you suppose a bird screams in a day?" he said "How many times do you suppose they think it necessary to scream over each fear of the possibility of misfortune? Why—" and away he went with his calculations. Your family have naturally talked over the chances of today's sale,* and remembered the availing prayers of their wise and honoured grandfather, wondering by what turn they will now be answered. It has been a most amusing theme, a new illustration of reckoning chickens before they are hatched. Each has laid out plans; Mother's are too characteristic in every point to be imagined by any other mind, I have said nothing but have died with joy as I silently contemplated them from an artistic point of view. Father and I have had a wide range for the imagination, but being at heart very old and wise birds, we ended by "drawing the feet of covetousness under the skirt of contentment" and planning that if we made our fortune we would visit your stationery shop and get some more paper and envelopes. Mother and I are reading the end of "Off the Skelligs" at last, and I am not yet displeased with it. Mother & Edward will go to Framingham on Thursday.
E. T. E.

Concord July 15th 1874

Dear Edith,

We kept Edward's birthday beautifully. Since he was thirty I thought it a shame to let so important an age pass without peculiar notice. So we had lilies on the breakfast-table, and I sent notes inviting Mr & Mrs Keyes & Annie, and Madam Keyes to dine. I received answers that raised my spirits they were so cheerful, and Mother arose to gather all the roses and lilies in the garden and adorn the house. Also we donned

*The Jackson heirs had owned valuable property on Court Street in Boston, and this was sold to good advantage in 1874 (see Vol. I, p. 534, and Rusk, *Life*, p. 482).

our best attire. The guests arrived (alas! I knew it would be so! But I don't know how to help it.) long before the dinner did. I fear we didn't sit down till twenty m. of two. But then we were all having a good time; only my pride and conscience suffered. We had a good time from beginning to end, perfectly delightful, and Mrs Keyes departing thanked Mother for her boy. At 5 o'clock the party broke up, and Edward & Annie went out on the river. In the evening I had promised Father, and was just giving him a reading of your letters about your reception when Mr Chamberlaine, just returning from Europe, rang, and made a call on Father. He & his wife have rapturously returned to Concord bringing presents of rare & valuable botanical works for Concord Library, and for Father photographs and a book which they heard him say was lost in the fire. After I had gone to bed I had a short visit from Edward who expressed satisfaction with the celebration and his presents. Emma Goodnow shows some improvement under Edward's care, the family are too much encouraged, and Edward is thankful he can save her from fever. She had very bad afternoons till he began with her. But he cannot make them put her out of doors. The next day I went to see Helen. She lay almost as white as the bed, very much altered. We had a delightful hour. She was to go to Portsmouth that night. She made cautious investigation whether I would visit her, and of course I ardently promised that if ever she sent for me I would try hard to come. I came home at noon, found my new friend Mr Westcott in the cars, and he told me he & Mr Reynolds had arranged a joint S.S. Picnic at Walden for Lexington & Concord, to come off next Friday. On Sunday we had Mr Barnes of Woburn & Miss Leavitt was here. Uncle George and Mr Channing came to tea, also Edward & Annie. On Monday I had a little walk with May Alcott, who related that Mr Munroe had ordered one of her pictures, and that Mrs Howe of Manchester had sent to ask to see her oil paintings with intent to buy. She was very happy. In the evening Mother went with me to Teachers' Meeting. Hardly anyone there, and for that very reason apparently it was particularly delightful. Seldom does Mrs Hoar talk so freely, and never hardly was there so intimate and serious a talk at the Class. Afterwards we all went out to look at the comet which was superb, I think we shan't see it so well again. When we left Father he was waiting for darkness to see the comet; when we returned he had forgotten it. He willingly put on his hat and crossed the hills to see it with me, it had already begun to bury its nose in a cloud, and he was disgusted with its behaviour. Coming down it was

— 1874 —

just like walking in a dream, seemed like many dream-experiences & not like day-time ones, the silent careful shuffling down the hill in light that was & was not. Mother exclaimed yesterday that she was quite in the notion of going to Naushon, and seemed to feel happy that the time was fixed. She begins to think that lily is going to be a beautiful white one after all, and has had it set out pot and all. The paper this morning tells of Lady Amberley's death. We are very sorry. Then the new fire in Chicago. The paper is rather sensational in its words but so very cool in its tone that I hardly understand whether or not it is a great fire. Give our love to our darling baby tomorrow on his birthday.

E. T. E.

Concord July 16th 1874

Dear Edith,

We have remembered the birthday of our Baby. These splendid crimson carnations which you have sent Mother shall be his flower. They arrived last night, in very good order. Last night was one of those heavenly hot nights with yellow west in which shone the new moon and evening star. Father called to ask me something and I saw he was putting on his best kid gloves. This he explained was to keep the musquitoes from biting his hands while he was looking at the comet through his spy-glass. When I heard of the comet I went too. But there was none. I have been reading to Mother all day so couldn't write.

[Unsigned]

Concord Monday July 20th 1874

My dear daughter,

I think about you very often but haven't written because last week I was trying to write to Charles & Therchi, and couldn't bring even that about, though the week was very quiet and domestic till Friday when we & Lexington had a S.S. Picnic together at Walden, beginning at 9.30 and lasting till 6. I think it proves that my strength has come back that I could be on my feet and labour there all day without any evil consequences. And I had a truly delightful time, anyone can enjoy a picnic who goes to work, but it makes one shudder to think of the tediousness those must suffer who go expecting some indefinite delight in it, and sit round or walk about waiting and hoping to be amused. To get dinner ready was one of the most sociable businesses of the day. Then did the ladies of both parishes have a chance to get acquainted. The day was

— 1874 —

most beautiful and I showed the various glories of the pond not only to strangers, but to many Concord people who really had never seen it near enough before to know anything about it. Then Saturday I went to Dorchester and spent the morning with Miss Dabney & Edith; and wishing to visit the J. R. Lowells in the afternoon and yet unwilling to go to Cambridge for nothing I cast about in my mind where I could find out about them, and had the happy thought that Lilla would know. So to Park Sq. I went and found that married pair in a little parlour upstairs, Lilla very prettily dressed in white, and Mr Perry resplendent in a seersucker suit. They assured me that I should find Mrs Lowell, and Mr Perry brought Lilla's Elmwood Album and was very amusing in showing it to me, and trying to preclude all possibility of my mistaking the house or the right way to the right door. And he succeeded. I went quite straight and found Mrs Lowell and had a good time with her before 'twas time to go.

Wednesday 3rd. Waltham.   I didn't think this would wait so long. I am making my visit here. Oh what a beautiful place, and what delightful people and children! And the night before I came I got your letter. It was a feast to the aunt's heart, indeed to the ancestral heart generally. I should think on the subject of doing and not doing it would be best to say to Edith [E. Forbes], that you will go or not go anywhere as she wishes, of course, but when she asks you you will always answer by inclination without side considerations influencing you, and then if your inclinations and her plan don't agree you can tell why you don't wish and she why she does and it can be arranged according to comparative weight of reasons. I have always found that a more comfortable state of things than having people try to be silent and considerate and self-denying. In short, to tell one's will but not be strongly attached to it. Then plain daylight shines all round. I'm sorry you are away from church for so long. Set your Sunday and keep it to the letter. Make sure to have enough, so that it shall have its full legitimate influence on the week. Otherwise you will suffer by degrees, more than you know, for we deaden very fast. Keep my books if you use them. When you have done with them send them. Our great lesson is Thy will be done on earth as it is in Heaven, that is the way we must do our work, that is the way we must receive what comes to us, never stopping at second causes. When you read the Gospel and Epistles never limit them, believe they really promise all that. I think almost no one believes it. We must believe and seek the whole.

E. T. E.

— 1874 —

Concord Aug 4th

Dear Edith,

The comfort I received from your letter was very great, and your parents were delighted. Also with my daughter's account of the five bears, which was true to the life and showed them pretty good. I'll try to write again to her & you before I come. My present idea is that Mother & I will go to Derby's Crossing and take the Framingham & Mansfield train to New Bedford at 8 minutes past 1 and come down on the 4.15 boat from New Bedford. I think Father & the trunks had best take the usual way, as cheaper & saving the long ride to D.'s Crossing. Write if you think there's any objection. Father is very likely to relent and stay his whole fortnight. Mr Lowell and Mr J. Holmes came here Friday, also Judge Hoar. Great play! No more today.

E. T. E.

Naushon August 11th 1874

Dear Edward,

The absurd time-table at Concord Junction had a misprint, that was all. We arrived in New Bedford at 3.58. I was not quite at ease, and as Mother said to Father "She conversed with the Conductors all the way, I never saw such flirtations. She said she found them very civil." At Mansfield I peeped into the Boston car, and saw Father and Mr Cabot sitting cosily together. I thought it a shame to disturb them and told Mother not to speak or disclose herself till we had found a seat and arranged our things, but Mother couldn't help stealing a shy glance at him as she passed and he caught it, and endless riot and disturbance instantly ensued. For I had remembered that I had never told him to inquire for our trunks and bring them along, so now I asked him for them. Of course he hadn't thought of them, and I had to run and telegraph for them. And he and Mr Cabot wished to give Mother and me their seat, and we wished them to sit together, and so they stood and expostulated, and I found Mother a seat elsewhere, and I tore round about the trunks, and Father wasn't settled in his mind till that was arranged, and then he wished me to take his seat—Mr Cabot standing all the time—and I wouldn't, and couldn't because of open windows. And suddenly from somewhere in the car appeared Mr Oliver of Fayal to offer his seat and urge it upon me. Now the seats I coveted, the brakemen's seats by the front door were occupied, the one behind the door by a fat man, the other by a tall man. So I addressed the tall man

— 1874 —

and receiving a favourable answer I seated myself quickly, and the turmoil subsided at once. At last the fat man, who had a five-year-old daughter, whom I envied him, a charming child, not handsome and sound asleep, but with such promise in all her features as one seldom sees, shook the innocent awake and got out at Weir's. I took his place, Mother came and sat near, and I looked out of the forward window. Baggage-car door opened and Haven appeared. I rushed into his face and eyes the moment he got into our car. As soon as he had spoken to Mother he said "Well, I'll bring Edith", and departed. Presently he came again carrying a blue waterproof from which stuck out long stalks of wild red lilies, and followed by our sister. They had come up to Weir's on purpose to dig up these lilies for the Naushon garden and for Haven to meet us. Father was much more astonished at both these arrivals than even we. Then Edith said, "Has Mr. Cabot brought his boy?" and Handasyd, now ten years old, turned up. Our party grew from little drops of water to a considerable stream. We were landed at Naushon itself by 5:15, and from the upper deck descended Alice, Sarah Mac., Annie R. A., Mr. Sedgwick of Syracuse, and Mr. Hughes of England, younger brother of dear Mr. Hughes. Dolly awaited Father and me in a single wagon. We ran and called her by name, expecting her to testify surprise and rapturous affection. She continued grazing. Father hauled up her reluctant head that she might behold us. We thought she would certainly rush into our arms. She could hardly be made to glance at us—only tried to return to the poor dry grass—and we called her ingrate and unnatural, and got into the wagon. We saw Violet straying home from the Mansion-house, and when Father threatened not to turn up towards the bear-garden, Ralph's rough head and Wood's Hole voice at once began to call our attention to the right road. He also called out, "Cam is real big," and proceeded to yarn on, "SOMETIMES WHEN I SEE HIS HAIR I THINK IT IS FIDIE." And Cameron scrambled up from all-fours in the flowerbed in front of us and smiled and jumped very prettily. The young E. W. in his Mamma's arms awaited us on the porch, and while I was eating him up, Edith presented John head downwards with his kiss all ready as I sat on the piazza. Violet was next introduced in the middle of a sentence just a yard long about some appleseed mice that Aunt Alice had lately given her. But I can truly say the child is lovely. She followed me up into Mother's room and talked away with pretty smiles that made a dimple in her really plump and rosy cheeks, and was neither conscious nor

— 1874 —

flippant; and when the ale was brought, Ralph delighted Father by teaching him how to draw the cork with a huge new mechanical corkscrew, and Violet ran with the tumbler, and both appeared to great advantage.

Handasyd is most attractive. He and Ralph like each other, and expect utter bliss. Mother is doing very well. The advantages of milk diet show on a journey—her meals aren't irregular as formerly. Edith's knee very bad. Poisoned bairns nearly well. My daughter in clover and succeeding. Haven and Edith asked eagerly for Annie. Haven left us in New Bedford for N.Y. Love to Annie.

E. T. E.

Aug 17 1874

Dear Edward.

I was sorry to hear Annie has been sick again. I hate to have it happen. I also have a poor account to give. Mother has been sick from the beginning. It is of no use for her to go away from home unless she can have a splendid time every minute, she grows sick and low-spirited away from her accustomed places and labours. I am afraid Naushon will do her no good till she gets home. Then she is likely to feel the benefit. Worse still Edith has water on the knee worse than ever. Some-times she languishes in bed, anxious, away from house, children and company; sometimes she overtires herself downstairs, rather than be *hors du combat* any longer. Otherwise all is most prosperous. Father is well and has truly enjoyed himself with Mr Cabot, and with Edith. Parnassus gets on steadily, though Edith says a fortnight more will hardly finish it. Father hasn't once found a moment to say "it makes me want to go home", he is delighted with the bathing every day, and his appetite increases. The children are all good, and I have a story or two to tell. For instance the following conversation. Ralph. "Handasyd, do you ever swear at your father?" (in a tone as if he thought it w'd be very funny & charming if he did.) Handasyd (laughing, and with an air as if 'twere impossible) "No! Do you?" Ralph. "No. But sometimes I feel as if I should like to." Handasyd. "So do I." The innocent little niece rode home from the bath with me. "See my stones! There, this is the prettiest. I always choose one with a fine band of white all round it. I like those, and I like fine-spotted ones. There! there's some succory, lots of it. I love succory, it is blue, that's my favorite colour, and it has such a pretty name." Every bit of her chatter was about the beauties of nature and it seemed perfectly original and sincere. Cameron is very satisfac-

— 1874 —

tory. Little Edward was never so homely, but healthy and good. His strong stiff hair is brushed frantically in all directions to give it a curly appearance. Alas! how vainly! Farewell. Miss Coombs comes over to dine tomorrow.

E. T. E.

Concord Friday Aug 28th 1874

Dear Edith,

We came home with great ease and comfort. Nothing at all went wrong. I have a friend in the conductor of the Middlesex Central, who always treats me as if I were under his especial charge, and last night when Mother and I were at tea in the Lowell depot refreshment-room he suddenly appeared before us and told us that the train would be ready in twenty minutes. And he carried our bags and helped us out at Concord. Between Lexington and Concord I chanced to turn round and Anna was behind me! She at once came and sat with me. She has been in Lenox a fortnight, and before I asked about the Hoopers, I had to ask for Lenox, and she had taken in its glories, and praised it to my heart's content. We arrived at Concord all too soon. Dr Folsom was with her. It was one thorn of this brilliant rose that I was stealing part of her ride with him. Mother sends her love, and says she had a good time at Naushon and a good time coming home; she especially enjoyed the boat transit from the island to Woods Hole, she looks back on it as a festivity. I saw the President, but she missed him. I was sorry. We were charmed with the crowd of children from the Azalea. Anne of course had everything comfortable for us, but Maggy alas! is still drinking and everything in her department is out of order. I have seen Annie this morning and Mrs Keyes, and Lizzy Bartlett and we have talked much about the wedding. I have told Edward about the presents from me. Father & Mother will give Annie a Davenport, and to Edward what he shall choose. Mary & Col Russell are to be asked, I am glad to say. Give my love to my daughter, and to Will, and come as early, all of you, and stay as long as you can at the wedding. And write soon a word how you do.

E. T. E.

Concord Sept 14th 1874
Mother's 39th Weddingday

Dear Edith,

I am going to send some pears to the Keyeses for the wedding. I heard Annie say her Father had told Barrett to bring pears and grapes. I am going to send the pears now, so that they may tell him in season that they have a fund to fall back on, and he may bring the fewer. While I was getting them ready I thought of your vineyard. If you think your grapes are ripe enough, wouldn't it be a good plan to propose sending some grapes for the same reason. This is a humble suggestion. Presents shower. It is amusing to see how it makes Annie want to cry, she says she grows smaller and more ashamed of herself every day. Why everyone the moment they have made her a present, she says, withdraws only to come again the next day and give her another. I rebuked her for feeling ashamed of such a delightful thing, and she said "I should like to see it tried on you! You don't know how it feels till you've tried it" I wish you were here Come soon! To live with Edward is a continual feast. He is so bright Father and I are dazzled. The quotations are as numerous as Valentines, and we are speechless and helpless most of the time that he is in the house. Your letter this morning was a treat to your family. We are going to borrow Mr Staples's horse & wagon to help ourselves up to the wedding, for the Concord people will depend on Penniman, and Mr Keyes too in a measure. I trust my daughter and the bigs will arrive Fri. noon at Concord Junction, and you by 4.15 tr. ready to go up to see the presents first thing. Aunt E. told me she meant to give them a gravy-spoon. She says Kate is occupied heart & soul with this wedding.

E. T. E.

Concord Sept 15th 1874

Dear Edith,

Many many thanks for the invitation, but that is the time of my visit to Mrs Lowell. Father says he left at Naushon Milne's Poems, Sesame & Lilies, and some other book from the Athenaeum. Please let them be returned by the earliest opportunity. I think you have the ballad-books that were sent down. Haven't you? Edw. says in Childs' Collection we should find the truth about the Lykewake Dirge. Father hasn't yet begun on the preface, or on finding the mottoes. Yesterday came a thousand dollars from Court St., a great comfort to him. Yes indeed Court St. & Parnassus are great presents on their 39th anniversary from you & Will, and I think this is a momentous month. Father, Florence, Alicia and I have dreadful colds just beginning, and Annie is still in the middle of hers, but we think she may be through with it before the wedding. Lily makes an amusing imitation of the way the family will cough, sniff & use hoarse tones in receiving their guests. Mother is not half well yet. Do be well yourself.

E. T. E.

Boston. Oct. 1st 1874

Dear Edith,

I received your letter as I was coming to the depot this morning, read it through in the wagon and returned it by John to my eager parents. It was a delightful letter. I am rejoiced that everyone had such a good time. Of all the tales of festivity I believe I am most impressed and flattered by the hoisting of the flags in our children's honour. Thank Annie for her note. It tasted good. Tell her I know Mother'll be quite relieved to hear Edward hasn't been snappish with her. I am, I find, much dismayed at the prospect of their not coming home to our house. I wonder if they didn't get my letter saying I was making no visit, for she recommends me to finish my visit in peace. Your family's wedding-cake's not going is a grief of mind to me. I beg pardon. All is gone now except a piece I meant for John.

E. T. E.

Concord Oct 3rd 1874

Dear Edith,

This brings my love and congratulations on your ninth years weddingday. And as this day nine years ago we lost our bride out of the house, today we are to receive another bride into the house. It is very interesting that it should fall on the same day. I hear that you cannot celebrate the anniversary in any very lively manner, Edward says you are both on crutches. I am very sorry for you. But do be faithful to them now, and get all cured. I went down to the depot to meet the pair last night, and found them already arrived and approaching the buck-wagon. Seeing that we had two single wagons I proposed to Annie that she should go with her father and I should take Edward home to his friends and let the passers-by in the street draw their inference, but she didn't want to. So she and Edward went in one wagon, and Mr Keyes and I meekly followed with the baggage. Arrived at the Keyeses, not without being rained on, we sat down in the parlour while the sun exhibited every imaginable firework and dissolving view as he made them his parting bow. We told them of the boxes & barrels and parcels that awaited them at Bush, and Annie danced at the word. Edward declares Annie is feeble, and was worriting over her then, and when he came down in the eve^g to speak to his parents looked over his medicines and hurried away because he wanted to look after her. I was sorry for that. Shall I now send you some w. cake? Tell Alice I've found her slippers.

Concord Oct 17th 1874

Dear Edith,

We heard with immense interest, woe and terror of your overturn,* you would enjoy the comments. Edward is chiefly concerned about Norma, Father about the Ediths, Mother about the general practice of driving on side-hills, Edward & Annie about who-was-the-driver, we critically reviewed the letter to ascertain, and decide it was Will. All are glad the youngest was at home. And, dear Edith, my daughter and I are literally burning up inside with the wish to be on hand to help you. It is always my desire to be with you when you are moving, and after the lameness and accident of course more than ever. If you do need me say when and I'll try, though I can't quite promise as there may be need as great here, though I can't think there will be, for Annie & Edward & Anne are here for Father & Mother and you have only Jane for you & babies both. We are in extremest peace though the horizon is lowering. Maggy said at once after her first grief was over, "I'll stay till you get a girl no matter how long, and I shan't take any other place this winter, so if ever you are hard up send for me. I wouldn't for the world have you or Mrs Emerson in any trouble I could save you from". And she redoubles her pains in cooking, cleaning, washing & ironing ever since she was dismissed, and is so gentle and sad, I am more than ever heartbroken about her. The little M. is as cross, as affectionate, as faithful & diligent as ever. I begin to look for a new cook next week. Yesterday Mr G. B. Emerson came & spent the day & night. We enjoyed it very much. Edward & Annie & I took him to Easterbrook. My daughter came at night. She & Uncle G. to tea. Today Mr & Mrs Cranch come to dine. All are very well & weather perfect. Mrs Bartlett, C. Cheney, S. Richardson, A. Wheildon, Henry Brown, Mr Reynolds & Alice R. & I had the

---

* J. M. Forbes wrote in his *Letters and Recollections*: "Will managed to upset his Beverley with his wife, servant and 4 children upon a bed of rocks near Sentinel Tree . . ."

— 1874 —

happiest of journeys to & from the beautiful, hospitable, joyful Greenfield. Coming down we got hold of George Bartlett's last.* I showed it to Father who says it is "excellent, most ridiculous, everyone would relish it! It must go in the facetious poetry." With ever so much to say & ask I must leave you now, darling girl.

E. T. E.

Concord Oct 19th 1874

Dear Edith,

This morning I expected to go find a cook, but Anne on Saturday night said she was going to stay, and yesterday morning Maggy came to Mother and said she would like very much to stay. Mother said she would think about it, called Anne and said M. had asked to be tried once more, and Anne said M. was pleasant and they were on excellent terms, and she dreaded a new one and would rather she would stay, and advised Mother on our account and M.'s to keep her, so then the little M. was called and told, and behaved like a wild northwind for half an hour and then settled to clear shining, and Maggy was told we would keep her till next time and no longer. And universal peace now reigns, except that Mother was taken very sick yesterday afternoon. She is much better this morning, thanks to Edward. I'll come Saturday to Milton, and spend the day with you. I have invited Mary, Sarah & Mac from Thursday to Saturday. Many thanks for your dear good letter. How wonderful that Don wasn't hurt, and how cunning was Cameron! The usefulness of the bairns pleases me very much. Give my love to dear Will and my blessed children and Alice. How glad we are that Dr Abbe came!

E. T. E.

Mother sends her love and says she feels a great deal about your accident—a very great deal—and is most thankful that you are safe.

Milton Monday Oct. 26th 1874

Dear Mother,

When I reached Milton I found Edith Davidson and Mrs Kelly & little Edward had come down with Martin to meet me. Little Edward looked as usual, half pretty and half not, he condescended to sit with me and stolidly endured my conversation all the way home. We found

* G. Bartlett's poem "Mignonette" is in *Parnassus*.

— 1874 —

Edith sitting in her window-seat enjoying the pleasant day, she had moved up on Friday. Her back was no worse for the journey and yet it is still very weak, she seems a little forlorn and keeps her bed or couch all the time. She had a headache but it went off after tea. Sunday Will drove her over to Squantum. I found Cameron & John playing with the wheeled chair, Violet placidly enjoying her own room, sitting alone there in her little rocking-chair reading. Ralph invited me into his room both Saturday & Sunday at dusk, lighted his gas & read poetry to me. The baby on being called to come to me coquettes with charming smiles, he approaches, but when near he turns & runs away, and does it over & over again. He is quiet when played with but terribly active & devastating when left to himself.

[Unsigned]

Concord Nov. 3rd 1874

Dear Edith,

My will to write thee a letter is very good, if I could. Oh I'm a hard-worked girl this week I assure thee. I'm afraid it is very uncertain about Mother's being able to come at all. She was very unwell on Sunday, had another attack of that dizziness that Edward doesn't like, and has not left her room since. But it is over now, and today is lovely, so she is going out again. The kitchen is very happy still. Little Margaret told me she was going to be very good, real pious, and she laughed out. She had just come home from church and told me 'twas All Saints Day. I asked her if going to church three times had made her feel so good, and she said "I don't know, but going to church isn't much unless folks is good all otherways too. I know people that don't know how to read can't be so good as people who do—they don't know so much." I was sorry for the dear child. I want to teach her, but when could I? I have thought about it before. Father found when he went to see Mr Osgood that he could not have his five additions put in where they belong naturally in any of the divisions whose proofs have been already printed. But he hunted up places good enough in coming divisions. Father exclaimed yesterday "Correcting these proofs is work that pays well. Selections made long ago, and forgotten, keep rising, each as fresh as a star." He is proud of the book. Mother sends her love to you and says she wishes she could come but is quite unable at present. Annie & Edward remain with us till Friday. They are very much disappointed that the carpenters don't begin on their house till the last of this week. Mrs Keyes is

1874

going to give Annie a bay-window in her S. parlour. Edward has been busier than a bee racing & riding from 7.30 often breakfastless except for a slice in his hand till he came home at 8 or 9 in the evening to supper, this was partly professional, partly political, he was delegate to the district caucus, and partly in the service of the town, in the Centennial Committee, and Comm. on new school-house. Town meeting came off yesterday so two of those services are ended for the present. His knee is still a little lame. The Manse bay-window is finished. I think it is all right, and am resolved to be pleased, as I am with ours.
E. T. E.

Concord Nov. 8th 1874

Dear Lily,

The sight of a letter from Mr von Hoffman gave me great pleasure and so did every word as I read it. I am so thankful to hear of the approaching baby! What a comfort it will be. We are all very much interested in the coming of the Theodore Lyman's new baby in the same way. I never have seen Mrs Lyman till last week I was in Milton and dined with her at Mary Russell's. I have made two visits to Mary this year and she has been once in Concord, besides that she and Col. R. came up to Edward's wedding. Dear Tom [Ward] came too, of course he did, I must tell you all about that. The night before the wedding while we were at tea, Edward was called to the door, and did not return. Of course we concluded that he had gone off with a patient, so when we had done tea we didn't wait for the bridegroom but were adjourning to the parlour when we met him with his old Wife—the name Tom goes by with him—both with a broad smile of delight on their faces, coming out of Edward's room, he now has the downstairs bedroom. All of us jumped for joy, and I had the pleasure of giving them their tea, and hearing Tom tell of Monadnoc. He had left New York the night before, spent the day on his beloved mountain, found some golden-rod, Annie's favourite flower, and brought it and some mountain cranberries to her, and arrived at our house at about seven. In the watches of the night I still heard those boys talking. At the wedding itself I saw little of Tom, though in the beginning when people were assembling, he was near me, and asked who people were. He was interested to see Malcolm Forbes's wife, and I particularly enjoyed showing him the dear little Sarah, for she is a treasure, a source of constant delight to every member of the Forbes family, and to ours in our degree. You

— 1874 —

came to Edith's wedding and Annie's was just like it, the same minister married them and with the same service, and Edward & Annie stood just as Will & Edith did, facing the minister with their backs to the company, and turned round after the wedding. They stood before a long window looking out on the Keyeses' back-piazza, and a pillar of the piazza just before the window was covered with golden-rod, and 'twas perfectly brilliant, shining in like sunshine, it was a very rainy day and we needed the yellow light. Annie wore white muslin, and looked lovely, and both spoke audibly, though Annie's voice shook, and I thought it was exactly like the faithful child; she is often afraid, but she never will turn back from her duty. She is a dear generous child, always pleasant to have in the house and missed when she goes away. She and Edward went of course to Monadnoc for their wedding-journey, and afterwards to Naushon. They had heavenly weather all the time, and Annie wrote home that no one could imagine the beauty of the institution of the wedding-journey who hadn't tried it, it was exactly the right thing at the right time, absolute rest and freedom after excitement and hurry, so that there could be full enjoyment. They came home to us, and spent a month with us, then a month with Annie's family, and that is almost finished, they will go to housekeeping in a few days. Their wedding-presents have almost furnished their house.

Dec. 12th. I am determined to send this letter today. It is just two years since our visit to your house. Father and I were talking of it this morning, and remember it with great affection. Edith has been at home for Thanksgiving with her flock of five. Ralph is eight & little Edith seven, they no longer seem babies, they are school-children, and the increase of sense and reason is so welcome to me in them that I don't regret their departed infancy. Cameron & John are four & a half and three, inseparable companions, and very handsome we think, and innocent & charming with their imperfect talk, there are some letters they can't yet say. Little Edward is 16 months, very large, active and given to devastation. The moment he enters a room he runs with unerring instinct to the place where he can do most harm. He is devoted to his Grandfather Emerson who thinks always that the youngest child is the best. This one has lived more exclusively in the nursery than the other children did for Edith has been much troubled with water-on-the-knee. For three or four months she has spent most of her time on the sofa, though she could go about a little with wheeled-chair or crutches. She and Father have at last sent "Parnassus" to the publishers. I don't remember whether I ever told you about that book. Father always had an intention of making a collection of poetry very strictly selected, and used to talk with Edith about it when she was a little girl. She became very much interested and saw that Father hadn't time to copy himself, so when she was fifteen she began to do it, and has never given it up. She has regularly seized his leisure moments and made him look up and mark what he wanted copied, and has done mountains of writing, and made Will help her sometimes too. This has been going on now seventeen years and at last the work is done. We were all at Naushon for a month this summer and the whole family gave most of their time to it. Indeed every guest this summer has helped in some way, I think. Ida Higginson was there with us, and she took an interest in it most reviving to Edith, who has a real respect for her taste in poetry, indeed so has Father, and Ida made herself especially useful by her classifying skill. She helped decide under which heads the poems should go. Father never liked settling that, and it was a great comfort to have Ida's help. From that time Edith has consulted her about every detail of getting up the book, and though Edith devises all, Ida's is the casting vote. Their taste in the binding agrees very well. We are going to send you a copy as soon as it comes out. Lizzy Simmons drew the laurel wreath for the cover. Pauline Shaw has had a terrible fright this autumn, Mr Shaw had a very severe attack of pneumonia, the doctors despaired of him, and Ida said it seemed as if Pauline saved his life by her courage and ingenuity, never giving him up, and from moment to moment trying new things, watching and saving every advantage. And we have had the mildest finest autumn, and winter so far that was ever known, which has been a great blessing to him and helped his recovery. Everyone is so thankful. Dear Nina Lowell has lost her Father [Francis Cabot Lowell]. He was my Father's classmate and a great loss to him. They were dear friends in college until the last year when different interests began to separate them, and then Mr Lowell being a Whig and Father Anti-slavery made the separation increase so they seldom had anything to do with each other though the old affection remained. When the war had removed slavery they began to meet oftener and in the last two or three years they were dear friends again. Nina has set up her solitary housekeeping in W. Cedar St. and Edward Lowell and his little daughter & two sons live close by on Mt Vernon St. & Mrs Coo-

— 1874 —

lidge on Chestnut St. so all the young nephews & nieces are within her reach, but it must be a sad winter for her nevertheless. I rejoice to say that Father has been well and strong ever since our return, he no longer gives lectures, but he gives much time to the College of which he is still an Overseer. Except Edith we are all well, and my old strength has in great measure returned. I am now able to work all day and it is a great happiness and freedom. I see I must stop. Give my hearty thanks for his good letter to my friend, your husband, and Oh! my dear Lily, you may be sure I delight in both of you.

E. T. E.

Concord. November 9th. 1874.

Dear Edith [Davidson],

I suppose that the finger of destiny has reached that point on the dial of time which marks the close of this beloved correspondence, so we will make no fight but lay it down in peace. We will write when we can but must feel no duty about it, for a supposed duty that one cannot fill is a galling yoke and I think we have a broad and solid ground of real relationship which will not tremble at this change any more than it did at the change, more than nine years ago, from the spoken word to the written word. Now the written word must give place to the understanding silence, and that also is a blissful phase. That is the way I live with all my other dearest friends.

I have often quoted Cousin Phoebe's words to you, "Though we should be separated by two oceans I know we should be conscious of each other's existence," and I have also told you as years go on and I see less and less of Ida and Pauline, I only find when I do meet them that we have grown more united since last time, and that without letters, except on business or occasions. And so it will be with you and me, and every step in the Christian course infinitely increases this happy nearness because it brings us into the Communion of Saints. I thank you for this good long letter all the more because it was so hard to find time to write it. Yes dear, work hard at your teaching. Try always to train the children in application and to teach them to use their minds. Parents almost never do. I suppose they haven't time. That heavy responsibility falls on the teacher. That Sunday here you promise will be a blessing to me. I shall try to do none but sociable work if I can, but Thanksgiving will be very near. Goodbye. You must know, but I'll tell you again that

— 1874 —

your letters all these years have been to me the wine that maketh glad the heart of man.

E. T. E.

Concord, Nov. 10th, 1874

Dear Lucy [Jackson Hartwell],

I was very much pleased to have a letter from you on the occasion of Edward's wedding. It is as you say a marriage which seems to promise happiness pretty surely—they both are such sensible people and so good and true. They spent a month with us after they returned from their wedding-journey, and now they have gone to the Keyeses' to spend another month. The third they hope will see them settled in their own house. They had the most satisfactory wedding-presents; and their house is said by the tenant and the boarders she had to be a particularly pleasant and convenient abode. 'Tis old-fashioned and each room has the wooden side that one sees in all houses over 70 years old. It is altogether small and humble in its look, which will be a great advantage to a poor couple. They are likely always to be rather poor, and the first years, until the house is paid for, they must live very modestly indeed. Mr. Keyes, for his wedding-present to them, has arched up the chambers into the garret to give them a little more breathing-space and less rubbish-room. Before they were only 6 feet 8 in. high. Edward is charmed and thinks this one of the best of the presents. It is much pleasanter having him a doctor than I had imagined beforehand—convenient for us in the house—and then it is so interesting to have people coming to the door daily in haste for the doctor, and the successes are so exhilarating to us all, when he has them, and I am surprised that he does have so many. His practice increases with cheering steadiness. He and Dr. Bartlett are partners, both very happy in the partnership. Whenever I meet them in the Doctor's chaise they have a look like our two babies coming hand in hand to have a piece of orange, and it makes me smile every time. You know that Court St. is sold, and we have nearly double the income from the price that we had from the estate while we owned it. I hope your family will too. It will be as great a comfort to Aunt Susan to have the additional 700 as it is to us. Our latest news is that Haven Emerson has a second boy. Then we are told that Ned and Sally Bartlett are expecting their baby in February. This is an occasion of joy to everyone con-

— 1874 —

cerned and to Annie & me also. Give my love to Lizzy. I am sorry you are so far away, both of you.
E. T. E.

Nov. 17 '74

Dear Edith,

I sent you the telegram, hoping you'd get it before you heard of our defeat [in the election at Glasgow] otherwise. Mother is most thankful, Father is relieved and so am I. It isn't half so interesting as being elected, but it is far safer and happier, now we can be more settled, and Father can lay out his winter. Parnassus has reached the 459 page. Father has struck out "God Save the King" and substituted "Bonny Dundee".

Now for business. When will you come to Thanksgiving? Mother I think is rather improving in health than otherwise this week, but I am not sure that 'twould be advisable to send her down to you, as unluckily that always involves getting ready, and getting ready hurts her, and she seems afraid of it, and Thanksgiving is so near. She sends her love to you and hopes you will come soon and stay long, and says that therefore she will not come, though she concludes "Oh if I could only travel like the dogs and the pussies how quickly would I be in Milton!—this very night!" I had last night a lovely letter from Sarah Malcolm, I shall write to her. Edward & Annie have bought all their carpets, and Mrs Beal is making them. Edward says he & A stand lost in admiration of their own good sense and good taste all the time when they go a-shopping. I have seen nothing except the bureau I had made for Annie as yet. On Sunday afternoon we entered their house and I was surprised at its size, and more than ever convinced that Mr Keyes was making them the best of wedding presents in raising their rooms. How do you do? How is your knee? How are Will and the children?
E. T. E.

Nov 21 1874

Dear Edith,

Your family send their love to you on your birthday and look back over your three times eleven years with affection and delight. Your Mamma sends you a Bible Atlas, thinking you may like to use it with your children, and hoping you will like to have one in the house. I have a humble gift here which I do not send. Judge Hoar stopped his carriage

and said the kindest things about Glasgow. He said the vote was larger than he expected, really wonderful, and he thought Father must be delighted with the result, so great a tribute with no troubles resulting, to have the honour and not the rectorship, and he and Aunt Lizzy were thankful not to have him go away. Then two such beautiful letters, a lovely one from Mr Lowell, and a funny one from Mr Forbes on the subject, and three newspaper articles, have made me highly contented with the result. How glad we are that you are coming! Our preparations go on very smoothly. I hope to go to church Thanksgiving Day.
E. T. E.

Milton, Dec. 22nd 1874

Dear Miss Dabney,

Your note was a great comfort, and when it came I thought I was going to answer it that very day, but no indeed! a time of hurry began, which wound up yesterday by Mother's and my arriving in Milton. We finished Concord preparations for Christmas first, and now are enjoying that delightful long breath after a piece of work accomplished. Mother is going to stay ten days till after New Years. Father is left all alone at home, but he promises to come down for Christmas Eve and day, and again for New Years. He likes very well to have an empty house to himself sometimes to do his work with a free mind. We have just had the pleasure of seeing Parnassus come out. It has alas! many little mistakes in it which I shall have rectified in your copy before it goes. See what a pretty laurel-wreath there is on the cover, Lizzy Simmons drew it. Edith wished to have only blue books, but the publishers prevailed on her to have also red & dark brown, and I think the red is so much the handsomest that I think I must send you a red one though brown is your favorite colour. I was very glad to hear what you told me in your letter of the pleasantness of settling in Cambridge, and the more because it seems as if Mrs Dabney would now stay in America. Alice sent me back the "Patience of Hope", I am glad if you liked it. The last book that Mother and I have been reading is Miss Yonge's Recollections of Keble, the first chapters of a book called "Musings on the Christian Year". I believe you don't know the Christian Year very well, and therefore may not be so much interested in Keble as we are, but if you come across the book, do open it and look at these opening chapters. It is a year since you came, since I saw you at the Forbeses' last Christmas. I wish you were here now. I dined with Mr & Mrs Forbes

— 1874 —

and Alice yesterday, they were all cheerful and delightful, and a letter from Sarah came while we were at dinner so she was not altogether absent. Goodbye! I wish you a Happy New Year. And in it you must give me a visit, remember!

E. T. E.

Milton Dec. 23rd 1874

Dear Father,

Edith begs that you will give Ralph Parnassus. She says he is entirely wrapped up in the book. Ever since Friday the moment that he comes into the house his first question is "Where's Parnassus?" and he reads his favourites, and asks his Mamma to read to him. When they had read the Relief of Lucknow, the Royal George, etc. Edith thought she would give him some new friends, so she began with George Nidiver, and both children said "Oh we know that, that's in the Fifth Reader." Only think of it! They both like it, are well acquainted with it, and didn't know till now that Aunt Lizzy wrote it on purpose for their Papa to read to them. This discovery interested them very deeply. Then Edith read them Alice Brand. Ralph was taken at once with it, but Violet said she didn't understand it, and didn't like it. Edith was beginning to explain it when Jane came to say it was bed-time. The next day Ralph came home from school with the request "May I have Parnassus, and read it to Eestar & Cameron?" Edith gave him the book, and away he went, collected his audience, and carried them to his own room. In about quarter of an hour there was heard such a fearful noise, a roaring as of many lions, and Ralph quite scarlet with rage and distress, dragged in Violet crying loud with passion. He burst out "Mamma, Edie won't listen to Parnassus, and she *says it's silly*!!! And I told her it was *Grandpapa*'s book, and then she had to say something else. But she *won't* listen to it." Violet at the same time was saying "I don't like to hear Parnassus, I don't understand it, and that's what I meant when I said it was silly. And I want to read 'The Nursery' and Ralph won't let me. And he says *that's* silly. It isn't! And I don't want to hear Parnassus." Ralph had been trying to read Alice Brand to her. Cameron didn't appear. No doubt, Edith said, he had cheerfully accepted whatever Ralph chose to inflict, and then during the fight, had fled to his dear Don. Yesterday morning there was a tempest of joy in the house. Cameron was allowed to go to school with Ralph & Violet, Miss Crosby had invited him. One couldn't choose which of the three was most

— 1874 —

proud, excited and brilliantly happy over this great event, Ralph beamed as much as Cameron. At dinner-time when we asked C. about his adventures he had no chance to answer both his elders were so voluble on the subject. He had been very good and might come again. Edith says a New Years Present which Will would like very much is a wall map of Mass. Have you been able to get all your books to send away from Osgood? Edith can get none. She hopes you'll come out by the 2.40 train on Thursday to E. Milton. She is most thankful to you for coming.

    Bring some postage stamps.
        E. T. E.

January 1875 – November 1876

1875. Visit in Boston. Trip with RWE to Philadelphia. Centennial Celebration of April 19, 1775, in Concord. Lecture trip with RWE to New Hampton, New Hampshire and the White Mountains. 1876. Visit to the Cabots in Brookline. Trip to New York, Philadelphia, and Centennial Exhibition with RWE. Oration at University of Virginia; trip to Charlottesville. Visit to Washington, D.C. Charles Emerson born. Emma Lazarus visits.

---

22 West Cedar St. Boston
Jan 7th 1875

Dear Mother,

I saw Lizzy Weir at the depot, and told her of the waiting Parnassus, and I think the next time John goes out it might be well to send it to her. I went first to the dentist who laboured over me for an hour and now I feel much better; then I did errands, paid for Woman's Journal $2.50 & .20 for postage, and came to Nina's about one o'clock. I found a note saying the Beacon St. house was just sold and she was obliged to be in it today removing last things, so I must take possession of my room and make myself comfortable. She came home to lunch at 1.30. I found Mr Sears's new book on her table, she said Mrs Paine (whom Father will remember seeing in her phaeton last summer in Concord) had brought it to her and had read her the sermon "No more Sea". Then after lunch she read Vaughn to me a little while till 'twas time for her to go back to Beacon St. I have spent the afternoon with dear Mrs. Hemenway. She has been sick for three weeks, and is now sitting in her wrapper by her dressing-room fire. She had just been reading the "Memorial of Charles Sumner" and was full of glory about it. I told her about the days after his death—she was in Cuba then and lost that great uprising. It is worthwhile to hear her talk. I wish you had been there. While she has been sick Edith and Augustus have been keeping house and giving dinner-parties, and she has enjoyed hearing about them and their plans for what they would have for dinner, but "Best of all! they had no wine. They told me they thought it was better for young people not to. I was glad of that. It pleased me to the heart! The older I grow

— 1875 —

the stronger I am on the Temperance side. But when I have it on the table all I can do for the Temple is not to touch it myself."
Your affectionate daughter
Ellen T. Emerson

22 West Cedar St. Boston
Jan 8th 1875, Friday.
Dear Edith,

I don't know what you think of the manners of a sister who never wrote to tell you that she and your Mother got home safe with all their pretty presents, and without fatigue or any bad result. I had a multitude of small errands and scraps of business to attend to, and more than a dozen little notes to write which filled in the time. Coming through Boston Mother had time for an interesting interview with Rogers which at last terminated satisfactorily, and the slippers will be made to answer, so her mind is at ease. Father met her and they went up by ex. train. I followed at seven and went to Bible-class, where we had a good lesson and after it Alice Wheildon walked home with me. What a blessing are my business relations, they ensure me brief but frequent interviews with that handsome and engaging creature, and with several other people whom I have a great affection for but could never hope to meet otherwise. When I reached home I found Maggie had gone to bed before Mother had done tea; Anne unpacked the trunks and we ended that day. Tuesday morning Father and I went to the Bank together in great style, I paid my note, he his, then we paid bills, and did errands. I visited Edward & Annie, found them both on the floor in the bay-window carpentering. They agreed to come to dine, and did, and Edward described hearing Mr Cook preach the day before and was very interesting. After dinner Parnassus occupied us for an hour in the Study. Then Edward and Annie read aloud to Mother and I like Satan walked up and down in the earth for hours. Oh what a horrible light dawned on Edward and me that day. A month before we had been entrusted with the charge of S.S. children's New Years party with Mrs. H. Keyes and Lucy Barrett as coadjutors. This Tuesday was the day we had appointed, and here the day had arrived and we had utterly forgotten it. In the Annals of the Town no Committee has ever behaved so dreadfully. Weighted down with shame I started for Lucy Barrett's. She

— 1875 —

met me. This very hour the same horrible truth had struck her, and she had set forth to see if we hadn't done it without her. I went the next day and confessed to Mr. R. *He* didn't mind, but it does seem as if the Committee were almost the only people in the parish who forgot the subject. In the evening Father went to the Social Circle and Mother sent for Maggy, whom she had not yet seen. I from my room heard her say at Mother's door, "Did you want to see me, Mrs. Emerson?" and the voice showed desperate fear. Mother told her all her sins, like the Day of Judgment, and she confessed unwillingly but confessed, and is to stay till next time. Wednesday noon the School-Children came. Alicia helped me prepare. There were only twenty. Mother knew eighteen by name. They sang and were pleased with their things. In the afternoon we had an hour's read of Dress Reform, then a meeting of the guilty Committee at Edward's. Evening Lyceum lecture and I packed to come away. Here I'm having a very good time. I saw dear Mrs Hemenway yesterday. My time is gone for today. How do you do? Come and see me if you are in town.

                                        Your affectionate sister
                                        E. T. E.

                                        Boston Jan 9th 1875

Dear Father,

    I hoped to have seen you here yesterday. I think you must have been in Boston. Did you have a visit on Thursday from Mr Spring? May Alcott told me to tell you he was coming but I forgot. I am just going out to call on Mrs George B. Emerson, and Sylvia and Mrs Parkman. I have not yet found time to hunt up the remark of Schiller on Napoleon; that poor Mr Burrell will hardly get his answer in the time he asked for its coming. Yesterday my daughter came to see me with a message from Mrs Elliot Cabot. She was on her way to dine at Mrs Parkman's. Dr Hooper just came here to invite us to dine with him tomorrow, and meet Miss Hale and Mr Gay and hear about Egypt, but Nina doesn't feel well enough. Mary Blake came to see us yesterday while we were out. I helped Nina at the Beacon St. house a while, and met all the family there, and Mrs Coolidge came here in the afternoon. Last night the young George M. Barnard and his wife who was Ellen Dutton Russell spent the evening with us. They told us some stories of Henry Dalton's children, their mother was Elise Russell, Mrs Barnard's sister, and she died some time ago. Mr Dalton's second wife, Florence Chapman, has a newborn baby, a boy, and when the little Elsie, who is six, was told she had another brother, she was silent. On being asked whether she was pleased she said "No." "Why not?" "In the first place I don't like boys," she answered "and then I found enough to do taking care of one. Now I shall have two." The *one* who gave her so much trouble was her only brother, two years older than herself, Harry. "It was a most characteristic answer" Mrs Barnard went on, "The other day she and Harry came to play with my children, and when they came I gave them some molasses-candy. Harry had a habit of asking which troubles his father, who does all he can to cure him of it, but quite in vain; and he very soon wanted some more. I told him I had given him at first as much as his papa would wish him to have, and refused. Presently he came again, and I refused him again. After a little while I felt some one behind me. I turned round and there was Elsie. 'Aunt Ellen, I hope you'll excuse Harry. I'm sorry he was so rude. But' with a sigh— 'he has no idea of manners.' " Remember that this child is six, and Harry is eight. Now I am going to Osgood's to see if you are in town.

E. T. E.

January 18th, 1875.

Dear Edith,

Father has gone to Boston to-day to see Mr. Elliot Cabot and Mr. van Brunt, to beseech them to come up and see the "boulder"* and give their opinion whether it will do as it is, or can be fashioned into another pedestal, or they must begin at the beginning and find a new stone. I have charged him if they can come to invite Mrs. Cabot too. He says that at the Committee-meeting the other night, called to express sentiments after seeing the boulder, every man was sad and blank, either sure that it wouldn't do, or not sure that it would, and all eagerly agreed to his proposal to call in these umpires. Edward and Annie dined with us on Saturday (because we were going to have a goose) doesn't that sound like youth & home to you? and we had an opportunity to exchange our views on the party the night before which was a great pleasure all round. Father was expecting a Senior to come by appointment to ask advice, and E. & A. were expecting a call from Miss Brown of Factory Village, so we separated early. Edward at dinner told

---

* The "boulder" was to be considered as a possible base for Daniel Chester French's statue of *The Minuteman*.

— 1875 —

some lovely tales of his Billy. He makes him shake hands before he gives him his grain. The other day he left him untied and Billy found the meal bag, emptied it on the floor, and helped himself. Edward gave him much exercise and no water, and allowed supper-time to pass unnoticed. When he went in to put Billy to bed, B. immediately lifted up his foot and held it up appealing all the time Edward stayed to remind him that he wanted supper. It was Billy's halter that was used for the Vestry bear. Edward told him he trusted to his honour. Nevertheless he found him on the barn-floor when he brought the halter home. "William! Where are you? Go to your place!" he said sternly, and Billy hastened back and stood in his stall. Mother sent me yesterday morning with a hundred copies of "Our Dumb Animals" to distribute in the pews, and she had the satisfaction of finding that most of them were carried home. She has just gone down to enter a protest against the bleeding of calves, armed with a copy of laws and instructions-how-to-proceed furnished her by the Society. Saturday afternoon I was reading to Mother when Father came for me. I must bring down the pedigree. The descendants of John Topsfield had turned up, and sure enough there was Edward D. Emerson, younger than our Edward, great grandson of J. of T. I accused his ancestor of having been rich and therefore dropped by the poorer branches of the family, and he said it was quite true he had married a rich wife and had received besides an enormous grant of land. He said he had been acquainted with many Emersons of different branches of the family, and he thought the family characteristics well-marked and well-preserved. They were principally these: 1) A great shrinking from people. 2) Independence of mind—they can't let anyone else do their thinking for them. He asked me if I didn't agree. I told him I had never known but two, my Father and Uncle, well enough to judge, so I couldn't answer, but I privately thought Father seemed to have them. He further said that the J. of Topsfield race was uncommonly long-lived and healthy, living to be 85, 87, 93, 101 years old and in perfect working-order, always to the last. When these had gone Father and I set out to walk but met the belated senior. I told Father it was his man. We turned back. The youth had also taken the same thought and turned, so I left them. Edward's S.S. class of one nobly survives and Edward faithfully teaches it. He & Annie are coming with Mr Hale to help mourn your & Will's absence.

Your very devoted sister
E. T. E.

— 1875 —

Concord, Monday Jan. 18th 1875

Dear Edie [Davidson],

As is usual in visits there was less and less time to write; on Wednesday came the Conference, and at night I went to Milton where all day Thursday I helped get ready for the great engagement tea-party of the evening (Alice Forbes to Edward Cary); and on Friday I came home, went to a dinner-party in the afternoon at Mrs Chamberlaine's, to Parish children's party in the evening and Saturday settled myself back, so you have waited a long time for your letter. I am glad you had a good time in Milton, I think you must have liked to be there as it were in the midst of the engagement. How surprised everyone was! No one had thought of it. I found it very interesting to go to Milton and see Alice and all the people involved. Nothing touches one more than to have a glimpse of the solemn and momentous side of an engagement. Then the joy seems all the clearer. Alice mentioned with pleasure her note from you, and I was pleased on both sides that she enjoyed it and that you wrote it. January 21st. I have just had the happiest twenty-four hours. Mr. Hale came last night to spend the night—Mr. Edward Hale. Edward and Annie came to tea. Did you ever stay in the same house with Mr. H.? A man with such multitudinous irons in the fire is a mine of delight. Everyone feels a desire to tell him everything, and he has on his side everything to tell you. The amount of conversation crowded into the hours of his visit was astonishing, and there is one delight in it which reminds me of ten times one is ten all the time. He is one of that sect himself truly. He came to read a story at the Lyceum. It was "In His Name." I was disappointed and anxious at first, but was carried along very soon and found the audience enthusiastic. Then at home came the chance to tell him all I had thought and ask all I wanted to know about it, and get very full and satisfactory answers. He was clear comfort all the time he was here. He went at ten. At one came Mr. and Mrs. Elliot Cabot!!! and spent the afternoon. It was perfect happiness to have both of them. The vistas of possible conversation that opened on all sides made one's spirits rise almost out of sight. Thank you for sending the stretcher back. I hope little Lucy is well again. What teacher for yourself have you got? I am glad you have more time. Don't work yourself too hard however. Mary Blake says Lilla is convinced that she has overworked herself, so take warning and be a tortoise willingly. You must always keep a reserve of power.

E. T. E.

— 1875 —

Concord, Wednesday, February 3rd 1875

Dear Edith,

Last night we had a grander feast than usual. Whether from gratitude for Edward's election (to the Social Circle) or some other motive, Father was anxious that we should ignore old customs and do our best. Dear Mrs. Sanborn came and helped me through. She stayed from four till ten, and washed and scalloped all the oysters, and whipped the cream for the chocolate. She has just come home from New Bedford, where she had such a peaceful visit. She saw Quaker ways for the first time, and was charmed, and among other things she says the low quiet voice which they find sufficient for ordinary uses surprised and captivated her.

Did Edward tell you that he contemplates a crusade against the "Concord quark," as he denominates the tone of conversation used among us? Mrs. Sanborn will be a ready helper. So will I, if I can bring my own voice down. Wouldn't it be good if any change could be effected?. Mother alas! is sick abed. She would come down yesterday to arrange the flowers and cut the cake, but otherwise hasn't left her bed since you saw her. Edward and Annie came down this morning. They had had a proud and happy four days with you. Father went up with Judge Hoar's letter to show Aunt Lizzy. He came home excited and enchanted. He had seen my London photograph framed and hung up. He had never seen it before since it was taken, and had forgotten its existence.

E. T. E.

Concord February 15th 1875

Dear Haven,

This is the first regular *letter* that I have written this year. January was filled up with visiting, and I have been trying what it was to be sick abed and have the new doctor in the first days of this month. I can't tell to this day whether I *was* sick, only his new methods removed much of the suffering and shortened the time, or whether he put me to bed and had me play sick because he thought in general it was advisable to make me do so. I had a very good time, and except that it does bring some arrears of work to perplex me now, I have nothing to say against it.

— 1875 —

Annie calls him "the lightning-cure doctor", and the success that has so far attended him is delightful to us all. He seems to me to have a great many patients, but I believe he doesn't think so. His glory this week is having cured a valuable mare of Mr Hubbard's, which was very sick, and at first Edward thought there was no hope.

Feb. 23rd. I have just half an hour and I'll give you a news-summary and amplify later if there seems to be time. You have not heard much about Parnassus; Will's going to Chicago; the letter from a lady who had by means of Aunt Lizzy's poem discovered George Nidiver himself in California; Edith's visits to Concord; Father's proposed journey (and mine) to Philadelphia; Edward's going to housekeeping; our relations with Mr. George B. Emerson; and then I ought to thank you for sending us the article on Glasgow—which reminds me that I don't know whether you have ever heard of the winding-up letters from Glasgow, which were very interesting. You sent me also a Tribune and an article about the Glasgow hero which I have not yet read; something prevents my ever reading or writing this winter. But I am keeping them to read, and when this week of school-examinations is over Mother and I hope to sit down as of old and then we shall read. Now to begin on the heads I proposed. Mr. Forbes is having a great battle for righteousness in the R.R. business which he wages with his usual skill and has won rather than lost so far, I hear. But it wears on him very much, and Will watches and accompanies him perpetually to save him from fatigue and trouble as much as he can. And besides, Will himself as trustee has made good and difficult stands, we are told, and we are very proud of him. Now he has gone to Chicago, while I think his Father stays at home, and again we are puffed up that he should be sent to do such important work. Edith is all alone. I am going there next week. She is still pretty lame, though she seemed to limp less when she came in February to hear Father lecture than she did when she visited Edward and Annie in January. Father gave his usual Lyceum lecture in Concord, and to our surprise the world made much of it. There came an extra train from Manchester, N.H., bringing from there and Nashua and another town 300 people to hear it, and it was advertised in Boston papers with the trains. The result was that the Town Hall was really filled, gallery and all. Father looked beautifully, everyone tells me, and read with his old ease and confidence. I didn't go. Edith came on purpose and Aunt Lizzy took tea with us. On that occasion we read aloud the letter about George Nidiver.* It came some days before, and Father and I kept it a secret till we could assemble the family. Edward and Annie failed us when the time came, and lost the pleasure. It was such a surprise, and if you could have seen Aunt Lizzy and heard the general shout when the climax was reached, you would understand that that letter was a real event in family history. We are all also happy in having a cousin in Mr. George B. Emerson. He has come up once since Edward's wedding and spent a day, and I have been at his house and had a beautiful time, and last week Father went there to dine, and now we are all comfortable and pleased, and before it was the other way. We have had a great deal to delight us in the coming out of Parnassus—the letters on the subject, the reviews in the papers, the quick calls for second and now for third edition—and we have also endured great anguish of shame and useless regret over the extraordinary mistakes and the number of mistakes in it. The second edition was a decided improvement. We hope the third will straighten everything out. The greatest pleasures about the book, however, were various little anecdotes which came to us by word of mouth, and Ralph's pleasure in it is a source of glory as well as amusement. Edward's share I shall have to leave to tell you about till I come. This *shall* go tonight. This week we are examining schools. It always makes me remember how Uncle William used to do it so beautifully that every minute of the exercises we felt entire confidence that all would be skillfully conducted, and when he came to speak, every word satisfied by its justice and surprised by the minute observation and clear memory it showed. I think he will never be equalled by any successor. I have been longing for him.

My love to all the family and to the funny little Haven (for you always describe him as funny) especially.

Ellen T. Emerson.

Concord, February 17th, 1875.

Dear Edith,

Did you see in yesterday's Advertiser Father's letter to Mr. Stirling? Isn't it good. I am glad to see it, for it went unseen by anyone, only it is a

*Elizabeth Hoar wrote at least two poems. "George Nidiver" was about a man in California who successfully confronted and faced down a grizzly bear after using his last shot to kill a second bear which was attacking the boy who was hunting with him. "Story of a Bridge" was about a young man who crossed a partially wrecked bridge to warn the approaching train on which his sweetheart Mary was travelling.

shame the A. doesn't mention where it got it. It makes it look as if Father had inserted it. Did you see the remarks on Concord and Lexington in the same paper? Mr. Reynolds was here yesterday and it was enchanting to hear him & Father talk on that subject and the past & coming 19th. Father asked Mr. Reynolds to write an article for the Advertiser to counteract yesterday's. I hope he will. Father came home very much pleased with his visit to Milton, especially charmed as usual with little Edward, but interested in the relations of the little span, and delighted with the parents, and interested immensely in all Will had told him. He has had lovely letters both from Mr. Childs and Mr. Furness, also one from a minister of N.H., enthusiastically thanking him for having published Parnassus. Edward had the Social Circle last night. I went down and was in the fun a little, but was afraid of fatigue so did nothing. The rug was spread and looked beautifully, the alabaster and sconces lit, the fire brilliant, your ivy did duty on the supper-table, and vases of geraniums and azaleas from Annie's & Florence's plants the parlour table, and supper-room mantelpiece. Everything looked charming, the newness of the silver was apparent. Your slop-bowl & Sarah's pitcher were for sugar & cream for the chocolate, Annie's sugar-bowl & A. Damon's pitcher for the coffee. Everything they had came in play, the owls were out, and all the salt-cellars and the castor, the cake-baskets & tall dish, the best tea-set, and the common, and the India china, and the glass, all the coffee-spoons & everything. I whipped the cream for the chocolate, and half a pint made the brown pitcher A. K. B. gave Annie piled full. On Saturday Father's lecture to the fair ones comes off. I shall go with him. Can I meet you at 12 and buy sack & bonnet with your advice and assistance? I shall bring $7.00, you have 10. for me so I think we can buy both with that. Mother is getting better in both ways, the cough less troublesome, and her strength returning. The theatricals made 83 dollars, but to the surprise of all concerned the expenses proved to be 50, so there were only 33. to send. If you like I will come on the 3rd of March and stay till Friday night.

E. T. E.

Concord March 15th 1875

Dear Edith,

We are to go to Philadelphia on Wednesday night at nine. I mean to come in at 10.20 and do shopping and make calls. If you are to be in

— 1875 —

town 'twill be pleasant to meet. Secondly tell me how to equip myself for a sleeping-car. I have no idea. After having heard your letter read three times Father took to reading it himself, and liked it better than before. The other day his study had to be cleaned in the afternoon. He waited in the dining-room—I was spending the day at Edward's—and chanced to take down "Round the World in 80 Days." Ever since he seems pleased to find breakfast a little late, and seizes the opportunity to read a little more. He has got two-thirds through, and often exclaims that he shall be likely to read the whole. Then he laughs to himself at the memory of it.

No more time.

E. T. E.

Copied from EEF edition.

March, 1875.

Dear Edith,

Yesterday was Sunday. I wish you had seen Father's face when I presented myself at four o'clock. He was so innocent, so surprised, so rebellious, so piteous, so enraged when he found himself submitting; and he kept it up through the walk, always knowing a shorter way home. He is immensely funny and frolicsome. Again you should have been present when the subject of the new hat was introduced. He is resolved he won't have one. He gave me a dollar today and I told him I would save it towards the hat-fund. This aroused Mother, who inquired what was the matter. I said, "Why Father ought to have a new hat." "Ridiculous!" exclaimed Mother with emphasis. "Now what a shame!" said I. "It isn't half so ridiculous as it is for me to have a new bonnet. If you could only see." "No, no," said Mother, "of course he must have a new hat. But for *you* to save money to buy it!" "What is it?" asked Father. "What did your Mother say? I'm all ready to be aggrieved if it was cruel. I didn't hear. What did she say?"

Philadelphia, March 20th, 1875

Dear Mother,

I lamed myself in Boston and haven't been able to keep my shoe on since I came. Very inconvenient. I can't go anywhere without a carriage. And the care Mrs. Furness has lavished on my foot! She did it up two or three times a day at first, always herself, and took so many steps

— 1875 —

about it and devised so many reliefs that gratitude alone should make it get well. Still I hardly expect to walk much while I'm here. Sunday night. I expected to write a letter but couldn't. The lecture came off the very night we arrived—of course. I thought in vain, "What can interfere with a grand success!" Nothing! The lecture was to be Eloquence. I knew it was straight and Father was fond of it and familiar with it. He had slept in the afternoon and felt well. I couldn't call up any gloomy possibility. He didn't even care for reporters this time. So with cheerful mind I went. It was to be in the Academy of Music. The Furnesses and I were to sit in the stage-box. We entered. I was placed in the front seat. Down went my heart. Here was a theatre almost if not quite as vast as the New York A. of M. I sang to myself Will's verse, "Cheer up Sam" and thought of Father's skill and the quality of his voice. He began and made no efforts, and I narrowly watched the distant galleries. The people looked as if they were listening hard, but not as if they had given up in despair. I saw Father's "science and power combined." Not a shout. No one would know he felt any difficulty, but he made longer intervals between his words. Motionless as a country audience the three thousand people heard the lecture. Only one man could I find whose face followed all the turns. He alone laughed at "Blasphemy." Not another smiled. Dr. Channing elicited a slight general laugh. The Earl of Carnarvon had its natural effect on the whole house. Nothing else. And it is true the marvellous charm of the lecture was missing. Still I looked quite cheerful and hoped no one else knew. But the next day Father and I were together three minutes and he said he might almost as well have been put in the open air to speak; it was impossible to give anything its right rendering when one had to consider whether one could make one's self heard at all. He did not feel very badly, but of course we are both sorry. I haven't heard the lecture mentioned since —that is, not *as a lecture*. People have said they "enjoyed hearing my father." No one has suggested his reading anything more. They wrote and asked him in good season to make arrangements. Now it would be too late.

We have been feted and petted. Have been exceedingly happy. Father shows unusual pleasure in the society of Mr. Furness and Mr. Bradford, and went with enthusiasm to be photographed with them. He has stayed over Sunday to my amazement just as if he meant to when he came. I want to stay longer, but he won't. We go to N.Y. tomorrow. How do you do?   E. T. E.

— 1875 —

Concord, March 29th, 1875.

Dear Haven,

I write quickly before making the plunge into preparations for the 19th of April. We heard as soon as we arrived one or two pieces of news about it which somehow or other set Concord hearts dancing with a sense of festivity and grandeur, and a recognition of patriotic feeling.

Carlisle held its Town Meeting two weeks ago and somebody rose and inquired whether it was possible that the letter to the Town which had been confidently expected from the Town of Concord, inviting her sister over to commemorate with her the fathers of both who fought side by side a hundred years ago, had never been received.

After some hesitation one of the Selectmen acknowledged that there had been some such letter in their hands, but they thought it would cost the Town something to take part in the Celebration, and therefore they had just put it away and kept it quiet. Carlisle was shocked, threw out its board of Selectmen, chose a new one, raised $500 and sent word to Concord that she would come as a Town, bring the Chelmsford Cavalry as her escort and guests, and have her own tent and dinner, as Concord ought not to have the whole expense of the day. Wasn't that pretty? That was one story. The other was that the Portland Blues, who are a crack company of Maine, like our Cadets, were invited to come to the 19th and have answered that they mean to come Saturday night as they wish to spend Sunday in Concord and go to church in the old meetinghouse, and they request the parish to allow them the use of eight pews for that day. We now see distinctly that those who wish to enjoy all the glories of the occasion must finish their preparations on Friday 16th and have nothing to do but parade and stare after that. The pedestal of the statue [*The Minuteman*] is finished and put in its place, and under it is the regulation copper-box containing a History of Concord, the pamphlets printed after every anniversary or celebration ever kept here, the photographs of Ebby Hubbard and Dan French and of Concord itself, the whole history of Bridge and Statue, the newspapers of the day, which by curious good luck had nothing about the Brooklyn trial in them, and I remember nothing more, except the names of all concerned and the plans for the Nineteenth. Yesterday, no Saturday, I went to Boston and was lucky enough to meet Edith at Will's office. I delivered the Easter Eggs with instructions as to which was to whom. The day after our return Edward & Annie dined here. They asked all sorts of questions about you and the family. I like to hear Father talk

— 1875 —

about Willy. He would be glad to have him in his arms every day. The photograph of "the Three Boys"* as Father and Mr Furness call it has come, indeed there are three different ones. Very good indeed, and interesting. You shall have one if you ask for it. I saw Aunt Lizzy at church yesterday, and Mrs Edward Hoar too, but little of course was said. The snow was deep and the sleighing excellent when we got home, but the clear sun even without any help from So. wind is doing great works, the noise of waters far and near is heard from ten to six every day, and then the night freezes everything hard again. Edward's Billy has sprained his ankle. What if it shouldn't get well before the great day! He wouldn't be happy on the stupid unwieldy Christopher. My love to all, and make your plans to visit us in force this summer
E. T. E.

Concord, April 24th, 1875

Dear Haven,

I wonder what has been the tone of the newspapers you have seen on the subject of our great day. The one or two that I have come across have been rather flippant and awakened my wrath. I haven't time for much detail, but I'll give you a little general idea of how it was. I think the labours of every inhabitant for a month beforehand were herculean, and one of those who took it hardest was Edward. He was on the decoration committee. He no doubt did the whole, as head, though some of his committee helped well. He found mottoes for the dinner-tent, the houses, the roads, the Ball-room, and they had to dress everything in flags besides. You see it was a kind of housekeeping that included all out-doors. Enormous! Well, the result was perfectly satisfactory. The town had a festive air. Every house, tree and corner was labelled with its history. The Ball-room was described by everyone as the handsomest ever seen. Father and Aunt Lizzy say as much as the youngest about it, and Emily Russell Pierson, who has an eye for such things, said she had never danced in a more beautiful one I am told. It was the Cattleshow Hall dressed by a professional decorator with flags and made glorious with designs of guns, sabres and bayonets at the ends. The Arsenal lent them. Just when Edward was most wanted in the preceding week, when days were growing to four and three, came an uncommon rush of practice, and every time he entered his house he

*RWE, William H. Furness, George P. Bradford.

heard someone had sent for him. Then he would exclaim, "Faint *now*! Sick *now*! This sickness doth infect the very lifeblood of our enterprise!" He said Dr. Bartlett had told him his very highest average had been five dollars a day, "And here am I with an average of six dollars a day right along, *now* at this very moment when I ought to work twelve hours a day for the Nineteenth and have no thoughts for anything else." He was in despair, but he did manage both. At his house he and Annie had Emma Pratt and Alice Curtis, Col. Pierson and Emily, and Maj. Higginson. Ida couldn't come because Pauline was just starting for Europe. At our house we had Mr. and Mrs. Curtis and Frank, Effie Lowell, Edith (Will alas! was in Nebraska) with Ralph and Violet, Col. Theodore Lyman, Edith Hemenway, Edith Davidson, Oscar, Eugenia and Lidian Jackson, and Helen Cabot. Does that seem many? I thought it a pretty fair houseful when I asked them, for I never thought of crowding people, but when I heard what other houses did I was ashamed of my small list of guests. The Cheneys had twenty-five on Sunday and Monday nights covering all their floors and sofas with people. Miss Emeline Barrett had forty. The coming of the guests on Saturday, the sound of bands in the street, the decorations going up, the continual procession of carriages coming into town, the crowds getting out of every train made everyone excited and happy. The joy of the occasion began to dawn upon us, and with every hour it increased. We liked our company and they liked each other so much, and the mighty concourse was so inspiring. Then when Monday came it was at first so bright and we had great hopes of the weather, but there was a strong freezing wind under a black sky most of the day, perfectly horrible. Yet the crowd was as great as could be dealt with, and a lovely day might have brought one three times as great, which would have involved us in endless confusion. So the weather was probably the best we could have had, as it interfered with nothing. In most houses half the family stayed at home and received and fed strangers. At the Manse 400, at the Keyeses' 2 or 300, at our house and most houses 50 or 60, and all who thus stayed at home were happy and enchanted with their day. The other half with some guests went to the tents, and huddled together and somewhat defended by the canvass from the wind, were not quite frozen and heard and enjoyed so much that they forgot discomfort and pitied those left at home. The poem and the oration were grand, the dinner excellent, the after-dinner speaking the most interesting I ever heard. I was one of the tent party. Of course one of my great pleasures

— 1875 —

was seeing Edward as Marshal. I felt as glorious as a sister could. Then the coming home and comparing notes was delightful all round, and the Ball was a great success. So I end the day with the paper—will only say more that Edith was handsome at the Ball, Annie didn't go, and Edward was tending a dying baby all night. On Tuesday everyone went. We hated to lose them but had the satisfaction of a brilliant festivity to look back on. I wish you had been here.
E. T. E.

Concord April 30th 1875

Dear Miss Dabney,

I have known all along that I was neglecting to write to you but oh! when one is involved in a Centennial Celebration one can do very little else, and think of very little else. Probably no one outside can quite estimate the vast and overpowering magnitude of our Nineteenth of April celebration as it seemed to our green unaccustomed selves. A year ago we regarded it as the rest of the world did, as a great day and an interesting one. But when a town spends a whole year in preparations, and consultations, and when the effect of these consultations upon each man concerned is only to increase continually his appreciation of the colossal nature of the tasks before the town, till a feeling of awe, and almost of blind despair takes hold of him, the womenkind naturally infer that the indoor labours must bear a proportion to those of the citizens, and they go to work with frenzy. The amount of work done in this town in the last two months is amazing, for the absurd little trick of the human mind which Mrs. Whitney talks about in Patience Strong (that if people are in any especial hurry and stress of work they will always go out of their way to do any little difficult or tedious odd-job which they never before could find time to do) showed itself in every house, and all the rubbish was looked over and disposed of, and the most retired corners were cleaned out. All the broken furniture in the garrets suddenly moved down to be renovated, and everything in the domain was attended to, as if the day of judgment were at hand and order were the saving virtue. The result was that every blacksmith, carpenter, mason, painter, cabinet-maker, paper-hanger, harness-maker, cobbler, in the town was driven and persecuted night and day; and you can understand how every soul in every house and every creature they could hire was worked. I think sleep even fled almost entirely from every responsible person, and between ten and twelve at night each was in the habit of thinking, "I'll just lie down and ache a while, and then I'll rise and fight again." You should have seen Edward's indignation when a patient came at half-past seven in the morning and his girl told him Edward hadn't appeared and she guessed he wasn't awake. "Why," said he, "I had been out attending to my busines an hour or more and was just coming home to breakfast." He was on the Decoration Committee, and to dress and label a town is a very serious undertaking. He has wondered for three months how we should feel when we waked up sometime and found it was the 20th of April. It was impossible for anyone to imagine what we should do and not do, and where we should be when the Nineteenth should come. I believe our ideas began to settle about ten days beforehand, and the vague immensity condensed into some kind of shape, and we managed at the time to accomplish somewhere near what we ought to. I was strictly forbidden by the sage and cool-headed who manage me to invite a soul, since our house was on the Committee of Reception and must be used only for Town guests. I obeyed. I have been sorry since. I think that recklessness is often rewarded by a kind of success, and I wish I had been hairbrained. We had only thirteen to spend the nights and forty or fifty in the day. At two houses smaller than ours they had 25 and 40 for the nights. At the Manse they fed 400 that day. I should have liked that a great deal better, and I was prepared for 18 by night and 150 by day, and the prudence of my controllers lost us the pleasure. Yet the pleasure as it was was immense. There couldn't be happier days than Sunday and Monday were to Concord people, and the Oration and Poem and Statue were worthy of the occasion. It was glorious. I hope to see you soon and to find you well & prospering and then we will set the day for your visit to which Mother & I are looking forward. I hope you are also keeping it in mind.

Ellen T. Emerson.

Concord June 14. 1875

Dear Edith,

Mother at present means to come down on Wednesday noon, and stay with you till Friday or Saturday. She thanks you for sending for her. I wish I could come with her, but now is the time she must come, and Mary Blake, in the most lovely manner, has invited me to come Wednesday and see the shows of the 17th with her from the windows of her family on Beacon & State Sts, and I have accepted with joy. Our schools close day after tomorrow, and that removes one care. We are so happy Father & I in the hope of your company on the 28th or 29th. Do get well and make it sure. You would have enjoyed hearing your own letter read, when it arrived Saturday night. Father & Mother were so seriously interested in the experiment of laying on of hands, as well as so cut to the heart by your sufferings. Poor little dear! I hope the improvement continues. On Saturday Mother's double cousin Mrs Whitney with her daughter Mrs Burton & her husband & baby spent the day here. We liked them all, and Mrs Whitney told Mother *she*! had all those long-mourned lilac Windsor chairs from Mother's mother's parlour and would send her two. We are delighted. Our cook doesn't do. We are at sea again. Oh dear! And the worst of it is she is so excellent & willing but has no *head*, and forgets & spoils & never gets through. I fear it will be a blow to her. If it isn't I don't care.

E. T. E.

Concord & F. R.R. June 21 & 2

Dear Edith,

I think you may dismiss all uneasiness about Mother's coming home, she did not catch cold, and then she had a good time. To be sure, I neglected to force her supper upon her, she omitted it, didn't sleep, and has been frightfully sick ever since, (not sick abed but wretched & worried, which is in some respects worse). But that I lay to my door on Friday night not to the journey. We long to have you & the children come. Father will start on Tuesday morning I think, and though I hate to miss your visit I am glad Mother will have you while I am gone. Mr Alcott is now holding weekly conversations in Concord and Father & Mother enjoy them and declare he never before talked so well. The Severs are all here at Miss E. Barrett's and we had a tea-party and they came, on Sat. night. They were most delightful. Our S.S. Anniversary came off on Sunday with much enthusiasm, outsiders like the Severs and the childless townspeople seemed enchanted. But I want to tell you of the 17th. I have seldom known such a day of glory. One more interview with Our Country, one more sense of our relation to her. So many pleasures at once, and that at the heart of them all. If only I had had Father & Ralph with me to see that they saw all that I saw, & knew all that I know, it would have been perfect. On Friday I found Father had seen the soldiers with advantage among those who knew much, but all

— 1875 —

that kept him ready to cry with joy & wonder for the rest of the evening while I unfolded it, assisted by the papers, he had missed.

E. T. E.

Pemigewasset House, Plymouth, N.H.
Thursday July 2d, 1875, 11 a.m.

Dear Edith,

Father did not go to Cambridge on Wednesday morning, but spent his time in Boston buying a new map of N.H. and disguising himself so effectually in a vast new felt hat, positively glittering with newness, that I recognized him with difficulty. I, unmindful of you, spent the half hour I had to spare in getting toothbrushes and catering. When the hour of one found us at Lowell, I produced a milk-biscuit. Father ate it without a word, but when I laid a second on his newspaper said, "No, thank you." I had only placed it there as plate to a cake, and mollified by the appearance of the cake he ate both that and the plate. Next I tried a cake alone, and seeing that that was taken with more duty than delight I got out a bunch of bananas. These were a most gratifying surprise. "You are artful in your management," he said. "You wouldn't have persuaded me to eat a cracker if I had known what you had in store." I got him to try cracker and banana together, and he seemed to like the combination, and repeated it. We had the Merrimac beside us all the way, a lovely companion. It is called Pemigewasset till it reaches Franklin. There its name changes to Merrimac. Mr. McIntyre received us at Bristol at about five o'clock. He had a carryall for us, and we first drove by one of the finest falls I ever saw—indeed two, one on each side of the bridge—which made us scream aloud for our Ralph and Violet, and then for you; and then through enchanting scenery under a perfect sky for about five miles to New Hampton, where we stayed at Mrs. Dyer's, a place after my own heart. Mrs. Dyer is a lady and does her own work. Mr. Dyer is a most kind and worthy man, one of the trustees of the [New Hampton] Academy. Their only child is grown up and lives in Boston. Such a good table and comfortable house! The only trouble was that I couldn't go right to bed. A thought had struck me in the cars. I didn't know what the lecture was to be—had paid no attention to it. I therefore looked it up and read it diligently till I heard a band of music. I sewed it quick, and had hardly time to get my bonnet on before the procession of the Germanae (the girls' literary Society), the Social Fraternity, and Literary Adelphi (the boys' societies), headed by the Con-

— 1875 —

cord, N.H., band, stood at the gate. A marshall with portentous baton took Father, and a humbler one with pink ribbons on a cane took me, and assigned us our places in the procession, and we marched in unbroken silence with infinite solemnity to the Academy, where we were asked to sit down in the "Office" and wait a while, and there we talked—Father with the Elocution master, and I with a young lady, we supposing them to be the Teachers, Principal and Assistant, and in a manner our hosts. When it turned out that one was a visitor, the other a man just come from Boston two weeks ago to polish the delivery of the graduating class a little, all our conversation and behaviour to them seemed funny and misplaced enough. We were finally brought with much pomp into the Hall, which was very well filled. On my right sat a man who heartily entered into the lecture, invariably appreciated it as he should. In front of me sat his foil—a man who took everything exactly wrong, and worried me as much as one man could. But when Father told the story of the Sociables at the Town Hall that went to the heart of the uncomfortable creature. He said he thought that was a good idea. When I came out and inquired, I found my r. hand neighbor was an Orthodox minister; the other was a musician, plays a violin in a band. The audience was unusually responsive for a country audience, and a universal scream of delight hailed Miss Fanny Forbes's speech about dress, though Father trembled a little beforehand lest they should be too orthodox and strait-laced to bear it.* When we had been marshalled home, a pile of autograph-books was brought in from the Academy. I asked what time we should have breakfast, and Mrs. Dyer said, "Any time you choose—seven, or half-past six, or"—I hastened to say seven, and fled to bed, for oh dear! how tired I am! The first thing after breakfast the band of music and Academic Procession appeared at the gate and carried us once more to the Hall where they had regular Commencement Exercises till one o'clock. Mr. McIntyre had won our hearts driving us over, and he appeared today the most charming and *generosus puer* there. He was first scholar and had the Valedictory. Then we came home to dinner. Mrs. Dyer had a houseful of company, among them Mr. Emmons, a youth who looked as old as the first class, who are all, even Mr. McIntyre, quiet and shy. To my astonishment he

*In the essay "Social Aims" RWE wrote: "I have heard with admiring submission the experience of the lady who declared that 'the sense of being perfectly well dressed gives a feeling of inward tranquillity which religion is powerless to bestow.'" The remark was attributed by the family to Miss Fanny Forbes.

— 1875 —

talked freely at dinner. It appeared he had graduated years ago here. Next he informed us that he took care of the Fitchburg Co.'s boats at Walden three summers ago and knew all about Concord, and saw our fire. Later still he proved to have taught the High School at Stoughton, Massachusetts. I no longer wondered that he knew the use of his tongue. At three o'clock Mr. Dyer introduced Mr. Bray with a horse and carryall at the gate ready to take us to Plymouth, and away we started, and oh! enjoyed Mr. Bray greatly. Never before have I heard the Yankee dialect in such perfection. "That 'ere clover, blowed out, looks kinder splendid, don't it?" and he said "leetle" and "hoss," and when he told us about having bought this hoss last week, his infant grandson at his side turned gaily round and said, "Yes! he pretty nigh cleaned out his wallet." This unexpected news from a babe of Cameron's age, who hadn't before opened his lips, upset all alike—Father and me and the proud grandfather.

We took the cars at Ashland, and left them at the Pemigewasset House at Plymouth. There we took tea, went to walk, saw a most lovely sunset, and I went to bed before dark you may be sure. The next forenoon we went strawberrying, and right after dinner took the stage for the Flume House. We had the box seat with the driver. The day was perhaps the most heavenly ever seen—clear July glory—and I being dressed for a sleigh-ride was able to forgive the coldness of the wind, so there was no drawback, and Father enjoyed every inch of the way and could not have done praising everything. He thinks he never had such a delightful drive. Mr. Joseph L. Bates was in the stage, and he and Father occasionally shouted a few congratulations to each other. Mr. Bates left us behind and went on to the Profile House. I stood on the piazza while the stage stayed. Father meanwhile was getting rooms. I thus picked up the knowledge which way to go to find the Flume, and the moment the stage went started forth.

Happily a sudden oblivion had removed from Father's memory his former visit here. He wondered at my wayward folly in setting forth without asking questions. How did I know how far it might be, which way to go, indeed what was it we were going to see? "What is the Flume?" he asked. "Is it a mountain or a river, or a tree, or a rock!" I never guessed that he had really forgotten, and told him I knew nothing about it—I was going to see. We came to where the brook runs under the road—he liked it very much—then following the path we met it in full glory, and he was delighted indeed. He said he remem-

1875

bered having admired something long ago, and this was it, and worthy! All was as new to him as to me. It was an interesting expedition. We spent much lamentation on your inability to come, and I think the Flume would be perfect if five young Forbeses arrayed for the bath were crawling its floors and tumbling in its basins. Father wants Mother to see it and everything, and I tell him we'll bring her next summer.

Fabyan's. Sunday night. Father has a very good time. We walk, sit round falls, two to six hours a day, and have such excellent cooking that he can't help eating, and I keep him surrounded with all the snares and gins I can devise. The Hotels are most comfortable and very handsome. Father has proposed never going home, once. And I mean not to arrive till Thursday night, though it is impossible yet to say when. I think we shall use the whole hundred dollars. If it will only benefit Father 'twill be well spent, but when I see how pale and thin he is, I fear a week will do very little. I send you an oxalis from the Flume in case you'r unacquainted with it. My love to all my dear family.   E. T. E.

We're to take stage for Franconia at 1:20. We mean to spend the night at the Flume House. We have bought a mug and tin-pail that I may go strawberrying. This amuses Father. He almost dies over it. He is very funny, very dismal, very unwilling. He feels very rich, however, with the New Hampton money, and we are going to blow it out straight and have all the luxuries. He paid for the tin-pail with pleasure.

Concord Sunday morning July 11th 1875

Dear Edith,

I'll beguile the minutes while Christopher is being harnessed by writing to you. Father is up early dressing to go see if he is a grandfather, he went last night but brought home no news. I went at noon yesterday and saw the nurse eating her dinner. She said that A. had been in labour seven hours, and had made good progress. I was allowed to go to the top of the stairs and speak to Edward. He said Annie was under ether, and I heard her groan once or twice. He rushed back into the room, then came back & finished his directions about Mother. He said "We're going on well." I went again at 8 in the evening. I saw Mrs Keyes. She said it was a pretty serious hard pull all the time, then she corrected herself and said Annie slept and got a good deal of rest between. That Dr Bartlett also was with her, and said he should not

— 1875 —

interfere before twenty-four hours. ———Well we have been there. Edward looking exceedingly seedy appeared at the door & invited us in. His smile looked so weak one couldn't tell what it meant, but he said "yes". I called Father to get out too & Edward said "I'll show you" & rushed up stairs. Coming down he said "We've got a basket full of childer" and I hoped. Alas, but one. Very cunning, head all out of shape.

Dear Edith,

I hated to leave off just when the inexorable train made me. Edward was bringing down a square champagne-basket rigged with pink & white muslin, containing the flannel bundle usual on such occasions. He told us 'twas a boy, we didn't like that at first and thought we'd send him back and change him at the shop, but we've decided not to. But his grandfather was heartily glad it was a son. I proceeded to uncover him. He has the upper lip of Annie & Prescott, but when he shut his mouth he reminded me of the looks of Edward himself at the same age, large-featured, with rather full lips. I told Father not to tell Mother till 'twas time for her to wake, but he delayed not an instant. She soon sent for me and said Father said "the baby was pretty & looked like its father & like its mother". When I saw him after church again, I concluded he wasn't a bad-looking baby, his colour is so pretty, and when his face is composed just right he does very well.

E. T. E.

Concord July 13th 1875

Dear Sally,

Edward's & Annie's little son was born on the 11th. He weighs 8 lbs, is what I call thin, but Mrs Keyes says he is plump, and describes him as a tidy little baby. His countenance is, of course, if we speak the plain unvarnished truth, hideous. But compared with other newborn babies he is quite good-looking. Two of Edith's were uglier. I think he looks as well as Don did at his birth.

July 17th. I still send this to show I began to write but we have lost the little boy. He died the next day. He hadn't been definitely named. Edward wished to name him William, as the family name, and because his associations with it were so pleasant, but hesitated because of Haven's Willy. He gave him the name when he died. He was considered & treated as the heir of our name. I thought it generous of the Keyeses. He was brought here as soon as he died, and buried from here like the

other William Emersons. I had the pictures of the four generations over his coffin. He used the two days that he lived after I saw him—for on Tuesday I was refused and on Wednesday I went to Milton—in improving very fast. So when I came home and found him lying in state here, his little head was in much better shape, and he looked beautifully, and most pathetic. We all mourned for him, and how many people cried at his funeral! I think it was the sight, he looked so little & innocent & sweet. Annie of course is much grieved, but she bears it rightly, and is doing well. She and all of us are thankful he lived, and that we had real comfort of him for those days, and that he saw us all awake, and really looked at us.
E. T. E.

Concord July 21st 1875

Dear Edith,

Tomorrow I'm going to Beverly, and tomorrow the Essex Institute (of Nat. Hist. or Science) is coming here. Father is sorry I am to be gone. Uncle George, Mr Reynolds, Lily Keyes & Edward seem most interested in it, and other people talk about it a little, the Chamberlains have gone into it heart and hand, Mr C. is a Salem man, and both are botanists. July 28th. They came yesterday, had a beautiful time & said they never saw such a town, never were so well received before. On my return from Beverly where I was most happy, except for the fear about Cecile, who is very feeble indeed, and they are so bright and silent that not till Mrs Agassiz came on Saturday and confided her own anxiety to me did I guess how great is their alarm about her. They are afraid she is in consumption. And the moment I heard that I put many things together. Now I am anxious every day to hear about her, and yet dare not write to Ida to ask, and show that I was frightened, and take her time to answer. I saw dear Mrs Cabot, performed my errand, and it prospered, saw also Clover, Marian Jackson, Mr Higginson, Fanny Morse, W. James, all the Parkmans & Mary Felton. On my return I heard your letters to Annie read in family conclave. Mrs Bancroft has written to invite Mother & Father to Newport. To Edward's & my deep regret, Mother _will_ _not_ go. Father says since it is they that ask, he'll go for one day. Annie is sitting up now daily, yet I have to neglect her entirely. Edw. has just done a stroke of school work night & day, looks dreadfully, but I rejoice to say got a 10-hours sleep last night. Don't mention Naushon yet. Father won't & I oughtn't to come till daylight can be

— 1875 —

seen at the end of the book-tunnel. When it is I'll write, and then you'd ask with a chance of success.

E. T. E.

Dear Edith,

I am setting forth for Beverly, and shall come home tomorrow. Mother went to Boston yesterday and had an interview with Dr Parker, she and he are not congenial souls, but she says it was as satisfactory as could be expected—with him. Annie seems bright, when I went in yesterday I saw that she lifted herself several times on her elbow. Mr & Mrs Beck came up and dined on Wednesday. Father asked Uncle George to come but he was going to Boston, and I asked Aunt Lizzy. I found her in the garden picking currants for jelly, and she was in a most characteristic mood, declaring it was utterly impossible, but the impossibility was wholly inward. We asked Edward who promptly replied as he does to everything "No. Annie." so no one came but Mr & Mrs Beck, and we liked each other exceedingly all round and talked very fast. Except alas! we did get onto Woman's Suffrage at dinner. I don't enjoy that subject. But the Becks seemed truly enchanted to see Mother mounted in glory on her most ungovernable war-horse, prancing or rather bolting forward to conquer or die with all her banners spread. And if in the afternoon Mr Beck said anything about homoeopathy, spiritualism, or woman suffrage or anything that lead that way while Mother was out of the room, Mrs Beck would exclaim "Oh I wish Mrs Emerson were here. Frederick, you must repeat that to her" and generally had it repeated on Mother's return. When Father ordered the wagon, and I came to see them off, for Mother, it appears, has never seen Minute Man or bridge, and resolved to ride too, she & Mrs Beck expressed such grief that I should be left at home, that when they offered to ride 3 on a seat I accepted, and thus we all went, visited the Manse, attic & all, saw Cousin Mary, Lizzy, Cousins Gore & Fanny & saw monuments & everything & then left our guests at the train. Mary gave us a dinner that I was rather vain of. I got some raspberries for dessert & when I went to pay Mr Henry Shattuck for them I found him & Mrs Shattuck in such Arcadian employment in their garden, it did seem bliss realized. I believe they are not even bothered with a servant in their house, and all their pleasant days they spend together in keeping their garden a real Paradise & their fruit-house a most charming

— 1875 —

lucrative place. And they both were so agreeable. We mourn for your domestic troubles.

E. T. E.

Concord Aug 16th 1875

Dear Edith,

Mary Blake's last letter said Cecile became unconscious on the 5th and makes all the resistance she can when they try to make her take any nourishment. James Higginson was with them. I have tonight a note from Nina saying Dr Ware calls the disease tubercular meningitus, says there is now scarcely any ground for hope left. She may live another week. Book [*Letters and Social Aims*] moves slowly along. It is interesting and painful like most work. I find it easier than three years ago for two reasons: I am better acquainted with it, so feel less blind and helpless; and I have now not the least scruple about showing Father things, while then I couldn't bear to because it was the beginning and I hated to shock him with the sense that his memory was failing him. But as fast as one hill of difficulty with this book is ascended I come in sight of another twice as appalling, so my spirits are seldom high about the business. Father's, however, rose as soon as he began to feel the cable draw and perceived that I was really helping him along. He is evidently more cheerful ever since, and often sings praises and proposes writing to the Advertiser that a partnership has been formed. He doesn't like to summon Mr. C. [James Elliot Cabot] to this, but I foresee that 'twill be necessary. Your letter came last night and gave us all great pleasure. Edward and Annie are well—dined with us last Friday for the first time. They are the latest converts who have appeared at Mr. Alcott's conversations. C. Hoar told me Edward talked a great deal and without his usual hesitation—talked fast. And she added, "Mr. A. sometimes tires me, not when he is saying anything, but talking along to fill pauses, and I was tired last night and leaning my head when Edward began, and that freshened me right up and everyone else too." Father stayed his one day in Newport, and saw many people beside the Bancrofts. He says Mrs. B. reminded him constantly of Mother when she talked. He supposes it must be the Plymouth in both. Schools begin on Monday, we are up to the elbows in business. Father greatly rejoiced in the part of Mr Lowell's poem that referred to Washington, and laughed over & praised Dr Holmes's. Mother sends her love to you & says save her no pink 4 o'clock seeds, she has them too. She'll save you yellow & white & orange & scarlet. I'm glad you are so well & gay & so are all. My love to your whole family, send a few general remarks on your children & mine.

E. T. E.

August 20th 1875

Dear Edith,

I send Mrs Agassiz's note. How very kind it was of her to write to us! I suppose the paper this morning will tell about the funeral, and I mean to go if I can. It is just a year ago that they were at Naushon with us, and Cécile ran down with Cameron & Don to meet me coming from the other house, that little run which was so delightful that it has made them remember Cécile with pleasure ever since. My daughter was written me a beautiful letter about your babes, in which Violet shines like a little star with beams that revive the hearts of her grandparents & aunt.

E. T. E.

Dear Edith,

Mr Cabot is coming on Friday to spend the night and begin his task. Our spirits are high. I don't clearly see that Father and I shall come to Naushon but we shall if I can compass it. Mother often talks about going, she says she never wanted to so much, and never felt it so possible. I am quite pleased to hear her say so, though I don't trust it much, for she is as likely as not to hold back if it should come to the point. Edward & Annie mean to come down on Monday for three days. Annie was yesterday so alarmed for him that she used all her eloquence and to my joy when I went to see her just now she said she had persuaded him. Twenty is rejoicing in three little kittens and the big ones are still frisking prettily in the grass. Mother is not appalled, rather pleased. Last Saturday, no the one before, I had my children's party. It was chiefly the fruit of pain about children's morals. The only way to get at them that I could think of was to teach manners and discipline and games that they might enjoy by themselves, at parties. So after much reflection I visited every mamma in the district and invited our school & the last class that went up. It succeeded beyond hope, and I want another. Tomorrow is dear Don's birthday. I hope his present reached you whole. His grandmamma sends him a box of sugar plums and a hug. How do you do?

Dear Edith,

Dear Mr Cabot came on Friday, and all was as I hoped, the visit delightful, the task accomplished. He was easily able to do, what I never can, take a broad view at a glance, and say "needed" and "not needed". Today we send an instalment to the printer. Your great long letter has given various happy hours to your family. We mourn our dear old Dolly, Edward most of all, you see he hoped to see her this week. I readily believe no pen could paint the Baby's glories but your anecdote seems to show that table discipline is suspended. Don's calmness between Cameron's ambition & Edward's ardour is likely to be stirred up, well for him! So thankful you can walk! And Mother & Aunt Lizzy revel in the thought of your garden.

E. T. E.

September 8th, 1875

Dear Edith,

I have made a little call on Mrs. Cabot just to report how matters went in Concord. When I told her how Father had really enjoyed Mr. Cabot's taking hold, I said, "He looks forward now to his coming again. He dreaded it naturally at first; he was frightened." Mrs. C. thought I meant Mr. C. and said, "He was thoroughly frightened." "No, I meant Father." "Well they both were till they had tried. What a mercy it is that there are women in the world to arrange for men!" And so we rejoiced together, I telling how much had been accomplished and she how Mr. C. had returned positively refreshed from the labour, though she says when he came home he told her he hadn't been of the slightest use. Then her heart sank, but she took a thought and questioned him minutely about what had been asked of him and what he had done, and found after all that was only his way of putting it. So her conclusion was that he had accomplished something. I assured her it was all that was hoped. We arranged that he should spend a week with us the last of the month. Heaven sends help just in time. Father could not have done without this. The fatigue tells. He won't be able to do so much towards finishing it this month as he was last, but it shall be carried through somehow and be off his hands by Oct. 15 that it may not do him fatal

— 1875 —

harm. Not that I am quite sure it hasn't already. Yet I think working straight on is the best course for him. Happily he doesn't suspect how tired he is, and seems to feel good courage and sheer satisfaction in Mr. Cabot's share. Oh I have been at Ida's. When we went up to get ready for dinner, there was the nursery, and in Ida's room in the corner Cécile's bed with its netting drawn over it. Her high-chair stands as it always did at her place at the table. Nothing was said about her. When Ida was asking about you and the children there was a little sound in her voice when she came to Violet that made me remember that Cécile had fallen in love with her last summer.

Wednesday. Edward and Annie stumbled on unconscious me at Fitchburg Depot on Monday p.m. Edward had a proper tan, but neither had picked up as much as I meant. Edward asked after the schools. I was able to give a cheering report. You never knew a better state of things, each school in order and fond of its teacher, and every question that had arisen Mr. King and I had settled, so no arrears for him. "Next, patients?" When I told him that two out of the three had died it was evidently a severe blow. He seemed positively to feel guilty. Recovering, he said "Anyone else sick?" and when he had to hear that Madam Keyes was in great danger, though not despaired of, he exclaimed that it didn't seem to be right for doctors to take vacations if such were the results. He & A. then embarked on the recital of the Naushon news, telling how well you seemed, how charming R. had been and how Don fell on his uncle's neck & asked for a sword & Cameron wanted a picture of a girl. The baby they said was a full-fledged barbarian. "Now Ralph with much of the same loud, rude & wild nature always had a streak of innocence that excited your pity, not so this young rough." I think it was lucky they went to Naushon when they did. They seem both to have felt so tired & weak that they just lay still and did nothing and only began to come to themselves at last. We found Mother & Madam K. both better. Mother is still in bed, but comf'able.

E. T. E.

Concord Sept 14th 1875

Dear Edith,

Your last letter most delightful. How we all did enjoy Don's birthday! Today we are to have Annie & Edward & Prescott to dine on occasion of our fortieth wedding-day. I hope you are coming to Florence's wedding, and will keep Mother's birthday with us. Our dinner was brilliant. Mrs Edward Hoar walked home from the Depot today with me and said she couldn't believe it was 40 years. Why she remembered Mother's first call when she wore a straw bonnet and a green ribbon. I repeated it to Father and he said "Your Mother never wears green ribbon. She wears black." "Oh, not then!" I said, "She was a young lady then. She was younger than Edith is now." He was amazed, and so was I, to think she was so young. Every story of your bairns is sweet. And I'm so glad you are well and had a good day at Gay Head. Book advancing and I am cheered to see that though slowly Father really does get along.

E. T. E.

Concord Sept 25th 1875

Dear Edith,

Mr Cabot came and work goes on. Something has been accomplished. When I bragged at dinner-time of some of the neat corrections "we have made", Father said "You remind me of 'How we apples swim' said by something that couldn't swim at all!" whereupon I didn't quite "simmer" after all, but Mr Cabot was highly entertained. It is good fun to hear him laugh when Father tells him he hopes he'll be rewarded in heaven. I never have said a word to you about keeping this assistance a secret. I have been careful, ridiculously so for me. Have you let people know? The S.S. Committee finally returned my class to me deciding 'twas a pity to let them go out of S. School. I haven't seen E. & Annie since you went. Mother has rejoiced much over your visit, so do we all.

E. T. E.

Concord Oct 12 1875

Dear Edith,

Life has been most interesting and eventful. Mr Cabot stayed the rest of that week, and then again came last Wednesday, and so at the same time did Georgy and Louisa Schuyler and G. sang. Such a happy day! They went at 4. Then acute delight working on the book. Then Thursday Lord Houghton came and Judge Hoar dined here with him. Again what a happy day! Lord H. was charming and Judge Hoar! he kept us all laughing and admiring from beginning to end. Lord H. gave us one tale of visiting Mr. Carlyle after Father's visit in '33 I think, and Mr. C. said, "That man came to see me. I don't know what brought him. And we

— 1875 —

kept him one night and then he left us. I saw him go up the hill. I didn't go with him to see him descend. I preferred to watch him mount and vanish like an angel." Spiritualism was much discussed. Judge H. is as decided as Mr. A. Agassiz, but in all he says so much fun. At last as Mother went on finding with astonishment how immense his prejudice, she asked what he should say if he saw any of these things done with his own eyes. "I should conclude I was insane, and unfit any longer to attend to business." "But what if you were not insane?" "I should think it time to retire to Sleepy Hollow." Mother finally told him she had heard it said that Judge Hoar reserved his credulity for the Christian Miracles. He smiled, waited a minute, and then said very soberly, "I am rather a believer in Miracles." Then he went on and laughed, "But for this form of what Miss Hannah Moore might have called 'practical piety' I have nothing to say." Mother related that once the spirits had said that if Miss J. Whiting hadn't sat obstinately skeptical beside her they would have put her in a trance, and that she had always been grateful to Miss Whiting for preserving her from talking nonsense. And Judge Hoar replied, "I am sure Mrs. Emerson would always speak good sense." Well, I can't tell you anything of all the good talk & pleasures. Then Friday Lord H. went at noon, and Mrs S. Hedge Davis came at night, and Saturday noon Mr Cabot went, and Aunt Susan & Lieut. Calif came for afternoon & to tea, and Mrs Davis stayed till Monday noon. In the afternoon, a meeting. Tuesday Rose & Mr Lathrop to dine. Mr & Mrs Dale came after dinner & stayed to tea. We have been getting along with a girl & a half, one girl, no girl, new girls. So you see I could not write, but I have been exceeding well and the days were each like a novel running all up & down the scale of bliss & tragedy, & surprises every moment. Book advances. Edward is better than he has been. A. just recovering from a cold. Our family pretty prosperous, and all enjoying dear Mr Cabot every minute of the day. He has just returned for a new session. The book done I must pick up my shattered affairs at home & school, and then if our kitchen prospers propose to have a week of delight with you. It *looks* utterly impossible, but I believe it isn't.

E. T. E.

Concord, October 15th, 1875

Dear Edith,

    The work of revising the book is finished and dear Mr. Cabot went today. Father came in to dinner after driving him to the depot and said,

— 1875 —

"Well Queeny, Mr. Cabot, the spotless, the perfect gentleman is gone. He is the born gentleman. In all his life he never did, nor thought of doing, anything that didn't belong to the perfect gentleman, and therefore he never has to put on the gentleman as most people have to." And afterwards, after dinner, he began again to sing his praises and ask what could anyone who looked for the ludicrous side of people do with that man, a person so clean, so simple, so exact that no one could find a point to take hold of. But here I'm sorry to say I can't at all recall the words. This is October 15th, the appointed day. And the main body of the book is in Mr. Osgood's hands. Nothing is now to be sent except three articles which I must copy from the Dial. When the proofs are to be read, and when we have collected enough, Mr Cabot promises he will come once more to read them with us. When you invite us to come it opens a door to a delightful prospect, towards which I will plan and labour. We have such good girls! But they quarrel and won't live together. I think it will be November before I can come. I have abandoned all school duties for so many months that I must make a thorough round before I go away at all. Mother seems better, and she & Father seem to seriously intend coming to enjoy your hospitality.

E. T. E.

Edw., Annie & I begin our singing lessons next week.

Concord Friday Oct 23rd 1875

Dear Edith,

You ought to hear oftener from us. The grapes & bundle came, and Father & Mother are very glad of the grapes, eat them with real pleasure, and Mother is delighted with her new bulbs. Now to tell you the sad events of this most tragic week. Edward lost one patient that he was very sorry for, Mrs Brennan just a week ago, and on Sunday Ida Smith whom he was carrying through a very bad typhoid fever with great success, had alarming symptoms which made him very anxious. On Monday she was much worse, and he telegraphed for his dear Dr Ellis, and called Dr Bartlett. The consultation, though most satisfactory to him as physician, gave no hope for Ida. From that moment Edward stayed by her, working and watching with all his faculties till seven the next morning when he called all the family to see her die, and fled broken-hearted, their grief hurt him more than all he has ever witnessed before. And oh! just think of it. The suddenness. She had always been so well, and she was such a dear good child, and to Emma all you are to me. The whole town mourned. The next day Father and I worked

— 1875 —

till 'twas too dark to see, on proofs to send, and then walked down to the mail. I stopped at the door of the office, and listened with horror to what was being related, that Mr Keyes had tried to drive across between the engine and the car, and the car struck the wagon, and Mr K. wasn't hurt, but Mr Hudson was, no one knew how much, he had been carried by in a hay-rigging with the conductor & Dr Emerson, and he was lying wrapped in a buffalo. It was only five minutes ago that they passed. It seemed the most terrible story we ever heard. Even if Mr Hudson were only a little hurt it was very bad. You see we thought of course that Mr K. had voluntarily run the risk. But in the evening Uncle George came in and told us he hadn't suspected that a car was coming. The expressman brought the news in the morning that Mr Hudson was dead. At noon I visited Edward who was watering the lame & sick Billy, he asked how we were at home, and when I said "well" he exclaimed that he was thankful no calamity had befallen here for him to hear of, and then related that he & Annie set out last night to walk up to the Keyeses' and as they approached the crossing the train passed, and then they saw the General and the buggy coming, and close to the track, and a car dropt by the train and following it just coming onto the road. To their horror the General came steadily on, they shrieked & waved & ran, but it was almost dark and they could not make themselves understood, and the flagman was wildly dancing & shouting all in vain, then they saw Mr Keyes whip the horse and then the car struck the buggy and it absolutely disappeared, the horse was left, nothing else. They ran as well as they could and presently saw Mr Keyes, far off, get up, and then Edward ran "to find what was left of Mrs Keyes", and presently saw Mr Hudson rising, but he was very much hurt. Mr Keyes walked back and got his buckwagon, and Edward stopped the first passing wagon and took Mr Hudson home, and presently Mr & Mrs Keyes & Annie came & Dr Bartlett. They found no symptom of internal injury, only bad bruises and a cut on his head, and they bound him up and went away quite hopeful, & Edward visited Willy Barrett whom Mr Collier's dog had bitten in the leg so severely that he has to stay in bed. When he came home he went once more to see Mr Hudson. He was vomiting blood. So for another night Edward fought in vain for the life of a patient, and I think Dr Bartlett too, and Mr Chamberlain came over and helped all night but in the morning Mr Hudson died. And here is poor Mrs Hudson absolutely dependent on her husband who had even to feed her, left not only a widow but as an orphan baby. Mr Keyes's hurt from the accident is only a bruise, but a bruise so severe that Edward says it is as bad as a broken leg, and he is more anxious about it. Poor Edward with only one night's sleep for four terrible days, and this anxiety still on him, weighs most on my mind, but the whole town is sad and there are so many people to pity. No one smiles now in meeting in the street. The book goes on wonderfully. I think it should be all ended a week hence. Father isn't well today, but yesterday he worked grandly. Mother goes to 39 Somerset St. to board for a week and see Dr Parker, next Monday. Annie looks handsome & delicate as she does after a fit of sickness. The shock of the day before almost killed her Edward said. Florence is at home and well, and can help to comfort her mother and nurse her father, and Prescott is at home. And now I must go and see how they all do today.

          Your affectionate sister
          E. T. E.

         Concord Nov. 9th 1875

Dear Edith,

 The book still lingers. We are within two chapters of the end, but must send for Mr Cabot once more. How soon will you come to Thanksgiving? The sooner the better. Mother is going to Boston to Dr Parker tomorrow. John has a little girl, born on Saturday, much to his delight, and everybody's. E & A both very well and have had a ride on horseback. Aunt Lizzy has come home. Too distracted to write much. Remind Will, Edward says, of a request in his letter concerning setting a day for him to come down & dispose of the noble Christopher. Cousin Mary has been here, with refreshing tales of our children.
         E. T. E.

     Hovey's Store, Boston, Nov. 15, 1875

Dear Edith,

 Mr. Cabot came last Thursday. I had meant not to send for him again, but on Monday reading "Greatness" in print for the first time I saw I couldn't straighten it alone, and wrote for him. And from Thursday noon till Friday night we had one steady stretch of work, and did wonders. On Saturday morning Mr. Rice came for me to do the Unitarian begging at 9 o'clock. Mr. Cabot asked me what he was to do. I told him the book was ended, there was nothing more, and instead of clear relief and triumph which I expected, he showed a little disappointment

— 1875 —

and said for his part he was sorry to get through—he had had such a good time. Father and I were charmed. I had asked him at breakfast if he would go straight on as soon as I could get the book together, and we planned two more books which I hope we can do this next year. Father was aghast at my audacity, amazed and consoled to see the eagerness even which Mr. Cabot felt to do it. It lifts a weight off all three of us. We had rather do it, and Father have it done, in his lifetime than to wait. And our hand being in, it is easier now. When will you come to Concord? Monday? Please stay a fortnight. Fri Dec 3rd some theatricals at Int. School. Edw. thinks they will be cunning when do you want us? How are you getting along?

E. T. E.

Concord Dec. 8th 1875

Dear Edith,

Mother will go from here tomorrow at 12.45. If it is a stormy day she will come straight to Milton. If it is pleasant she will visit Dr Parker and take the 5 train out. I have been instructing Father to bring materials for making up with you the new book of poems. Eugenia [Jackson] & Mr Dodge came yesterday and we are all thoroughly pleased with Mr Dodge, he appears to me a real acquisition for Thanksgiving or any Carnival I may hereafter hold. And he plays and sings. Lizzy & Annie Bartlett and our Edward & Annie came to dine. We had a very good time. The Intermediate School have decided on a statuette of General Washington, and large heads of Father & Mother to spend their money on. Should you be willing to have your crayon photographed? Father was charmed with the Baby's good-bye.

E. T. E.

Thursday

Dear Edith,

I began a letter but have lost it. Father & Mother won't come to Christmas. I am sorry, but I don't see how they can. Mother proposes coming next Wednesday and I mean to follow on Thursday noon. Father is invited to give the oration before the literary societies of the University of Virginia next June. I should like to go. E. & A. had Social Circle this week, and last night we took tea with them with Mr Pickering, lecturer, and the Chamberlaines. On Saturday I had a party for the

Intermediate School. It was delightful. I go to E. Gurney's tomorrow, shall do shopping in the A.M. in Boston.

E. T. E.

I was pleased with Mrs Cabot's note. Father feels better about the Reading now.

Concord Monday Jan 10th 1876

Dear Edith,

Please tell Will the barrel of flour has never come. We left behind the coveted bear; also, I fear, that sermon of Father's which Mr Bartol *lent* me. Perhaps Aunt Lizzy took it with her, but if she didn't and if it was left, will you read it, and see what you think of having it printed, and send it, the opinion, & the bear to town by Will on Wednesday when I am going to Boston and will stop for them at his office. Also I desire to know what day Mr Osgood wants the poems. If we are put up to a date, we can be ready. Are you coming on Wednesday to hear Mr Conway. We are all well except that Father has a cold, not a bad one. Edward & Annie went to the French Theatre with Mr & Mrs Chamberlaine on Saturday. Fanny Hubbard is engaged to William Wheeler the engineer, a "Corner Wheeler", whose solid virtue has been a subject of congratulation in his native town ever since he grew up, he is as good as Emma Smith. I had a new S.S. scholar yesterday, now I have twelve, attendance 8. Miss Mitchell said today that Mary Clahan is a brilliant little scholar, can always be relied on to know and to understand her lesson.

E. T. E.

Concord Feb 17th 1876

Dear Edith,

I think it doubtful whether Father comes this week at all. Your flowers came and pleased Mother very much, she was pleased with the lilies of the valley particularly, and Annie was charmed too when I gave her one. Mother is sick and has been growing worse. Edward is such a "conspirator" as she calls him that I cannot guess how sick she is, he thinks it best that people shouldn't know, nor what is the matter either, especially Mother herself. But I am afraid it is diphtheria, and I am afraid she is very sick, for Edward spent last night here, and was up and busy most of the time, and the things he does are things that are

— 1876 —

done for diphtheria, and at midnight I think he was scared, for he scared me, and for several hours I had a realizing sense what it would be to lose her. And since, he has said at four and at six that she was a great deal easier so now the immediate fright is gone.

7.40. He has just come and said Mother is *a great deal* better. But of course we are not out of the woods yet. Aunt E. charmed with Violet's poem.

[Unsigned]

Concord Friday

Dear Edith,

Mother is doing very well. Edward spent last night here. Unhappily the poor fellow had been up all one night this week at a confinement, and the night of Wednesday made him rather tired, still he manfully visited schools yesterday, and last night sent me early to bed and undertook another night's watching. And Oh! wasn't it good? When he had settled Mother and prepared all his traps for steaming & broth etc. which were to be kept up all night, he lay down for a minute's nap, and both of them, both he & Mother slept, and waked not. I got up at four and when I was all dressed I peeped in and seeing all quiet & the fire gone out, I started for some kindling, but I had disturbed them. Edward was shocked & frightened at his behaviour but happily no bad results. He found Mother had been so warm & well tucked in & the furnace so faithful that all was safe, and by five we had her steaming again & partaking of suitable meals. I hope he was safe in his house & bed at six. Valuable information about poems you give. Father is for leaving out May Day. Aunt E. has been choosing new poems & today I hope to send them for Mr Sanborn's opinion. Father says he values it very highly.

E. T. E.

March 3rd 1876

My dear Edith,

I began this morning by telling Father that eleven years ago today it poured; which caused him to laugh and to say "Oh?" and to inquire exactly what kind of weather was it twelve years ago today? I couldn't answer that, but if he had asked ten years, or nine I could have told him better. Next I related the history of that blessed third of March, and it interested him very much [date of Edith Emerson's engagement to William H. Forbes]. And beloved, I hope it will be celebrated by special peace & pleasure with you. Give my love to Will and tell him that we all feel here that it is a day to be remembered, he has been so good and dear to us all ever since, and Father sang a doxology at the thought. I am not quite happy since your letter, but I think it best to go to Alice next week, though Father is to lecture in Lexington. Then on Tuesday to come home from Mrs Cabot's to Father's Social Circle, and stay only one day, come to you on Thursday and stay till the next Tuesday, March 21st, when I will come home and spend one night and day to see about Father's lecture, and return on Thursday morning to stay till Saturday morning. That Sat. Father will lecture in Boston. If all is going well at home I will then come back on Monday and spend the week with you. That will make a fortnight in all. Then it will be April and time to begin Spring cleaning. Write me if you feel any discontent at the programme. I have succeeded in getting the Poems question into Mr Sanborn's hands. Study May Day yourself for rearrangement.

E. T. E.

Brookline Mar. 11th 1876

Dear Father,

Edith rode over with Alice [Forbes] & me yesterday when Alice brought me and my baggage over from Milton to Mrs Cabot's in her carriage, and on the way I gathered much interesting news of home, only I could not learn how the Lexington lecture had prospered, and I felt more eager about that than about anything else. When we arrived at Mrs Cabot's she asked A. & E. to stay to lunch, and first we visited the greenhouses which were more gorgeous than any I have seen for years with brilliant flowers all in bloom, and have several marvels, old African acacias covered with blossoms, big trees they are now, planted by Col. Perkins fifty years ago. Mrs Cabot said she desired to have Mother see them. On our return to the house Mrs Cabot said "I'll show you your room and you can entertain Alice there, I will take Edith to my room." And so she showed me my room with a vast glowing fire in it, and while Alice & I 'pared for luncheon Alice looked about with an affectionate satisfaction saying "Oh my dear what a pleasant room, I'm so glad you are going to have such a beautiful fire, and a couch in your room! And you'll sit in this chair to read—oh my dear it will be so pleasant!—and you'll write your letters at that table, I shall imagine you tomorrow morning." This is a visit unparalleled for petting. Alice spent every moment in devising comfort for me while I was with her,

— 1876 —

and now Mrs Cabot is doing the same. Is there not a hot water bottle in my bed, and a hot stone in the carriage when I take a drive? And that is a sample of the whole day. We went down to lunch, and found only two of the boys at home, No 4, Charley 9 yrs. & No 5, Richard 7½ yrs., the tidiest sweetest little boys ever seen, and after lunch we begged for the twins. We heard their voices in the entry, the door opened and in they rushed, one chanting aloud, and bringing up at his Mother's knee, the other dancing with the agility of a squirrel & flourishing gaily across the room till he was caught by Alice who succeeded easily in getting him to talk. They have long ringlets and wore little light plaid long-sleeved dresses and scarlet sashes & stockings. They are three & a half. Mrs Cabot says Philip, the one who sang, is the quiet & firm one, and Hugh, the dancer, is the volatile one. They are a charming spectacle whatever they do. After a while Richard fell on the floor and Hugh sprang on his back with the sudden quickness for which he is distinguished. Richard took the hint and set off on all fours; whereupon Charley presented himself on hands & knees before the other twin who lost no time in bestriding him, and exclaiming "Philip is a great deal the best rider", trotted round & round the room. It was as funny as it was pretty to see this circus, and we all laughed hard till Alice & Edith had to go. (Will & Edith however are coming today again to dine.) I could not help exclaiming at the quick movements of all the children "I am used to slow children" I said. "Oh yes!" said Mrs Cabot, "I know it. Oh what a delight to me Ralph's slowness was when he came to Beverly, a real relief. I think he has had a permanent effect on Handasyde, and he has never been such a tear-coat as he was before Ralph's deliberation made such an impression on him." "Ralph is bully," cried Charley from the floor "I wish he'd come again, Mamma." "Yes, we must have him again," agreed Mrs Cabot. "Oh bully!" said Richard "Ralph's bully. I like him ever so much." Then I gave Mrs Cabot a piece of information gained from Alice, that 6 mos. after his visit to Beverly Ralph slowly said to her "I think I *ought* to have gone with Handasyde *one* of those times." At this Mrs Cabot laughed. On that visit, whatever Handasyde had planned for him he had refused to do, and poor H. had had wild fits of rage & despair, which had failed to move the cruel R. Mrs Cabot said she had insisted on hospitality & told Handasyde he must give up his cherished plans. But Mr C. had, on being appealed to, decided to let each go in his own way & both be happy apart, which cut the Gordian Knot, and they were happy apart. In the evening I told Mr

1876

Cabot about your poems, and that Mr Lowell had asked you to remove The Mountain & the Squirrel. Truly it would have done your heart good to see his horror at the idea. Then I made him get the poems and see what he thought about leaving any out. He agreed very well with Mr Sanborn, thought that on the whole it was as well to leave none out, but was perfectly willing to part with To Ellen at the South, Suum Cuique, From the Persian of Hafiz, Ghazelle, and perhaps with the Park. But he insisted on keeping the Ode to W. H. C., Forbearance, Berrying, and differed from Mr S. in believing the Eros, and perhaps To J. W. should go. I found him quite unfamiliar with the poems in May Day, but he remembers the Adirondac poem and does not care for it. When Mrs Cabot came back he told her of Mr Lowell's proposal & exclaimed "Why it makes me quiver to think of it!" and Mrs Cabot said "What? That poem? Why every child in this house knows it by heart, and last Christmas Richard decided that the very pleasantest thing he would do for his papa was to take a handsome sheet of note-paper & copy the Mountain & the Squirrel in his very best handwriting, and then draw a red line round it, for his Christmas Present to him." And she turned to Mr C. and asked him if it wasn't now pinned up on his study wall, and he said "Oh yes." I'm going to look over May Day with them before I come home, if I have a chance. You ought to see the show of boys. The oldest, Frank, is handsome & charming, just the kind to be crazy about with the most beautiful hair. He is sixteen. Edward who at fourteen is almost as large & looks larger, he is plain, very full of spirits & noise. Our dear little Naushon friend Handasyde, now 11, is the third. He grows handsome, and when he came home the other day just after Edith had gone he exclaimed "Oh I'm sorry! If I'd known cousin Edith was here I shouldn't have stayed to play after school." Then Charley, the good boy, the gentle little saint, whom Handasyde above & Richard below would each like to have all to himself, just Ralph's age, 9, very pretty, and with all his first teeth still so that the dentist considers him a great curiosity. Then Richard, the musical, the violinist, volatile, innocent & pretty, and then the twins, Philip & Hugh.

I'm coming at 11 tomorrow

Concord Mar. 16th 1876

Dear Edith,

The other day in Father's absence I lent Lily Keyes the Desatir, and when I told him, he seemed to feel as if the earth trembled. The Desatir

— 1876 —

lent! & without his express consent!! "Why," he said, "I'm willing if a young lady wishes to borrow a book that you should lend her Scott's Lanes of an Old Countryman, but not the Desatir." This I preserve because of the lovely guess at a title. Mother is better, but getting up still seems far in the future. Friday night Nina invites us to spend the night before Father's Boston lecture. If Mother gets well enough to spare me on Tuesday I think of going to Hatty then, to the Norton's on Thursday, and to Nina's on Friday. Then I would come to you Monday and stay till following Tuesday, then come home for a day or two, and when Will goes return and give you seven more days, only Sundays at home. How is that? Father has gone to Boston to a meeting of the Historical Society on the anniversary of the Evacuation of Boston by the British. He has had a letter on the Boston Ode from Mr Williams, our Concord minister, which he values very much, containing criticism & suggestions. He accepts two. I didn't know how many friends I had in Brookline till I went to church. Mrs Moses Williams, Mrs Judge Lowell, our cousin, & Judge Lowell, Charles Ware, Agnes Poor & her mother and Aunt Adams's family came to speak to me. And Mr Brown himself I had some talk with. Give my love to my daughter if she is with you. And oh dear Edith I shall delight to come when Fate allows.
E. T. E.

Concord Thursday

Dear Edith,

Mother was worse yesterday but a severe course of obedience has worked well, she is again better today. Oh no, there is no need of your coming. I gather from Father's talk that the lecture in Lexington was a real success, but he stopped short when he fancied the hour was over and didn't give the "bang". I'm sorry for that. I can't guess when I can come to Milton; I hope, still, next week. I was delighted you & Will had a good time and that he appreciated the army of boys. Fine show in the pew on Sunday too. Mr Cabot so enjoys Mr Brown, why don't you & Will drive over & go to church there some Sunday?
E. T. E.

Concord Monday Mar 20

Dear Edith,

Mother seems to go on in the right direction, though very slowly, she hasn't yet been up. Edward is persecuted with schools, two new teachers just beginning, & infuriated parents labouring with him still by the hour! and he is writing a paper to read before the Medical something; add to which everyone is sick. So his wrath is towering, and he interrupts his prescription to snort like Friyja, & girn terribly at the past & the future. Our singing lessons are ended & the last was dreadful, we never did so ill unless on the first day. Hatty accepts me, I go tomorrow night. Father had a very pleasant day at Hist. Soc., and made a little speech. Mr Pierce died on Saturday. A week from today I hope to come to you. Could you meet me in Boston & do the shopping? If you come to the lecture Sat. will you go afterwards with us to Mr Thayer's office?

E. T. E.

Concord Tuesday

Dear Edith,

Father & Mother and Annie all heard with pleasure and gratitude of the apples, which John saw at the Depot last night but has not brought home on account of the storm. What a glorious storm it has become tonight! I hope you are all enjoying it. I have seen nothing like it since Ralph's infancy when he & you were snowed up here & Will came at night. I enclose Mr Higginson's letter & Nina's too. Edward came this morning & for part of dinner-time. He seems to feel able to bear his troubles which are of far greater magnitude than Father knew, or rather told us. The Town passed a vote of "dissent from the opinions inferences & sentiments of the Superintendent", and Sam made a cruel attack on him, and Mr George Tolman was very insulting, and of the whole School Committee not a single one said a word. Annie said he was very much hurt and they could not sleep last night. The trouble was that he told in the report of the lying & cheating, the impertinence and general baseness of the children in very plain terms, but I think not a bit too plain. The children, the teachers & Mr C. Walcott, who all know, (and no one else does) admit it to be exactly true. What hurts is that Sam should use such a tone, and that the sch. comm., even when called on wouldn't say one word. Annie wishes him to resign. I hope he won't. Mother glories in his persecution and says it must follow righteousness. And oh I am proud every time to see how he never does shirk explicit statement of disagreeable truth when it is called for.

E. T. E.

— 1876 —

Concord April 1st 1876

Dear Edith,

When I came home I found that Mother had caught more cold and had been in bed since I went away, and Edward met me and said I must not leave her any more, so I have sent for my valise. I found Mother in a very cheerful frame of mind. Your catalogues she received with enthusiasm. I haven't yet showed her Violet's picture. I am husbanding my resources. Catalogues of plants seem to furnish her and you with amusement for days together. Curious fact! She seems pleased that I am going to stay at home. I will come to you as soon as I can but oh! when will it be? I am exceedingly disappointed. I bought my dress at Chandler's, 20 yards. Last night we had our meeting with great success, arranged much, and went home at 9.30. But Edward walked home with me and worried away, as he does in the evening, as if nothing ever could come right again. He must send in today his subject to the Medical Society, and he has no more idea than the Man in the Moon what his subject is to be. But except his subject I think he has no cause for discontent whatever. Oh dear Edith goodbye. I have enjoyed my two days with you very much.

E. T. E.

ETE to Haven Emerson, April 5. First page of letter missing.

On June 26th Father is to deliver an "address before the Literary Societies of the University of Virginia". I have learned that when we are going anywhere Father takes no interest in proceeding, and I may loiter and turn aside, but on the homeward journey he chafes at an hour's delay, so I mean to start as early as possible. Mr Sam Bradford has invited us to his house in Philadelphia. There I mean to have three days, then two for Washington, and then on to Virginia. If Father will allow me I mean to make an equally interrupted return. But I cannot count on that with confidence. I hope you are intending to bring your children and make us a visit at last this summer. How long it is since I have heard from you. Is there no photograph of the Baby yet? He must be walking about in the Park with Ruth & Willy who I suppose are getting tanned as they did two years ago. I am looking forward with pleasure to seeing their little brown faces. I hope Susy is really well, and you too. I don't know where to begin with Concord news. I suppose the doctoring is what you will first think of. All the month of January there was "a perfect dearth of sickness" as Dr Bartlett said. Edward used his

— 1876 —

leisure in visiting the schools. He really accomplished something there, but he takes everything hard and frets more than is good for him meanwhile. The labours and torments of a Superintendent of Schools reach their climax between Feb. 20 & Mar. 20, and at that very time patients set in, so that in that month he hardly had one regular meal, and lost many nights sleep and every time he came home from visiting schools & patients he found infuriated parents awaiting him to scold him and demand redress. I think he suffered all he could bear. And at Town-Meeting this week he got it again, his enemies were violent, the School Committee held their tongues, and he had a miserable day. Father could not bear it and came home. I hope Edward will go on however. He has the opportunity and the power to improve the schools and the opposition is to be expected. Annie is very well and they are blessed with a capital servant, and the horse does better than he did last year, so at home he considers himself prosperous. Will is always lame with his heel, otherwise that family is in high condition. Edith is lame no more and the five children never had more flesh & colour. I am happy to say that Cameron & Don at last are learning to read. Ida Higginson, who lost her little Cécile last August has a little boy born this week and there is great rejoicing over him. Also Malcolm and Sarah Forbes have a little daughter. I hope they'll name her for the grandmother Dorothea Murray. Few people have the right to so uncommon and interesting a name. Here at home we are very well, Father has been particuarly well since Mr Cabot first came in September. All his worries being lifted off once for all has made a difference in his health as well as in his happiness. Cousin Abraham and poverty being removed by Will,* and afterwards all troubles about booksellers, for Will has done that too with great success and unlooked-for results; and all troubles about the book and M.S.S. by Mr Cabot, Father considers himself now a truly happy man. This winter he has three times read a lecture at a private house, and once in Lexington, and once in our Lyceum, and each time it was an enjoyable occasion to him and the listeners. I hope he will within this year get another book ready, and that will be a care more off his mind. Aunt Lizzy spent a week at Edith's at New Years, and then went to Miss Belinda Randell and stayed some time with her. Then this month she has been making various visits, and has just come home. She is well, and whenever we see her it is a delight to hear her talk. I am off

*Refers to WHF's role in helping LE manage certain family business affairs, most notably the sale of a house on Court Street in Boston. See note, Vol. I, p. 534.

the School-Committee now and mean to be of more use at home. Edward is sorry to lose me, and I hate to leave it, but it has become evident that I am wanted here. Now in return for this letter I expect a long one with accounts of sayings & tricks of each of the three children separately and of yourself and of Susy to whom I send my love.

E. T. E.

Concord April 10th 1876

Dear Edith,

I don't wonder when you say your meditations on the subject of your sister's clothes occupied whole hours. It has shocked me each time to see what a devastator of the day these books prove. I have spent long periods of this day over them and your letter. If Mme. Rey makes my Polonaise she can furnish pattern, if we don't like the one we buy. I have sent for four. I don't wish to trim the silver grey particularly. I desire to have it the plain, plain dress that its predecessor was. Most of the ways you suggest are too elaborate for my idea of it. I accept the last, plain fringe, rather than the others, but I would really prefer no trimming whatever or a single row of a trimming, light & thin in its effect. Now shall you see Mme. Rey, or shall I go to her? An event occurs daily between Fast-Day and April 21st, and I promised Mr Cabot to send for him in April. Truly I don't see how I can keep the promise. I'm quite taken up with house & clothes & can't give myself to literature. Then my millinery! I must find a day. Tell Will we should like to know if one day or week is better than another to send down Christopher & carryall. I believe we are prepared to take that step and for my part I am anxious to see it taken. Oh Edith! life is very interesting and delightful. I have beautiful times. I do enjoy my own town every day of my life and it makes a great difference both in the kind and degree of pleasure one has in the world whether there is a little public element in it. My new friend Mrs Damon is on the School-Committee as well as Edward, I feel pretty sure I shall still hear enough to follow the fortune of the schools pretty well. I suppose Annie has written about how the School-Committee sent for Edward to tell him they had reelected him unanimously and then passed a vote of thanks for his Report which they fully endorsed. And in general people are beginning to praise the Lord that he makes even the wrath of man to serve him, and is turning the fuss into a conviction that there is great evil in the Schools and something must be done, and that it is a blessed thing that Edward sees the enemy and calls it by name and is prepared to fight it. And all the teachers have come to say they enlist under his banner, and the School-Committee said "We'll join you in any measures", and the children who alas! are always first consulted, confess it is all true and give a faint sign of content in the exposure. It has been a great experience to Edward. He was touched and cheered. Isn't it pleasant to have spring come? Yesterday at breakfast-time Father & I watched a large flock of birds between the September & the Dutch Codling picking up something, and we saw them with dread, Their manners were like those of City sparrows & their size. We thought the Reg'lars were upon us. But after breakfast we found them as numerous in the grove and there in the shade we saw they were the Monadnoc snowbird, dear creatures! So this morning we took pleasure in their numbers & diligence. Father wondered where they were bound. Northward. "Strange taste!" he exclaimed.

E. T. E.

Concord April 14th 1876

Dear Edith,

We have had our convention, and have enjoyed it. The Teachers said it was a very good one and they learned much, also that Concord seemed a most hospitable town, they had never been so well cared for. Edward says however that the motto of most of the speakers seemed to be "Men may come and men may go, but I go on forever", and he shook his head in despair. When I was repeating this to Father he exclaimed "Edward's conversation is a delight, from the surprise and the brilliancy of his quotations and songs, one wonders where he got them. Very rich he is in them!" Father gave a 35 m. lecture to the Teachers last evening in the Hall to wind up the day. It was capital. Mr Fay Barrett and I, who sat together and had waxed confidential, enjoyed every word. Mr Barrett's exclamations & responses, from page to page, as Father went along doubled my delight. Rounds of applause came in occasionally and I held my head high to think how much Father had done this winter in this way. He was rather humble & distressed when I met him, but he believes our assertions. Mr Thayer's visit was most happy. Cousin Gore and Cousin Fanny & Aunt E. dined with us. At tea-time Mr Tower brought a horse for our inspection. Father, Mother, Mr Thayer & I stood as judges, I fear we didn't amount to much. I met Edward trying the animal today, and he stopped to glorify Father's

lecture, and tell how Concord boys, Horace Walcott, A. B. C. Dakin and C. Richardson had been reached and delighted by it. I hope you'll be here May-Day. I'll take the bairns Maying at four o'clock if you'd like. I have sent for Mr Cabot and he is coming from Thursday night till Saturday. Mother is now advancing, she once more ornaments the streets of Concord, Aunt Lizzy and I look at it in that light, and she went to church yesterday, Easter Sunday, and enjoyed going. The congratulations on Edward's report come in a steady stream, and he is in as much danger now of being puffed up, as he was at first of having his heart broken.
E. T. E.

Concord May 8th 1876

My dear Edith,

I'm going to Boston tomorrow to Dr Sewall who says I shall be well by July if I'm good, and there's nothing to speak of the matter, and to Miss Melcher whose choice of flowers I fear you'll hate. How I wish you were to be there! (I'll leave my bonnets for you to see & have altered if you wish.) and to Mme. Rey. Then to Nina's & B. Tudor's, and shall come up at 2.45. Mrs Hoar says her African rose was all transplanted last fall and she thinks it is not this year in good condition, but in the autumn she'll give you some. Miss P. has sent the anemones, she says they spread. I'll bring them to Boston tomorrow. I had a delightful visit to Edward & Annie, we studied Trojan antiquities. E. as usual was anxious about his patients, and daily exclaimed "Wisdom is the principal thing, therefore seek wisdom! and a knowledge of Medicine is necessary to the practice of it." Martha Derby is a lovely Concord flower, and gives me more pleasure every week. I would like to show her to you, with her pretty youthful slenderness, and lovely colours, her beautiful manners and easy speech and her faithful nature. Last night as I contemplated my Sunday Scholars coming out of church, rank after rank, I was filled with joy and admiration, all so good, so many with beauty or air or remarkable intelligence, and some with all. Cousin Gore came to church yesterday for the first time, he is much better. What a summer day it was! Did you all enjoy it?
E. T. E.

Mother is gardening, Father & I are at the Oration [to be given at the University of Virginia in June], Mr C comes this week.

— 1876 —

Milton, May 24th 1876
Still as it will be read tomorrow
I speak as if it were May 25.

Dear Father,

If I were at home this morning you should have a birthday present, and however you may feel about it *I*'m very sorry to be away on this occasion, and it isn't quite my fault that I am, because it was circumstances not I that made this the only week I could come to Edith. Your burly little favourite has been very amusing since I came. I first saw him in the entry, being dragged upstairs by Mrs Kelly, in spite of repeated declarations "I want to go out-doors." He doesn't call himself Baby any more, though when his brethren were teasing him by quoting some early remark of his "Hot burn Baby!" and he had been roaring, first at one and then at the other, "Don't staid it!" and was pretty furious, Ralph said "What are you, Baby? Are you a boy?" he replied indignantly "No!" at which I asked "Are you a girl?" "No!" "What are you?" "I'm a BABY," he said with emphasis as if he was very proud to be one. The latest event in the family was Cameron's birthday on Sunday, and I had descriptions of it from the children. Will came home last night and he says the tone of the Southerners is certainly improved from what it once was, and the South looks better. He came up in the cars with an ex-Confederate soldier, and had much talk with him. The man said he should vote for the *best man* for President. If the Republicans put up a better man than the Democrats he should vote the Republican ticket. Two years ago when Will & Edith came home from the South, Edith said the sight of the country and the talk of the inhabitants always made W. so wretched that he couldn't bear to go. Now, though quite alone, he has come home cheered rather than disgusted. He went to see a Mr Tomlinson in some Southern city, who had much to say in praise of Governor Chamberlain, he said he knew in the beginning he was a good man, but he was continually a surprise, doing better on each occasion than had been expected. There was a convention before the State Election (on which it in some way depended) and most of the delegates came hostile to Chamberlain. He was there, and some question was asked, or something was said, which gave him a chance to make a speech. And he carried them all with him, and they gave him a good majority. Don't forget about carrying those Errata for "Letters & Social Aims". They are in the light green copy of the book on the small table in my room. And do acknowledge to Mr Ainsworth, the Flosh, Cleator, etc., Mr Martineau's picture, before I come home. Goodbye, you may have three cups of coffee, if I were there, I would pour them out.

E. T. E.

Concord May 29th 1876

Dear Edith,

Mother is quite well again as far as habits are concerned, comes to meals, and spends her days on flowers and the interests of the garden. Of course she doesn't feel quite as strong as before. Our sky, in the house, is quite clear again. Mrs Gregory is worse. I keep going over there. Edward thought last night that she would never leave her bed again, but the cooler weather has revived her. Alice Hooper appeared at the 12 o'clock train today, but no Anna! alas! Then I saw Mrs Hooper following her, and was as much consoled as I could be. Mrs Hooper & Alice are perfectly charming. We have enjoyed their visit to the full. Annie came down to dine with them, but Edward was away, he spends his days in Boston reading. The oration has been set aside since I went to Milton. Tomorrow I am going to Boston, and coming home to decorate. Then I shall begin the oration, and try hard to stick to it. Tonight I suppose you are in Philadelphia. I would that I were there. Mother is just coming up from the garden with a handful of lilies for our baby's grave. If I had strength I would pick some pansies for our other graves. Aunt Susan & Uncle William used to care very much for pansies. Mother in the prettiest manner contrived to thank Mrs Hooper & Alice for their present to our house, and we showed it to them, den & all, yea kitchen & closet and all. Aunt Lizzy came at three and spent an hour, and told many a tale. And she & Mrs Hooper delightfully capped each other's reminiscences of youth & education, and Mrs Hooper sitting by me on the sofa was shocked to see me put pins in my teeth to hold, though I didn't put them 'way into my mouf. And she told me a thrilling story of Mabel Hunt's late escape from dying of a pin.

E. T. E.

Concord June 2d 1876

Dear Edith,

I don't write because of oration. Poor thing! it has many hindrances, what will become of it? Mr & Mrs Lyulph Stanley are coming today for two days, and an English Unitarian has brought letters to us and will come next week, and dentist & doctor take another day, so out of ten small days devoted to it, 'twill get but five. Your New York letter filled me with delight. I keep a-reading it to the family. Mother is quite well and dined with the Alcotts and Mrs L. M. Child last night. Father went to a Free-Religious Lunch yesterday and enjoyed it, and oh! I mesel' tasted for the first time the sweets of anniversary week. I went to the doctor & by taking 7 o'clock train went to the Hollis street morning meeting, and had afterwards a beautiful long walk & consult with Mr Huzzey, one of my fellow-officers. Nina says Philadelphia was beyond her hopes. Ida Higginson better & about. Baby intelligent & full of spirits.

E. T. E.

Providence June 17th 1876

Dear Edith,

Edward has got through with schools, and with the Medical Essay. His Essay we didn't hear, but Annie said it was very interesting, and Edward seemed cheerful about it. He told us beforehand that it wouldn't be inspiring to read it in the great Lowell Institute to a circle of ten or fifteen while all the rest of the supposed audience were conversing and going in and out. He was appointed to read at three. At three he arrived and found the President, Dr Cotting, on the platform; Dr Wood in one of the front seats with an expression of loyalty and attention, and perhaps three other people in the hall. So he talked with Dr Cotting for ten minutes, and by that time the audience had increased to 15 or 20. Then he began and there were fifty or sixty when he ended, a good many of whom undertook to listen, and the President didn't ask him to omit, but allowed him to read his whole paper. Also a young doctor and an old country-doctor rose afterwards and asked him questions. So it was quite as successful as he had expected, perhaps rather more so. We had Mr Brown last Sunday and every soul of us greatly enjoyed his visit as well as his preaching. Father diligently attended church, and the sight of him edified various members of the congregation, while he took the usual comfort in being there. I think he loves to go to church almost as much as I do. Edward sat in our pew for once, and that gratified me. I mourn for him. You know he sits since his marriage with the Keyeses. Cousin Gore said he hadn't heard a good sermon before for twenty years, and it was a pleasure indeed. Cousin Fanny came to church in the evening and asked Mother to borrow that

— 1876 —

sermon that Cousin Gore might hear it too. Accordingly Mother asked for it, and Mr Brown left it. Whereupon a wide jubilation arose, and everyone desired to see it, Father especially. He said, "I felt all the time as if it might be the beauty of his voice that made it seem so fine. I should like to read it and see if it really is so good as I thought it was." The next day he said to Mr Cabot at dinner-time "Mr Brown seems unconscious of all his power. If he really understood it, and used the riches of his voice, it looks as if it might be prodigious. That voice is great luck."

Do! oh do! send me photo of Ralph & Cameron in Scotch.

E. T. E.

81 Madison Ave. N.Y. June 21st 1876. Wednesday.

Dear Edith,

I haven't heard a word from home since I came away. I hope there is no despair about what Father shall bring, or where his things are, or on his part as to *what* he is going to do. I came on the Stonington boat on Monday night with Col. Russell, Marian, Sally, and E. Hallowell. I enjoyed meeting them very much. Haven met me, and when we came home the children were racing round in a great state of joyful excitement. The baby is just like Ruth to my eyes, and has the same pretty sweet voice. He couldn't get through saying to me "Goodmorning Elly" this morning till some time after breakfast, with the voice of a bird, and joyful smiles. What a reader Ruth is! She is busy with a book all the time. Her caressing ways are very pleasant. I hope to find everything at home in sufficiently good train to leave, and if I do I'll come to you to help you, and move down with you, and stay till the 13th or 14th. But all of course must depend on how matters stand, and not only at Bush but with Annie. For do you know? Annie gave me the greatest delight by saying that she hoped we should be at home when the baby came for the thought that Father and I were pleased, and were waiting with genuine impatience to see him, rather than to have her get through was a great support to her, for her own family thought nothing of the dear lamb and only suffered for her, and she wanted people who thought of the baby. Our address in Phil. is 1628 Walnut St. We leave Mon. noon. How do you do?

E. T. E.

— 1876 —

Phil. June 23rd. Fri. eve. end of our
first day at the Exhibition.

Dear Edith,

We arrived at 6.30 last night, found immense hospitality, welcome & comfort, and all rejoiced to hear that I could visit the grounds. Dr Furness appeared before breakfast and has never quitted Father's side in the whole day. I had a chair, and hardly put my foot to the ground. Saw *Norway*, *Russia*, Japan, *Turkey*, Italy, *Mexico*, New York, in A.M. Tried 2 circuits of grounds in R.R. cars, French Restaurant, Govt. Building, oh! Arizona oh! Colorado! Did you see? Env. machine, postage stamps. Frigates. Antietam & Dante. Sea Lions, whales, whaler, bears, torpedoes, bridges, lighthouses. Though I sat on one seat most of the time, I had a chair 50 m. Father seemed more pleased than I expected. He is dazzled & astounded, had no idea of the glories. I had. Dr Furness amused himself & me with aircastles & plans of showing the whole to Mother. He says he has resolved she shall see it yet. To Wash^n. Monday, to Va. Tues. Back to Washn. Thurs. Rigg's Hotel is our address there.

E. T. E.

Philadelphia June 23rd 1876.

Dear Mother,

The Bradford family are kindness itself. Just a short account of our day. Dr Furness has gone through it side by side with Father, from before breakfast. Now Father is going to take me over to call on Mrs Furness. And every time Dr F. got a chance to talk with me, he desired to hear your views on his views, and he talked to me about Jesus for a long time. We saw a picture of him, and Dr F. looked at it a long time, and then said "When anyone has truly known Him as He is, then he may evolve a picture of Him from the depths of his consciousness. Till then we can have no true picture of him." When he was not talking on these subjects, he was making plans to get you to the Centennial. Father was electrified at the first sight of the Main Building yesterday, it was beyond any expectation he had had; and so all day today he has been lost in admiration and amazement. The thing that made me cry was this inscription on the Egyptian Gate. "The oldest People in the World sends Morning Greetings to the Youngest Nation." Everything is quite up to its fame and the wonder is that all is so easily done that here I am at night untired after a whole day of it.

E. T. E.

University of Virginia
Wednesday June 28th 1876

Dear Mother,

The day has come, the oration is to be at 6 o'clock this evening. I shall write you tomorrow how it sped. We arrived yesterday afternoon and were received in the train by Prof. Holmes and three students, Mr Thom, Mr McKinney and Mr Page. Mr Holmes brought us to his house, which is very pleasant and we are most kindly entertained. The university seems to be first-class, they are infinitely proud of it. The students are, as far as we have seen them, charming boys, and Mr McKinney to whose care I am committed is a very agreeable fellow. I cannot write much today, I never do find any chance. Father seems willing to stop at Philadelphia again coming home so we aren't likely to appear before next Tuesday. I hope the darling baby'll wait for me. I spent on Monday an hour with Cousin Phoebe at the Convent. It was delightful to be with her, and yet she seemed more changed than other people have told me in her feelings, she is a nun more than anything else now. Sometimes I wondered if she was embarrassed, but I always concluded, no she is a nun. Father had a letter from you yesterday, which he lost unopened, much to my despair. I'm going to have a hunt for it now. I wasn't by when he received it. There is much company and something always going on. My love to Cousin Sarah.

E. T. E.

June 29, 1876

Dear Mother,

We are on the R.R. between Culpeper and Manassas coming home. The oration, as you know, was beautiful, and Father delivered it beautifully, but the Hall was large, a hard one to speak in, and was packed with people—principally students of 17, 18 and 19, each attending fair visitors, perhaps two to a beau—with a large sprinkling of children from four years old upwards, and a due proportion of parents and Professors' families. The uproar of people coming in late and hunting seats continued some ten minutes into the address, and I saw with dismay that Father's voice seldom rode clear above it, and all the young

Letter from Ellen to her mother about RWE's oration at the University of Virginia, June 29, 1876.

— 1876 —

and gay perceived the same thing, and like the audience at Mr. Adams's oration at the Dedication of the Memorial Hall, concluded they couldn't hear very well and had better enjoy themselves, so the noise rather grew than decreased. Eight front rows, two knots of students, determined to hear, who left their seats and came up the two aisles and stood; a like knot above on each side hanging over the gallery railings; and as many of the faculty and "joint-committee-of-the-literary-societies" on the platform as were on a line with Father or before him, heard. Here and there people strained their ears in vain; and the larger part of the audience whispered together, while some talked and laughed aloud all the time. It was too bad. Father thinks if they would only have been quiet he could easily have made them all hear. I don't. I think he could not have reached more than two thirds; his voice didn't sound strong enough. A few people afterward spoke to me about it very pleasantly. I know the oration was appreciated by some of the hearers, and in introducing Father and in a speech made afterwards, things were said such as I desired—that it was a sign of re-union, his coming down; that "It was fit that Virginia should hear the Sage of the North," etc. We have been treated with every attention, and have seen people from every southern State, and I have enjoyed all very much, particularly Mrs. Holmes, our hostess, who is just the sincere, peaceful, friendly kind that makes one feel at home. We have heard speeches from two young men. One annoyed me by speaking of the South only as his country, but there was much that I liked in what he said, as for instance that God was showing poor Virginia that he wounded only to heal, and that she would soon be able to be thankful that she had learned that industry and education were the basis of true prosperity. The other youth, a Peyton, suddenly in his speech threw up his arms and praised the Lord that Slavery was abolished, and every sentiment he uttered was delightful to Father and me. I diligently hearkened and watched to know whether many people felt as he did. I concluded he stood rather alone, but I have slender means of knowing. If the oration had been my first thought in this visit I should be disappointed, but as I regard the expedition principally as a right hand of fellowship, I am contented.* Tomorrow to Phila., Atlas Hotel, Centennial Grounds, next to Hawaii. Your letter never turned up. I am unhappy not to know what it contained.

E. T. E.

*See Appendix, p. 663, for another account by ETE of the Charlottesville visit.

— 1876 —

Washington June 30th 1876

Dear blessed Edward,

What a pleasure to get your letter last night, the first news for a whole week, and all good news! I am bursting with the desire to impart information, but where's the time to do it in. As we rode up to the Capitol this a.m., or rather entered horsecar with that intent, Father was seized with such affection by his righthand neighbour and showed such pleasure himself, I wondered who. He didn't introduce me, so I sat and forgot till I heard, "I'm going to show Ellen the Capitol. Why Ellen, here! Here's Mr. Bret Harte." So sure enough it was. As I lost my heart to him in Concord, I did again today. He said presently he had passed the place he was bound to, and should go with us. He was talking all the way of the beauty and perfectness of the Capitol. "Oh!" he said, "It gives you the whole genuine Fourth of July feeling. The first time I saw it I went alone, a gray winter morning. All my friends wanted to show it to me, but I was glad I had crept away by myself. For a little while after I first came near and really saw it I didn't want anyone to speak to me." He walked up with us and showed it to us in a solemn affectionate manner as if it was the ideal of our country, with occasional bursts of joy and admiration. "How a man can look at THAT and dare to enter it with a mean thought *in* him," he cannot imagine. We enjoyed every minute that he stayed with us. He promised to come and spend the evening with us, but he didn't. After he left us, Father and I visited Mr. Spofford, the Congressional Librarian, inquired into the state of copyrights, saw the library and views. Then Mr. Spofford, who is fond of Father and very pleasant, showed us all about, and that was worth everything to us. He took us into Senate, where we saw Mr. Sumner's desk, and House, where we heard part of a good speech by Mr. Frye of N.H., then to old halls and showed us where Mr. Sumner was struck by Brooks, and in the Representatives the statues contributed by the different states. Meanwhile we were losing our dinner and train, but Father scornfully rejected any proposal to consider them. He was really interested, delighted to see and to have me see, and all day yesterday was ten years younger than he has been since we started. Upstairs and downstairs we went, and wound in and out through labyrinths, and saw pictures and views and marble and people. And when we returned to the Hotel, Father was charmed to think the train was gone and an afternoon and night, an oasis of quiet, lay before us, and for the first time was able to listen to questions and plans and understand them. He has arranged to spend the Fourth with the Wards if they want us. Then we shall take Stonington boat on the 5th and get home Thursday morning. I shan't come, however, myself, but go straight to Naushon with Edith as I promised and return the following Thursday, 15th, which completes my month of absence.

E. T. E.

Washington July 1st 1876

Dear Edith,

We have had really hot weather for a week, but it appears that Virginia is not hotter than Massachusetts, the thermometer has not gone above 93, and though flies are troublesome, we hear no musquitoes, at Charlottesville they are unknown. Much as I love heat, it does not add to the pleasure of a R.R. journey, and we had six hours of R.R. Monday, eight on Tuesday, and six on Thursday again. But the delights of seeing Father's innocent pleasure in drinking water have amused me from Monday till Saturday. He has forgotten all former summers, and feels as if he had never tasted water before, and had just made the discovery that it is the best thing in the world. He never remembers that he can have it, and every time I bring it to him he is so glad of it, so pleased with my sagacity in having discovered such an agreeable amusement for him, so full of entertaining addresses to the element and panegyrics on it, all new every time, that I wish you could all see and hear. And when I get a great pitcher of ice-water in his room he feels that luxury can no further go. Also ice-cream, which abounds here, as I never saw it before, is an unexpected refreshment and delight to him every time. When we were almost dead with hunger and fatigue on Tuesday, about two o'clock, a black man offered it at Gordonsville. I snatched at the chance. He was gone for it a long time, but when he brought it it was two great tumblers full, and as the conductor was just saying, "All aboard!" he told us we could give the dishes to the brakeman when we got through. That was a treat—plenty of it and no hurry. It set us up amazingly. Then the fun which no one but I ever has, as I am the travelling companion, of seeing all the world burn incense to Father was never so great as now, just because it is the South. To hear him constantly called by name. He asks a question of somebody, who instantly with respect answers, "It is so and so, Mr. Emerson." To see people come and stand before him in the aisle of the cars and gaze at him, and bring their children and ask him to shake hands with them. People from Tennessee, Alabama, Texas—it is a sort of earnest of

1876

civilization in those states, as well as pleasant on our side. I have looked with toleration, even with favour, on the autograph-albums presented. Mr McKenney & Mr Thom & Prof. Holmes, the Professor of History, met us in the train [at Charlottesville]. And I think Mr McKenney particularly a charming man. He took charge of me. He and almost all the students, like those at the Newhampton Institute we went to last year, first teach to earn, then come and study at the University till their money is all gone, then teach again and return, and you can see how good it must be for them. Their pride in their University is immense, and with good reason. It is excellent. They believe that for hard work and thoroughness and high requirements there is nothing in the country to compare with it, and that their degree of M.A. is worth more than that of Harvard or Yale.

It is a beautiful and romantic-looking set of buildings, and as utterly different from any Northern University in the whole arrangement of its houses and grounds, as it is in its plan of education. It is very large and the outer square is built round only on one, two or three sides, I forget which. Everything without exception is built of red brick with white pillars. Outside the gates are many more students' houses. There are no annual classes, no curriculum. Boys may come for any three studies and receive "certificates of Proficiency" in them when they have finished the courses and passed rigid examinations answering 80 per cent of the questions. But they can only receive the degree of M.A. after having received such certificates in nine studies: Latin, Greek, History, Literature, Chemistry, Mathematics, Modern Languages, Natural Philosophy, and I've forgotten the ninth; and if they wish a Law degree they must have had three courses of Law—International being one—besides six other studies. They have no vacations, except the summer, and they study very hard, boys and Professors both attest. The houses are 50 years old and built with a certain grandeur, which however is not kept up in all details; large high rooms, but poor entries and stairs.

The society seems delightful. Innumerable Professors with their families called on us, who were not only most friendly but attractive-looking at first sight. They seemed like Boston—not like backwoods—people too. I mean they were like people who were accustomed to seeing a large and varied society, and the students too gave the same impression. The number of people I have seen and the states they were from I cannot count. Alas! of course it all overwhelmed and confused

— 1876 —

Father, so that he hardly knew the inmates of the house, much less could distinguish and remember callers. The oration was finally perfected to the last comma, not a pitfall left in it, but it took till 6 o'clock on the evening when it was to be delivered, and then I went over to the Hall with the Committee, to whom I had previously made known what would be needed, and saw to everything—two capital lamps blazing onto a very high, cushioned desk. I didn't dare to hope for the great happiness of success, but nothing, nothing! was omitted that could be done. I knew the oration was perfectly beautiful, and that Father couldn't find a place in it to stumble at. I knew the desk and the light were right. I dressed and saw to him, he took a walk, and dressed, and looked well. The audience assembled and was large, all looked prosperous, but I'm glad I did not hope. It makes me cry to think of it. The gay boys & girls found it would be hard to hear, and they preferred to talk and laugh. For a long time Father hoped to overcome it and "fully expected to make himself heard before long", but the uproar never subsided. I think it may have been heard by a hundred people. Oh! he read it beautifully, never better. And when he saw there was no hope and skipped, he skipped well, so that it didn't hurt the thread. I'm glad I didn't feel too badly about it then. It has seemed more sad since, in looking back upon it, and finding how disappointed Father is. They say it is a particularly hard hall to speak in. Then, dear Edith, the oration wasn't all, the friendliness to Virginia boys was the main thing and that has been showed. Afterwards Mrs Holmes had a party that lasted till one, and I enjoyed it exceedingly. Professor Gildersleeve (Greek Prof. now just going to Johns Hopkins University) is a particularly agreeable man. We have invited the Holmes family, Prof. Southall, and Mr McKenney to come to Concord. I hope they will. We stayed yesterday to see Washington, and today our trunks went to wrong depot and I have stayed behind to collect them, and Father has gone to Phila. to find rooms to spend Sunday in. I hope he'll forget me, and go to see the Exposition, but he may imagine all sorts of troubles and not take a moment's comfort. No news from home later than Monday 26th but that was good. Father rec'd one letter from Mother in Va. & lost it unopened! Did you ever!

E. T. E.

Concord, July 12th, 1876

Dear Edith,

I reached Concord at one and betook myself to the baby's house.

1876

Edward was harnessing his horse outside, and when I called to him manifested surprise. He quickly waltzed me up to Annie's room, and she seemed, and he declared her, perfectly well. He told me, "This was the Ninth Day, so called." She looked very pretty and very fine in your Paris present and her yellow hair. Then I rushed to find my nephew. He has a very good little head and his ears are glued tight to his head, luckily. I kissed his delightful cheeks and Edward brought me home telling me that my donkey had come the night before and had excited the greatest curiosity and amusement coming down from the depot (Willie Bean rode him) and had refused to take a step beyond the library. When we reached home, John spied me and rushed forward eagerly. "Has Miss Ellen got home? Look over there Miss Ellen, and see what you see there!" It was dear Miss Graciosa, the prettiest soft gray coat, white legs, and neat little black boots, and such a pretty face as no donkey ever had before. Father and Mother were dining, and, hearing my voice, came running, not believing their ears and scarcely believing their eyes. Edward stayed a minute and then went home to his own dinner. I visited my nephew once more in the P.M., met Alicia & my Emma S[mith]., called at the Manse where Cousin Sarah Ansley was spending the day, told them about Cousin Phoebe, made my congratulatory visit at the Keyeses' & stopped on Florence's doorstep, and came home to tea. Unpacked. Cousins S. & Elizabeth & Edward were here in the evening. Next day began letters. Alicia & Emma spent the A.M. with me, I on my couch, and endlessly did we chatter & enjoy. Baby very cunning with open eyes yesterday. Love to Edie. I hope to go to Mrs Cabot's tell her.

Concord July 15th 1876

Dear Edith,

Did I leave my brass shoehorn, my treasure, behind me at Naushon? You don't know how beautifully Annie gets up. She already sits in a chair, and feels so perfectly well, it is delightful. The baby, Mrs Whitney says, is just coming to a proper condition and appetite, certainly he is better-looking. Yesterday morning the girl came upstairs while Edward was away and was very saucy, and then packed up and left. Happily Mrs Barber had gone away for some weeks and told Mrs Keyes before she left that she wished someone wanted a girl for a few weeks & would take her. So when Edward came home he went and got her, and she is happily installed. Mother takes great comfort in Cousin Sarah, who, I hope, will remain long. I have been of no use since I came

— 1876 —

home. I have had so many calls, and my return from so many visits required so many letters, the donkey four, and oh! the accumulation in the month of absence. Aunt Lizzy is in Cambridge. How do you do? How is dear Susy, and do she & the children go into water? My donkey is on exhibition & has numerous visitors daily in the E. yard.

E. T. E.

Bedford (while Edward visits typhoid patients)
Monday July 24th, 1876

My dear Edith,

I wish to know several general facts 1. how you do, whether you are any better than you were a year ago. 2. whether little Haven was sick long. 3, how Susy seemed to enjoy & profit by her visit. 4. how our two sets of babies got along. When I came away they hadn't mingled much, Emersons were always together & Forbeses together, except when Ruth & Edith had paired off, or Violet or Cameron was rejoicing in Willy. I hope they all dovetailed at last so well that there was no distinction of family. When I go to see our little boy I often hear him called pretty which I am very glad of. You should have seen the charming air with which he leaned his little head against Father the other day. Edward always calls him Sonny, but he uses the same appellation to my donkey. Cousin Sarah and I ride the excellent Ciosa about the yard successfully. I haven't yet ventured into the street and Edward says I shall no doubt be more or less stoned, as well as hooted after. My Sunday-scholars are each to have a ride tomorrow afternoon and tomorrow morning (Alice and Francy Dabney will be here), I think of taking donkey to the cliffs. Cousin Sarah and Sally and the two girls and I make five, one for Ciosa and four for the wagon. July 27th: The Cliffs expedition was successful. Graciosa set out on a trot which soon became a canter, and felt more disposed than not to exert herself all the way. I was in the saddle from home to the parky place, and Alice from there to the end of the journey. Francy rode her home. My dear! the bliss, the luxury of proceeding peacefully all alone through the beautiful woods on that heavenly morning on my pretty beast (I was a good way ahead of the wagon) was all my fancy ever painted. Both the girls were glad to ride on a donkey again too. I am pleased to hear people's remarks on the Dabneys. They made a great impression. Prescott & Alice R[eynolds]. came & made a call on me, and talked to me in the most sociable & confiding manner, and when I wanted to take the

— 1876 —

ETE holding her donkey, Graciosa, near the East Door. The rider is probably Mary Sage.

Dabneys & Sally out on the river they sent word that they'd each bring a boat & take a passenger. And so they did. Prescott's shining face, & attentive manners, not to his Alice only, but to us all, and his exceeding thoughtfulness, made our party so delightful. We carried our tea. The next day P. & A. went with me to the Unitarian Picnic, and again I enjoyed them. Aunt Susan Jackson came and spent Thursday night & she & Sally & I invited Lizzy Bartlett, and went out and had a picnic on the Pond. Then I have been at the most delightful stand-up party at Judge Hoar's where Marny Storer was funnier than ever, and to tea at the Manse, and last night to Mrs Sanborn's tea-party, and have refused 3 invitations since I came home besides.

My donkey and I tried the Main St. and everyone was at door and windows yesterday morning. Kate and Cary Hoar each took a ride on her, and appreciated her. Everyone doesn't. Lily, for instance, and Clara. Jenny Barrett does.

I wonder whether you have heard our baby's name. It is Charles Lowell Emerson, so named out of the enthusiastic hearts of his parents. I didn't know it, but it appears that Gen. Lowell has always been Edward's hero, and he teaches him to his Sunday School Class perpetually, and Annie who hears the Life read aloud annually has imbibed the same feeling, and they think that name will be more of an inspiration to Baby than any other in the world, and that they can thereby better teach and train him to be the kind of man and citizen they desire to see. I think it the most romantic and interesting way to name a baby, and you know I always did wish to have a baby named for Gen. Lowell. Yesterday when I visited the little Charles he made a sensible & really pretty face. Annie goes about the upper story, and has once been carried down to dinner. Dr Sewell says I must play disabled all summer. I'll come the moment I can, and try to have Father precede me, say on the 9th. Your pretty letter giving such a good account of all our Bears deeply interested your family.

E. T. E.

Concord July 25

My dear sister,

All is chaotic still, we can't guess what is to happen, and shall continue machinations. Father's opposition to original Naushon plan all words, he has asked Miss Lazarus here & in so doing particularly inquired of me when he was expected at Naushon. Mother has been sick again, and seems to me more feeble than usual. Cousin Sarah goes today & will return if F. & I go to N. on 10th. Mother gives up going at all & I myself consider her not fit to try. So thanks, we abandon new invitation & cleave to old, or F. does, I if poss. Dabneys here & charming, also charmed.

E. T. E.

Naushon Aug 8th 1876

Dear Mother,

Ever since I came I have been hearing cunning little remarks and beholding funny little scenes with a view to writing you about them. But ah! no chance to write. We are all in apple-pie order now & ready for the steamboat. Every room looks pretty, and the garret where the

— 1876 —

three boys are to sleep interests us most of all. The interest of the children in the apples and pears was very amusing. I found Ralph seated beside the basket of pears looking them over. "Oh!" said the Aunt. "Mamma said I might," said the nephew. The darling Don clave chiefly to the Sopeywines, and he wanted one that was "all red", and had it to put under his pillow. Ralph is as usual most charming.

Wed. A.M. The party has arrived. [Mr. and Mrs. Elliot Cabot with four sons.] Thank you for all my things. I haven't touched the bathroom divan key. It hangs on Nursery looking-glass. The key of Father's trunk was on his own ring in his own pocket, the key of Edith's room I always put behind shutter of front entry window & I piously strove to impress that on you. I enjoyed your wrath but I am blameless. Tell Margaret the beef-tea I brought has been a great comfort. I found my child [Edith Davidson] sick & needing it, and if I hadn't brought it she would have had to wait two days for it. It lasted till more came. Father is enjoying Baby Edward.

[Unsigned]

Naushon Aug 11th 1876

Dear Mother,

When Mrs Cabot came she said the dream of her youth had been Naushon, but it had never been realized till now, and she likes it every minute. Yesterday Will took her the long drive in and out through the woods, and she said it looked just as she had imagined; today they have all gone on a picnic to the West End, so she will see that. Two wagons, and two cavaliers made the party. The cavaliers were Handasyde on Jara, and Edw. C. on Cricket. When Baby saw them getting in to the wagons he rushed to his Mamma and said "I want to go". On being led into the house he began a dance of despair. Edith says that is his usual way of expressing his feelings. Presently he flung himself on the floor. But seeing the wagons about to start, he rose in fury saying "I *will* go!" Alas while he wrestled with the door they departed and when I came in I found him roaring. He might soon be seen however trying to push Don out of the hammock, and covered with smiles when he succeeded. My daughter is better. Father seems contented, happily he got caught with a novel, and he is pleased with the snare. He tasted this morning "the unblest joys of cup the third". The apples & pears are very popular cooked and raw. Father is hoping for a letter from you. This morning Ralph stole up into the garret to wake Handasyde, and presently the house began to shake to its foundations, and "cascades of laughter" to pour down, which really inundated the house with delight. Ralph & Handasyde and the two big brothers had a pillow-fight. And truly the middle-aged hearts on the second story experienced a blessed refreshment from the noise, as all bore witness at breakfast-time after the offenders had been excused. Father who sleeps in the Schoolroom didn't hear, and Will said "Well, it sounded as if that noise must reach the cellar, and if Mr Emerson didn't hear it, it shows how much was absorbed by the ears of fond papas & mammas under it. I can answer for one, I drank in the whole of it." Violet sleeps with me, and is a sweet and entertaining little creature. She told me of all the fun between the boys she had heard yesterday. "Oh! I like so much to listen to them! I'm not one of the talkers", she concluded. She delights in stories of Ralph when he was a baby.

E. T. E.

Naushon Aug 16th 1876

Dear Edward,

Thankyou for writing me such a good long letter. I have been proposing to write to you & Annie ever since I came down, but everyone knows how hard it is to write at Naushon. Everyone asks about you & Annie & Charles, and we are all delighted to hear the heir proves a true scion of the race & like his parents loves the water. The Cabots have been daily more delightful than words can tell. Frank is a youth of a fascinating cut, everyone sings his praises. Edward just the other way but gains in interest every day. He is much taller & broader than his father. He sketches, he delights in the conversation of the elders more than Frank does. Sometimes he talks a little himself. Father cannot help laughing when he tells us how they, F. & E. & Handasyde played together in the water every day at bath-time. He has enjoyed that as Mother does her kittens. The greatest glory to my mind has been to hear Mrs Cabot say she was studying housekeeping, and the dressing and bringing up of children, and hoping never to forget what she had learned of Edith. She says Will is the best father she ever saw. They have gone now alas! and Mrs Cabot says the night before they went Mr Cabot heaved so deep a sigh that she asked what was the matter, was it, *was* it that he had got to go away tomorrow, and he said yes. Mrs Cabot has cut out patterns of her boys' clothes for E[dith]. & of our boys' for herself, and talked and instructed, and praised, she is so bright and

— 1876 —

funny, that we are kept laughing. Dear Mr Cabot has worked with us over the poem question, and has been the same kind of quiet delight that he is in Concord. I was delighted with the School-Committee news, and the Bedford news. If I could know just what it means, and if it means the right thing, it is good that Charles [Emerson] is coming home. I mean if he will stay & work.

E. T. E.

Concord Aug 23rd 1876

Dear Edith,

Going on agreeably from day to day. Nina is here, domesticated. Call this morning from Sarah R. just going to the Centennial, later from Mrs Sanborn, May Alcott, and Lizzy Simmons. Excitement of Emma Lazarus's approaching visit great. Edw. & Annie & baby dine here tomorrow with Aunt Lizzy & we go to tea at Cousin E.'s at night. Love to my dear child and tell her Mrs Cabot says the Doctor won't listen to Colorado and still prefers Mentone & Egypt. How do you do? Is Will there? Don't forget rubber-ball for Don on his birthday. Little Charles's head grows half at a time & looks dreadfully funny, face meanwhile improved. No time!

E. T. E.

Saturday morning Aug 26th

Dear Edith,

Miss Lazarus came last night & looked different from my expectation. I count she is 27, but she looks nearer my age, I thought she was little and she is large. She is very pleasant and has plain natural manners so I expect a cheerful time, and she! of course she is at the very summit of delight & joyful anticipation. And it is worthwhile she should come. You ought to have seen Mother & heard her first hour's conversation last night with Miss Lazarus. The innocence with which she walked right into every dangerous subject made me dance with amusement, I was happily rather out of sight, or I should have had to keep my countenance, but Mother was so innocent and ardent that she never remembered till she came up to bed, and then she appeared in my room alarmed at her conduct, but I assured her no harm was done. Kate Hoar sent word that she thoroughly enjoyed donkey though unable to ride her & when too sick to look out of window had Ciosa bro't daily into her chamber!

E. T. E.

— 1876 —

Concord Wednesday Sept 6th 1876

My dear Edith,

Mother is sick again, but not very. She has been one day in bed, and I think today she will get up. Nina's visit was on the whole just what I wished it should be, we kept her quiet most of the time, but Miss Bartlett took her out on the river once, and often visited her, and she saw Cousin Elizabeth, the Sanborns, Aunt Lizzy, Lizzy Simmons, May Alcott, Sarah Richardson, and received a delightful impression of Concord society evidently. One wise arrangement was made in the beginning, at 8 o'clock I broke up the evening, and saw Father in his study & Nina & Mother in their chambers before I went to bed. The result was that neither Father or Mother complained of fatigue in the whole lively fortnight of company that we have had, a result as new as the arrangement. When I invited company to tea I asked them to come from five to eight, and all worked smoothly. When Emma Lazarus came I told her that we separated at eight, and I must ask her to go up stairs at that time too. She was very complimentary about it, but ah! when the time came the first night, she begged hard for a respite, so I gave every one quarter of an hour. Then I came to the head of the stairs and called Mother and Nina. When Mother came up she said Emma had asked whether Father was going to bed too. If he was going to sit up, mightn't she sit up too? And of course Mother's civility made her consent. I fumed a little and feared it was a bad precedent, and she would tire Father. He said the next day he was alarmed at first, but very glad afterwards to have had that talk with the poor child, and she went up by half-past nine. The next day she accommodated herself in all things to our customs and never again proposed such a thing, just of a piece with her lovely sweet-tempered part in our correspondence. But that first day she must have had real disappointment and trial. I don't believe it ever crossed her innocent mind that she was invited to be my guest. She supposed herself Father's till she got here. In the morning accordingly Nina told me she established herself on the front door-step to be handy, and having waited patiently till half past ten or so, came and asked Nina where he was. Nina replied, "Oh he is always shut up in the study till dinner-time." At eleven I took her to ride to the cliffs, and the view there seemed to surprise and satisfy her very much. Living only in New York and Newport, she is unaccustomed to this kind of scenery, has seen none since her visit to the White Mts. seven years ago, and we had a pleasant time together. She told me I was a great surprise to her,

— 1876 —

from my letters she had gathered that I was so severe and she wanted to know if I was equally surprised at the difference between her and my idea of her. I couldn't tell. I rather think not, now. She was in most respects what I knew already she must be, and I had a little romance too in my feeling about her before which I find is only increased now she is gone. Well when we got home she said "What will Mr Emerson do this afternoon?" I replied, "Oh he always spends his afternoons shut up in his study till he takes his walk." Edward laughed when I told him the tale, to think how relentlessly I had shut her out of hope for morning, afternoon and evening. But she had all her disappointment at once and in the beginning, and bore it nobly. After that everything seemed only to fill her young enthusiastic mind with utter happiness, and her youth and happiness were elixir to us all. She enjoyed Mother exceedingly. It was one of the highest entertainments I ever had to hear them together, her ardent persistent questions sometimes and Mother's utterly unexpected answers, which surprised now by their unfathomable innocence, now by their erudition. She got at many a corner of Mother's mind never before visited. Then again Mother's sudden walking right into and onto all Emma's supposed feelings and opinions with such lofty unconsciousness, and the pretty frankness with which Emma would take it. Father and she were also a novel spectacle. The peaceful directness of her questions astonished him she didn't see how much, and she got answers out of him that I should have declared he wouldn't give. Not that I think she succeeded in getting at what she wanted to, but he wouldn't have treated anyone else so well. Then think of what nuts it was to me, old S.S. teacher that I am, to get at a real unconverted Jew (who had no objection to calling herself one, and talked freely about "Our Church" and "we Jews",) and hear how Old Testament sounds to her, & find she has been brought up to keep the Law, and the Feast of the Passover, and the Day of Atonement. The interior view was more interesting than I could have imagined. She says her family are outlawed now, they no longer keep the Law, but Christian institutions don't interest her either. The three pretty, joyful letters she has sent to us three since she went home gave us uncommon pleasure. Mother sends her love to you, aches to see you, is wearing the big woollen stockings with thankfulness, wonders how you came to think of getting them for her.

E. T. E.

— 1876 —

Naushon Sept 9th & 10th 1876

Dear Mother,

I came down with Will & Sarah, Augustus Hemenway & Col. Morse. We found the Azalea waiting for us, Edith & my daughter & Ralph & Violet on board. The Azalea was crowded with passengers, Clifford, Malcolm, Will & Col. Morse with their wives. We were promised that she'd "go down like a scalded mouse, with this wind", and so she did, they all said. Mac was perfectly delighted. Ralph in Scotch cap, blue nautical suit, and bare brown legs covered in patches with black & white paint won from the Azalea in hard tussles of climbing. He was very active and appearing in all sorts of places at all moments. After his departure to the bowsprit his appearance became a topic of conversation, and the question arose which of his relatives he most resembled. Someone said there was a look of Malcolm about his mouth, and Sarah Malcolm said "Yes, I see that. He has a way of shutting his mouth from below that Malcolm has when he isn't going to say another word, only to watch the wind, and the jib-sheet." When we landed, Violet and I walked up from Will's wharf. We heard a shout, and beheld struggling up the rocky hillsides, three little highlanders not much bigger than the huckleberry bushes, and Baby appeared the stoutest of the three, though he tumbled down oftener. Cameron shouted "I've learned to drive cows!" and tore after the cows again to show off, but Will ordered him home. Edith D. has gained strength certainly but her voice is gone, and she coughs still, so I don't dare to think much of her improvement. I told John if a rainy day came he must pack bottles and sweep down spiderwebs in cellar. Ask Father if he goes to Boston to carry the bathroom clock back and tell them it gains 12 m. a day instead of 3.

           E. T. E.

Concord Sept 29th 1876

Dear Edith,

Only a note in acknowledgement of your beautiful great letter full of pleasure for us all. Mother is still in Boston. Our dear baby came home much improved by his Monadnoc journey it is said. They all had a beautiful time. Father is still at work on the new poems, and I am not helping. Edith [Davidson] is very feeble this week I am sorry to say. I'm glad she goes so soon. Dr & Mrs Cabot declare I'm not hopeful enough, and say they think she has a very good chance. Her maid Mrs Utassy is good-looking and says she will do anything & everything, be courier, maid, dress-maker, reader, musician, nurse, and asks five dollars a week. She was the fourth one who offered herself, answering the advertisement Will wrote. Thank him again for it. Edith likes her. She comes tomorrow to pack the trunks. Edith's presents from Annie Anthony & Sarah Malcolm have just come. They are beautiful, and she is enchanted.

E. T. E.

Oct 9 '76

Dear Edith,

Mother has had a carbuncle on her hand, and in some inscrutable way it has prevented me from finding any time at all to write. Edward gave her ether when he found it was a carbuncle, and cut it. Funny, characteristic scene from beginning to end. Mother afraid to take it, and sure her hand was better, Edward firm, but saying "I'll make it as easy as I can for you. I'll let you hold the ether yourself at first." "I intend to" replied Mother. She began taking it, and kept saying "Not yet", for a long time. When she came out of it, she wanted to know when we were going to attend to her hand, and couldn't believe it had been done. It has been doing very well since. Your letter came the next morning, and gave us endless delight, such pretty stories of our babes. Everyone according to their views exclaims over Don's sensible remark on sailboats, Edward triumphant, Father astonished, Mother exclaiming "the darling!" I am enchanted with your method of dealing with Violet. The letters from her & R. were looked upon as curiosities of literature, and Uncle Edward exclaimed that Violet's showed it was a feminine production. The behaviour of Baby was of course the dearest theme to Grandpapa. Thank the sweet for his letter to his aunt who must write no more tonight.

E. T. E.

Concord Oct 12th 1876

Dear Edith,

Forgive me that I write so little now, I'm tired & busy. Can't get to bed before ten nowadays, so have no head but I'm pretty strong & consider my back cured, so I shan't return to Dr Sewall. Now about Therchi. *Do* call her by her first name, it is your business officially, to do it, and not to do it would be so pointed that it would neutralize everything else you could do. I beg you to do that. Annie & Edward have done exactly what I think is right, received her as a stranger with no past, one they know nothing whatever against, but in a friendly fashion, & by her first name, as their cousin's four years' wife; and all goes smoothly, yea merrily. They come to our house today. We had Social Circle night before last. Mrs Sanborn came & helped me. All went well. Mother's hand is healing, and she is very comfortable. Edward was chosen at the caucus to go to a Groton convention to elect, or nominate, or something, a member for the Senate of the General Court. He came home last night. Edie's letter by the pilot says only 7 cabin passengers, all totally uninteresting, says her stateroom is all finely rigged with her possessions, and the afternoon is lovely. Thank you for new long letter.

E. T. E.

Concord, October 18th, 1876

Dear Edith [Davidson],

The papers provokingly omit mentioning the arrival of the Wyoming at Liverpool. Yesterday I spent the day with Pauline [Agassiz Shaw] and she told me to give her love to you the next time I wrote. She gets better very slowly, she says she feels how *un*able she is, every time she does anything. I had good talks with her, we agree so well it is a comfort to talk together,—about dressing plainly, about truth. You know, don't you, how much more I have thought about the truth lately, and so has she, and she said just what you said and I think—that it is such a great task set us as we never before imagined, instead of being natural; and then how to teach children so that they will be always learning to do it better, instead of slipping the other way. And we thought the right way to feel was that the truth is positive, not comparative as some people say, and cannot be altered. (We agreed we had a sort of feeling in fabricating an artful statement of it, that somehow it was really altered to suit our wishes, and in trifles no harm was done). And that it is august, holy, and like the stone in the Bible whosoever falls on it shall be broken, but on whomsoever it shall fall it will grind him to powder. So we hope by taking hold the right way now to learn better, and Pauline has so many children to teach. Then I felt so glad you had been told about yourself before you went. I think I should have been uncomfortable if you hadn't. I'm going to tell Edith about looking out for Violet, indeed all our children, so that they may regard excuses as lies. She came to Milton yesterday. I expect to hear on Monday from you.

E. T. E.

— 1876 —

Concord, October 23rd, 1876

My dear Miss Dabney,

To think that I have never told you of my donkey's charms! She is all that I imagined. My only grief is that I can't use her enough. I can't go out on her when it is cold or rainy, and sometimes I have no more errands than just enough to do on my feet. But of course there are occasions when she is just what I want, and I am always perfectly delighted to be on her, and sometimes I get a chance to lend her. She obeys very well and has an easy gait, and she is so pretty she is always a charming sight in the pasture. The days of schools are over for me. I wish I could have had her then. I feared at first that all the boys would hoot after me, but on the contrary, they have been only interested and delighted to see the little creature. I never had the least shadow of trouble. The first four or five times I went through the town everyone ran to see and call others to see, and we enjoyed her together, the town and I. Have you been to Philadelphia yet? Have you seen the Centennial Exhibition? I hope you have or will. Everyone goes from Concord, or at least 250 people out of 2500 inhabitants, and that is a large proportion. We are all enchanted with it. My daughter has gone abroad, to spend the winter in Mentone. The doctors assured me that she wasn't beyond hope, though not out of danger. She knew all about it, but she felt quite sure she should get well and no girl was ever more utterly delighted at the chance of crossing the water. Pauline Shaw provided her with a maid, three of her young friends sent her companion, and her uncle paid her expenses. Tomorrow comes our Conference. That reminds me, did you go to Saratoga? I had to lose it again. Edward said I wasn't strong enough. But I have picked up since and now I am very strong. The red hood you gave me is admired whenever I wear it. Everyone is immediately interested in it. I always meant to tell you.

E. T. E.

Concord, Sunday Oct 29th 1876

Dear Edith,

Our dear Edward has broken his leg. Lily didn't appear at church, came to S.S., sat by me crying. After S.S., waited for me and told me. Edward went to Bedford in the night on horseback, and coming home Billy had fallen and broken Edward's leg under him. I went straight there. Lizzy S. by Annie's invitation came Friday night to spend Sunday with them. I found her & Mrs Keyes in the parlour. They went late to bed last night, had only been asleep a little while when about 12.30 a man called Edward to go over to Bedford about a boy. So he went, and Lizzy thought it was only a few minutes when she heard Edward and someone else calling Annie, and presently Annie called to her that Edward had broken his leg, and she came right down, and Mr Barry, teamster, was there and helping him, doing everything. The bed was happily still in the north lower room which was let last summer, and all made up. So they put him to bed there, and he fell asleep at once. It was about four in the morning. Mr Barry went home, Lizzy moved into Annie's bed to take care of the baby, and Annie went to bed below. Neither of them slept. Baby waked at six. Annie came up & nursed him, they dressed, & still Edward slept. In his sleep he must have moved his leg, which was comfortable at first, but hurt him when he waked, and till Ned Bradford came. He thought himself it was broken half-way between knee and ankle, but when Ned examined 'twas found to be just two inches above the ankle, both bones. I came home to tell the tale to Father & Mother. Poor Father couldn't bear to hear it. What a terrible thing it was to hear! Now that I'm used to the idea, it doesn't seem so bad, but the first hearing was dreadful to each of us. Mother's strength was all taken away; she couldn't lift her head for a long time. The dinner-bell had rung, and I told them all the yarns at dinner. After dinner Father & I visited Edward, and had the immense satisfaction of hearing his own account. He hopes to be round in his plaster cast in two or three weeks. I asked Lizzy what Edward was fed on and she said "Oh he has his dinner like the rest of us." Ned Bradford stayed to dinner and drove away about three o'clock. Flory & her husband & baby came while we were there. Then Mr & Mrs Keyes, then Madam Keyes, just to inquire & depart.

We are all so thankful that you threaten to come, beloved. Do! Mother wants to see you more than can be told, and she wants a grandchild too. Annie says, "Wasn't it lucky I was here? Think if I had stayed and let him come home alone! I never should have got over it." I'm sorry she should be confirmed in her notion of never leaving him. I've had no chance to hear about their visit to you yet, but I know it was delightful.

E. T. E.

Concord Oct. 30th 1876

Dear Haven, and Charles,

Edward & Annie came home prosperously on Saturday, but Edward was called out in the night to go to Bedford, and went on horseback.

— 1876 —

Coming home about half-past one, Billy tripped and fell, and Edward's leg was broken between the wooden saddle and the edge of the raised bank on the side of the road. His right leg, it is, both bones. He rolled one way & Billy the other, when he stopped he lifted his leg, and felt the crepitus, as he feared. Billy picked himself up, came to Edward and stood still by him holding up his leg, which is his way of asking. Happily they were close by a house, and Edward shouted that his leg was broken and he wanted help. Happily also the people were not heavy sleepers and in a very few minutes Mr & Mrs Barry & their brother came out to him. They were as quiet and ready to wait for exact orders as they were eager, and everything was done in the best manner. Mr Barry tore slats off his henhouse for splints, and drove E. home in his own buggy, while the brother followed on Billy. They brought him into the house and set him on the bed in the room opposite the parlour without waking anyone. Then he had the door opened into the front entry and began to call Annie. It was a long business waking her, and instead of coming down the front stairs to him and having no shock as Edward hoped, she ran half-awake to the dressing-room window which looks out on back-door & barn. There she saw two strange men & two horses, who the moment she appeared began to say "Come down, your husband wants you to come down". There was a bright light in the kitchen too, and she thought they were robbers who wanted to make her show them where the silver was. She tried hard to see with her sleepy eyes and at last recognized Mr Barry. Then she knew something had happened to Edward, and rushed down, not knowing what she should see when she opened the kitchen door. To her relief she heard him call from the lower bed-room. She heard the tale, and then ran for her clothes & called Lizzy Simmons who was to spend Sunday with them, and Thomas. Thomas made the fires, and went for Prescott Keyes, and Mr Barry stayed and did the lifting and with Lizzy and Annie got Edward to bed with his leg in the fracture-box, and Prescott came and Edward sent him to Boston for Ned Bradford, one of his young doctor friends. Then Mr B. went home, and everyone went to bed, but no one but Edward went to sleep. He did immediately and didn't wake till breakfast-time. And Prescott brought Ned Bradford to the door at ten o'clock, so that the leg was set, Dr Bartlett also being present, and made into a plaster cast before dinner, and before any of the family here at Bush knew a word about it. We were all very much grieved at first hearing it, and I think Father won't quite hold up his head again till Edward is well. Edward declares it is a very valuable

1876

experience, and he is glad for once to be at this end of the leg instead of the other. Also that surgery is not so painful as it is said to be, that breaking the leg isn't bad, and setting doesn't hurt at all. Annie looked as if she had gone through a great deal, poor child. The baby didn't choose to confide to me his sentiments. I hope the journey to New York was pleasant, and that all are well.
E. T. E.

Concord Nov. 2nd 1876

Dear Edith,

We have been flattered by you and Will with such promise of visits that it rather has prevented my writing. Edward looks better than he did at first. He is bleaching already by confinement, but he looks strong and is hard at work studying history, and painting between. His delight in both pursuits is overflowing, and he has many an extract to read if you will listen. Annie has just been here and says he had solid sleep last night, and is up at the window today and thinking of crutches. Will you bring Will's for him to try. Mother asks you to bring the pinking-iron too, please. I hope you'll get this before starting.
E. T. E.

Concord Nov 14th 1876

Dear Haven,

I am very much obliged to you for writing to me so fully. Every word of your letter was as interesting as it was sad. And I am afraid you are right. But on the other hand it is possible that Charles may find here in Concord a garden to work in, and they may succeed in getting a few scholars, and if they do so much I shall be quite contented. I have, more than you, closed my eyes to what Charles might have been. I simply look at him as he is, and think it possible that since he longs to *do* something, he will stay by any chance of gardening which is not a losing business, and teaching which pays even a little, and that Therchi since she will see all her neighbours doing the like will be content to do most of her own work as she has hitherto. They have taken rooms at Miss Lavinia Bates's opposite to Dr Barrett's house. Nov. 17. They came to see me this morning, not very cheerful, both eager to feel settled. I want to have things go smoothly with them this winter. Florence Hoar came in yesterday and said the Prichard family had found them very charming when they took tea there. Charles is at work translating he says. Annie found him spade in hand helping Miss Bates in her garden the other day. Therchi is pleased to find Miss B. can speak nothing but English, and tries to talk with her. Edward is as well as could be expected except that he doesn't sleep properly. He is delighted with the chance to study history, and full of lore to impart when I see him. He goes out to drive and will dine here tomorrow. Father & Mother send their love to you & Susy and your descendants, and hope you will all come to Thanksgiving. I wish you would; it would be perfectly delightful. Edith has been here for a week with her youngest. How we should like to have the nine descendants together! Give much love to Susy, tell her not to say no, but to consider it and say yes.

E. T. E.

Concord Thursday Nov 16

Dear Edith,

I should be sorry enough that I didn't come last night to Milton and stay a week and take my ease with you, if I didn't have a stronger persuasion than ever that I ought not to leave home at all. You know I went to Boston yesterday to make 3 calls. Father went too, to overseers meeting. As I came home I thought I'd buy a steak, feeling pretty faint myself. When tea-time came it proved the saving of the family. Father & Mother, 20 miles apart, had shirked dinner and were intending to take one mouthful of bread for supper. And today Mother desired to play the same game, but isn't allowed. C. & T. are settled and happy at Miss Bates's. When I went in day before yesterday to see Edward he was drawing the map of France & gave me much instruction in it. I learned and I enjoyed. How do you fare? Oh Edith how lovely it was to have you last week! And the dear baby. Little Chas. visited us yesterday but was homely. Virtuous of course. Edw. can't sleep yet.

E. T. E.

Concord Nov 20th 1876

Dear Edith,

With joy we hailed your letter on Saturday night, and found particular joy in your having seen Cousin Lucy Lowell, in Violet's doughnuts, in the poetry-lessons, and I am delighted moreover to hear that Will was well and funny, and that there is a dancing-school. I have letters from my daughter & Susy, which I have just sent to Mrs Davidson and hope to have back in time to enclose. Last night we had our first circuit-

— 1876 —

meeting. I couldn't go, and 'twas too rainy for Mother, but Father went, and when he came home Mother visited me to tell me he had been delighted. So I made him relate his adventures to me this morning at breakfast-time. People don't sit in their own pews in the evening, but he had found his own and sat in it because he had rights there, and no sextons or wardens would drive him out, and being quite safe he felt proud and held up his head and looked round. Three ministers came in, and the congregation, and Judge Hoar was there. Mr Guild made a good Christian speech, but not quite up to my brag. But he was perfectly sincere and told a straight story. That other man, the official one (Mr Shippen, Sec. of A.U.A.) spoke more easily; very good, very skillful, but he isn't so much in earnest. Your minister did better than either of them, he is more Christian, more human, and put his heart into it. The meeting was intended to give our parish an idea of what the Association wants money for, and what it has been doing, and we had the Sec. and 2 directors to set it forth.

The other day when I saw Mrs Bond (Miss Powell) she was talking about her health, and she said several things that seemed to me very good. She thinks women ought not to go into public work at all till they are pretty old and sure that they are strong, and sure that they have a right to their own time "because public work is imperative, it has to be done whether or no, so it has to take precedence of private duties". I liked very much the doctrine from beginning to end, and accept it as an argument on your side. You see I can't altogether agree with you when you scold me usually, and now I see why. You never admitted this one point that public duties are imperative. Anyone who has done them as Miss Powell and I have feel that they are, and that they do by force take the precedence of private duties. Still the very fact that they do and ought to is the reason why Mrs Bond abjures them, and now that she puts it so before my eyes I am ten times more ready to abjure them too, for the present. Charles & Therchi came to church yesterday. Mother meant to go to Boston this afternoon but is prevented by the rain. Cousin Elizabeth has made us two lovely calls this week.

E. T. E.

Concord Nov. 27th 1876

Dear Edith,

Thankyou for sending the photographs so soon, and for your letter. We are glad to hear of little Violet's advancing more & more as eldest

— 1876 —

daughter, and of your presents. Please send word about Thanksgiving as follows: when we may expect you & what you think of following distribution, Red Room, Aunt Susan & Eugenia [Dodge]. My room, Violet on couch, Lidian [Jackson] & I. Nursery, Mrs Kelly, & J & D & C [John Jackson, Don and Cam], D in crib and C on trundlebed. Ralph in Sarah Gately's room. Mr Dodge, C. & O. [Oscar Jackson] up garret. Can you & Will set the table places at an early day? Mr Channing will come. Uncle George & Cousins Gore & Fanny will not. All the rest will. Please bring with you two blankets and my silk dress. We need more blankets because there is more sleeping alone & therefore a larger number of beds than usual. Also please bring carving knife & fork and half a dozen little knives. I think with Annie's big ones we shall get along. Mother is getting better. She went to church last night.

E. T. E.

January 1877 - December 1878

Concord activities. Stay at Naushon. Aunt Lizzy visits. Sickness in Concord. Annie sent to Milton. 1878. John Emerson born. Visit to the Ward's in New York. Aunt Lizzy dies. Work on RWE's lectures with James Elliot Cabot. Trip to Niagara with RWE; Saratoga Convention. Dean Stanley's visit.

Concord Jan 5th 1877

Dear Edith,

I shall send Mother's brush by Father tomorrow. I came home just in time to unpack, and pay my bills, and put away the clean clothes. I have now settled to sedentary employments. I send you a bottle of cream, and Mother must bring home the bottle. Father came home last night and said the wonder of life only increased as it went on, that if it were not so old we should all feel what a mystery this existence is, most people don't feel it, but he does more the older he grows. Then he talked about the age of the planet and how with the aid of its inhabitants it was always improving its face, and how convenient it was for them and all its great elements are on their side, though now and then to be sure a great wave does come whopping into a town of respectable people. And everything he said was very pretty, and more about what he himself thinks, and how he feels than he often tells. I wished you were here and I wish now I could write it, but I don't remember the words, and the things were beyond my understanding. Edward came on horseback yesterday morning and showed himself to his proud family, and today he & Annie came in a sleigh bringing Effie's lovely letter & New Years presents to Charles Lowell Emerson. I hope they'll immediately send you the letter, which will tell you all the pretty, affectionate care she has taken to send him everything he will like to have; a facsimile of Col. Lowell's silver mug, a photograph, the oration, and a jacket she knit for baby herself. They were charmed, and so are Father & I.

E. T. E.

Concord Jan 5th 1877

[To Edith Davidson]

This, dear little cheated girl, is the rest of your letter. Father & I went

— 1877 —

to Milton on Saturday and I hoped we could do the ideal thing, finish our preparations that night, rest Sunday, yea, keep the Sunday, and then have New Years easily and punctually on Monday. I can't say we quite did it, or did any better than usual. I think it was quarter of ten when we began with the presents & about half past one when we got through. But it was good to have Sunday between. We are having a winter such as I love, an ideal winter, snow on snow, and oh! my child, the glories of that Sunday out of doors cannot be exaggerated. The whole world was not only spotless, but strong hard crust, polished to the last point, the whole landscape shone and gleamed in the sunlight & moonlight for it was full moon,—think of that!—and it was just cold enough not to melt in the least, but to us seasoned by long cold weather it felt balmy like summer, large flocks of very soft happy white clouds, which evidently enjoyed the day as much as we did made the clear enchanting blue all the more brilliant, and kept quite out of the way of the sun, for I don't think they cast a shadow once all day. Well, we rode to church together, Ralph & Violet on the front seat, and Cameron in all his beauty between Edith & me. In Milton they have settled a new minister, a Canadian, Mr Frothingham. His sermon on the old year filled me with surprise from sentence to sentence, stretched my mind, interested me very much. Dr Morison told me after church that he was a great acquisition. The afternoon & evening were uneventful, except when Father & I went into the green room and saw Edward's various performances in the way of presents. Being lame he had made everything, such a theatre for Violet, such armour for his nephews, such paintings for Annie & Mother. I admired, and as for Father he could not sufficiently gaze & wonder. You are well-acquainted with the proceedings before breakfast New Years morning, Will writing for dear life, and here & there another stray poet, and the sudden calls for more white paper & the ribbons. The solemn bundles with all their colours coming down by armfuls, the perplexity as to where the different people's piles are. Aunt Lizzy wasn't there alas! she is sick at Mrs Storer's. And I was very conscious too that you weren't there. I missed you a great many times. The first ceremony was new. Violet brought the little boys' baskets, and Baby took a basket full of small presents tied with green ribbon and ran round with it to give us each one, standing with stolid satisfaction to see it opened. He had an egg-cup for Edith & Will held him while he presented it & read the following poem which W. had written:

— 1877 —

> "The man who has the shortest legs
> His present offers up
> And asks that you will eat your eggs
> Out of this little cup!"

Then Don took his basket of presents tied with blue, and trotted round, all smiles & dimples & made his presents, and then Cameron who seems to me more brilliant than ever brought his. After the children had received their other presents Edith called back the little ones and produced your letter & cards. They were delighted with them and so was everyone. I gave Mother your tidy. She was properly affected, and sends her love and her thanks. We dined in the hall, the children in the dining-room. We never had such a gay dinner before. Col. Russell & Malcolm were in unusually high feather.

End of letter missing.

Concord Jan 23rd 1877

Dear Edith,

Thankyou for sending for me, and I should delight to come, but I must not turn to the right or the left for the next 3 mos. if I wish to make any progress; the number of daily small things that interfere and my own slowness are obstacles enough. I have succeeded in doing 2 or 3 hours work since New Years. I visited Mr Wesson at once and he lent me in the most friendly manner the source of his wisdom and allowed me to copy the directions for the three dances. I imagine there are fifty in the book. The Steamboat Quickstep is called "Washington Quickstep" in the book, this I mention as it may help you in finding the music. You ought to see the gorgeous turn-out provided for little Charles. Scarlet sleigh-sled, the deerskin mat Alice gave E & A lining it & hanging handsomely over sides and back with its scarlet edge, and a small white fur robe made of the best remains of Mrs Keyes's old fur cloak. It is quite killing. The sled belongs to Roger, Mr Walcott bought it of the Surettes and painted & varnished it new, but as Roger is still too young, Charles will kindly take the shine off it for him. Mrs Thayer died on Saturday, and Mr Thayer seems so feeble they are anxious about him too. I hope he'll live. I can't bear to lose our old standbys. The news that Violet's hair is parted gives unmitigated satisfaction to us all. Now she must have her photograph taken. I enclose Uncle George's account of his visit to Edie. I have sent her today's letter to her

— 1877 —

Edward Waldo Emerson, left, and RWE holding little Charles.

Mother. She tells of a talk whispered to Jane, and says she often had to "hesitate for breath". I don't like that statement at all. It is much the worst thing I have ever heard. Edward & Annie & Baby interrupted me and I have had a good visit from them. Edward walks upstairs like a

gentleman, he rather chassezs down. Mother has a cold and is under Edward's care today. Goodbye, much love to you and all.
E. T. E.

Concord Feb 1st 1877

My dear Edith,

Today Edward & Annie dined here with little Charles. That baby's virtue I begin to see is in great measure due to Annie's wise education, and you know how glad I am to learn that. When he is laid down he has got to lie he knows. If he cries Annie doesn't take him up, and the result is that he either falls asleep or finds some way of amusing himself. Annie has for the first time in her life been holding forth to me on the subject of discipline, and its beauties and advantages, also how easy it is if you are unyielding. The Weirs dined here with them and seemed to enjoy the baby; they said it had a strong resemblance to you & Edward when you were babies. But I have sad news of Kate Hoar, she has diphtheria, and Edward thinks she may die. I have not heard this morning how she is. Father has gone to Boston every day this week to the dentist, and has never expected it from day to day. If he had known it beforehand I should have got him to go to Milton and spend one night. Mr Cabot is coming on Monday to work all next week. Mr Reynolds lectured on Wednesday night and everyone praises the lecture. It was talked about yesterday at dinner, and everyone desired also to magnify Charles Walcott's extempore speech. The week before Miss Georgia Cayvan was to give a reading here. She is an agreeable very handsome girl 18 yrs old, who stayed with Florence on the occasion and won everybody's heart. She had a cold and brought a gargle with her. Learning from Flory that there was no dressing-room at the Hall she said she would use her gargle before starting and asked for a spoon, which Flory having brought she poured out a spoonful, threw back her head and began. Suddenly she threw bottle and spoon across the room and screamed & flew. Alas! she had taken ammonia, and of the strongest kind, brought to sniff away a cold in her head. Flory sent for Edward. Poor Miss Cayvan had completely skinned her tongue and part of her throat. Of course there was no reading & Mr Walcott went and explained that Miss C. had met with an accident and dismissed the audience. All the world at once concluded she was drunk at the Hotel, so at Mr Reynolds's lecture Mr Walcott arose to rebuke the charitable rumour, explain exactly what had happened, and where. Edward's soul

— 1877 —

was delighted by the severity and skill with which he characterized the imagination of Concord. I said "Flory ought to hear". "Oh Flory would only say 'Why, of course' " said Annie, "She knew it all before."

E. T. E.

Concord Feb. 2nd 1877.

My daughter dear,

I think you have never been told to how many friends your letters go, how many people send for them. They go to Edith, to Mrs Cabot & Lilla, to Lily Keyes, to your Mother & Will, to Lillie Bowditch and to Annie Anthony. They are sometimes almost worn out when they return from their journeys. I wonder whether you have ever felt any interest in Moody & Sankey. They have come to Boston and interest Concord very much. It has seemed to me such a practical thing to have inquiry-rooms, and to have it made easy to go. I think you would agree with me, that one great desideratum with poor sinners is a chance to ask a saint a few questions. Then besides the natural usual interest in all that concerns religion, I have had a great increase of feeling on the subject from the fact that our S.S. subject the last two weeks has been the Conversion of St. Paul. Set many people to talk on that subject under circumstances that open their hearts a little, and it is pathetic, it is terrible, to see the amount of dark despair there really exists where the "clear sunshine of the Gospel" is supposed to lie. So I was thankful to hear that these Evangelists had come, and hoped everything. On Tuesday I went early to Teacher's Meeting, and had a long talk with my dear Mr. Reynolds about it. He looked quite sad—I don't know why— and he kept asking me questions about whether I believed this and that, and why, till finally I had given him all my views on the whole matter; and then he began to give me his. The other Teachers were coming in all the time and they were all equally interested to hear. Mr. Reynolds says that unhappily the people chosen to superintend and work in the inquiry-rooms are not always proper persons; that of them all he knows only two, but those two lead lives not half so good as the lives of "average sinners," and that makes him suspicious of the rest. This was a blow to my best-founded hope. He says moreover that letters from England say that the great excitement M. and S. [Moody and Sankey] produced there was succeeded by an ebb of life in all the churches, and in general more harm than good was done. And so on, with many a fact, and many an instance, till my hope and enthusiasm were pretty

— 1877 —

thoroughly killed. He said he heard Mr. Moody preach in N.Y. or somewhere, and that he is coarse-grained and holds an antiquated theology, which Mr. R. considers in itself degrading, but he is a sincere, honest man, and as he speaks so he believes and does. To my surprise, Mr. Reynolds wound up with saying that he should be unwilling to put a straw in the way of the movement, because the man was a good man, the melancholy state of things which he came to improve was quite as melancholy as he thought it, and though to Mr. R.'s judgment he was attacking it in a mischievous and mistaken way, still he was attacking it, and it might be he would do good. Presently he said something about the deadness of religious interest in the community, and I, again surprised, told him I thought—for I do think—it was never more alive. He gave for answer, "Why suppose I should undertake to hold a religious evening-meeting of the most interesting kind and with ministers to help me, and suppose something else of an interesting secular kind were going on at the Town Hall, where do you think the people would go?" Of course they'd go to the Hall, but I wonder, does that show religious interest is dead? You don't know what good times we have now at Sunday School. Alice Linder joined my class in the autumn, and her presence I suppose it is, has transformed the whole character of the lessons. Now it is the girls that talk—I sometimes less than any of them. We often get at the very kernel of the chapter quite early in the hour, and seldom have I heard such practical, such affecting discussion, though we always of course are interrupted and dispersed at the end of 20 minutes. But I am content and much more. It is impossible that they should forget it or leave off studying and discussing in their own minds for a day or two, I am sure. My poor kitty, cut off from Church and Sunday-school, how do you feel? Do write me and tell me how hard the famine is. Mr Reynolds once said it was a useful experience, and faith and piety maintained in solitude without a single external support was solid and true, and had its great reward when it was again allowed its natural expression and the fellowship of the church. Goodbye my dear. Mr Cabot comes again next week, perhaps you'll come off short.

        E. T. E.

       Concord Monday Feb. 5th 1877

Dear Edith,

  Our dear Kate Hoar died on Saturday morning of diphtheria. Sam asked Edward on Friday to stay all night and he did. She was quite unconscious Edward thought, but Sam thought she was sensible that he was there and that he never stopped trying to relieve her. At five she died, and Edward says it was some consolation to see the beauty and peace succeed the look of desperate suffering in her face. Judge Hoar drove Edward home and talked to him about her in the loveliest way. The news broke Annie's heart and made her positively sick. But yesterday she was better and they came to dine with us and brought the darling Charles. Your letter came on Saturday morning and filled an aching void. Our dear Violet's woes made our hearts to bleed. Mother & Annie feel the deepest comfort at hearing that Don does go to dancing-school. I'll tell Mr Reynolds about R. Morison but now he is preaching in Washington. Yesterday we had Mr Schermerhorn, next Sunday Mr Shippen will come. Write me just what you will do about Father's lecture week. Mr C. comes tomorrow for good, that is to begin the main body of the work, which may keep him a month. Goodbye dear good girl, and come for as long as you can.

E. T. E.

Concord Feb 17th 1877

My dear daughter,

I actually forgot you yesterday for I was occupied with the pleasures of having Edith and baby here. The real reason however was that I was very tired. Mr Cabot was here the week before and I was very busy doing with him and finishing what he left me to do. Then Lizzy Brown from Framingham came on Friday and that afternoon we spent wrapping up the candy in tissue-paper for the school-children who came after school. They came as usual, and sang, beating time, and spoke two pieces, and I carried round one basket while Mother did the other, and said "What do you say?" and all went off delightfully. Lizzy stayed to tell Mother that they had been as affectionate as could be all day, had had on their best clothes and best manners, and it had been the easiest day of the whole term, from the great expectation of half past four. That over, Lizzy Brown and I had much talk till eight, then I had to go to copying. Saturday I went to spend Sunday in Brookline and had the pleasure of an hour with Aunt Lizzy, who is now dressed in a flannel gown and sitting in a chair. She says her weeks of utter weakness were weeks of rapture, every beautiful glorious and entertaining thing of her whole life returned to her in full vividness, she could hardly believe that a single life could have contained so much delight. And the wonder still remained, but as she grew stronger the rapture passed away. Behold me just at dark arriving at Mrs Elliot Cabot's. They never received my note announcing a change of plan, so having expected me since morning she had just gone with 3 eldest to a party. Mr Cabot received me however in the loveliest manner, and I had such a good time at tea with Charley & Richard talking flags. We were all learned & interested in the subject. After tea Mr C. read aloud to them the Pearl of Orrs Island—very amusing to me his frequent skips. The boys went to bed. Out came my M.S.S. and we worked an hour. Then I went upstairs and just as I finished undressing dear Mrs Cabot came home, and made me a short visit. The next morning was a heavenly spring day, warm, clear and still. We all walked to church together, and Mrs Cabot talked about Moody & Sankey, and said she was uncomfortable, neither disapproving nor heartily approving. She was going to hear them but rather dreaded the excitement. Mr Brown preached a sermon very interesting, but intellectually rather than otherwise, to me. After church I saw Agnes Poor, Mrs Brown, Cousin Lucy Lowell & the Judge & Mr Harry Lee who walked home with us, most of the way with me, and he was immensely entertaining. The gayest lunch, to which he didn't stay. No one present but the 7, their parents & I. The seven discoursed, the 3 listened. On Wednesday Harriet Putnam came, she came at 12, and her husband & W. at night to hear Father's lecture. Father gave the Boston lecture which is a favourite of mine. Hatty & her family went on Thursday, Edith stayed till yesterday. I have had no letter from you this week but I'm quite content. Mrs Cabot sent me hers, so I have heard from you. Goodbye my child.

E. T. E.

Concord Feb. 22nd 1877

My dear Edith,

I sent by Charles the Life of Hayes which Concord people like for Will to look at. He told Mother he thought he should be interested in it, and she has never forgotten it. Last night we were hunting for our Lyceum tickets in wild dismay when your note brought one. The other hasn't turned up, but Father pushed in unmoved without any. They greatly enjoyed the occasion. Mr Cabot is here and I'm in a great hurry. I have received a note from Susy Willard [Edith Davidson's companion in Mentone] which almost puts an end to hope. You shall have it as soon as Dr Cabot & Mrs Davidson have seen it. How I hate to send it to

— 1877 —

her! How can she bear it! With it is a gay letter from my good child herself.

E. T. E.

Concord Feb. 27th 1877

My dear Sally,

You shall have the letter you have long deserved. The first thing I wish to write about is Charles & Therchi for I know your interest remains though you have been so cruelly treated. I see them often, but never to purpose. But they are pleased to have their own furniture and possessions about them, though they don't like the American house so well as the French apartment. They are often invited to dine or to tea or to make a visit, once to go to a concert in Boston. Charles always hastens to refuse and seems to prefer utter solitude like an old man. Happily Therchi loves to go about, accepts for herself and him, and takes him with her. Therchi has joined the sewing-circle and is in a fair way to get acquainted with people. Charles has two German scholars. Edward & Annie are prospering. Annie looks very well and feels stronger than she has for a long time; Edward's leg is well healed, but not yet quite what it should be. His ancle-joints aren't limber, but they will become so. Their baby is in full glory now. You wouldn't know him. Mother is well, better than when you were here. I wish you could have heard her discourse upon that inferior creation, the Man, last week to Mr Cabot when he dined here. It was unusually amusing. She goes to Boston alone almost every week. Yesterday she discovered a wholesale toy-shop, and the bundle that came home with her showed how pleased she was with the find, and made Father exclaim "Why I thought Christmas was past." She is looking forward with delight to the blooming of a whole table-full of tulips in pots. If they will bloom next week they shall adorn my party. I have just felt a breath of youth and am going to invite all my old set, of twenty years ago, all that are left, to come and dance cotillons to the sound of a fiddle as we used to, and have no supper. They all seem more than willing to try such a sport. You asked me in one letter how we could let Father leave out "Goodbye proud world" from the new volume. We were sorry, and several friends begged for it, but Father disliked it so much himself that all persuasion failed. Your pickles have been luxury to Mother ever since they came, and when the peaches were eaten up she took the vinegar and scalded canned peach in it, which she hopes will prove half

— 1877 —

as good when she opens it next week. My donkey is lame. She stood and looked pathetically at us from the barn bars. I congratulated her on the beauty of her ears & crest. Father said "Why I was looking to see what was on her head, it looks as if several large birds had lighted there." Looking at her with that idea, I could see it so, and it made me scream it was so funny. I hope you have many scholars and not too many and that you will be well enough to enjoy your garden in the spring.

E. T. E.

Concord Feb. 28th 1877.

Dear Miss Dabney,

Thankyou for remembering my birthday. I enjoyed hearing about your new brick house and I hope you will tell me all about it sometime. I no sooner think of keeping house however when the serpent enters the Garden of Eden, to wit a servant. But I hope you will have one who will love you like your Amelia, and that will restore Paradise. Don't think I am surrounded by serpents now. I have two good good people, who have made me happy for a year. It is the first oasis since 1869 though, and I don't forget what a time I have had most of my life with the kitchen. Tomorrow I am going to Mary Watson's to spend the night and enjoy a little party which she is going to have. It is a great while since I have seen her. They are living in Boston this winter. Our School examinations are going on this week, I mourn that they no longer belong to me. I mean to go to two of them however, and don't I wish I could sit with the committee and hear what they say to each other! Few relations are more delightful than the relations of a committee among themselves, they are so intimate, and full of the delight of the common work. Yet they fall to pieces in a moment when you leave the committee. You are at once an outsider and no matter what the disposition of your old associates may be they no longer have a right to open their minds freely to you as of old. My Sunday-School Class has been better this winter than it ever was before. As the girls grow older they naturally talk more, and a new idea possesses them, the desire to hear what the whole class thinks. It is no longer a talk between me and one pupil at once. It is a furious burst of question and answer all round and my new office is that of chairman in an excited meeting, deciding who shall speak and keeping the others still. Each is crazy to hear, and at the same time eager to interrupt. We come down to Sunday School with the certainty that we are to have a taste of bliss, and we part with the feeling that it is like a flash of lightning, so bright, so soon over, and seven days must pass before we can have another. What we have had a glimpse of today we can never look at together again; for we are part of a system, we study the general lesson, and there will be a new one next Sunday. It is good for us though, we can't but return to a subject that has been made so interesting, and I'm sure each thinks and thinks it over till the new lesson drives it away. I trust you will be here to go to my next Conference with me. How do you feel about Moody & Sankey? They interest Concord very much, and the tone of the Christian Register about them is so friendly we are delighted. My donkey is lame still. I hope she can be cured before spring, I am impatient to ride her again, so are all her friends. Shall you have one come from Fayal for you, to be part of your farm? Alice Cary wants one if mine does well.

E. T. E.

Concord Thursday Mar. 15th 1877

My dear Edie [Davidson],

Last night's party was a happy thought that had a happier execution. Some of my friends blazed into great enthusiasm on being invited, especially Sarah Richardson and Abby Gourgas and Cary Wheildon, and others took it more quietly, but it had on the whole a very hearty reception from the invited. I laid deep plans, I began a week beforehand to have Sarah sweep the carpets with tea-leaves that all dust might be eradicated; I sewed carpets of unbleached cotton, and thought where I would stow the furniture. My especial aim was to be punctual, and though I failed in that at tea-time and wasn't dressed when the Bartletts came, and sat down at 6.25 instead of at 6—at 7 I came out gloriously. Come, my daughter, and take a look at the rooms. I think they have a truly festive air. White cotton all over the study & parlour except a foot or two on each side, and down the front entry from the register to the pantry-door. Nothing left but a chair or two & Father's cabinet of drawers, and rosewood book-case in the study. In the parlour *such* a vase of red & white flowers on the mantelpiece, with four candles, my elephants bearing two; and a parterre of tulips in bloom, with the *moderateur* towering over all, on the pier-table, and the piano tricked out with flowers & candles. All the Thanksgiving green up still. The dining-room had both red sofas and some extra chairs, the red cloth was on the table, and two large round Fayal baskets of cookies were on one end, on the other the graphoscopes and all the large pho-

— 1877 —

tographs, the sideboard covered with tumblers & pitchers of water. No plates. Dining-room open all the evening and there wasn't a break in the eating of cookies from 8 to 10 apparently. The guests arrived in flocks; about 40. Married pairs. How. H. Walcott, J. Smith, H. Smith, T. Todd, E. Bartlett, King, Tuttle, Whitcomb, Brooks, Sanborn; Bachelors, John Gourgas; Girls 2 Wheildons, Sarahs Richardson & Perry, M. Weir, 2 Bartletts, A. Damon & J Loring. Annie Damon was the little girl of the company and she made the most of the position; the indescribable flutter of youth and joy & excitement in "my *first* party, you know" that she kept up was as pretty as it was amusing. In one cotillon Sarahs P. & R. chose to be huffy, to take it as a personal affront when any mistake was made, and to dance or not as they chose. You wouldn't believe that two people could make that conduct so funny. We reeled and shrieked with laughing all the time. Then in the Ladies' Triumph, which Edward expounded to the ignorant. "First lady runs away with second gentleman, her own partner pursues & she returns in glory between them, and then goes down the middle again with her own partner to make all square with him, and they all right & left together with the second lady. Then first lady repeats the escapade with third gentleman" The air of the pursuing partners carried out this programme and how we did laugh. Indeed the intimate feeling we all had together of ancients playing young; and not young, after all, only because we had known each other for so many years, was as pleasant as the general gayety. When they went at ten o'clock C. Wheildon said "Goodnight! I'm the lady that has enjoyed this ball the most", and I knew every mortal had been perfectly happy. Mother says she never saw such a delightful assembly in her life. Today Pauline Shaw is here, with Robby. I had no letter from you this week, one from Susy telling the San Carlo plan. I hope you went and enjoyed it. Your pincushion adorns my bureau all the time this winter. We have letters announcing Lucy Jackson's engagement to Lieut. Spencer of the Regulars. I'm sorry for his business, but hope he'll be a man good enough to comfort me. They say he is some 8 years older than she. Goodbye dear child.

E. T. E.

Concord Mar. 26th 1877

Dear Edith,

When will we go a-photographing? I wish very much to send the pictures to Edie while she lives, and therefore I would like to avoid

— 1877 —

delay as much as we conveniently can. N.B. I say conveniently. It is doubtful work writing to her now, first whether she will ever get the letter, and besides whether she is still deceived and would enjoy the ordinary news letter, or has been told, and thirsts for sympathy & recognition of her dying state. I have decided finally, till I hear, to write two by every mail, one of the usual kind to her, the other to Susy to be given to her if she wants it. Today is the day I usually get my letter from Mentone; there is none. I'm sorry, I hoped I could forward some later news to Will Davidson before he sails. He spent Saturday forenoon with me and I liked him very much. I haven't seen him to talk to before since he grew up. To have him go straight from me to her and carry absolutely nothing to the dear child from home seemed too bad, but I thought in vain, there seemed to be nothing in the world one could send to anyone so sick that seemed fitting. But in the night I thought of my gorgeous new piqué sack, so I have sent her that, just lent it to her, to sit up in bed in, and I'm perfectly delighted. I know that will be useful if she only lives a week after it comes, and it will please her to wear it as mine even more than if I gave it to her. My poor little girl! it seems so pathetic, so few people near her who even know her by sight. Cousin Elizabeth asked me if I regretted her going. I don't. She wished it and enjoyed it more than anything we could have done for her, and that it has failed needn't make us repent it. Will Davidson thinks he shall go out on the Dakotah. Your letter Friday night was delightful, except as it brought word of your fatigue and Will's headaches. Twenty has 3 kittens. I send a note from Mother to me (sent down by Sarah yesterday) to excuse herself from dining with the family. I succeeded however in getting Twenty down cellar, and Mother seeing how gaily she trotted off with me, consented to come to the table. Tomorrow (Tuesday) your whole Bush family dine and spend the night at Nina's. If you are coming to town let us know.

E. T. E.

Note in pencil from LE enclosed in letter: "The cat cries so piteously in the closet and will not stay in her box that I should be unhappy to leave her and could not of course be agreeable. Besides it would be cruel to abuse Kitty's confidence in my affection."

Friday.

Dear Edith,

I have been shut up by a cold and such bad weather as really must

— 1877 —

delight Mark Twain, coming directly after his remarks upon our spring to the New England Society. I believe we have had only two warm sunny days in March, and one bright one, with a bad East wind, in April. We all mean to come to Boston tomorrow. Father & I will rendezvous at Metcalf's at 11. A & E & C at 2 o'clock Letter from Mentone of Mar. 19th came yesterday, saying in two weeks Edith had lost flesh very fast, and was so weak she no longer sat up. She no longer feels able to read to herself but she has made friends, who care, who come, who will do anything. That is a great piece of good news. Mail-time.
E. T. E.

Tues.
My dear Edith,

I had no chance to tell Ralph more. Edie died at half past ten Sunday morning. I had letters yesterday up to April 2nd, so did the Cabots. Arthur [Cabot] arrived Mar 29 [in Mentone] with the purpose of staying a week. He brought quantities of foreign photographs & one of Lilla, and Susy said he had an endless provision of delight & amusement for Edith. So they were perfectly happy together, and Edie had heard her brother was on the way, and it created in her no question of "why?", nothing seemed to suggest danger to her, she was that day making plans about her summer clothes. Her uncle had visited her. Balm to me as to the Cabots is the thought Arthur was there. I dreamt of her last night for the first time. It was good. It seemed as if she had come & company or business had been in the way, and at last we were quiet and she came so glad and put her arms round me. Now I would rather have had that than other kind of dream.
E. T. E.

Concord April 30th 1877
Dear Miss Dabney,

I have just heard that Mr Dabney has come in the Fredonia, I mean the Azor. I hope he will have time to come out to Pomeroy and see you & Frank & the little house, where I hope you are now living. Have you heard that my daughter is dead? She died two weeks ago in Mentone. She has been a delight to me every day of her life these twelve years; and yet her death gives me no pain at all. It interests me very much, just as everything connected with her always has, but I do not feel any sadness either for her or me. To her family I can see it is a most bitter loss, though the doctrine of "the Gates Ajar", that people after they die can teach and help those they leave behind, seems to me so reasonable and possible that I cannot help applying it here. She has had a painless, very steady, decline, and has been kept in entire ignorance of the truth, believing she was improving all the time. Her brother went out to her and arrived five days before she died, and Arthur Cabot, one of her oldest and best friends was travelling in Italy, and hearing of her state came to see her about a week earlier. Susy Willard her companion was all one could desire, all Edith's friends must be always grateful to Susy for the perfectness and ingenuity of her care. Everyone in both houses where they boarded became interested in Edith and did everything they could think of for her, so that Mrs Cabot, who loved her like an own child, said she was surrounded with love in her last days. I do not wish to ignore the homesickness she must have felt, and the wearisomeness of the solitary winter to a poor child, but I feel as if on the whole she had happiness & mercies showered upon her all the time, and best of all Arthur & Will came just in time to make her last fortnight delightful. We have not yet heard about her death. I know you have seen her and will want to hear about her so I have written you the whole. My sister Edith, and Will, and all the children have been here for a week. It has been a great festivity. While children are growing how interesting and delightful they are! And we have had beautiful spring days and Edith has enjoyed taking her little boys to her old haunts and finding the old flowers. I hope you are having a very happy housekeeping and that you will not forget when you write me to describe the house as you promised. But don't write till the Azor is gone and you have leisure again.

E. T. E.

Concord May 2nd 1877

Dear Haven,

We have been most grateful for every detail you have given us about Susy, the children and the babies, and besides Miss Amelia Prichard has related exactly how the trio [Julia, Helena, and Elizabeth] looked and seemed, with a pleasure and enthusiasm that quite satisfied us. It sounds to us, with our ideas, quite alarming that Susy should be about so soon, but I suppose you know. We should be afraid she would get too tired. Edith has just gone back to Milton with her little army. I find the children at this age far more agreeable and interesting than at any previous age, and am surprised and thankful that it is so. I supposed since the youngest is nearly four that they had all *passed* the charming age and were on the way to the "uninteresting" time. This is the first time I have seen much of them for nearly two years. When I go to Milton they are at school or at play and I am otherwise engrossed, and when they have been here I have been too busy to look at them. Edith is the tiredest most driven creature I have seen for this long time, she needs a sister very much. I wish I could go to her. Will was delightful, he stayed here three nights, which, Edith says, made his father quite homesick. He can't bear to be separated from him a day. One night we went to tea with Charles & Therchi and had a very pleasant time. Charles works very hard in his garden and Therchi thinks he tires himself too much. He has several pupils and teaches also in the High School. I think they are pretty well placed but I wish I could do a little more for them in the way of social life than I do. I hear as good news as ever of Aunt Lizzy, they say she does gain a little, and we hope she will make us a visit before she goes home. Mrs E. Hoar has gone to see her today. My dear Edith Davidson had a very painless decline, we have not yet heard how she died. We all feel that everything was done for her that man could do, and her behaviour has been noble and lovely from the beginning, always enjoying her blessings, and cheerful and affectionate, and when she learned that she could not live she was ready to die. Give much love to Susy and all the dear children.

Ellen T. Emerson.

Concord May 5th 1877

Dear Edith,

Susy [Willard] has written me all I so wished to know, just how everything happened, how my darling looked and what she said; and the whole story of the way her death came on is the most beautiful I ever heard. I won't spoil it by telling you anything till you can see the letter. Mrs Cabot writes that when Edith talked to Arthur that night when she had been told, "she showed a wondering curiosity at first, and then went on to thinking of the friends she was to meet". His letter has gone to Mrs Davidson and is coming to me next. That interests me very much, the "wondering curiosity", I think it is very natural. Eugenia is a real delight, she gets better daily. Yesterday she had a sad tumble just as she was trying to get onto the donkey, by his starting when she was trying to jump and I had her feet to push her up, down she

came full length on her back on the grass & her head struck very hard, but happily the only result is a very lame neck & chest & shoulders today. Mr Cabot has been here. I couldn't go with Father last night, but Mr C. did & Annie & Therchi & the Chamberlaines. Father saw you & Will, & said he "exchanged distant but kind regards with you". Annie says the Concord hymn was a failure but Boston was glorious. Can you come next Tuesday? Do! Goodbye, beloved, I send Violet her stamp.
                                                            Ellen T. Emerson.

Concord Wednesday May 16th 1877
My dear Edith,
Mother sends her love to you and says she and Father will come next week and spend a week with great pleasure, and Father says he should be so glad to—but he believes he is very much engaged, and for the present quite unable to leave home unless for such a visit as you made him last week, coming after tea & going before breakfast. Such are the speeches and I prophesy that they will both come, but Father will soon find his way back to Concord, where all shall be prepared for his reception, company and dressmakers & Mrs Beal, all day every day, and a social party every evening in the study, and I am going to Jamaica Plain to visit Cousin Abby, with the keys of his cabinet in my pocket. Dr [Asa] Gray came up yesterday and spent the day with the Chamberlaines, and they invited us to join the botanical excursion to Easterbrook. We had a delightful time. I heard Mr Edward Hoar talk for the first time. Mrs Cabot comes tomorrow, aren't you coming too? I expect you, of course. Mr Gam Bradford comes tomorrow to give a lecture to the club. You & Will are invited. Your stories about the children are delicious. Goodbye for I have no time for more.
                                                            E. T. E.

Saturday
My dear Edith,
Mother seems very likely to get off on Tuesday noon, but who can tell. Father is as naughty as usual, we ply him with instruction, exhortation, reproof, threat, and blandishment. No one can yet predict what he will do. Mrs Cabot has been as delightful as always, and has assisted me in making Father eat his breakfast. We took tea at Edward's last night. Edward & Annie said they had been so much improved this week by Dr

— 1877 —

Gray, Mr Gam Bradford & Prof. Bôcher that we could not get them to come home with us at 8 to Mr Alcott's conversation at our house.

E. T. E.

Concord June 2nd 1877

Dear Edith,

Father had very interesting adventures yesterday. He couldn't tell whether you put the right address on Jane's basket and letter but I think you probably did; and he says he sent the basket and paid for it. He carried the tickets to Aunt Susan and she seemed glad of them, and expressed satisfaction in the results of Eugenia's visit. He bought his book of Osgood and then went on to the Free Religious Anniversary. He saw Mr W. H. Channing on the platform and sent a man to call him down. The man first put him "in a private sort of a hole", and then sent Mr Channing to him there, who was affectionate and happy and promised to visit us later but not for a week or two. Then he returned to the platform, and Father remained "in that hole" while Mr Alger delivered his very long oration, and then went out and sat among the audience to hear Mr Channing's, which he said was very bold and very personal, right to people's faces. But no amount of cross-questioning elicited the name of anyone whom he mentioned to his face except Dr Channing & Theodore Parker, who both are dead, Father admitted, so I guess who was the present and living. Then Father went to Parker's & dined, and came to the Old South, where he seems to have had a pleasant afternoon, was satisfied with Mr Clarke & Mr Hale and charmed with Dr Holmes, especially when he recited Old Ironsides. "He stood there with the look of a man whom the Lord is touching and filling with many words, and as if he forgot his audience and gave himself up to it, and went through it in a glorious dream". He also praised his "coquetting with that picture of his." He didn't see Aunt S., thinks she wasn't there "for there was so much social life round the platform afterwards I think I sh^d have seen her." They gave him a bunch of roses. There, no more time, but I thought I must after so long a silence write you a little letter.

E. T. E.

Concord Saturday June 9 1877

My dear Edith,

Our week has been very interesting. Monday I spent on my daugh-

— 1877 —

ter's letters, and read them to Mother. Tuesday was to me a grand gala, we had so much company. Mr R. Laird Collier had caught Father the week before and asked him to set a time when he would see him and Father set Tuesday. On Saturday he wrote asking permission to bring an English youth who is at Cambridge in the Divinity Sch., up with him. Father consented. On Monday we had a letter from an Englishman enclosing his letter of introduction and asking when he could come so we arranged thus—the same day and the same dinner should do for both, but Mr Collier should have Father to himself from 12 to 3 o'clock dinner, and Mr Carpenter should have Father to himself after Mr Collier's departure and stay all night. Well they came, Mr Collier and Mr Norman at noon, and oh! what pleasure to me was the talk! I had to leave the table to go to Teacher's Meeting. After the meeting I had one of those consults with Mr Reynolds which are very satisfactory. Coming home I stopped in to see Aunt Lizzy. Father had seen her on Saturday, Mother on Sunday, but I hadn't till now. She looked well and told me some stories about Aunt Mary that I had never heard. And finally she began to extol the Psalms which had expressed all her raptures for her all the spring. She is coming to Bush this next week. On reaching home I found that Mr Collier & Mr Norman had gone at half past four and Father was sitting with Mr Carpenter. When he saw me he came up stairs and said "It is long after six and he doesn't say a word about going." Poor man, he had quite forgotten that Mr C. was invited to spend the night, and poor Mr Carpenter rather! Father had been ostentatiously exhibiting his fatigue to remind him that it was time to go to the train. Did you ever? I had tea with speed, and after tea the wagon, & Father & I in front, Mother and Mr C behind rode about till 8.30. It was warm and pleasant. We saw the Minute-Man, stopped at Edward's, and then we went to ask the Chamberlaines to dine the next day. The next morning Mr Carpenter went to see Louisa Alcott and then took the 10 train. He certainly had a funny visit, and behaved beautifully through its extraordinary scenes. I wish I had time to tell you how this family behaved. Wednesday came the Chamberlaines and little Charles and his parents. General conversation seemed impossible at dinner, so Annie and I, side by side, had a peaceful confidential chat. On Thursday noon Mr Cabot came, and for the first time since February I had the pleasure of working too and knowing I was helping. He only stayed till Friday afternoon, but something was accomplished, and he said he felt now that we were getting hold of the task. Today Edward

— 1877 —

is in the agonies of Examinations, tonight at 6.30 and hereafter for some time, imagine him a prey to infuriated parents. Goodbye darling. Tell me how you do yourself.

Your loving sister E. T. E.

Concord June 28th 1877

Dear Edith,

I should prefer coming to Naushon in July and I agree that it would be better for Father and Mother, but it must depend now on Cousin Charlotte's convenience. I sent a note to her this morning. I think there is no doubt that Mother will come with us, and I am glad she should come once when she is comparatively well. Father is much more sure to remain peacefully there when no one is at home. Aunt Lizzy came last night, and took tea with Mother and me, for Father went yesterday to Commencement and to dine with the President at the City of Boston's dinner. He stayed all night and goes today to the Phi Beta Kappa, hoping to hear an excellent poem from Mr Stedman, so Mother and I were alone. Aunt Lizzy makes many pretty speeches. Once when I was tired she said "If you were to break off suddenly and go to heaven, I don't know what I should say, seeing that your Father and Mother and I are close behind you. It isn't that I dread for you. But what I do dread is that you should have lonely years of helplessness to bear, and I dread it for Edith too. So I hope you will both be careful not to do too much now." I thought I had remembered more of her speeches but they have escaped me. Day before yesterday Father visited me in my room and made a tour of it, beholding with fresh interest every object in it, for he hasn't been up there for months. On the closet-door are pinned the pictures Cameron & Don made me, and as I described to him how they were made I was again struck with the fact that Cameron is endowed with the faculty of invention. Father did enjoy those pictures exceedingly. I find that an old letter from you is always a great card, and that the new ones bear reading aloud once a week or so. We never get tired of the stories of our bairns, and Father forgets so fast that they are new to him every time. That day in my room he was pleased with every photograph and looking at himself & Mr Forbes with Ralph he exclaimed "That is excellent of Mr Forbes. How well he always looks! You can't put him so that he doesn't. It is because the Lord made him so. He never appears to disadvantage."* Aunt Susan Jackson is moving up here, dined here today. So did Mrs Tileston & Lily Keyes, and the

*See photo, Volume I, p. 487.

last two and Mother have gone to a Conference at Walden. Lizzy Storer was a delegate to it. We suppose she will come home with them.
E. T. E.

Concord June 29th 1877

My dear Edith,

 Last night Father came home very happy from Cambridge. He didn't arrive till 7.30 and I went to bed at 8, and talked myself a great deal of the time so that he might eat his supper, if he had talked he wouldn't have eaten. The delight to me was that he was just like other people, truly overjoyed to see Aunt Lizzy & Lizzy Storer, eager to tell them, charmed with their words, tasting for once the delight of society, instead of feeling so hopelessly withdrawn as he usually does. He had seen Mr Stedman and talked with him. He dwelt much on that, evidently felt that it was an event, the long-desired point on both sides finally reached. Still there has been no description, no expression of pleasure in the man himself, and the poem he said was not a telling poem. Neither does he feel any impulse to describe President Hayes, he says they acknowledged each other's acquaintance, but there is no burst at all on that subject. While every mention of Mr Bayard is accompanied with some words of commendation. "He is a pleasant man, he means what he says", or "What a pity he should spoil his oration by making it so long! His manner is perfect, natural and quiet, he simply speaks as to friends in a parlour", or "he is evidently a beloved man, like Samuel J. May." The City dinner he is truly enthusiastic about. Never comes to that without some cry of joy. I hope it may be because he succeeded with his own speech, for Aunt Lizzy says the paper affirms that he made one. I haven't asked him if he did, But I think he couldn't feel so happy if he had made a failure. The real source of his enjoyment however was Dr Holmes who sat by him "and having no one else to speak to he devoted himself to me. He is a wonderful creature! Always admirable!!" There darling I've told you all I yet know. Now I desire to return to Lizzy & Aunt Lizzy. Did you know Charles got two teeth last week?

Thy affectionate sister
E. T. E.

July 7 1877

Dear Edith,

 I will surely come on Tuesday morning by a nine o'clock train, and it looks as if I could do no more. Mother exclaims this morning that she will not go to Naushon, she dreads the journey and would rather see you in Milton. Father she says is of a willing mind and when she proposed inviting a lady he dreaded, said to her "You had better do it while I am at Naushon." Lizzy Storer has gone. Eight happy days we have had. Mother has especially enjoyed her sympathy, for she is by nature on the side of Woman, Dumb Animals, and the marvellous, and our friends so seldom are. I have been struck by the quickness of her mind. It is equal to Aunt Lizzy's. We have had great frolics several times too, and each mortal in the house has taken comfort in Lizzy in our separate ways. I wish you could have come. Edward Simmons is here, very charming. John Jackson had a little son born June 17th, He came up to spend the 4th with Aunt Susan and help her move in.

E. T. E.

Naushon

Dear Mother,

We have been so on the go since I came, or receiving calls from the Mansion-house that I have had no chance to write you a letter. I haven't yet bestowed your presents on the children. I am waiting for a rainy or other vacant time. Edith & Will seem very well and happy. Ralph is positively a big boy, rather rough, but I think very charming and actually handsome. To see the true mariner expression in his burnt countenance and blue eyes fills me with pride. The dear Violet is brown and stout, affectionate and useful by nature, such a faithful follower to her aunt and assistant to her mother, it is perfectly satisfactory. Then Cameron's manners are still perfect. He took tea alone with me and the grace with which he offered me everything before he took it was very striking. There was a piece of chocolate-cake. He offered it to me. I refused. "Won't you divide it with me then?" he asked with a most attractive smile. "No, but I'll cut you off a piece of it," I said. "No, thankyou, if you won't take any, I don't want any." Now don't you think that is manners? I thought it remarkable.

[Unsigned]

Naushon, August 8th 1877

Dear Mother,

Give my love to Father and tell him he made a mistake in going home so soon and leaving the comforts of this house, the sight & hearing of these charming children, the health of the bath, and the variety of the guests. If he had stayed one day longer he would have seen Edith & Will go off for a ride on horseback, could there be a more agreeable sight? Will has bought a new horse named "Montenegro" and Edith went thereon. I wished you had come yourself. When we were at Gay Head I wished for you, and thought you ought to see it. The fact is you could, if you only thought you could. To be seasick doesn't injure people. Our dear babes were all there acting out their natures. Ralph climbing cliffs and jumping out to rocks which the surf broke over, with Jim Russell and Handasyde, Violet trotting beside her aunt and carefully collecting the various "little rubbish" (as her parents call her stores) which she thinks pretty, but always keeping an eye on the scenery in general as well as on the scraps of shell & sea-weed. Cameron & Don and Baby tearing along in the neighborhood of their parents, C. & D. disdaining to be led, but Edward quite willing. The Mamma often obliged to turn round and say "Now if any of that red clay goes home, REMEMBER, if you touch it without a blouse on, you'll lose it all, I shall throw it away." "Stop, stop! I can't have any of that clay hugged up to those jackets" etc etc. I met Don with a large partially decayed crab in each arm. He laboured along with them through the deep sand for some time. At last I heard both drop and turned round to help him pick up his treasures, but he smiled with the air that said "I have outgrown such follies", and we embarked without them, while Violet brought home every bit of her collection. Mr W. H. Channing came yesterday to the Mansion-House, and Edith and I are to dine there today. Mary is there with all her flock. Give my love to Cousin Charlotte & to Edward and Annie & blessed Charles.   E. T. E.

Concord. Aug 9th 1877

Dear Father,

Will confesses that he intercepted at Wood's Hole the proofs of "Perpetual Forces" and sent them to Concord to you without my seeing them. I wish you would keep them till I come home next Tuesday, for I want to see them. You might meanwhile send them to Mr Cabot for him to see your corrections and add his. I have several remarks to make if I could only remember what the places are. One is on p. 9 near the top; is "crowner" a real naturalized word fit to appear in "a prent book" over your august signature? Then don't you think the remark on "Bonaparte" reading the geogr. of Europe like telescopes etc etc, too ellip-

tical altogether? I do. Please write me a letter and tell me what you think of the article in print. How do you like the beginning? I think it is confusingly abrupt and varied, for a page or more; after that it becomes perfectly satisfactory, and on the whole I am proud of it. There are two versions in your own hand of the sentence about nature's having a fore-looking tenderness & equal regard for the next generation
1 { and the next and the next and the fourth & the fifth
2 { and the next and the third and the fourth & the fifth
Which do you like best?
There I believe that is all I have to say on business. Now I will tell you some tales about your beloved Baby & Don. Yesterday morning Baby was naughty upstairs and his Mamma below had some inkling of it. Therefore as she, passing through the entry, saw him coming down after the storm was past she asked "Have you been a naughty boy, Baby?" He looked up in despair to his nurse who was near the head of the stairs,—"Adelaide, *what* shall I say?" "What shall you say? Why, tell the truth." And Baby very humbly made his confession. In the afternoon I saw two very small brown creatures in disreputable hats some way off on the hills, apparently eating berries. So I walked in that direction, and when I reached them I found they were Baby & Don and that they had a pail with them which they had nearly filled with excellent berries, not a red one, nor a stick or leaf to be seen in the pail. "Aunt Ellen," said Don, "when both are talking at once, and the oldest is saying what is most important, oughtn't the youngest to keep still?" Why, have you and Baby been talking both at once? "Yes. When you came Baby and I were nearly cross. Because we were both talking, so *nobody* could hear, and what I said was important. And Baby was telling about a little Indian boy that wanted to sell us stones at Gay Head and I knew as much about it as he did, and more, so it wasn't important. And it made me forget what I was saying." Baby didn't seem to hear the recital of this woful tale, he was wholly occupied with the bigness of the berries he had just found, and presently said "Don!" "What?" "Weren't you kind, Don, to show me this splendid place? Weren't you?" Don agreed that he was and said "There has got so many blackberries here because it's Blackberry Hill. I believe *I* knew this place when I was born almost." He afterwards explained "I knew it last season, & the season before that, and the season before that, and I guess I was a pretty small baby then."

E. T. E.

— 1877 —

Naushon August 15th 1877

Dear Miss Dabney,

You see from my date that I am making a visit to Edith, and enjoying all the pleasures of seeing my sister and watching the employments and behaviour of the five little bears. When I first came Sarah had not been home a week, and I was very much shocked by her appearance. I find Will & Edith are as much afraid as I am that she will not live long. She looks a little better now than she did at first but has to be always careful. The other morning she took me to a pretty place in the woods called the Deer Parlour and we sat there two or three hours. She told me stories about her English visits which were as interesting as reading a novel. Then one afternoon she spent here while Father & Mr Cabot were here and told them about her months at Virginia Springs, the place, the doctor, the Confederate General, the rebel ladies, the negroes. We felt as if we had seen it. When Father & Mr Cabot were here our family went on the Azalea to Gay Head. That is the best excursion that there is from here I think. Mr Cabot had never seen the place, and I wanted him to see it in splendor. When the colours and the grand forms suddenly came in sight, I had what I wanted, he enjoyed it as he ought to. The last time the Azor came in I had a very kind letter from Alice Dabney about my daughter. It was after I wrote to you that I received the account of her death. They did tell her she was going to die a day and a half before. At first she couldn't believe there was no hope of getting home, and asked if it was wrong to think of it. But very soon her thoughts all turned forward and they said she spoke sometimes with a sort of wondering curiosity, sometimes with pleasure (at the remembrance of those she should meet) of death. The next morning she attended as far as she could to what she wanted done, and wished them all to stay as much as possible by her bed. The next morning at ten she was unconscious and died before eleven. When I first came to Naushon where I have found her always of late years, it brought her back with delightful vividness. August 16th. Alice [Forbes] Cary is coming down today and I hope I shall hear some Fayal news from her. I am very fortunate in being here when she comes, and Mary Russell is here too. Our guest at this house is Effie Lowell and she has Lotta with her. She is a treasure, and Lotta is a charming child. I hope you are beginning to think of coming to make some visits in Massachusetts. Do you read the Unitarian Review? They have sent it to us lately and we are delighted with it. Since Effie came down we have taken to "improving our minds" by learning about Montenegro etc. Such things you always know. I am glad you do. Do you have time to read much? Don't feel it proper to postpone writing to me very long.

Ellen T. Emerson.

Naushon August 17th 1877

Dear Haven,

I have been reading your letter to Edith and enjoyed every word of it. I have begun to knit three jackets for the trins, but as it will be long before I finish them I am rather aiming at the size they will want a year hence than what they want now. Effie Lowell is here and is teaching me how to knit the ornamental border. I can't tell you how happy we all are in her visit, she is so handsome besides having all the virtues and glories. She came to Concord to see Edward's baby, while Aunt Lizzy was at our house. Little Charles Lowell E. was christened on Friday July 13th at our house, by Mr W. H. Channing, who christened Edward & Edith. He came to make us a visit, and had a public Conversation with Mr Alcott on the Wednesday evening before, and everyone was delighted with all he said. Edward was present, and as he listened with joy and sympathy, he suddenly thought he should like to have his baby christened by this man. When he consulted Annie she was pleased. Edward appeared at breakfast-time the next morning and proposed it, and everyone rejoiced. The next day Father and I went to see Mr & Mrs J. R. Lowell off to Spain on the "Parthia" and, with hosts of other people, went way down the harbour and returned on the tug. Hatty Putnam was one of the friends present and she said "Effie meant to come, but she gave out this morning." I at once asked if Effie was in the neighborhood, and Hatty said "Yes, she has come for the summer." We sent at once for her and Hatty and had a most beautiful visit from them. Effie was the perpetual feast that she always is to me, and Aunt Lizzy set her as high as I wished she should. She said that it was seldom one saw that grand cast of person whose smile was as noble and beautiful as her repose. Aunt Lizzy's month with us was a beautiful one. Always when she is talking I wish every word could be kept. She told me many stories of the family in old times, before our day. I wish she could write them, but I suppose she wouldn't be willing to try, and if she did try she might find she wasn't strong enough. You know that Mrs Storer considers her hopelessly ill, and perhaps she is, but practically she is as well as ever by day, though she seldom has a good night. She walks and rides and sews as much as ever; and works at home. The day I last saw her she had swept her two parlours herself. And she is happier than formerly because she is now considered sick and nothing is expected of her which is a daily comfort, when a person feels unable, and that is what she has felt almost all her life. Mother has been unusually well all summer and Father too. I think the constant company has made them eat better, and partly accounts for it. Father is just publishing an article in the N.A. Review. He came down here the last day of July and Mr Cabot and Handasyde with him. They stayed a week, and went to Gay Head, seeing it to great advantage. Our children are growing into the second stage of life, no longer babies, though in fact there is a good deal of baby in every soul of them, even Ralph who is now eleven. Violet has been made very happy by Lotta Lowell's visit, she appreciates the comfort of having a little girl to play with. They have pleased all their elders by taking long rides together on horseback. Violet has never before been really glad to go. Ralph is allowed to take them out sailing. He is so cautious that his Aunt often fears he will be a coward, but his parents are content because they are sure that he will run no risks, and they can safely trust the children with him.

Canton Aug 23d   I didn't have time to finish my letter at Naushon. Edward & Annie came down and brought little Charles, so we made a large and laughing family. There was a great deal of carrying-on till I came away on Monday morning. The baby was the delight of all his little cousins, and Effie took him very often, and carried him to and fro, and exclaimed that he was a most huggable child. There, I hope you will call this an old-fashioned letter. And still more I hope that hay-cold may bring you to Concord this month. Love to Susy, the children & our twins.

E. T. E.

Concord Aug. 29th 1877

Dear Edith,

The time of silence is past, this week I shall be able to write and you shall have letters. Monday night Mother walked into my room and said "I have a great yearning for my dear Edith. Why doesn't she write? Isn't it a great while?" The next morning I felt extreme comfort when the good fat letter came. Seeing it was to Mother I forbore to read it, but when she did wake and my work was done I went in and lay down by her and we had a good time over it. I was very much impressed by

— 1877 —

Baby's conscience and religion. It is a wonderful instance—that right seed received in good soil and coming up so hopefully when you never knew you had planted it there. Oh Edith dear, Ralph seems to me unfaithful still. It does look as if the one virtue of real faithfulness was all that was wanting to make him a most promising child. And—I'm going to tell you what I think because Pauline says she is glad when people do and she thinks we owe frankness to the people we love, and then I told Ida she thought so, and Ida said she agreed, she felt as if living without hearing your friends' judgment on your life was like carrying on a study without having any chance to recite, you never knew whether you were doing well or ill, so I proceed—I feel as if faithfulness in him could hardly be cultivated without immense faithfulness in you, e.g. if you desire him to be faithful in dressing the only way to make him so, to bring him to a clear sense of what is required of him is to show an exactness and regularity in looking him over, corresponding to that which you expect him to use in doing, until he proves to have formed a habit which may be depended on enough to allow you to alter your form of vigilance to another a little less wearing on you and showing more trust in him, but serving as check or stimulus enough to keep him from going back. I think he needs first of all to be put through one or two dressings under your own eye to get a distinct idea of the order of performances, the manner of doing things, and the diligence with which they should be done. I don't think any one of these points is very clear to him, or could be made so by mere talking. He doesn't seem to appreciate at all that a precept is to be kept in mind and acted on; he needs to learn this, and how can he except by finding that you do perpetually care for it, and not only at moments? There is one more thing I thought of several times. We ask of each of the children serious efforts at self-control, whether it is of Ralph to stop scratching, collect his scattered powers, and set to work in earnest, of Violet to keep back her contemptuous words and be agreeable when she feels hateful, of Cameron to stand still and bring his wandering mind to bear on the subject in hand, or to lay down the sceptre he has unjustly seized, but feels so at home and so glorious in wielding, and we have no real right to do it when we are not exercising as vigorous a self-control ourselves, and successfully, so that power and peace and help are in our commands, and on this point I want to tell you a little tale Lily K. told me. She was up at the Tilestons and the children rushed into the room bringing one to their Father for justice, she having just been guilty of cruelty to a younger who was of the party, screaming and showing her wounds. Mr Tileston was enraged, he started up and towards the offender, but didn't touch her, stopped and sat down. He didn't speak nor stir, he was struggling for self-control. Absolute awful silence succeeded, Lily was frightened, so were the children, the screams stopped, nobody dared stir. At last he smiled upon the trembling wretch and took her in his lap and began to talk to her. Lily said she learned such a lesson and thought the children did as nothing else could have taught of the wrongness of anger. On this point, one thing more. When children's cheerful rolling round upsets ink or does other great and unexpected harm, it seems just to me not to be angry, as that was not a sin, and they had better take the trouble of attending to it, but not get a word of the same severity as when they tease one another, disobey etc. My own dear pussy-cat, I want you to understand that I feel that I need to put all this in practice as much as any one, and that I am delighted on the whole with your management of the children, and have a good deal of doubt about writing it at all, for I wouldn't for the world have you feel that you have a critic round when I have the privilege of being with you and the children. Now to return to your letter. Don's birthday was beautiful, and he certainly seems to have a Sunday-child's character. When the presents were given Mother felt unhappy that she had sent nothing. She did mean to send "the Children in the Wood" by me to be ready for this occasion, but couldn't find it. Mr Forbes's speech, and Don's pretty bow to Mrs Emmons were special sugar-plums to me, and Mother also fully appreciated them. Now I'll tell about Eugenia. She came down Wednesday night with Annie Kent to get the donkey for a little ride. I asked her how she was getting along about her wedding, when it was to be, and where. She said she had pretty nearly made up her mind on September, but there seemed to be great difficulty about where. It couldn't be at home, the room was so small, and to invite her friends to so remote a place as the Lincoln church and yet have no party or spread seemed forlorn. Mother at once offered our house. Eugenia smiled much pleased, said she would ask her mother and Mr Dodge. I jumped at the idea. What a pleasure it will be! Father on being consulted said it was a very proper thing, and he had no objection. The next time I saw Eugenia she said Mr Dodge never seemed more pleased with anything in his life, and that this prospect had changed the occasion from forlornness to festivity. Aunt Susan brought Lucy on Sunday to dine with us. Annie & Edward surprised us by driving up and staying to dinner. Cousin Mary Simmons came to tea, but then our dinner guests were gone. She listened with zeal to my account of the approaching S.S. Convention, said she should stir up their parish to attend. Monday came Mary Watson. We rode the donkey, we went on the river, we quarreled, and sewed and discoursed. Lizzy Simmons took tea here Monday and oh! how I enjoyed her & Mary's talk on D. Deronda, after hearing Mr Channing's & Sarah's & Effie's. This is all I can say today. Are you any better? Your loving sister.

Concord Sept 13th 1877

Dear Edith,

My hopes of writing to you haven't been realized, have they? I am doing a marking and making a visit to Mother, and she wakes pretty early, and the cold renders me unable to write much till the sun gets high. My hand trembles I don't know why. This is a specimen of my hand-writing 30 years hence. I hope you will succeed in making all your little visits, and your new household I think sounds promising. Mother has been very weak and has more suffering than usual these last ten days, she looks very white and delicate. Edward has taken her in hand and I hope she'll improve. Last night Mr Dodge's Father & Mother came to visit Aunt Susan and Mother and I went up to take tea with them. I carried her beef-tea in a bottle. You ought to have seen Mother all the evening having an argument with Mr Dodge, she was in her element. I sat off and viewed the scene, and sometimes felt like supporting Mr Dodge's side of the thing. Father is always saying delectable things. I just looked into the study and he said "I just heard screaming of boys out yonder and I went out for I thought they were after my toad—my long-tails—but instead of boys I brought in these things." This means that he was afraid it was someone trying to catch the donkey, and found he was mistaken, but being out he brought in some pears. Mrs William Reynolds was here working on carpets and he was altogether too funny for her; when she heard his report of his day in Boston, given in the above style, she got to laughing so that she didn't know what to do. Many a sentence I mean to lay up for you but I forget. I'm personally deeply disappointed that you aren't coming, but you are right.

E. T. E.

The Emerson house with RWE standing near the East Door and the donkey Graciosa in the yard, late 1870s.

— 1877 —

Concord Sept 18th 1877

Dear Edith,

Your letter I have just received at breakfast and read to Father. We find it a succession of tales of surpassing interest and delight. How good that the baby [Malcolm Forbes] is a boy and all right, and what fun for Mrs Forbes to make her secret preparations so beautifully and seasonably and have them not in vain. How is Sarah Malcolm? That you leave out; is she scared or glad? I'm glad you are going to Mt. Desert today. Father I hope will see you. I hope Ralph will come to the wedding [Eugenia Jackson to Mr. Dodge]. Of course I shall *take* time to dress the lamb. Yesterday we spent the day in a store on Summer St. viewing the procession. C. & T., the Bartletts, Mr King & Cyrus Hubbard & I. It was a most happy day. We had more windows than people, opera-glasses, orders of procession and a capital view. There was an elevator and in the halts of the procession we amused ourselves riding up & down, and once I visited the roof with Charles & enjoyed the beautiful harbour, Milton & Dorchester heights etc. I was anxious a little about Father, who would not stay with us. But at night he came home having been carefully watched and cosseted by his body-guard every moment and having seen from the platform on the Common the arrival of the procession and its various windings & unwindings into place around the monument, and the addresses of Cols. to their veteran Regts. & many other interesting sights. Mother is better. Aunt Lizzy took tea with us

[Unsigned]

Dear Edith,

Absolutely no chance to write. Ralph's coming & behaviour were delightful indeed to Father, Mother, Annie, Edward & me. But not to himself I fear, as no other boy was there. The house looked beautifully, the day was perfection, the bride & bridegroom were all that could be desired, the monk as Edward called the priest was a most pleasant easy gentleman in the company and read the service with seriousness & heart. But he wore his black & white robes, and a black rope round his waist. Eugenia wore Lizzy's & Lucy's wedding dress, Kate Hoar & Annie's veil, and had colour in her cheeks and looked well. Cambridge friends & neighbours congratulated our family upon acquiring Mr Dodge, with much affection and even enthusiasm for him in all they said. Aunt Susan & Oscar were hardly able to keep back their tears.

— 1877 —

Fanny Brown alone remained over night in this house, oh no! my dear Ralph who helped me to move back the furniture. Mother was able to come to ceremony

[Unsigned]

Concord Sept 24th 1877

My dear Edith,

I never thought that you didn't know Mother was sick. She was taken sick the morning before the wedding. It isn't very severe but she hasn't been out of bed since except that she went down, saw the ceremony, kissed Eugenia and came straight back. Now I'll plunge into some description of the wedding. Frances B. & Lidian came on Wednesday and washed vases, filled pincushions and candlesticks and put your room & redroom into their best dress; Thursday Lizzy Bartlett and Therchi, Lidian & Annie Kent, also Oscar were here by ten, not long after George & Bradford Bartlett & Alicia arrived. Mr Bradford Bartlett rehung the dining-room curtains, Lizzy cleared out the pantry, and did errands and then helped him. The amount of scarlet flowers collected for decoration was amazing. The parlour long-window-curtain was arranged as it was for you, and the bower over it was made of a vine with huge green balloon-seed-vessels and white gilliflowers on an evergreen background. At dinner time many went home and as the caterer had the dining-room we dined on the back-piazza. It was very pleasant. I made the great mistake of not going up to dress till people began to arrive. I thought it would take but a few minutes and it was a long process. So I didn't come down till Eugenia was actually ready, and received none of the guests, and had no idea who they were, many of them, a state of things which may or may not have been queer and uncomfortable as far they were concerned but certainly oppressed me with a sense of shame and failure and put me at real disadvantage from beginning to end. Eugenia arrived in her travelling-dress looking extremely fresh and pretty, and dressed in my room, Mr Dodge asked me where he was to be kept. This very serious question had never occurred to me before, I strove in vain to remember where Will was kept 12 yrs. ago. Lizzy Bartlett & Lidian were dressing in the nursery, Eugenia in my room, Mother & Father in theirs, guests were already arriving and taking off their things in redroom & your room. The garret was too hot. Aunt Susan thought the red-room-closet would be

[Unsigned]

— 1877 —

Wed. Sept 26th 1877

Dearest girl,

To go on where I left off I decided to put Mr Dodge in the dining-room. Was that right? Then Kate & Sarah Gately dressed Mother in the new black silk wh. Mme. Conneau brought from Paris and Jane cut, and Sally's present of a pale blue crocheted shawl, and she went down. Father met her at the foot of the stairs and escorted her along the entry and through the aisle opened for the bride and placed her in her chair. I thought she looked perfectly lovely. Immediately after Father & Mother came in, Mr Dodge & Eugenia descended. The aisle from the ceremony to the fire-place was kept open, as at Edward's wedding, so everyone saw very well. There was a cricket placed for Eugenia, and when the time came she knelt. Mr Dodge had, naturally, no thought of doing any such thing, and stood. The priest waited a minute and then asked him to kneel, and he did. All the young men present felt for him. But as the priest said the prayers as if he meant them, and blessed them with affection, we felt better, and hope Mr Dodge did. My dear Ralph escorted me up to speak to them, and was introduced to Mrs Dodge Sr. Then I lost him and saw company for some time. After the spread we signed the parchment, and when our dear Ralph sat down to write, the deep silent interest and amused shaking of everyone in the room, during the ten minutes which that very neat signature occupied was delightful to the aunt, as they were chiefly strangers. The little children who could walk danced and played games on the grass in the E. yard, with Miss Bartlett and made a pretty spectacle for the cake-eaters in the dining-room. Mother came down to dine today. She's almost well.

Concord Oct 18th 1877.

My dear sister,

I am still busy and active, but must express my sympathy with your sickness by writing you one real letter. I wonder whether you are at home. Tell Will to write me word. You know Edward belongs to the Fortnight Saturday Club. It was at his house week before last. Mrs Sanborn told me the Club had a delightful meeting, and she was amazed to hear how well Edward read, "he promises to read as well as your Father." I asked if Father was there. No. So I came home full of wrath and found the poor man hadn't been told. He was disappointed indeed to hear what he had missed. Mother said she went and that Edward had read extracts from Froissart etc, lovely stories she had never heard before. I have had the pleasure of riding to Bedford one day and found his spirits were high. He was pleased he said to take me over that road to show me the extent of his practice. Almost two thirds of the houses call him their doctor. He told me of course many stories, and when he found me writing a letter he scolded hard. I had seized the opportunity while he visited a patient. I said my brother and sister were both great puzzles to me, I couldn't understand in the least the philosophy that guided their actions. He said "Oh some work is interesting and some work is merely tedious. All public work except School-Comm. work I find tedious, alleviated sometimes by the society in which one works. But all these little corners and fragments of time should be redeemed from work altogether and devoted to pure recreation. When I get one I always read, and a little read of ten minutes cheers one up and is the best thing one gets." I wrote to Eugenia and asked her from you whether she would like a clock or preferred something else. Mother is going to Boston today to buy a new cover for the study-chair which spent last year up in your room. Kate is covering mine with the green moreen and exclaims "If it does be right when it's done I don't care, but if it don't I shall be crazy" and when she had covered the arms—"There! his hands do be dresht, if the rest of him don't." On Tuesday night I was invited to a drop-in at Sarah Perry's. I had a beautiful time. First I was gentleman and danced with Alice Rattray Wheeler. Next I danced with Mr Jonathan Wheeler in "All the Way to Boston", and was very much pleased that he should dance. Next a cotillon with Mr Blanchard. We had a great deal of fun, and flattered ourselves that we had danced very well. Then I danced Merry Dance with Mr King and had a great frolic, he looked as serious and mild and behaved as antically as he could, and we contrived to get various extra down-the-middles and scandalize the other dancers. He said he had been much depressed since he drew the map of the Seat of War for me, for the next time he saw a map he found he had made a mistake. I strove to cheer him. Father won't wait another minute.

Thy sister.

Concord Monday P.M.

My dear Edith,

Edwin Barrett is to be married again on Wednesday and I have made up my mind to go to the reception. I propose to wear my light silk and to wrap myself up in Mother's cloak, and wear my brown plush hood, go in the horse cars from Nina's where I will dress & return thither at 8.00, take 9.30 train to Milton & stay a few hours with you the next morning, coming in at 11 or 12 to meet Father. There is no *need* is there of a wedding bonnet? Shall I look too familiar & too much at home without any bonnet & shawl? Answer me at Will's office. I shall go to Boston early on Wednesday morning to buy me the cheap winter bonnet which must be my best till January, and do a little New Years shopping. If I *must* wear a bonnet to the reception will you send me one to Nina's, that is if you have one which will be the thing, or shall I borrow something of Nina, or Mary Blake? and shall I wear the white silk shawl you gave me? You see I don't know anything. We have just bought a new cow, a Jersey. John went to E. Lexington for her. "Is he going to drive the cow home in a carriage," asked Mother in entire earnest, "or will he walk with her?" It sounded so like a question about a bride, that we were seized with laughing and haven't yet recovered. He did walk with her for 3 hours. Emma (Hatch) Kellum has a little boy. Julia Paine drove Georgy Schuyler over here last Wednesday for half an hour's visit. 'Twas very good of both of them and we enjoyed it. Aunt Lizzy is reported as much better, Mrs Storer is encouraged to think she may live and be well I hear. Uncle George is just leaving Concord for the winter. Mr Channing went to church with us last night. I didn't know it was his first appearance there, but he told Mother he had never heard Mr Reynolds before. I wish every one had been there the sermon was so good. Tuesday I went to tea at Mrs Edward Damons, beautiful family, good time, Mrs Williams sang.

Goodbye beloved. E. T. E.

Concord Oct 30th 1877

Dear Aunt Lizzy,

Thankyou very much for writing to me. The letter arrived in the midst of the pleasures of the Sunday-School Convention which was as happy an occasion as I expected it to be, but oh! so short! The meetings seemed much shorter than they usually have and the time at home like nothing. We had Mr & Mrs Hussey of Billerica (Edith's room), Mr & Mrs Tiffany of W. Newton (Red-room), Mr & Mrs Brown of Brookline (Nursery), Mr Weston of Warwick and Mr Gibbs of Athol. These last, billeted on us, were as much a part of the delight as anyone; Mr Weston, a little Plymouth boy when Mother was married, she doesn't remember, but he regarded her as the glory of Plymouth and so did his elder sister whom Mother does remember with affection, one of her Sunday-scholars there. He was a quiet gray-haired man. I was a little afraid the first day he wasn't having as good a time as the rest but soon found out how happy he was to see Mother, and he proved to be at the height of enjoyment all the time. Mr Gibbs was so young that I took him for a teacher, but he made friends with Mr Brown and told him he had been formerly a Methodist minister, but at the end of his first settlement felt he didn't belong and made up his mind to leave the Conference but the U^n. Society of Athol sent for him. Mr Channing came and Mr Hall of Worcester and you can guess how shocked Mother was when she found where I meant to put them—Mr Channing in the little room over the kitchen & Mr Hall in the passage called the lower bath-room. She said I shouldn't, but then she failed to contrive any other place for them, and when she saw the rooms she was reconciled. They looked positively pretty, and Mr Channing expressed great delight in his. Mr Hall was moved into Edith's room after the Husseys went and he said to Mrs Bartlett that he "hated to leave that funny little room." She and I occupied the S. room at the end of the wing, and heard Mr Hall & Mr Channing when they came up stairs rejoice that they were side by side. In my room we had two beds for teachers, two ladies from Canton and Miss Hussey slept there on Wednesday night, and the next night Mrs Elliot Cabot and Mrs Walter Cabot. Mr Quimby of E. Bridgewater was here by day and at Mrs Whitcomb's by night. Then the second day we had Mr Muzzey and four teachers to dine, and Mr Reynolds, Dr Stebbins and Mr Shippen to tea, besides various ladies. That was all the company we had, and it seemed only too small, and far from anyone's being tired we were all rested by it. It was much less work to get ready for than a Thanksgiving because there was no pie-baking, and not such a grand & various dinner, and as there was no responsibility whatever, and the days were passed sitting peacefully in church, there was no fatigue for me at the time, and very little for Mother, except she was anxious at meal-times for fear people wouldn't be helped. Our visitors all brought the true Convention-high-spirits, soon made one happy family, and seemed to think they were having one of the best of meetings. Of course I only saw them at the table, I don't know what went on in the parlour, but I can testify that they were very gay, sometimes frolicsome at the table. I changed the whole arrangement of the company at every meal, and that seemed to amuse them. Our Kate Rouse was here to help and she liked the spree, and

— 1877 —

told me "Margaret don't like company very much but Sarah do like it fearfully." And sure enough when all had gone and Sarah set the tea-table for three again she remarked "It looks lonesome here tonight, looks dreary." I hope to go out to Milton tomorrow night. I haven't seen Edith since I left her sick at Naushon. Sarah Malcolm's baby is the smallest I ever saw, and is very pretty though his nose is too large. She got up perfectly well, and he is thriving. Father is well, he eats his meals very easily, more so than in the summer. His talk on the occasions when he can't remember the word is enchanting as usual. I wonder whether you saw my letter or ever heard of Bret Harte's meeting Father & me in the horse-cars in Washington when Father took me to see the Capitol, and how enthusiastic he was about the beauty and moral effect of the building. The other day Father recurred to that and said "How well he behaved that day he found us in the coach, that day that he went with us to see the—United States—survey of the beauty of eternal Government." I thought this was a most glorious leap in the dark. If he could have got at Capitol he would have said nothing else, but struggling hard to describe it he brought out the story of what it evidently was to Mr Harte, though what had been said that morning was so different, that it was in no wise a memory of even a single word. I hope you will appreciate this, Mother doesn't. She is very well and has done plenty of gardening. Mrs Myrick has sent her some poems which she is diligently reading to all comers. The Club met here last night, but it was rainy & no one came but Mrs Hoar, Miss Prichard, Mr Whitney, Mr Channing, the Sanborns & Edward & Annie. Father was asked to read something, Shakespeare was suggested, but he collected a whole set of accounts of Mr Thoreau from his old books and read them. I thought his undertaking that showed he felt well. Edward is busy and happy, Annie exceedingly sick and uncomfortable, but as brave as ever. She is hardly able to manage Charles at all. Edward has to tend him a great deal. Charles is the portliest baby in town, his occupation is principally opening & shutting doors & boxes. We are glad you are not suffering agonies at Rome. I understand you are to come for Thanksgiving and hope you will. Mother & I can't come to Clifton much as we should like it. Thankyou for wishing for us. We all send love.

E. T. E.

Nov. 12 '77

My dear Edith,
    Father did go to the Museum as arranged but Mr Loring was out just

the hour that we were there. Of course to the Aunt it was an occasion of bliss and great glory, and so was Violet's little visit at the end. Father beheld the outside of Trinity Church that day for the first time. Have you ever been right at its foot and looked up? As we came out of the Museum I showed him the Second Church, it is exactly opposite. He said "Well, that is better than it was in my time." He thought the new Old South was "gay". We bought a catalogue of the Museum, you must send for it when you go. Coming up that night was like a Ball or at least like going out to tea. It was the 5.30 train & so crowded we had to stand. Then lovely Helen Van Voost insisted on my taking her seat and I had a long talk with her aunt and we recalled our days in Rome. By & by Helen came to show me that Father had now found a seat for me. It was beside dear Mr George How. Of course we plunged into consultations, and came later to astronomy. He told me how very near Jupiter & Venus had been to the moon the night before. Oh dear! I hadn't seen it. At Waltham I descried one of my children, Ida Davis, far forward in the car. I beckoned and she came running. I had a most satisfactory talk with her, for she is not shy and she is really interested in Sunday School on the side of intellectual curiosity, not otherwise. We reached Concord all too soon. After tea I displayed to Father & Mother my purchases which amused them (and Sarah too). They eagerly picked up every crumb of information respecting you & our bairns which I could give. Friday morning I sat down to the M.S.S. Edward came to dinner, Annie was dining at home at her Father's and he hadn't been able to finish the operation he was engaged in till now, 1.30, when their dinner was over, so he had come to us. After dinner he invited me to ride to Bedford with him and of course I couldn't resist such a pleasure though there were other plans for the afternoon. We had a good ride and he was cheerful. Coming home we had glorious skies all round, and we were going westward, it was constantly changing magnificence of two kinds, the soft warm south-wind clouds, gray & rose, and the hard bright N.W. wind clouds, red & gold, and clear sky in all shades of blue green & yellow behind, with a brilliant young moon dodging in & out. And Edward's explanations, deductions etc. were very instructive and mixed up with much reminiscence, perfectly delightful to me. After leaving him I visited Ida Bryant, the baby was 20 days old. I found her on the sofa downstairs, though I'm afraid it was imprudent. On Saturday morning the Advertiser brought us the news of Frank Dennis's death, Mabel's brother. He has always been perfectly beautiful in every feature with the family yellow hair at its prettiest, the finest blue eyes

— 1877 —

and the most perfect complexion in town. I have known nothing of him but his beauty, but I hear now he was a good boy, had supported himself since he was 14 or 15 and had this last summer begun to help his mother. He was virtually engaged too already, everybody says, to a little girl of sixteen, who was dressed in black and sat with the mourners. They had the funeral in the church and it was crowded. Everybody felt it. There was much crying of people who only knew the boy by sight. Father has received a reminder from the Old South Committee that he is to repeat the lecture on Boston, and a request from the Derry Haskinses to read a lecture in Derry. So now I'm doubly set to work with them & Thanksgiving. There's John for my letter.
E. T. E.

Concord Nov 22nd 1877

Our dear little Girl,

We wish you joy on your birthday morning and send you our love and two presents which no doubt you have by this time and which were not ceremoniously tied up alas! I forgot that till too late, they might have been. Forgive! Mother sends you a pair of scissors and I have made a shoe-bag intended for the pink room, but ready to be used otherwise wherever it is needed. We wish fate would ever allow you to be with us on your birthday, but it seems always impossible. Come as soon as you can. Edward & Annie had the Social Circle last night. Alice Reynolds has spent a week with them, and stayed one day over to help them through that. Lucy Spencer came Sunday and is spending a week with me. I am having a good time with her. Tonight comes a coffee-party at the Town Hall, I am on the How-do-you-do Committee. We are all going. Lidian is to be a waiter. Lucy went with me to Bible-class yesterday and proposes to keep on going. Mr Cabot comes tomorrow till Saturday. Mother's Cousin Edwin is here, appeared last night. Mother went to Boston yesterday, no, Monday, and did the Thanksgiving shopping. We came home from Henry V much wiser and happier and I am most grateful for being allowed the pleasure of seeing it with you and the children.
Thy affectionate sister
E. T. E.

Concord Nov 24th

Dear Edith,

If you & Will & Eugenia & Mr Dodge and all the Thayers & Simmonses will stay till Saturday of course Aunt Susan's family and the Ripleys' and ours with the addition of the Bartletts would make enough to have a family dance to Mr Wesson's fiddle on Friday evening from 7 to 9. Mother & Aunt Susan agree to dance, and I think all the Ripleys & all the Bartletts except the Dr. will. Ralph & Violet are old enough, & 3 Thayers. I have written to Sophy & Cousin Mary, and Mrs Bradford Bartlett & Eugenia to make sure that every one will stay and I think the only grief will be the shortness of it. When can you come? Don't forget silver knives, carving knives & nutpicks. I think Annie's spoons & forks will be enough. Mr Cabot didn't come, he had a bad cold. Cousin Fanny came yesterday to say she and Cousin Gore depend on being here at Thanksgiving, and she approved of the party. She will come too perhaps.

E. T. E.

Concord Saturday Dec 8

Dearest bairn,

I wonder how you will get along with this Fair on the top of everything else. Mother was charmed and cheered by your note, she knew you hadn't said goodbye and it was a real pleasure to her to find you knew it too. I sent this morning your Hymn in two copies, Father made a mistake in the first, and didn't write the second nearly so well. I sent with the Hymn the Studies in Religion, the tube and Violet's toothbrush. We find besides a light blue Afghan and a top-string. Jenny Mills is better. Mother will probably come down on Tuesday, I on Friday afternoon on my return from Derry, or on Saturday. We have 3 Complim^y season-tickets! Lucy & C. & Therchi called on you as soon as you had gone. Mr Cabot has made us a lovely visit, Father has read us 2 lectures. I dined today with C. & T., very pleasant time, exceedingly. Goodnight. Much love to all my darlings.

E. T. E.

Concord Dec. 24th 1877

Oh Edith dear, I have sad news to tell you, our Flory [Keyes Walcott] is dead. She died last night at half past six. Philip was born on the 11th, the next day Flory was very well and happy & bright, the next came fever. Edward never let her see anyone, and the nurse always said she was well, which puzzled everyone. Edward began to be anxious. Then Charles Walcott had a very bad ulcerated sore throat, sent for Edward in the night & E. had to work over him almost all night. He was very sick for two days; at the same time Flory grew worse, and Edward exceedingly anxious and yet obliged to conceal it owing to Annie's condition & Charles's condition and Mrs Keyes's being tired with the care of Roger [Walcott]. The moment Mr Walcott was better Edward told him and asked for a consultation, and Dr Baker came. From Thursday till last night Edward has remained by Flory night & day, now he is here, poor fellow, for he dared not go home for fear of carrying fever to Annie. Saturday night the change came and it was for the worse. Florence was delirious and violent and they had a terrible night. Early yesterday Edward sent again for the best doctors from Boston, that they might feel that nothing had been spared, but he told them there was no hope left. I went to see Annie. That good girl! I admire her every day more. She looked so haggard and so piteous, and she was so brave and natural and open. She & Lily stayed at her house, Prescott & Alice took care of Roger at the Keyeses', Mrs Keyes stayed at Florence's and Mr Keyes went to & fro all day yesterday. The doctors came at noon, but everything was vain. She became unconscious and died without coming to at all. When Edward came here last night he hadn't seen Annie and was so hungry & chilled & exhausted it made us feel dreadfully, and he said "We're all ashore now. I can't attend Annie." I don't know how much he meant, I hope he only meant if she should be taken immediately. He is still asleep. Do you want my help one day this week I'm at liberty for one day.

E. T. E.

Concord Tuesday noon

Dear Edith,

Edward begs you will ask Dr Holmes if he knows of any comfortable and apparently safe house in Milton or nearer Boston where Annie could go to have her baby. For the poor boy has decided it is safer not to take care of her himself. He says "Tell Dr Holmes that though Concord is not unhealthy this month the character of such disease as there is is bad, diphtheria, erysipilas etc." and since his patients have such troubles he can't go near Annie in peace. Why, when he went home this morning and Annie ran out, he had to tell her not to come. So if Dr Holmes knows of a house out of the way of these diseases or any infectious fever where they would take her and Mrs Whitney for a month or so, and take her at once, please telegraph & write. Edward is going to Boston this noon to ask Dr Reynolds to attend her and to ask Storey

— 1877 —

and write to Dr Faulkner to see what chances there are in Jamaica Plain & Brookline. No more this mail. I have seen all but Lily.

E. T. E.

Concord Dec 26 1877

Dear Edith,

No one ever saw a dearer better girl than Annie. When I go to see her she always treats me like a sister and tells me all the things I want to know, and to hear what she says and to see how she behaves is a blessed privilege. Indeed all of them are lovely and sensible in the midst of such trouble. The first day after Flory died when I was alone with Annie she cried, and she tried so hard not to and seemed to think it was wrong, but she said Charles had kept moaning all night so that she couldn't sleep, for Edward was away and she was anxious lest C. was sick. Mrs Keyes came and I saw what a comfort it was to her to hold Charles and hug him. She said Roger couldn't sleep last night either till after midnight. Roger stays up at the Keyeses' and Mrs Keyes says the care of him is such a comfort, she cannot imagine what she should do without him, it seems like doing for Flory still. They had their Christmas dinner yesterday just as they meant to. Edward & Annie and Charles went, and Charles Walcott when they asked him said yes he would rather come, which touched and pleased them all very much. And Annie said they had a lovely quiet pleasant time, it was not trying it was refreshing, and dear little Roger was so sweet and cunning, sitting beside his father and behaving with the eminent propriety natural to him, that they couldn't praise him enough. I spent an hour with Annie yesterday and to my joy she talked over Edward's plan of sending her away. She said she could not go, she couldn't give a reason why it seemed to her wrong, but it does, and she cannot get round it. "It surprises me," she said "that I can't do it to please Edward when his heart is so set upon it. But I can't. It isn't the trouble either to me or to others, it isn't what people say, it isn't anything but the difference between right & wrong, and while I feel it clearly I don't know what it is that makes the right & wrong." It is impossible not to respect her decision, it is impossible to find any fault with it. I feel so, and even poor Edward feels so, anxious as he is about it. He says his conviction that there is no other way to do is as clear and strong as hers that it is no way for her, and he hopes something will change her mind. Her Father agrees with him that it would be wise, but thinks her choice ought to be

— 1878 —

left free. Mrs Keyes has not been consulted. I have received your telegram [inviting Annie to Milton] and am carrying it straight to them. Thankyou for the fly-flap.   E. T. E.

                                               Tuesday noon
Dear Edith,

   I enclose Mrs Clemens's letter which gives us all great pleasure. Father hasn't written. I am trying to make him. Winter gave us a sad bite last night, 22° below zero, and as we found the house bitter cold with a feeble furnace-fire, no amount of wood in the chimney did much good, Mother has caught a little cold and today we can't bring the house up to 60° when it is 2 o'clock at noon, so she is kept in bed. Last night when I came home I ran right up to see Mrs Keyes. The squeals of the sleepy Roger were heard in the lower bed-room. Mr K. came when I rang, and asked quickly how Annie did. I said "Beautifully" and he cheerfully went for Mrs Keyes who came forward through the parlours with a really happy smile and said she was delighted to see me. We sat down for about 5 minutes, I to tell her I had seen Annie [at the Forbeses in Milton] and descant on the perfections of my new nephew. Ask Annie what she thinks of naming him George Henry. I'm sure they are two good names. Mrs Keyes told me Dr Barrett had Sun. ni. a better night, that Edward is driven but seems very well, that he slept at home and that day had taken all his meals there, that he now was in Bedford on their horse, & would be home at 7.30. Then I trotted home & met the depot carriage at the Court House sent for me by my anxious parents. Father had had his tea. Mother & I had ours and I told him my history of Milton. No more now. John is waiting.
                                                            E. T. E.

                                      Wednesday Jan 9th 1878
Dear Edith,

   Edward came in for a little while last night. Mother began to extol the baby and I added my voice & praised his beauty. "Yes," said Edward in an affectionate voice "some of us like Charles." "No, no," cried Mother "I'm not speaking of Charles, I'm speaking of the new baby." "Oh!" said Edward "he isn't much of anything yet." I suppose he can't be to him inasmuch as he hasn't seen him. Then he struck his hands suddenly down and said "*Why* wasn't he a girl!" I assured him that such a pretty promising boy was as good as a girl. He has now been heard of in Concord, and everyone I meet inquires for him and I receive congratulations. I have read Aunt Lizzy's letter to you and mean to enclose it herewith, but may not. Mother has a letter from Cousin Charlotte announcing & explaining her approaching marriage to Mr Cleveland's brother of Orange, New Jersey. Jan 16th is the wedding-day. Edward dined with me. No Doctor has yet come to his relief. He says he has a great deal of work, but his very sick people seem to be all Irish and not acquaintances of ours. Dr Barrett he says is a little better today. I am just arriving in Boston. Give much love to Annie.

[Unsigned]

Concord Saturday Jan. 12

Dear Edith,

Edward left his rubber cape & gauntlets in Milton. Please let the cape go to Jane, and let Will take the gloves in and have them at the office. Then the next person that goes to Boston will bring them home. Please send me back Mrs Clemens's letter. I haven't showed it to Edward. He has help in the shape of Dr Carvelle who has had experience, and doesn't look too young. Edw. feels well he says, and he gets his sleep, and would be doubtless all prosperous but for his neck, something painful is coming there, a carbuncle he fears. He doesn't want Annie told. Mother is pretty well. I have had a good visit to Mrs Cabot's. I mean to come to see you on Wednesday if possible. We have Social Circle on Tuesday, and on Thursday Mr Cabot is coming, and it may be I can't get away between. Give my love to Annie, my nephews & my niece.

Concord Jan 21st 1878

Dear Puss,

I enclose Mr Cabot's letter. Look here! Edward *can't* come till this carbuncle is healed, because all doctors think they're not improving neighbors to lying-in women. Not that it ever was a bad one, the healing has begun, the new flesh is growing, and Edward moves his neck more easily, and has more appetite. He hasn't once been out in the night since Dr Bartlett died. He looks pale still, but I think everything promises that he will be well as soon as he ought to be with the thing. He says Annie will not, must not, move till after the baby is four weeks old, and if she is well then she shall come. I read him Aunt Lizzy's letter and she asks anxiously about him you see. "Tell her," replies Edward, "that I have been clucked over till the welkin resounded with the cluckings." Oh! we are so infinitely happy in having him every day we almost die of joy all the time, and he keeps us & Dr Carvelle too in fits of laughter. Except Johnny Whitcomb his patients are all doing well though the Hoseys plague him very much. Lily won't give a truly satisfactory description of the Alexander of my affections, but she praises Charles and oh! what pretty stories Annie writes to Edward about him, and his holding the baby! Do you want Father to come & spend a night? I find Alexander draws a little more every day and so does "that boy" and I think he will come if you want him. Don't be hurt at the last sentence, you know it is always the thing that has to be carried that he enjoys rather than the ambulant creature with plans of his own. Give my dearest love to Annie & to yourself.

E. T. E.

Bush. Jan 29th 1878

Our dear little girl,

We all feel badly about you, your papa's consternation on hearing that Will was sick was a delightfully characteristic mingling of grief & sympathy such as any papa might feel with amazement and perplexity that sickness should dare to touch one of his elect. The powers above must have made a mistake, what could they have been thinking of? to have allowed one of the intellectual, one of the handsome, his own son-in-law, to have the Scarlet Fever! Your mamma often groans over poor Edith, and we all think you are worse off than if Will was an ordinary incapable man, because you are so used to his helping and taking care that you miss him practically as well as have the fright of his being sick. When I went to Edward's and heard about Will my whole attention was absorbed in that. And when I had come home and told your parents and they after eating that bitter morsel next inquired about Ralph I had nothing to tell, so all the evening Father after shaking his head about Will would say "And you don't know how that beautiful little boy is getting along?" and Mother would say "Darling child!" Mother is thankful that you have a homoeopathic doctor. Do send a postal-card daily.

Father is better today. Mother & I have just visited Annie and Alexander whose name seems likely to be John. I think it would be eminently proper that it should be, and Edward seems to, and Annie wishes to give him the name. He is a charming little creature and

— 1878 —

makes faces more than most babies do. I've had a beautiful time with Annie, have seen Cousin Mary a minute. Caroline Cheney's mother is very sick and Caroline almost worn out. Mr Cabot will come on Thursday to prepare Father's lecture for the Concord Lyceum Feb 6th. Have I told you that Lucy's little boy came along on Friday morning, 10 lbs. Goodnight darling.

E. T. E.

Concord Jan 30th 1878

Dear Edith,

Many thanks for your letter telling us that Will was better, a delicious mouthful received with eagerness by each in turn. We enjoyed the thought of Will & Ralph's meeting and spending a social hour at a sort of nooning upon the long journeys they were taking respectively to their own beds. Give our love to them. I haven't visited Annie today, nor asked for the baby either. Father is mending, but doesn't yet go out. Mr Rice of the N. A. Review called last night, and Father was what I thought dangerously frank with him. He forgot that he belongs to the publishing fraternity. Mr Rice came in the happy belief that Father wrote Perpetual Forces last summer fresh *for* the Review, this belief I meant to leave flourishing, but Father innocently chopped it down and let every cat in the house out of the bag, told him he never did anything about it, that Mr Cabot & I compiled these things etc. etc. And I sat quite peacefully & listened but within I was stamping wildly about, tearing my hair & uttering ever new shrieks of surprise & dismay. Still it was all true & truth does no real harm. Let me have at least a card daily.

E. T. E.

Father thankfully eats your oranges.

Jan 31st 1878

Dear Edith,

I have just come home from Annual Meeting of the Bible Society; we have had a really glorious time at Mrs Edward Hoar's, 29 of us. A little book was exhibited dug up by Cousin Elizabeth in the depths of her garret recording the foundation constitution & names of the "Mite Society" in 1810. They pledged themselves to bring in one cent a week for the support of the Evangelical Missionary Society. The names deeply interested the company, Miss Lucy P. Fay (Mr Heywood's mother you know), 6 Miss Thoreaus, Elizabeth, Sarah, Jane, Nancy, Maria and one other, and in general the maiden names of all the oldest ladies of our childhood. Mr Cabot came this noon and we have had much to consult over. There is a paper on Sovereignty of Ethics which has been on the stocks these eight months which interests us very much. My sentiments are mixed, I love one sentence & abhor another all the way through, how Mr Cabot feels about that he doesn't mention but we both think it wants continuity. He carried it home for the third or fourth time and arranged it more satisfactorily. Moreover he gave it to Mrs Cabot to read. She was deeply interested & thinks some of it superior to anything yet! We are trying to get up a splendid one on Education, and to make the Fortune of the Republic for the Old South a first-class lecture. I am sanguine about both, more than Mr Cabot is. I have your letter, full of meat for me. Every symptom & detail gratifies me to know. I'm glad you're getting straightened out. How is your back? Father is better. I've seen Edward today but not for conversation. Couldn't go near Annie. Shall send your letter to Edw. in the morning. Many thanks for it.

E. T. E.

Concord Feb 1st 1878

Dear Edith,

What a glorious snowstorm! I am *almost* satisfied with its depth. Mr Cabot and I have been hard at work all day on three lectures, each of which I flatter myself will be very good. Mrs Cabot's eyes seem to have exercised a blessed magic upon "Sovereignty of Ethics". I like it much better today than I ever have before. Either this is a much greater storm than it looks or the Concord people are growing effeminate. Not a sleigh has come past the house today, two sleds and one or two foot passengers are all. John won't allow me to stir out of the house. He says it is too awful, "I sh'd get tuckered out, and should get my feet wet, no matter what I'd have on 'em, and then most likely I should fall down." I'll tell you! it's because we have gone so long without snow that people have forgotten about it, and are as much terrified as the English. My year of fasting from the society of my class having fully expired I invited them for Saturday P.M. Emma Smith & Jenny and Lotty & Lily of my old class came & Lulu Everett of the new. We had a beautiful gossip first of all, and there is this advantage over old times that now we know one and all how unbounded is our mutual admiration there is the fre-

— 1878 —

quent outbreak of delight at being together which makes the meeting all the freer & happier. At Mother's request I read them Jane Taylor's "Display". Did you ever read it? It is very interesting, and to my children's modern ears so old-fashioned that they kept exclaiming about it. Last night at Mrs Hoar's Miss Prichard poured out tea. She asked particularly about you all and said she had a rather sad letter from Aunt Lizzy. Your postal-card has come, thankyou. I'm glad all is quiet.
E. T. E.

Concord, Feb 4th 1878

Dear Edith,

I went to Edward's yesterday noon. He had on a collar as of old, some colour & flesh on his cheeks, and was a very agreeable sight. Annie was bright, had dined with her Mother the day before. They asked us all to tea tonight, Father to bring his Lyceum lecture, Education, "because" said Annie "tell him his daughter-in-law isn't able to go to Lyceum." Mr Channing took tea here last night, baby's name canvassed. I go for Ralph Waldo, Thomas Ward, Peter Bulkely, Josiah Bartlett, Abel Adams or *somebody*'s name. Mr Channing warmed to Peter Bulkely. Mother thinks Henry Roland. I thought of Henry Thoreau & think Mr Channing did, but I prudently held my tongue. This morning I went to Aunt Susan's & heard the really piteous tale of poor Lucy's being abandoned, & Lucy never complains to her mother or anyone, which distracts Aunt Susan. The lecture absorbs all my time now of course so I'm short today. Many thanks for your good letter of Saturday night.
E. T. E.

Concord February 6th 1878

My dear Edith,

I didn't write you yesterday and I hope you didn't write me. I am dismayed to find that you have many and fatiguing notes to write and have such a conscience about me that you write to me though you have written to Edward the same day. We all see the notes. Write me no more now except you wish to communicate something, or ask for something. We have been busy with the lecture. Father read it at Edward's on Mon. ni. It took just an hour which pleased him and he said he understood it better. We all liked it "Education". Father can't possibly remember for a minute the subject of the lecture, asks what it is every minute. This amuses him very much. He also thinks it rather

— 1878 —

high-soaring for a Concord audience, and laughed today and said "A funny occasion it will be—a lecturer who has no idea what he's lecturing about, and an audience who don't know what he *can* mean!" I do however expect success. Mailtime.

E. T. E.

Friday Feb. 8th 1878

Dear Edith,

When I went to Mrs Washburn to have my sack tried on she confided to me that she was going to the lecture tonight for she had never heard my Father lecture, and she was afraid this might be the last chance. Miss Prichard & Mrs Hoar & Mrs Tileston I met, and I believe they all remarked that it was a fine day for the lecture. I came home with a sense that the whole town took an interest. In the afternoon I got Father to read it to me once more. Near the end his voice failed, he coughed and afterwards for an hour or two he made signs rather than speak. I was anxious. We made great fires, brought his thickest clothes and lined them with wadding, and done up in every wrapping John drove him to the Hall, and he was furnished with cubebs to chew. His voice sounded to me very hoarse and as if it hurt him to speak, yet he used it freely, as I thought heroically but who can tell? I expected every moment would be the next, as Will says, that he would cough and be incapable of proceeding and yet he got through to the very end about as well as he began. The lecture itself was a perfect beauty, and beautifully delivered, and I enjoyed it all the way through. So did everyone. (Monday.) Enthusiasm ran very high that night, and indeed ever since. I am used now to hearing that each lecture is the best, but I don't wonder to hear people say it of this. Dear Miss Bartlett, who is laid low by her Father's death, said to me "You don't know how I enjoyed your Father's lecture! Enjoy is a word I haven't used for a long time." Dear bairn, I've been sorry to neglect you, company and errands have unexpectedly snapped up my days. Meanwhile how have you prospered? Are all the well four still well? How is Will? How is my dear Ralph? Father has gone to Boston today. I'm going to N.Y. 7th or 11th Mar probably. Mother is well & her hyacinths begin to bloom and please her. Her portly kittens chase their horse-chestnuts gaily about on her floor. How pretty her voice is when she talks to them in the entry "Come,

— 1878 —

kitty!" Little Charles sat up to our table & dined with the family for the first time last week. Blessed Peter was left at home.

A affectionate though
dumb sister.

Concord March 5th 1878

Dear Mrs Lewis [Miss Waterman],

I sent months ago all our photographs for two or three years back to Alice Arthur and asked her to keep them a month and then send them on to Lizzy Barber with instructions to send them to you when she had done with them. I don't know whether they have yet reached you. I have had a letter from Alice about them, but nothing from Lizzy. I am just about to write to Alice to ask whether Lizzy has had them. If they have not reached you yet they probably will very soon. Now the rest of this page must bring you all the news it can of your friends in Concord. I suppose you have heard of Dr. Bartlett's death in January. That is the greatest change that has happened in the town. Everyone misses him, and his daughters feel the affliction as of course they must, though all was beautiful. He hadn't in the least lost his mind and had more work than ever. But he was very infirm and suffered very much and they think he would have suffered only more & more if he had lived. And Miss Bartlett is a saint as you know, and a cheerful one. She & Annie & Ripley are at home now, and Lizzy has gone to Washington, and has visited Cousin Phoebe in her convent. I did myself once. Edward is just leaving the School Committee and we all think he does right, he has now practice enough to be obliged to neglect his school work and he has often had to take it out of his meals & sleep. But we also regret it. He loved it and did it well. His little lame Charles, 20 mos old, doesn't walk or speak but seems strong and intelligent and we think he will do both as well as other babes of two in another year. John, named for his grandfather though without the Keyes, is a sad cryer, cries most of the time, though improving in health and a little in behaviour, he was born Jan 6th at Edith's in Milton. All at her house & ours are well. Dear Florence's children are one at each grandmother's. My last minute has come. I want to get this off by this mail, for Mrs Ward, Tom's mother, has sent for me to come to see her in N.Y. next week and I want to show her the photographs, so if you have them please send them to me there, I shall be there till Mar 25th, 2 Washington Sq. N.Y., Mrs S. G.

Ward. Lucy Jackson has a baby 3 weeks younger than our John. Flory's Philip is 3 weeks older, she died when he was 12 days old. Charley Emerson has lived here in C. for a year but now returns to Paris. Goodbye. How do you all do, espec. your twins?

E. T. E.

Concord March 11th 1878

Dear Aunt Lizzy,

Tomorrow Father is going to read his Education lecture at Mrs Storer's and wishes to come to see you so I have made up a packet of the letters on the Old South lecture and some others to send you. I can't bear not to see you see them, I am sure you will laugh over one or two of them. Father is going to try to have the Nez Percé poem printed in the Atlantic and copied into the Advertiser. It was a comfort to have you say about it what you did. The Bartols have asked Father to repeat the Fortune of the Republic as you'll see, and he will on the last Saturday of this month. Would anyone from your house like to come? Please ask them to come if they like, 12 o'clock. Perhaps I shan't see you till after that, on account of going to New York. Annie is getting along better with her crying baby, he now wakes her only once in the night usually. Little Charles pities him when he hears him cry and tries to console him. Edward is just beginning his school-report, he has resigned and is no longer on the School-committee. Mr Cabot has finally put Sovereignty of Ethics into shape and we feel that the work advances really though never very fast. I send you a set of newspaper accounts of the lecture for you to see the kind of remarks they throw in. It isn't true that there was a single call of louder from the galleries. One lady after the lecture when he was reading the poem asked him to read louder, he didn't hear and I called to him. That is all.

E. T. E.

Mar. 13th 1878

Dear Edith,

I'll go back and give you a little family history since we parted. Father & I went to see Nina and found that it was Alice Lowell's birthday and she had gone to her party. Then I undertook to bring Father back to Mr George B. Emerson's as I promised, but he was recalcitrant so I finally allowed him to wing his arrowy way to Parker's and went alone to apologize for him. Mr Emerson was kindness itself, asked for Edward, assured me that he was the finest fellow he ever saw, and wondered how he ever found time to write such an admirable report, the best he ever read. I then returned to Father, and we went & bought tickets to the Museum. Then I dined at the Hemenways', Edith, Mr Eustis & Augustus were there, and great pleasure I had. Father came for me, we went to see Adrienne Lecouvreur. Horrid play, painful, confused & immoral. One of the Body Guard was in attendance and had brought an opera glass on purpose for him apparently so Father saw very well, but he was in haste to get away and we left soon after nine. The next day I found he had enjoyed the handsome dresses on the stage, and that was something. He sent me home in a carriage. In the morning we visited the twins before breakfast. They seemed to me decided Hemenways, and were charming, five mos. old. Edith and I had deep discourse all the time we could get. I went at ten with Father to photographer. Found it would take two of us at once to succeed. Then to the Art Museum where Mr Loring devoted two hours to us, and happy hours they were to me. Father too was perfectly happy, never hurried at all, and seemed loth at last to go away. I came up at three and had a very agreeable visit to Charles & Therchi. The rest of that week I have forgotten, except that we had Bible Society on Thursday here, thirty-two members present, and much pleasure, and that I was trying all the time to work up the lecture for the Atlantic, and had added much beautiful material so that Father and I thought it far better than when it was delivered. On Tuesday I had Belle's birthday party, Julia Wood, Grace Wood, Lizzy Surette, Riba Johnson, Mary Tileston, Grace & Mary Keyes, Edith Heywood & Gerty Tuttle. It was delightful, their manners were good and their youth & playfulness affecting to the aged ma'am. On Wednesday I think came the Atlantic's letter refusing the article, but Mr Cabot and I worked it up just the same, and it is now ready to print. Then the Bartols invited Father and I did my best to get him to accept their invitation & Sophy's and to my joy he did, and he has really had a good time at Sophy's. I hope you can come to the Bartols' Mar 30th. I rejoice that you were there last night and saw Aunt Lizzy today. Annie went last week. I can't go to N.Y. before Tuesday. Edw. has just finished his Sch. Report, sat up all night with it. Little John still a bad cryer. Lily Keyes spent yesterday here. I enjoyed her extremely, she grows more of a sister all the time. C. Cheney still very ill and the doctor says she will recover slowly. Mother is well and walks out often in good weather. Is happy in a hyacinth show. Thankful for your letters, rejoice Will is Town Hall Comm. chairman.

E. T. E.

2 Washington Sq. New York Mar 22nd 1878.
[At the Wards']

Dear Mother,

I have half an hour in which to begin the better letter. First I want to tell you about little Loulou Thoron [daughter of Anna Ward Thoron]. She is like King René's daughter or Miranda. The most delicate greenhouse flower that ever bloomed, so carefully tended and wisely watched, that while she has everything and lives the centre of so many lives in the house, indeed of all, she is utterly unconscious of it. She is as innocent and unconscious as she was born and as her grandfather says "has a great deal of conversation", and with lovely ease does every polite thing, and sits at the head of the breakfast table, pours out, and gives directions to the French man in French so that she seems as finished and capable as if she were grown up. She comes down to breakfast all ready for school with her sachel in her hand, and after pouring out she eats one piece of bread without butter, takes her cup of milk with tea in it, slips out of her chair, kisses her father's forehead, he never appears to notice it, and says good morning to me, and goes to school to a convent of the Sacred Heart, where she dines and has two sessions of school. Then she goes to riding-school. She loves horses, understands them, has regular lessons about their anatomy & points, is taught to leap and do all sorts of things, comes home to her music, is dressed and visits her grandmamma, and perhaps finds her way into my room. She enjoys "Little Women", likes to talk about it. Mrs Ward has taken pains to give me as many hours as possible, and I have done all the talking in those hours, which has its disadvantages of course, but she always started me, always showed a faithful interest inquiring out each point as I went along, and I judged from what Tom or someone said that she liked to have news to ruminate on in the hours she was shut up. She was more lovely than ever in one way, she talked about religious subjects often, but scarcely brings in a word about her own church, and her stories always had a beautiful moral. She was more eager about Aunt Lizzy than almost anything else. The sights I had of Mr Ward were less satisfactory than usual, he seemed to talk more about things he didn't really care much about than he sometimes has,

— 1878 —

but he was very kind. Tom and I sat together at dinner twice and that was all I got of him. Sally came to see me. I went to see her. She is pretty well, and is doing well with her painting. Mr George Ward was very polite to me. Emma Lazarus was very affectionate and inquired much about you as well as Father and sent a dozen times her love to you & begs you won't forget her. She had her sister Josephine with her. Seeing Emma at her own house I found she was still a little forlorn, but Josephine said "Well a little thing often cheers her up." "Yes," said Emma, "sometimes when I have sent for Tom to come instantly and he has expected to find me in a terrible state, I'm all restored before he comes. What a true spiritual physician he is! wonderful!" There this is all I have had time for. I shall come home Thursday night.

    In the cars coming home from Boston, Mar 30th 1878
My dear Miss Clara [Dabney],

I have been in N.Y. as Roxa will tell you and came home Thursday night, and today Father has been repeating the Fortune of the Republic lecture at Dr. Bartol's house. I started early and went to see Aunt Lizzy. Mrs Storer looked very grave when I came in and said "Aunt Lizzy is still alive, we none of us thought she would see this morning, we sat by her all night." At first I thought I was too late, but Mrs Storer said she was now mending and might have several days of comparative ease, and I might come in the afternoon again, and should see her she was almost sure. So I went into Boston and Father gave the lecture. We had a beautiful time and after it stayed at Dr Bartol's to dinner, Edith & I. Father read a poem about the way we treat the Indians, which some one sent him, and I must send you that, as dear Aunt Lizzy says "That is a part of the history of our country that is always grieving & shaming me, and this trumpet gives no uncertain sound, and ought to be blown wherever there are ears to hear. I am glad your Father read it." Then I went to see Aunt Lizzy and thankful indeed I am that she has lived to see this day. Certainly there never was a more satisfactory interview, she was full of fun and play, full of instructions and maxims. "It would be a pity" she said "that I should have all this experience and not leave the results of it to anyone." She can't breathe, gasps & struggles for breath and is eased every instant by ether, and she told me what helped, and kept saying "Remember when you have the care of anyone in this condition." I wish I could write all the bright and wise things she said. Thankyou for both those letters, I shall answer them yet. And may you

1878

have the best birthday yet. It must be good with so much of home & heaven as Roxa brings you and you to her. Give her my love & I send it to you.

E. T. E.

In the cars, April 2nd, 1878

My dear Edith,

Since I fear you didn't see Aunt Lizzy this afternoon, I will write out for you every word that I can remember of my visits to her. She looked exceedingly thin and blue and kept her eyes most of the time shut tight. On Saturday afternoon she was sitting almost erect propped up on pillows, and Lizzy Storer sat on the bed by her with the ether horn and held it before her all the time. Sometimes Aunt Lizzy would put her face right into it for some minutes; sometimes she would only have it held close for a moment now and then. "I like to have you see how the day goes on, darling," she said. "This is the whole order of performances. And I want you to remember what a comfort ether is, and to know that it is only the first sharp freshness of it that is the comfort. After that is gone off, though the napkin may be as wet as sop with it, still it does no good; it gives only a sort of carbonic-gas that rather injures the lungs than helps. So when you administer ether, give a few fresh drops every few minutes. I don't know any more about all this (she meant the approaching death) than you do. I am learning it step by step, and" Here she put her face into the horn. "She has courage," said Lizzy Storer to finish the sentence for her. "No," said Aunt E. energetically, coming out from the horn, "She hasn't courage nor anything else. The Lord has it all." "The Lord gives her courage then," said Lizzy. "It is the same history all the way," said Aunt Lizzy. "First a need, an agonizing need, and I scream, and relief comes, real relief. So far it has been sure." Fanny came in and sat down a minute and Lizzy said, "Yes, Aunt Lizzy knows that the ether will help, & it is a great support to her when distress comes on." "I have at last found a comparison for myself," Aunt Lizzy went on. "I am a bumble-bee turned over on his back and kicking, and kicking—or a fly—Ellen, be kind to flies! Never leave one in the milk. Take him right out. Flies have awful times." "Oh Aunt Lizzy, did you always feel so? Or did you come to it?" "I have come to it. *By experience*," she answered. "Ice." Fanny brought a piece. "Put it in with your fingers," said Aunt Lizzy, and opened her mouth. "Natural methods are the most direct. Remember that Ellen. Ice is another

— 1878 —

great comfort. When people are wretchedly uncomfortable and don't know what they want, give them ice, and *with your fingers*. Sometimes the elegant Fanny forgets herself. She is so used to doing things with propriety." We all laughed and she did too, and then finished, "And of all detestable things, a piece of ice slipping about on a teaspoon is the worst. Isn't it wonderful? These four people understand me so perfectly! If I grunt out of one nostril they know what I mean; if I grunt out of the other they know what that means. If I shake my head they understand; if I say, 'You Goose!' they understand that." Lizzy laughed and said Aunt Lizzy said the other day, "*Don't* be judicious, Lizzy, do *something*!" "I want to hear everything you know," said Aunt Lizzy. "Tell me about Haven's babies." I did and ended up with praises of little Elizabeth, telling her how sociable she was with me and that Susy said she had much the quickest mind. Aunt Lizzy had the ether over her face, but nodded her contentment, and when she came out of the ether sent messages to Haven. Then she said, "I want you to hear my epitaph. You know my brothers have a great taste for inscriptions, and I know that presently they would have to lay their heads together to record my virtues, and as I have no virtues that I wish recorded, I thought I would save them the trouble and make my own. Tell her my epitaph, Lizzy." Lizzy began, while Aunt Lizzy put her face to the ether-horn, but instantly lifted it and said, "No, no, that isn't right! You haven't a literary mind!" at which we all laughed, and Aunt Lizzy went on. "You know the whole history of my Father and Mother is given there. Well mine begins 'Elizabeth Hoar, eldest child (not daughter) of Samuel and Sarah Hoar,' aforesaid, I always *say*, but of course that would look ridiculous on the stone. People can read all their virtues in full on their monument, and can infer from them what mine were likely to be—'the great joy of her life was in her nephews and nieces, among whom she numbered also the children of William and Waldo Emerson,' That is my epitaph." I don't remember what came next. I said, "I hear Mr. Cabot came to see you." "Yes, a very pleasant visit. I couldn't tell him all he wanted to know of your Father's early life, but I told him he always shared his Mother's cares and his Mother's poverty, the care of Bulkeley, the cares she had, he never felt that he belonged to himself. Neither did anyone of them—they all took their part—except your Uncle Charles! He grew up like a lily! You never saw that dear creature! I am sorry for you that you didn't." I said that Mrs. Keyes had talked to me about him and that Alicia said her Mother was positively

1878

indignant when she presumed to imagine that our Charley might equal him in business or Edward in virtue. "Oh no!" said Aunt Lizzy. "They do not. I have never seen anyone like him—never have seen any elegance, any form of grace, that could approach his, so that I could once say, 'That is like your Uncle Charles.' " And she said more of the same kind, but I don't remember the words, to make one feel that he was unique, and that his beauty and manners were a creation allowed to dazzle mortal eyes just once, and never would be repeated. When I came home and told this to Mother and Miss Fanny Prichard, they eagerly added their testimony to the same effect. "He was a seraph." Lizzy Storer said while Aunt Lizzy was taking the ether and resting, "There was a book." "Oh yes," said Aunt Lizzy. "I wanted to tell you of a book, 'The Spirit of St. Francis de Sales'." Of course I couldn't help interrupting that I classed that as one of my own especial books, and we eagerly exchanged remarks for a minute or two, making sure we both meant the same thing and agreed entirely about it, and then she went on, "There, that brings me to another of my comparisons. What the ancients accomplished by means of those arches that still make the Campagna so beautiful, the moderns have accomplished by a single pipe, laid underground. And it amounts to the same thing. When we see the water springing up we want it. And," here she opened her eyes for a minute and looked earnestly at me—"it makes no difference, Ellen, whether the water came over the arches or underground." Then came more religious talk. And I have utterly, utterly forgotten what she said, and what it was about. Forgotten! It seems strange to say that, about the best of all. I remember the feeling, and how she looked at me, and how I understood and agreed, and knew she knew it and was satisfied, but I have vainly tried to bring back a single word.

That night when I came home Florence Hoar and Miss Prichard came to ask about my visit. Oh! I remember one or two more things that I have omitted. She said she had enjoyed Mother's visit and Edward's, and had told Edward details about her disease which she thought might be interesting and useful to him professionally, "For Aunt Lizzy," put in Lizzy Storer, "thinks she knows more about her sickness than all the doctors." At which Aunt Lizzy nodded that she certainly did, and went on, "and I was glad to recognize Edward as a Medical brother, in my life, once." Presently Dr. Tarbell, (one of her young cousins who calls her Aunt) came in, and Aunt Lizzy said to him, "No not now, I shan't see Ellen again. Fanny will tell you what a lively

— 1878 —

time we had last night. So come, darling, and give me a good kiss, and then go right away. You have been the greatest comfort to me. Good-bye! when I am dead I want you all to form an Aunt Lizzy Society." She delivered into my hands a bundle of Father's letters to her. Then it was time for me to go.

The next time I saw her was Monday morning the first of April. Mrs. Storer said she had said to her once in the night, "I *know* in whom I have believed." She had asked the nurse whether she should die in the night, and Mrs. Ogilvie said No, and she said, "I am glad. I feel as if I should like to see another day. I want to see Marny's baby again." They said she was having a very hard time, but they thought she would soon come out of it, and I had better stay, she knew I was there and wanted to see me. Very soon I was called up. "Tell your Father," she said at once, "that I am waiting till the grain is taken off my tongue. Don't you know what that means? Don't you know that pretty story of Chaucer's? About a little boy that sang a hymn in honour of Christ's Mother as he passed through the Jew's Quarter to school. And it offended the Jews and they killed him and threw him into a pit. And his mother came to look for him and heard him always singing, 'Alma Redemptoris Mater,' and found him in the pit. He was dead, but even when he was lying in the church before the altar, 'with his throat all cloven' "—and she indicated the cut with her finger, "he still sang 'Alma Redemptoris Mater,' and when they asked him why, he said, 'When I was killed, our Lady came to me and told me to sing this song in her honour, and methought she laid a grain upon my tongue; and I must sing, nor shall my body be at rest, until the grain is taken off my tongue.' Ellen, I don't want you to be troubled at seeing me so and think that either you or anyone else has the same thing to go through. We always used to feel as if lock-jaw was a fabulous disease; and then John Thoreau you know had it, and died of it. And then we never heard of anyone else's having it again. And hydrophobia we consider almost a fabulous disease, but one person may have it within our knowledge, and yet no one ever have.

End of letter is missing.

Concord Apr. 6th

Dear Aunt Lizzy,

I was to have spent two days with Mary Blake this week, and meant

— 1878 —

to pass through Cambridge and ask to see you again, but I wasn't well so have had to stay at home. Mr Cabot has been here and "Sovereignty of Ethics", the paper you & I read together last summer, has been our principal business. It is coming out in the next North American, the proofs came yesterday. Father had one to read while we worked on the other, and at dinner-time he came in saying "If I had been asked I never should have allowed this thing to be offered to the magazine. Why it's a long sarmint." The next time I saw him he said "I like this better as I go on, the beginning was bad, but where I am now—why, it's very good!" In the evening he said "I don't know where you found all this, but it improves upon acquaintance, and the improvement works backward as well as forward, even the beginning turns out at last to be good too." So Mr Cabot and I, besides the great delight of the work itself, have the delight of success with Father himself. He was really uneasy at first thinking the paper was tedious, and now he is proud of it. I thank you for every word you said to me, I delight to remember it. Your affectionate niece

Ellen T. Emerson.

Yes, and Father & Mother were eager to hear all you had told me, and your messages were real consolation to Mother, and Lily Keyes was most grateful for hers.

Concord April 8th 1878

Dear Haven,

Aunt Lizzy died yesterday afternoon. Cary Hoar came to see me this morning and said her Father and Mr Edward Hoar drove to Cambridge yesterday, so that they and all the Storer family and Dr Tarbell were with her all day. She was able to talk and said she was all ready now to die, she had done all she wished to do, and said all she wished to say. The last thing she said was "I have never been deserted either by God or man." When Dr Tarbell saw that the end had come, he gave her ether enough to put her to sleep, and she did not wake again. I went to see her the day after I got home, the 31st of March. She had ether every moment, and spoke breathlessly and with interruptions, but she was happy and full of talk and fun. I have been trying ever since to write out all she said for Edith, and when it is done and Edith has read it she will send it to you to read. I went again a week ago today and sat with her more than an hour, and as before every moment of it was an added privilege. On Tuesday I went in for ten minutes more of delight and wonder; she was stronger, sitting up straight, and talking freely without ether. Since then I have been tied at home. The funeral is to be on Wednesday afternoon at three, here from her own house in Concord. I wish you could come. I have seen Charles & Therchi once or twice since I came home. They are selling their things, trying to pack up and living in the melancholy & confusion of a prolonged moving, which is depressing & irritating to both. Edward's babies both have scarlet-fever. Charles has it lightly but it holds on fast. Little John smiles and is as good as usual, though as red as a lobster. Edward and Annie are both pretty tired. Father has lectured once in Boston since I came home, and will next week. I enjoy these occasions and so does he I think. Aunt Lizzy liked to have him do such things, too. My love to Susy.

E. T. E.

Concord April 22nd 1878

Dear Edith,

Good morning! I am at Edward's taking care of John, and he has condescended to go to sleep, so I'll improve the opportunity and write to you. Charley & Therchi came to spend two nights with us before they went away. They made me magnificent presents before they went, shells, and their beautiful copper saucepan, and zinc hot-water pitcher, and a zinc pail and a little funny Hungarian earthen pitcher that I always took to. Thursday was their last day. We went to the Cliffs. T. had never been there, nor Charley since his youth. Both were very glad to have seen the pleasant place before they went away. Then we engaged Edw. & Annie to come and we had a very gay dinner-time. Edward as usual was full of stories, one shocking one if you looked at it seriously, why, a good deal like "Finnegan's Wake", a story of his practice, told in brogue, enchanted Charley, who exclaimed that if he could have practice like that he would be a doctor tomorrow. Then at three o'clock they started, and we are all sorry. Mother has told me today a little story I never heard before: that when she was born her Aunt Lydia visited her and not being of a cordial nature and perhaps like me given to speaking her mind about babies, exclaimed "How she glares!" This hurt our grandmother's feelings and when Aunt Lydia next asked "Who's she named for," grandmother was so provoked that she said "Lydia Shaw." Said Miss Shaw was a friend of the family and when she first saw mother she said "Why you little dear, if it wasn't for the name of mouth I shouldn't know you had any!" These with the other story of

the "black satin head" make three facts about Mother's personal appearance when she was born, and I'm delighted to get them.
E. T. E.

Concord April 29th 1878

Dear Miss Dabney,

Today at last I have time to begin my letter. It has been a busy month for Father, he has given two lectures, and he has an article in the N. American, the proofs of which had to be attended to, as well as those of the Fortune of the Republic. Then we have had our cook sick of diphtheria, she got off very easily and was only in bed four days. Still it made a week's break in all other business for me. Then Edward's Charles has been having Scarlet Fever and sequels for more than a month, and two of the weeks has been sick enough to make us anxious, but for the past three days he seems to be getting well, and we are very happy. The young baby also has the fever but has never been very sick. You don't know what a pleasant and romantic thing has happened to me. When I was at boarding-school at Mrs. Sedgwick's in Lenox I was in love with Bessie, the eldest daughter at home. She was altogether the most efficient and brilliant person I had ever seen. She kept the house, and taught music, and sat always at one end of the long table to help. We almost never saw her except at meal-times, but it was our great delight to hear her talk and laugh, she had a most beautiful interesting voice, and she was funny. Sometimes she read to us in the afternoon when her mother could not and we considered it a great good fortune, and one Sunday she read the Bible to us, I thought it the best reading I had ever heard. And the natural quickness of her motions was one thing I admired with reverence. I always have that feeling for quickness. I wish you could have heard her run up two flights of stairs. It was an event of my day every time she did it. Well, it will be twenty-four years in October since I came away, and in that time I have not seen her except two calls that I made with Julia Gibbons at her house in New York in the first two years after I came away from Lenox. I suppose it is twenty years now since I have seen her. And the other day she spoke of me to Mary Watson and Mary told her I had never forgotten her, and she asked Mary to bring me to Lenox next week with her to make her, Mrs. Rackemann, a visit! I am greatly interested. I would rather return to Lenox so than in any other imaginable way. I have never been there since I left school. It is going to the same old house though altered; and it is to see her again, which may be delight or not, but I desire it. And Lenox is beautiful, and of course I love it. I shall tell you all about it the next time I write. Oh give my love to dear Roxa, I hope you and she are able to enjoy this beautiful spring to the full. Unhappily people seldom are, they are often prevented by sickness and usually by spring-cleaning, and all sorts of indoor cares carelessly manufactured, but I hope it isn't so with you, and that sun and grass, and morning and evening and moon and stars, and leaves and birds really give you the pleasure they can. I often puzzle myself with the question whether our houses in which we shut ourselves up with dust and paint and carpets and furniture are an absurd willfulness on our part, and living principally out of doors and enjoying all that is there provided for us is right; or whether these same boxes and their contents are the indispensable nurses of virtue. Certainly I feel a sincere respect for the poor women whose whole lives consist of weary sewing, house-cleaning, cooking and clearing up, and not half so much for those who choose driving and boating and sitting on piazzas for their occupations, yet the one existence seems wickedly thrown away, and common-sense recommends the latter. You combine both, you are a worker and yet you always have an eye on the things outside, and they seem to come home to you. The rest of this week I shall have company. One of my own Sunday-scholars for one. That is a great event. Tell Roxa my Aunt Lizzy died on the 7th of April. Beautiful and happy to the end she was. I saw her three times. E. T. E.

May 18 1878*

Dear Edith,

Little Charles is a shade better today. Edward is now perfectly cheerful about him and says it is wonderful to see how strong he is and how he rallies as the feverfit goes off and plays with his foot-rule and other possessions. I wish to offer a few remarks to correct your ideas about the Fortunes of the Republic, and possibly allay your wrath. The "original order" was not Father's but Mr. Cabot's and mine. We have never changed his order I think where it could be ascertained. This is a collection of every general remark on the country from many lectures of many dates, each full of the moment when it was written and so adapted to that occasion and no other that scarcely a page entire could

---

*Dated in pencil in EEF's handwriting.

— 1878 —

be saved. When you first heard it at Thanksgiving it was most of it from the lecture named F. of R. which Mr. C. had already sifted but there was then no order at all. As read at the Old South it had copious additions from Moral Forces and some from other lectures, one on N. England particularly. As read at Dr. Bartol's it had been helped by all we could collect from American Nationality. So don't think this last is any more my version than all the rest for from the beginning I have done as much in arrangement as Mr. Cabot. And no change of mine which he disapproved of has remained. Father never had these things combined, so *he* never had any order for them. I thought and so did Mr. C. that the final arrangement was truer and easier for the mind, but maybe it isn't so. Let any person of judgment not familiar with the lecture read this order first and then the order in which the proofs were printed, only cut apart and pasted together again so as to look alike and rouse no prejudice, and see what his verdict would be. You see you are prejudiced by familiarity with one order. Each correction which you complain of was Father's not ours. He complained of the "chiefest" and wished it removed. I asked him whether it did to say "the care of the sick and the serious care of criminals," and he said "no, no, change one of them," and took it and wrote "judicious treatment". If you don't like it perhaps you can get him to change the first *care*. I agree with you that in every instance the corrections are painful, that it was written in a telling way, and correct enough to read as a lecture, but alas! printing must be exact and parse well so each loose point must be attended to, and Father is no longer able to correct with the same vigour with which he wrote. Each correction is his where he could understand what was wanted; in some instances I have showed him the trouble seven different days in vain. Then Mr. Cabot had to make it and he always does it in the modest manner of scratching out a word or altering a tense, or something that will leave it still Father's words if possible. How do you do?

E. T. E.

Concord May 20th 1878

My dear Sally,

Ever since I came home I have been desiring to write to you to tell you of my highly romantic visit to Lenox. For I have been there, oh! I have been there! and I feel as if that novel of my life so long closed, had

— 1878 —

been opened and a lovely chapter added. Mary Watson and I went the first week of May, and as the season was early things looked as lovely as they usually do three weeks later. With what delight I recognized the churches and the Hotel, all just the same! Caroline Cheney who was in Lenox last summer had prepared me for the changes in the house, so I was not surprised at going in at the wrong gate and stopping on the wrong side of the house. Mrs Rackemann thought of every imaginable pleasure for me. I slept in the Dummy, the bed was where Anna McLellan's used to be. Mrs R. offered to move it across to where mine used to be. By chance I sat exactly where I used to sit at the table. Mrs Rackemann took me over to see the school-house, and up to the church. I walked down the hill at recess-time as of old, and one afternoon to the Pinnacle. She took me to Mrs Farley's and to Mrs Tappan's, and naturally I sat much in "the little parlour" and looked round at all the books, the very books we had read to us, and saw upon the desk in our day. It was a daily new pleasure and wonder to hear and see that Miss Bessie was herself, had the old smile, the old voice, the old ways. And as to the dear children, they were not particularly in my thoughts before I went, but they were the best part of my visit. It didn't take two days to love those little girls. And Felix and Wilfred were lovely too. Mr Rackemann was there one day and was exceedingly friendly and agreeable. The beauty of Lenox was greater than I remembered. I saw everybody almost. Mr H. Sedgwick and his wife & daughter, Mr & Mrs Minot & Alice, and Mr & Mrs Joseph Tucker. I came away thankful and much contented, but I only want to see them again the more. I have had a letter from Charley at Hamburg dated May 16th saying their voyage was better than when they came out, all but fellow-passengers, but saying nothing of their plans. All are thriving here. You will find Charles if he goes on as he has so far, looking as stout as if he had never been sick, and the baby is a full moon with plenty of red in his cheeks. Cousin Elizabeth says you are coming in July and Mother and I expect our visit as usual. Cousin Hannah is coming some time, but Cousin Sarah says she won't. We hope she'll change her mind.
             Ellen T. Emerson.

                25 May 1878
Dear Edith,
  The Charlotte Russe came last night I saw what it meant. Unluckily it came directed to Father & he at once recognized what it was,

1878

whom it must be for, and the occasion. Dear Mr Cabot was here & spoke of his birthday this morning. He had the Charlotte Russe for luncheon, the rest of us for dinner. Alas! they were sour. Such a possibility never entered my head till I tasted them. But Father ate his all up (with wine on it) & never found out. Charles pretty well today, cup & letter magnif this P.M. Rec'd with joy & emotion. Proofs revised.

I'll try to write you the rest of my letter. At dinner we had one present ready for Father, Mother framed one of his pictures, an engraving which he bought out of pure delight in it, of a child creeping up to a dog and saying, "Can't you talk?" while pussy who was following the baby stops because he has stopped and surveys the scene, rubbing herself against the door-post. Both Father and Mother enjoy looking at that picture with never-ending enjoyment. When Mother exhibited it as his present he was rather taken aback for he knew he bought it and paid for it himself, and he didn't notice the frame, but he was brought to understand the point afterwards. I couldn't make my present in time. By the noon mail came an adoring poem from Lois Laurie, South Acton, "To R. W. E. at Seventy-Five." That is all that has been done for him here. E. and A. have not been here for days and have forgotten all about the birthday and since Margaret is pretty sick today I couldn't invite them here or have any company, as otherwise I certainly should. It is his club Saturday, but he wouldn't go just because it is his birthday. He's afraid some one might remember it.

Tuesday morning (28th). Edward did remember his birthday and came after tea. He said Mrs. Dr. Reynolds had just died and had been under his care. Howard and his lovely wife had come home. Edward said it had been a wonderful and affecting spectacle to see the little pygmy Eliza taking care of her Mother who was more like the Cumaean Sibyl than an ordinary woman. Howard he says is all he ever promised to be and he enjoys him every moment. Father has restored "serious care." I haven't left time to write more on that subject.

[Unsigned]

May 28th 1878

Dear Edith,

We were made happy by your letter this morning except that the health bulletin is pretty poor. We accept with thanks the offer of Adelaide, Don & Baby, and the hope of the rest of you. Edward's rhymes please his grandpapa, and encourage his belief in the child's uncom-

— 1878 —

mon endowments. Sarah is coming on Thursday and I am glad. Pauline has agreed to come and make me a visit before she goes to Lenox. If I can I shall go home with her for two days. I gave Mr Cabot all your views & Will's about the article and he has retained short-coming and unbecoming and Father has restored serious care, but he said a careful reading and comparing of the two orders convinced him more fully of the wisdom of each correction and change. Sometimes I really do not agree with him, though my rule is that he knows best and shall decide, but this time I do agree with him, and therefore feel sure the essay is better than before, though I should like to have you satisfied. Oh dear! Mr Cabot isn't coming again for six months. We are very sorry. He advances wonderfully. Next winter at this rate will see the M.S.S. all sorted, sifted & ready for use. It is nearly a finished job now. That apron was made by one of Mother's Cotton aunts, Mary, her Mother's eldest sister, born about 1750, married a Mr Jennings, had no children and died early. One of Mother's sisters was named Mary for her, but did not live more than a day or two. This Aunt Jennings was a famous embroiderer, Mother thinks none of the other sisters were. Edward & Annie came to dinner & brought John. He looks a little prettier than he did a month ago and has more colour. He is now about middling. I think no one would remark him for anything. Charles from long seclusion is very bashful. He always however shows joy in Father. The other day he saw the Southworth big photograph for the first time, presently he smiled & as they looked at him hung his head & blushed. Annie asked him what he saw, trying other things first, and at last asked "Grandpa?" whereupon Charles said yes with emphasis and reached his arms toward the door, signifying he hoped Father would come. Edward came to report. Father hurried to see him. But he returned disappointed, saying "Just the same silent child, can't do anything but grunt. They are like people that have a parrot." The Fullers opposite them had their first baby on Sunday, Edward being doctor & Annie nurse till Mrs Whitney arrived. To Edward's black despair poor Mrs Fuller has today broken out with Scarlet Fever. He feels as if somehow it might be supposed to come from them, though the Fever with them is now past for more than 3 weeks. It is 3 weeks since their fumigation. Poor Edward is hardly strong enough to bear the dismay & anxiety of his profession. Give our love to Ralph. We are sorry about the ivy-poison again. How do you do?

E. T. E.

— 1878 —

Concord June 17th 1878

Dear Haven,

Cousin Hannah is coming on to spend a month with us and means to start June 30th I believe. I hope Ruth will come with her. I am making all my visits before she comes, except a long one to Edith when I shall take Ruth with me. Edith's little boys are here, and Ralph & Violet are coming today to spend a week. Edward & Annie are well & Charles has an amazing appetite and is beginning to walk a little. He makes less progress in talking than any child I was ever with, but he understands any talk in any words they assure me. Even when they use long words to mystify him, they say they are sure he isn't mystified. The small baby has now a great round face and red cheeks, white eyebrows & eyelashes; homely but hearty & jovial. Father and I have just come from Exeter where Father read the lecture on Education at the Academy. We had a very good time. I was truly delighted to hear you had named Elizabeth, Elizabeth Hoar. They are all in the family Bible now. Give my love to Susy. I hope her courage doesn't fail about little Ruth.

E. T. E.

B. & P. Depot June 24th 1878

Dear Mother,

I haven't had a moment to write before. Going out to Canton I was in the same train with Pauline and her children, and had a most interesting talk. When we reached Ida's she & Lucy Russell & *Nina* were on the piazza. A gay afternoon full of conversation, disturbed by the delightful uproar of the five children occasionally, and Pauline carried her four home at 5 o'clock, Ida took her baby up to put him to bed, and Nina & I studied Greek for an hour. Then came a walk with Ida, tea, and all the evening a discussion on Sunday-Schools. Ida deeply disapproves not only of their faults but of their existence. Sunday morning, very pleasant breakfast & flower-arranging, I went to church alone. I stayed to Sunday School & enjoyed it very much. Mr Savary preached on the actual and the ideal Sunday-School and when I was coming away he said "I should like to talk this over with you, I think I'll come over to Mrs Higginson's and see you." In the afternoon we sat among the hay-cocks with the baby a little while and Ida and I took a walk. When we came home we found Mary & Mr Blake sitting with Nina on the piazza. We joined them and were having a delightful talk when steps were heard

— 1878 —

on the gravel. We turned round. 'Twas Mr Savary. Mary seized my hand "My dear! a minister! is this one of your convention friends?" I said yes, and Mary laughed, highly amused. So he came up onto the piazza and the subject soon came up, and was interrupted by tea. After tea we all sat down solidly to it. Ida agreed very well with Mr Savary and we got at the experience of everyone. After he went we continued the discussion a little further, and Ida seemed as we came to a better understanding a little less otherwise-minded about it. Today Monday Ida came to Boston to the dentist and I to the Conference Officers' Meeting. Our Meeting was very interesting, practical and I think important. But Mr Tiffany & Mrs Lowe were absent, also Mr Peabody, so I did not have perfect joy, though I enjoyed my old friends who were there very much. I haven't yet written to Cousin Sarah, but don't know what to say. Can you pay her fare without paying Cousin Hannah's too? My address is Mrs Henry L. Higginson, Canton, Mass. Write me a note on the subject.

E. T. E.

Concord July 6th 1878

Dear Edith,

I was sorry enough to hear from Mrs Kelly about your cook's disappointing you. I visited Mr Osgood but he was on the main, en route for Europe. So I saw Mr Garrison, found myself utterly powerless to cope with him. He seemed to think that publishing the book at all was a queer idea, and that I little knew how much money it was going to cost to do it & advertise it. I rather wished I hadn't gone. I gave him your message about Parnassus and he didn't see why its own wreath couldn't be retained, but then he said that wasn't his department, he would tell Mr Ticknor. I told Barrett to dye my dress yellow. I found Louisa Alcott in the cars and she told me that the torchlight procession of boats on the river had been beautiful on the Fourth. Afterwards there was an alarm of fire in Mr Tuttle's store, formerly Mr Brown's, and it burned through into Mr Whitcomb's before the engine arrived. Once on the spot it poured in a deluge that extinguished the fire and did plenty of damage besides. Father, Mother & Cousin Hannah are full of inquiries about you all. Goodbye with love to you & all.

E. T. E.

— 1878 —

July 12th & 11th 1878

My dear Edith,

Your letter this morning was a great pleasure to your family. We are particularly glad your cook has come. Ruth does better here than she did in Milton. Her virtues appear when she is set to work. No child could be more pious than she is in her sewing-hour, and as I get more acquainted with her I am deeply impressed with the admirable training she has had. Her naughtiness passes so quickly and easily and the good below comes out with many a wise saw and pretty allegory which she has learned of her Aunt Ruth and her Mother. She declares alternately that she is very happy and very homesick. When I read her stories she is delightful, she screams with joy and excitement. We have read through Narnia the Princess and have begun Flowers for Children. Her sewing is very neat compared with our children's. Cousin Hannah is her playmate out of doors. Oh Cousin Hannah is a flower herself. I contemplate her character and her history with reverence and delight. Her little stories are so pretty and surprising I must tell you one or two. "The only remembrance I have of Grandmother Ripley is of my Mother's taking me up into her room to see her, when I was five years old. They set me down on a high chest, and my grandmother gave me a sheet to turn. I sewed the whole seam before I got up, and I remember they said I had done very well." All her little tales show the wonderful strictness of the old times, and her own pious submission. Tell me about my dear Ralph's birthday, Give my love to him.

E. T. E.

Friday July 12th 1878.

Dear Susy [Emerson],

I have had company today and left myself little time to write you about your bairn [Ruth]. She has a good time quite often every day, and on such occasions exclaims "Oh I'm glad I'm here!" and quite as often every day when she has her hands to wash, her sewing to do or any other slight rub, she exclaims "Oh I'm awfully homesick. I knew I should hate to come here." But I have no doubt that she is on the whole happy. I enjoy reading to her and hearing her scream with delight over the story. Last night she remarked that it was singular she should have fallen so in love with Cousin Edward & his wife. "He is such a nice dark man. I always expect to love dark men. And then Cousin Annie has such a nice strict face. I always like strict people. My Aunt Helena is

— 1878 —

very strict indeed." I was surprised at her calling Annie strict. Today at dinner Cousin Hannah was narrating a case of discipline which she considered wickedly severe, but I didn't, and, again to my surprise, Ruth burst out "Oh good for strict people! You like it because you're strict!" She seemed to sympathize. I have never given her any dusting because I saw she would make a fuss over it, and I wished to avoid it, but she has taken hold on peas & raisin-picking, and such things quite often. She learned her hymn with surprising readiness. You don't answer me about Sunday-School. Mayn't I try her there some time? Your stories of the other children are delightful to us all. I am glad to hear the babies are gaining colour. And I beg to have as many particulars & remarks as you can give me about all the five.
E. T. E.

July 18th 1878

Dear Edith,

Just a synopsis, for no time for more. Last Saturday night Mother went to her club and found Mr Alcott had two philosophers & 3 philosopheresses from St. Louis here. Ever since Philosophy not only reigns but pours. Sunday night great conversation here, this morning Plato Meeting at 10 at Mrs Sanborn's, tonight Philosophical Tea here. At the other extreme my donkey patters to & fro on her pretty pins with Ruth & Maggy Ames's & other children with great exultation & outcry. Ruth remarks "Everybody stops to look at the donkey as much as they do at the triplets." Cousin Hannah left us Monday night, and we long for her return. Sally is at the Manse. We took tea there last night, Ruth & I. Tomorrow Maggy & her children spend the day with us. Father is having his crayon portrait taken to be engraved in Scribner's, by Mr Eaton an artist Edward met in England. Fanny Hubbard married yesterday. Adelia Hobson & Charles Bartlett engaged, also Cora Myrick to Ben Brown. Mr Nathan Stow very dangerously ill. Annie & Edward donned their own wedding-apparel to go to F.'s wedding, and looked beautifully. I'm going to Boston Monday, can I serve you? Love to our five-year old, to all of you & to Alice.
E. T. E.

Concord July 26th 1878

Dear Edith,

Your anxious family had counted that it was ten days since they had

— 1878 —

heard from you when your good thick letter arrived, full of moving information. Imagine the shudders of the grandparents when Ralph faced the Hole [Woods Hole] alone for the first time! This reminds me that Ruth came in terrified last night and said Johnny or Eddy had solemnly assured her that "something lived on the road to Mr Keyes's that somebody would give five hundred dollars to have killed!" The indefiniteness of this information made it seem mysterious & horrible to the last degree, and I have smiled over it ever since; its ingenuity, simplicity & fearfulness are admirable. I hope Violet's return was appreciated. We are always sorry to have you tired and plagued. I hope you are come by this time into smoother waters. Today little Charles who has been sick proved to have an abscess hidden under his bushy hair. Annie has two new girls but they are not quite a success. Father received this morning a bill for Fortune of the Republic which I enclose to Will. Father doesn't know what to make of its coming before the book appears. Yesterday Judge Hoar called first on Edward and then on us and surprised us all by a legacy of a hundred dollars from Aunt Lizzy. How lovely! Charley had his before he went, and Haven's is now to be sent. I have been elected delegate to Saratoga. Father actually half agrees to going with the Hoars & me. Sept. 14th to 21st. I hear from Annie that you have the Piersons & Bowditches this week. It sounds very pleasant.

         Your sister.

         Concord Aug 3rd 1878

Oh dear beloved Edith! how happy are the Grandmother & Aunt! We begin to count our chickens and rejoice in our new comfort. I shall rigidly call him Alexander, for my mind strays more than ever towards little Rosamond. His bands shall be my loved employ. Sally is here & Lizzy Simmons with her. Also Frances Browne. I find no time to write except to Haven & Susy who must receive reports of Ruth. I wish I had a chance to write you a few yarns. Oh how I want to see you all! When I think of R. one pattern, V. such a different one, our blessed C. again, then the uncommon D. and the big E. at the end, each so different from the others, the idea of still another fills me with rapture.

         E. T. E.

         Monday Aug 5th

Dear Edith,

Father will come on Thursday. E. & A. hope to come next week. Do

— 1878 —

you want me at the same time? I suppose not. If they don't come I shall by the 15th arrive with Ruth in my pocket. You expect her with me don't you? Haven writes that he shall try to come next week and spend a few days. Please send Castle Daly by Will to the Office. Mother wants to read it, and Father will get it there. I like your idea about Aunt Lizzy's hundred very much. Ours are as follows: Edward means to have an oil painting of Annie. Father is not decided. What he chronically wants is a telescope, but he doesn't seem to want to actually buy one. Edward & I suggest things but he hasn't agreed to anything. Mine I mean to put in the Savings Bank.
E. T. E.

Aug 9th 1878

Dear Edith,

We have had a little picnic at Easterbrook, the Bartletts & Simmonses & Uncle George & we. We had a beautiful time, and the dear donkey went along, so that it is to be called "the donkey-picnic". But she was naughty, broke her tie-rein, and strayed away, was thankful to be found, yet was frightfully kicky when they saddled her again. May Morison rode her up & Lizzy Bartlett rode her down. M. M. liked her as I do, but it amazes me to see how few people do. We had a good conversation on Conversation, the different kinds. Cousin Mary said their family's manner was to talk all at once, so that no one was left to listen. Will came last night in the shower and was a real delight to everybody every minute that he stayed. He as usual brought good counsel. Cousin Hannah comes Wednesday; Haven's coming is doubtful. I will come on Friday, or even Thursday, and stay a week, or I won't come, just as you say. I have been using my fly-flap today successfully. Don't mind not being able to write letters, though we do like to have them. I hope you are feeling comfortable.
E. T. E.

Give my love to Father and tell him Mr Ben Brown's bill is paid. It proved to be all as it should be. The letters are of the usual absurd kind. Beg him to stay till I can come. Mother missed him very much the first day, but she is getting used to his not being here, and believes in his staying.

Aug 12th 1878

Dear Father,

Mr Dakin has brought the money for the bossy; $8.02. We wonder

— 1878 —

whether you had the same thunderstorms that we did last week. On Thursday Florence Hoar went to Lincoln to stay with Helen Van Voost, and at ten in the evening the house & barn were struck by lightning, and immediately, Florence says, every room was filled with smoke and a strong sulphureous smell. The family naturally concluded that it had been set on fire by the lightning, and though they couldn't find any blaze or heat sat up all night. In the morning they found the lightning's autograph outside the house, but absolutely no harm was done. The barn was a little broken. On Friday night we were all interested & scared by a portentous green cloud, but nothing came of it more than heavy rain, except a few mild hail-stones. On Saturday we all went to Easterbrook and had a pic-nic. We were driven home at 3 o'clock by a little shower. Since then we have had more peaceful weather. This morning Sally & I went to the Cliffs. The view is magnificent, with river so high. She is gone now, she was called home and went this afternoon. Little Charles & John came to see us in company this morning for the very first time. John was full of jumping. I carried him up-stairs and Mother cried "Whose baby is that?" "Mrs Dick Barrett's" "Oh bring him here! I want to see him." I placed him on the bed. Mother donned her spectacles & looked hard at him. "Why! How *much* he looks like our baby! Don't you think so?" "Does he?" I asked very innocently. "Why, *'tis* our baby! Isn't it?" And I had to confess. Charles immediately crept into the front entry & asked for DaDa! Edward hopes to come day after tomorrow to Naushon, and bring them. Don't come home till I get there. Have you carried "Fortune of the Republic" to Mr Cabot? I hope I shall come before he & the boys go.

E. T. E.

Naushon, August 17th 1878

Dear Father,

Only think of it! Here are little Charles & John and their parents, here are the Five Bears and their parents, here is little Ruth and her satellite, the present writer. If you and Mother were only here the family would be complete. You little know what amusing discourse from Will & Edward, what songs from little Charles, frisks from John, and pretty smiles & speeches from all your grandchildren you are missing. All the way down in the cars Charles watched for that great ocean of water which had been promised him. Edward says that first Walden Pond, then Stony Brook, then Charles River were substituted, and every brook or pool they passed had to play their part, but he was content with the quantity & variety of water that was offered to his sight. Since he came he hasn't been homesick, as he was last year, but takes great pleasure in seeing once more his Aunt Edith & cousins, but his main joy is the hall-floor & the piazza. Annie says "he thought they were made on purpose for him, and the first day he came he scrabbled breathless from end to end of the piazza over & over again as if he couldn't possibly have his fill of scrabbling, and was afraid if he didn't improve the opportunity to the utmost he should repent it for it couldn't possibly last." Scrabbling is a word that very well describes his furious creeping. He has learned to bow to the company, a funereal bow it is; and when his head is once down it seems as if he meant to keep it down till the assembly is dispersed, but it does come up at last. He has a new word; he says "wa-wa" for grandma. I met little Edward coming down stairs this morning holding the fly-flap on for a tail as I supposed, but on asking I was answered "Vis is nofing but my rudder. I am blind & can't see my own way", accordingly at the turn of the stairs the rudder was put hard a-starboard, and he came nobly round. Will came home last night very late in the evening, and jollity has very much increased. I went into the study this morning for my pen & found my brothers closeted there. Edward asked me if I could guess what they were doing. I saw no indication to guide me, and gave up. He said they were composing together a new Eclogue. I hope it is true. We had a heavy thunder shower in the night and today is a rainy day. Effie Lowell is expected today at the Mansion-house with Carlotta, and we all consider it a great piece of good-luck. She was here with Edward & Annie and me last year. We like to have her see little Charles, as well as to see her ourselves. If Mr Osgood sends you any copies of Fortune of the Republic please put an inscription into a copy for Mr Cabot and leave it at the Athenaeum for him. I sent him a copy by Edward hoping E. would find him here, but he had gone and has no copy yet.

     Your affectionate daughter
     who wishes you were here
     Ellen T. Emerson.

           Naushon August 19th 1878
Dear Mother,
 When we arrived at Woods Hole we found Oliver Grinnell waiting to bring us right over. On coming in sight of the Mansion House wharf

we beheld Edward & Edith waiting for us & Cameron climbing down onto the float, followed by Baby Edward. So we were received with great kindness and found Annie in the wagon just above the wharf and drove up to the house all together. We were in good season for dinner and much fun we had. The next day came Effie & Lotta to the Mansion House. Mary Russell and all her children are there & with Effie came Hatty's son William Lowell Putnam. I went over there to dinner. Alice was so good as to ask me. When I came home Ralph invited me to play squails and took great pains to teach me and to play badly himself to match my inefficiency. Effie came over to see the children. Charles was shy but did pretty well. John was brought down and she at once took him. He roared right out, and she put him back in Annie's arms. Annie hugged him, looked at his face red as a peony and grievously distorted and couldn't help holding him screaming up to the company, saying "Look at that face! Did you ever see anything so funny?" There was a general laugh. He flung himself upon Annie & cried louder still and was inconsolable. Long after he stopped screaming he held on & sobbed, and he didn't smile again for an hour or two. His feelings had been hurt. Today he is all smiles & jollity. I think he is more interesting for having feelings.

Your affectionate daughter
Ellen T. Emerson.

Naushon August 23rd 1878

Dear Father,

All the Mansion house family have come home now. Mr & Mrs Forbes arrived yesterday, and are most thankful to get home. Mrs Forbes asked about you and said very affectionately that she counted her summer incomplete since she had lost your visit. She wishes you would come and make a visit to them at the Mansion house. Sarah seems much better. I am very sorry to say that our stay here is nearly over, and we are coming home tomorrow, Saturday. Edward & Annie probably in the train that goes up at three, and I in the 4.30. Will & Ralph have been out plover-shooting this morning and have killed one plover. Today & yesterday have been exceedingly cold, and little Charles has lost his baths, a great disappointment to us all. I went to Woods Hole in the rowboat that carried the mail the other morning. As we passed Will's wharf, I saw Cameron there all alone leaning over the railings, and remarked on it to Henry Cook. "Oh I guess Ralph is

1878

somewhere round," he said. Sure enough, a little later we saw him sailing in his little boat, and further on we saw John playing alone on another island. Ralph was sailing towards him. I saw what beautiful plays they have with an island apiece & a boat to ply between. When we returned they had all been diving from the wharf and were dressing. There, they've come for the mail. I can't finish my letter. Your affectionate daughter

E. T. E.

Wednesday Aug 28th 1878

Dear Edith,

Your good luncheon which you gave us was as tidy, as fresh, and as good when we came to eat it as when you and I sat together at your breakfast-table. The party ate it with joy and gratitude. Little Charles behaved moderately well, little John squalled his loudest whenever he wasn't sleeping or eating. In Boston we took an ambulance for the useless sisters & brethren, which conveyed them to the Fitchburg Depot while E. & A. went shopping. Ned Bartlett & Dan French came up in the cars & were nowise ashamed of the party, even helped to dislodge us in Concord and stow us into the family vehicles which awaited us. Annie's parlour gaily dressed with golden-rod, sunflowers & hops by Alicia looked very cool & cheerful and a smiling new cook waited in the background. Mother had sent a loaf, a pie, & a basket of pears for them. We parted, & Ruth & I came home. Father met us at the East door, Mother was lying down, and Cousin Hannah was reading to her. We went in there a moment then Ruth departed to the barn and I sat down to write. Edward came to see Father, I went down in the Study & remained till tea-time. Thither came Mother, and I described to her & Father each of your family. The next day was Sunday and Cousin Hannah couldn't go to church with us for fear she should cry. She had just heard of the sudden death of Prof. Bardwell, Lola's husband. Lola is left with no property except a house-lot & her furniture. The little girl is two. Cousin Hannah doesn't know whether to go to Kanzas, or send for them, or whether she had better stay here & they there. She is impatient to go home to consult about it, so she goes tomorrow. Haven telegraphs that Ruth must come with her. On Sunday Mr Moors of Greenfield preached. The text was "O Lord send I pray thee whom thou wilt send." A shower came up, darker & darker it grew, the preacher could scarcely be discerned, but through the deepening shade

— 1878 —

he was seen to lift his sermon to his eyes, & hold it on this side and on that, and he went on. I longed for a lamp & looked round for the sexton. He was gone. Oh dear! And that lamp is right down in the vestry, I could get it so easily! Why don't the standing-committee feel called on to do something? But the standing-committee sat still. "When you feel that a thing ought to be done", viciously said Mr Moors "don't wish the Lord would send some one to do it. You are the one that ought to do it, if it is by any means in your power. Sit still no longer, praying the Lord to send whom he will send; understand that he sends you." In spite of these very plain directions I remained in the pew, I hated to do it because I was a woman. "I doubt if the Christian church would have survived the first century," said Mr Moors "if it hadn't been for the interest of women *** and in these days ** let no one say that this or that is not the province of women ** and you, my sister, don't fear to carry on the work that is in your heart because you are a woman." But I was obdurate. Tell me did you ever hear a sermon in which a cap fitted you better? I have since heard that Mr Moors said that darkness was so great that he was afraid he must stop altogether, that he struggled so hard to see at all that the perspiration poured down his face. I have also heard that Mr Geo. How went down & found the study lamp but it wasn't filled, and he didn't know how to do it. You see if I had gone I could have filled it and Mr How would have brought it up. Ruth was a very good child all day. Father took her & Cousin Hannah to the Cemetery in the afternoon. In the evening came the Sanborns & Pres. Gilman of the Johns Hopkins University of Baltimore, with his wife (who was Miss Woolsey, the Elsie, we think, of Katy-did) and the Manse family, but I was in bed. I have just come up from dinner alone with my parents. I have been airing the Saratoga scheme and planning the journey, and Father seems willing to go still. He thinks he might go further in search of George E. Tufts. We saw in the paper that Will had a Convention in Worcester & was chairman of a Committee for drawing up Resolutions. Father & I have felt puffed up ever since. This morning Mother called me in to read her all about it. Not far had we gone when we learned that the Resolutions were not passed. The dinner-bell rang and interrupted the reading. In the middle of dinner Mother said "Do you know I have all the time a load at my heart because those Resolutions were not accepted?" "What resolutions?" asked Father. I explained the discovery so painful to our pride which we had made. "No, no! it isn't my pride," said Mother, "it is much more than that. I know that Will stands for righteousness and that his resolutions embodied righteousness. Now I fear that the Young Republicans have rejected righteousness." We are going to read on farther presently, and I hope we shall find it is not so bad as that. Cousin Hannah is enjoying an introduction to Cov[entry]. Patmore. She has never heard of him before. Father & I have spent the evenings in directing the "Fortune of the Republic" & getting it off to his European friends. Give our love to dear Don, we remembered well whose birthday it was.

Ellen T. Emerson.

Dear Edith,

As I came home from the apple-bee I joined Father at the Library and we found the P.O. open so stopped in, and there was your letter. When we got home I read it first to Mother & then to Father. How good & consoling it was of Mrs Forbes to come over & move your things and let you lie down. Tuesday. I began this letter at Mrs Walsh's while waiting for her to try on my dress, that business over, I got my bonnet from Miss Melcher, and gave her the blue velvet to make my winter bonnet. Then I went with Father to Mr. Stodder to learn the art of using the "telescope." I believe I wrote to you that he had bought one. It is the littlest thing that ever bore the name, but very light and charming and convenient. We enjoyed our hour very much. We looked (from Devonshire St.) to see if there was a spider-web on the eagle on the top of the City Hall, and plainly discerned one strung from his beak to his breast and very dusty. Mr. Stodder said he could see a fly lodged in it the other day, but at this hour the sun on the roofs agitated the air through which we looked so much that we didn't see the fly. He says our t. will show Jupiter's moons, and Saturn's rings, but won't do much more astronomically. I think that is enough for us, cold nights scare us and we shall use our friend more by day than by night. Then I went to Waltham and found Annie at the photographer's. We got the baby ready and had him taken six or 8 times, but he wouldn't be still, and the photographer was, like most of his race, so sorry that we had opinions & plans & that he had yielded the slightest deference to them that he couldn't get over it and harped upon that string continually. Then we visited Madam Keyes's sister Mrs Leland and came back to meet the 4.30 train. When the conductor took our tickets he told us Father was in the rear car, and I went and told him what joy & honour he might have by coming forward. He did & held the excellent rosy smiling compan-

1878

ion all the way home. Oh let me not forget to tell you he is always called Gummy. I never say it myself but Oh! the pride & fun of the voice with which Annie introduces him when visited by relations "That's Gummy!" Or when exhibiting him she says encouragingly to him "Now Gummy at 'em." I almost roll on the floor with delight. I haven't said half, nor asked anything, but want to know all.

E. T. E.

Concord Sept 12 1878

Dear Edith,

Have I ever told you that Mother is going to stay at the Manse while we are at Saratoga? She is looking forward to it joyfully. She is having one of her sicknesses however, the first for a good while. It seemed to be brought on by going to Boston with me and spending a whole day. But we accomplished much in that day & enjoyed it exceedingly. Your letter of Tuesday was a great pleasure to us all. Very good news it is that Don is well & the trunks packed. Also that Miss Tozier and the children are welcome at the Mansion House. How good they are! Mother was waited upon the other night by Miss Jane Hosmer with the request which I happily nipped in the bud before Mother heard it that she would "give a Conversation on Swedenborg before the Club" at her house. I felt as if Mother's lovely innocence would be spoiled by such a proposal. I cooked it a little and carried the message that they wanted her to read them that article on S. in the "Commonwealth" which she had praised. I was sure the Conversation would be forthcoming whether or no if they led to it. Edward said the other day, "Conversations seem to be Mother's natural field. I regularly hear when there has been one either that 'It was a failure because Mrs. E. wasn't there,' or 'Oh yes they talked a good deal about cats and rats and sealing-wax and whether pigs had wings, but at last Mrs. Emerson spoke, and then all the fools were silent.' " I always hear the same thing. People tell me they were "thankful for every word my Mother said the other night, & they do rejoice when she speaks." Father exults greatly, he often is present and hears her, and says "I like to see her security and I know that whatever stranger is present will soon recognize the weight of what she says. She is equal to anything they may bring up." Mother is really a great belle, she has more invitations than she can accept. I was quite curious about the Swedenborg conversation, but alas! it rained & Mother wasn't well. It was given up & Edward read instead, it was

— 1878 —

something good & Mr Sanborn helped and there was a very gay evening, though few were present, the Hosmers living so far away.

Your affectionate sister.

Niagara Falls. Monday P.M.
Sept. 16th 1878

Dear Mother,

Truly we have had a good time. On Saturday morning we occupied a Parlor Car and after we had recovered from the shock of having left our tickets behind us, and met Mrs Bartlett at Ayer Junction we found ourselves quite gay. At Fitchburg Judge Hoar bought our tickets & posted our letter. The girls were all frolicsome & Judge Hoar was very funny. I supposed it was his normal state till Cary said it was lovely to see her Father in such good spirits. It was the loveliest weather imaginable and we soon found ourselves in beautiful scenery. At noon we ate our luncheons & bought some capital ice-cream in the car & had it at leisure as we journeyed. At Winstown Saddleback stood out close to us without a fence or building or tree between to mar our view of it. At 2.30 we arrived at Troy where we were to change cars in an enormous and perplexing depot with trains coming and going all the time. As Father and I were slowly preparing to leave the car the black porter snatched most of our property and jumped out; we naturally following. Father exclaimed that his umbrella was left behind. Instantly I jumped in again for it followed by Judge Hoar and Mrs. Bartlett. I thought I made sure that it wasn't there and the porter and Father readily gave it up with the idea that the p. should presently return and look. So with many a hair-breadth escape we crossed the depot to a Ladies' Room where our six small pieces of baggage were deposited and I found Judge H. and Mrs. B. hadn't come with us. The porter took Father to recheck his trunk to Niagara instead of Saratoga. Cary and Fanny Storer went to walk. I remained alone to guard the baggage. Time passed on. What would Father do, I now began to think when the porter left him? So since I was anchored by my charge I stood in a conspicuous position and remained a prey to anxiety. At last Mrs. Bartlett appeared straying forlorn and hailed me as a port of hope, we stood together and finally after 5 m. more saw Judge Hoar, who bore down upon us with Father's umbrella in his hand saying he had been entirely lost, having got turned around in seeking and finding the umbrella. He had hastened as he thought in the right direction, brandishing his prize, but at last after

— 1878 —

a mile's walk, seeing a youth of intelligent countenance had asked him where was the depot and was told to retrace his steps. I told him my fears for Father, and he set out in search of him. No sooner had he gone than Cary and Fanny hove in sight dragging Father in their wake. They had crossed his lonely path as he wandered without an idea of where he might find his baby. We peered about for Judge Hoar, and dimly discerned his hat just fading in the distance. A party was detailed to bring him back, while the main body remained stationary as a beacon. When after all these adventures we were reunited the dames made curtseys, Judge Hoar spread his arms and removing his hat bowed all round, Father clasped his umbrella to his heart, and we were about to vow to separate no more, when I remembered we hadn't bought our tickets to Niagara. I delivered our baggage over to Mrs. Bartlett while we sought a distant ticket office. Returning we found Judge Hoar waiting to show us how Mrs. Bartlett had fulfilled her duties. "See!" he said, "There it lies and Mrs. Bartlett has only stepped through two rooms and out onto the sidewalk to speak with a friend. If it hadn't been for me"—He was interrupted by a shout from Mrs. Bartlett who came running hard like a little girl across the long Ladies' Room which made him laugh with delight. "I had just about decided," he said, "to carry it all off and hide it, and see how you'd look when you came back." They reviled each other for a few minutes and then Judge Hoar said we must take our train, theirs would come 15 m. later. "Goodbye, we shall see you again at Saratoga,"—then, viciously remembering the umbrella and the tickets he added, "with as many pieces of baggage as may be left at that time." So we parted and clouds came over the sun, and for ten hours more of afternoon and night Papa and I rode, at first quietly, then patiently, then grimly. As it neared midnight Father began to say, "We go fast, but the faster we go the more nowhere do we arrive." But when he heard the falls at last he shouted for joy, "Oh! well! Yes I hear! We had supper and got to bed at 2.30 A.M. Slept till 8.30 and again last night had a long night. Your affectionate daughter
Ellen T. Emerson.

On the road, Rochester to Saratoga
Tuesday, September 17th, 1878.

Dear Mother,

I will try now to tell a little more of my story. I forgot to mention that we passed through the Hoosac Tunnel, and that interested the party very much. Several other small tunnels in the neighborhood had to be passed through, and Mr. Woodbury of N.H. who was talking with Judge Hoar exclaimed "Tunnels, tunnels everywhere and not a drop to drink!" At one place where a train was backed up to hitch our car to with a sudden push that almost upset us all Judge Hoar smiled encouragingly and said "A bumper at parting is the rule; we have one also at meeting." All these little jokes afforded Father amusement, and we were as I told you a hilarious party. At Niagara when Father and I arrived we heard the splashing of the water as we entered the Hotel, and found a good fire which I was very glad of we were so cold. Father had declared all the last part of the way that the cars were capering off towards the Pole, they had forgotten the way to Niagara and the temperature showed which way they were bound. I had his winter surtout there with us all the time, but he was displeased with me for bringing it, and so wilful and naughty about eating, absolutely refusing to taste a mouthful through that desperately long afternoon and night, that I didn't unroll it for I thought he would sooner die than put it on. I couldn't even persuade him to use it for a pillow to rest his head against. The consequence is that he has had ever since a little hoarse cold, but he denies it. I am so thankful I did bring that coat, for he was equally naughty about going near the fire, wouldn't do it! So I had his feet tucked up with it when he went to bed, and sent for more blankets so he did have a warm night and the next day he had forgotten that he was angry & as it was pretty cold he wore it in his room & I felt all the time that it was saving him from a severe sore throat. I duly made his bed both nights, and he had that over him besides the blankets. The weather happily has grown steadily warmer ever since Sunday morning. I caught a sore throat too but it has given me no inconvenience, such as they often do, and is getting well. Well, on Sunday morning we found a dining-hall and a very good breakfast, and Father was frisky and proposed to remain always where he was so well treated. I put on my things to go to church first of all as it was 10.30 but learned that 11 was church-time, which discovery was balm to Father's soul, he was so scandalized at my going to church leaving the Falls unseen. This gave us half an hour and we walked towards them. I had thought over the ways of man and wondered whether the craving creature wouldn't manage to prevent our seeing the Fall without paying for it. Too true! Who would have thought it could have been compassed, seeing the Falls are so vast? But so it is. I have amused myself prospecting and

— 1878 —

peeking and poking to see if there isn't any spot in all out doors where you can get a glimpse of them without paying quarter of a dollar for the privilege. Not one! High board fences and all other devices are used. In my youth I read in a torn newspaper K. N. Pepper on Niagara, and laid to heart these words, "The 50 cts. it cost me to ride over here when I might just as well have walked!" They stood me in good stead, I always preferred to walk, and I looked about well before doing anything so we haven't a 25 cts. to regret. We went into Prospect Park. You can see the rapids from the Hotel and from various places but the Falls you can't see except from Prospect Park. We ascertained that 25 cts. would allow us entrance for the day and we might go in and out. So the 50 was paid and we hurried in. You see a little point juts out just at the shoulder of the American Fall. Thither we hied and got as near as we can anywhere to it, you could reach it with a clothes-pole, and you see the Horseshoe Fall also very well. The muddy water curled white was very interesting as showing the best that Nature could do for muddy water and there was a plenteousness of the muddy water which was agreeable to the mind, though it was muddy. Again there is a certain solemnity in the great array of white columns, and the motionlessness of them though they were all rushing, and the splash is very fine though I mourned bitterly that there was no thunder I had heard so much of it, and there was naught! Then close to, the fine embroidery of pearls on the falling mud is pretty, and the clouds of spray under you are white as snow itself and more beautiful than I imagined, their softness and solidness and rising and curling. You see I looked at it with coldness, and of course I was sorry for that, I had heard stories of its being overpowering and hoped it might touch me in some way, but it didn't in the least. The rainbows added very much to it, and gave Father the usual pleasure. Whenever we approached the edge he held on to me with both hands and said, "I'm afraid you'll jump over." I have often felt it on bridges when I was sick or very weak, but I was quite well now and the idea never occurred to me. Father probably felt it himself, and so he thought I must. He went to church with me and played he was going in, but didn't. After church we again walked the shores of Prospect Park till dinner-time. Again in the afternoon. I had made up my mind that Goat I. was the place I wanted to go to, but Father said that was too expensive, (50 cts. apiece to see that) so I thought we would content ourselves with Prospect Park since we had purchased the liberty of that! But how was it K. N. Pepper could have walked over? On that I studied, and

— 1878 —

proposed to Father to visit the new Suspension Bridge. We did, and found that you paid 50 cts. for the privilege of *walking* over that. It would tire Father and cost as much as Goat Island. I looked over to the Canada side and saw that from there, even from the river's brink at the foot of the Precipice you must see the face of the American Fall which we couldn't get on our side and a better view of the Horse Shoe. Then paying diligent heed to the placards I ascertained that we could be ferried over for 25 cts. apiece. So I proposed that. Father thought not. He said he had contented himself all his life with what we could see from where we were, and he thought I might. So I waited and thought it over, finally making up my mind that it would be folly to save those quarters. The next time I requested Father to treat me to this spree, and said I had decided it would be absurd not to see the whole when it cost so little. Father yielded as an indulgence to his baby and set out very otherwise-minded indeed. But the new and better view soon converted him. I meant to walk up on the other side and leave him to wait for me, but a carriage offered itself for 25 cts apiece, and as Father hesitated I said we would take it. Far from repenting it he soon became enthusiastic and we were lucky in having chosen the late afternoon for the expedition for now the rainbows were all on the Canada side. It was very fine, and very satisfactory. We drove way up, even to touching the Horse Shoe Fall, a half mile or more with the view improving all the way. The H. Fall is *the* Fall, the American is small in comparison. We walked back and the river-side, the precipice, is beautiful in itself, from its height its handsome rock and the beautiful trees and vines which partly cover it. We walked back reviewing and admiring and Father said he wouldn't have missed it on any account, he had never seen it before from that side. I think, however, that he has. We both thought all the way that the view on the American side was as nought but getting back to it we found it better than we remembered. It has its advantages too. We sat down awhile to see it, and Father said, "I think I shall remember what I have seen today while I live in this world, and in the next too." "Yes," I said, "you can tell the Lord you saw it." "Yes, and ask Him to please to tell me now what it means. It seems certain that there is a relation between Nature and the God of Nature to explain these facts that are so important to man." I don't believe I have got the connecting clause of that sentence right. I don't feel sure that "to explain" was what he did say. He seemed to be more struck with the endlessness of the supply of water than anything else, every time. The next morning he wished to hurry out to see if it hadn't diminished a little. So we did, paid again, and took our last look. He went at noon to Buffalo, apparently not afraid, but I am. I cried with fright seeing him go off all alone. If some member of the body-guard isn't in attendance I can't imagine how he will find his way. And do you know! not one has reported since we left Judge Hoar; I never have known a case before of his being a single day without one. I committed him to the care of the conductor, who promised to take charge of him and deliver him to some one in Buffalo. I am not distinguishing myself meanwhile in the care of myself. I committed my fortunes this morning to the Hotel Porter, and his wits were wool-gathering. He sent my trunk to Saratoga and put me on the train to Clifton. But I'm straightened out now. E. T. E.

Concord, September 23rd, 1878.

Dear Edith,

We came home Saturday night at 9; visited Mother a few minutes, and then reentered Bush which had been deserted (except by Margaret) for a week. Father was very unhappy that Mother wasn't here, and has spent most of the days and evening at Edward's with her. But Edward gave us leave to bring her home this afternoon and now she is taking her first nap in her own bed. I didn't take in how sick she has been, both she and Edward say it seemed a dangerous illness at first, and she is still pretty sick. If it is as bad, and is going to have as much of an effect on her as my illness of 1867 which lasted me 7 years, I may well tremble. I don't yet know. She is full of admiration of her doctor, thinks him very thorough and devoted. And Annie has been lovely to her. Father enjoys Annie more and more; in enumerating Edward's virtues & endowments he always brings her in in one way or another, and seldom hears her name without some commendation. You know from my former letters how we went to Niagara, and all about that. On Monday P.M. we separated & Father went to find Mr Tufts, I to Saratoga. The joys of Saratoga socially & intellectually were all that had been promised. My child you had better go yourself next time. To dwell in a fairy palace, in the best & gleefullest of company, to see every friend lay or clerical from every part of the world that you almost ever had raises one's spirits continually. Then I don't know what your ideas of conventions are—I imagine you think them like after-dinner-speeches, wearisome, but work isn't wearisome, and conventions mean

work, and work enlivened by the gayest play. The essays are so fine you feel proud of your race, the business is carried on like a game, and life is so exciting and full that a day seems a week. When I arrived every mortal had read in the Sunday Herald that Father was to attend the National Conference as a delegate! You can understand the pleasure I had in improving the opportunity offered me almost hourly of denying the truth of this statement and assuring his friends that he was far away. Not till Friday morning did he come and then, all zeal to go to the Conference, he wouldn't stop to rest after his whole night of sitting up forlornly in the train, was hardly willing to eat at breakfast, and if I hadn't insisted on feeding him first he would have rushed from the depot to the church. He greatly enjoyed Mr. Curtis's essay. After that I thought two more essays were coming and advised him to go home and go to bed. He did. And couldn't forgive me, nor I myself that I let him go, for he slept through the rest of the Conference, which was sprightly and delightful but he enjoyed your dear letters and all the company.
E. T. E.

Concord Sept 25th 1878

Dear Edith,

When Monday came I thought of Ralph beginning his career of Boston school-boy. I hope it will do him good. Your picture of him in your birthday-letter to Mother was delightful. She sends her love to you and thanks you for writing, it was a great consolation to her she says. She is still quite confined to the bed, but enjoying the comfortable feeling of rest which usually with her accompanies sickness. I haven't begun to tell you all about my adventures, and I want to. Our party at the U.S. Hotel was Judge Hoar & Cary, Fanny Storer & Miss Prichard, Mrs Bartlett & I. I sat usually between Mrs Bartlett & Miss Prichard, and used to confer with them, when the uproar of dining hundreds made general conversation impossible, and sometimes Cary & Fanny & I would sympathize over Essays, Reports & speakers. At the table below us sat Mr. E. E. Hale and his daughter & delegates, the James Freeman Clarkes & Brooke Herfords at one diagonally next us. Mr Hussey's party & Mr Westcott's in sight, Mr Reynolds & the rest of Concord farther down. Mr Hall of Worcester in our near neighborhood and there was occasional communication all round. The first time Mr Hale spoke to me he came with humble head and feeble voice saying "I have bowed to you three or four times, but I haven't shaken hands with

— 1878 —

you yet. Perhaps you don't remember me. My name is Hale, Edward E. Hale, pastor of a church in Wisconsin." Of course at this place I saw again some of my beloved long-lost friends, now preaching in distant places. Among those I most longed to see was Mr Flagg of Bernardstow. I was coming home on Sat. believing he hadn't been there. My dear! I sat with him in the cars an hour or more and had real conversation with him. When I repeat to Mother all the talks I have had, all the serious sincere religious discussion which I have heard she wonders that so much happiness should fall to the lot of one person in one week. My dear Mr Green introduced me to a cousin of his, a young very radical Unitarian minister, who had with him in the cars as we came home another of the same stripe, and for an hour or two they talked out "The New Ethics", Mr Everett's essay, to me. This was my first encounter with Radicals, and it was infinitely interesting to me to learn their theory of life and religion. Of course they kept firing sentences out of Father's Essays at me, it was very pretty to see them laugh with joy at their patness and the sensation that they were quoting them to his daughter. Father sat by but didn't hear a word. Now to return to Father's leaving me on Monday. Of course I feared he would have trouble. If he did, he has forgotten it. It is curious to hear him tell his story, and notice the intervals in it where things made no impression on him. He succeeded in finding a friend and former employer of George E. Tufts who remembered his writing the letter, and told him G. T. was now 38 yrs. old, distinguished for his utter incapacity of getting a living, having a way of doing everything backhanded and loving only to write, but producing no effusions of a kind that publishers would take. He also gave the present address of G. T. to Father; not more than 40 miles off he was, but Father was tired of hunting, abandoned the chase, and came to Saratoga. He doesn't remember anything about one of his nights, the other two he can tell the story of. By means of newspapers, tickets and memoranda, in his bag we have made sure of where he was part of the time. But when he did turn up at Saratoga, cindery, pale and thin after his night's journey, instead of being more forgetful than ever he was uncommonly clear. It has done him good to find his way alone. Someone had said to me, "No people would be so glad to see him as the Unitarians!" And so it proved. Never has he been so sought and watched and followed as he was every minute of the time he was there. People introduced themselves and each other and almost stood in cue. I in all possible ways prevented his escape and sometimes succeeded for an hour at a time. He was bright and able to talk, and I thought since it was good for him and pleasant to them there was no reason why it shouldn't continue. I left him at the foot of a stair-case to his room packed with seated ladies, and followed my own pleasure. Mrs. Bartlett came to me and said he had hailed her from afar and asked her if she couldn't show him any way into which he could glide unobserved. She pointed out the elevator, "Then they could look at me all the way up," he objected, and she fled. Soon after I observed him swiftly darting through court and corridor, and since he had once freed himself I took pity and showed him the darker quieter stairs that led to his room. He had a beautiful time at dinner. He sat between me and Mr. Curtis who was between him and Judge Hoar, and they had some talk all together, and part of the time Mr C. and Father talked. Then came Dr Bellows and leaned over between Mr C. & Father, and there followed a very lively play which everyone at the table enjoyed and Father not least. The next day the Conference was over and gone, all the delegates had departed. Father & I took a buggy and went to call on "That Lady". Alas! when the girl came she said Mrs Putnam was at Far Rockaway. Father liked Mr Putnam very much. He seemed to me a very quiet bashful man but Father was so much pleased with him as to surprise me; I wondered whether it was because he was "that Lady's" husband or whether Father saw his real character. He told us that the waiters at the Hotels said these Unitarians were a very different class from what they usually saw. This seemed to me very natural, and I said "Of course. These are almost all very humble country-church people." "The waiters say it is a much better class." he answered. A chambermaid, Mrs Bartlett says, addressed one of her friends as she entered her room with the remark that it was nothing to the chambermaids to do their work with this houseful to what it had been all summer. "We get our work done this week by the middle of the forenoon, and usually it takes almost all day." By this we understood that the Unitarian ladies clear up their own rooms.

E. T. E.

Concord Oct 12th 1878

Dear Sally,

In your letter you tell me about Willy & our trins, but you wholly omit my poor little Ruth. I hope she wasn't naughty when you were there. Susy & Haven have written me just the right kind of letters

— 1878 —

about her since she went back. Edith is moving up from Naushon, but I can't go to help her this time as I hoped. Little Charles walks as well as any child just beginning, we were overjoyed to see how serviceable his twisted foot is without a particle of apparatus on it. His best achievement so far is five steps at once. He advances a little in talking too. John is magnificent, but homely almost as ever. Annie & Edward are particularly well and happy. It is weeks since I have been at the Manse, I am sorry to say. I took tea at the Bartletts' last night and Miss Bartlett was delightful. So were they all. Annie Emerson is going to take Philip Walcott for the winter, and Mrs Sanborn says if she does she (Mrs S.) shall take John Emerson.

Ellen T. Emerson.

Concord Oct. 16th 1878

Dear Puss,

If I thought I could spare it I would enclose to you Dean Stanley's letter. He says he will come Oct. 28 or thereabouts. How are you getting along? Did Will ever say anything about Mother's wood-lots after receiving my letter? Annie has come home from Worcester. She brought us down a fine roast of venison which Will had sent to Edward. The Shakespeare Club meets at their house tonight. I hope for at least a business word from you very soon. I am full of regrets that I have been of no use whatever to you, darling, and see no prospect of coming soon to you since there is this break in our 3 years prosperity in the kitchen. Mother is better, begins to assume her usual habits.

E. T. E.

Concord Oct 17th 1878

Dear Haven & Susy,

I have most beautiful letters from you, and should have answered before if Mother hadn't been sick. Though she has been very comfortable most of the time it has prevented my doing many little things. When we went to Saratoga I did not forget to consider whether we couldn't take New York on our way, but Niagara & the Conference could only come into one week by careful arrangement. It was my first sight of the Falls and I was disappointed even more than I had expected, for I was pretty sure beforehand that water could not have the effect on me that I had always heard described by people coming home from Niagara. Still I hoped till the last minute for some effect, and felt

— 1878 —

none. I have one excuse, the Falls were very muddy. We had delightful days there, Father enjoyed them and talked with me more than usual. On Monday Father abandoned me voluntarily for the first time for many years and set forth alone to wander in Western N.Y. to look up a correspondent of his who ceased to write to him years ago, and I went to Saratoga, quite anxious about Father and wondering if I had done right to let him go alone with his incapacity for remembering a name, but he wasn't afraid, and I wrote him a guide-book. You will have heard from every Unitarian what bliss we all revelled in for four days at Saratoga, it was almost the same joy we have at Monadnoc in being all together utterly away from care & in the highest spirits, and there was besides the sense of being instructed and improving the instruction. The last day came and no word of Father. I thought it time to write to Edward on the subject. So I did, before breakfast, and as I carried my note down I met my Papa coming up stairs! You don't know how much good his travels had done him. Though he had been riding all night he was uncommonly clear and able to remember, and to talk with every one. All the Unitarians wanted to shake hands with him, and sometimes he had suffering hours when they cornered him, but I smiled at his woes. We came home Saturday and found Mother sick at Edward's. Edward is really happy & prosperous and pretty well nowadays. Annie is magnificent, so rosy and shining and always subjugating her family-in-law more & more. Both the boys are in fine condition. Edith has just moved up from Naushon and all her family is well, Don having recovered smoothly from scarlet fever. Our present deep interest is Dean Stanley. Nothing could be funnier than the way reports perpetually spread here & apparently over the country that he is staying with us. Letters from N.Y., Conn. & Mass. come to us for him. We were made glad two days ago by a letter from him promising to come by Nov. 1st. Give my love to Ruth and thank her for her letter.

E. T. E.

Monday Nov. 4 1878

Dear Edith,

I send you two letters and a Christian Register. Be sure and read every word of the opening two paragraphs of "Conference Gossip" and Father & Mother & I have enjoyed the whole piece so much that we expect you to also. I went to get my blue velvet bonnet Thurs. and hated it so Miss Melcher is making it over. Then did I go a-shopping, and had

— 1878 —

great pleasure in towel-buying. Now that the handsomest towels cost only 25 cts. one can buy them. I went in the afternoon to Alice Bartlett's wedding and first to Mary Blake's to change my collar & brush up. Mary was in New York but the little Marian received me with hospitality, and zealously assisted at my toilette, full of sympathy & anxiety about my hurry. I was in excellent season finally and saw all that there was to be seen of the plainest kind of church-wedding. Going out I met Marny Channing Loring & Cary Channing Cabot and was very glad to see them. Father had a letter from George E. Tufts, a very interesting one. Father is very apt to comment on the beauty of his coffee-cup and he commended the butterfly handle the other morning saying it was better than others, and wondering at the ingenuity which contrived it. Have you seen a little notice in Adv. called "Emerson's Old Age", from Scribner? If not I'll send you that.

E. T. E.

Concord Nov 6th 1878

Dear Edith,

I fear from the few figures I have seen that Butler has even more votes than his enemies feared; he seems to have 75 or 80 to Gov. Talbot's 100 though the Advertiser is crowing and trumpeting the signal victory of hard money and says the green-back vote is insignificant. John voted right, as usual. Edward told us at dinner that Mr Staples went for Butler, but Sarah Richardson said last night that he told her himself the day before that he should vote for Gov. Talbot. Mr G. F. Hoar spoke here on Saturday night, and all his friends enjoyed the occasion. Father thought it was one of the best speeches he ever heard. Edward said there were plenty of men of the other parties there to hear. I forgot to tell you that I went to Mr Hawes the other day and paid for Father's daguerreotype, and have his receipt, so we at last own the original thing. Did you read about the Dean at the Century Club? We did. It was very pleasant. We have invited Mrs Hemenway & Augustus for next week, Wednesday & Thursday. I hope they will come. Our news in Concord is principally as follows: Edward Reynolds is engaged to a lady from out of town, a niece of Mr Haskill the cabinet-maker up by the depot; Mrs Chamberlaine has bought the house opposite hers, the one that used to be Mr Channing's and is coming home this year instead of next. Annie tells me Edward's portrait has come home. We haven't seen it yet. Father & Mother are invited to visit it tomorrow. How early can you come for Thanksgiving?

E. T. E.

Concord Nov 11th 1878

Dear Edith,

I am glad you are on a journey, and Southward too. Your basket came on Saturday and was very welcome to me with my Freedmen's barrel so soon coming on & my two families of children all so needy. Father is really working very hard to write the preface for Sampson & Low. I am most anxious that he should succeed, but he thinks he cannot get it done in time. Annie invited us all to tea on Friday to see Edward's picture which was an entire surprise to Mother & Father—and to me, for it wasn't the picture at the Mechanics' Fair, but utterly different. More distinctly Edward, and looked exactly as if Mr Hunt had painted it. Mother & Annie give it unqualified praise. Father liked it. I didn't at all. To me it is as bad as Mr Hunt's picture of Will, it has a look of stony hopeless misery. Then we went down to tea, and having admired the baby-show and asked which was Philip and which was John, we saw each infant put through his accomplishments. John cries from 10.30 P.M. till 4 A.M. and Philip often begins at 5. Mother was as much pleased with the chrysanthemums & the—is it broad-leaved myrtle?—as you could desire, and they are beautiful. Who wrote me that pretty letter from Naushon? Don? But whose chirography is it? So clear & neat!

E. T. E.

Concord Dec 10th 1878

Dear Edith,

Poor Edward & Annie are having a hard time, all the children & themselves too having a hard cold. Annie is hoarse and as wretched-looking as I ever saw her. Roger, Edward thinks, has Scarlet Fever. He broke out this morning. Lily's cold has finally driven her into her bed. So they are all in doleful dumps. At Bush we are well and frisky. Dec. 11th. Roger is so much better today that Edward doubts about its being the fever. Annie looks as sick today, John hasn't improved, Philip has. It is his birthday, poor little boy. I dispensed the bounties in the way of old clothes, which you brought with you, to various grateful recipients. Ann Byron especially prays that your children may prosper. I have

— 1878 —

wanted to write before, and have been grateful for your letters. Mr & Mrs Forbes & Sarah made us a delightful visit. I could desire no better time, except for our fathers. Mr Forbes often seemed to wish himself away, and Father was correspondingly frightened. But Mr Forbes was a perpetual treat nevertheless to us all, and sometimes seemed to enjoy himself too. I consoled myself when he didn't with the knowledge that it is natural to the masculine mind to desire home, and that it is good for it to be sometimes thwarted in that desire. I wish I could know that it did no one any harm to come. I was very glad to hear of the dancing-school and that you saw the Mrs Cabots. Maggy Ames has moved into her house, and is happy to be keeping house again. I went to Boston on Monday and liked my bonnet *pretty* well. I poked round through many shops, spent much time & money, brought home vast bundles, and enjoyed a glorious "opening" when I got home. Your letter about New Years awaited me. Would either of your little boys like a velocipede? So rejoiced to hear that E. Bartol has succeeded with Don! How is Cameron?

E. T. E.

Concord Dec. 24th 1878

Dear Edith,

Thank you for your answer. If you think best Don can have the bow from Frank and the train from Father. The little engines now on the train may be kept for little Charles in the future. I saw a beautiful chair at Paine's which would be lovely for V. if it comes within. For if Will has bought the 5. worth of things for Ralph as I said there'll be only about 5. or 5.50 left for V. beside her bow. When I go to Boston I'll see. It is called "Venetian", black wood, cane seat & back, broad seat & tall & stately back. I thought it the handsomest mine eyes had seen. Mother's trunk is to go on Thursday if poss. and she I hope may be able to come Friday. If not Saturday. Annie has neuralgia in her face for a certain number of hours, but is cheerful about it. Edward is hard-worked. The children are well. Goodbye, if my feet were free how quickly would I skip to Milton.

E. T. E.

January 1879 – December 1880

Waldo Forbes born. John Emerson dies. July 4th Celebration in Concord. Grove meeting at Lake Winnepesaukee. Trip to Concord, New Hampshire with RWE. 1880. Visitors. Circuit meeting in Concord. Ellen Emerson born, and Charles dies.

Concord Jan 11th 1879

Dear Edith,

My dream seems pretty true about Roger, though not about Charles. He is in the same state C. was last winter, but so wasted & weak that there seems to be less ground for hope than there was with Charles. It is abcesses. Mr Keyes & Mr Walcott have no hope left. Mrs Keyes & Annie don't quite give up. Edward is very anxious & can only say "He has a chance." This I heard at the party & in the cars coming home. I'm just going to Edward's to breakfast. Mother I hope is safe. All went well with us, and we found the house extra warm & polished to receive her. But John is sick in bed & Father went away yesterday into the w[ide]. w[ide]. world, leaving word he might not come home till today & he hasn't. So no one came to the train for us, & if Mother's admirers hadn't turned out in force to stop depot-carriage we sh'd have been in trouble. Dear Edith I mourn for you & so does Mother, we want to see you again, beloved. And greatly have we enjoyed Will & the Bears & everything. Your most naughty but affectionate sister.

Ellen.

Concord January 14th 1879.

Dear Alice [Jackson Arthur],

Aunt Susan took tea here on Sunday night and told us about her Guild, and the Service they have every Sunday, and of her hopes that you would soon come and live a year or so with her, and of her desire to come and take Mrs Barber's house and live next to Maggy Ames. I never knew a greater success than your family's coming to Concord, they seem so snugly established in church & social relations. I send you a letter or two of Frank Browne's, and Edith's Christmas letter that you may get a little news of other branches of the family. (Please return them.) Ralph is now twelve, wears long trousers, and goes to school in Boston. Violet is eleven and when she is good which is about three quarters of the time she is the dearest most affectionate exemplary & feminine of girls, with natural tact and perception, and a faculty of making bright speeches. When she isn't good she contradicts & criticizes her brothers too much and her tongue is a little too sharp. She idolizes her mamma and is very useful to her and I take as much comfort in her as if she belonged to me alone. Our three small boys are the wonders of the world for sweetnees and goodness, but Cameron though a flower of beauty & with the most winning voice & manners, is as impractical as Miss Elizabeth Peabody, to the daily despair of everyone who has anything to do with him. Don & Edward are much better in that line, and so innocent & affectionate and humble, they seem to have retained their babyhood a great while. Edward & Annie are happy & well, except a Doctor with many patients some of whom are in the most critical condition must always be a harassed man. Their floor is alive with creeping infancy, and their two own sons are very promising. Poor little Roger [Walcott] has lain at death's door with Scarlet Fever for a week or ten days, but seems to be gaining now. Mother is so well & charming I wish you could see her. She is so free & happy now that you would wonder, who only remember her in her evil days crushed with care & starved to death with no one to look out for her. Aunt Susan Emerson first suggested to me that such was the case about the time you were married, and the moment she learned that food was not poison a new era dawned for her which has been at its noon for the last year or two. She is as delicate & suffering as ever, but now she has food when she needs it, she never, or almost never, goes on to those fearful distresses that were so common, and she goes much into company, and enjoys it greatly. She is a regular belle. Father is well and gay at home but shuns the face of his fellow-men alas! because he forgets words. Now you must write me just such a yarn about yourself & your family.

Ellen T. Emerson.

Saturday Jan. 18th 1879

Dear Edith,

Roger died last night. Lily came to see me in the afternoon and told me the disease had gone to his lungs, and she thought he had better die than live for he was paralyzed on the right a little and she thought his brain was affected too. He was buried this afternoon. And people talk and say "His Mother was drawing him away." It sounds very pretty to

— 1879 —

me, and it is pleasant to outsiders to think so, but I suppose Mr Walcott & Mr & Mrs Keyes would say that Flory never would have thought of taking away their great comfort. Charles came yesterday and visited Mother, and today and visited Father, and seemed pleased to come and unwilling to go away, his cold still hangs on and so does John's. But John's spirits are at their right level once more. Annie brought him to dinner on Tuesday. He crept about & explored like all his predecessors, and the moment any door was opened set forth at full speed to go out at it, but was uniformly prevented.   Monday, Jan 20th.   Is it only sixteen years since the Cavalry Party? I thought it was twenty or even more. Well Ralph and Jim [Russell] have come and gone, and they stood it about as well as I expected. Ralph was as obedient as he could be, even when he did hate to obey. I shall have to qualify my statement a little. He might have done better as to promptness once or twice, when I told him not to *stay* in Jim's room, and he remained 3/4 of an hour. Still I suppose he knew that I was not unconscious of the fact, and that if I thought it a sin he would hear himself called, and left the care on me. So I didn't blame him, and let it go, though I shouldn't actually call that obedience. Yesterday morning head-ache, stomach-ache, nausea, langour, misery, set in one after the other, a new disease every half hour, augmenting in violence as church-time approached, and Jim earnestly represented to me that he had a head-ache and Ralph was "very sick". But having seen and heard many things in general and much of Ralph in particular & reflecting that J. also had a head-ache and proposed to stay at home, and that *I* shouldn't hesitate to go to church with a head-ache or any other disease not catching, I offered much commiseration & alleviation, but when staying at home was proposed replied that church was a warm quiet place, safe for invalids, and that as far as Ralph was concerned I had orders & orders I carried out. So we went to church in perfect health & harmony all together, and Ralph stayed reluctantly to S.S. but I found at night that he had been sufficiently interested in Sherman's teaching. Roger, Annie says, was perfectly clear to the last moment. He followed Mrs Keyes with his eyes whenever she moved about the room, as he always had. Edward didn't want Annie to go to the funeral, and run the risk of bringing the fever to Philip, but she said her Mother had more need of her than ever before and Philip must take what little risk there was. Edward himself is still very much driven, but holds out pretty well and there is no one else at death's door now. He said when he came in one day "To lose two patients in one week is very bad. Annie and I are going to take the babies to be photographed some day this month." Father has consented to read a lecture to a South End class of Mr Alcott's, ladies, I believe. It will be on Jan. 31st at 3 o'clock at Miss O'Leary's 75 Chester Sq. Can you come? Your sister

E. T. E.

February 13th 1879

Dear Edith,

I saw Mrs Tower at the Lyceum last night and she told me that Mr S. D. Kent is still a book-binder. Send the books straight to him Marlboro' Mass, where his bindery is, though he lives here. How interesting that Will is an Academy Trustee! I hope they'll have a good housewarming at your Town Hall and that the people will like it. I should like to come if it weren't for lectures. I am sorry to write so little, but with lectures how can I? We go to Amherst Feb. 28th. Didn't you think that least distinct picture of Father reading his newspaper was good? I did. Infinitely better than the present published one, the dire. Wouldn't it be well to tell them that they may, if they must publish, use that? Much delight was given in Concord by C & D's pretty little letters, which we shall soon answer. No more time!

E. T. E.

Milton Feb. 28th 1879

My dear Mamma,

Yesterday was the first day on which the baby might be expected, and while we hoped for it, and Edith said that it would be a great inconvenience to have it choose March 3rd on account of Town-Meeting, she yet felt sure it would come that day, & we made up our minds to that. Then did I begin to bite my chains and howl with fierce remorse that I had so early abandoned my parents, and to consider whether I wouldn't go home this morning. But when morning came I found Dr Holmes and Will already at the breakfast-table, so I gave myself up to joy and could hardly keep sober enough to pour out, and eat my breakfast. However about ten o'clock Will & the doctor were tired of waiting down stairs and came up to see Edith, and presently the doctor drove away. Before eleven Will came to read to Edith and I descended to the study where I am writing.

Later.   The note I sent to Eugenia I hope has reached you saying that M. was paid up to yesterday, and tonight you owe her 4.57, tomorrow night $5.14. I haven't—I was going to say heard from Edith for 2 hours—but Will has just come down stairs, 3.21 P.M., saying "Well, you're an uncle, Ellen!" It's a little, a big boy rather. Edith is comfortable.

E. T. E.

Milton Feb 28th 1879.

Dear Haven & Susy,

I have been driven with work the last month at home and in January I was making visits all the time so that I have been very slow in declaring what joy and food I found in Susy's letter of December. I have come to Milton to spend a month with Edith and Dr Holmes has just come in and gone up stairs. I trust this letter will have beautiful news in the end. Father is very well this winter. He has read two lectures in parlours with more security and pleasure than he did last year, and next Wednesday he will give one before the Concord Lyceum. He was to have gone to Amherst today to read in a parlour, but he has cut his hand with a razor, not deep, but it doesn't heal, and Edward forbids his going. Mother too is well, goes out more in the evening than she used to, and is a great belle. Miss Peabody lives in Concord now and has started a class in Philosophy. Mother goes to that, and since she has studied about Socrates, she thinks perhaps he was less hateful to Xanthippe than she had supposed, and he stands a little higher on her books. Edward bears this winter much better than he did last winter, he looks thin and old, and his hair looks sick, but he seems in better order nevertheless than he was a year ago. The three boys have worn on Annie a little, she is thin and has lost too much sleep, yet she bears it wonderfully and has her usual cheerful courage and keeps her colour. It is a real comfort to her to have Philip [Walcott], she knows he is properly taken care of, she can see to his morals, and he is so happy with his cousins. Charles & John have been a forlorn pair most of the time during December & January, teething and having colds of the heaviest kind that lasted & lasted, and abscesses, ear-aches, & C. had to lose his great toe-nail. In the last month they have picked up, can now breathe, sometimes smile, and even laugh, and we hope the walking which has languished all winter is about to begin again. Edith's children, at least those who had scarlet fever last year have had all sorts of colds & headaches & small woes all winter too. Edith has been very well and has set

— 1879 —

her house in order to the last point. Will is well & working very hard. He has been chairman of the committee to build the new Milton Town Hall, and that was finished a week ago, very satisfactorily, for a few hundred dollars *less* than the appropriation. He is newly elected Trustee of the Milton Academy, and in Boston a Director of the Bell Telephone Co.

A big boy has just been born, 3.20 P.M. Edith had a very easy time, the doctor came at 2.

E. T. E.

Milton March 8th 1879

Dear Mother,

This may not have to be a business letter, I hope not, I'll tell you about the children. The little baby has cleared up his complexion, and has more neck than he had a week ago, and holds up his head a little already. Edith seems delighted with him and can't praise him too much, she says he is one of the cool leisurely kind that she likes. Cameron has cheered up and got well since I went to Concord and is bright as a bird. His daily business is to build a fort with chairs. He is also interested in stamps. He & Don have a joint collection and keep it in a heap on the nursery window-seat. Occasionally they brush it all onto the floor & lie prone, stretched at full length beside it, sorting & counting it. This morning Violet and the little boys went to ask Mrs Forbes if they might pick violets in her cold-frame. She gave them leave not only to do that but to take some azaleas, and they brought home to Mamma very pretty bouquets. Edward at first wished to keep his for himself but when all the others had given theirs, and he had retired to the nursery with his flowers he either felt uneasy or the others prevailed upon him to lay them on his Mamma's altar and they were brought in with much delight. Then came Mrs Forbes to make a little call and she had a crimson rose, a blush rose & a Cherokee rose for Edith, so the room is now a flower garden. Mr Forbes sent a telegram from Georgia yesterday saying their train had been smashed up and their party was saved only by their Pullman car & three happy accidents. The paper doesn't give any light on the subject this morning. Ralph went to Boston this morning to spend his holiday playing with Powell Mason & Harry Curry and the Sears boys. Tonight Jim is here and is playing "Puss, puss in the Corner" with our children in the hall, very quietly as to feet on

account of Edith, but with very hearty laughter. Edith is doing well, has good nights and naps every afternoon. Will is very amusing with the baby. Ask Father if he has answered the Ch. of the Messiah about that hymn. If not please see that he does today.
E. T. E.

Milton Thursday March 27th 1879

Dear Mother,

I have neglected to write to you; there have been business letters. I am very sorry you are sick. This weather is so bad that it is perhaps an economy to use it to be sick in if you must be sick. Edith sent for Dr Holmes today to ask whether it was time to try sitting up, but he says "Not yet". Miss Fanny Forbes came this morning to make a call. When I met her at the door she exclaimed in a wilful manner, "I shan't come in", with an air which showed that *I* was the reason why. However she proceeded to come in, and when I asked what was the matter she said "What? you! Is it you? I thought it was Edith, and I considered the whole a very improper proceeding, when she ought to be lying on a sofa in her wrapper." As she went into the parlour she began again "I do not choose to recognize the creature that has come here". "I hope you don't mean our Baby upstairs" I interrupted. "I only accept girls," she continued with decision and set down a box on the table, "but I brought this to see if Edith thought this might do for him to wear at Naushon." So we cut the string and the box proved to contain a little blue jacket. I ran up to tell Edith she was here and to put on the Baby's best blanket though Edith said "It's of no use, Aunt Fanny always shuts her eyes when she looks at a little baby." But when I took in Alexander's general effect I thought it was enough to soften a heart of stone. I felt sure the most infuriated enemy of little men-children wouldn't refuse to look, and to continue to look at the spectacle. So I invited Miss Forbes up, and she contrived not to discern him for a good while, and talked very gaily with Edith. At last he creaked and Edith pointed him out. Miss Forbes promptly rose and approached the basket. She did not shut her eyes, but came quite near and said "What big eyes you have!" Then she pointed to her veil and said "Don't you like a Shetland veil?" By lucky chance he turned his eyes upon her veil with a considerate expression. "You do like it, don't you?" He gave an affirmative grunt, which she accepted & quite converted, said he resembled Ralph and was a good child. She even looked at his feet and said as she returned to

— 1879 —

Edith "Usually I shut my eyes when I see a baby." She laid the blue jacket over him and crossed its sleeves. Edith was much pleased with it. Her whole visit was delightful. As she went away the children came home from school, and strode into the hall. To my dismay Violet looked as if she was going to pass her by, but just as I began to say "Say how do you do", she gave a spring, threw her arms round her Aunt Fanny & cried "Oh Releaser!" Instantly Don followed her example, and after the embraces such a din of conversation began, each child crowding and screaming to be heard & beginning every sentence "Releaser! Do you remember—" or "Releaser, have you seen—" or "Releaser, we've built such a big dam." This continued till her wagon came. Violet says that one summer at Naushon they played that she was Lady Zuleika and Edward couldn't say the name right & called her Releaser, and they all gradually adopted the name. I shall come home Saturday by the 6 express. Your affectionate daughter
Ellen T. Emerson.

Concord Mar. 31st 1879

Dear Edith,

I trust I finally did such errands as I accomplished on Saturday right. Mother was delighted with the flowers and uttered many a heartfelt Oh over each rose & striped carnation. As to that great pink camellia her surprise at its size and admiration of its beauty were great and lasting. It spends its days on the front entry table and is ceremoniously brought into the dining-room at every meal. She & Father delight of course in every morsel of news or narrative of you or any of you. I make them laugh most of all by any tale of Will. Edward was here yesterday. When I asked him about John he said "Well, he has latterly consented to slumber lightly in the night if one of his parents will sit beside him with a lamp." Father looks tired out with his preface and has stayed in the house too much. I am glad he is going to Boston today. Much love to you all, I hate to leave you. Ida was suffering very much when I saw her on Saturday. Chas. & T. are coming to Bush today.
E. T. E.

Concord March 31st 1879

Dear Miss Dabney,

I hope I shall get this letter or perhaps only note to you on your birthday. It is just ten years this winter since the winter I spent in Fayal.

— 1879 —

I am going to tell you about Dean Stanley now for fear I shall let it slip away and never tell you. We first heard of his coming when he was already here. We were at Saratoga at the happy National Unitarian Conference; and when we came home he had left Boston, and we pursued him with letters. In England you know how good to us he & Lady Augusta were, but though I felt acquainted with him it was wholly an outside acquaintance, & with Father this was still more the case. But when Father published "Letters & Social Aims" and sent a copy to Lady Augusta, she was dying, and Dean Stanley wrote us a letter, as to friends. Then when we joined the subscription of her American friends to her Memorial Westminster Training School for Nurses, to our surprise he wrote us again, a lovely letter. You shall see his letters, they are illegible, very short, but his heart is sure to come out somewhere, if only in one word. And when at last we got his answer to Father's invitation, it was again just so. Edith & Will came to enjoy his visit with us. He brought his two friends, a young pleasant medical student, and a confiding cheerful lady-loving gentleman who wasn't young, Mr Grove. They arrived at nine at night. The next morning Dean Stanley came to me when I was alone in the dining-room after breakfast and shook hands with me just as if he hadn't seen me before and said "I am *very* glad to see you again", and then his face all gave way and he turned quickly and went out of the room. From that beginning all the rest of the visit I could see how wholly occupied with the thought of Lady Augusta he was, it was clear that he loved everyone that had known her, and everything that happened showed me what an infinite irreparable loss to him she was. After he went away I read the sermons that he preached here and they were interesting and touching now that I knew what he meant, how he had learned what was in them, and how thorough and sincere a man he is. He asked to see our battle-ground and showed great information, and a surprising interest to see & zeal to learn about the events of 1775 here. Mr Grove on the contrary knew nothing about it and the whole story was new to him and touched his susceptible heart; he came home and followed me round the house about my work, telling me about their visit to the Monument and Minute-Man—"and oh my! how I cried when I read that about 'the embattled farmers!' " Then Judge Hoar came to dine & he & the Dean talked about American libraries, newspapers, schools, habits. I was between them & heard it all. I want to tell you but I can't. I shall tell you one more thing. Dean S. said to Mrs Cabot "I enjoy my visit to America

— 1879 —

more than I can say. I meet so many friends of my dear wife, and I constantly feel by the way they treat me that they recognize who is always beside me." Everybody in the house became personally attached to him while he was here. They were two very happy days. Now goodbye, with much love and many thanks for your beautiful long letters.
Ellen T. Emerson.

Concord, April 9th 1879

Dear Edith,

Thankyou very much for all your sendings to Ida. She had some of the water-ice and liked it, just before I was there the last time. I was there on Monday, and on Tuesday, but she didn't know me. Annie is coming to Boston to buy herself a new brown dress directly and means to snatch also a visit to you, but Charles is sick just now and that delays her. Give my love to Don & thanks for his letter. Mr & Mrs Cabot came on Monday afternoon & we worked while she read & went to see Jenny Mills. In the evening work again for us & the family in the parlour read Louisa Alcott's Transcendental Wild Oats. Tuesday morning I gave Mrs Cabot all that I have read these two months that I cared much about, to read, and she read it all and found time to talk it over before she went away. Meanwhile Mr Cabot finished the Preface and began the lecture on preaching which is to be delivered to the Div. Students in May. They went at noon, but I felt fortified & consoled by having seen Mrs Cabot, and the Sampson & Low business was all done & will go next Tuesday. Dan [French] dined with us on Tuesday with Edward, Annie & Philip. The bust is nearly finished he says. He is a charming boy. Father met Edward yesterday & was asked to visit Charles because he was sick. He said when he came home that he did go, "but my little boy was quite indifferent, he wouldn't look at me. He was entirely occupied with his own interests." "A book?" I asked. "Yes, perhaps it was. So I took up the other thing." "Was he affable?" "Yes he was willing to be held, but mine sat immoveable, and I came away." Charley & Therchi are very pleasant company. They have at last seen Eliza Reynolds, bought her furniture and hired the house on this side of it for a year. Mother hopes to come before May 1 to see the baby, and any day when I can persuade her to start we'll turn up without sending compliments. Did I write you how Dr Hedge's sermon on Sunday was a town experience? You ought to hear how people talk it over. He sent me the proof sheets of it. I read it yesterday with my class. I just met

Mrs Hunt seeking a laundress, and she told me she had been pleading my cause at 92 Carver St, telling Miss Jackson to serve me her prettiest and offer me no doubtful characters.

Saturday.

Dear Edith,

Ida died on Thursday morning. The affection she showed for all her family and the pleasure she expressed that the end had come, the perfect confidence that she was going to heaven that she showed, and the look of happiness that came immediately she died make them all happy.

Our John is very sick today, abscess under his arm, 4 double teeth coming. Mrs Keyes said when I said I never heard of abscesses before, her children had them when teething.

E. T. E.

Monday night 6.30 P.M.
April 14 1879

Dear Edith,

I lost the noon mail. John has been no worse all day, but I just went there and listened at the door, having asked my question, for an answer. I smelt brandy strong & they didn't hear me, they were moving, flying fast, and Annie crying was asking Edward something to which Edward answered in haste "Wrap him in flannel". I'm just going back, I didn't like to go in then, for I saw Mrs Keyes below so I knew they wanted no one. If I hear anything more I'll put it in. I am afraid at that moment they thought he was dying.———

He died just then
Ellen T. Emerson

Concord April 15th 1879.

Dear Edith,

I did want you here today to see your dear little nephew, and to represent the Emerson side. Father and I only could do it, for Mother isn't so well as usual, she is having another sickness. But she arose and was carried with precautions to see the pretty little creature before the funeral. The utter beauty was gone, as I think I told you today, but though he looked sunken & unlike himself he still had the lovely look of a dead baby. He was dressed in his pretty white flannel wrapper, trimmed with white silk braid. Round his neck he had one of Charles's finest and prettiest ruffles, and on his feet the cleanest tightest little white angora socks, and no shoes. I thought he couldn't possibly have been dressed in a more affecting manner. He lay on the centre-table, moved up between the front windows, his head towards the book-case. Annie sat at his head & Edward at his feet, and all his relations round the room. Annie & Mrs Keyes hadn't their things on, and after the service was over they went upstairs and when everyone had looked at the baby and he had been carried out to the carriage, they came down and Edward & Annie rode alone with him. Everyone went to the grave and he was let down into it by Edward & Prescott. Father & Charley also got out of their carriage & stood by, no one else got out. He was buried beside little William. I have had long talks with Mrs Keyes and Prescott since he died, and I find that the only people that didn't appreciate him were Edward & Father & Mother. Every one of the Keyeses considered him not only an uncommonly promising little fellow but the one in whom their pride was centred, the one that by nature attracted them. It was a comfort to me to find he had been valued. Annie valued him, and knew him as well as Charles, but Edward, like the rest of the world, had never got acquainted with him.

E. T. E.

Concord April 28th 1879

Dear Will,

This letter is to Edith but I suppose you want an answer about Pinafore before you go out of town, so I begin it to you. Father had just received three tickets to the Carnival of Authors at the Music Hall next Saturday afternoon when your invitation came but we have asked Edward & Annie to attend him there, and Mother and I want to come with you very much. Or to put the fact more exactly, Edward is going to take Father if possible, but patients may prevent, and in that case Annie & I shall go with him. Then would it do for me to pass over my ticket to Therchi? To go with all the Forbeses to see the Pinafore seems to me one of the pleasantest proposals imaginable. I think Father would enjoy it more than the Carnival of Authors. What do you say to the morality of accepting the tickets from Miss Putnam and then passing them on to Edward, Annie & Mother or me and going himself with you? I fear 'twould be a sin. He, innocent man, will go whither he is led not knowing at all which he would like best. Two engagements in Concord—Charles Stewart to the sister of Adelaide Foster's husband, Miss Gertrude Jacobs of Dorchester! and Amy Bean to George Houghton both of Concord.

Mail-time.
E. T. E.

May Day 1879

Dear Edith,

Father & Mother agree with you & Will that they are at liberty that he is at liberty to go to see Pinafore in spite of having accepted tickets to the Carnival of Authors. Edward & I don't agree with them and are glad that you & Will do. So, unless Mr Cabot is coming or the lecture needs *me* at home we'll all three come on dromedaries & ostriches with banners flapping in full glee to see you & the Pinafore, and I think Father & Mother whether or no. Mother can't combine it with a visit to you this time, but will try to come the next week. We will thankfully accept some apples. Ours are gone. I have a cook who came Monday night, and it looks as if she might be perfectly satisfactory. That beautiful letter about Will & the baby never acknowledged! My hair stands on end at the thought. It was because little John died just then, I'll tell you about it on Saturday. Mail-time.

E. T. E.

Concord May 7th 1879

Dear Edith,

Lidian [Jackson] has just written to Frank Bigelow to break her engagement and Aunt Susan is afraid if he comes to see her he will overpersuade her to renew it, so I have asked her to come here if she likes, and I will carry her to Milton with Mother & me tomorrow to have her out of the way. Mother has been a great support & comfort to the poor child & Aunt Susan on the occasion, and the little girl is good. If Mother can't come I'll telegraph as early as possible. Of course with her everything must be doubtful, but I expect to come out with her at 2.30 to E. Milton tomorrow & return, since Edw. doesn't want Father left alone all night, by 4 o'clock train, and to come again on Saturday & bring her away. We went to Cambridge on Monday & called on Mrs Storer and saw all three girls & little Roger, magnificent in strength & spirits, first teeth & red curls, running & talking. Then we went to Mrs James's &

— 1879 —

saw her & Mr James, met dear H. Putnam & Mrs Agassiz on Quincy St. and returned to Sophy's charming house where we had a beautiful time. I thought the lecture excellent & well read, but there was some boggling at words, and a wicked choking cough set in towards the end, so that it was almost impossible to finish. The audience was affectionate & appreciative. Dear kind Dr Hedge came and poured balm on Father's afflicted soul the next day, for Father was as unhappy as usual. He had a very sick night alas! so we had to give up our glorious plan of calling on Miss Sarah Clarke the next morning and dining with Aunt Adams, and sneak swiftly home instead. He has gone today to Overseers' Meeting. When can you come? May 24 to be here on the birthday? Dan's bust is finished, we are satisfied.

E. T. E.

Concord June 10th 1879

My dear Cousins Hannah & Sarah,

My first errand and earnest request is Will you both come as soon as you can and give us a month? Mother & Annie have been constantly asking me to hurry and present this petition. I hope I am not too late. As to time, any time when you can! I suppose you have heard of our events this winter & spring, that Edith did have a charming little blackeyed son, born on the 28th of February, and that he lived and prospered and only benefited his mother, who is in better health now than she has been for some years. We cannot yet get over our delight at this great blessing. His name is to be Waldo Emerson. Oh how glad we were that he was only a year younger than blessed little John at Edward's, and would be a cousin of fit age for him to enjoy! and how we planned a procession of descendants for Father's birthday in May! And on the fourteenth of April at sunset Edward & Annie called me up into their chamber to see how beautiful little John was after he was dead. He looked so strong and handsome and serious and superior, and the wind blew his white hair just enough to be pretty, not enough to tumble it much. To Edward he was nothing like such a loss as Charles would have been, but nothing can help his being a terrible loss to Annie. The good brave girl keeps a cheerful face and voice and goes on exactly the same. Father is waiting for the letter. Goodbye. Much love.

Ellen T. Emerson

— 1879 —

June 11 & 12 1879

Dear Haven & Susy,

Edward & Annie and I have been talking over the cemetery monument and especially the stone it shall be made of. I don't like granite of any kind, I don't want a speckled stone. Slate which I prefer Edward & Annie hate because it can only be faces and must be filled with something else. White marble we should like well enough if it didn't mould and stain so badly. "Then black marble!" says Edward. "*Too* black!" say Annie & I. Edward proposed various sandstones, but posterity, distant posterity, is my chief thought in the matter. I desire that this monument shall last and be a precious authority upon the names, dates & relationships of the family for the whole nineteenth century; so sandstone doesn't please me at all. Edward says we mustn't quarrel it out alone till we have heard what you & Charley say. That is my first business, and my second is to ask for Ruth for a week or two again this summer if it can be managed. You will mortify me and punish me very severely for what all the family consider my ill-judged frankness in telling all her sins last summer if you don't let her come this year. Please remember that I told you all the time that I liked her and liked to have her, and that I do want her again. I hope it is always in both your minds that we want to see the six here, and that a Thanksgiving ought sometime to come when you all, & Sally, & Charley & Therchi, should join the family festivity. Edith & Will were here on Father's birthday with all their flock and Edward & Annie brought Charles. We all missed little John. Though we saw him only seldom, of course he was counted in every moment in all our thoughts & plans, and so we perpetually feel the change and the something wanting, and I am glad we do; it would be much more sad to lose a baby and to have it make no difference. The baby across the road came across to play with Charles yesterday and Annie thinks C. thought it was his brother. She says he showed more joy than she ever saw him express before, and when little Percy was carried home Charles cried. She keeps Philip still, and that prevents C.'s being solitary. They are planning to go to Monadnoc if Edward can get away about Midsummer-Day. Prescott Keyes's Class-Day comes June 20th and Annie is going and has a very pretty new muslin for the occasion. I mean to go too. I wonder whether you have heard that Dan French has made a bust of Father. It is good. I have no fault to find with it. We all consider it a piece of great good fortune. I

— 1879 —

Bust of RWE by Daniel Chester French, on the front stairway at the Emerson house. At left is a portrait of RWE's great-grandmother, Phebe Walker Bliss, and on the right is a portrait of Lidian Emerson.

am not sure that Edward is satisfied but Edith & I are and Mr Cabot said "I never expected to see anything so satisfactory". Charley & Therchi seem well pleased with everything, especially their house. Charley is a most faithful worker in the Telephone Office and received a word of appreciation the other day from one of the chiefs which was very pleasant. Father is very well and has had a visit from Dr Furness & Mrs

Furness which was delightful. I see that in some respects he loses, it is always in the same line, of words and of power to fasten on his point in any disturbing circumstances, but every day brings proof that he doesn't in other things. He remembers plenty of the events and speeches of every day, and after any sermon or lecture, perhaps days after, he will make remarks upon it showing that he kept its thread all through and judged it every moment, as for instance "Every part of his sermon was powerful in itself, but *the whole* wasn't powerful enough. It wasn't finished in proportion", or something very like that, I am not sure I have his very words. After Uncle George's lecture on Brook Farm, Mother said to me "I wish Dan French could have seen your Father while Uncle George was reading, he looked just as I like to have him." I said I thought he had. The next morning Edward Simmons came down to see the bust, and said "I noticed Dan's expression last night, and then I saw he was sitting exactly opposite Mr Emerson; so I went round & whispered 'Dan, if you're like me, you're at work'. And he answered 'Hard at work.' " Presently Dan arrived & I told him Mother's speech. "Oh! of course I saw it," said he, "the very expression I struck out for when I began the bust. And then it changed to the expression I have on the bust, and I saw the difference. It is hard to think it is too late to put it on." All these speeches I repeated to Father afterwards who listened with interest. "Did he want a particular expression? Why didn't he tell me? I would have put it on." "Put it on! Oh Father! You couldn't possibly *put on* an expression." "Oh" said Father smiling at my surprise, "an old cock can." Nevertheless I believe he couldn't.

E. T. E.

Monday June 23rd 1879

Dear Edith,

The Fourth begins at the Town Hall early in the morning. Father is to read the Declaration of Independence. A vast choir including half the town is to sing the patriotic songs. We then proceed to the boat-race at Flint's Bridge. In the afternoon come athletic sports, and the River Carnival in the evening. Do come or contribute somebody if you can. Mother will not come. I think I forgot to mention that in this morning's hurry. The Chamberlaines have come home and brought a cargo of beautiful books to the Library. To Mother they have brought

— 1879 —

the most charming lapis lazuli box. And Lizzy Barber has brought her a handsome China vase. I have had a pleasant note from Mrs Davidson.
E. T. E.

July 5th 1879
Dear Edith,
Edward & Annie did attack me about Father's reading and I surrendered the matter at once into Edward's hands, only I told him Father had already begun to study it by himself, and that must be taken into consideration. This, Edward said, altered the aspect of affairs, and he let it go. Father read it perfectly well I thought. I sat on the platform behind him among the singers. Edward had alarmed me so that my heart was in my mouth, and Father's voice was very low I thought, but Miss Bartlett tells me she sat on the back seat and heard every word. I have heard great enthusiasm about it since from his friends. Great clapping when he rose. Shouts of "Up! Stand up!" The whole house rose, and continued great applause. When he sat down another tremendous clapping and G. Bartlett called for "Three cheers for the man whose voice is heard round the world." So they cheered. Miss Leavitt cried "Why? *Why* aren't the five Forbeses sitting on the front seat where they belong?" When I surveyed the audience I found the Hall was full. This I hadn't expected and it was very inspiriting. I saw everybody I knew and many strangers. Then came the procession. J. Melvin at the head with a fine white baton with new satin ribbons brought in Father, then other marshalls brought Judge Hoar, Mr Reynolds, Mr Alcott, the Committee followed. When they were seated on the platform in front of the choir Judge Hoar was introduced as the President of the day. He made a beautiful speech, which filled all hearts with joy, about the meaning, the use, the moral of Independence Day, and introduced Father as the grandson of our Revolutionary Minister. Then came those demonstrations I wrote about. Oh! I forgot the singing. Judge Hoar introduced the choir before he spoke himself and we sang "Speed our Republic", then after his speech which led naturally to the sentiments expressed in George's ode he introduced the Ode & invited us to sing it. Then came Father, and then didn't we stand up & holler the Star-Spangled Banner! all four verses. After that the concourse was invited to join the choir in singing America. And that was the end. We were very sorry. Everyone wanted to go on! Father & I drove home, and seeing symptoms of an egg-dance, I asked why, since all had gone

— 1879 —

so well. He said it was because he had studied the Declaration faithfully for the last three days and knew every point in it he supposed; and it was hateful when he came to read it to find a new document without a word in it he had ever seen before, so that he almost feared he had begun in a wrong book. I couldn't persuade him to go with Therchi & me to the Regatta, nor Charley either so she & I went alone. We saw Sherman & Rocky Hoar win a dory race, and John Keyes win a paddle race, then Sherman come in 3rd in a wherry-race, Charley Richardson second, & one of the Silas Hosmers first. Then a dory race with cockswains followed & in this race Sherman & Rockwood were beaten. Finally a tub-race, the finest I ever saw, Steddy & George Minns. Steddy just mounted his tub & paddled with his hands straight across the river & back again with no delay or accident at all. G. Minns was less successful but he got across & half way back before his tub capsized and then he swam ashore with it. Usually the tubs founder half a dozen times before the boys can get started at all. By this time it was noon, and as the crowd came back to town the noon bells rang. We came home to lunch. Cousin Sarah welcomed us, she had arrived at about 10 o'clock. The girls had gone out so Therchi & I put the luncheon on the table, and then we had a very agreeable dinner all together before the thunderstorm came on. I went to bed after tea, but Father & Mother & Cousin Sarah went to Edwin Barrett's new house to see the River Carnival and they said when they came home that it was as beautiful as last years. Cousin Sarah said "It looked like a sea of fire, and all these rainbow colours shining in it. I don't know how many boats there really were, but I felt as if there were thousands and thousands." Mother & Father said less but seemed almost as happy. The next day my Sunday-Scholars came to read and we read a little of the Angel in the House. Their appreciation of it warms my heart every time I read it to them. That night we went to Mrs Sanborn's to tea. Mr Charles Dudley Warner was there, Miss Leavitt, and Mrs Edward Hoar who brought with her Mr Whitney's sister. We had a beautiful time. After tea the whole company except I went to the club at Mrs Cheney's. James K. Hosmer gave the lecture. Mother invited him, his wife, and the Cheney's to tea on Sunday night. Much did they praise Mother's funny high-flavoured strawberries, and in the evening we had to have a great fire it was so cold. My days have been full of events, but not of a kind very interesting to you. Most of this has been written in cars & steamboat going down to Nahant to visit Nina & Julia Paine. I had a beautiful

— 1879 —

time. We discoursed in the house round the fire most of the time and not once did I go off the piazza. Julia's affection for Miss Yonge and familiarity with all her works was like yours. We had a very sympathizing conversation about them, and Julia says Harriet Curtis has always wished to write to her and tell her how much they are valued by Americans & *Unitarians*. You know Nina is going to Amherst. The Hotel where the pupils & many Professors had engaged their rooms was burned on Saturday. Coming home I found Cousin Sarah returned from Monadnoc. Tomorrow morning I go to Lenox. Goodbye beloved.
                        Ellen

                                          Lenox July 9th 1879
Dear Mother,

Nothing could be more smooth and prosperous than my journey, and Tom [Ward] himself met me at Pittsfield. Sophy was in the shops, and when she had done her errands we drove gaily home. When we came in sight of the house Wardy Thoron on the porch was first seen. Then on the tennis ground in front of the house I saw Loulou & Mr von Hoffman. Then Lily rushed out and began beckoning and waving, and they all came round to the porch, where also Mr Ward & Ferdy appeared. It was a great family. All behaved in the most hospitable & affectionate manner, and Ferdinand on being introduced said How do you do? and then took my hand & kissed it, his foreign manners, you know. The glories of the house now began to dawn upon me. It is very beautiful and interesting. Then they showed me my room, and I wish you could see it, it is so pretty, and has a most perfect view of the Stockbridge Bowl, Monument Mountain and even the Dome. Then Sophy & Tom & I dined & Sophy's sister Nina, an amazingly bright & frolicsome girl sat with us meanwhile. Lily is lying down. Now while I write Mr v. Hoffman, Sophy & Loulou are shooting with bows under the window. I'm going down to be with them. Goodbye!
                    Your affectionate daughter.
                            E. T. E.
Please ask Cousin Sarah to water the daphne.

                                      Lenox July 11th 1879
Dear Mother,

Yesterday morning Lily invited me to walk with her, and first we walked through the lower regions of the house, and visited the laundry where two women were ironing whose presence embarrassed me so that I didn't examine into its arrangements, then into the cold room where stand the big refrigerator and three or four wire safes. Then along a broad entry where the barrels stood, and a vast paste-board leaned against the wall to the kitchen which was most interesting. From the kitchen opens the people's dining-room on one side, and on the other a large light room studded with closets which stood out in it like wardrobes. Beyond was the milk-room, and finally the wood, coal & furnace cellars. Then as we came out we met Mr Ward & Mr von Hoffmann and Philip & Ferdy. We all took a little walk through the domestic wood of very fine tall old oak & chestnut trees behind the house. The little boys picked raspberries and kept coming back to us. Ferdy speaks English to Mr Ward & Lily, German to his father and Italian to Philip. He is eight years old, a charming little boy. Mr Ward has been most kind and lovely to me, never was more so. He treats me both ways combined all the time, he is as exact and attentive as if I was an old lady and a stranger, and he calls me dear and treats me like a child. Beautiful talks I have had with him, about trees, about courage, about Tom. Mrs Ward I have hardly seen but when I do see her she is as affectionate as she always has been. I had the pleasure of sitting by Tom one day at dinner and chattered away with him to my heart's content but that has been my only chance. Tonight he has gone to N.Y. He enjoyed Edw.'s Monadnoc letter as I expected. I have just returned from dining with dear Mrs Rackemann who sent her warmest regards to you & Father. I shall come home in the 5 o'clock train on Tuesday night. Ask Cousin Sarah to send those two nursery chairs and any other 2 you choose to Mr Alcott's house on Monday or Tuesday morning.

In great haste.   E. T. E.

Concord July 18th 1879

Dear Edith,

Father & Mother seem to take very kindly to Philosophy, and of course Mother's first move was to invite all Professors & shining lights, and all her particular friends to a great Conversation last night. It proved uncommonly poor, and we all felt very unhappy. Mr & Mrs Keyes were here, which is uncommon. The Chamberlaines sent us down a box of rhododendrons from Monadnoc wherewith we adorned the rooms. Edward & Annie also came but in the course of time Annie strayed up into my room and saw me to bed. We had a good time

— 1879 —

together. Miss Peabody dined here today. Father and I can come to Naushon just as well on the 11th as on the 4th. I am thinking of going to a "Grove Meeting" up at Lake Winnipisogee next week with a party of Concord people. Everything is favourable, Cousin S. here, everyone well, no company, and no reason why I shouldn't. You ought to see how pretty Dan's studio looked when we took Miss C. to see Father's bust, but the bust is never so perfect to me since it is in plaster, as it was before. I find I don't get over the disappointment. I have invited Effie Lowell at one time & Emma Lazarus at another to visit us before we go to Naushon.

E. T. E.

Weir's N.H. July 22nd 1879

Dear Mother,

We all met at Nashua and came in high spirits to Lake Winnepisagee. We landed on a platform right over its waters, and felt all that sense of coolness & stillness & relief of getting out of the cars into beautiful nature that we have all often enjoyed. A friendly voice cried "All who wish to go to Concord Building, follow me", so we all followed, presented our credentials which were received with laughter and pocketed unread, because they said we didn't need any, and then we were told the evening meeting was just beginning. The Meeting consisted of a welcoming address from Mr Powell of Laconia, who said he was chairman of the Reception Committee appointed by the N.H. Unitarian Ass^n. as their representative, as such, servants of all who arrived, to take good care of us, and that they would do it to the utmost. Then one from Rev. Mr Beane of Concord N.H. telling us about the last Grove-Meeting, and that all who attended it learned the lesson that religion was more a social & less a solitary sentiment than they used to think, and that the cumulative effect of making it the business & study of a whole week night and day had been very great so that not only in general the Unitarians of N.H. had been more active, zealous and mutually attached ever since than they had been before, but that individual men had felt through the whole year the lift they got here last July, it was true of him, and he believed almost all who were here would be able to give the same testimony. So he congratulated us that we had come, and said we couldn't help expecting much from this week. Then some notices, and we were dismissed and brought by Mr Powell to our present abode, Mrs Lovett's house, quite near the Ground on a hill

— 1879 —

overlooking the lake and having a fine view of the Gunstock Mountain on the right and Ossipee Mountain on the left, a most pleasant & comfortable abode. The cooking is admirable, and there is plenty of new milk. Of course the mountain water is excellent. We arrived just a little late at the 8.30 morning prayer-meeting. There was the "Rev. Jenk. Ll. Jones" addressing us, not from the stand but down in the aisle. What he said was good and in a quiet sincere voice. Someone else spoke. Then there was silence, and Mr Powers said "If the Spirit doesn't move us, we will close the meeting." Notices were given, a hymn was sung. and Mr Jones gave the blessing. We were told that Mr Tiffany would preach at 10.30. Mr Beane of Concord N.H. came up to me and introduced himself and after a little discourse said "The Communion Service which I handle every month has on it the inscription 'Presented by Ellen Tucker' Did you know that? I presume you bear that name from having seen your signature." We were pleased, I of course most of all, that dear Mr Tiffany was here and we enjoyed his sermon. It was "Physician heal thyself", learn something before you attempt to impart. In the course of it he couldn't help saying that Mr Emerson was an example of the true way of teaching. Then arose his brother ministers and "hackit him in pieces sma' " (not on the point of Papa) except Rev. J. Ll. Jones who had a great deal to say about Father, in much the same strain as Mr Tiffany, and what did the man do, but standing within a rod of me insist on looking me in the eye all the time he was speaking of Father. I stood it a little, but kept him out of focus a great deal. I shall meet you at Mr Hawes's on Thursday. I hope you are thriving. Give my love to Father & to Cousin Sarah.

E. T. E.

Boston Concord & Montreal R.R.
Thursday July 24th 1879

My dear Edith,

I have this good chance to write you but no ink. Today I have arranged to meet Cousin Sarah & Mother & Mrs Sanborn in Boston and we are going all together to have Mother's photograph taken at Hawes's. I told Cousin S. to bring some flowers so that Mother might have her favorite accessories. I have great hopes for the result. Edward told me to secure Mrs Sanborn for the occasion as her society is particularly exhilarating to Mother and may give more life to her expression. After the martyrdom, as a lump of sugar, Mother is going to choose a

— 1879 —

Lidian Emerson in 1879.

new study-carpet, and perhaps one for the dining-room too. So we expect a very happy day, and how perfect the weather is! Do you know I went to the School of Philosophy on Saturday and found it so excellent that I'm afraid I have done very wrong in not arranging to go all the time. To be sure it was a great day, Prof. Pierce day. You ought to have heard the unintelligible introduction to his lecture, it gave me a queer sensation to hear my native language and receive no clear idea when one evidently was expressed. It sounded a good deal like "'Twas brillig & the slithy toves". But after a while a light began to dawn, and the religiousness of all he said was very apparent, by & bye it came out above all the rest, it made the end of the lecture a sermon, and everyone in the room could understand and was refreshed. Then did the philosophers begin to question him, and I gaped upon them. Did those questions really mean anything? What learned men! Where did they dig up the amazing words they used? Did they understand them themselves? I didn't wonder that they hesitated & sometimes said they hadn't ended the sentence as they meant to when they began, and went back to try again, but they would come into port at last and appear satisfied. Then with what curiosity I looked to see whether Mr. P. had been able to follow their recondite march and knew what they were after! Yes! He did! He invariably made them a reply as if they had asked him whether he used salt with eggs. Sometimes he said Yes or No, sometimes he would answer in their own jargon, and question & answer would go on, all equally mysterious till they would come to a perfect understanding evidently, sometimes without my getting any guess what was talked about, & sometimes descending within my reach. Mr Pierce was charming, we all enjoyed him, and he said often "No, no. That is metaphysics. That isn't my department. If I answer that at all I must answer as a mathematician." He was sometimes asked "Can you tell us such & such a thing that you referred to in your lecture in plain language that everyone can understand?" and he would say "No. It could be done, but it would take too long", or "Yes, it is a little difficult, but I can give you some idea", and when he said he could, he did, and we sucked it in. Saturday afternoon Father walked all round the Pond with me, and wasn't at all tired. I always wanted while I was in Lenox to tell you what happy talks I had with Mr Ward. One day he said "Your Father has unsurpassed courage. He takes his position without second thought, and holds it, quite careless of other people's assent." I told him that Father had said to Jones Very that his position was constitutional, he *couldn't* take any other. "Certainly it is," said Mr Ward. Then I had many a drive & walk with him, and he told me about the trees, the landscape, lights & shadows, the picturesque. Opened to me a little the way the artistic being looks round and what he sees, and why. It was nectar & ambrosia. Once when we climbed Bald Head all the grandchildren started with us, but before we came near the top the Governess said they must go home for supper. So they started back. "It is worthwhile to start with a party!" exclaimed Mr Ward, "they look so pretty in the landscape!" We watched their progress as they skipped down across the pastures into a lane, and it was beautiful to see them. "That's the part of the landscape one doesn't own," said he. Someone had reminded me in the morning of Father's saying "My neighbours own the land, but I own the landscape," "Unless someone cuts down the trees in it!" cried Lily. And I suppose Mr Ward referred to that. Now this week I have been up at Lake Winnepisogee. Mrs George Clark, Mrs Nancy Holden, Mary Beal, Mrs Jas. B. Wood and I. The Farm-house where we dwelt was a model place, board $5 a week. Capital cooking, Jersey milk, berry pastures such as we never imagined, heavenly view, lake & mountains, pleasant rooms, the people the true salt of the earth. Why to hear them talk did you good through & through. The only drawback was the feather beds, one hates feather beds & quilts in summer. I have here had a chance to see the Western Unitarian Minister side by side with the Eastern. They are the most different creatures imaginable. Of course I have had many an amusing and interesting adventure. On the whole my hero is the Rev. Jenk Ll. Jones. I wrote to Mother about the first day and I suppose the letter will be sent to you. The evening after I wrote Mr Jones spoke on the subject of the afternoon "Is Life worth living?" I heard more clearly now than I had before the advantages, the joys, the light of Unitarianism. It was a beautiful, beautiful speech. The next day it rained and we had the meeting in the "chapel" a sort of barn with four planks running its length. At 10.30 we heard a Western preacher. He talked almost as fast as Phillips Brooks and it was very interesting. The discussion that followed approached the standard of the ideal conversation. We broke up reluctantly & the 5 Concord ladies went home & found dinner going on. I was ware of two men just coming up to the piazza. They were the Rev. Powell and Rev. Jenk Ll. Jones. Oh wasn't this a pleasant surprise? Mr Powell was already a friend, who considered himself responsible for us all. He said "Of course it is quite unnecessary to introduce you & Mr Jones, you must have met already", but it was necessary and I was very glad it was accomplished. In they came and Mr Lovett discerned them from afar and went into the parlour with them. I went to the table where already were seated our party and two good-looking young men from Camb.port who had just arrived. Mrs Clark at once with match-

— 1879 —

less innocence introduced me "Miss Emerson let me introduce these young men. I'm sure I don't know their names." The youths smiled & bowed but wouldn't utter their names. "Miss Emerson lives on the same street as I do," went on Mrs Clark, "she's the daughter of Mr Ralph Waldo Emerson. I know you've heard of him." "I may have," said one of the young men "but if I have, I don't remember it." Mr Lovett here looked out of the parlour and said to the waitress "Are you ready?" "In a minute," she responded—she was setting chairs for the ministers. At last all was ready, the ministers came, and we had a very cheerful time with them.

B. & L. Depot.   As I walked up the depot a man, a farmer, came up to me and said "I'd be glad to give you $2.00 for them notes you've been writing as you come down in the cars. All the folks thought you was crazy—'cause you was writing. I thought they'd arrest you. But I knew you was all right." Oh dear Edith, why should I be thought to be crazy? Perhaps I'd better not write in the cars any more.

E. T. E.

Naushon Aug. 12th 1879

Dear Mother,

Poor Father had a journey filled with anguish of mind on his part, and delays on the part of the train, even long backings which indeed were to him the most welcome part "for they may possibly run us all the way back to Boston, and then we can go home, and I can get my keys, and my eyes, and all the things,—and *stay* at home. It is a crazy thing for poor old gentlemen to be dragged out of their own corners and carried off to make visits." But we were really very comfortable and arrived about quarter past four with every piece of baggage that we started with. As we rowed across in the boat Father asked me about his umbrella. "I'm afraid after all we have lost that that goes over my head." I asked him if he knew what its name was. He meditated for some time and said "No, but I know its history. Strangers take it away." We keep it on the table in his room that he may continually behold it. After dinner Cameron & Don eagerly invited us to row on the harbour and Father and I went. Violet & Edward also. Then did Don man the oars, & Cameron pushed off, and Edward in the bow nursed Don's little schooner which was to be dropped by and bye to sail beside us. Violet steered. All the children showed immense nautical experience, and behaved in a friendly and cheerful manner among themselves. In this immense boat the party of six took little room, and I thought it showed a good deal of strength in dear little Don to row us unassisted. At every stroke the oars pulled him quite off his seat, but his little brown hands & legs looked so vigorous, and he seemed to enjoy it so much that it was all the more pleasant to be rowed by him. Ralph presently sailed near us in the Catfish, the little Mayflower was dropped and sailed away. "I'll race her," cried Ralph, but the Mayflower bore down on him instead of going straight, and he picked her up. In a few minutes he climbed into our boat and then we had all the gr.children except the absurd being who in pink streamers and white worsted was spending the afternoon on the wharf. Father says there are pears in his cabinet drawers. In a hurry.

E. T. E.

Naushon Aug. 13th 1879

Dear Mother,

I haven't yet begun to tell you about our arrival etc. The faithful Violet of course was sitting on the end of the wharf awaiting the boat that brought us, and Cameron & Don were climbing about not far from her. Ralph was sailing away in his Catfish. As he passed us, near enough for us to see his burned red eyes in his very brown face, he said "How do you do, Sir? How do you do, Aunt Ellen", in a manner as if he was resolved to do his duty, but without a smile, or a motion. On the wharf however we were met with kisses and smiles, and Violet was eager to show the square knot with which she had tied the horse's halter. Father and I sat behind, the children and baggage in front, and Cameron drove, though Father was uneasy with so small a driver on the rough road. We found Edith & Sarah Malcolm with little Edward, and littler Margaret drawn up on the piazza. Malcolm had gone to New Bedford and Will is in Boston. The baby has been growing pretty in some points but in others is alarmingly homely. I think he is going to have a strong aquiline nose. He is very happy, and kicks, and talks and smiles, as much as a baby need. Today there is to be a yacht race, the N.Y. squadron is at N.B. and the Azalea is bound to race too. Mr Forbes was standing by his horse on the wharf last evening, and Henry Cook's dog rushed out barking, which made the horse prance, and she pranced right upon poor Mr F.'s toe. He was laid up on the sofa and in much pain when Mrs Forbes came to tell us about it, but this morning he drove over before breakfast, to say he was going to the race and ask

— 1879 —

Father to go too. They have just started, Edith and the baby to go to New Bedford and come home in the steamer, the two grandfathers & Malcolm to enjoy the race. Father seems to be having a tolerable time of it. He is pleased to see Cameron & Don dashing over the plain and through the woods upon their steeds, pleased to see the nautical nursery when out in the boat, pleased with Ralph's size and devotion to sailing, pleased with his dear little Edward who sits in a chair before him and recites to him poetry and stories with earnestness. The dear Violet also touches his heart, and he said to Edith "One would think that little girl must be inestimable!" Edith fervently responded that she was. Malcolm & Sarah sang to him last night, he has a pile of Littells in the study and reads them. Lily's letter and the eyeglasses came last night, and were most welcome. Father's soul has rest now that the keys are put away, and the tickets & eyeglasses are in his pocket, and the bank-book in the bank.

End of letter missing.

Naushon Aug. 14th 1879

Dear Mother,

Father has become uneasy and I suppose will hardly stay another day. He had a good time on the yacht-race, and returned very deeply impressed with Malcolm's valour, power of command and of taking responsibility, said he seemed a greater man than his father! He is very much burned by the day's wind. The Azalea came in third or fourth, and had a very close race with two sloop-yachts. I think it was as good a chance as Father could have had to see a race. Handasyde Cabot came yesterday. Edith & baby who went up on the yacht found themselves in the way, for they came late, the yachts were all in line and ready to start, so Mr Forbes said "We can't put you ashore, we shall have to take you on the race!" Edith was aghast, for the yacht might not return before 9 at night and the baby's food had just been spilled by a lurch of the boat. Happily a steam-tug hove in sight, and Edith and train were transferred to that, so she had a glorious day of performance & happy hits and returned at three. Meanwhile Don & Edward asked to go to ride and disappeared to catch their horses. Later as we rode to bath we met John on Katy-did & Edward on Countess. Edward presently climbed into our wagon and told his morning's adventures. "How do you fink we got froo ve gates? Don got off, and tied Katy-did, and opened ve

— 1879 —

gate & untied Katy-did and led her froo, and I went froo, and ven he tied Katy-did and shut ve gate, and untied Katy-did and got on again." Thorough and excellent Don! In the afternoon Ralph went sailing with Handasyde, and Sarah and I went with Margaret, Edward & Don to pick blackberries. We wandered on the N. shore hills, and little Edward cried "Vere's ve Azalea!" Blackberries were forgotten. The Azalea was flying home and very near. When she was gone we returned to our work and brought home two or three quarts. "The Preacher" ought to go to Will on Friday.

E. T. E.

Naushon Aug 15th 1879

Dear Mother,

I hope you'll have a good time tonight with your tea-party, and I exhort you to make a daily meditation on the necessity of prudence, and abstinence from all offers, promises and plans in the beguiling presence of Miss Peabody, seeing that your lamblike innocence, soft heart and gentle unsuspiciousness are exposed defenceless to her attacks in the absence of your natural protectors. Let this daily meditation precede her visit, and be followed by consultation with the clear-sighted Lily, who had better supervise the interview every time, and let *her* accompany Miss P. to the door, so that you may never be left alone. Father is watching the horizon for a friendly sail that may waft him back to his study. Never was any prisoner more eager to get away. He is kept only by every appliance of force and fraud. Ralph looked at your photographs and said "The sitting one looks as if she were sad about something in the past, the standing one looks sad & displeased with someone at the present moment." Edith, when I said you really half inclined to come, arranged on the spot an elaborate plan to get you down this week, but I nipped it in the bud, I don't think it best to bring you when I couldn't attend to your preparations & journey. No time for more today.

Your affectionate daughter
E. T. E.

Concord Aug. 19th 1879

Dear Edith,

When we had time to discourse Lily told me this beautiful tale. "It was lucky Mr Emerson was away this particular week, for multitudes of

The study in the Emerson house. Probably the earliest picture available.

people of all sorts came to see him, and it was particularly lucky that he sent word that the study must be locked up for fear philosophers and strangers might find it easy to dodge in there, for Miss Peabody sent word that she was going to bring a lady at five in the afternoon, and Mrs Emerson needn't disturb herself in the least, for she didn't want to see anybody, she only wished to spend an hour alone in Mr Emerson's study. It seemed to her that the greatest pleasure she could have would be to lock herself in and meditate an hour in the scene of Mr Emerson's meditations. But Mrs Emerson decided that in the face of Mr Emerson's instructions she *couldn't* possibly allow it, and sent word to Miss Peabody not to bring the lady except to see her." Let me caution you, Edith dear, about the use you make of this sugar-plum. It is too good not to spread like wild-fire if once made known, and might return with fearful bitterness to the ears of the sentimental Unknown. We must remember that. Oh how Father shuddered and how fervently he thanked Lily for locking the room!

Mother is better but it's likely to last 10 days or so.

Concord Sept 8th 1879

My dear sister,

Last week I neglected you. On Monday I had a meeting of my committee the only one to which I belong and a delightful time we all had. On Tuesday Edward & Annie came to dine and with them we invited the Amherst philosophy student, Mr Smith, you remember, the senior who invited us up to Amherst, and took such good care of us there. He has remained behind all the other philosophers, and says he inclines to go this autumn to the Harvard Divinity School. I hope that business "crisis" of Will's will culminate soon. Of course we are very proud of the Bell Telephone success. Do move up soon. I'll come and help you if I can. Father really has some idea of coming down to stay a day or two more with you, to be away from home a little, I have so much company. So invite him if you have room while the Cabots are there. Mrs Lewis and her twins were here Friday and Saturday, and it was very pleasant; the children are pretty and good and charming together. Last Thursday all the Sam Bradfords were here, and we had a very good time. Father especially enjoyed it. Charley & Therchi come tomorrow to stay till their house is finished. Mrs Lesley & Mary we hope will visit us, and

— 1879 —

that visit Father must be at home for. With much love to you & the bairns I must leave you now.

E. T. E.

Concord Sept. 18th 1879

Dear Edith,

I wish I had asked for a postal-card to tell how Father arrived. I hope to send tonight the gushing man's letter about Sampson Low's preface, which has come since I saw Mr & Mrs Cabot, and which I want them to see, as well as you. It is at Edward's now. Therchi sends her love to you. I am having a very good time with her. I have been thankful every minute that Father has escaped the present turmoil. His study has been the theatre where carpet-matching, sewing, scouring and window-washing are the play. The parlour with the dancing-cloth down is the carpet-sewers home. The dining-room has been Mr MacDonald's work-shop. All the furniture of these 3 rooms is in the two entries. Charley & Therchi have the redroom. So the only spot in the house to receive visitors in, and I have had plenty, is the front entry, and stairs. The dining-room is done.

Concord Sept 20 '79

Dear Puss,

Send me quick Mr Channing's letter that I sent you some time ago, back, and show these if they are there to Mr & Mrs Cabot. Much have we enjoyed your story of sweet Don's return from N[ew]. B[edford]. Father though he asseverated that "a broken person *can't* enjoy anything" yet laughs as he tells of reading Brook Farm, and rejoices greatly in the thought of the baby, seems also to have had other pleasure. Lizzy Simmons will be here Monday to spend the day. Mother's birthday today.

E. T. E.

Monday morning

Dear Edith,

Do you & Will want a copy of Dan's bust of Father? It is all ready for you if you do. Write about it as soon as you can, and if you want it, say whether in Naushon or in Milton. Do you want to come with the Cabots & Plumptres?

E. T. E.

— 1879 —

Sept. 29th 1879

Dear Edith,

I am glad you do want the bust, and Mr Cabot too. So two are properly disposed of. I think Haven & Lizzy Barber are also proper people to have one if they want, but I don't know how Mother will decide. Let me know as soon as possible when you shall move. If you come up on the 10th I'll try to come down on the 8th. The Plumptres call themselves Plumtrees and turn out to be not travelling but making a visit in Salem, and bound to snatch a week for Niagara, which they find it hard to get because the Salem people are so eager to keep them. I understood Mrs P. that they would have stayed here as we asked them to, but their friends wouldn't hear of it. Mrs P. was one of the lovely and affectionate kind, not overpoweringly English, there was no bar between her and us, and Dr P. was strikingly humble, which was very attractive to me. Both were very comfortable people to get along with and seemed to enjoy everything they could see or hear. They were only here five hours. You don't know how good it was to have Mrs Hemenway here. Augustus came the next morning to carry her home.

E. T. E.

Mother's plants have come & are set out. She is much pleased.

Phenix Hotel, Concord N.H.
Tuesday evening Sept 30th 1879

Dear Mother,

We arrived here at 3. In the train between here & Nashua we encountered an old abolitionist, Father has forgotten his name, but he recognized Father who sat with him, and talked to him all the way to Manchester, introducing him to another man by whose advice we came straight to this Hotel. When Father undertook to pay for the carriage the man bowed and said "Free carriage, Sir, as long as you stay at this Hotel". As we came inside the door we met Col. Wm. Kent, eldest son of the old Col. Kent,* who seized on Father with delight, introduced us to the Manager and told him to take *good* care of us. We had rooms, then dinner; then Father and I walked out in search of old landmarks, but as I expected not one was to be found, so we returned to the Hotel

---

*Col. Kent married the widowed Mrs. Tucker, mother of Ellen Louisa Tucker, RWE's first wife. He met her at the Kent house in Concord, N.H., when he went there to preach in 1827.

— 1879 —

to take a carriage. Father thought the driver would know where houses stood fifty years ago. Happily we met Col. Kent once more, and he said "The house where you boarded is gone, the South Congregational Church stands on the spot where my Father's house used to be, and the house is moved way up to a back street, but it still stands, little changed I think. Our church is on another piece of ground of my Father's which he gave to build it on; it is one of the handsomest in the United States; I'll show it to you." So we set forth once more, saw the church, just new frescoed for its 50th Anniversary, and the new chapel just built with kitchen, parlour, dining-room & Sunday-School rooms, to be dedicated tomorrow. Mr Beane, the minister, was there, the minister I met at the Camp-Meeting, you may remember. He showed the parlour with an air which made me think he didn't wholly believe in having one, and I heartily sympathize with him if he disapproves. When he spoke of the Parish it was clear he enjoyed it and was proud of it. He said it was the most thoroughly democratic one he had ever seen. Mr Kent he told us was the only surviving member of the church that was gathered fifty years ago. He is now 87 years old. There was great activity all about us as we talked, the Sunday-School Teachers and children were putting the library in order in its new home, the ladies were attending to various details, the sexton was sweeping the church, the gentlemen, some in their shirt-sleeves were helping with the library and the ladies' work. Everybody was in high spirits, very busy, and having a beautiful time. The church has a long green yard in front, with several maples in it. After we had seen it all, Mr Kent showed Father the site of his former boarding-house, and of Ellen Tucker's house, and then left us, promising to take us in the morning to see the latter in its new situation. Then Father and I walked out into the country, crossed the Merrimac and saw a gorgeous sunset and moon-rise, and returned just in time for tea. Goodnight.

E. T. E.

Oct 2nd 1879

Dear Edith,

We are on our way home from Concord N.H. where we have been petted as much as possible. You know Ellen Tucker's step-father was Col. Wm. A. Kent, and his eldest son Col. Wm. Kent was staying at the Phenix Hotel where we were. He took a barouche yesterday morning

— 1879 —

and carried us to his Father's house, now moved far away from its original site, altered too, with a French roof. But at my request we went in. The porch evidently was the old porch with its Ionic pillars, the staircase & hall were unchanged, the parlour on the right of the door had on a violent paneled paper of the common taste of 15 or 20 years ago, and was very scant of furniture. Col. Kent said his Father had enlarged it to its present size in 1822 when he married Mrs Tucker, had torn down the old-fashioned wood-work of the whole chimney side of the room, substituted a plaster wall and a marble mantle-piece, the very one still there. In this room Father was married 30 Sept 1829, just 50 years ago the night before. I didn't ask him where he stood, I am sorry I didn't, though I think it very doubtful whether either he or Col. Kent would have remembered. We then went into the sitting-room on the left hand of the entry with its genuine chimney side woodwork. That Col. K. said was as it used to be, and he and Father visited also the side door, and "portico", as they called the piazza, and the dining-room with much greater satisfaction than any other place, expressed in little ums of sad affection on Father's part, and on Col. K.'s with many a "Yes, yes, this is the same." The lady of the house pointed to a door between parlour and dining-room and said "I have been told that door was cut to entertain Gen. Lafayette. I suppose you remember, Col. K." "Yes. I had the honour as a military man to command the escort that received him. Yes, he was my Father's guest in this house for three days."

Oct 3rd. Many good wishes and congratulations to you & W. & your flock on this anniversary. What a lovely day!

E. T. E.

Oct 4th 1879

Dear beloved ill-used Cousin Sarah,

I am fully sensible of the hatefulness of my conduct, and yet, yet! I don't know how to do any better. We are at this moment seated in the dining-room, Mother on the throne which she usually occupies when sitting for her picture, and Mrs Noa is working on it. Mother gave her two sittings yesterday, and two today. It is 3.45 P.M. and she hasn't lain down yet, sat from 12 to 1.30 and from the time she left the table till now. I conclude she likes it very much, or perhaps is stronger than she used to be when you were here. Mrs Sanborn is reading aloud to her & Therchi also enjoying the reading. The new carpets which we meant to

— 1879 —

choose the first day you & we went a-photographing waited a long time, but one day early in Sept. we triumphed. The carpets were chosen on Friday, and the next Friday the dining-room smiled in a bright green carpet and a crimson one glowed in the study. The Weirs got the old dining-room carpet and were pleased with it. Father went back to Naushon for the days when carpet-women, mops & hammers reigned, and all the furniture of dining-room & study was packed in the front entry. He & I have just come home from Concord N.H. where they have been celebrating the semi-centennial of their U. Church. Father was one of the first ministers who preached to the infant soc. in a hall in 1827 & 8, so they asked him up, and he went with zeal. It was the last day of Sept when we went up. Not till I waked the next morning did I remember that Father & E. L. T. were married Sept. 30th 1829. On the 50th anniversary exactly he had come back to show me the place! Wholly by accident. He was very much interested when I told him. The next morning we found the old house, guided by Col. Kent, and entered the very room. Yesterday was Edith's 14th wedding day, she & W & R. & V. have gone to Pigeon Cove for the first time since W. & E. went there for their wedding journey, to keep the anniversary. Annie & Edward's wooden wedding was kept with much wooden-ware, Sept 19th. Charley & Therchi stay here while their house is rebuilding. I have no more time now, though much to say.

E. T. E.

Concord Oct 13th 1879

Dear Haven,

Mother wants to know whether it would give you positive pleasure to have a copy of Dan French's bust of Father, photographs of which I send. If it would she will despatch one to you at once, but if you would simply tolerate it, or find it an inconvenient piece of furniture, it would be well to avoid inflicting it upon you. Father and I have lately been in Concord N.H. celebrating the 50th Anniversary of the founding of the Unitarian Church there, to which he ministered in early days. He enjoyed it very much, and great pleasure was expressed by the clergy present, and the old church-members at seeing him go up into the pulpit and read the hymn, they said "It seemed as if he was formally closing his ministry." Next Tuesday we are going to Edith's to the christening of the little Waldo. Charles & Therchi have left us today to

— 1879 —

set up some sort of housekeeping in their unfinished house. Give my love to Susy & Ruth, and the others. I wish you ever could come here.
E. T. E.

F.R.R. Dec 5th 1879

Dear Edith,

Father and I have just been reading your letter at the breakfast-table. We hate to hear of Will's being sick so often. Can't he help working too hard? The account of your cheerful kitchen was very pleasant. Father & I are now going to Boston to see about Parnassus and to buy a Typewriter, then the Art Museum will fill the rest of the day. Unless perhaps we do the New Years shopping. I did go yesterday to the Ordination at Wayland. I sent to ask Mr Reynolds whether the 1.30 train wd. be a safe way and he answered that he was going alone and would take me with him. You know it was the most lovely warm day, so the long ride was a positive pleasure, and of course the chance to talk was an infinitely greater pleasure. We considered the subjects on which I am teaching my class all the way over. The church is new painted outside and looked very trig. Inside it has a new carpet, but it is otherwise unchanged from what it was when last I came there more than 17 years ago to hear Mr Sears. How it reminded me of him! Dr Bellows conducted the services, and preached the sermon. Mr Waterhouse ordained Mr Lloyd, and he alone placed his hand upon his head. Mr Reynolds gave him the charge, Mr Guild of Waltham the Right Hand of Fellowship, and Mr Tiffany made the address to the people. I wish you could have heard the two last. I send herewith your little scissors. Your books are at W.'s office. Your thimble shall come next time.
E. T. E.

Dec 8 1879

Dear Edith,

Mrs Noa's address is 69 Bickford St. Roxbury Mass. Her studio is in the Studio Building opposite the common. Father had a very pleasant time at the dinner. He liked Amelia Holmes S. who was his near neighbour, and Rose Terry Cooke seems to have been agreeable. He ran away at the moment when he expected to be called on, supposing too that it was about 9 in the evening. Still he thought he would try to get home, went to the Fitchburg Depot and asked if any train wd. go to Concord. To his surprise & joy he was shown into one which was soon

— 1879 —

Family group at the East Door, Thanksgiving, 1879. Standing, from left, Edward W. Emerson, Edward W. Forbes, Ellen T. Emerson, little Edith Forbes, RWE behind Cameron Forbes and Lidian Emerson behind Don Forbes, Edith E. Forbes holding little Waldo, and Ralph E. Forbes, far right. Seated is Annie Keyes Emerson with Charles.

to start. It was the 5.30 and only one other Concord man was in it, which confirmed his idea that 'twas the midnight train. He came in while we were at tea and was utterly amazed. It took him a long time to readjust his ideas of time. He expected to find the household gone to bed and Mother eating her eggs. If not yours whose can that thimble & those scissors be? Alice Cary invites me for Wednesday & Thurs. I think I'll come.

E. T. E.

Dec. 23d 1879

Dear Cousin Sarah,
   I thank you very much for sending me the letter about Cousin Thom-

— 1880 —

as's lecture. Also thank you for the newspapers about Bishop Whittingham. Mother and I have read some of the articles but not all. Mrs Noa's picture is finished, and is much better than I expected, or than anyone else did. It is remarkably true as to features, and has a delicate look, like Mother, and after all is *better* than portraits are apt to be. If you saw Alicia's exhibition of bitter hostility to the project, you will understand that Mrs Noa has really made quite a success when I tell you that Alicia, in a cool and reasonable voice indeed, says "Yes, it really is very good." It is, as portraits go, but after all it is weak and prosaic compared with the Mamma herself. Edward, who had a worse fit than Lily when he heard of it, likes it very well. When Miss Fanny Prichard saw it she looked at it a long time, and then said "I could cry!" she was so much disappointed in it. All are thriving, and Annie looks for a baby in April so you must look forward to the delights of holding it next summer as well as we. Merry Christmas and happy New Year to you and our dear cousins at the Rectory and Cousin Charlotte. We enjoyed seeing the account of Cousin Samuel's fortieth Anniversary.

[Unsigned]

Jan 6th 1880

Dear Edith,

Safe home, and I hope no sickness will follow. Mother feels very weak and good-for-nothing tonight, but I hope to restore her. She sends her love to you and says she has enjoyed her visit and that you have done all that a good daughter could to make her happy. We are all perfectly in accord as we count over and praise our Milton relations. I thank you for doing up that last big bundle. Marigold is happy enough to turn herself inside out at the sight of Mother. Jan. 8th. I found Mother was very bright yesterday morning and planned to go to Boston. So we accordingly did, all three. The clock was bought, and Mother's bonnet properly fitted to her head by a Boston milliner. It looks beautifully. Ann & Nelly are as we are overwhelmed by the magnificence & number of your presents & send their thanks.

E. T. E.

January 17th 1880

Dear Edith,

Your letter came on Friday night when Mr & Mrs Cabot were here. It was very pleasant to hear how you were, though the news was not

— 1880 —

particularly good. Be a good girl! Mind Miss Sewall, and lay up all the strength you can. Mr & Mrs Cabot came on Friday afternoon. When the sleigh came in sight I knew that all the black crape meant just what it looked, and I noticed how whenever there was an interruption to general conversation, so that Mrs Cabot was left to her own reflections, the heavy sigh soon came, or perhaps I ought not to say heavy for it was silent, perhaps she didn't know it, but it was invariable. She was just the same as ever, as of course she would be. I attacked Mr Cabot on the subject of publishing a new book, I had rather decided that it was best to do so. He was evidently of the opposite opinion. We talked a long time. I told him that my main object was that stimulus which publishers give. If we had to have the work done at a certain time we should, and as we had been doing hitherto it wouldn't be accomplished in years. We are not sure of living to do it, and why not do it now while all conditions are favourable? He replied at length that he did not need any publishers for stimulus, that he was ready and able to go to work and arrange everything without. That he did not incline to print another book, for this reason; that no book Father has ever printed since is equal to the Essays, and the lustre of his Works is dimmed by each succeeding volume of second-rate ones. Those papers that are still unprinted were most of them written before "Solitude & Society" was printed, and it is evident that Father in those days thought them inferior to those he did select for "Sol. & Soc." Practically he decided against them, and we should be wiser not to reverse his decision. Mr Cabot also said that he meant to ask Dr Hedge and Mr Lowell what they thought about it. He was sure that Mr Lowell would advise not publishing a book, and not collecting Sovereignty of Ethics, Perpetual Forces, etc. "What then?" I asked, and he said "Why they were already printed. Anyone who cared for them could hunt them up." And Mrs Cabot said "Posthumous publications the author isn't considered responsible for, they are received with pleasure as the last people can get who are in the mood to be thankful for anything." Then I said if we didn't finish and publish now and were prevented from doing it hereafter, our chaotic work would fall into other hands and be most severely judged with reason too if we only derange without rearranging. Mr Cabot said he was willing to finish & polish our work but was not clear as to the wisdom of publishing. When he went out Mrs C. said "There, dear, you've had a good talk with him." She said she sympathized with me, and would advise that I should make a written statement of what Mr C. & I had done & how we came to do it and put it with our work, our apology to our successors. She added that Mr Cabot acted only in Father's interest, and perhaps didn't consider enough the needs of the world which might be instructed and pleased with what he proposed to withhold. I feel now quite satisfied and happy and hope to work hard and steadily and keep Mr Cabot coming twice a month.

Jan 19th P.M.   I have been sitting with poor Edward a little while. He is distracted when he thinks of his patients. He says they need him absolutely this very day and he *cannot* be sick. At the same time he *is* sick. He means to be up tomorrow. Meanwhile Annie has sent word to Jim and Ned Bradford, and hopes to see one of them before midnight, and that they will forbid his stirring. I took Mother the other day and left her at Mrs Williams's door. When I came for her Mrs Williams opened the door herself and smiled. She looked handsome and noble but more worn than she had at the funeral. Mother said that when she came in she told her that she had wanted to see her so much that she should soon have come to see her. And then she had talked out, and Mother had really answered her, and Mrs Williams said "You comfort me." I took Mother a second time yesterday, and it was just the same. Mrs Williams can tell Mother how she feels and Mother can help her. I never see her without being surprised and touched anew, and it goes to my heart to see how much Mother is to her. Jan 20th I'm just going to see how Edward does. I'll keep this open and put in the report.

Jim came. He is better.

[Unsigned]

Concord Feb. 19th 1880

Dear Edith,

I have had very kind invitations from Mary Watson and Alice Cary and have had to refuse them both. It's too bad. I suppose I had better expect nothing but to refuse & lose till Mr Cabot goes to Beverly, or I shan't get the work ahead at all. I have looked for your fountain-pen but in vain. Violet's visit was a great pleasure to us all. I took tea with Miss Leavitt on Tuesday and had great fun with Mrs Leavitt. She always gets me into a frolic. Did I tell you how Father said "Your Mother ought to have her picture taken with her cats round her"? But he didn't say cats but some other cunning descriptive word, just as when V. was here he said, seeing Marigold asleep in a red chair "I don't like to have that *little person* in that chair." I told you I had some stories about Mother. When we were packing the Freedmen's box, she kept coming down with contributions, and brought once a quantity of toys. "Oh Mrs Emerson," said Mrs Sanborn, "you forget that Christmas is coming. You'll want all those toys for presents." This she said to stay her hand, but Mother never heard the end of the sentence, but exclaimed, at the word Christmas, "Yes indeed, so it is! I hadn't thought of it, I'll see if I can't find some more", and hastened away to bring down as many more. The other day she said "Send some money for me to Gen. Armstrong." "Why Mother, you don't know how well I'm doing for him. Did you know Edward gave me $10.00 for him?" "Did he! The dear boy! Well give 10 for me too." "Why I was thinking that since Edward had given ten, & Father—" "Yes indeed, I think so too. Give 20 for me." I never finished my sentence, but you see of course what I meant to counsel. And she didn't do it for fun nor for contradiction but in the innocence of her heart. I made no comment. I hate to spoil her unconsciousness. Annie is quite right when she says "The way your Mother *slings* money round ——"

Your affectionate sister
Ellen T. Emerson.

Concord March 4th 1880

Dear Edith,

Cousin Mary departed on Tuesday afternoon, we enjoyed her visit. Charles had one of his frightful-looking adventures just as she went. He was running to the dining-room window and tripped and put his head into the pane with such force that it broke a great hole in the middle, and we all thought he must be cut to pieces himself. Poor Annie was sitting by the fire, and it seemed a great while before she could get to him. Edward was nearer. As to Charles he was neither scratched nor scared, he regarded it as a part of the ordinary course of life. Did you get your fountain-pen? Father declares solemnly that I never gave it to him, and he never delivered it, but it went in his pocket, tied up and addressed to you, 30 Sears Bg. and never returned. Have you seen Rev. George W. Cooke on Father? He wrote the article advertised in the Commonwealth. The C. also published Edward's letter to Alfred Ferguson of Indianapolis. I was sorry. I hate to have the family appear to rush into print about the matter, but Father said he was glad, he liked to have the truth told, and later he said "It's a good thing to have a son, who when anything detestable is said can defend his papa."

E. T. E.

— 1880 —

Concord March 6th 1880

Dear Sally,

I often think of you, often think I must write, only I can't, and Cousin Elizabeth has brought the purpose to the point of duty at last by bringing to Mother your kind present. The pickles were opened at once and Mother partakes of them with great satisfaction. When Annie dined here last week she seemed so glad of them that Mother is going to send her a part of them to "growl over" at home—favourite word with Edward since Uncle Adams gave a vivid and affectionate description of the pleasure the ninety-year-old grandmother (who was a pet in the house like a little child) took in picking a chicken-wing. She dined up-stairs when they had chickens so as to have this delight in full all by herself. Edward hearing this, summed it up to us with "she loves to pick it and growl over it all alone", and thenceforth it has meant the height of happiness in his vocabulary. We are saving the plums for the next great festivity we have. So Mother and all send thanks and admire your culinary skill. I met Miss Sever in the horse-cars the other day and she told me you were busier than ever with lessons. I am glad of it, only I hope you won't get too tired. Here we are just as usual, all very well, Annie suffering rather less than she did with little John, and expecting the baby by the middle of May. How long it seems to wait! But she says if she can wait she supposes I can. Edward has his hands pretty full, but it is several months since I have heard him exclaim "I *hate* the practice of medicine!" so I think he is in pretty good spirits. Charles's tongue is much freer than formerly. He is no steadier on his feet and has the most alarming-looking tumbles daily. Charley is now the Treasurer of the Continental Bell Telephone Co. which he says is a mere rise in name, not in pleasure nor salary, but he seems pretty cheerful when we meet. Therchi occasionally says "I am very happee. I like my little house very much", but she also says "The next time I go to Europe" and a year ago she used to say "Never! I will never take another voyage." I meet Cousin Elizabeth occasionally as she plies her course between the Manse & Maggy's house. Mother is full of zeal in Woman's Rights, happiness in her Club, admiration of her cat, anxious cares for the bossy and the donkey, eager anticipation of gardening weather; as well as usual. And Father seems to grow stronger this year. My pretty silver pin is a treasure, and I am vain of it. This year I must contrive to get my visit from you.

Affectionately
E. T. E.

— 1880 —

Concord, Apr. 3rd

Beloved Edith,

On Tuesday we take the 3.30 train for Newport. Father has cheerfully consented to my asking Mrs Edward Damon to go with us, and she has agreed to go. I expect much pleasure, no I don't either, I see *possibilities* of uncommon pleasure in this plan, for Father likes her, and she is very much interested in Mr Channing, and if his address is fine, both she & Father will be happy, I think. I like her and have enjoyed every snatch of talk I ever had with her, and yet I know well that opportunity often seals one's lips and mind. Many things of the past I want to tell you about our doings since we left you, but no time. The experiment of going to Brookline was successful, Mother enjoyed & didn't suffer. We dined happily at Aunt Adams's, went to Nina Bangs's wedding, explored Trinity Church, saw Nina, & Frank Lowell, also Mr Brooks, Mother & Father both were charmed with everything.

Alas! tonight I come home to sad news. Mrs Heywood's little Prescott died today of diphtheria. I hadn't heard that he was sick. He was about six years old.

E. T. E.

May 11th 1880

Dear Edith,

I have lost my mind and waste my days so that I haven't found a chance to write to you. I didn't get the note you sent me in season to keep the ink, or buy your cloths. I'm very sorry. Now today comes your invitation, and how gladly would I accept it, but till Sat. 22d I can't come to Boston, and must wander hatless all that time. I am full of glee about this programme: Wed. tomorrow, Circuit meeting, Rev. & Mrs Tiffany, Rev. & Mrs Wilson, 2 W. Newton delegates, 2 Waltham delegates to spend the night; Thurs. U.B. Society meets with Mother & me; Wed. 19th, Dr Faulkner, Cousin A. & Mrs Larkin to spend the day, Dr & Mrs Furness till Friday. I am expecting uncommon fun, and Mother who has Mrs Williams in the parlour this evening is quite unconscious of it. She knows there is a circuit-meeting and looks forward to it, and has said "I suppose we shall have some of them here" but she doesn't seem to realize that it comes tomorrow and vaguely expects 2 instead of 8. Of U.B.S. she is ignorant. She also knows vaguely and with entire approbation of Cousin Abby & Dr Furness, but not when. She says she is uncommonly well. She went to Boston with Father yesterday in that hot gale, and come home very tired. She said "I waited & waited for a horse-car, and at last when I saw one and hailed it, my sunshade suddenly turned inside out with the wind, so the car which was just stopping went on without me, and I wasn't affronted, for of course they couldn't tell *when* I might get through. I took a hack, and I thought I would never take a sunshade again—I was so plagued with my heavy bag, and all my weight of clothes, and my sunshade getting in my way all the time, and the heat!" Every word of it was so characteristic & funny as she said it, I wished you could hear. I'm very sorry about your coil and wish I could help you.

E. T. E.

Monday May 17th 1880

Dear Edith,

I didn't forget either on Friday or Saturday but couldn't begin a letter till now. First let me congratulate you on being able to walk again, we all feel the better for it. Next I want to say Mother had a wonderfully well week last week. From Monday to Saturday she exclaimed daily "Why! how well I feel!" but yesterday without any assignable reason, and today too have been very suffering days, though she was about her usual avocations,—not sick. I had company on Wednesday & Thursday, and the ecclesiastical division came on Mother's mind so gradually I never could tell when she did fairly understand it for the first time, it cost her no anxiety at all; while for my part I was really vain of our four elaborately ready rooms. I drove up to meet the Tiffanys at the 3.23 train, and they brought with them their daughter, Mary, & Miss Bessy Thurston (daughter of your Mr Jas. Thurston) for delegates. Here occurred a difficulty foreseen indeed, but unprovided for because I knew not how, four & myself to ride in the carryall, we had to put in the 3 ladies on the backseat. Then we changed at home the c. for the open wagon & went to Walden with Miss Tiffany between her Father & me. It was a heavenly day and the woodroad had a blue carpet of birdsfoot-violets for Hilda to trot on. This our guests beheld with great admiration. They took a gratifying interest in every object, and Mr T. meanwhile told me that Storrow Higginson is at present doing very well, and detailed to me how they had invited him to read two lectures on Mr Thoreau in their parish parlour, had taken pains to gather a first-rate audience for him, and raised 70 dollars to pay him, and a young man of the parish, himself a reformed drunkard, had adorned the platform with plants. And poor Storrow had written a

— 1880 —

most grateful letter to Mr T. and told him it had all helped him in every way, money the least perhaps, needed as it was. By degrees we waxed very sportive, Mr T. is as playful as Mr Sanborn, and we had great delight. As we came along by the Bowery on our return I saw Mr Guild & his two delegates (Mr & Mrs Warren Emerson of Waltham, a young and charming pair) walking along towards our house, so Mr T. drove me home & left me to receive them, while he took his family to call on M. Ames, & to see the river & monument. At 5.30 appeared Mr & Mrs Wilson of Quincy, and our circle was complete. At tea, "Mrs Emerson, have you any children?" "Two boys." "It is a great thing for brothers to be born near together, then they have the chance to fight all the time," said Mr W. Emerson. "True; they don't have to go out of the house to seek a quarrel," said Mr T. The enormities of infant boys became a delightful subject of conversation. "With my 2d son," said Mr T. "the lying stage and the stealing age happened to coincide. On one occasion I succeeded in recovering what he had stolen & learning all the particulars. I called him and questioned him very carefully, and he answered me, looking up in my face—he had beautiful blue eyes!—with such frankness and celestial innocence, a lie every time! he looked the image of honesty. At last I produced the article, and told him all I knew, and he had nothing to say. 'Do you know, if you go on in this way, what will happen?' 'Yeth thir.' 'What will happen?' 'I thall go to thtate P'ison, and then I thall be hung,' he cheerfully replied." And so on. We had a charming string of stories. Then our Meeting. I wish you could have heard Mr Guild! The rest were good, but I don't think Mr Ph. Brooks, nor anyone, could have gone straighter to people's needs that he did. Then cake & milk in the parlour, and very general talk till nearly 11. The next day a general scattering. On Wed. Mrs George Clark called me and said she meant to bring me a loaf of sponge-cake for U.B.S. I told her I should tell the ladies that she & I were joint entertainers. While we were at dinner on Thursday she arrived with the most perfect imaginable loaf, and said "You mustn't say anything about it to the ladies, not a word. I'd rather you wouldn't. Because Dr Emerson says its bad for little boys to praise them up; it makes them vain. And it's just the same for old ladies." I thought it was the prettiest little speech! After dinner I confessed to Mother what was about to happen. She took it very easily and I was properly ready. First came Mrs Houghton, Amy's Mother-in-law, and presently three other ladies. We all talked over the wedding, the meeting

I'll come tomorrow at 10.15 to M.L.M. [Milton Lower Mills]

— 1880 —

Concord, May 21st 1880

Dear Sally,

Your letter was delightful, it came when Edith was here, so she too had the pleasure of it. Your day in the woods which you told us of seemed a great thing. I hope it has been repeated since. When Father and I visited Annie in her chamber the other day she had your blue shawl over her. I hadn't seen it before and at once fixed upon it as the prettiest thing in sight. My niece is a baby to be proud of, has a good skin and wholly escaped the "red gum" which has disfigured my other niece & nephews, and never turned yellow, has a glorious appetite, and best of all a curly head already! She weighed 9 lbs to begin with and gains with surprising speed. I confess with grief that she inherits her aunt's foot of generous build and a hand to match. We all like her very much.

Letter left unfinished until June 11.

Concord & many railroads May 30 to June 2

Dear Edith,

To go way back, when I came home from Milton I had just time to get ready for Cousin Abby & Dr Faulkner. Edward came to dinner and the eager manner in which he & Dr F. plunged into medical discourse was amusing to me. He & Cousin Abby were both much interested in my printing-machine, and in Mother's picture. They said they hadn't seen the Minute-Man, so we took them there, then up on Ponketasset to see the Great Meadows, and I thought the view never looked more lovely. After this we brought them to see Annie and the children and left them there, I hastened home & Father went to the Depot to meet Dr & Mrs Furness. We had a very good visit from them, and Dr Furness read aloud to us one morning his discourse on Dr Channing, which was delightful. They went on Fri. morning, having seen however one Concord show, Dan French's tableaux on Thursday evening. These were perfectly beautiful. Beth was "The Puritan Maiden", and again Charlotte Corday. Norville appeared as Judith with the head of Holofernes, and Florence Hoar was something and looked perfectly beautiful. Mother says Dr Furness praised them and in speaking of "The Puritan Maiden" said "One hand was very finely in shadow." I thought that was a regular artistic remark. After the Furnesses went away at 10. Mr G. W. Haven brought George at 12 to spend the P.M. That was a very pleasant occasion. George is 19, very large & tall, and behaves just right. He always attends to all the conversation, never speaks unless spoken to, but then is very ready and pleasant. Edward came to dinner and found plenty of common ground with George of course. In the afternoon they took a drive and went at 6. I don't remember any event after that until Father's birthday when he & I took a morning train to Boston (it was Anniversary Week) to attend the Unitarian Anniversary and hear Drs Furness & Hedge & Mr Channing speak on Dr Channing. This was the first Anniversary Meeting of any kind I ever attended. Near me in the aisle was Mr Hall, who duteously as usual paid his respects, and then introduced me to his sister Harriet, who sat by me till Father came. Behind me was Mr Tiffany, and not far off I discerned my Buffalo of the West the Rev. Jenk. Ll. Jones! When Father came it proved that I had chosen a seat too far back. He couldn't hear half, and finally gave up trying, so I lost much of the pleasure I expected. When Mr Channing ended, Father made a rush for the door, but in following him I captured Mrs Jas. B. Wood, and we three dined together. I found Father not very anxious for another meeting, so I promised to join him at 4.30 train, and Mrs Wood & I went to Unitarian Women's Meeting. What a happy surprise awaited me! We picked out our seats and when we reached them, there sat my especial friend Rev. J. B. Green! Of course I called him to sit by me and had a good time with him. Next I saw Mrs Caroline Hoar and called her, and when she came our party and our comfort were complete. We had a very edifying afternoon though what it was all about I fear nobody knew or knows yet. Five women made interesting and amusing speeches but 2 said they didn't know the object of the meeting, and none of the others gave us much light. Meanwhile we four in the seats caught occasional chances for talk. It was so hard to hear that we finally moved forward, and passed near Rev. J. Ll. J. who was there also. He reached out his hand with a smile as if he deeply felt the fun of the meeting. When Father & I got home at night Judge Hoar brought us down in his wagon, and made a little formal birthday speech to Father, very pretty & kind. I forgot to say that Mr Channing in his speech in the morning had sung his little song of pleasure that it was his birthday & Father's birthday. We found that in our absence the Chamberlaines had made their call, and left a framed photograph of Cromwell, and that Mr Lathrop had brought a bouquet of Solomon's Seal & Lady's slippers. Edward presently brought Annie, out for the first time, and Edw. & Mother compared notes on the visits to each house of an Advertiser Reporter who had come up to report the "village celebration" of the

— 1880 —

great day. Oh! how glad I was he found nothing! He did his diligence to collect all he could, and made a little paragraph for the next morning's paper. I received on Saturday night from Mr Todd, a copy of the "Literary World" with its ten or twelve pages about Father, and he had one with a kind little note from the publishers, on Monday. After supper— it was a hot still evening with vast piles of gold cloud from the West more than half way up the sky—we all ascended the chariot and returned Edward & Annie's call, and saw Miss, who however was asleep in A.'s lap in the parlour, and wouldn't wake. She has the curliest of hair on her crown, her front hair is straighter. She grows fast and is fat. Little Charles is very hoarse and croupy. He seems as he did two years ago after scarlet fever, snores hard all day & night, and often squeaks high in his breathing, and Edward is almost as much frightened as he was then. They keep him steamed all the time. Edward was up all Saturday night with him, sent for C. Putnam on Sunday, was up again most of Sunday night. Monday he was a little encouraged, but lying down last night for a little rest, he fell asleep and slept like the dead for 4 hours, during which time a thunder-storm came on, and the weather changed, and he waked to find C. relapsed. Poor fellow! Annie's fright on Saturday and Sunday told on her so that he dares not let her know how anxious he is today. He doesn't leave the house at all, and watches C. every moment. Father & Mother have gone to Boston, and I have dined at Edward's and have just come home. He says Charles breathes better, and when I came away the child was gaily despatching a dinner of bread & meat at Annie's knee, as if he were the healthiest boy in the world, so I hope the worst is over, and Edward will be relieved tomorrow. Now to return to last week; on Wednesday I went again to Boston to the Children's Mission Anniversary, and Father by the same train to the American Academy Centennial. I stayed at Nina's all night and had a good time with her, and liked her nephew Frank Coolidge who is staying with her. The next day Father, Mother & I went to dine at Mrs George Russell's. That was a delightful occasion. All the daughters were there, all just as kind and charming as they could be, and Mr Ames was there too, and Father got a little acquainted with him. We all had a beautiful time. I never was in the house before. That evening we had our last Friday Evening Meeting at the vestry, and read the last chapter of Ecclesiastes. It was delightful to have it all thoroughly and systematically explained. Everybody enjoyed it so much that it has been much talked over ever since. On Saturday, according to invitation, our Wis-

— 1880 —

consin cousin Bessy Howe came at noon & brought a boarding-school friend. Wasn't that a good idea of mine? Cousin Edwin Cotton unexpectedly accompanied them. They drove Father and me to the depot, and amused themselves the rest of the day. I found out that there were so many possibilities of difficulty for Father that I went with him to the Parker House, and sent for Mr Parker. I told Mr P. to send someone to Brookline with Father who could instruct the driver who took him to Mr Winthrop's to go again & get him for the 9.45 train, and to send to the Albany Depot to meet him when it came in. Also to show him the list of preachers Sunday morning, and then after church put him on horse-car or train for Milton with his bag. How faithfully did Mr Parker do his part! But Father, invited by the Boston gentlemen at Mr Winthrop's to return with them in their carriage, forgot his driver engaged to come more than 2 miles to get him, and accepted the invitation. He paid his share. But what shall I do about that Brookline carriage? I was delighted that Will came for him, and he had a good time in Milton. When shall we go round together? What day shall I spend with you?

E. T. E.

Concord June 7 1880

Dear Edith,

When C. Putnam went away this morning he said Charles was a long way from being out of danger yet. And Oh! my dear, in the middle of the forenoon came on a savage attack. I suppose there is no hope any more. Violent struggles at every breath, perpetual attempt to tear his clothes away from his chest, fading colour in his eyes, no attempt to speak or look. They sit with him by turns, Edward, Annie & Lily, who alone understand all his signs. Where Annie & I are sitting Edward comes in & says "he has asked for milk & drunk several swallows and doesn't seem sickened", and then he sat down in front of Annie and said "There is no reason yet why he shouldn't get well if only the inflammation would begin to abate." "And is there no bound set where it must begin to abate?" asks Annie. "No, except that everything has a tendency to get well." The last time he passed through the parlour he said to Lily & me "It seems as if our little boy were fated to have no chance. Look at the weather." Mrs Whitney is a blessed comfort, watches & helps and straightens out everywhere, takes care of Annie & baby, and often of C. 5.45. C. & J. Putnam have just arrived which consoles everyone. Dear blessed Annie is keeping back the crying with all her strength.

I can't come to Boston for 10 days.

Concord, June 8th 1880

My darling Violet,

I should like to have you come either this Sunday or next, you and Madge [Cunningham]. Next Sunday is a little better for me, and is Anniversary Sunday when the Sunday School has its service up in the church. If our Charles is alive he will be better. If he is dead I still think you would like to see blessed little Ellen and Aunt Annie and Uncle Edward ten days after, as well as three days after. Last week when I was with him he leaned back against the pillow, and said "I can't come to your house because I am sick; because I am not able. Because I am not able," and he smiled with satisfaction at using a new phrase. I think he had been studying upon it and this was the first time he had tried it. On Saturday afternoon he asked his Papa to sing a song about a troubadour who was going to leave his lady-love & go to the war. When it was finished he said "Why didn't she go too?" "Because when men go to war they are likely to get hurt." "Why do men go to war then?" "Because they want to get hurt." "Then why didn't she go too?" "Because he didn't want her to get hurt." "*Why* do men go to war?" "No one knows. My Son, it is a problem which has perplexed the minds of the wise for centuries, and does still." Charles smiled enchanted, he loves a string of words. One night when he was very sick he said "Papa, water." Edward gave it to him, he drank it, and slowly whispered "*Why* do men go to war?" and Edward remembered the answer, and gave it, to his extreme content. Come this Sunday, dear children, if you like it better. There can be no circumstances when we shouldn't like to have you.

Aunt Ellen.

Tuesday June 8th 1880

Dear Edith,

This morning he is just a little worse. He had a "quiet" night, that is he slept, and didn't struggle hard, but he can't lie positively still for a single breath. Now at seven they have thought it best to give him ether, I wondered yesterday why they didn't. I only saw Annie, who was in bed nursing the baby, looking very handsome and with her hair shining and her face pale; she said with difficulty that she hadn't seen him, only he was worse, she didn't know any further. I presently heard Edward's voice downstairs ordering the horse for the train, so I ran down. He looked hopeless, and with long pauses contrived to say "He is as he was yesterday. We are giving him ether. Charley Putnam doesn't quite give up the ship, he thinks he may live. Will you stay? Then will you make up a fire in the parlour?" And he hurried upstairs. When I cleared up the parlour the table was covered with ponderous English & German books on diseases of children, the doctors had evidently been studying in the night. Jim P. had gone to Boston to get a drug not to be had in Concord, and was coming back to Lexington where Johnny was to meet him with the wagon at 8. Ned Bradford was to arrive by the 11 P.M. train, so Edward had all his doctor friends to support him. Aren't they good? It is a sad time. I can hardly imagine any disease to be a more painful sight, but one thing is clear, that Charles has none of the agony of imagination that a grown person would have about breathing with difficulty, and that we have for him. Practically it is most wearing & he feels the wear, but doesn't attribute it to anything & think about it, as we should.

[Unsigned]

Concord, at Edward's, June 9th 1880

Dear Edith,

I don't know what Prescott wrote about C. on the outside of my letter. I told him to say "7 p.m. alive", but he was so elated himself I fear he wrote "better" too. I just ran up here to inquire, met P. coming out and asked whether Charles was alive. "Yes indeed, and breathing beautifully", he said with a joyful smile. So I carried home the good news that he was much relieved, though it wasn't yet time to hope with any security about him, put together what I wanted for the night and hurried back to find him dead & laid out, and Edward & Annie preparing what the doctors wanted for the autopsy. He lay as John did on a board across the top of the crib, white as he could be, and placid, but looking very sick. He felt warm and natural when I kissed him, but he looked dead, not simply glorious like John, he had suffered so much more, and so very long. I went straight home as soon as the room was ready and the doctors went in. Father & Mother were of course astonished and Father came upstairs to sit with Mother and me and talk about him. This morning Father exclaimed again when he thought of Annie, as he

— 1880 —

did last night, "The mother is always a beautiful child, to me. Full of all goodness! And sensible! No nonsense in her!" After breakfast he didn't want to come here with me. He said "Edward wants some one better than me, someone full of life", but finally came. We met Edward on his way, going his rounds; he said he had advised Annie to stay in bed. So we came to a silent house, and saw no one till Mr Farrar came down stairs and then he went up to show us Charles. Father and I were both much upset by the sight, he looked so beautiful I couldn't help crying. Mother cried much over him, but kept saying "How handsome he is!" He is to be buried in a high-necked, long-sleeved white flannel sack-dress, like his brown ones. Do bring at least Violet.
E. T. E.

End of letter to Mrs. Sally Emerson, begun May 21.

June 11th. I believe Cousin Elizabeth has told you of little Charles's death. I wish you could have been here to see how noble and sweet he looked in his coffin. He never could hold himself erect in life, and I never suspected how much beauty that defect concealed, till I saw him laid straight with his head beautifully placed, and then it all came out. Edward & Annie sat beside him, his coffin was placed on his own little table where it always stood in the bay-window. Edward closed it, and he & Will carried him out. There was no hearse, no trestles, none of the funeral paraphernalia that Annie can't bear. She and Edward behave beautifully, they always do. Everything, everything! was done for Charles but the disease pursued its course with fearful steadiness. Three doctors to watch him most of the time made no difference. Mother and I send much love to you. Mother sends ten dollars for the anti-vice-regulation cause, told me to send it a month ago, but I couldn't find the time. Affectionately
E. T. E.

Concord, June 15th 1880

Dear Mrs Lewis,

Our news is very sad. Little Charles died a week ago, perhaps you will already have heard of it. Edward from the beginning thought it was croup and considered it most doubtful whether he could be saved, but it was nearly a week before he appeared sick to the inexperienced eye. At last however on June 4th I could see that he was worse and by Sunday he was so changed by a terrible attack in the forenoon that we all began to give up hope. All Edward's young doctor-friends were most kind (one of them, C. P. Putnam, is the first baby-doctor we have) and one, two or even three were there daily & spent the nights, so that we know that everything was watched as it should be, and nothing left undone. He died at 8 Tuesday night. His goodness was as marked all the way through as it has always been, He obeyed peacefully every command. The marvel to me and to us all, was that he never took the slightest notice of his sickness, never showed in voluntary look or tone that he wasn't perfectly comfortable, never spoke of it—simply struggled to go on with his plays, and to talk about his playthings, and the music-box which was his last delight. In the last few days poor Edward & Annie could hardly restrain their tears but they struggled hard and behaved beautifully. You can hardly imagine how beautiful the child was after death. Annie had made him a little flannel sack-dress such as he had worn lately, but this was white, for him to be buried in, and it helped the beauty of the impression. She wouldn't have any flowers near him, but on Sunday someone had sent him a water-lily which he had enjoyed very much, and when they were putting him in his coffin his Uncle Prescott brought in some beautiful fresh ones, and they all felt as if Charles would like it so much that they put one in his hand, and it looked right, so it remained there. They buried him beside his brothers. The dear little baby was born April 28th and is as healthy and hungry a little girl as I ever saw. We are desperately proud of her, and so was little Charles. She is named for me, greatly to my satisfaction. We are charmed to find that her hair is curly. She is a prettier baby than Charles, not so pretty as John when he was born, but he grew homely very fast. Annie got up beautifully and was already downstairs before Charles was taken sick. Everyone regards her with new admiration for her noble and lovely behaviour throughout. Haven Emerson came on from New York to the funeral and spent two days with us. He says his six are in fine order. I hope to visit them this summer. I am very glad your visit East did you good. I hope you can repeat it very soon and bring Mary & Susy. Give my love to them and promise them donkey-rides and carriage rides if they'll come. I admire your courage & wisdom in undertaking French again, I hope you have kept it up. I shall remember the names of the books you have told me of and read them when I find them. Farewell.

            E. T. E.

— 1880 —

Concord, June 17th 1880

Dear Edith,

 I am sorry not to write but have been turning off several letters which weighed on me. Edward began as soon as Friday to take Annie a little ride every night and usually they stopped in here. On Saturday night as they were going away Mother said "Bring the baby soon. Why can't you come Tuesday and bring her?" This upset Annie and she ran out to the front door and Edward & I with her. As soon as she could speak she said "Go say I will, and I didn't mean to cry. Ask her to forgive me." By this time Mother arrived and told her to wait till she felt like it. And she kept saying "I didn't mean to. I'll come if I can." On Sunday Mother spent an hour with them after church and they talked about little Charles all the time. Edward enjoyed it very much, Mother said. She couldn't tell about Annie. On Tuesday Annie came in at the East Door, cheerful & smiling, with little Ellen in her arms, and no one would have guessed that it was a hard day for her & Edward, though undoubtedly it was. The baby was good but sleepy. Annie caught sight of the little red chairs from Newport, and said "I want you, if you're willing, not to give the baby a chair. I don't want to have a row of little chairs—" She had to stop. Lily says she is staying with her, and finds that her friends stay too long with her. On Wednesday, for instance, Esther Mann came after breakfast & stayed till 12, Lucy Chapman stayed 2 hours, Marcella 2 hours, Annie Lombard 3 hours. All these in one day, and Annie was very much tired by it. So now Lily makes it her business after 15 m. to call Annie to the baby and take her place, and Annie doesn't return. This P.M. I have my N. Primary party and Violet & Madge I hope will arrive. Tomorrow I shall of course help with the flowers. On Tuesday I think we can come to Milton & spend one night, perhaps two. I'll bring baby's dress then, & his chair, and Sarah Malcolm's. Mrs Davidson & Belle spent the day on Wednesday. Yesterday Aunt Susan Jackson had word from Oscar that he shall come home for vacation on Aug 2d & return for the winter. Can't you come up this Sunday too? Mr E. E. Hale is to preach for us. I have a letter from Cousin Sarah saying she'll come early in July. Edward & Annie hope for an invitation from Haven & Susy to spend next week at Rockaway. Annie says she is so tired all the time she doesn't know what to do, and a change would rest her perhaps. Mother's roses are more glorious than ever before she thinks.

             E. T. E.

— 1880 —

June 28th 1880

Dear Edith,

We are all very sorry you are sick, and I am impatient for tomorrow to come to you. Edward & Annie will come home just as I go. Last Friday Father & Mother went to Boston by different trains, and Mother discovered that she has added another to her list of beaux. Mr Gilman, the new organist, asked to sit with her in the cars. They had a most beautiful time, and he asked her to allow him and Mr Wentworth to come and sing to her. He was very devoted in taking care of her till their roads parted. Father thinks he shall have to get out his pistol. Saturday night Father & I walked out in the garden, he with the purpose of killing rose-bugs, and he found plenty of game. His utter unconcern about rolling them to pieces in his fingers is amazing. I showed him two big soft white worms, and he cheerfully rolled them up in the same manner. I couldn't believe my eyes, though I know he has had life-long practice with caterpillars. When we came in we met Mother promenading in the East yard to view some pink clouds, and we all came into the study together. Presently I caught a rosebug on my head and laid him down on a magazine on the table. He briskly moved about with a sense of danger. No sooner did Father see him than, as I had hoped, he swiftly reached out his right hand of extermination, but swifter Mercy in the shape of Mother caught sight of him at the same moment, and snatched him, magazine and all, away just as that fell finger & thumb were within an inch of him, and bore him to the open window. I deeply enjoyed the play, the more so as each parent seemed wholly unconscious of the intent or presence of the other, each simply and abstractedly followed their natural bent. On Sunday afternoon walk as I chose a place to sit down, most convenient for sitting, but not much shaded, Father said, "Isn't there too much heaven on you here?" Father actually went once more to the Club on Saturday, because Mr G. F. Hoar was to be there. He had a delightful time, he said. Don't you & your family want to come to see the procession of boats on the Fourth?

E. T. E.

Milton July 1st 1880

Dear Mother,

Edith doesn't seem to improve with hot weather, as I should think she ought to. We have cold weather this morning and perhaps that will suit her better. The baby is cutting some teeth and has a rash & feels

— 1880 —

rather forlorn, so that I am not seeing him to advantage, but when he clears up for a while occasionally he is charming. He has a way of singing his feelings continually. If he is happy, you hear a song of joy all the time as he wanders solitary all over the house, and if he is pathetic, you hear a steady worry, worry. At dinner yesterday the children and I made the party, and of all disagreeable subjects the digging open of graves had fascinated Edward & John and had to be discussed, but we had a delightful time after all. Edward & John to be sure desired to consider the object of the grave-robbers, the condition of their prey, the possibilities of being buried alive, etc., etc., and I didn't wish to shut them up with sharpness, but we got round upon St. Cecilia, the Etruscan Kings, and other more interesting tales, and the elders were charming. Upon a return to the original subject I gave them Uncle Charles's story of the fellow-student who personated the subject and spoke in the chaise. That gave each child unmingled delight. We spent most of the day in trying to bring Ralph to the business of folding his clothes & putting them into his trunk to go to Beverly to see Handasyde. It was rather amusing though enraging to see how impossible it was. There was about one hour's work to do, and it took six hours of Ralph's & my time, and two or more of Edith's. Let us hope his moral sense will wake soon. He was charming, goodnatured and friendly, seemed to think he was very funny and pretty good, all the long exasperating day. Violet took me down in the morning to the garden which is finally laid out according to Edith's plan, and if it were not for the drought and the look as if grass & flowers must give up and die it would be pretty. Coming back we heard shouts of "Aunt Ellen! Aunt Ellen! there are cunning little young ones in this nest!" I couldn't see anybody, but Violet pointed out a movement in the top of a cherry-tree, and sure enough there was Edward in a yellow dress holding on and peeping in, full of excitement. Will at first when he came to supper was in very low spirits, but gradually revived, and Ralph came in & lay in the Sleepy Hollow Chair, and soon he & his papa were in a high frolic. After supper, when Edith was down & we were in the parlour, he sang to the children, and they all three were in raptures, Will changing his song as "Come to my heart my dark-eyed one" into "my weak-eyed one", addressing Ralph, and pulling Violet's ears when she laughed. It was very pretty to see Will's joy in their absurdities, and theirs in his. The doctor is to come today and I'm very glad.

— 1880 —

Concord July 21st 1880

Dear Kit,

We were very grateful for your letter, every word of it, and particularly enjoyed the baby's entrance at dinner-time. I am glad he has been happily ushered into the ocean, too, and that Ralphy saw it, and everybody else. Sorry about your housekeeping troubles. I suppose we are just plunging into the like, after long comfort. Well, we must take our turn. How good of you to send me a photograph of each kind! I am very proud to possess them and keep them handy, to admire very often. Dear little Ellen had her picture taken on Monday, and succeeded very well in Nelly's arms but in Annie's she looks like a young barbarian of the north or like a native of the Guinea coast, according to which picture you take. The picture of Annie is pretty. Frances came on Saturday morning, and in the afternoon, Edward & Annie, Miss, & Cousin Sarah having been here to dinner, the last stayed with us and mended all my stockings and was perfectly charming, after Edw. had carried home the Baby & Annie. Frances & I went for Mr Brown to the Depot and then Mary Dakin came to see me and the rest sat on the doorstep, so that when I came down it seemed like days of old to see the doorstep occupied. We then discoursed on the dear subject of Education, till Father came and then the wagon and we rode up to the cliffs where we beheld unusual glory and as always hated to come home. The sermon gave deep satisfaction the next day, and Mr Alcott came to dinner with the intention of carrying Mr Brown off for the afternoon, but Mr B. wouldn't go, absolutely insisted on going with us instead, and we had a good walk to Walden Ledge. Father talked a little too. In the evening the Cheneys came in. I immensely enjoyed the Sunday, and Father said he was a pleasant guest. Then on Monday afternoon came Lidian and later Mr Channing, and both of them in their different ways have been thoroughly delightful. No fights yet, though they have come in sight several times. He goes today, and she has already gone. No more time now.

E. T. E.

Concord, July 30th 1880

Dear Edith,

We are as happy as can be with our company, Mr Channing all the time, and Rose Lamb, Lily Keyes, Mary Watson for me, and Mr Alcott,

— 1880 —

Mr Sanborn & other philosophers for him, coming and going, and Mrs E. Hoar, Miss Prichard & Mrs Jones to amuse Mother. Lizzy Simmons & the Howards to tea Tues. We go to the Manse tomorrow. Occasional attendance also of family & guests at Philosophy. Yesterday Mrs Howe lectured and came afterwards to dine here with Mrs Terry and Miss Whitehead, who is coming tomorrow with Lily Cleveland to spend Sunday & hear Mr Channing teach my class. Miss Whitehead's zeal of admiration for America has only increased since you saw her. Alicia said that at Philosophy she became so eager that finally she joined in the conversation of the great, and though crimson with the consciousness that she was speaking in meeting she carried through all she had to say. I have visited dear baby this morning. She is to be christened by Mr Channing on Sunday afternoon at her own house. This morning Father & I in the wagon were on the Mill Dam & Edward was standing by us, speaking to us. He looked up street and said "Turn in quick! turn in to the sidewalk!" We did. There was a runaway tearing down. It was Mrs Prescott Hosmer without her hat in a long open farm-wagon drawn by a large horse. She never looked up nor made a sound, her teeth were set & she was pulling with all her strength on the reins. Edw. jumped forward too late. A whole line of road-men & the superintendent were at the crossing but their efforts were ineffectual. Edw. however was giving chase and by their brandished shovels probably the horse was checked enough for him to catch on behind. I couldn't see the least sense in his doing that. Mr Rankin now failed to stop the horse. Edward was crawling along in the wagon, and I wondered why he got in. His weight made little difference to such a horse. Now he had climbed over the seat and was sitting beside her. I thought she would like to have him come but his intention never occurred to me till I saw him take the reins, Then I acknowledged that I had been uncommonly stupid, but it made him seem very bright to me, to have thought so quickly what else he could do when he hadn't stopped her horse. They turned out of our sight, but in a minute more there was a shout from those who could see of "It's all right!" He had turned the horse in front of the Middlesex into the Hotel stable. Presently Mrs Hosmer turned round & said "Why I had three ladies in behind. Where are they?" They were found in due time. One of them was in Dr Barrett's office with her arm broken, Edward went to visit his patients as soon as Mrs Hosmer was on *terra firma*. She hearing of the broken arm hastened to Dr B.'s office and seized her passenger, carrying her off with determination in spite of the arm, and sent for Edward to come and set it. He carried all appliances, ripped off the sleeves from the arm. It turned out to be quite sound. So all ended finely.

E. T. E.

Concord Aug 21 1880

Dear Edith,

I go to Prov. & Rockaway on Monday morning. When do you want us? I think I can't bring Ruth home this time. I'm sorry. Cousin Edwin is gone, Mother well, Cousin Sarah comes Monday, Mr Hall tonight. Oscar is engaged to Kitty Ellis of Dorchester. At the christening in Belmont we saw her. Mother wants to have some embroidery done for you, muslin or flannel or thibet. What would you like? In haste

E. T. E.

81 Madison Avenue, N.Y.
Wednesday morning Aug 25th 1880

Dear Edith,

I have an hour to wait for Haven and first of all I must write to you. I think often of you and all the children, and wish I knew what you were all up to, and how you seem. I take great pleasure in the crop of photographs you sent me and of course have brought them all along, and have been exhibiting them.

Our latest joy at home was Mr Edward Hall's visit. When Mr Blake of Worcester was at the School of Philosophy, he dined at our house with Mr Channing, and said "I go to Mr Hall's church. I enjoy him, I'm very fond of him. He's so handsome!" and he smiled most affectionately at the thought, and looked as if he thought it might be a weakness to delight so much in his beauty, but how could he help it! I find Father had a good deal the same feeling, and exclaimed with pleasure every time he was reminded he was coming because he was going to be such a goodly spectacle. I was a little disappointed in the effect he had on Father. He liked having him there, liked sitting in the room with him, but wouldn't talk. In vain Mr Hall directed his conversation to him, even distinctly addressed him; Father would smile and turn away as if it had been said to me, and he had no further concern than to hear my answer. But when I went to bed Saturday night I think he asked him into the study, and they sat an hour together. Really it was so great a pleasure I want to tell you all about it. From the first morning he was the same creature that begged to brush the crumbs in 1877. Just like a cousin brought up in the house, pleased to get home and be at home. He sported all the time. Mother sat at the table for the first time since she was sick, and had a grand discussion with him. Then after tea when Father had gone into the study we moved into the parlour, and I having thought over my own wishes, which at first sight seemed bold & moreover selfish, decided that they were reasonable and that I would venture, awkward as it seemed. My S.S. lesson for the next day was unusually difficult, and I asked him to teach it to me. He was as much surprised and abashed as I expected but saw also that it wasn't unreasonable. So I brought the Bibles, the Greek Testament, Mr Morison's notes, and Mother brought Campbell's Four Gospels. It was all exactly as I thought it would be. He did much for me that I couldn't do for myself. The Greek & the Latin which waste much of my time to precious little purpose were daylight to him. He wholly rejected all interpretations of difficulties known to me, dropped as useless what I consider valuable, but at the end all was clearer to me than it had ever been before, and I had firm ground under my feet. It didn't interest him very much, but he was perfectly willing and able. It was nuts indeed to me. Mother went to bed before we got half through. Father came in and listened to the last ten verses of the chapter, as if he thought it very pleasant too.

On Sunday morning which was the most beautiful morning possible we had a cheerful breakfast, and Father took him out to see the garden and pear-orchard. Then he went to his room. Mother & Father both went to church. Mother rode. On the way to church Mr Hall anxiously asked particulars that I couldn't give about communicating with the organist, but there seemed to be no hitch. My friends Rev. Mr Hussey of Billerica & all his family were on the porch and they sat in our pew. I hadn't expected such consolation in the service. It was not only superior in its whole tone, & beauty, which I knew it probably would be but it went to the heart of things all the way through. It seemed to rest one, and I thought I could feel the whole congregation receiving comfort from it. After church he went down into S.S. but didn't speak & soon went home with Mother. What a beautiful time I did have with my class! who were impressed with the difficulties I had seen, and gladly received the light I brought from Mr Hall. Edward & Annie came to Sunday-School to meet me and we all walked home together to dinner, a very uncommon thing it is for us to walk together. Annie & I were

— 1880 —

vain of ourselves & each other for we had on our best muslin gowns. Dinner of course was a festivity. The School of Philosophy was talked over, and the views of several pupils reported. Many an old family yarn was poured into Mr Hall's ears, and something recalled to Edward's mind a story which I never heard before. In 1871 he said a man with a crotchet came to lay it before Father. He (Edw.) went to the door & conducted the shaggy wild-looking man into the parlour. He sat down & kept on his hat. Edw. accompanied Father to the parlour to see what would happen. Father having said how do you do, said "Let me take your hat, sir". The man ignored the offer, sat down & was about to proceed to business, but Father repeated it. The man said "No Sir, I prefer to wear it." "Well then," said Father, "certainly! we will talk in the yard if you prefer it", and walked out into the yard, without waiting for any refusal, the man meekly following. Far Rockaway. Here I am. Children charming! Haven well, Susy suffering like you & me in the kitchen. I shall wait to finish next time.

E. T. E.

Far Rockaway Aug 26th 1880

Dear Mother,

This is written with a cold-water-pen. See in the date how the cold water gradually took colour. When I reached Haven's house he wasn't expected for an hour, so I wrote to Edith and presently Ruth came in from Somers. Of course she had grown, and her hair was a spreading mane of accidental ringlets, very becoming to her indeed. She looked handsome, and was affectionate and demonstrative in her welcome as usual. We had a little talk, very pleasant to me, and at nine Haven came. The moment I got to talking with him it seemed as if I could never stop, there was so much to discuss. But of course he had business, so Ruth & I, and my letter, moved out of his office into the dining-room and I continued to write & Ruth to read. Haven presently proposed a visit to Sally and I was thankful. I had a feeling of having alighted only for a moment, and it hadn't occurred to me that there was time for that. I proceeded straight to her house and spent 3/4 of an hour with her. It was very hot bright weather as I walked back, and Haven & Ruth amazed me by saying we must have our lunch quick if we wanted to get off before the rain came. We hurried and when we came out of the house it was a cool rainy day. It rained hard all through the journey but held up when we reached Haven's door. Susy is pale & thin. I feel very

— 1880 —

sorry for her, she suffers in her kitchen. She is lovely to me, and a model mother. Willy & Haven came down curious to see me, but a little shy, they hung their heads & laughed. It wasn't long before Haven brought in "his girl", that is always Julia. She was so big I was surprised. I supposed they were to be small-sized children, but they are not. Elizabeth waked next and was rather afraid and distant when introduced. Haven reminded Susy that late dinner-time was approaching, so I descended to my room to unpack, presently someone began a vigorous attack on my door. It proved to be Helena, very anxious to see the new arrival. She was exceedingly sociable, and liked the contents of my trunk, staying with me till I left my room. Haven, Susy & I with the older children went to see a swimming-race & a tub-race. Coming back we found the trio at their own table having supper. The evening meal ended, Susy took the boys & Ruth upstairs, and Helena, Elizabeth & Julia stood before me and with earnestness told me of a stuffed bear, of a broken fan, of a man who gave each of them two peanuts. It was as lovely an entertainment as could be imagined. Cousin Sarah's letter has come. Oh how thankful I was for it! All good news it brings, too. Do ask her to write again. Please also will she roll up & send by mail the twilled-flannel waist in my bureau drawer. Be regular at meal-times. Edward will have to tell you how necessary for yourself that is.
E. T. E.

Saturday. (4 Sept. '80)
Dear Edith,

Father has a stiff back and must consult Edward today. If that doesn't prevent—and it would be most awkward if we had to stay, so I shall urge going—we shall take the 12 o'clock train from O.C. Depot on Monday, he & I. Mother is not able, I see plainly. She goes to Edward on Monday & Cousin S. starts for home on Tuesday. Lucy & Capt. Spencer dined here on Thursday, and yesterday the Conways & Sanborns, Edward & Annie & the baby, who sat with me at the table and was charming. Tonight C. & T. & the Prichards to tea. Rose is here, in pretty good heart, and had a sitting from both Father & Mother yesterday, hopes also for another today.
E. T. E.

Concord, Sept. 7th 1880
Dear Puss,

I fear more and more that we cannot come at all. The desire to stay at

— 1880 —

home grows upon Father, and he has numerous "excellent reasons" for "denying himself the pleasure" of making the visit. I shan't give up trying till Thursday, but since I must be at home on Saturday, I shall not try for Friday. Since I hope for a girl on Monday I can't come after this week till Sept 28 or 29. Cousin Sarah has gone. I am disappointed not to see you at all. Much love to you.
E. T. E.

Concord, Sept 14th 1880
45th Wedding-day.

Dear Edith,

I can come as well on the 25th as on the 28th, and of course if I am of more use in Milton shall be doubly glad to come there. I will certainly spend Sept 30th & Oct 1st with you. I am judge of needle-work at Cattleshow which begins Sept 30th, and I had, happily before your letter came, written to the Secretary that I must be absent at that time. I say happily for I am incapable of judging needle-work. So I must be absent, having given Mr Brown that excuse.

I have enjoyed all your letters and wish I could have written some in return. I am glad R. & V. enjoy Miss Yonge, and I don't wonder that R. can't bear the deaths she allows, he inherits that from Father—do you remember how he wouldn't like Cranford after Capt. Brown died, and I know I wanted to stop in Daisy Chain. That Edward has learned to swim & that Cameron & Don can sail are facts that deeply interest me. Every mention of Violet is sweet to her aunt, best of all the news of her riding. Say to Cameron that if my chance comes I shall answer his letter to Grandma & Grandpa.

We have celebrated the wedding-day and the anniversary of going to housekeeping, more by words & reminiscences than in any other way, but last night Edw. & Annie, Chas. & Therchi, and Sally came to tea, and we had a very pleasant time, and they brought flowers & we circumstantially recalled the first teatime 45 yrs. before, which Edward told us he "remembered as if it were yesterday". Mother & I & Edward too are glad her patterns are used for the basket. And have I never said how happy I am that Waldo loves music?
E. T. E.

Concord, Sept. 18th 1880

Dear Cousin Sarah,

Thankyou for your letter. Very glad were we all to get it, Father

— 1880 —

included. I was of course interested in every word about all the cousins. What a good time you must have had that night you all sat up till one o'clock, naughty as it was! When I came from the depot after driving you thither and told Mother what you said she rejoiced very much that she *had* given you the money in your purse. We proceeded to the Manse to dinner and Mother enjoyed it, and so did I, so much that we only wished we could always keep going there. They were all sorry you were missing. The next day Father went too, and we again had a high festival, the third day Father and I went to Boston, the fourth & fifth he dined with Edward & Annie, and we ladies at the Manse. The fifth was Saturday, and Annie McLaughlin came home, so on Sunday we sat under our own vine & fig-tree, & have ever since. A. exclaimed that she was glad to get back, and went to work with a will cleaning and cooking. On Wednesday last, I went to Boston and brought home a New Brunswick girl whom I like very much, and hope to keep. Tuesday the day before was Mother's 45th wedding-day, and Wednesday was the day we are more likely to keep, the anniversary of their coming to this house, and beginning housekeeping. Sally & Chas. & Therchi, and Edward & Annie came to tea, and Mother had a present of a new pair of glass salt-cellars. We all had a very good time. Mother declares that she doesn't get well yet, but she does go up in town and appears as usual. Annie has sent away the little Nelly and means to take all the care of Baby herself. She is as well as usual now, and Baby is quite glorious. Tomorrow is Edward's sixth & Mr Keyes's thirty-sixth wedding-day and Father & Mother are to dine with both bridegrooms and the brides at the half-way house. Lily & I are not invited. We must dine together here. I have found a hdkf. of yours which I will send herewith. I hope you'll soon go to Cousin Charlotte's. Give my love to her, and Mother's, and to yourself we send it.

E. T. E.

Concord Oct 3rd 1880

Dear little Girl who left us fifteen years ago today, we all send our love to you, and are glad of your marriage today as we were that bright wedding-day. It was just such a day then as this now is. We rejoice as usual over the treasure of a son and brother you have given us, and as to those six beloved bairns, they are up to our old dreams of what pleasure bairns might be. I ought to have told you before I came away, how good my darling Cameron was, how heartily he was trying to practice his profession of caring for his mamma's pleasure as much as for his own. I trust by mercy to the child you were given the inkling which I neglected to give you, so that he received the approbation which little hearts need so much to help them in the narrow way. I am pursued with anxiety & remorse about my carelessness in this point. Be careful with your troublesome children to point out particulars in which they may please you, and notice and praise every instance of remembering, and don't allow yourself to make sweeping accusations in moments of irritation. It discourages them even when it doesn't put their backs up. Cameron always strikes me as peculiarly grateful for kindness & likely to dwell on it with great pleasure, and refer to it afterwards. I remember one or two instances of this with him, and none with the others. His grace of manner proceeds from a soft heart as well as from love of approbation. I hope I don't seem to blame you. I know how overburdened you are apt to be, and what a good mother you are.

Your sister.

W. Manchester Oct. 4th 1880

Dear Mother,

I came down last night in the cars with Annie (Hooper) Lothrop, and from her learned about a great many of our friends. Mrs Mason, Mrs Sumner once, is in England with Belle who is Mrs Balfour, and has a little daughter. Clover has been in Europe all summer & is just returning. Mrs Hooper is here with Annie and has hopes of getting Anna Folsom to spend the winter with her. Nina is in Boston hard at work upon her house. Ellen Parkman & Harry are keeping house down here in their Mother's house. I found Ida [Higginson] sick in bed, but on the mending hand. I think this house beyond all the rest that I have seen bears the bell for perfectness. How I long to show you my room where I have a great open fire burning all the time, with its beautiful mantelpiece, and tiled hearth, china tiles so gay & shining, and its washstand which seems to me the handsomest yet invented. The impression you first receive is of elegance & neatness, not at all of costliness & luxury, but as you study the details you see that such work must have cost, and this seems to me a very conscientious way of building a rich house, cultivating to the workmen and to those who live in it. I have a beautiful balcony looking out to sea, with a long window, and wire musquito-bars that fill the whole, but slide easily away to let me out, and another window looking out on rocks & woods. Mr Higginson said he came

— 1880 —

down in the cars with Mrs Cabot last night, as she was returning from the funeral of her last remaining sister. Ida thinks however I had better go to see her today and is going to send some grapes by me. Ida and I have had already very long good discussions, and are laying out for a day of photographs, letters, & bliss generally. I hope Father remembered to tell you of his cup of coffee in Boston. I shall come home at 5.20 Wed. P.M. by the 4.30 train. Let Maggy press my white muslin where it needs pressing, please. She'll find it in my large pine box at the end of the garret, in a big pasteboard box, which is wrapped in a crib-sheet. The while muslin petticoat to wear with it is either in the drawer of the skylight closet, or 3d drawer of Edith's closet, or hanging in E. entry wardrobe, or folded on my next-to-the-upper shelf of my hanging closet. That needs pressing too. Please look at dress before she begins & tell her what it needs. I am to wear it tomorrow, Wed. eve^g. I add a list of Wed. work for M.

Your affectionate daughter
E. T. E.

Milton Oct 28th 1880

Dear Haven & Susy,

Today Violet is thirteen years old, and I came to spend her birthday with her. She met me in front of the house, invited me upstairs, and to my infinite amazement and equal joy, opened the door upon a basket containing a sister born this very morning. Was ever anything so good? Edith is as well as ever, better than sometimes on the first day, never had an easier labour. Rosamond, as Violet and I still may call her, weighs 11 lbs in her clothes, probably more than 10 out of them, and seems to be a child of light complexion. Edward sick abed for the last two days, but not very. A neglected cold. Charley just getting about after being in bed nearly a week. Everyone else well & thirsting to see you at Thanksgiving.

E. T. E.

Nov. 3d 1880

Dear Mother,

Edith has had another good night, and Baby has also had a good night. As to her name she is to receive it on Father's next birthday, and Will says he shan't think of deciding it till May comes. He encourages us to think that Rosamund will have a share of consideration with others, but says the subject is one which demands a six months study. For looks, all her paternal relations say she is *very* pretty, which is true once or twice in the day for a minute or so. Lidian's letter has come and I am very much gratified, a letter is an unaccustomed luxury when I am away from home. I rejoice that Edward is better. I enclose Edith's list of roses. She says she has lately been told that roses do best when set out only a day or two before the ground freezes. Are you to mark 18 on this list & return it that James may send for yours with hers? I found wrapped up in another letter in my portfolio the "Beauties of Emerson" letter, and have sent Father's refusal. I said to Messrs. Houghton Mifflin & Co. about the "Birthday Book" "He's harmless, let him go." Will has had a letter from Mr Holmes in Plymouth saying he will contest your tax bill, and have it reduced to a proper amount. I dined last night at Alice's and she asked very kindly about you & Father & so does Sarah.

                E. T. E.

              Milton Nov. 3d 1880

Dear Haven,

I thought I had settled with Susy both these questions when I was at Rockaway. I certainly told her that you were *all to sleep at our house.* It seems to me that it will be uncomfortable to you to be separated from any of the children at night. Some years hence it will make less difference. I propose to give you & Susy Edith's room, and the trins and their nurse my room. Willy & little Haven I mean to put up in the den with Cameron, John & Edward, and to take Ruth and Violet with me in the blue room. Or if you prefer that Willy & Haven should not join in the wild revels of the den, I can put them in the little room over the kitchen. Of course you can have the matter as doubtful as you please till the last moment. I shall be ready for you and dreadfully disappointed if you don't come. I expect you of course to stay from Wednesday morning to Saturday. Edith of course will not be able to come, but she promises me Will and the six children we had before last Thursday. Rosamond, as we call her till she is named, is a very symmetrical baby. She certainly has a very round little head covered with the lightest hair I ever saw on a baby and a pretty good little face when it is still. We are all of course happy at the result of the election, though as Sarah Forbes says it is too bad about Solid North & Solid South. Our children here seem a great deal older than they did a year ago. What a good time we shall have three weeks from today if you come!

E. T. E.

Milton, Nov. 5th 1880

Dear Mother,

I have just received Cousin Sarah's note and Lidian's accompanying it, and am delighted with everything Lidian tells me; principally with your message about her. Oh, I was sorry to hear that Rose L. was going to Boston for the winter. But it was good news about Aunt Susan and Charley and about Edward, and I was glad to know about the pears. I think I shan't come home on Saturday, though at first I felt as if I must spring at the word of command. But in fact Lidian is just as good as I for you, and probably less likely to get tangled in conversation with the first-comers and never bestow a thought thenceforth on lamps, chairs, or any other hospitable point. Then I do expect to be positively useful on Sunday here more than on any other day; the absent three are coming home to spend Sunday and must be piloted through church-going and hymn-learning. I am coming home on Monday by the five o'clock train and going to a church-meeting in the evening. I shall stay till 1.30 on Tuesday, and then return, if it seems right, to stay till Thursday P.M. when my visit here will end. Mrs Forbes has just been looking at the baby; she says she appears to meditate busily even when asleep "like all the Forbeses", and poor Mrs Forbes has never seen her awake. When she is awake she opens her eyes quite wide now and looks about, and is sometimes as smooth in her features as a big baby, though she still spends most of the time in working them into the absurdest expressions. Every time Waldo appears he exclaims "Baby! Whak!" which last is a most discordant squeak intended to represent what he has heard that young creature say. I wish you could have heard Don talk today when he dined alone with me. When he said with sad simplicity "Nelson & Cam won't let me play base-ball with them, because they think I'm a— —fool" he hesitated a little before saying the word but when he did say it, it was with a tone of acquiescence in their right to judge, and with a soberness which showed that though he regretted it he didn't dispute it at all. He has just mounted Donald and trotted off in the rain to see Winny Clark. I am sorry not to come Sat. but don't you think I'm right?

Your admiring daughter
E. T. E.

— 1880 —

Concord Nov. 22d 1880
Your birthday
This year, our baking-day

Dear Edith,

How glad are your family at every thought of you and your seven beloved children and Will! This is the best birthday yet because of number Seven. How little we imagined last birthday that we should be so blest on this! I think if it were not baking-day I should have to come to see you with all your host. We all send our love to you on the anniversary and present our humble offerings by the trusted hand of our dear Violet. Mother sends a long-handled boot-buttoner such as Alice & Nina use for you to try. According to them it is a comfort, as saving stooping. I am skeptical, but you can keep it round for stout visitors if you don't like it yourself. Father sends a variety of tack-lifters and you can take any two or the whole. Ellen can't find the rest of her present but sends the Purple Princess one of the small cushions for her pocket meanwhile. We all want to see you very much. How did Annie like our little creetur? I thank you for the praises of Ellen and all your kind messages, Mr Cabot has been here and begun on the note-books.

Your affectionate sister.

Concord, Dec. 1st 1880

Dear Edith,

I have wanted to write to you daily to tell you about your dear bairns, but hitherto have had no time. Thankyou for writing to me about their return. Every word was what I wanted to know. The night they arrived here they seemed to fill their relations with pride & joy to an unusual degree. Mother & Father kept looking at each other and at me, and Mother afterward exclaimed "How *beautiful* they all are! and how *sweetly* they talk!" We all listened in vain even till bed-time for Susy's arrival. It was very pleasant to see how eager all the children were, and from the beginning even until now I am more & more convinced that we must hereafter always have Haven's family if we want a perfect Thanksgiving. It doubles our children's pleasure. Our dear little boys were sharply put through their practising the next morning by a relentless Aunt, but were so forgiving as to be willing to be very useful to her for the greater part of the day, breaking and putting up green in the morning, and in the evening doing the usual grating, chopping and picking. Edward desired to try his hand at each employment and after two minutes experience of it begged to be excused, but discipline was

— 1880 —

Annie Keyes Emerson and Ellen T. Emerson, seven months old, November 22, 1880.

maintained, and his brethren reviled him. Cameron has asked leave to scallop the oysters next year, and I have promised that he shall. We are both delighted with the plan. Don throughout has been obliging and

— 1880 —

useful and pleased me very much. As to our Violet she has been indeed a right-hand and a cushion of comfort. And Ralph was good & dear and cracked nuts for me in a shady nook under a table hour after hour. The children have told you no doubt of Susy's arrival while we were at tea, of the knock that startled nobody, followed by the little voices that filled all the longing ears, and of the wide-eyed glance & simultaneous rush all round the table, everyone climbing over chairs and all their fellow creatures too to get to the door first, while Grandmamma, bewildered, continued to cry out, "What is it? What has happened? What are you doing? Are you all crazy? Why don't you tell me?" and no one could spare breath or thought to answer till they had seen whether it was really true that the cousins had come. And in the entry there were the N.Y. family in battle array, Haven & Willy both arms out for embracing, with eager smiles, the babes shy though glad to get here, and Susy smiling over all with nurse Sarah behind her. Happily the rooms were ready, and the three cribs proved a fit. On Thursday, Thanksgiving morning, I early discovered that I could have my ball and that Mr Wesson would play. From that moment I trod on air I was so glad. Dear Ralph & Violet made the bower of bliss* and the old ancestors looked with grave approval on the piety of a new generation. It is funny now to see how Grandma Bliss & Mother have bent their adorning boughs together into a snug little bower for Father's bust which Violet has twined with club-moss. Eugenia & Susy took care of the salt-cellars. I went to church. It felt good. All our friends clustered round to inquire after the trins and congratulate me. Coming home I found Will, very kind and gay and we began setting the table very prosperously but in spite of everyone's kind assistance and all the planning I had been able to do the want of your head & hands was felt severely as the hours went on, and I confess to a pretty bad failure in all my part, though I believe the dinner was good and the waiting passable, and everybody as pleasant & indulgent as could be. I forgot the crackers & cheese, the pears, mismanaged about the pudding & the cream. Edward's absence was another sad stroke to the dinner. I have thought though, that he perhaps was relieved and would rather be engaged in hard & anxious work than trying to make merry without his boy who has made Thanksgiving a proud day to him for four years. Blessed Annie met it without flinching. She talked and laughed & helped play as freely as anyone. She took little Ellen home at six, and came back bringing Edward at eight.

*"Bower of bliss" probably refers to decorating with greens the portraits of the Bliss ancestors on the stairway.

403

— 1880 —

From the moment he came in Edward worked like a tiger to keep the children amused to the last possible point. You ask what the children wore, I suppose you mean the cousins, not our children. Little Ellen wore one of those dresses Mrs Forbes sent her, long-sleeved, high-necked, and with an embroidered ruffle round its long, long skirt. She looked very fine. The trio wore white piquet sack dresses, embroidered, but simple. Mother thought them perfection. Haven, a handsome black green & blue plaid jacket & kilt, stockings scarlet above and plaid to match below, and a dark blue satin neck ribbon. Willy a grey long jacket and knee-breeches, scarlet stockings and a gleaming scarlet cravat. I think Sarah had on a muslin tire over a blue dress, but am not sure. Dora had her hair braided in two short braids tied with ribbons, and I think her dress was a claret thibet. Willy is dressed like a young gentleman now. I think Ezra had a dark suit not very different from Ralph's. Minnie & Sarah managed the children's dinner, I believe without great difficulty and successfully. The babies all cried more or less however. Violet & little Haven were the only ones who enjoyed the full bliss of the Ball. I wish you could have seen Haven. His utter abandonment to the joy of every dance was a refreshment to all the old. My dear Don danced very well once or twice with me and once with Mrs Bartlett. Cameron's & Ralph's experiences I didn't see. Uncle Edward said the best part of the evening to him was the spectacle of little Edward labouring nobly through "All the Way to Boston". C. & D. & E. also Willy spoke however in most moderate terms of the pleasure of the occasion. On Friday afternoon Elizabeth Hoar & Elizabeth Hoar Evarts called upon Elizabeth Hoar Emerson. It was very pleasant. I have no more time. Mother thanks for flowers. She has a cold and keeps her bed. Will next Wed. & Thurs. do for me to come to you? What happiness 'twill be to me! We in this house have had a good Thanksgiving, and are not tired. We hope your knee will let you go soon. Delighted with the mention of baby.

E. T. E.

Dec. 21st 1880

Dear Edith,

What a surprise and pleasure the tintypes were to us! They are respectable though faint, and how different-looking from Waldo at the same age they show Rosamond to be! Mother says "She isn't pretty, but there is no reason why she shouldn't turn out so!" That is exactly what I

— 1880 —

always think when I contemplate her. Father made no remarks, but looked at it with great interest & pleasure. I am glad you are downstairs once more, and hope your knee will soon get well. Thankyou very much for asking me to Christmas. There is nothing I should like better if I can manage it, and probably I can. When do you want us to come to New Years? I advise you to let us know as soon as possible the answers to the questions on this page, that we may arrange accordingly. As soon as possible I'll send you a prepared list of what we are going to give to whom and the remaining questions. Annie has nothing for V. and I know V. wants one of those bottles, so I'll let A. give it to her. The other I'll give to Ellen and when Rosamond is twelve I'll try to find one for her.

E. T. E.

January 1881 – December 1882

Sickness in Milton. Forbes family visits California. Work on Emerson-Carlyle correspondence. Cooking school in Concord. Visits to Manchester, Naushon, Canton, and Providence. Search for a minister. 1882. Spring in Concord. RWE sick. Death of RWE. Alexander Forbes born. Mr. Bulkeley ordained minister. Conference at Saratoga. Florence Emerson born.

Monday, Jan. 10th 1881

Dear Edith,

Mother sends her dear love to you and desires me to tell you that all the time when she was with you and since she has felt as if you had come nearer to her than at any time since you were married. She has come home rather weak about you, and praises your looks, declares that your youth has returned and that she kept enjoying your countenance all the time. She is anxious for fear you considered her visit a failure, and says oh no! if I weren't so weak that I was oppressed by the terror of the packing to come home, and if I could bear to make so much trouble as I do I should have stayed till Thursday. Having finished her messages I remark that I left behind my candlestick from Alice and my veil & bashlik, and Mother's chuddar shawl. I'll come for them as soon as I can. We came home with all the property in great peace and safety. Mother unpacked herself, and went to church with Father and me in the morning to hear Mr DeNormandie of Portsmouth, who took tea with us with his hosts Mr Blanchard & Helen. And a beautiful time we had. Father praised his preaching. I liked him best at home. This reminds me that you probably are curious to hear Father's verdict on Mr Frothingham. This it was. "I thought when he began that it looked rather unpromising but I saw as he went on that he had a skill of his own." He said it approvingly. I have been sitting down by my beautiful new work-basket, poking it over and enjoying it. It is a great present, altogether too great and should have been from the whole family for both New Years & birthday. It goes to the right spot. I thank you. I am very proud of it. And my Sister Dora from my beloved Ralph is another very good present that I like very much. Then blessed Violet's immaculate match-box is going to be kept in pink cotton-wool in the darkest deepest corner of my dominion for great occasions and gala days. And

— 1881 —

tell my Cameron sweet that I have sat and gloated over my adhesive paper, especially my name written on it by his own hand several times. And Don's red handkerchief is of the exact colour that I love and made by Violet's pious paws did he say? And as to dear small Edward's little vase that will figure up stairs & down in every glorious and inglorious use till its or my death do us part. Mrs Sanborn & Miss Leavitt are coming tomorrow to

End of letter is missing.

Concord. Jan. 27th 1881

Dear Edith,

I want to know how you are getting along. I have engaged the Hall for my Ball on the 24th prox. and Mr Wesson cheerfully agrees to be my music. The list of invitations Lizzy Bartlett kindly made out with me. They invited me to tea last night and though George was away we laughed as much as if he had been there. Aunt Susan and Lidian are now domesticated there. They take great interest in my Ball. Annie & Edward have dined here and brought the big peony along. She was very gracious and delightful all the time. Edward & Annie have been also very kind and indulgent about my little plan, and Father seems amused. We are taking up carpets as if it was April. I have some idea of making my Ball an objective point and tearing the house to pieces & reconstructing every thread in it to be ready for so grand a gala, as we did for April 19, '75. Tonight I am invited to tea at the Cheneys to meet Frank Barlow and Mrs Julia Ward Howe.

I enclose a letter from Mr DeNormandie of Portsmouth. Can you answer its question. He took tea here when he preached here, and Mother & I enjoyed his visit very much. We are going to have a tea-party on Saturday for the Harrises, and Bishop Ferette & Grace Cook.

Give my love to all my dear measles-patients, and the candidates. I hope you are prospering yourself, and how is Baby? I am coming to your Ball Feb. 4.

Thy sister.

F.R.R. Feb. 2, 1881

Dear Edith,

What a time you are having! What a mercy that the measles have a short run. If this were to go on indefinitely you would be all worn out, everyone of you! This is the first time I have ever observed any inconvenience to having a large family. They seem to shingle along a little so that you have only two suffering cases at once and we will hope that most of them will be happily convalescent before Waldo and poor little Rosamond take their turn. I thank my stars that the 24th is still three weeks off for if you couldn't all come to dance at my bridal I should be most unhappy. Yesterday I dined at Edward's to revise the list to be invited and he increased rather than diminished it. Today came our conference, and I saw no reason why I shouldn't go, for the first time since Jan. 1877. Mother also abetted me. But Mrs Henry Hosmer came to Edward's yesterday to invite me to a lunch-party today. I was torn in my mind but considered the lunch-party a more unique chance, so accepted, and later was invited to tea at Mrs Emery's. While I was dressing this morning it suddenly occurred to me Why not go & come up at 11.15? So I went gaily down and have had all the good of the two opening hours. In the business meeting when I heard the ignorant and unpractical views expressed I almost leaped over all bounds and addressed the assembly. If I am going to keep my rule of not speaking in meeting, I shall some day have a hard time I fear. Happily all the directors know as much and are trained in the same school as I, and two of them were there and jumped up quick to avert the impending dangers. So all was saved at last, or I think I should have had to speak. Why they would have hurt the work of the Conference so that it wouldn't have recovered in years, and I having been absent so long didn't know who was in power, and what force there might be on the wrong side, and was more anxious than I need have been if I were living at the heart of the matter as I used to.

[Unsigned]

Feb. 9, 1881.

Dear Edith,

I came away very much alarmed about Ralph's ear & V. in general, she looked so livid and so weak, and last night I thought Sarah Forbes's note was to tell me how sick they were, but as she doesn't mention them I take courage and hope all goes well. Mother & I went to Boston on Monday and had another whole day from 11 to 6 there, bought her a new carpet, almost the old one over again, two pr. new boots, black silk, etc. and ended by a glorious haul from Whitney Warner & Frost's. Father is invited to read a paper on Mr Carlyle before the Hist. Society tomorrow afternoon at 3 P.M. He intends to do so.

— 1881 —

Poor Rose Lathrop! Everyone feels as if it was one of the hardest blows that ever fell. Mr Lathrop came on Monday to Chas. Walcott, he felt as if he must know what it was, and C. W. says he seemed wholly broken down. Rose is at Parker's sick. As soon as the child died Mr L. took her there and left the body in the charge of the undertaker & F. Lathrop who brought it here, and had it buried after a little service at Dr Peabody's. Mr L. was no more able to come than Rose. Annie feels it very much of course. And Mr Diman has just died suddenly in Providence. I hope for a note from you to tell how our seven stars are shining today.   Your sister.

Feb. 12th 1881

Dear Edith,

How thankfully did we receive your letter with its news of your patients. What fun though you must all be having shut up together thus, and how I wish I were there to help read! I hate, so do we all, to hear about your hand and foot troubling you so. What does Dr Holmes say? Some day soon you must begin a new manner of life to get rid of such torments. Father read an account of Mr Carlyle to the Historical Society on Thursday afternoon. It was a very pleasant occasion. I send you Cousin Abby's letter and the stork story. How kind of Alice to send me things!

Edith dear, I'm behindhand with letters, or I should write you a volume.   Affectionately

Ellen T. E.

Concord Feb. 17th 1881

My dear Cameron,

I am, as I told you, quite unable to send you any other Valentine than a letter, but I'll send you a letter for a Valentine.

When I came home Grandmamma cried out quick the moment she saw me "Oh! How are they?" She had felt all the morning as if she couldn't wait to know what news I should bring of all the six darling bears that are or ought to be on their feet, and the one little small wee Bear that kicks up her little feet in her cradle. So I told her all about everyone of you and she was just as much enchanted as I thought she would be.

This morning I lay awake and heard the clock strike four and very soon after came the sound of fire-bells. I jumped right up, because so many people had when they rang for our house eight or nine years ago.

— 1881 —

Then I remembered that every fire since but one had been put out before anyone could get there, so I lay down again. But in a minute Grandmamma came in to say "It looks as if the whole town were on fire!" Then I didn't wait any longer, and at half-past-four I was ready and trotted up in town eating my breakfast as I went. Of course it was a most glorious sight all the way, a great wall of smoke covering a quarter of the sky and bright red, and the Orthodox Church and all the buildings facing North had their north side brilliantly illuminated, so I knew that it certainly was this side of the Bank, and when at last I could see the fire it proved to be the Middlesex stables. The stable had been already pulled entirely to pieces, and every beam was burning merrily by itself, making a broad bright low flame covered by a vast smoke. All the town seemed to be there, standing silent in the street, and a few men on roofs had axes and a few more managed the hose. I stood by the hydrant, and heard the man who was at work on it explain to the Chairman of the Select-men the need of having four "gates" (openings) in it instead of two. I asked the man what he thought was catching now, and he said "The Stable is burned. Hatch's store is on fire. They're trying to save it. If they do the fire is over. If they don't, no man can tell where it will end." Then I came home to tell Grandmamma and Grandpapa, and Grandpapa was dressed and went back with me to see the fire. We walked up and down and saw the fine blaze on all sides, and especially interesting was the back view which we saw from the priest's yard. While we were there some pigs came right out from under the burning barn, and a gentleman told us that no one thought they could be alive, so there had been no attempt to save them, and at this last moment someone had heard them, and they had been successfully rescued. Then we walked back onto the Mill-Dam, and there Mrs Silas Hosmer came to me and said "Have you found your brother?" "No," I said "I don't know whether he's here." "Here!" she said "Why, of course he's here. He's been here from the beginning, they say, & working wonders, working far beyond his strength." "I don't see what he could do," I said, "I didn't know he knew how to do anything of this kind." "He *finds* things to do" she said, "& he does them. I'm afraid he'll hurt himself and I'm looking round to see if I can't catch him out and send him home, for if his strength should fail what would become of all of us? We can't afford to lose him." So she left us, and Father said he must go right home, but I thought I would go to tell Aunt Annie about Mrs Hosmer. I found Aunt Annie in the parlour with a good fire getting a breakfast for Uncle Edward. She said he jumped at the first stroke of the bell, and so did she, but he got away first. As she came to the Court-House, she said "I was going to find something to do, and the first thing I saw was a horse brought over from the stable, which was not yet on fire, but just catching from Mr Hunt's shop, and tied by the Court-house. The poor thing was frightened out of his senses and I got Mr Farrar & he held him while I untied him, and you never saw a poor creature so thankful to have somebody come and attend to him, and I led him over to Emmy's, and I met a man there who tied him to her post." Presently Edward came in and was wet through. He had to change all his clothes before he could sit down by the fire and have breakfast, and he was too tired to talk much. But he told us that he had been at the pig-rescue, and it was funny to see the procession of blackened pigs come forth, and that the men said two were missing. "By that time," he said, "I had a lantern and I went into the cellar for them, but there was too much smoke to see anything so I paced it regularly to be sure to cover the whole ground, and at last I got one out. He said it was warm and comfortable, he didn't want to stir, besides it was pleasant and secluded there for a pig, and the crowd outside looked kind o' promiscuous, but we got him out at last. The floor was on the point of falling in." At this point Annie exclaimed "I'll thank you not to go in again under burning floors that are falling in." I said he wouldn't run any risk, and he said he shouldn't, but Aunt Annie said "I don't believe your Mother's son would be willing to let a burning floor fall on a pig without doing something!"

Then I came home and the daylight was just showing in the east.

Give my love to Violet and tell her that her snow fort is still very pretty. And give my love to all the family & tell them I send them this valentine

Merely to say
I think of them always
When I am away.

Their Aunt Ellen

Concord, Feb 26th 1881

Beloved Edith,

I am as sorry as you that you couldn't come, and Ralph. Until Will actually came without you I had a hope that you might. Your letter saying how sorry you were was a balm to our minds. How pretty a

— 1881 —

Ellen Tucker Emerson, aged 40.

thought was your and Will's birthday-present. I am charmed. I had presents & flowers & kindness showered on me. I didn't succeed particularly in readiness or in doing a proper hostess's part, and was sorry, but I do think I could have done better if the day hadn't been so cold, and if I hadn't had a cold. There was too much left to do after everyone came when I ought to have sat down with them, and again I was late to

— 1881 —

tea. But they were all kind, and didn't mind and took care of each other, and gave me a regular ovation when I came down. You should have seen the glorious bunch of roses Col. Russell gave me. He was great fun all the time, to me and everyone. Will was very good to come, especially when he was sick. He was all the time a comfort & delight. He danced with me once, and I had some gorgeous down the middles, or rather up, with him in the Va. Reel. And he looked out for things & folks. I was extremely pleased with all the gentlemen for wearing their dress coats. I could not persuade Edward to do it, or to refrain from advising other gentlemen not to, he dislikes his so much. I could write a volume on the pleasure I had in folks's clothes that night. I thought it was a *pretty* party. Col Russell went to the Hall with me, and arriving 5 m. before 7 found Alicia already there. The moment the clock struck people began to arrive, and there was a whole hall full when Mr Wesson came, and we were dancing at 7.25. My friends had all laboured for me all the week, conspicuously Lizzy Bartlett, who undertook it as her own party, and attended to everything early & late, made cake at home, washed dishes at the Hall, and directed there the labours of Alice Linder, Alicia, Miss Leavitt & Lidian, spent Thursday in seeing to the washing of the floors & tables there & later in helping Sarah Richardson & me make sandwiches, then when the Milton friends arrived she returned to the Hall and took charge of the ice-cream-men and the supper. Neither Mother nor I went down stairs once till supper was announced, she took all the care, but she danced most of the time, in her blue calico which appeared to be a silk. Many a frolicking matron & grayhaired swain showed that the party was taking a right course, but alas! it's ending at 11 seemed premature for only at 10.30 did most of the mothers stand up to dance. But people began to go home at ten, and more than half had departed before we came to the Ladies' Triumph, the last dance, which waked an enthusiasm beyond my expectation. I think we must have another sometime, without any supper, to follow up the impression made by that Ladies' Triumph, and finish learning the other dances they didn't quite learn & most of all to get these mothers out in earnest earlier in the evening.

End of letter is missing.

March 3rd 1881

Dear Edith,
    I am hoping every day for news of you, but it seems that if no news is

— 1881 —

good news you are having a good time indeed. It will be a week today since my dear Ball and since I had the last word from you. A part of my mind is always occupied in looking into that muslin & lace-trimmed cradle, covered carefully with solid rows of diapers to see the blessed Rosamond smiling & cuddling there. I feel glad we have her, every hour of the day. I have delivered your presents to Edward & Annie, to E. Weir, and to Miss Andrews. All were greatly delighted. Tuesday night Edward had the Social Circle, and Father went, and really enjoyed it. Tell me, did we send you Kate's wrench for opening jars. Please send postal at once to say. Mother is enchanted with her jar of pears. We are thinking of surprising you soon to see the bairns. Thank Sarah Malcolm for her delightful letter. Mr & Mrs Cabot are coming today. I hope you are getting well and that W. & you & the 7 will have a cheerful day. Your affectionate sister and aunt.

E. T. E.

F.R.R. Monday morning Mar 7th 1881

Dear Edith,

Father and I are going to Boston to Mr George B. Emerson's funeral. I think the pretty plan Mother & I had of surprising you must be given up for a while. Last week was too rainy. This week is pretty full. I am glad that little Edward can be said to be *well* without any but. All the rest seem to have from one to half a dozen buts. What makes Rosamond too fat? Lying too still in her cradle? Well spring is coming and with that a chance for everyone to recover. I have sent you a Concord Freeman, and in it you will find a small account of our late fire. Mother is much troubled to see that Will & his Father and many of the righteous are inviting Carl Schurz to a dinner, at the very moment when he is convicted of holding in a pig-headed manner to the old, unjust & cruel policy towards the Indians, and trying to push the wrong to the bitter end. What does it mean? Why do they give him a dinner at all? Is it because they approve his Indian policy and wish to sustain him in it? Or is there some other reason, and has it nothing to do with Indians either way?

We had a most satisfactory visit from dear Mr & Mrs Cabot. Did I send you his letter saying he shouldn't write Father's biography? I must send you one from Mr Thayer saying it was high time Mr C.'s biography should be announced since G. W. Cooke is writing to Mr Hedge to engage his assistance in his. I read it to Mr Cabot & I asked him what he meant by saying he shouldn't. Edward & I had been dismayed by it. He proves to abide by his promise. He is going to use all the material he has & can gather & publish it in a sketch such as will be useful to the biographers who may arise hereafter. Indeed I don't see that he is likely to disappoint us at all. Only he wants us to understand that he doesn't call it a biography which last, he thinks, needs a perspective of fifty to a hundred years.

Tuesday morn. Father & I visited Mr Houghton yesterday, and he said that he had consulted Mr Forbes about sending "Power, Wealth & Books" in a gratis pamphlet to business men, and receiving no reply had proceeded & done it; when it was a thing of the past he received Will's letter saying he didn't wish it done. I showed some disapproval. The Parnassuses are said to be in Cambridge printed but not bound.

E. T. E.

Concord, March 10th 1881

Dear Sally,

I think the photographs are beautiful, and we all thank you for sending them, and have them displayed. I am very sorry to have been silent all winter, I have been planning to write, but have written less than usual. Why, I wanted to write and tell you when Rosamond was born. Alas! she is not to be named Rosamond, but we call her so while we can. She isn't very pretty. Edith agrees with me, but then we trust she'll do as well as the others and they are all well enough, as to looks, and she is an eminently peaceful and smiling being. All Edith's children except Rosamond have been having the measles, really a hard time for the parents. Little Ellen is a miracle of health and joyfulness. It is good too that she seems to be an affectionate little thing to comfort poor Annie. The painting of little Charles is nearly done, and Edward and Annie both seem entirely satisfied with it. Annie hopes Edward won't have much more practice than he has as long as he lives, he has such constant work, but he bears it perfectly well, indeed health seems to reign both at his house and ours. We are all wonderfully strong here, and have a most beautiful time. We all three seem to enjoy whatever turns up this winter to an uncommon degree. My Ball on my birthday was my great festivity, and to my surprise Father asked me every morning for a fortnight when it would come off, and as it approached asked if he could go, and still more to my surprise he went and stayed till within half an hour of the end, and remembered it as agreeable. Sophy & Mr

— 1881 —

Thayer came, and Cousin Mary and Lizzy, and all my Milton friends except Edith & Ralph and Malcolm's Sarah. Col. Russell came. He was full of play and politeness. Edward carried on the whole thing for me, and Annie says he had a good time too, which he had not expected, for he never loved dancing as I do. I wish I could have had you there if you love to dance. For of course it was the old folks, the people of our age, that had the floor this time, with enough of the young to adorn the occasion, and we, the old, enjoyed it more than they could.

It was very good in you to spring up and write me a letter, and not reproach the sinner at all. Thank you for your account of Haven and Susy and the six, I haven't heard from them before for months. You don't say how dear Julia is. I have no doubt the school is increasing, and I hope that doesn't wear out you and her any more than it did when small. Mother sends much love, and so do I, and we want to see you.

Affectionately,
E. T. E.

Concord, Mar. 23rd 1881
In the study after dinner.

Dear Edith,

Waldo is standing at the sofa with the Mrs Follen book like his own at home, very quiet and interested. Whether it is that sickness has subdued him, or that he has grown more reasonable, he is much more good-natured than ever I saw him before, and there is almost never a flurry of crying & "no, no"-ing. Minnie says he still eats very well, and indeed he seems as active and happy as possible. He has the blocks, and plays most with them, he has the remains of your tin tea-set and uses that a little. Annie brought him a horse of Charles's and a ringing rolling toy of John's, and he uses one in the Study and one in the Dining-room. He has your room, and our crib, with two mattrasses, two blankets and a shawl. Mother visited him at midnight, and thinks it was well she did as he had pushed down the clothes. She made over the crib so he couldn't, and will look in at him every night at 12. Father can't yet understand his talk, he is very eager to catch every word, and I believe the wretch talks inarticulate drivel almost exclusively when his poor grandpapa is straining every faculty to understand, though he speaks quite plainly to me, especially when he wants something. Mother constantly says he seems to her the most enchanting child we ever had. He spends most of his days in your room, but comes to the kitchen for breakfast & supper, to the dining-room at our meal-times, and sits in my lap sometimes, and sometimes beside Father in a chair, ready to have a drink of water, and oftener he runs about the room. Then he makes one or two visits to the Study in a day. Father comes for him and carries him down with delight, but feels it necessary to exert himself to entertain him and when I come to the rescue he is usually exhausted, and thankful to be relieved. He cannot think of any way of getting rid of his infant visitor, so today I found he had gone up to the Den! and left Master Waldo to enjoy the Study. In vain I explained that Waldo could at any moment be carried upstairs, it seems to be an idea he cannot take in. I shall be more on the watch hereafter.

I have a little story about Father. He asked me if I couldn't get Mr Brown of Brookline up here again. I said I didn't know exactly how. He said "And tell him you'll give him a hundred dollars if he'll stay here and preach all the time." After a few minutes he sighed and said "Yes! I wish I could have a minister." He asks every few weeks who is going to preach and when he hears there is to be an exchange asks if it is to be a good man. If I say yes he does not forget it, and follows me up about it on Saturday and all Sunday morning. Then he goes to church, and if he likes the appearance of the man and his voice when he reads the hymn, he is attentive, and pleased after church. If the man's voice sounds poor to him he hunches himself, scowls and looks down all church-time, will not listen to a word, and escapes fleetly to his study, and at dinner says "That man was never made to be a minister."

I have had great comfort today in speaking to Will through the telephone and hearing how well Ralph & Violet and Don are getting along. How thankful we all are! And all Concord is almost as much interested as we, everyone hails me to get the latest news whenever I appear on the street, and Edward says he is very much struck by the affectionate inquiries he meets all day long. The news from blessed Rosamond seemed as bad as that from the elders was good. We are all pinning our hopes on the fact that now her own mamma has been able to get to her, it has seemed so hard for you and Baby both that she should be sick and you couldn't go to her. Oh beloved Girly how do you do yourself? I hope you can get some rest, though while the baby is so sick I suppose you hardly can. Oh if I could help you! I'll look out for this child as faithfully as I can.

E. T. E.

— 1881 —

In the cars Mar. 28, 1881.

Dear Edith,

I will tell you about our morning. We had received a letter, and I enclose it, from Pres. Eliot, and repaired with it to Mr Norton, who said he was in England at the time Mr Carlyle made the arrangement with the University, and really was the one who talked, planned & finished everything with Mr Carlyle, and he never saw any list, nor heard of any. If you have among the letters, which doubtless are dated 70, 1, or 2, the letter about this, please get it out, and see if it mentions any list. As we departed Mr Norton reminded me—to my joy—that he had the letters to Father, and asked, "What is your wish or his wish, at the present time, concerning my keeping them, and printing them. For let me say if he, or you, have have preference—as to give them to Elliot Cabot—or otherwise, I am perfectly—smooth—on the subject, and have no feeling in my mind—or heart—against it, or that would be wounded by it. My own opinion is that this correspondence, on both sides, would make a complete and precious book, there has never been anything in the world quite of the same kind as the relation between these two men, and it would be a very proper thing to have their letters a book by itself, containing nothing else, except the necessary notes, rather than having them a part of a book." I told him that you & Will thought Mr Cabot ought to have them, Edward's wish I couldn't recall, and that I wanted them printed as he had said & by him and knew that Father had wished it when he gave him the letters. That I hadn't understood exactly why you two thought Mr C. ought to have them, and had asked Mr Thayer why, & he had said that anyone who was going to write Father's life would consider this correspondence as one of its most interesting treasures, he should himself, it wd. be a natural feeling, and you felt sorry Mr C. should be deprived of just this. Also that I had talked about it with Mr C. and he had thought with me that 'twas best to leave them with Mr. Norton. That I couldn't give final answer till further consultation.

Letter is unfinished.

Concord, March 30th 1881

Dear Haven & Susy,

I am afraid you may receive with this the news of the death of Edith's dear littlest girl. Up to Monday morning we had hope which increased daily that she would get well. She is worse now, the disease which had healed on one lung has appeared on the other, and without cause as far as we know.

April 1st   The telegram came, before I could write more. The baby died at two o'clock on Wednesday. I went down at once, for I was afraid she might lose her looks before morning as little John did. Oh Edith and Will have had a hard winter, sickness as poor Will says "piling up upon them"! Constant night work, new cases coming as fast as anyone got well, somebody always so sick that they were anxious, but the perpetual terrors of the last two weeks have been far more serious than anything before, and they do not begin to feel secure about those children who are recovering from diphtheria. They are as good as you would expect, but oh! so tired. You wouldn't believe what a loss to W. the baby is. Her long exile upstairs one would think would have allowed him little chance to be acquainted with her. She was all we could desire, large and strong and always smiling, beautiful blue eyes and the whitest hair. All the children say the loveliest things. We are all going to the funeral today. I don't know whether Will has written to you.

Affectionately
E. T. E.

Concord, April 6th 1881

Dear Edward,

You must be a good boy as Annie is a good girl. She sends a card almost every day. Mr Norton came up yesterday and brought Sally according to agreement. He read us a letter from Mrs Mary Carlyle about her uncle's last days which were very interesting. Mr Carlyle used to say, she said, in talking about his end that his idea of death was that it came "like cataracts of sleep" and so it did for him, he fell into a very heavy sleep and never waked. Mother had the mutton put to me for dinner and the moment Mr. N. saw it, he proposed to carve. I said Father wouldn't like it, but at that moment he started for the wine and Mr Norton seized the knife & fork and cut for life, for life, till he came back when he quickly subsided into his seat. He was thus kind and domestic throughout the visit; and I had a great deal of pleasure in it. Sally is very pretty and sweet. She had been the night before a spectator at the rehearsal of the Greek Play with her father and the Greek Professors, no one else in the seats. It was at Sanders Theatre and in costume. Mr N. said the students entered into it with enthusiasm, and

— 1881 —

delighted in declaiming their Greek, but that after all there was something modern about it, they could not act with the self-restraint of the Greek, it was a little the modern stage's rendering of the feelings, and it gave him a curious sensation to perceive the influence of Victor Hugo while he heard the words of Sophocles. This did not seem however to have impaired his enjoyment of the occasion. Mrs Agassiz spoke of it on Saturday, and Miss Annie Sever at Cousin Abby's. The latter said that Mr Paine had rather over-weighted the Play with music and had just come to Mr Goodwin to say that he must have three more violins. Mr Goodwin had refused, for the music was already costing a thousand dollars, and Mr Paine—think of it!—had replied "Yes, but consider the music is all that has obtained your audience." !!!! Mrs Agassiz said the next day at Ida's "Mr Paine is irrepressible. He is already on his thirty-fifth Opus for the Greek Play." She said that she didn't care usually for his music, but that one or two of these compositions were really interesting. Mr Norton too said that it was true the Play was pretty full of music, and Sally said that Mr Paine was now urging that the declaiming parts should be cut down a little to make room for more, but Mr Goodwin was of opinion that it would be better to cut the choruses down. Mr Norton like Mrs Agassiz said some of the music was interesting. After he & Sally went in the 4.2 train I was writing for the mail up in my room and Father came up for the letters. Since they were not ready he sat down upon the couch and waited a long time. My door & Edith's were open. At last he said "I am looking at this *beautiful* home", and went on to say that everything heart could wish was here—"and then the approach to the next room!" It was very pleasant. Lily came and spent the night with me night before last and I enjoyed her visit very much. Mother has got her roses out, and her garden into good shape, and is triumphant. Affectionately

Ellen T. Emerson.

April 12th 1881

Dear Edith,

Violet was with me when I bought the clock. I didn't look at the name, it was near Bromfield St. for while we bought V. & I kept looking over to W. B. Clarke's to see our little boys arrive, and did see them. The tongs came from the Murdock Parlour Grate Co. on New Washington St. I can come Friday, and again on Sat. or Mon. as you like. It is delightful to hear that the children look well again and were all together, I

— 1881 —

hope they enjoyed their reunion as much as you. The sooner they come to Concord, the better pleased their ancestors. And oh! how happy if you can come for Sunday. Your labours at present seem to show some return of your strength. How blessed to have had three or four beautiful days after the long hard weather. Today's rain is very much needed too, so we will welcome that. My theatre party will have to be on Saturday afternoon for Edward advises that it be to see the Vokes family, and that is their last performance. I suppose none of you want to go too. Annie will, & C. & T. I hope, Father & Mother of course. Edward & Annie have dined with us. The young Miss accompanied. I'm going to invite Alice & Mr Cary for the 19th. I hope some of you, or all, can be here that day.

Your sister.

Concord, May 4th 1881

Dear Edith,

I have had immense pleasure in your letter of Ap. 24 & 26 wh. reached us last Friday, and in the children's, and have only one fault to find viz. you didn't describe the arrival of Edw. & A. wh. I wanted to hear about. Our events at home have been as follows. Friday morning Pauline went, & Therchi & I accompanied her in the 10 train to Boston. We had time for an errand or two then went out to Jamaica Plain by the 11.40 train and were met by the carriage. When we reached Cousin Abby's Therchi was delighted with everything, the size of the rooms made a great impression upon her. We were showed into Aunt Adams's room, but T. was only allowed to talk with her five minutes, for she isn't so strong as when you and I were there, and Cousin Abby carried off Therchi immediately and left me with "the Aunts". They wished to hear all about you, and I told them of the California journey, which seemed to them—as it is!—one of the finest arrangements ever known, and then they wanted to know about Baby and I showed them the photographs. They cried at the sight of them, and when I showed them to Cousin Abby so did she. Everyone at Aunt Adams's greatly sympathized with Annie & all of us in the relief that this journey will be to Edward. Dr Faulkner exclaimed "It's a *great* vacation for a physician." All Concord seems thankful for the chance for him. Our visit was altogether pleasant, and we came home with Charley in the 4.30 train. I haven't yet told you about Pauline's visit, four happy days. I resolved that as many of my friends as possible should see her this time, so I

— 1881 —

made her live my usual life with me, and she lent herself to the plan perfectly. When people came to see me she saw them too. She went to Bible Class and appreciated that, and on Tuesday evening to a game-party at Miss Ball's where she saw A. Gourgas, E. Skinner, S. Richardson, A. Bartlett, the Norcrosses, Mary Wood, Mrs LeBrun, Mrs Wm Buttrick, S. Perry. Of course she joined in all the games, and showed how bright & how lovely she is, and I was as proud & pleased as possible. Wednesday morning she wished to visit the Lexington High School, and I asked Emma Smith & Jenny Barrett to ride over with us. We talked quartette most of the time, so they became well acquainted. Mrs Mann came to tea and Pauline ran to her most affectionately & never left her side. They talked Kindergarten. Thursday morning we asked Mrs Davidson & Belle to ride with us, but Mrs D. was sick, we took only B. and had a cheerful talk. In the afternoon came 8 of my Sunday Scholars. I begged Pauline to lie down, but when she found I was going to begin with the Bible, she declared she would go straight into my room and begin with the class. She took such interest in them, and in the books & the talk, she made it a glorious occasion. I forgot to say that Miss Leavitt dined with us that day, and that one day when hungry we sought rest and food at Mrs Sanborn's and had a beautiful time. On Thursday night Miss Bartlett came to tea. Once we walked to Rose Lathrop's on an errand, and once to the Weir's. Don't you think I introduced her pretty widely in four days? Of course everyone was grateful to me. On Friday night when I came home I found Edward's letter to Father, & yours & Violet's & Cameron's, riches, riches! when I came to the tea-table, and we read & read & rejoiced. After tea as I prepared for Friday-in-meeting I suddenly remembered that Mother was to take tea at Aunt Susan's and play whist. How shocked we all were! Mother hurried off & I to meeting. Alicia & Lizzy Surette & Miss Ball walked home with me, delightful! I got ready to go to bed, and heard Father setting out to go for Mother. Knowing that he didn't know where Aunt Susan lived I accompanied. We beat the streets, you might say. By the stable he went round and I went through, then we walked up street on opposite sides. Finally I heard a voice faint & distant, like Miss Bartlett's, listened sharply & caught the letter S given by Mother. I didn't know before that that was a distinguishing sound, but I recognized that S at once. Next I heard the other voice, now Lizzy's, not Miss B.'s, then Mother's again. Presently Father called to me that he had his prey on his side. Saturday morning I parted with my dear

— 1881 —

Maggy, recalled to St John's by her Father, and went to Boston to visit Ida. In the afternoon Mrs Agassiz came to see me, and Mr Alex appeared at luncheon-time fresh from Tortugas. Then the Morses & Fairchilds came to dine, and Mr Theodore Lyman looked in in the evening to say that the Walter Cabot children had just received a telegram that Mabel was now convalescent. Sunday morning at breakfast-time Mr Higginson came to say that Mr John Minturn had shot himself. He was engaged to come to dinner & get Mary & the children to come with him, and departed. When I came home from church Frank & his wife and two children were just entering the house. The little Frank, called Peter, and the little Mary Cabot were as fine a show as could be offered, he slender, refined & poetical-looking, & she like an apple-blossom and chunky & sweet. I read them Puss & Robin, and they kept a constant refrain of "Yes", in a very interested tone. Then Ida banished them to the nursery & I had a very happy time with Mrs Frank. Then Mary with Therchi & George who has a beautiful smile, & Mr H. came to dinner, and I left them to go to church, and when I came back they had gone. We ended the day by taking tea with Nina & Julia Paine. No more today.

Thy affectionate sister

Concord May 7th 1881

Dear Haven,

Many things keep me from writing as I should like. I remembered your birthday & the little girls', enjoyed Ruth's production sent to C. some days later. Poor C. & T. I pity from the bottom of my heart. C. looks worn & wretched and the dreadful process of pulling up stakes seems to be going on, both hating to leave what both consider the happiest settlement yet, each actually blaming the other for it, apparently; yet C. must know that T. isn't to blame for being afflicted with mania. Everyone who has to do with the poor child increasingly likes & respects her as far as I can find out, and but for this she might be happy and at home for life. I send the file of Edith's letters from the time she was called home from the Hotel in Boston where she was staying with Waldo to be near the ear-doctor till she went to California. The baby's funeral occurred April 1, but they had then no lot. They bought one next to Malcolm's and the day before they went away they buried the child. Mother & Father are both very well and enjoy life greatly. We are all going to the Greek Play May 17 and Father & Dr Furness are to sit together. Much love to Susy & the children. When shall we see you again?

E. T. E.

Concord May 11th 1881

Violet dear,

Your Aunt Ellen was entirely amazed and rejoiced at getting a letter from you written on the cars. And a long and beautiful letter it was telling me many a thing that I should never have known if you hadn't written it, and that I wanted to know. When I received all the three letters on April 30th I devoured them eagerly, and then sat down like a little dog who had had one piece of meat and wants another and have waited patiently, patiently, with my eyes rolled up & fixed on box 208 in the post-office and have trembled with eagerness four times a day ever since. Mr Wm. James when he was in So. America wrote home "Unless Alice affords me some tricklings from her gracious pen, I shall go mad, mad, mad!" Substitute Violet for Alice and you'll see how I feel neatly expressed. I can't get over my disappointment that there should have been so much sickness. I suppose that accounts for Mamma's not writing. Aunt Annie's story of the glories you saw from the car-windows is satisfying to the soul. And I'm sure that you & Ralph and Cameron must have had much of the same pleasure in it that she had. Aunt Sarah sent us word that a telegram announced that Grandpapa and Uncle Edward were going northward last Sunday. I wonder whether you will all go to the big trees and to the Yo Semite. Tell Mamma I have Miss Nina L. & Mrs Blake here, and Mrs Blake has just trimmed my rainy-day hat, and offered to buy me a dress hat. So I am going to Boston to buy it with her on Friday. Tell Uncle Edward that F. L. Higginson saw an old gentleman and three ladies in a carryall being run away with down Beacon St. with a pair of horses quite beyond control. The old gentleman had one rein and the lady the other and evidently they couldn't pull any longer, and he ran out & caught the horses' heads, and was dragged some way, but he stopped them. Mrs Blake thinks someone else followed & helped, but she hasn't seen him since, and has heard these two accounts. I send this to Uncle Edw. not that I ever want him to do the like & get killed, for I don't see why Frank wasn't killed, but because I like Frank & want to brag of him. His wife with whom he was walking had the pleasure of witnessing the whole. Give my love to my dear nephews, especially the sick ones, and write me just a little note once or twice more.

Aunt Ellen.

Concord, May 17th 1881

Dear Edith,

How thankfully did I receive your long San Francisco letter last night, and how much did we all enjoy it. We feel now as if we had had a good sight of Edward & Will, and know something more about Annie. And at least we have heard of Jim's coming and his & the children's pleasure in meeting. Your grand rooms, your roses from Mrs Ladd, your ride into the country & particularly *the pomegranate hedge*! interested us very much, and of course I know V. took as much pleasure in the vegetation as her Mamma. I'm glad Annie & Edward are at Lizzy Barber's. We are just setting off for the Greek Play. Mother has read it, and Nina read it to Father when she was here, but alas! our libretto went under ten days ago, and the most elaborate searches fail to unearth it, so I haven't read a word. Nina has invited me to go again with her on Thursday and I think I shall. We understand that it is decided that Mr Reynolds is to be the new Secretary of the Association. The interest Father takes in this news agrees with what he said before about wishing he had a minister. Every day, sometimes twice a day, he asks me if I am sure of it, and either bids me make sure Mr Brown is obtained as Mr R's successor, or sighs, "Then perhaps some one will come who will not keep me away from church." At this present moment I have rec'd a tel. from Edw. about Mr Cook's M.S. dated San Antonio *Colorado*. I trust it is a mistake. I still hope that he is going to the Yo Semite. I hope *you* will, and the boys. Mr Brown thought it was a great thing for children to travel, and I agree with him.

Thy sister.

Concord, May 21st 1881

My Cameron dear,

Your letter was full of just what I wanted to know, and I have read it four times over. I never have heard of those cable cars before, but you have made me understand so well that I feel almost competent to direct the laying of such a cable and the building of such cars myself. That delightful ride with Mr Barber and Uncle Edward I think of again and

— 1881 —

again, and the long walk the next day shows I think that you were not very lame after the 13 miles on horseback. This is your birthday and I hope you are celebrating it by some glorious good time or other. How old you are growing! You know that this week we have been in Cambridge to see the Greek play. Mr Goodwin said he had placed Mr Ko, the Chinese Professor, in the seat where in the ancient amphitheatres the Priest of Bacchus always sat in a gorgeous robe, knowing that Mr Ko's would be the most gorgeous dress worn on the occasion. We made inquiries about Mr Ko, and Mr Goodwin said "I showed him my rubber boots one day last winter when I met him in a snowdrift with nothing but his sandals. He was very much interested in them and the very next day the little Kos came to school with new rubber boots on." Mr Goodwin further told us that the effect of spending a year in Cambridge had been that first the little Kos tucked their queues inside their collars, and lately Mr Ko himself, who had always worn it dangling to his heels, had followed their example, and if you didn't look for it, you would hardly remember that he wore one. Goodbye, see everything you can & write another letter to your affectionate Aunt Ellen.

Concord, May 26th 1881

My dear Violet,

How glad and grateful your Aunt was when she saw that great thick envelope come out of the Post Office with her name on it in your writing! I waited just to get Cameron's letter off and then began to read as I walked home, and very much did Grandpapa and Grandmamma & I enjoy it all that evening. The next day I carried it up to Mrs Keyes who was very hungry for a little news of Aunt Annie and little Ellen, and when she heard something about them in the letter she shared in my joy. And then I sent it to Aunt Sarah Forbes after I had read it several times over, and Cameron's with it. I think she will have as much interest in them as I. Today I hope she will send them back. Yesterday was Grandpapa's birthday, and he began to get congratulatory letters the day before. Dr & Mrs Furness came too on the 24th, and they predicted rain. But no indeed! the sun shone and all the robins & songsparrows sang like mad, the garden was all tulips & narcissus below, the lilacs had an uncommon show in mid-air, and all the apple-trees which were not expected to blossom this year had on their best red & white muslins which they proudly rested on a background of fine blue sky. The lilies of the valley were out in two magnificent battalions on the grass behind

— 1881 —

the house and the Peter's wreath & flowering almond had as many flowers as their rods could carry. Dr Furness walked about the yard for an hour before breakfast. He said he hadn't heard the birds sing before this year. While we were at breakfast Mrs Chamberlaine appeared with her hands full of rhodora and immediately after breakfast Louisa May Nieriker came trotting into the front entry in a little white dress, accompanied by her Grandpapa Alcott & Aunt Louisa, the latter bringing a magnificent mound of rhodora, and saying that since May had always thought much of Father's birthday, Baby had come to pay her respects. They stayed a few minutes and the baby admired the Coon & the wastepaper basket. When they had gone a poem was found within the mound of rhodora

> "His own rhodora fresh & fair
> For Concord's honoured Sage
> Brought by the little Alpine Rose
> That crowns a friend's old age."

The mail brought birthday letters & cards, and in the afternoon Mr Harris came with a basket of roses from Mrs Harris & himself. Messrs Houghton & Mifflin sent up a birthday book for Father and Mother gave him some Pompeii pictures which afforded him great delight because they seemed to interest Dr Furness. The only thing wanting was a letter from California. How does your Mamma do? It seems as if she must be sick, she never before wrote so seldom. I am glad every moment that you are all seeing so much of the world's wonders, and in such a pleasant way, and I hope there'll be no hurrying home. Though I do wish you could come tomorrow and spend Sunday for Charles & Louisa Rackemann are coming.   Goodbye darling girl.
Aunt Ellen.

June 14th 1881

Dear Puss,

I have been much consoled by my visit to you and the sense that you were soon coming to us, and never since I left you have had a proper sense of the duty of writing you a word. I hope you haven't been disturbed by my silence. Annie & Edward are actually staying with us, A. very well, E. & E. not, but as for Miss you wouldn't know it, she is all smiles and talk, and has a round & rosy face though her legs are little. C. & T. came to tea and we had a beautiful time. C. Walcott, Maggy, Pres-

cott & Alice, & the Fullers called within an hour of their coming, all in raptures. P. & A. are to be married on July 5th,—all points to your being here on the Fourth. Next Sunday is Anniversary Sunday, and I should like full well to have all or any of you here. Give me soon some idea of when you'll come. Give my love to every dear soul of them all.
E. T. E.

Concord. July 5th 1881

Dear Cousin Sarah,

I have waited on the mail for a week with extraordinary assiduity and all in vain. So I wrote this morning to Cousin Samuel to ask what had become of you and when Johnny came home from carrying it to the office he brought your consolatory letter. When you reach Boston on Thursday morning, as I ardently hope you will, proceed directly to the Fitchburg Depot Telegraph Office which is in the Ladies' Room, and see if there is any communication there for you. If not, just sit and wait for me till I come bringing little Edward who tomorrow night attends Prescott Keyes's wedding with me, and possibly I shall bear you away to Milton with me to help Edith off to Naushon. At any rate you'll see that one scion of the family, believed by his two grandfathers to be the best of their grandchildren. I have been very much disappointed that I couldn't get you earlier. Will & Edith went off this morning and took away all the children. The house is now as empty as you usually find it. Annie & Edward are as glad as Mother and I that you are coming.
Affectionately,
Ellen T. Emerson.

In the cars July 16th 1881

Dear Edith,

Last night I was kept awake by toothache so I took the 7 o'clock train and called on Dr Parker this morning before he came down to breakfast, and now on my way home will write all I can. Lizzy Simmons came to me on Tuesday night and will stay till next Tuesday. Lizzy is very funny, and Father's delight in her presence is only alloyed by fear of her going away. He never meets her in the street, or even sees her hat on, without anxiety, and keeps saying "Stay always! See to it, Ellen, that she doesn't go away!" Mother says he sometimes asks with alarm in the night if she has gone. Cousin Sarah is as great a comfort to Mother, and life is very gay this week at Bush. Little Ellen comes to spend a day now

— 1881 —

& then. Lizzy thinks she is the prettiest & cunningest thing she ever saw. The School of Philosophy is in full blast now, but it seems to make less show than in former years. I imagine they don't have so many people. As I was coming along last night I met my dear friend Mr Francis Tiffany on his way thither, so it appears he thinks it worthwhile to come over from Newton, once, at least. Mother has gone to several evening sessions and Father went once, but I don't think he will try again. Cousin Sarah means to reserve herself for the lectures of the Episcopal Philosophers, Drs. Kidney [?] & Mulford. Annie says Edward is as well & strong as he can be now, and so is she. Mr & Mrs Keyes have gone to visit Prescott & Alice at Dover Point. Edward's birthday came on Sunday and I carried him two stalks of lilies in the morning. He seemed as usual surprised & affected that anyone should remember or value his birthday. Dear Cousin Sarah had waited for me at Miss Barrett's with Hilda and we rode home to breakfast. Father was looking out of the dining-room window & evidently felt that nothing could be depended on in this life, if his ladies had actually gone off with the horse before he came down to breakfast. On Tuesday Mrs Staples died, and when we followed her to the grave on Thursday there was a beautiful show of lilies at the foot of Aunt Lizzy's grave. Then I remembered that it was July 14th, her birthday, and I was very glad they had celebrated it.

E. T. E.

E.R.R. Depot Boston July 20th 1881

Dear Edith,

I'm waiting for my train and will use my minutes. I'm very glad you can take us on Monday, Aug 1st. Lizzy went home last night, I'm very sorry to lose her,—and so are we all. She has been so bright in all her little speeches, we have laughed continually at the table, and whenever she and I have discussed subjects it has been amusing to find how alike we think and how we have the same little habits. One blissful day, Monday, we actually went up to Easterbrook to dinner. Father & Mother wouldn't go, but Edward & Annie agreed to, & we tried for Lily. She had Grace Minns staying with her, and in spite of much urging refused. So Lizzy & Cousin Sarah & I set forth, carrying raspberries picked by them two, and the bread & thick butter with no meat to suit me, a sheet of cake and two bottles of water. Lizzy reviled me much for not being willing to depend on the water of the country, but I know better. She even went so far as to pack the bottles with intent to break them. When we reached Annie's L. & I jumped out and I dressed my beloved baby, who certainly showed no signs of affection meanwhile, quite the contrary, and Lizzy packed Annie's basket, as generous as ours was mean, with chocolate, sandwiches, milk, and gingerbread and Miss Baby's repast in a bowl in the corner. Edward didn't go with us, he promised to come soon, so when we came to the limekiln we didn't like to go far from the road, so we disgracefully sat down on the top of the limekiln not a rod from the wall, and thought it was a lovely place commanding as charming a view as one would desire to see, and really quite sylvan & retired. The baby approved of the situation and crept about happily. Presently we heard wheels, Alicia and Grace had early repented their refusal and followed on. In a very short time Edward came, and then the meal and the great fun began. We at one time had one of those times of laughing when no one *can* recover enough to speak. But alas! the rain descended on us before we had quite got through and Lizzy packed us quick into the wagons for home, though we all inclined to stay & see whether this was more than a shower. She was determined, and the rain never stopped at all, but continued till night. She was quite pleased, and apologized to Annie saying "I have had the care of youth for so many years that I have grown prudent and can tell the Doctor & his wife when it is time to take a baby home." I am now near my journey's end

Letter ends abruptly.

West Manchester
Thursday July 21st 1881

Dear Father,

I never came to say goodbye, or to remind you that I was going away, because my time was so short after I waked that I could only scramble off, and I felt very sorry, when I had really caught the train, and had time to remember, to think I had been so faithless. Ida's house where I am staying is perched on a very high steep hill, at the foot of which is the depot, so when I arrived I looked straight up into the sky and beheld above me the roof and windows of her house, and presently she appeared half way down the hill coming to meet me. Mrs Agassiz was here too, only for the day, and was not far behind Ida on the path. Oh how I wish all my family could come with me, to see not only the dear people but the glories of the hill, the garden, and the house! Such a wilderness of brilliant low flowers and tall white lilies and blue larkspur and red hollyhocks against a dark rock background, as we first came to, would have charmed Mother, and romantic rock steps up to a piazza with every kind of hammock, couch, long chair, and straw seat, and into the handsomest house I have ever seen. Pauline's daughters 15 & 18 were in the parlour Ida had built on purpose for them, and we all sat there together for an hour, and talked about college. Ida says boys have private tutors to help them through now, and she thinks it is an excellent plan, but Pauline jr. and Marian consider it outrageous laziness, and told with anger how their various cousins in college enjoyed society and loafing, cut their recitations, never opened their books, and when examinations were imminent, came to their tutors and made them prepare them to do the examination papers. I was glad to see that the rich girls at least hated the ways of the rich boys. Mrs Agassiz's train came at 5.30 & she returned to Nahant. Then came home Maj. Higginson, and his Father, and little Alex came down in his nightgown to accompany his Mother's piano with his trumpet, a very cunning performance, which anyone would like to see & hear. I am going to see Mr & Mrs Cabot today and shall come home on Saturday. Tell Cousin Sarah my bundle came safely at bedtime. I suppose she delivered to you my message that yesterday was John's day.

Your affectionate daughter
Ellen T. Emerson

F.R.R. July 23rd 1881

Dear Edith,

They forwarded me your letter from home this morning and it was full of plums which Ida enjoyed as much as I did. Now first of all I want to tell you that Effie's address to the Charities Convention will come off next Tuesday evening in the Representatives Hall at the State House at 8 o'clock. Ellen Parkman is going to come up with Mrs Elliot Cabot, & open her house, 16 Brimmer St., and has invited me to come & bring a chum and spend the night. Will you telegraph to me speedily if you will? There is a possibility, Effie says, that her voice may not be strong enough to be heard, and if they can't hear her some man will read it for her. This of course would spoil the whole, for us. I have just written this fact to Mrs Cabot. I shall ask Annie if you can't come, and Mrs Edward Damon for my 3rd choice. Effie begged us not to come, she says it won't

— 1881 —

be worth hearing, and we shan't like it, and then how awkward for her & for us! I hope Major Higginson will come. I have just talked with Annie, she won't come at all, on account of the baby, and of Maggy Ames who is making them a visit till We. or Thurs.

E. T. E.

F.R.R. Boston July 27th 1881

Dear Edith,

I was much disappointed when your telegram came to hear I couldn't have you for Tuesday, but glad that you didn't want me Thursday, for it would have been hard to manage that. Tomorrow night there is to be the postponed Carnival of Boats, and I have invited Mrs Lesley & Miss Hancock of Phila., also Mary Blake & her husband to enjoy the festivity. Thursday is also Pauny's 18th birthday and Ida is going to have a festivity for her in the shape of a picnic, and our Baby at Edward's will be 15 mos old. We suppose that is the occasion of this Carnival of Boats. Friday Sherman Hoar will come of age and celebrate his freedom by a grand Ball at the Town Hall. We are all invited. Edward & Annie & Maggy & Therchi came to dinner yesterday. Edward had adorned the button-hole of his new blue coat with some leaves already turned, and was greeted by my Lizzy Bean (who was staying with me) with "You look like autumn!" "Yes," said he "I feel that I am in the sere & yellow leaf, I suppose I do look it." Well I'm afraid I shall feel that when I come to Sherman's Ball, but if I can see the smallest chance to play gentleman I shall have a beautiful time. Then came my Sunday Scholars and were delightful. How different they are! Only two of them enter thoroughly into the beauties, dramatic situations, entertaining personal anecdotes, and accidental innocent phrases that add their share so amusingly to David's history, which we are reading—the others treat it as a task, dry as dust! I have pleasure out of them in one way & another, and then the different kinds of activity of which their minds are capable interest & puzzle me each time we meet.

As soon as your telegram came I telephoned to Mrs Damon & she instantly replied that she would go. So at four Cousin Sarah drove me to the depot; and there I met Mrs Damon and we came down together. I had been telling Lizzy Bean Effie's history and when I showed her the verses in the "Loyal Woman's No" that described her to me they seemed more beautiful than ever, and then the enchanting poem about Col. Lowell's end in the Biglow Papers. And since I have been thinking

— 1881 —

over those about Col. Shaw. Also Aunt Lizzy's remarks about Effie came back. So I was thoroughly prepared for the evening. Mrs Damon & I arrived . . . See next letter & go on with it [Letter is continued on July 29. See p. 435.]

Concord, July 28th, 1881

Dear Miss Dabney,

I have wanted to write you such a long letter that I couldn't begin unless I had a long time before me, and whenever I had a long time a multitude of business notes devoured it. To begin at home, everything in the house remains as exactly the same as it possibly can. I think this is very pleasant. Father & Mother just as well as ever, Mother not aging at all, and I as strong as I was when I was young, and all three as prosperous as can be. At Edward's the little Ellen is 15 mos. old and pretty and bright and sociable enough, she walks and can repeat almost anything we say after us though she does not talk on her own yet. It was a great pleasure to Annie to go to California, and it did them all good. All the Forbeses are safe at Naushon I believe. Edith writes a lament over the old Mansion House repaired into a new & ugly shape, and not, to her thinking, improved inside. It is not yet finished. Malcolm's family are to stay with her & Will, and the Mansion-house family stayed with them the first days after they went down. In those days to Edith's great delight Mr Forbes was struck with the virtues of our Violet. She will be fourteen very soon. Poor little dear! her birthday will be sad when it comes, for her sister was born on her last birthday, and she had thought what glorious double celebrations they should always have. Ralph has become so big and old with his fifteen years that he seems quite a stranger to me, and he has begun to accomplish something, which is quite new. The three little boys dressed alike, and with their hair cut alike, resemble each other sufficiently to make it necessary even for their relations to take a look at them to see which is which. This pleases Edith and she takes pains to make them as much like triplets as possible. They are all talkative, and when they spent a week with me lately I was in ecstasies with their appearance & conversation every moment except when they were quarrelling. Little Waldo is two and a half, and Don wrote to me yesterday that "he is very cunning and pretty cross too". They all take a great deal of pleasure in him, and all his brethren delight as much in bringing out the crossness by teasing him as they do in the cunningness he displays when let alone.

— 1881 —

This week I have heard Effie Lowell speak in public. That is my latest great event, and it was a great event. You know she is a member of the N.Y. board of State Charities, so that she was discharging a natural part of her business in speaking, or rather reading a paper, at the Conference of State Boards. Her paper was superior, and her style of reading was as sensible and beautiful as I expected. You perhaps may remember that Mr Shippen, the Sec. of the Unitarian Association, has become the minister of the Church at Washington. Well the Association has taken our minister Mr Reynolds for its new Secretary so that our Parish is left to choose a new minister. I find that my expectations are not high, it does not seem as if there were any young ministers in the denomination who were Christians, and how can I like to receive a minister of the modern kind who is distinctly persuaded that Christ was a man, only a man, and that, as two ministers have said to me, he was valuable to the human race, "exactly as Washington was, as a moral example." For a long time I had great hopes of the Unitarians, the tide had turned I felt, and they were becoming more Christian; but since I have learned *how* they have become more Christian I am only pained by their preaching. At least they have learned to study the Gospels and to own in Christ their best example and teacher, and to confess it plainly, and that is something to be thankful for, and for a long time while I regarded this as a stage I enjoyed it, but now the older men almost without exception have settled into the same place, and I seem to see that even if it is only a stage it is one that is likely to last these many years. Of course the first thing that occurs is, if the Unitarians don't please me why stay with them? Because I belong to them. I cannot find another home, in every other church the whole atmosphere and all the methods are strange and seem less healthy and right. I must stay where I belong and hope that the new light the Unitarians need, and that not I alone but most of the people I hear talk feel the need of, will shine in my day. The worst of the situation is that the ministers seem content and believe that they have what the people want. But the laity are hungry and find that the food the ministers offer does not satisfy. I call this the strongest ground for hope. Where many are so eager there will be something for them. I have read in the paper that a vessel sails tomorrow. I tried for time today to write more, but Dr Hedge lectured this morning at the School of Philosophy, so we went to hear him, and Edward & Annie came to dine, then came my Sunday Scholars who have only just gone. I am reading to them Mr Edward

Hall's Essay on the Bible read last autumn at the Saratoga Conference. It gives Kuenen's view of the Bible, which I hate, and I think it is really unsound. But Mr H. himself is in general scholarly and knows his New Testament better than any man I ever dealt with. I like him as much as I dislike his Essay. There I must leave you. Goodbye, with much love to you & Roxa, and Mrs Sam and Alice.

Ellen T. Emerson.

July 29th 1881

Dear Puss,

How maddening of me to leave you just as I was coming to what you wanted to hear! Mrs Damon & I arrived first at 16 Brimmer St. and waited till a carriage came bringing Mrs Cabot & Ellen Parkman with a woman and a trunk of bread & butter etc. Ellen unlocked the door, and in a short time invited us upstairs. We were not much more than ready when we were asked down to tea. Indeed speed was necessary for it was 7 when they came & the meeting opened at 8. Well tea was more getting something to eat as fast as possible than anything else and then we rode up to the State House because Mrs Cabot's foot was lame, her horse had fallen on it. When we came to the Hall of the Representatives I was disgusted to see a small audience. Effie & Lizzy Putnam were sitting together on the front seat, Mr Sanborn was in the chair, and people were scattered over the hall. When Effie was called and went up to the desk I saw for the first time how tall she was and she appeared to me then as beautiful in figure as in face. At Manchester she had looked pale and worn but by this light she was like a rose. She had on *spectacles*, to my horror & surprise, otherwise she was perfectly beautiful. She wore her bonnet. There was no doubt at all that she could make herself heard. We had to listen closely to be sure, but we lost nothing. She began her sentences in a high voice, very pretty and easy to hear; her low tones were harder to catch, but they were beautiful. I didn't know before how the whole of a person is drawn on to do what she was doing. Her natural endowments, her build, her voice, of course showed just what they were. Her position in society, her custom of talking with men, men who know letters, politics, laws, her acquaintance with her business, her experience in it, her good taste, her heart, her sense, *all* told. Oh how I enjoyed the sight of her as a spectacle. This wasn't against my principles, it wasn't a woman speaking in public, this was a member of a board of charities doing a member's duty at a meeting of boards of charity, so I was free to enjoy her beauty, and the beauty of her performance. The wisdom of what she said being far greater than mine I could only accept not judge. It commended itself. The experience and the power it showed filled me with admiration and the heart that came out here and there was one thing I had not counted on and gave me a new reverence for her and for her work. Then arose the gentlemen one by one and discussed this point & that point till at last Mr Sanborn arose and said that in considering details he feared people would lose the main drift of Mrs Lowell's paper, he therefore would remind them that she, first in this Conference, had presented a philosophically arranged *new plan* of administering public charities, whose general features seemed wise and practical though in some points he might differ from her. This speech of Mr Sanborn's pleased Mrs Cabot & Ellen & Fanny Morse and they gratefully alluded to it as we came out. This awakened Mrs Damon to praise him and to assure them that it was always so at every Conversation or meeting—he was always the one to remember what others forget, to see that nothing fell to the ground, and that the company was restored to the subject from every bypath it contrived to stray into. As I passed Effie, coming out, she said "I told you not to come."

Aug. 6th. I have had four tastes of Philosophy, it is very good. We had Dr Jones here last Sunday to read a lecture. He came to tea, I pumped him at teatime, and mastered a part of his queer vocabulary. Then I stayed up, and saw the hosts of Wisdom's children pour in, accompanied by a few of our friends and a detachment of the young & gay. I understood some passages of the lecture, and like them ever since. I noticed a fair one with golden locks. The next day I found the enclosed letter and a card. Mrs Sanborn came in and told me of the delightful philosophers and mentioned Miss Lowéd. I at once asked could that be Miss Loughead? It was, it was she of the golden locks. I have taken her to ride, and had her to dinner yesterday. The Howards, Miss Sophy & Miss Kate, dined here too. They and she are, all three, devoted philosophers, and it was very pleasant to hear them talk over the lectures. We had one of the pleasantest afternoons you can imagine and ended by mounting the wagon to be dropped at the several homes. First we took the Howards to the Manse, and all the inmates seated on the grass before the door begged Miss Loughead & me to stay. We did for half an hour. Cousin Sarah was there, she is making her visit at the Manse. Today I have dined at Aunt Susan's with the Episcopal Profes-

sor & the three Episcopal DDs who board with her, and it was great fun. They & Mother studied the questions What is Philosophy? Cui bono? I learned something. Then I had a ride with Dr Jones. Edward & Annie passed me with such derisive eyes that I couldn't keep my countenance, but I asked him questions and he *answered* me, he took the trouble to think what I meant, and to think what he knew about it, and I knew more when he got out of the wagon than I did when he got in.
E. T. E.

Naushon, August 19th 1881

Dear Mother,

We came across with Alice and a Mr Isaac Hinckley who is a naturalist. He said "There, those tern have laid their eggs and fed their young on that little islet all summer. Probably a good many of those that we see flying round it now are this year's birds." Then presently he pointed out a loon sailing at a distance. Next he descried a night-heron sitting on a stone close by us on the Nonamesset shore, which he pointed out to us. He says night-herons have three curious spots on them when they are plucked, on each shin and a larger one on the breast on which no feathers grew, but a sort of greasy down, and that when the night comes and the creatures fish many a fisherman has seen them with these spots shining bright for they are phosphorescent, and serve as lanterns to attract the fish. By day they can cover them with their feathers. But they can lift away the feathers, and let the lanterns shine.

When we passed Will's wharf we saw Cameron & John just untying the catrig and presently they sailed after us & actually caught up with us, brown faces, bright eyes, shocking hats which they wave above their close-cropped heads. They landed on the raft first, all ready to kiss us when we followed them, and they invited me to join them in their boat and have a sail instead of going up to the house. This I refused. Edith opened the door to us, and little Edward appeared from somewhere with a little mite of a pair of trowsers on that come almost in sight of his knees, and suggested that he had done a deal of growing. Then Waldo was brought in fretful and unwilling to lift his head. Edith said he had been sick for a day or two. Dear Sarah Malcolm came downstairs with little Gerrit in her arms, looking as fresh and clean as her babies do. Violet was taking a painting-lesson of her Aunt Sarah at the Mansion-house. When she came home she made her usual jump at her

— 1881 —

Aunt Ellen. She looks brown & heavy & strong, is a perfect nurse & comfort to all the little children—Waldo and Malcolm's Margaret and baby. I share her room. Ralph is big, and sportive as far as words go. I enjoy his shut mouth every time he shuts it. Cameron spoke "Alice Brand" to Father very well, but every time Ralph turned his eyes on him he stopped and laughed so hard, so joyfully, & Ralph with him that I thought that entertainment was as good as the speaking.
E. T. E.

Canton, August 26th 1881

Dear Edith,

I couldn't write yesterday. I was in a hurry to tell you that you needn't have any fear that weather, or even sickness, injured the pleasure of our visit. We were delightfully entertained all the time, and weather was made of no account whatever. Father remarked the other day that this visit had had a curious effect on him, he didn't know since he came home whether he was at home or not, he had to take views of the study and look into the various rooms to see whether this was his house or someone's else. I was rather sorry to hear it. He hasn't said anything about it since, so I hope it was only the state of one day.

Now to consider the questions I want you to answer concerning religious literature:

1   What are your ideas of what is Religious Lit. for Children.
2   Is the Unitarian Church, as such, bound to furnish it for its own.
3   It must do it both by writing and by furnishing library
4   Suggestions as to writing
5   The library—what it should contain, of course in broad classes named by a model book of its class; what qualifies a person to be library committee; new books and old books.
6   Duties of teachers about the religious reading of their classes.

There, I think that would make an essay of sufficient scope and natural unity, and if you will tell what you think it will be very valuable and interesting. If you would add a chapter about hymns as a transept to your construction, so much the better.

I have had a beautiful visit here at Mary's and admire her children. Not that I have seen very much of them,—I haven't a faculty for seeing & talking with bairns when I have no business relations with them.

Mr Higginson has been out here, and I have had the pleasure of hearing him & Mr Blake mourn over the President. He has some hope that the Vice President is yet capable of being a good man. Henry Higginson, when I was at Manchester was saying that all good men ought to hold out their hands to Mr Arthur & show him they had hope of him, and convince him that if he would take high ground he would have a strong support. He wanted them to write him up in the papers, and prepare him for his possible Presidency. I wonder whether he has done it or had it done.

Now I am going home to drive up the cooking-school. You don't know how kind Mrs Hoar has been about it. When I visited her she told me that she & Judge Hoar had visited the school-house and arranged for its fitting up. Then she had counted the cost and found it w'd be $200 besides what we pay Miss Corson, so she was going to make the gentlemen subscribe. I see every day I should be nowhere without her head. How are my dear Cameron, Edward & Waldo?

E. T. E.

Tues. Aug. 30 1881

Dear Edith,

I am very sorry you are having such a hard time, and wish I could come to help you. I trust you are coming out of the woods. I'll give you a fortnight yet before you *begin* to think about children's religious literature. I don't want the letter for five weeks. I am not sure but suppose that there is an idea abroad that there should be Unitarian Religious Literature for children, and I should like to have that dealt with reasonably & decidedly. If Sarah Forbes has any constructive views on the subject, get at them. I found Cousin Sarah sick abed on my return, but she is getting well. The Cooking-School will keep me from Mary Russell at present. Little Ellen was sick yesterday, but is better today. Love to my blessed Don who has had a birthday and no letter. And to my Violet. And to Sarah Malcolm.

E. T. E.

Fitchburg Depot Sept 2nd 1881

Dear Edith,

I have just come up from Manchester where I have had a beautiful visit to Hatty and Effie. When I arrived the girl met me at the depot and said Mrs Putnam was at the beach and thought I might like to come down and get a bath. The thermometer was at 90°. Naturally therefore I acceded with a hop skip and a jump and in a few minutes Hatty,

— 1881 —

Lotta & I with Lucy Russell and a Miss Headly her cousin rolled in the broad Atlantic. It was a real beach too with surf on it, like Lynn Beach. Of course the water was like ice but it looked like the true thing and wasn't sandy nor full of weeds. In a short time I froze stiff and coming out into that air of 90 and walking up the baked sand was most delightful. It was, though short, one of the most satisfactory baths I ever had.

When we came to the house Harry Cabot was with Effie. He had come to plan a picnic with Lotta. And *I* was invited—do you hear? I was surprised but I accepted. This was the most wonderful visit in one way. It was to well strong people, who did things. I cannot remember any other for some time. All my visits are to those who can do nothing out of doors except sit on piazzas and drive, the only chilling things in the world and therefore the only things I cannot do. Here they did neither, life was active, and I could join in it all, and felt like other folks and able and joyful. Usually I have a disabled apart feeling because life is divided when I am visiting between walking all alone, and trying by many shawls to keep alive while sitting still in the wind. We had plenty of good talk and I read them your letter about the yacht days which they liked. The picnic was very interesting. Godfrey Cabot, Edward & Richard Cabot, Harry & Elise Cabot, George Cabot, Elliot & Joe Lee, Will Putnam, Effie, Miss Headly, Lotta & I. The evening was warm & dry, the water glass. We rowed out to Little Misery and had games & supper, and then rowed or rather floated & the boys sang college songs in parts. The phosphorescence in the water was in some places very pretty. The crowd of Cabot boys astonished Miss Headly.

Concord Sept. 8th.   Business letters have kept me from finishing this. Your beautiful letter yesterday was a succession of treats. Cousin Sarah went yesterday. I miss her. She is a lovely inmate. Miss Corson comes tomorrow night I think and our School begins on Monday. Did you have that amusing *yellow day*? I only wish the yellow had lasted till sunset. Your pink larkspurs refreshed in water please us all very much. They came by morning's mail and had recovered by dinner-time. Mother sends her thanks for them & the letter.

E. T. E.

Sept 14th (46th wedding day) 1881

Dear Edith,

Miss Corson has come. The cooking-school began yesterday. Fifty-one $3 pupils. She talks very slowly while she prepares her meat &

— 1881 —

vegetables, and we write down the words of wisdom. Annie McLaughlin attended with me, with great & intelligent zeal, and at the end reported "She's a sensible knowing woman." I am gratified by that. Suppose she had turned up her nose, I should have lost the benefit of sending her. You shall have my notebook to read. The free classes Wed. & Sat. P.M. & the dollar-class wh. is small on Mon. & Thurs. I am utterly swallowed up in it necessarily. It takes all day, morning & afternoon, to attend to its various requirements, and quite as much of Mrs Hoar's time as mine. The enthusiasm was greater than I expected yesterday among the ladies, however, and I feel quite happy about it. Last Friday afternoon Edwin Barrett came to ask if we could take the minister. He was not a candidate. This was to have been the first Sun. of hearing candidates, but the man invited was prevented, so the Divinity School had come to our aid, and was to send up a 2d-year-student. His name was Bulkley. He came on Saturday afternoon, a minute fellow, with feet smaller than mine, as I saw when I carried his little shoes in from being blacked. He was somewhat innocent, didn't always know what was wise & what was unnecessary to say, but was as happy, sociable and easy a boy as ever came to a strange house. I hadn't done my errands when he arrived and so walked him out with me. He is an 8th grt.grandson of Peter Bulkeley, though he doesn't pronounce or spell his name right. I showed him all the sites & memorials connected with P. B. and he was sufficiently interested. After tea I told him we shut up at 8, and I gave him leave to remain in the parlour till Father fastened the house. "Oh then I'll stay here" he said, "perhaps he'll come in to fasten these windows, and then I can bid him goodnight!" He talked Divinity-School & preaching & the priest's office freely with Mother & me and of course we had a very interesting time with him. When Sunday came & we went to church it rained & Mother stayed at home. I was occupied with seating Father & the Sanborns and saving a place for Therchi & didn't follow the boy with my eyes to the pulpit. And there is enough of similar work with hymn-books at hymn-time. When the prayer began I heard his heart beating in his voice, and sympathized, but that was over in a moment; there was a real voice of prayer that I had hardly heard in my life, it stilled & lifted me at once. When he stood up for the sermon I didn't look either. But when the sermon began to take hold on me and amaze me like the prayer I looked up and small & young as he looked in the house, it was nothing to what he appeared in the pulpit—not more than eighteen and little at that. And his absolutely natural

— 1881 —

delivery and the absence of any rhetoric were most refreshing. In all the service there was a little of the innocence that appeared at home; he hadn't an intuitive exact taste, but the thought, & above all the religion, the practicalness, & high help of the sermon were uncommon. Not since I last heard Mr Guild had I been so reached at church. I purposely refrained from saying a word to any one about him, that I might notice whether anyone spoke to me. No one did except Mrs Sanborn & Miss Stow, who did feel as I did. Since, I have collected many more opinions. Cousins Elizabeth & Mary, Mrs Tileston & C. Hoar, thought it good for a student, but so youthful they couldn't bear it often. Mrs Hoar said all I could desire, though as a critic & without enthusiasm. But there is a storm of admiration of his singing. So I am very sorry we cannot have the boy. I was mourning yesterday, and said "I wish he could come and board with us!" and both Mother & *Father*! said they should like to have him. "He's a good boy. I like him," said Father. Sally came on Saturday to the Manse, and came to Ripley Bartlett's wedding which was on Sat. PM. at the Orthodox Church. Mother & I had been received at the door by George and placed on the front seat—actually in front of the family! We objected to that, for if Ripley & Myrtle were to stand exactly in front of the pulpit-platform they might find my toes in the way. So I was relieved when he at last returned and said a side seat might be better. Mr Adriance, Lizzy Whitcomb's husband, & Mr Grant married them, with a service recalling the King's Chapel, but a little different. Then they walked into the Vestry, & everyone followed to shake hands. Myrtle had on a navy blue woolen dress & velvet bonnet. Her cheeks were like roses, and she looked pretty & very young. Sally Bartlett just returned from the sea-shore for the occasion, looked better than when she went away, pale & handsome instead of pale & altered. After the wedding our Sally came to speak to us. And on Monday morning after taking Mr Bulkeley to the depot, Therchi and I drove up to the Manse, and brought her & Lizzy Simmons down. Sally came home and spent the morning with me, and then went to Edward's for the rest of the day. Miss Corson is staying at our house, and has with her a Miss Brayton, her doctoress, who seems to be to her what Lizzy Simmons is to Carry Brewster, absolutely devoted & ready to be hands & feet & everything. When Edward & A. came to dinner yesterday I put Miss B. beside Edward, but I carefully refrained from telling him she was a professional sister for he has a strong prejudice against such. I first ascertained that she belonged to the regulars & was no kind of a pathic.

— 1881 —

Mother wants you should know that she has a mauve & a lilac larkspur like your pink ones. Cousin Sarah left us a week ago. Kate turned up yesterday, and how thankful I am! For Abby leaves us tomorrow. I have written this in cars & waiting at Intelligence Office today, and have no success so far. Tell my beloved Don that Aunt Ellen is charmed with his pretty letter, and will write to him as soon as the cooking-school will let her write again.
E. T. E.

Concord, Sept. 28th 1881
I paid .80 for Rudder Grange

Dear Edith,

Once more a short note in a train to say that my mind often writes you a letter, but without a girl, and henceforward with a girl to train, with cooking-school taking daily from 10 to 12 & from 2.15 to 6.15, I can't get it onto paper. The cooking-school ends Monday, Tuesday we have the social circle, Wednesday I have asked the Hemenways, & Mrs Hemenway to stay till Saturday. Then I'm going to send for Cousin Abby. After this I shall devote myself to training my new Maggy, except for the three Convention Days of October. And then as soon as she is taught I should like to spend two days & a night with you. I was very thankful for a letter from you yesterday. Mary Russell is coming up day after tomorrow to see the cooking-school and the sewing-school, & bring a child. We had beautiful town services for President Garfield. Judge Hoar read his letter consenting to come to Concord & made a beautiful speech, reading also the verses which Gen. Garfield had read at Lincoln's funeral. Father enjoyed it all. All are well. Kate is with us.   Affectionately
E. T. E.

Oct 3rd 1881

Dear Edith,

I never get over the feeling of the preparations for your wedding, and know the approach of this day from afar, as of no other. Your wedding really seems to have been the crowning festivity of my life. I was counting last night that we have lived here forty-six years, and only a little more than half that time did you live here. I was surprised, for it seems more, say four fifths. It is rainy, I am sorry, I always want it pleasant on this occasion. I send much love to you & Will and all the

— 1881 —

beautiful & beloved nautical nursery. Your letter & Essay have afforded extreme satisfaction to your immediate family, and I'll gladly help with the Yearbook. Mail-time!

Affectionately
E. T. E.

Concord, Oct. 7th 1881

Dear Sally,

You left me a beautiful present which touched my heart very much, and yet the old incurable disease of never writing has lasted to this moment. That is, the cooking-school has eaten up every moment till Monday, and Tuesday the Social Circle, Father's Club, that eats a supper, met here and yesterday we had dinner company, so that only now have I got hold of my pen. The sunflower is very handsome and just what I want. I hoped to go to the train to see you off, but could not manage it at all. I had much satisfaction in the time I did see you, and we talked about many of the things that I wished to discuss with you. I went up to the Manse yesterday with Father to inquire for Cousin Gore, and found Sophy and Mr Thayer there. They had just come up for the day, and with a second nurse for Cousin Gore, who was, Cousin Elizabeth said, a shade better. Sophy went right up stairs, and while we were there Mr Thayer was busy with a legal paper, so I got little good of them, but Cousin Elizabeth gave me her views on the situation in our parish with great & sincere vehemence. I enjoyed the interview immensely. Our Cooking-School ended satisfactorily. I believe people think it was a good thing to have, and Miss Corson seemed to have a pleasant time. Annie & the baby have made a short visit at Naushon, and have come home improved. Edith is to move up this week. Everybody is well. Mother sends much love to you and so do I.

Affectionately
E. T. E.

Concord. Tuesday Nov. 8th 1881

Dear Edith,

Mother is reading "Poor Papa" now with delight and admiration. She thanks you for sending it to her. Last night a Parish Meeting was held and to my surprise & joy, it was proposed immediately to call Mr Bulkeley and many rose to praise him and endorse the proposal, and a large and eager vote to "extend to him an invitation to settle with us as

— 1881 —

our Minister at the close of his present term of study at the Divinity-School", was the quick result. Nobody contrary-minded. Of course we can't guess what he will say, but it is an early forward step and even the prudent who are disposed this morning to be shocked at our sudden proceeding say "but then I am pleased". It was specified that he was to be informed that it was a settlement for life, and must be so regarded by him. The formal concurrence of the Church is to be asked by the Parish next Sunday, and then a committee consisting of Judge Hoar, Mr Blanchard & Mr Henry Hosmer are to prepare the letter of invitation and wait upon Mr Bulkeley with it. By Thanksgiving we ought to know. Lizzy Storer and Cary Hoar spent the day with me yesterday and we had a truly glorious time. Of course we talked nephews much and equally we talked church a great deal more. I hated to have them go away. I don't believe I have thanked you for your letter. We were very glad of it, and thought the notes sweet.

On the R.R. Dec. 7 1881

Dear Cousin Sarah,

Thankyou for the letter on the postal-card. I am just on my way home from a little visit to Aunt Adams who is now very feeble, often uncomfortable, and hardly able to enjoy life any more. This is the last time I am going to spend a night away from home for a long time, except when we all go to Edith's at New Years, for we begin to think it is too bad when Father is so sad every time I depart. First however I made many visits. On Monday I went to Mrs Hemenway's, on Tuesday to Edward's & stayed till Thursday, on Saturday to Edith's for Sunday, on Monday to Providence to Emma Diman who is a good girl and under every weight at present except that she has a good son and two charming little girls. Of course they make much happiness for her though she is in such affliction. On Tuesday I came home, and yesterday ended my catalogue of visits by going to Aunt Adams's.

Friday morning. I came home to find John at the depot with the news that the lecturer of the night before was to dine here with Mr Harris & I must ask Mr Alcott. They were quite enterprising in my absence you see. So I asked Mr A., and stopped at Edward's. Mary said he was coming to dinner and Baby and her Mother had gone to Milton to call on Mrs Forbes & Sarah who are going to California for the winter. Our dinner was pleasant, we liked the young Englishman, Mr Clarke. Mr Harris agreed to read a paper for Mother's next club. Mr

1882

Alcott insisted on Mother's reading her Transcendental Bible after dinner. My Sunday Scholars came, so I was upstairs with them and didn't hear it.

Dec. 13th.   Your letters to Mother & me were very thankfully received. Mother has never got her watch. There isn't a pretty and interesting one in Boston, they are as alike as peas, and prosaic. Edith is going to look in New York. Haven's little Elizabeth has had Scarlet Fever resulting in heart-disease. She droops like a little flower, Edith says, rests her head somewhere all the time. They—and we—are very sad about her. I believe Mr Bulkeley has answered to the call that he will not accept it for life, but for an indefinite period, and cannot promise two sermons weekly, but wishes liberty to have his evening service as he can, with an extempore sermon. I suppose a Parish Meeting will be called to hear the letter, and I hope they will take him on his own terms. Mother sends much love. Affectionately

Ellen T. Emerson

Dec. 13th 1881

My dear Edith,

I rejoice that your trunk has been found. I visited the F.R.R. inward Baggage-room to look for it and made sure it was not there. As for Violet, dear child! my idea was that Father, Mother & I all together should give her the toilet-set, but I suppose since she wants a Parnassus it would be well for Father to give her and Don, & Edward each, one at New Years, for by next year he may not be able to write their names. Waldo too? I had a good talk with Mrs Cabot about all the subjects, and we have agreed to push steadily for this one end that Mr C. shall this very winter get the book started. I hope Violet is enjoying life. How is Ralph? Are you going to New York before Christmas? Mother says don't forget her watch. Tonight a play at the Hall. Tomorrow night a tea-party. Mmes Hawthorne & Ameling & Harris & Mr H. & some others. Father said with joy the other day "There is no shawl today, all greatness!" Meaning no cloud, all clear sky.

Your affectionate sister
E. T. E.

Concord, Jan. 4th 1882

Dear Mother,

Father mourns for you a little, but not enough to distress you. When

1882

he comes into the dining-room he says "Isn't Mamma coming down? Oh! To be sure! Mamma isn't here!" Judge Hoar sent me his and Mr Bulkeley's letters last night. Father enjoyed them very much with me, and read them over again to himself. He praises Mr Bulkeley's letter, and says "And is it, the boy, the small boy that slept here? It speaks well for him." Your Dec. dividend still untouched is 330, and your Jan 180, so you have about 500 to carry you through to April. Your plants have borne your absence perfectly. I had a delightful afternoon with Therchi yesterday and Charley was charming in the evening. I have heard one piece of news, that Miss Blood left her tall clock to Annie Bartlett. I hope you are well, and going out daily. Do go call on Lizzy & William. Your affectionate daughter

E. T. E.

Friday, Jan. 13th 1882

Dear Edith,

What a good time we did have the other night! [At Mrs. Hemenway's.] I am very glad you came. After you went the Parish Correspondence found a sympathetic and appreciative hearing, and Father, Mother and I were delighted. Then when bed-time came Violet and I made the most of the permission to choose from five rooms. We explored them all and invited everyone else up to see illuminated Boston from Lotty's upstairs room, and from Augustus's. We did sleep in Lotty's first room. It was a very happy visit, and Mrs Hemenway finally sent Mother & me to do our errands at Hovey's in a carriage, and came down to see us out of the door. The errands were all amusing and we bought a vast table-cloth, that is vast in width, for one leaf added to our table, for we haven't a single handsome one for that size. Mother has gained very much while with you in health and in courage. She is much more willing to do things, and far from saying as she usually does that the visit or the journey has tired her more than she knew she has felt none but good effects, and is all ready to go to Boston again. I am going to Boston on Tuesday morning. Could you meet me at Miss Quimby's? I'll come down to the telephone at half-past five or so on Monday afternoon for your answer. I heard yesterday that young John Moore has married Miss Sarah Baker, a handsome young daughter of Mr George Baker. Mrs Elijah Wood has just died. We had a great pleasure in Edward's coming to tea, with Annie, quite unexpectedly last night. Edward had stories to tell of the Social Circle, and of Mr Staples's rem-

— 1882 —

iniscences as called forth by Mr Sanborn's questions of having Mr Alcott, Mr Lane, and Mr Thoreau in jail; also of other prisoners; and finally of Mrs Thoreau, and Mrs Hoar. "I tell *you*, they could use their tongues too!" Last night I went up to Mrs Sanborn's and she showed me a vase of most beautiful roses that Beth had sent to Victor. Mrs Hoar is better. Mother says you proposed to get us a buffalo. Don't do it. We don't need it. We have two more blankets, that we use only occasionally. The sleigh was not fitted out fully the other day. I absolutely refuse to have any such thing added to our store this year. We have enough and more than enough. Ask Mary Watson whether she will come also to Miss Quimby's, please. Bring in two vols. of Ralph's Emerson and I'll bring them home for Father to add the inscription. After Miss Quimby can we go together to Houghton & Mifflin's? Or don't you want to?

E. T. E.

Concord Jan 21st 1882

Dear beloved Edith,

Mother and I are delighted and thankful. Indeed I am so thankful that I care very little whether it is a girl or a boy I am so glad to have another baby. Mother came home with no suspicions at all, so she is as much surprised as gratified. And she says she is the more surprised as you seemed to her to be very well. I am so glad I shall be inclined all the time to dance and sing Goody! goody! goody! GOODY!!!

I wish we could get you for Sunday. I won't come Monday, after all. I should like to but really I ought not to. Something absorbing happens every day, and I don't take a step for Mr Cabot. I have asked him and Mrs Cabot to come early next week, and I must be prepared for them. When can you come in on Tuesday? Early? Bring with you an old dark blue book & an old claret one. So will I, and we will visit Messrs Houghton & Mifflin together, and put that business through. *Old* books, to show how they have faded.

Your rejoicing &
affectionate
E. T. E.

Concord, Jan 31 1882

Dear Edith,

I wonder whether you have ever opened the bundle of work for Mr

Cabot sent you in November. Please, if you haven't, do at an early opportunity. I have corrected finally all my papers here, and if you are hopeless of getting to yours send them back and I think I can do them. Mr Cabot is actually demanding at present, instead of waiting to be demanded of, and I am thankful. What a time of death this is! Yesterday we heard of three deaths. Mrs Beal, Mrs White by the church, and Charley Bartlett who died of congestion of the lungs on his wedding-day. They had been married only two years. Adelia also is sick of pneumonia, and there is danger that the poor baby is to lose his mother also. The teacher of one of the schools, a patient of Edward's, has scarlet fever, and another teacher was nursing her not knowing what it was. So two schools are closed, and the six other teachers in the same house suddenly have to find a new boarding-place. All this gives us a feeling of being a sick and upset town which I suppose we shall presently recover from, but oh! how they tremble at Edward's & the Keyeses' about Philip & little Ellen! Then today's Advertiser tells of Mrs Perkins, Mrs James & Dr Bellows. I think I shall go to Mrs James's funeral, and from there to see Therchi. Tonight the Social Circle meets with Edward. I am going to spend the afternoon with Annie to make preparation. She is coming back with the Baby to dine; and Edward if he can, but he is driven now. He was almost distracted with patients yesterday. We hope today he will be allowed time to eat his dinner.

[Unsigned]

Concord, Feb. 8th 1882

Dear Cousin Sarah,

I'm sorry to starve you so long. Now I'll do my best to give you a full meal. Here is a letter from Edith, and the precious Parish letters too. You can keep them long enough to send them to Cousin Hannah and Cousin Charlotte, for I know they will care. I have been reading a little in the history of our Concord Church, and find that our grandfather was chosen minister in Feb 1765 (Grandfather Bliss having died in May 1764) but was not ordained till Jan 1st 1766. He was then 23 years old, or near it. So the Parish has once before chosen as young a minister unordained, & had to wait nearly a year before he could be prepared to come to his charge. This precedent pleases me very much. Meanwhile we are exceedingly happy in having a new preacher every Sunday. We all agree that it is a luxury. Most of them are excellent. Edward and Annie dined with us yesterday, Tuesday, as usual, and brought the baby,

— 1882 —

now quite a grown-up girl. Her beauty departs as she grows older, but her colours are still enchanting. Her blue coat and the full white ruffle inside her hood are very becoming. Today she has gone with her Mamma to spend the day and night with Edith. Edith is to have a game-party this evening. Nobody could rejoice in more absolute health than we do. Father, of course, Mother sleeping better, and suffering less, both going out zealously to church, lectures or parties whenever they have a chance. I a Hercules, Edward getting along bravely without colds, Annie & Baby each had one, but both bloom like roses. Edith wonderfully well and active and oh delight! expecting No 8 to be ready to exhibit to Mother with her garden next June. Ralph rather oppressed with growing & with colds, but Will & all the other children well all the time. Violet goes to school in Boston, and boards on Beacon St. from Monday till Friday. She is growing taller and is as good as ever. Madge Cunningham, her only friend, went to California for a year last April and died suddenly Jan. 24th of Scarlet Fever. A hard blow to dear Violet, as well as to her family. Madge seemed to me one of the most perfect creatures I ever saw. Charley now lives at Edith's. He is happier there than here. The house is shut up. I went to Somerville one day and saw Therchi. She is homesick and feels outraged, but she has pleasant quarters, pleasant company, and says she goes into everything with all her might, sewing, conversation, billiards, dances, drives, "to keep from thinking". Charley is not only homesick for her society, homeless and heart-broken, but cannot bear the thought of how it all looks to her. He isn't willing to have the subject named or written about. Our fear is that he will give way and take her out. She was talking about him far & wide so that people were afraid to see her yet afraid to dismiss her, and at home was more constantly brooding upon her insane idea. It was high time to send her to the Asylum, but that she can never know. Cousin Fanny Ripley is still all broken down, nerves and health as well as spirit. It is very sad. She has been boarding at Mrs Goodnow's, but is now trying the Manse again. Her sister has come to stay with her. I have been having a most beautiful time this week introducing Mr Cabot to my ancestors, a risky thing to do! they are so interesting to me that when I begin upon them I can't stop, and they are not likely to be so interesting to him. Still he seemed to care sufficiently and so did Mrs Cabot. I gave him our bundle of antiquities to carry home, and Mrs C. writes "Elliot was so fascinated with his bundle that he found it hard to get to bed." My memory isn't half as good as it was. Cousin Hannah must certainly come with you this summer and we will tell each other everything we know & write it down for posterity. Mother's heart is set on her jays & their meals at present, and on her hopes of next spring's flowers. She is as much of a belle as ever. Tonight we are going to take tea at the Sanborn's. Mother sends her love to you and thanks you for her beautiful Christmas card. She, & Father too, admired it very much. She is depending on seeing you next summer. So am I. Please give my love to my cousins.

Ellen T. E.

Wed. Feb. 8th 1882

Dear Edith,

Mother and Annie are perfectly delighted with the wolf-skins and John not less. We had the sleigh got up with all possible glories to suit you when Mr & Mrs Cabot came on Monday. Mr Cabot wouldn't be tempted by the new fur but insisted on walking. He did ride to the depot when he went away. He has been reading the antiquities in the big brown paper bundle, and the papier-maché tea-chest, and says he feels quite intimate now with all our ancestors. I read to him and to Mrs Cabot the History of Concord, and told them the Moody stories and had a most beautiful time myself. Dear Mrs Cabot took her usual interest, but she couldn't keep the innumerable ancestors & collateral branches sorted in her head; while Mr Cabot did completely, never seemed confused for a moment. Then, when Mr Cabot went off with Father she and Mother and I had great rejoicing together over you and a good domestic talk in general. I found, and read to them, a thorough journal of all Uncle Edward's visit to Lafayette, which they appreciated, and Mr Cabot says it must be copied and given to the Historical Society. My green dress came and on Tuesday when Annie came I opened the box and exhibited it to them. Both applauded, and applauded you. Mrs Cabot thinks you are a good and efficient sister as well as daughter. The moment that Mr Cabot gets the mass of materials into his hands, and that ought to be this month, Mrs Cabot says will be the time for an advance upon him from all sides. You & Will must visit him or get him to visit you, Edward and I must make stringent requisitions; she will throw all her weight in our behalf, and Nina Lowell is to be invited to urge and exhort him. for she is on our side and he values her and her opinions. The best way I think would be for you all to assemble here and hold a Congress around him, he & Mrs Cabot being first secured. After Mr & Mrs Cabot left yesterday E. & A. & baby came to dinner and brought Annie Lombard. I told Edward how pleased you were with the glorious second snow-storm, and I too, and how ardently I hoped that the skies were preparing another and far heavier one. His disgust was delightful to see. He does have dreadful struggles with drifts, and cold winds across them. As usual he sighed for a better world, one where he should have time to reason with me. He fled the moment he left the table. The Annies & Mother and I betook ourselves to the opening inspection and trying on of the green dress. If you only like the dress as much as I do we shall be quite happy henceforth, and I'll have my summer dress made the same way. I rejoice in Miss Quimby—but—the Bill hasn't come yet. Last Saturday night in the height of the snow-storm Mother & Father, nothing dismayed, went in their own sleigh to Edward's Club. Mr Sanborn contributed the entertainment, the first chapters of his book on Mr Thoreau. They all say it was nectar & ambrosia and provocative of endless & delectable general talk. Neither Father nor Mother nor anyone else that was there can get through rejoicing over it, and lamenting that I and all their other friends were not there too. Sunday morning Father & I waded to church and found a very small congregation, three ladies in the Keyeses' pew, two in another, Miss Matilda Brown and I were all the ladies, and I don't think there were more than twenty-five gentlemen. The evening service was omitted. 'Twas a pity, for in the evening it was fine weather and good walking. The minister however was not of the right kind for me, so I bore it better than I could have otherwise. I have had two short visits to dear Cousin Fanny Ripley. I love to talk with her. She is coming tomorrow to see Mother. Mr Lathrop is to lecture tonight on Spain, & I'm just going to ask the Hawthorne family to tea with us. Tomorrow we take tea at Mrs Sanborn's. Next Wednesday Wm. Goodwin is to lecture on Schliemann's discoveries. Don't you want to bring up Ralph & hear that? Your affectionate sister

Ellen

Concord, Feb. 25th 1882

Dear Miss Dabney,

Your letter came about ten days ago and the capote by the same mail. I opened the letter then, but kept the capote for my birthday. And yesterday morning I solemnly opened it with my other presents in Mother's room. I am very much pleased with it, thankyou. Dear Miss Clara, I have been hoping all this time to get my letter to you started before I should hear from you again, but in vain. My niece Violet came up and spent the night with me last night because it was my birthday

— 1882 —

and brought me a pitcher which she had painted with ivy and holly. Mrs Cunningham has been teaching her to paint on china. She is beginning to grow tall at last. Oh how thankful I am! Last year I was afraid she was going to be uncommonly short. Nieces are great possessions. I am so glad of Violet every day I live! And my cunning little junior I expect to enjoy in the same way. I can't get acquainted with Edward's children early because I am never in the same house with them. Edward & Annie are well, and as to Father & Mother they seem to grow more strong & able every year. We are all always remarking that we do have a beautiful time in the world. In our church we have a new minister every Sunday which is elixir to Father, and to me too. They are almost all good preachers. Perhaps we shouldn't enjoy them so much if they were candidates; but they aren't! Our choice is made, and we are so happy about it that we always say "Oh didn't you like the minister yesterday? But after all I'm glad we are going to have Mr Bulkeley and not him." We were going to begin to hear candidates in Sept., and the first one suddenly sent word he couldn't come so they sent to the Divinity School for a student. And the student gave us preaching and a service such as we had hardly had before anywhere. He proved also to be a descendant of Peter Bulkeley our first minister who brought our forefathers from England to Concord. After hearing candidates for five weeks we said "Why do we hear candidates? let Mr Bulkeley come once more." He came and it was just as before. Miss Bartlett said "Other people give us good essays but this boy gives us preaching." We waited two weeks and then suddenly met and resolved to ask him. His answer at New Years was that he would come, and it was sent in a letter that made everyone value him more. Mr Reynolds rejoices in Mr Bulkeley. He says (when people say our choice was rash after two Sundays, without knowing anything more of the boy than the testimony of his teachers and fellow-students) "Yes, you were rash but I looked on complacently. I knew you were wiser than you knew in your rashness."

Goodbye, give my love to Roxa, to Mrs Sam and to Alice. I shall try to get a chance again to write.

Ellen T. Emerson.

Feb. 27th 1882

My Edith dear,

Your note and presents gave me great pleasure and I thank you very much for them and for the thought of coming. Violet's visit was delicious though brief and I think you must let me have the darling for a

— 1882 —

Sunday sometime to make up for my disappointment. I like my little box and my lychee nuts very much, I never had any before, and find plenty of people who never saw the like. Dear Violet's pitcher is a beauty and every body envies me when they see it. Annie & Edward gave me rosebuds, azaleas, geraniums and a wilderness of mahernia. Mary Watson sent me a card with beautiful rice-paper flowers. Miss Loughead sent me a beautiful flower-pot. Clifford and Susy sent me a box of violets, marguerites and daffodills. I have taken immense comfort of them. Yesterday morning Father as usual was full of joy and eagerness "It is the day of Heaven today, isn't it? And can we go to the Cambridge—to the House?" Of course I entirely sympathize, I was as thankful as he that church-time approached and Sunday-School was to follow. Mother for once didn't want to go, so Father and I set forth early and I carried Ellen Parkman's vase with its far-shining daffodills which Clifford & Susy had sent, in my hand to offer to the flower-committee. We met all the Catholics coming home from church and they all fixed their eyes upon them. Everyone at church smiled as they came in sight. But they were snubbed by the flower-committee who had just reared a highly artistic pyramid on the altar of pink & delicate flowers, which would be quite put out by the blaze, so I took them over to the Weirs' to spend the morning. I returned to church shorn of my beams and heard there a minister whom I shall always desire to hear again, Mr L. G. Ware. After S.S. I went to the Weirs' for my daffodills, accompanied by Alicia. Miss McClure came to see me on Saturday and enjoyed them. She is a vision of delight. Happy are they who can behold her! She borrowed our Egyptian images to show her infant class an idol. They were deeply interested, she says. Bob James has settled here for the present at Mrs Cutter's. He is rather domesticated at Edward's. He and Annie say he is a most entertaining guest, and lovely to the baby, who is captivated by him—Annie can stop her crying by reminding her that Mr James will hear. I hope you will like your bowl and pitcher sent by Violet. I had a pretty note from Therchi in her own hand, a capital sign, as well as showing great kindness, and with it she sent slippers which she had made for me and for Mother, beauties! Mother thanks you for the tea.   Affectionately
                                            Ellen

                                            Concord, Mar. 8th 1882
My dear Edith,
    I thank you for your beautiful long letter. Waldo's magic house is

— 1882 —

very interesting to us all. Father is delighted whenever I remind him of it. I am glad you had the pleasant visit to Naushon, and the mentions of Malcolm's house are very exciting. Your letter, saying you couldn't come, destroyed a secret blissful expectation, but it was such a direct delightful bit of intercourse I felt better for it all the evening. I wish I could have had you. I believe you would have enjoyed it. I could write a volume about it. Mother was desperately frightened about it, afraid about each detail of lamps, rooms & supper as she hasn't been of late years, and my spirits were very low in consequence, for I couldn't help being influenced & besides her fears my own conjured up a dead heavy time, silence, awkwardness, incompatability. Mother kept imploring me to abandon the project, but I reminded her that this was the 53rd week we had tried to have it, and was the first when nothing seemed to prevent. So we remained firm though scared. Edward declared that the guests were ill-assorted, and Annie nobly reassured & sustained us. Let me gratefully record that Miss Munroe & Mrs Henry Hosmer received the invitation as if it were a real delight. How kind of them! I hope in future I shall look at invitations in this way. I do really, but my habit is to look gravely at them in a business point of view, what they will interfere with and how much strength they will take, and let the pleasure come in sight after everything else. Well I remembered that Mr Reynolds once told me that in Jamaica Plain society was organized on a plan wholly different from that of Concord; viz. here we invite by ages, there they invite by families; if they ask the Father & Mother they invite all their children who are of society age or approaching it, and the grandmother or great-uncle who lives with them. This information took root in my mind, and I saw the method had excellent elements. So I did the same this time. I invited 58 persons, of every age, & 43 came. When Mother learned how many I had asked she said all former fears were now destroyed by the giant fear that the rooms wouldn't contain them, and she frightened me still more. I never suffered so much as I did from Sat. night till Wed. morn. on any occasion of this kind. Wednesday morning my spirits rose. The preparations are always delightful to me. I felt as strong as a lion, and everything began to seem like "folks & things & a door",* spectral terrors had disappeared. All worked smoothly and I walked out to borrow the 90 tea-

---

*The reference is to a story about Edith, as described in RWE's journals in 1851: "Edith's opinion. Edith, when a little girl, whimpered when her mother described the joys of Heaven. She did not want to go there, she 'wanted to stay' (and she looked round the room) 'where there was folks, and *things, and a door.*' "

— 1882 —

spoons. Alicia met me & invited me into her wagon. We collected all needed dishes & spoons. Lizzy Bartlett saw me & bore down on me. "Ellen, I feel anxious about your party tonight. I don't believe you're doing things successfully, so I guess I shall look in this afternoon & take hold!" How enchanted I was! She came at 2. We had a glorious time all the afternoon. I wrote to Mr Bulkeley on Monday, proposing that he should come, and he appeared at 5.30. I love the boy already, it was good to see him. He is so happy and unconscious, and enjoyed the evening. I imagined beforehand introducing him and seeing that all the people knew him. There was very little of that. He behaved as our Cameron would, took to company like a duck to water, skirmished eagerly about on his own hook, remembered everyone he had seen before, made himself useful and agreeable in every direction. After people were gone he addressed Mother and told her how he felt about having been called here with a serious joy that I hadn't looked for. At breakfast I had a long talk with him, and Father was not addressed. I feared he thought it tedious. But three times since he has said "That is a good young person. I like him. I like his talk." To return to the party, dear Annie told Mother, who always says she needs to be in five places at once at tea-time, that she was going to pour out tea for her. Mother was charmed, she beheld Annie administering with pride & vanity. She thought it was just as it should be. People came, and came, and came. They didn't depend on me to take care of them at all, they took care of themselves uncommonly. The buds didn't stick together particularly, they talked with their elders. I began to feel happy. Tea-time was great fun. Why, it seemed like the days of Mr Sanborn's school. I began to have an ecstasy of social pleasure such as teaparties gave us when we were young. The company began to retire to the parlour, Father came for his supper, Mrs Sanborn & Lizzy Bartlett drew near and sat by me, and Anna McClure, Edward & Annie & Mother were there, and at last no one else. We had a very gay time and laughed very much. When I returned to the parlour I carried my dear Lychee nuts, and how they stood me in stead. Almost no one had seen them before, and they added a halo to the occasion, gave me an excellent reason for moving from station to station, and an agreeable introduction to the young. I never was more grateful to you for a benefaction. People began to go at quarter after 9. At 9.40 not one was left. So we went early to bed. But I could not sleep for sheer bliss, I lay awake and enjoyed every minute and laughed and laughed over the jokes I had heard. Everyone else seemed

— 1882 —

to have had as good a time as I, and the burden of all the congratulation that continues to reach me is "And it was so lovely to have the children too!" Annie says she & her Mother each had such a personal good time that they are fired to go & do likewise, have an enormous party of all ages. The manuscripts have come, thankyou. No more time tonight.

Thy affectionate sister.

Cambridge, March 27 1882

Dear Miss Dabney,

I met Mr May yesterday and he told me Robertson James was just setting forth for Fayal, and it would be a good chance to say how-do-you-do to you, so I just write a little note. I envy Bob the sight of Paradise he is to have after two weeks of misery, the beautiful island, the advanced spring, the donkey-rides, the gardens and everything. I hope he will also have the pleasure of getting acquainted with you all, and I am sure you in turn will enjoy him. He used to go to school with Edward in Concord, and he was an officer of the 55th Mass. Vols.—colored regiment—when he was only seventeen. I think he ended the war in the cavalry however. Since he has been sick he has spent a few days with Edward and Annie and the Baby who were delighted with him every moment, especially the Baby. We went yesterday to Mr Longfellow's funeral. People did not go up to look at him, I don't know why, but as I could see him from where I stood it seemed as if he must look very beautiful. I think he had a happy end, his illness was very short. Father says he wanted he should live at least as long as he himself should, he was very sorry to have him die first. We went to the funeral with Mrs Agassiz, and she said it was the greatest comfort to her to stand with Father by that grave. He was one of that group of friends, almost the last, and he himself was half gone to heaven. It seemed good to her to think that the burial, and all this side was dim to him. That interested me very much. Dear Miss Clara, & Roxa, and Mrs Dabney, and Alice, I send my love to you all. And I wish I could see you. Miss Clara dear, if Bob had only gone a week ago he could have brought you this on your birthday!

Ellen T. Emerson.

April 5th 1882

Dear Edith,

With rapture we rejoice to think you're coming home so soon. I'll tell no one in Concord but Edward as advised. Please bring with you your Southworth daguerreotype of me. And bring the copies of the Carlyle letters. I write to Sophy by this same mail. Edward dined with us as usual on Tuesday and we talked of Mr Emery's beautiful paper on Culture read at Geo. Bartlett's on Saturday night. Of Mr Emery Edward said "Singularly enough Philosophy has led him to believe in Doctors, he thinks there is a healing art, and he sends for me for his own troubles and those of his friends, he believes in me and thinks I can cure fits." This was agreeable news to the family. You don't know how much Father likes my looking-glass. He admires it sometimes for a long time together, viewing from all points near and far. Tell my darling boys that I mourn that their Saturday is to be spent in Boston. I meant to take a holiday with them. I hope we can get the Cabots and Thayers. I rejoice that Will is coming.

Thy affectionate Sister

Concord 11 April 1882

Dear Edith,

Cousin D. G. Haskins sends us invitations to his daughter's wedding on Thursday. I enclose yours without its envelope wh. is addressed to Mr & Mrs Forbes. Julian Hawthorne and his wife dined with us & Edward & Annie today. We had a truly good time. When I came home last night I went to tell Edward and Annie of it, and only Baby was at home. When she had looked at me a minute or two, she began and as fast as I answered fired a new question. "Mamma's gone. How's grappa? How's Don & Cam? How are all the boys? How does Waldo do today? How's Edie?" Her business-like manner was very funny. I visited Houghton & Mifflin and had the satisfaction of seeing that my wishes were understood after some hammering. They have no distinct intention of acting accordingly 16[mo ?] set in cloth costs *us* 90 cts. a volume = 9.00. H & M said they took off 40 cts on a dollar from their usual price when selling to us, on everything. I am a little afraid my new bonnet may look startling, and mean to write to Miss [Stone?] to make the brim a quarter of an inch less broad than the mulberry velvet all round. I hope you have no objection. I am sorry you are gone, you singular and plural. And wish I knew how to make your visits pleasanter to you.   Your affectionate sister

Ellen.

— 1882 —

Concord, April 15th 1882

Dear Susy,

The photographs are beautiful and I have been watching from day to day for a chance to write and thank you for sending them to me. When Eustace brought them he told us that you could hardly bear to part with them. I am the more grateful. Charley & Therchi were pleased with theirs, and Edith who spent last Sunday here with all her children was delighted to receive hers. She was well enough, but very uncomfortable, and each of the six had a bad cold so they were not as cheerful a family as usual, but we had some beautiful times nevertheless. We spent one forenoon at Easterbrook, and the boys found Dangerous Islands in Enchanted Lakes, got into the water and came with shining shoes and eager explanations to see what their doom was to be, and Violet climbed rocks, and found cranberries for her Mamma and Waldo. They all went off on Monday morning. Violet is growing up, and more valuable than ever to her mamma and the small boys. You didn't tell me quite enough about Ruth in your dear letter, every word of which I valued. This is Haven's birthday. Give my love to him. Tell him I almost never forget it now, though I don't always write. Edward is now in all the agonies of writing an oration for a Doctors' association. If it only proves first-rate I don't care very much if he does get a little too tired. But one can't help feeling that writing done between 11 P.M. & 4 A.M. on strong coffee will be far below the natural capacity of the author. The baby is the most grown-up girl of two years that I ever saw, and Annie thinks she will always be an interesting and difficult problem and lead her parents a most eventful life. Charley & Therchi, so far as I can see, are having a smoother time than before Therchi went to the Asylum

April 19. Edward has today delivered his oration at the Doctors' Meeting and returned at five in high spirits. He enjoyed delivering it and they voted to print it. I don't know how regular a thing that may be. Perhaps it is no special compliment. Mother and Annie are pretty sure that it is. The baby seems much older, like a girl, not like a baby. Yesterday she climbed upstairs, walked up to Annie and took her hand saying "Come right down into the parlour and see what a naughty baby I have been," "What have you done?" "I have broken papa's mug." And so she had. She maintained a show of decent gravity while Annie mourned and picked up the pieces, but on being blamed she flippantly

— 1882 —

replied "I'll give him mine instead. That will do." We think she is going to be dreadful to bring up. I wish you could come to see us, dear Susy. Give my love to Ruth & all the other bairns.

Affectionately,
Ellen

18th April 1882

Dear Edith,

The milliner says the agreement between the bonnet-frame we chose last Monday and the one the plum-coloured velvet is made over is something uncommon. She was urgent that I should keep the rounding brim as belonging to this year's fashion so I consented. Send for me on the day when I can best help you and I'll come out and spend a day with you. I always wish, dear Edith, that I knew how to behave with you. Your flowers came last night in good order and pleased Mother very much. Mrs Cheney and Caroline came to tea and they seemed to like them too. I am surprised at the cost of the fire-pans, but think they are quite worth the money, and desire to pay for them myself and make you a present of yours. Then I still owe you 2 dollars on Mother's account. So I will some day send the 6.25. Tell Violet she left all her marbles, and Cameron that I found our insect-book the day after he went. I hear nothing from Mrs Cabot yet. Mr & Mrs Storey and the three elder children were here on Saturday, and we had a beautiful time. Mother & Father went to hear Mr Harris lecture on "Sartor Resartus". Mother came home saying she had supposed herself to be too old to be capable of the vivid pleasure she had had in hearing it. Her one object now is to get him to read it here. I find all the children's rubbers are here, and will send them home as soon as I see a chance.

Ellen.

20 April 1882

Dear Edith,

I don't think we can have the conference so soon as Monday, and I suppose it is doubtful whether we could get Edward to Milton, and he is the important person. I'll ask him. I'll write to Mrs Cabot to come here on Monday. Father is sick today but Edward isn't anxious about him. Edward's oration went off gloriously. Mail-time.

E. T. E.

— 1882 —

Concord, 20 April 1882

Dear Puss,

Shall I send the rubbers? 2 pr. Probably Don's & Cameron's. Last night I went to a delightful calico Ball. Tonight with Charley & Therchi to an Inspection of the company. Miss Adams of Waltham has written to Cousin Elizabeth that her brother Faneuil came home saying Edward's oration was brilliant, and as to eloquence Father's mantle had evidently fallen upon him. Isn't that a sugar-plum? C. Walcott stopped me in the street to express his joy that Edward had enjoyed it & succeeded in it, and apparently not so much out of civility but because he was so pleased himself, which affected me very much. Friday morning. Father is as comfortable as can be, but Edward actually means to have him stay in bed all day! I wonder whether he can be kept there.

Ellen.

Concord Saturday morning 22d April 1882

Dear Edith,

Father just now said "The Power of our life has been very kind." I said, yes, we had all been well and happy. "And not one rascal among them!" he said, meaning his children & grandchildren. He has asked whose house this is several times, but on looking round always says "Why yes, this is Mamma's house," and the point where he always finds this out is when his eyes reach Mrs Hildreth's crayon of you & me. He then begins a song of praise that he should be at home, with good people, where he can have a fire, and have

Letter is unfinished.

Concord 22 April 1882

Dear Cousin Sarah,

I'm sorry enough to have left your letter unanswered so long. I have in some way or other been prevented each day. Your roses came in wonderfully good order and gave Mother great pleasure. Father is sick today, and I am sitting with him, so I have taken my pencil out of my pocket to write to you. Edward is inclined to think it is the beginning of the end. Of course Father regards it so himself, he always does whenever he feels sick at all. At first he said when he felt very sick downstairs, and couldn't walk across the dining-room without staggering, that he didn't wish it to come in this way, he would rather have fallen down cellar. But now he is comfortable in his bed he is only glad that he is at home in his own house and that he has had a happy life and likes his family so much. I shall write to Haven tomorrow and ask him to send word to you. I do not feel sad about it. Of course I would rather he would get well, but it would be simply beautiful for him to die now while he can still speak and understand, and live his own life in a measure, for I have thought lately that in a few months he would no longer be able to do any of these. Everyone else is well, and Edward had success and joy with his oration before the doctors of the So. Middlesex Association. Affectionately

Ellen.

Concord Monday 24 April 1882

Dear Haven,

I suppose Edward may not have told you so I write before the 7 A.M. mail to say that Father has pneumonia, and of course the chances are against him. Dr Charley Putnam visited him Saturday night and last night, and Will says he told him it very probably was simply old age taking this form. He said to me "It is strange to see him without any of the distress & pain that a young person would have." For he simply feels sick & feverish, but declares whenever he wants to go into the study that he is perfectly well, and though opposed both by force & guile did dress himself Friday morning & go down for all day & come to the table, and Saturday afternoon he went down, but I took tea with him in the study. At bed-time he locked the windows & the shutters, raked down the fire, collected all the letters of the day for his breast-pocket, and then nothing would do but he must carry his study-lamp up to bed, and moreover *run* lightly up-stairs on the tips of his toes, but he did stumble frightfully at the tenth stair which disgusted him. Yesterday he tried for the study all the forenoon but we succeeded in diverting him, he was probably weaker, but insisted on sitting up in a common chair, nothing could induce him to take any other, all the afternoon. He has more trouble in making us understand than ever, but there are moments when he gets out a smooth sentence. He knows everybody and is interested & amused by talk, part of the time easily, part of the time the meaning of what is said doesn't reach him and he is polite, like deaf people, but inaccessible. Will & Edith, Cousin Mary Simmons & a nurse make easy & pleasant days, and Edward has put aside everything & sleeps here besides being here twice or 3 times in the day. Please send my letter over to Cousin Sarah, 223 Ryerson St., and Sally will want to see it. My love to you all and them.

Ellen.

This letter inserted slightly out of sequence for description of RWE's last days. See Appendix, p. 670, for another account.

Concord, & Milton, May 13 & 19 1882

Dear Miss Clara.

I know you will all have heard that my Father has died, and I have been wanting to write you all about him. It has seemed to me that in this last year he has lost a little faster than in former years. Last summer I noticed it, and much more this winter. It had even become hard for him to understand common things that were said to him, and it was very little that he could say himself. But he was particularly strong and well and much enjoyment was still possible for him. I think I have told you that church-going was a delight lately, and many little club entertainments, readings of papers & discussion afterwards, that he has been invited to, have given him so much pleasure that he was always sorry if he heard that there had been anything of the kind which he had missed. He had walked more than usual too, for sitting still in the study had become a weariness to him, I began to think. We are glad to think that there never was a time of sadness & helplessness, and there was not, but it seemed to me to be coming very near, and I was often tempted to look forward with fear. Though how thoroughly I have been taught day by day through all these years how foolish and needless that is! Every lion that I have seen before me all the way has proved to be chained when I came to the spot. I never have once said to myself or to Mother "What shall we do when this or that becomes necessary?" and in that way distinctly impressed myself with a particular fright, that I have not remembered the question when whatever it was did become necessary, with reason to adore the gracious Providence that had prepared all for it just in time, so that there was no sorrow, no fight, no trouble of any kind. Yet the fear of all that might be when speech had wholly ceased could not be kept entirely down, though I knew it was naughty, and when after Father had been two days sick Edward told me on Saturday April 22d that he probably would not get well, it seemed a very solemn word, but not sad, I could only praise the Lord. Edith & Will came on Sunday and stayed till Tuesday

— 1882 —

morning, and Edward gave up every thing but sick babies, so that he was with Father for hours every day. So that most of the time he and Will could do everything for Father, which was a great comfort to him and them. Then Edith's confinement being very near, Edward thought she ran some risk in staying, and Will took her home, but she sent up Ralph & Violet on Tuesday, & V. spent the night, and Cameron & Don came on Wednesday & Don spent the night. The sight of the children each time they came into the room was sure to make Father smile, and he could say "Good boy!" "Good little girl!" always and sometimes a little more. I don't think he was ever delirious, though confused enough to think he was not at home, and to want to be carried home as fast as possible. Still he often recognized that he was at home, almost always knew us, and evidently had many natural cares on his mind, for one day when he had been talking long and trying vainly to make me understand, he at last succeeded, and I found it was the present finances of the family that he was thinking of, and when I told him that the April bills were paid, and John was paid, and that there was money in the bank as well as in the house, he was entirely content, and said no more. He was perpetually grateful for everything that was done, and often smiled and understood for a minute or two what was said. Edward saw that he liked it when Cousin Elizabeth Ripley came to see him, so on Wednesday he sent Judge Hoar, Mr Alcott, Mr Channing & Mr Staples to see him. To Mr Alcott he spoke perfectly clearly, to Judge Hoar so that it was easy to understand, and Judge Hoar said when he came out "His face is as the face of an angel." To Mr Staples I am sure he meant to say "We have been good neighbours together", but it was not clear. Mr Channing did not come till evening and we could not gather anything from Father's talk to him. The next morning when Don went Father said "Good boy! excellent boy!" "I'm going Grandpapa," said Don. "Where?" "I'm going home." "Are you going to teach or to be taught?" "I'm going to school", said Don. But after that Father did not seem to be awake to much that was said or done, much of the time not to see us or to be conscious that we spoke to him. He asked once for Mother but when she came he did not look at her. Up to that time he had been more thankful to have her with him than anyone else. But sometimes through the day it was evident that he did know us. We never asked him. At noon Mr Cabot came. I made a loud and joyful announcement of it and Father said "Who?" When I told him again he said "Mr Elliot Cabot! Praise." Edward gave him brandy & Mr Cabot came in. Father showed the old joy when he saw him, and tried to say

— 1882 —

"This is that good man who has done so much for me", but it would not come out straight, and soon what he said was no longer to be guessed at. At four Mr Cabot went, he said Father was looking beautifully. Dr Putnam arrived & Mr Sanborn came to bid Father goodbye. Father smiled and said "This is a man that is a man," but could not say anything else, and seemed to be more uncomfortable. so that Mr Sanborn went. In a few minutes great pain began, Annie ran to call the doctors up. They tried in vain to relieve him, and finally gave him ether. Every time he began to come out of it he seemed still in pain, so that they renewed it, and at 10 minutes of 9 he died. Edward sent word at six o'clock to Charley Emerson and Judge Hoar and Mr Keyes and they all came. And everything that could be done for people was done for us. Dr Furness came the next day from Philadelphia. The papers will tell you about the funeral. It seemed to us most beautiful, most affecting, the great concourse, and most of the things that were said and done satisfied us. What a kindness it seems when people come to a funeral at one's own house. It never seemed to me a kindness to go to a funeral. But when people came to the funerals of our babies, and now to Father's it seemed to me so friendly, so lovely of them, it did me great good. Our little Edward Forbes was very sweet. He sat during all the service at the house with tears running down his face, and after we had gone up stairs to put on our things he asked Edith's leave to go down once more to look at his grandpapa, and Mrs Cabot said he seemed not to know there was a soul in the room, he came and leaned on the coffin and looked and looked. When we came to the grave we found it all lined all the way down, with little hemlock twigs, and a bed of green at the bottom. Some of the young people had thought to do that! I had never seen anything like it done before. Now come letters, lovely letters. We have been most thankful for them. Dear Mother says she always thought she should not want to live another day after Father died, but now she feels determined to live as long as she can, for she sees how it would leave me forlorn. At first she seemed very much changed and weakened and did not sleep, but since her sleep has returned she has begun again to seem like herself, and she isn't sad, we none of us are. I have come to stay a few days with Edith for number eight has come! A dear little scarlet boy with very light hair. We are enjoying him very much, and I don't think people who are blessed with a perfectly satisfactory boy ought to waste a minute in remembering that he isn't a girl. I send much love to you & Roxa & Alice & her Mother.

           Ellen T. Emerson.

— 1882 —

2 May 1882

Dear Edith,

Mother was very weak all day yesterday and didn't get a nap, but last night she slept well, and is better today. She has moved back into her room. Cousin Sarah was here a great deal yesterday; today only for an hour. We tried our first evening alone last night, and felt the house rather silent. This morning I went to breakfast at Edward's. He had received a beautiful letter from Mr Lee. We had such pleasure—he and Annie and I—in being together, and having a chance to talk that I think we sat three quarters of an hour, and I'm afraid we should do it often, but Cousin Sarah's coming puts an end to that plan. I have had thirteen letters this morning, which were a pleasure to Mother and me. Especially a beautiful one from Ida. Nina & Mrs Cabot are coming May 11th, so implore Alexander to wait till the 18th or 19th. Lizzy Bartol sent me some beautiful roses last night. Mother and I often notice our mercies. Eugenia & Elinor came for a call this morning. Many thanks to Will & you for coming and bringing the bairns—or rather I mean it was a great pleasure. Alicia says Tom cried hard at the grave, and Edward got him to stay with him to see it filled, and they were a comfort to each other. Tom walked from Framingham Sunday morning with a large bag of books, read two hundred pages of ———'s Philosophy on the way, walked round Walden incidentally, and said to Annie "Strange how it wearies one." Did you get home smoothly? How do you do?   Affectionately

Ellen

8 May 1882

Darling Girl,

I'm afraid you were surprised and displeased that I did not write a word to send you with all those letters. Now I will make up for it by sending you at least a little letter. Mother is getting better all the time. She has been once at church, and after church she and Cousin Sarah visited Father's grave. She is sad, but in an entirely lovely and peaceful way. A few people have come to see her. Last night the Prichards came. How good and dear they always are! And Louisa and Mr Alcott with tears and tributes. And the night before the Chamberlaines. Mrs French who has seen something of Mrs Bancroft in Washington came with messages from her, and stories of her delicious to Mother. On Friday Mr Bulkeley came up to hold Friday evening meeting since Mr

— 1882 —

Reynolds was away, and of course we sent for him to stay here. After we came home he said "Your Mother doesn't go to bed so early as you. Shan't I see her?" And Mother went down, and in spite of warnings beforehand and reminders later she sat up till ten in the parlour. They are very congenial souls and had everything to say. The next morning he asked if I was too busy to allow him to stay till ten and talk church. Of course I wasn't, and we had a very good hour. On Thursday night Mr & Mrs Sanborn & Mr Alcott came with Dr Bartol, who wished to rehearse before us his Sermon on Father for the coming Sunday. Edward arrived in time to hear the end. It was most of it satisfactory and extremely interesting. Whatever we criticized he was quite willing to change. On Friday afternoon I had a visit from Carry Wheildon which was oh so sweet to me! She said she had asked Alice to come with her but Alice had said "I can't. I feel too badly." Yesterday as we came out from the Communion Service Alice asked to come home with me, and stayed some time, a very interesting and yet perplexing visit, which must I think lead to something further. Edward & Annie and I have had a journey to Boston in company and met and dined together. A delightful day! Yesterday Mr Hussey preached and came to see me in the afternoon. That was also a very good time. I'll send you more letters directly. Nina & Mrs Cabot are coming on Thursday for a round week, and Mr Cabot for one of the days. Your letter was a beauty. Every word about the children was eagerly devoured.

Thy Sister.

8 May 1882

Dear Haven,

It was very hard to be able to see so little of you while you were here. I don't believe you felt so sorry for it as I did, but it could not be helped. Meanwhile your presence was an abiding pleasure. That Sunday was to me throughout far more beautiful than sad. Everything was as I wished or better than I had thought. Indeed all, all! from the beginning, has been touching and lovely. All the week a steady stream of letters has made me glad. People have written beautiful things to us. On Tuesday Mother began again to sleep, and since then she has been picking up. Yesterday she was able to go to church and afterwards she walked over to Father's grave. Cousin Sarah is with us, and is a comfort to us both. Edward is getting a little rested, Annie says. For me, I had no fatigue that one night's sleep did not carry off. Charley & Therchi have been

very kind and attentive. You didn't bring me the photographs of Ruth and Haven, or did you bring them and forget to give them to me? Give my love to my dear Susy and tell her I want them.   Affectionately
Ellen T. Emerson.

Concord 16 May 1882

Oh forgive me my darling that I haven't written sooner to tell you what you already know, the joy and eagerness with which they all—Mrs Cabot not least—received every detail that I could give them about that round ruddy enchanting baby. We are all so thankful to have a Baby that we do not ask whether it is a boy or a girl. I visited Charley last night and learned that Will had brought only good news of you and the minute being. Mother sends you a great deal of love. I may not come till Friday morning, but probably Thursday on 4.02 train from here and 5.30 or 6 from Boston. Mrs Cabot, called home yesterday noon by apparently mortal illness of her cousin Mrs Storer, will not return, and Nina & I miss her sadly. Dr Titcomb is engaged to Miss Fanny Rodman, and William Goodwin to Miss Ellen Chandler, Mrs Lyman's adopted daughter. Mrs Cheney will send your violets this week.
Ellen

Milton, 18 May 1882.

Dear Mother,

I came out at three with Will & Mac & Jim Russell in a fine hail-&-rain-storm which they regarded with indignation. There was to have been a lawn-tennis game in Milton this afternoon. Mrs Curry, the boys' music-teacher drove up in the carry-all with us. She said Cameron had surprised her by doing so well this winter at his practising. He reads his notes easily and his *time* is very good. Edward seems to have the best ear, but not a proper sense of time. When we entered the house the whole six proved to be at dinner. Mrs Curry bore Cameron away. All were surprised to see me and still more to learn that I was going to stay, so you see I can come home when you want me. Will ascertained before he came to dinner that Edith was having her nap. I haven't yet seen her. But after dinner when Violet and I came upstairs we heard the squeaks of Alexander and went into the dressing-room to enjoy them. Miss Brier did him up in a new flannel blanket, an old one outside, and an afghan over all, while I was informed that far from being the biggest, he was the smallest boy we have had,—only 9½ lbs. Humiliating dis-

— 1882 —

covery! I have ventured to say in Concord that he weighed perhaps 11 lbs. Where shall I hide my head? On carrying him into a good light and surveying him at leisure I feel prepared to say that he is the prettiest baby, except Annie's John, that I remember among the whole twelve I have had the glory of receiving.

Affectionately, a devoted daughter
E. T. E.

Milton, 20 May 1882

Dear Mother,

All are well this morning, and yesterday the baby subsisted entirely by nursing, never cried nor worried, nor spit up one drop,—so we think he & Edith both deserve a prize. He was discovered by Edward all alone in the dressing-room in his basket, wide awake and silent, rolling his two eyes thoughtfully about. Now all my experience with Edith's babies is that when they are awake and not entertained they cry. So we are very proud of Baby. Will calls him Francis, but this makes Edith indignant.

Last night came Violet's present from her baby-sister, the most carefully planned and carefully made table ever seen. Its cupboard doors are carved in high-relief, one with violets, and one with wild roses, and in another place the initials E. F. and E. R. F.* are carved with little laurel-leaves & berries round them. It has elaborate claw feet, and drawers of several sizes, and is made of amaranth wood. Will and Ralph and carpenter Cameron opened the box in the garden-room then carried it up to Edith's room. Violet walked up to the table, all the gas was turned on and the candle lit, Will delivered the keys to her, and she and all the boys together fell upon the task of fitting them. The carving was explored and admired. Then Will & Ralph lifted it and the procession was formed and marched to Violet's room. As he came back, Will said "Cam, I entrust to you the business of taking the box apart. Put all the nails away together, and pile the boards—but not in the garden-room—in the barn." "What does he want to build now?" said Edith. "He has planned a château for Chimo." "Ambitious little fellow!"

Please give Maggy some white paper for drawers from the sky-light closet drawer.   Affectionately
Ellen.

*The baby had finally been named Ellen Randolph Forbes.

— 1882 —

Milton 23 May 1882

Dear Sally,

I am glad to see an opportunity to write to you. I have treated you very ill, but I could not help it, and I know by long experience how charitably you treat my silence. Last summer the Cooking-School prevented my writing, this winter the fact that I could not get my room warm interfered very much with it, and kept me behindhand. People think I shall now find leisure and feel my occupation gone. Oh no indeed! Dear Father! He took hardly a minute of my *time*. He had the fewest wants possible to man, seldom wanted even company, so that I never had to sit with him or go with him, unless he was going where people were. Whatever I had to do for him still remains to be done, or its equivalent does. I thank you for coming to the funeral, and for writing me and Mother such a dear letter afterwards. I am glad you thought that Sunday beautiful. It seemed so to me, all of it. And all the affection for Father that has been showed is lovely. I hear that every week the grave is dressed afresh. And pilgrims still come to the gate and go away again as they did when he was alive. Mother is well again now, and Cousin Sarah is cosseting her while I am here with Edith, so that I think she hardly knows I am gone, except at meal-times. Edith is doing beautifully. Our sixth boy, born on the 14th, was smaller than any of his brethren. They all weighed ten pounds, he only nine and a quarter. But he seems to be the healthiest and most contented baby yet. All his Forbes relations are in California except Malcolm & Sarah. The Russell relations have called on him assiduously. The other children are properly pleased with him.

24 May. I have just taken the baby for his first walk. He behaved beautifully. We called on his Aunt Sarah Malcolm who is expecting her baby in a few days. Tomorrow will be Father's birthday, and I shall go home for the day. Mr Cabot wants one day in Concord this week and naturally I chose that for it will be less sad for Mother. When are you coming to Concord? You must give me your two weeks this summer. Let me not forget to thank you for your letter in the winter telling me about John Diman and his Mother. I am always glad to hear of Emma.

Affectionately
Ellen T. Emerson.

Concord 31 May 1882

Dear Edith,

Judge Hoar called on Sunday evening. He was very kind and pleasant

and I showed him the profile of Uncle Charles Emerson. He said it was good. As he went out he said "Mrs Emerson, I have a greater apotheosis than I ever expected to have, in being mentioned in Mr Emerson's will. I would rather have had it than ten thousand dollars." Blessed chance! No one dreamed of its being a pleasure to him when it was put in. I am coming out in the ten o'clock train tomorrow morning, Lizzy Bartlett with me probably. We received your letter with delight. I am very glad Sarah's baby was exactly right, punctual & all. Mother and all of us have enjoyed Dr and Mrs Furness. Well, I'll talk tomorrow instead of writing today. Affectionately
                                                    Ellen.

                                                    5 June 1882
Dear Edith, dear bairn, you seemed so under the weather when I came away I feel very anxious to hear that you are better. I sent Dr Parker to you. When I reached Concord Jessy Barrett Dennie drove me home, as I had not been sent for, and was very pleasant and affectionate. No sooner had I arrived and settled myself than Mrs Dr Jarvis called. Mother was lying down so I received her. She was very pleasant and kind. I think she had not been gone ten minutes when Mr Reynolds brought an English pilgrim. I had a truly joyful and exciting visit from them. They did not stay long, and were almost immediately succeeded by Mrs Richardson who had actually walked all the way down here for the first time in ten years I think. I was very glad to see her and show her various things. Then Mother came down, and presently I heard Edward in the entry. He said he had come to meet Dr Rollins, the young gentleman who photographed the study, for Mrs Cabot had telegraphed that he would be here by the 5 o'clock train. After tea the door-bell rang again. This time it was Mr & Mrs Emery, and Miss Prichard. Mr Emery said Mr Bulkeley had been in the Metaphysical Club with him and he felt quite acquainted with him, and should be surprised if he turned out mediocre, for he always received from him an immense impression of superiority and promise. On Saturday Lidian came to spend the day. And we had a very happy hour or two before dinner. I have once or twice in past years said things to her about her church which the next moment I regarded as very offensive and never begged pardon. So when we had become quite well-acquainted and sociable I confessed my faults, and she told me she had been changing herself, and when she was among bigoted High Church people, found herself revolted by their sense of exclusive possession of Christian

truth, so that when they said that Unitarian heretics would be damned she was impelled to reply she should prefer to be damned with them to being saved with the bigots. This of course gratified me. She told me Mr Phillips Brooks would preach at Lincoln last night, and I promised her and Cousin Sarah the horse & wagon to go. In the afternoon we all went up to the Manse to hear how Miss Ellison did. She has pneumonia and is in some danger. She was a little better. Then we brought Mrs Sanborn home to tea, and she and Lidian studied my new dress & bonnet, and tried every colour of ribbons with them, rejecting all but purples & cardinal. This employment, delightful at the time, and very useful to me, does however cause regret in the end. We might have had so much good talk in that hour. Miss Leavitt came later and we had a delectable tea-time, and laughed and frolicked our fill. Yesterday as it rained I was the only church-goer. Mr Reynolds preached to us in the Town Hall because the carpenters are at work in the church. My dear class was as good and as exciting as ever. And in the afternoon when Cousin Sarah had gone to church I read Mother Mr Brown's sermon of April 30th which had been lent to me in the Christ. Register, and we had some discourse about it. We sat piously in the parlour till 9 o'clock to receive visitors and were rewarded by a very pleasant call from Julian and his wife. They were to start today for the sea-shore with 6 & 7, numbers 1 to 5 having preceded them, then Rose & Mr Lathrop are to return to take possession.

Thursday June 8th. I forbore to write an epistolary word for two days hoping to advance work in the study, but to no purpose, and feel as if I had sacrificed you for nothing. There is only time for one story, and I will choose a purely domestic one. Edward came to call on Monday evening. He had already risen to go and was almost at the door when Mother left her chair, and he immediately said "Come here, Mother!" then commanding and encouraging "Come here." So Mother slowly came and he put one arm round her and took her hand, Mother standing with that half-faint, abstracted, stately air, her head up, her eyes down, that I am sure you will remember as characteristic, as if she felt too sick but was ready to pay attention to whatever was coming, if it proved sufficiently interesting. "Now" said Edward "we are about to give an exhibition of a military character, partly scientific, partly popular. Come, Mother!" and he began keeping time "Now! hay-foot, straw-foot! March! Hayfoot, strawfoot!" And they advanced, Mother still abstracted, stately, without lifting her eyes, but setting down her

feet with that elegance and precision that is natural to her, and lo! as they alternately appeared "Look at Mother's shoes!" cried Edward. She had on a vast knit slipper stuffed with many soles and a boot. It was so funny! It took quarter of an hour to recover. Dear Mr James came yesterday to call. Mother was happily dressed & in the parlour. How do you do? We are going to Boston Sat., any errands?
E. T. E.

Concord, 19 June 1882

Dear Will,

I enclose a copy of Mr Norton's letter in answer to my question whether we should ask leave of Mrs Carlyle or of Mr Froude. On Class-Day he will show me Father's [letter] I hope, I shall ask for it. Doesn't it seem to have been very thoroughly attended to eight years ago by Father & Mr Carlyle themselves? And Father really thought of it and carried it through unassisted by me, he still had plans & memory in those days. Have you seen Mr Cabot? He has two things to say on the subject. First that his idea of his book excludes correspondence *en masse*, he means it to be a sort of *auto*-biography of Father made up in great measure of self-description in characteristic phrases collected from all writings, printed & manuscript, and that it shall give one clear sharp impression of the man himself.

Second, that Carlyle is the dominant figure in the correspondence in question, Father effaces himself very much, and it would belong better in a book about Mr Carlyle than in one about Father.

Can you not write me so that I shall receive it tomorrow morning or tomorrow noon your & Edith's decision? I have Edward's and mine, and I half expect Mr Norton to dine tomorrow. Also say whether you agree with him that there is *no* need of asking leave of Mrs Carlyle.
E. T. E.

F.R.R. 27 June 1882

Dear Edith,

We came home very prosperously, and Mother says she had a thoroughly good time. She speaks with gratitude and joy of a good long talk with Ralph. I feel sorry I didn't get hold of my Alexander once yesterday. When I came home I found the Sanborns getting out of the cars, and carried them home. Mr S. gave me his book about Mr Thoreau and I am carrying it down today to show to Mr Cabot. Mrs Sanborn thor-

oughly agreed with me about Julian's article, and Mr S. who thought it wordy, yet liked it very much. Then as I drove down the street I overtook Miss McClure and Mrs James Wood, two very dear pals, and got them to get in, so I had a beautiful time both up & down the street. The wagon—I mean carryall—is all restored and varnished and looks very fine. Mother & Cousin Sarah stayed behind in Boston, would not come out with me, or rather couldn't, because the milliner had Mother's bonnet not half done at my last minute, so they had to let me go, with such terror & anxiety lest they should get lost as was almost amusing. But as I expected when they came home they had had a delightful time, done so many errands, experienced such leisure, to say nothing of the glory of taking charge of themselves that it was quite evident comfort stepped in when I stepped out. In the evening I took a little walk with Miss Angelina Ball, how affecting it is when a shy person ventures to tell a little of what she thinks & knows, especially when she has so good a mind & wide an experience as this noble creature. When I came in we unpacked the trunk and Mother & Cousin Sarah & I had quite a frolic. I am glad you are doing pretty well, and will come to you as much as I can.
            Ellen

                 Concord, 3 July 1882
Dear Edith,
 Cameron is both happy and very good. He has plans, ambitions and pleasures of his own, and falls in readily with any propositions of mine. Whatever he says he doesn't want to do, he presently informs me that he has done. The longer he stays the better we shall like it.
 Mr Bulkeley came yesterday to spend Sunday at Mr Reynolds's and returns to Cambridge this morning. After the ordination Mrs Bulkeley who is invited to the Reynolds's for the 12th will come to our house to spend Sunday. We shall have no guests at the ordination, except Grace Minns. Send word what days you want me, and very likely it will prove that I can come. Of course I shall delight to.
            E. T. E.

                Concord, 10 July 1882.
Dear Mr Cabot,
 We all of us, though we enjoyed the manner of your letter more than we can tell and all the side sentences of it were very sorry for your decision announced in it, and we beg you to change it. All you say is

perfectly true till you come to Father's plan being hyperbole. We were all greatly delighted with it, and we wish the boys to take the money. When we were young we each had a thousand dollars left to us, and we have each enjoyed having it every year since,—Father knew how much. So he hoped your boys would take the same pleasure in this. And he had enough, thanks to Will's good care, to do it easily, and we have enough. So please let it stand just as he left it. It need not diminish in the least your joy or ours in the splendor of the good fortune that Father and all of us could have you to do all this work for him; changed by your taking it, from a load and an anxiety to a constantly new wealth and delight.

Mother sends her love and says these are her very sentiments.

I shall send this week the note-books and copy you asked for, and probably some questions.

Ellen T. Emerson.

13 July 1882

Dear Puss,

I send Cameron's leavings and the veil you lent Mother. Our Violet's presence was delightful to me at our Ordination. To pick the services to pieces would show I think that only "the charge" was as beautiful as at Mr Washburn's ordination, but take it all in all, it was as touching and elevating as we could wish. Dear Mr Bulkeley! His feeling showed itself in every movement. When he entered the church with Mr Reynolds talking to him, there was the look of perfect freedom to enter into external details because of the settled solemnity within which these could not disturb. He sat down in the front pew, and was lost sight of among taller men till Mr Hall went up into the pulpit and began to read Father's hymn, then he rose and walked up the steps, there was a humbleness, an awe, and yet an assurance and peace in it, that made you feel that he assumed the whole responsibility of his calling with the trust that he was to be baptized for it of the Holy Ghost. Then they both sat down. Mr Hall and he alone were in the pulpit for the ordaining prayer. It was beautiful, but I missed the ceremony of three. First Mr Hall came forward and as he said Let us pray Mr Bulkeley rose and came to his right hand. Dr Briggs' charge brought his tears, and he could not keep them quite back. Mr Hornbrooke's prayer & the Ordaining Hymn were all we could wish. At the Hall when he spoke he was pale, and as everyone says, his face was as the face of an angel. His coming so at such a moment endeared him to his people incredibly.

Now they feel that he wanted them to know, wanted their sympathy, and they have given it. I have ten times more to say but no time.

Concord, 29 July 1882

Dear Edith,

Your letter about the journey gave utter delight. Chimo's adventures were funny and melancholy. What a time poor Cameron must have had with him! The only reason why I should not come to Naushon is that I haven't yet written a letter in answer to Father's friends since you went away, except one to Mr W. H. Channing, and that Mr Cabot and Mr Norton are both waiting for material. I mean to go to Manchester to see Ida, and to Jamaica Plain to see Aunt Adams, and plan no other visits. Mother is pretty well, but suffers a little from confining herself strictly to the house. If I attend to my work I omit her. If I attend to her I do nothing else.

Mr Bulkeley is a daily delight to her. She is always looking forward to her next talk with him. He is engaged and Miss Warren dined with us the other day according to a plan he & Mother made. Miss Warren seems a very good mate for him as far as one can guess by an hour. She is as innocent, cheerful & unconscious as he, as little too, and as young, loves her church and her Sunday-School Class, and her parents, and behaves very sensibly with her lover. She was pleased with the donkey and rode it when she went away as far as Aunt Lizzy's, Mr Bulkeley following highly enjoyed the spectacle. I have everything to tell you but not a minute. Mr Cabot asks for all letters to you during Father's sickness.   Affectionately

Ellen

Concord 8 Aug 1882

Dear Will,

I have a note from Mr Norton saying that he has consulted Harpers, Houghton and Osgood, that Mr Osgood offers the best terms, the stereotype-plates to be made at his, O.'s, expense, yet be Mother's property, and a royalty of 20 percent on retail price paid her on all sales. These terms he has accepted, so Osgood will be the publisher. Mr Norton says he is now looking up the subject of copy-right in England, and suggests that the royalty on copies there should be assigned to Mrs Alexander Carlyle. I think that would be no more than decent, yet I am

— 1882 —

afraid I never, never should have thought of it. It is a long time since I have written to Edith or heard from her. I don't know where you are, but hope this will reach you in some sort of season.

E. T. E.

E.R.R. 11 Aug. 1882

My dear Edith,

    I went yesterday to spend the night with Ida and had various happy times. First Major Higginson was at home and he sat with Ida & me and talked with us for an hour before dinner. After dinner I went straight over to Mr Cabot's and had an hour of work & play with him and he walked half way home with me. I brought him an old letter which told about Father's going to an examination, as a sample, and asked him whether such things were what he wanted. He read it and said "Oh yes! all such things." So you may whenever in any old letters you come across descriptions of any of his doings, mark each on the margin and send it to him. We all went to drive when I got back to Ida's. Col. Harry Lee & Mrs Lee & Mr Cabot came to tea. We had—*of course*—one of the finest times imaginable. After tea they talked about the War all the evening. Mr Lee said "They talk about our indecisive battles! Indecisive they were, *because nobody would run away*. They would stop fighting whenever fighting ceased to be worth while, but never thought of running away,—on either side." This Major Higginson agreed to "Now at Cedar Creek," he said, "we found men going to the rear. When we asked them What for? they said Because things were going badly and no one seemed to be directing, but the moment we told them" (I forget exactly what) "they were all ready to turn and go in again" They praised Mr Newhall's book, and Major Higginson said he considered Gen. Sheridan the best field officer alive, anywhere. It was all nectar and ambrosia. Then this morning Hatty Putnam came to see me and brought her two daughters and Mr Cabot came again & now I am going home.   Monday. Concord. I found your beautiful long letter at home. I am most thankful to know about you once more. I greatly envy you Effie's visit, though no, I would rather you should have her than I, I care so much about your having friends. Try hard to get well and if you find you need me any time tell me and I'll try to arrange it. Mr Hornbrook preached here yesterday and stayed with us. We had a happy time. All four of us took hold and studied Galatians Saturday

— 1882 —

evening, and with Uncle George we read Romans XI on Sunday evening. That was glorious. Tonight we are going to tea at the Emery's.
Thy affectionate sister
E. T. E.

Concord, 21 Aug. 1882

Dear Edith,

I have spent my writing-time for the past few days in what might be called a desultory attack on the huge pile of letters due, and have advanced from one to four pages on those to Frank Nash, Hermann Grimm, Emma Diman & Pauline Shaw, besides getting two sheets of my account of Father's illness written for Mr Cabot.* Mother has felt better the last two days. Cousin Sarah goes this afternoon. Your letter to Mother gave us great satisfaction, & that & your other two letters have each been read several times over. Last Monday Mother, Cousin Sarah & I took tea at the Emery's and in the evening Mr Emery got out his Emerson's Essays and read us from its fly-leaves his record of Father's talk with him in 1866. This set us all talking and we had one of the most beautiful evenings people ever have. On Saturday Mrs Sanborn spent the day with us, on Friday Mr Bulkeley came home unexpectedly, and we were delighted. Alicia, Grace Minns, Annie Lazarus & Emma Smith dined with us & him & we had a happy day. Alice & Cary Wheildon took tea with us and Alice & Mr Bulkeley sang. Great joy.
Last minute.

At Aunt Adams's. Thursday, 24 Aug. 1882

My dear Edith,

Cousin Abby is receiving a call so I write to you. Your remarks about coming up early are encouraging. Do seriously entertain the idea. The one drawback to my joy in going to Saratoga is that I shall be away on Mother's 80th birthday, and it is only too possible that we can never celebrate another. If you come up early you can be here. My dear Lizzy Simmons has spent one day with me and departed. The dear Miss Prichards are the most lovely watchful and steadfast friends. They come to see Mother in the evening and she likes it better than almost anything, and they bring her beautiful bouquets. I see the sentimental use of flowers this summer very clearly; when the Hosmers, the Prich-

*See Appendix, p. 670, for this letter.

— 1882 —

ards, the Emerys, Alice Wheildon, the Norcrosses, or George Bartlett bring her flowers I see how good it feels to her, to them; yea, to me also. I have been guilty of carrying some myself to several people. Mrs Sanborn is very delicate, very suffering, I cannot bear to see her so thin, so black and white. She spent a day with us, and was as enchanting as ever, but seemed feeble all day. On Monday night Anna McClure invited me to row on the river with her and take tea up the N. Branch somewhere. Edward & Annie invited Mother to tea with them, and truly it was one of the pleasantest things that could be, that row. Almost the first I ever took without having to watch the minutes anxiously. It was clear and still, and moon large enough to make perceptible moonlight. The river really is as pretty as it ever was, in spite of all the lamentation about Vandals & R.R.s. I had the rowing too, coming home, and that was delightful.

Ellen

Concord 1 Sept. 1882

Dear Brethren and Descendants,

Mother and I are having a beautiful life. Mother to my surprise announced that she didn't mind company any more, she had got used to it and liked it. Then Mrs Sanborn stopped in and invited her & me to tea on Monday night to meet Mr Channing and Mrs Emery, and Mother willingly walked all the way there. We had a beautiful evening, all of us. Mrs Sanborn and I talked peacefully as in solitude upon the sofa, and, whenever we stopped to listen, the talk of the other three was serious and delightful. We all came away together. The moonlight has been uncommonly glorious this week. I might have died of the rapture of seeing it that night and the next if it hadn't been so damp and chill that I hardly could feel it at all. Mother walked all the way home too. As I expected she said in the morning that she had had a capital night's sleep. On Tuesday Anna came to tell us that Miss Gage was to sing at their house in the evening and asked Mother to come to hear her if she liked. Mother unhesitatingly accepted, but ordered the carryall. After tea Mrs Fay Barrett and Lucy appeared, and brought a pomegranate. They went punctually at ten m. of 8, and Mother & I rode up to the Emery's. Oh I do love that family. I am utterly at home with every one of them. And they do cosset Mother as she likes and needs. No guests except Miss Gage and the Whaleys. Mr McClure sang the Friar of Orders Grey, that was wholly satisfactory. Miss Gage played so that it

was a pleasure to see her, her hands were pretty and she had no tricks. When she sang it was all very well though a little tempestuous, but Mother couldn't catch a word and innocently thought to herself that perhaps the lady had gone crazy, and wondered, as she is wont, that anyone should indulge in such sharp shrieks in the name of music. At nine I brought her away. On the way home each night she seemed very feeble and very sad, indeed if she walks out in the daytime it is the same. She walks very slowly and says only sad things. She wishes every day that it were all over, and many things make me feel as if she would not live long, but whenever anybody comes, and a great deal of the time, she is ready to talk and bright so that we enjoy life every day. She is having very good nights now that she walks. Mail-time has come. Affectionately
                                        E. T. E.

                    F.R.R. en route to Saratoga
                         18 Sept 1882   Hurrah!
My dear Edith,
  You shall have a word from your silent sister, oh no! when one is riding through the finest scenery in the State perhaps one's duty is to look at that instead of at one's relations and one's paper. Sept. 21. Last night I wrote to Mother instead of going to bed, and now I am staying at noon in the church to save money and time so I can write for a few minutes. Church lasts from 9 till long after 1. I am seeing my many friends and comparing notes about the meetings all the time between that & 3 when it begins again. I have to be sociable even if I didn't consider the society the fine nectar that I do. All my minister friends are here. Mr Jones has just shaken hands with me with a grasp and a might that show he is a lion indeed physically. This is the third time I have seen him and he came both this time and the time before without a word, only shining right into my eyes the sense "we are intimate friends just the same though we never have had the chance", and away he goes borne by the various businesses he is driving. I have made the acquaintance of half a dozen new ministers, ten or twenty laymen, American and foreign, and more ladies than you can count. Everybody is full of zeal and joy. We passed the contribution-box yesterday to get money for New Orleans and 1581 dollars were put into it! Yesterday was a better day than today, more discussion and less reading. The Hungarian delegate is an interesting man and has that *very precious*

air Don used to have. It is as captivating in the man as it used to be in Don. Everybody is taken with it. I am in the highest possible feather, and only wish life contained for everybody such an exceptional draught of joy as this is for me, and to dear Miss Ball. Goodbye till I can get home again. I hope your visit at home was brilliant.   Affectionately
Ellen.

Saratoga, Methodist church
Thursday 21 Sept. 1882

My dear Violet,

Your aunt is sorry that so interesting a letter as you sent her has not yet been acknowledged. What a pity that Waldo and Ellen should fight so! Isn't it curious that the two names should come together again? forty years ago it was my brother & I, now it is my nephew & niece. I am sorry to miss your visit in Concord. Here we sit all day long to listen to the history of the churches, and yesterday when the New Orleans church was to be given to we had such interesting speeches you would have rejoiced to be here and hear them. We have had glorious times. A temperance resolution was introduced tonight, a total-abstinence resolution, and that caused a most lively discussion, some people didn't want it voted on but cries arose in all directions. I like nothing better than an exciting subject in a crowded house! and this was just that—whenever one man was talking the rest would say "Amen", and "No" and "Hear", and "Don't stop, go on!" and when he sat down six would rise, and Governor Long quick as lightning would say "Mr ——— hasn't spoken before, he has the floor", then five would sit down. At last someone proposed that for this question everyone should vote by rising and standing to be counted, this was agreed to, then someone asked Gov. Long to read the rule as to who had a right to vote. Finally we were called to stand to our principles. I didn't know what to do. *I* am total abstinence and fully believe the doctrine but Uncle Edward says I am wrong, and I don't know that he isn't right. At last I decided to get up with the total abstinence people, there were 125, and 3/4 of them were men. The people who didn't believe in it got up afterwards, about thirty, four or five women among them. I was pleased to see that total abstinence got the vote and that so many men believed in it. We have had many meetings as eager and busy as this, and so much fun, we have laughed harder than people do at the theatre, almost at every meeting, sometimes there were 1500 in the house to sing and to laugh and to applaud together, and the more the delegates found how delightful the meetings were, the more they were sure to be at every one, so that each day the church has been fuller, from dawn till dark. Come and see your old aunt when you can, and bring Mary too sometime.

Your affectionate
Aunt Ellen.

21 Oct. 1882

Dear Edith,

I desire first of all to thank you for your beautiful letter telling of the hymn-singing. I hope that will become an institution. Has my dear Violet joined the singing-class, and did she enjoy it? Tomorrow Alice Bartlett is coming and will stay through the week. The English Mr & Mrs Carpenter have arrived in Boston, and I have written to ask them for Wednesday & Thursday. I promised to tell you about Ellen Parkman's wedding. She looked as pretty as possible and was affectionate and lively, no bride was ever better, her dress was truly beautiful, and when she went down to the dining-room to cut the cake, the dear little Elliot Cabot twins bore her train, instructed by their Mother, and we thought it the prettiest of sights. Her veil was bought in Brussels by her Uncle Edmund Dwight long ago, he gave it to her Aunt Ellen Twistleton for her wedding-veil. She sent it home to be Mrs Cabot's wedding-veil, and now it was used for the third time. I had a good time with Ruth Cabot, who is a Sunday-School teacher, and afterwards with Marny Warner who was so funny as well as interesting that I hated to leave her at all. She sent much love to you. Mrs Cabot said her next pleasure was to be coming to Concord. Edward and I have written to her about Father's bequest. Last Thursday I went to the Framingham Convention—prevented at the last min. from going on Wednesday night. When I came home my dear Ida and Pauline were already here, both looking well and young, and delight for me began. The only disappointment was that the great show I planned for them had to be given up. Anna McClure was going to take us up the river. Now Friday was a cold day, East wind, hard clouds all over the sky and an occasional ten minutes of pale sunlight here or there. So I went to tell Anna we would come in the afternoon if it was better, and then we walked to the Cliffs. That was satisfactory, the colours of the trees lighted the world without the sun's help, the distance was clear, walking kept us warm. I had a hope that the weather would moderate by afternoon, but it

— 1882 —

didn't—it grew worse. So we stayed at home, and alas! at night Pauline went. The next morning it was almost as bad, and Edward said with my cold I must not go on the river. Miss Bartlett took Ida a little way, so she got some idea, and I meanwhile went to ask Mrs Sanborn, Miss Leavitt, and Mrs Capt. John Brown to dine on a roast goose with Mother. They agreed to come and it was a great pleasure all round. I picked up Ida at Miss Bartlett's and oh what a blessed time I did have with her in the remaining hour before she went. I learn from her in almost every interview. Edward & Annie to see us yesterday with little Ellen. I suppose Annie considered it the farewell call before her confinement. Edward brought your letter telling of Will's return. We are very glad that he is at home and has gained something by the vacation. Mother seems to me pretty well, though Edward says she is looking badly. Last Sunday she walked up to Mrs Sanborn's and home after church, and went to church again in the evening. Maggy looks out for her very prettily, warms her shawl for her, and runs to open a door for her. Mr Bulkeley seems more and more a member of the family, brings things to read to us, takes pains about Mother's dinner, tells us his plans. We have a very good time with him.   Affectionately

E. T. E.

Concord, 28 Oct. 1882.

Dear Mrs Lewis,

I am glad at last to sit down with confidence that I shall be able to write you a letter to thank you for your generosity to me. Three times you have sent me a letter full of lovingkindness since my Father died, and I have been grateful for each one. Mother was as much interested as you hoped in the account you gave of the meeting your Society held in memory of Father. I am glad you cared so much about Judge Hoar's address. How beautiful it was! He is farther from hard and cold than any man I know of. He is very bright, can snub people gloriously, and does it with innocent delight on every occasion, not knowing apparently that it hurts them as much as it pleases him. But except for that he is all affection and tenderness. He came like an uncle to help us in every way, and when Edward told him he would rather hear his voice at the funeral than anyone's else, he said he didn't believe it would be possible for him to speak and not break down. But he did and every word seemed to us the fittest thing that could be said. Why, Judge Hoar is the heart of this town, he plans and leads everything beautiful & fraternal that is done in it. We too were very much interested in what Julian Hawthorne wrote, We didn't know that he knew so much about Father or felt so much affection for him. Poor Julian! he & his wife have lost little Gladys, one of the most exquisite babies the world ever saw, I thought, and of course they did. She was buried here a month ago. The photographs returned in good order, and I enjoyed your remarks upon them. How good that you appreciate our Don. He is one of the sweetest steadiest brightest of children. Edward always thought him the best of the boys till an intimate acquaintance with little Edward rather shook this conviction. I am happy to say I think each one is far the best when I am looking at him. The little Alexander is no exception. Annie is expecting her fifth, today or tomorrow, I shall keep this envelope open to put in the announcement.   Sun. 29 Oct. Little Florence Emerson was born this morning at nine. She is a round little creature, looks much like Charles & little Ellen. We are entirely satisfied with her & her name.

> Affectionately
> Ellen T. Emerson.

> 8 November 1882

Dear Edith,

Last night Mr Harris came to tea. He talked philosophy at first. I never heard him before, I was interested and understood very well. Then he talked about Father with Mother while I was upstairs, and when I came down he was saying that Father felt that people were looking at the form and forgetting that the thing itself was the point, and had set himself to show them the thing again, and most gloriously and beautifully he had fulfilled his work. Then he said that he believed the Correspondence between him and Mr Carlyle would be the greatest book that has appeared for fifty years, because in this, besides its being the interchange of confidence between two great souls, one thing that Father had carefully removed every trace of in his printed work—his personality—must appear. In every book so far we have only seen the light, now surely we are to feel the fire itself. I remembered that Mr Cabot had said that Father had utterly effaced himself in this correspondence, so that it would be properly placed in a life of Mr Carlyle, but not in one of Father. But I thought it prudent to withhold this view, as perhaps Mr Harris would find in the letters more of what he hoped for than Mr Cabot's words would lead me to expect. I am sorry I haven't

— 1882 —

written for so long. Frances Brown has been here this week, and will stay till Monday. Our new plumbing is in progress and will be different from the old. Little Florence on Thursday was so bright and cunning I got a very charming impression of her. Annie is almost well. Mother is very thriving. I hope you have been successful in New York and have had a beautiful time with Mrs Bowditch. My green bonnet has had a new harvest of praise on occasion of its first appearance yesterday when I went to Mr Russell's Ordination at Weston. I hope to hear from you, and from Violet, soon. Dear Miss Roxa made us a lovely visit.

E. T. E.

22 Nov. 1882

Dear Edith,

I am sorry I cannot see you on your birthday. How seldom I do! Last year I did. Aren't you glad you were at home with your papa and mamma on the last birthday you ever could be? I think that was very good. Mother and I send you our love. Your Mamma says she would write you a letter if she were able but now you will have to imagine a beautiful and affectionate letter and read it to yourself in your mind. I think you and I have had very pleasant times this last year, and I will try not to be so thorny in the future as I am apt to be even to the present day. I am looking forward all the time to your coming next week. Oh! Mother begs you not to make Will come here if he wants to go elsewhere. She is very much afraid he will be dragged in this direction against his will, whether she thinks his fierce wife or his conscience will do it I am not certain. I want him to come for my part. If he does, bring music along—especially "I'm very fond of a social glass". Singing is becoming common here, with Mr Bulkeley. Mr McClure sings bass and came down to sing on Saturday and was so able and agreeable. I'm sure you would both like him. Then Will Barrett is another great musical friend of Mr B.'s and we could easily have "I'm very fond of a social glass" on Wednesday or Saturday evening. Your New York letter was very welcome and very interesting. Annie Damon's Mother died on Saturday. We have been at the funeral this afternoon. Annie Emerson is down-stairs today. Mother and I are invited to dine at Mrs Sanborn's on Thursday, I am perfectly delighted. Today Miss Warren is coming to spend the day here.

Affectionately,
my dear Edith,
E. T. E.

1882

10th Dec. 1882.

Dear Edith,

Mother ate with thankfulness the quails, and rejoices much in the parsley. I have spread some to dry, but she uses much of it for green in her vases. Edward came on Thursday evening and read Brook Farm with us. Mother was arranging said vases with all the flowers you sent, and arranging them—oh dire! you will say—with the parsley, and called on him for sympathy with her admiration of the combination. He said it was pretty. The next day he exclaimed when he came again & saw it "Colours seen by candlelight Do not look the same by day!" and became as violent against it as you had been. Mother disappointed & aggrieved remained staunch to her standard of beauty. The Cabots came. Mother adopted Mrs Cabot as a daughter, and agreed to call her Lizzy. I had meetings on Friday night as you know, and that was the time which was chosen for Edward to read Father's "Amita" to the cousins and try to incite them to reminiscences. He told me that he considered the evening very successful and when dear Lizzy came up to bed she said all I could desire about Cousin Hannah & Cousin Sarah both. Yet the visit was a failure in a business point of view. Mr Cabot brought his arrangement of Education for us to read, and we couldn't. He carried it home again. Absolutely nothing accomplished there. Edward submitted his arrangement of Aristocracy but Mr Cabot couldn't look at it. He carried that home. In future he shall have the garret to work in if he likes. I learned that the present method of four in the study at once is bad. Cousin Hannah enjoyed the days. At breakfast she said "I don't know whether you want to go into so deep a question, but I often think it over. How do you explain it to yourself that among Uncle's children there should have been three such geniuses and in all the rest of the family in all its branches mediocrity or something below mediocrity? Yes, whichever way you look, stupidity, ignorance & insanity." I think she was very hard on the family, but there is some ground for her view of it, and when we looked about we found we had several insane relations. Today I came to Boston with too many errands to come down to see you.

Much love to you.
E. T. E.

January 1883 – November 1885

Quiet winter. Mr. Cabot works on RWE's writings. William James lectures. Picnics and social life. Fires at Walden. 1884. Matthew Arnold visits. Trip to Plymouth, Milton visit. 1885. Social life and parties in Concord. Circuit meeting and visiting ministers. Family visit to Plymouth.

Thursday, 18 Jan. 1883

My dear Edith,

You have been very long-suffering and I have felt it. But my conscience has not reproached me much for I have been trying hard to be of use to Edward with "Education" and have given him some solid time and accomplished something. Certainly I have rigidly kept my vow of inviting no one even to tea so far, and it is well I made it for the temptation has been strong. Tomorrow I transgress for the first time, and I don't mean to again. I have asked one of my scholars to come and have a talk at five o'clock and go to Friday meeting with me at 7. Mother has been getting well gradually, but has not yet gone out. She volunteered permission to go to the Frolic Club play that night when I came home. On Sunday morning Mr Bulkeley preached uncommonly well, it was one of those sermons, which he is capable of, which are like a poem with a refrain that delights you, and returns always unexpectedly and with a new point. As I came out of church no one spoke of it—though many have since—but I had a particularly happy progress, so many people were waiting to speak on business or something. Mrs Hubbard desired to tell me of Annie Wetherbee's engagement, a piece of news most refreshing, poor solitary child! Down in S.S. good time with my girls, and the pleasure of seeing Mrs Bulkeley & her brother-in-law & father-in-law drawn up in a row and suddenly remembering what the occasion must have been to them I felt doubly thankful for the beautiful service. On Monday I visited the new house & household, and carried milk. Lizzy Bartlett looked out of the window and cried "Oh I'm so glad to see some cream coming! I was just wanting it. *Ellen*!! Are you carrying that to the new minister? Now that's what I call mean,—going back on an old friend when you get a new one. The heathen don't do so, Martha says. If you had been a heathen you wouldn't have done it. But see how these Christians love one another!" She shut the window and withdrew. I enjoyed my visit to the new family nevertheless. That day I dined with Edward & Annie & the next day Edward went to Brookline & Annie brought both the little girls to dine. Mother is uncommonly captivated by Florence. She holds her much more than she usually does a baby and watches her every minute. We had a beautiful time. I took tea at Mrs Reynolds' for the first time in my life. The Hungarian Unitarian delegate to our Saratoga Conference was there, and of all the easy social strangers none could be desired more lively than he. I shivered a little in my skin, as I remembered experiences with people who couldn't talk English, before I went. But he could! I shouldn't dread having him on my hands a whole day. The next day he came and stayed an hour here and I really was sorry to have him go. Cary Hoar, Alice & Prescott, Mr & Mrs Bulkeley were the other guests and we had a little of them all, but talked most with him. At 7.30 Cary Hoar & I bade goodnight and hastened to the Frolic Club at Alice Wheildon's. It was very exciting to see people bearing down on the gateway from behind us, from across the street, from down town, yes even sleighs arriving. Annie Bartlett waited on the door, Miss H. Buttrick was usher, Lizzy Bartlett sat on the arm of the sofa sparkling with malice, Louisa Alcott occupied the other arm; between sat the deaf. Sister after sister shone upon the sight, and many a sister's mother, yes Mrs Rockwood Hoar was there, and Mrs Joe Brown and Mrs Richardson, in one row sat the Miss Balls their eyes beaming with serene delight, in the next the married sister; Mrs Buttrick had brought a married friend, dear Mrs Humphrey Buttrick; there further forward were the Weirs, and Susy Brown behind them. Miss Leavitt & Mrs Sanborn were in a distant corner, Abby Gourgas & Cary Cheney & her mother I saw. It was great fun finding out who was there. The play was only too short,—*very* funny!—some of it admirably acted. If only they would have begun it again and acted it right over I should have been better satisfied. The great actors were Miss Carleton & Louise Norcross, Anna McClure was the young lady, Cary Wheildon had about as much to do as she, a little less to say, and was so full of airs & graces, & quick like a squirrel in every movement that she made every one laugh all the little time she was on. The others, Sarah Richardson & Abby Brown were much heard of but hardly appeared at all. Alice wrote the play & was stage manager. Wonderful child! Yesterday the Bulkeleys first reception came off. I didn't go, but in the morning I went to see them; Mrs B. showed me the house in glorious newness & order, and Mr B. brought his cat, his own cat, to exhibit. The fattest of Maltese kittens. Dear Puss, all my New Years presents are delightful, my shawl is the pride of my heart, and so is the tie; so is the pincushion. Please don't give me three New Years presents at once again. I like *one*. Mr Brown of Brookline will preach, and stay with us. Don't you want to come for Sunday?

Your affectionate sister
Ellen

Concord, 19 Feb. 1883

Dear Edith,

Let me attempt to express my gratitude for your letter which has at last filled all the yawning voids. It seems very long to me when I don't hear from you for eight days. It came Saturday night at ten when I was just falling asleep surrounded by so much wide open window and darkness that I concluded to wait till morning. Sunday I found this great treat spread for me, and I may say I spent the whole day in reading the letter. I read it before breakfast, I read it at dinner-time, I read it all through again after dinner to Mother, and selections at six o'clock to Aunt Susan & Lidian. I am sorry to hear that the baby has been so sick, poor dear Edith! what a fright it must have been! The story about Cameron is indeed thrilling. When I read the tale to Edward & Annie, Edward exclaimed "Why that speech of Cam's is exactly like Father! sounds as if it were Father!" What a jump of joy that gave me! for I agree. That reminded me that Mr Harris, who with his wife & son & daughter took tea with us Fri. night, talked again about his confidence that C. will resemble Father. I told Mr Harris that some of Mr Carlyle's letters to Father were missing, much to my surprise. Mr Harris said "Possibly loaned to someone." I said I hardly thought that could have been. After a minute Mr Harris burst out "I know where those letters are! I remember! Your Father told me once that he lent several of Carlyle's letters to Mr Goodson and never could get them back,—that he had asked for them without success." Perhaps it isn't yet too late. I wrote to Mr Norton about it the next day. I am thankful that Waldo is improving at Aunt Alice's; and oh! how glad I am that some of the boys will come up on Wednesday. If they bring company tell them your rules distinctly and send them by the boys to me, written. I look for them by 4.30 train Wednesday. I am interested in the domestic revolution

— 1883 —

Edith E. Forbes and her children, late 1882 or early 1883. Standing at left is Cameron, then Ralph, Edith ("Violet"), and Don, far right. Seated are Edward, left, Waldo, and EEF holding Alexander.

downstairs and hope it will be followed by long peace. Mother sends a great deal of love. Come soon to us.

Thy affectionate sister.

Concord, 24 Feb. 1883

My beloved Edith,

Our boys were nectar & ambrosia to us at tea on Wednesday night, and since. We hated to let Edward & Don go. Tell E. his arctic was found by Mr Reuben Rice's place lying lonely in the road, Cameron shall bring it home. He & Nelson [Perkins] are happy & good and fill our hearts with joy. Where's my Violet? I am grieved that you should be lame again. Mother is enchanted to have a letter and thinks the story

a beauty. Mrs Sanborn is here making life additionally delightful. Last min.! Affectionately
Ellen.

Concord, 3 March 1883
F.R.R. rather. Saturday morning

My dear Edith,

This day has come round to be rejoiced over now the eighteenth time and I rejoice anew and send much love to you both. I desire to thank you for bringing me so good a brother, and both of you for all the kindness and the happiness you have given me, and all the pride and glory I have had in you. I hope to meet you today, but I am afraid your lameness will prevent your coming to dear Aunt Adams's funeral, and I will utilize the time on the cars to tell you that Cameron and Nelson were two dear good boys, and seemed to me to be only a beneficial influence on each other while they were here. I learned that Cameron is the only boy that, like Violet, loves Bush and Concord, and that he does, and considers it a pleasure to come. How surprised I was to find that Nelson sympathizes with my tastes and likes church and Sunday-school. I had expected him to be more averse than my nephews rather than less. So he was not a bad Sunday guest but a perfectly delightful one.

Monday.   I saw blessed Violet, oh how dear she looked! She promised you for the end of the week, oh joy! All I wanted to tell you must wait. I had no time Saturday. Thy affectionate sister
Ellen.

Concord, Monday, 19 Mar. 1883

Dear Edith,

I have just received your telephone and would come oh how gladly! but don't you know I can't? I never go out to tea even unless Mother is invited too. There is no one who can come you know to take my place for Alicia is in Boston for a month and Mother will accept no one else. I could come for the day Wednesday if Mother were well, but she has been sick ever since you went away. I don't know whether she is sick to amount to anything or not, but since she comes down and eats her meals I don't send for Dr Titcomb. She only doesn't feel right, and says she is very babyish and can't bear to have me out of her sight. Though she does when Miss Andrews is here. If she is pretty well on Wednes-

— 1883 —

day I'll come by the 9.03 train and stay till the 3.55. Your boys left "Captain Castaguette". I'll bring that along too. Mother is particularly happy in her jays' behaviour today. Last night she thought she would throw them out her egg-shells and see whether they would peck them. This morning at six I saw one of those jays carrying the egg-shell down into the garden, there he growled over it with delight and sucked & pecked at it, carried it to another spot to enjoy it with new surroundings, and when he finally left the garden he bore his dear egg-shell with him. Mother is going to strow the whole feeding ground with eggshells now. At this very moment with gladness of heart she has found one in her closet and thrown it out of the window hoping to see a jay come with the swiftness of thought. This morning Edward feels better, yesterday he coughed more. They were delighted with your present of fruit and ice-cream. He sent Mother four Tangerinas and they spoke to her condition. You ought to have seen little Florence this morning, she looked desperately cunning. Have any of your larkspur-seeds come up? Draw me the shape their cotyledons are when they appear. Charley & Therchi and Mrs Sanborn dined with us on Saturday and we had a beautiful time. C. seemed anxious to come and to stay as long as he could. He was very affectionate to Therchi, and she was very pleasant to him. I have found one or two little leavings of yours, hdkf the largest.
Affectionately
Ellen.

Edward's parlour   Concord. 24 March 1883

Dear Edith,

Last night Annie was very much alarmed about little Ellen and said Dr Titcomb seemed to be, but she is better this morning. Philip has a cold and that keeps Mrs Keyes at home. I have a cold and our cook has a cold. Colds seem to be the order of the day. On Thursday I wrote to Mr Norton and asked him what had been said to Mrs Carlyle about her share of the profits of the Correspondence and told him we liked the idea of her having the royalty on what was sold in England and looking out for it herself; of making an arrangement once for all which would save continual care and letters and business relations. He has not yet answered. Last night I carried to Ann the little shoes & arctics which she graciously received. She seems to me a little more prosperous than formerly, actually has managed this winter to do the washing of two of the teachers besides all that has to be done for the nine children. Mary

Ellen I suppose does much baby-tending for her. To her joy John Hugh has a place in the market now and regular wages. Alice Wheildon is to have an opera or cantata called "Ruth" at the Town Hall on Wed. April 4. If you are in the neighborhood, or Will, and would like to come to it, do! Everyone asks for you. Tonight we have invited the Chamberlaines to tea. If there is a scare about little Ellen tonight and I am wanted here it will be awkward. Unless Philip is very sick though Mr Keyes can be here in the evening.

Miss Bartlett just came to inquire for little Ellen and went up to see her, she says she sees no indication of measles, and thinks she looks fairly comfortable, and Alice Reynolds Keyes has been here; and my sweet Marion Keyes, she stayed and I had a delightful little talk with her, good child! How it does blow! A gale almost every day this month! This has been a typical March, may April be kinder! Have you kept in mind Father's monument and that some day you are to write a letter to Edward about it? It is time to go home to Mother now. I'll mail this on the way.

A pretty poor correspondent but affectionate sister,
E. T. E.

Concord, 30 March, 1883
I remember our baby

My dear Edith,

I have just finished my paper for the Parish Association. I didn't believe I should get it into shape so soon. It had four beginnings and two endings, all quite voluminous, and there was no body for these extremities but when I had three or four hours to give to it it worked up like so much dough into a good round little loaf, at least I think so and so of course does Mother. To think that now I must wait till my cold gets well before I can lay it before Mrs Hoar! I hope she will consent to it as it is. The news from Annie's yesterday was that little Ellen was down stairs and the baby was coughing as badly as she had been the day before. Today I have not sent but shall before tea. Since I am the link with the outside world when I am shut up in the house we soon drift away from any knowledge of our friends, but I haven't been shut up twenty hours yet. Our festivities lately have been as follows. Last Saturday night we had Mr & Mrs Chamberlaine to tea and had a lively and amiable time. They asked whether Mr Conway's book could be depended on and I told them I saw much that was true, much of which I

— 1883 —

couldn't know whether true or not, and much that wasn't true. They asked for instances and when I mentioned the description of Father's study Mrs Chamberlaine rose—we were in the study—and made a tour asking the history of each picture. Then Mother brought out all the old daguerreotypes to show them. On Sunday we went to church in the morning then over to Edward's where I saw little Ellen lying in bed looking very pretty, but Edward didn't think so, he couldn't bear to see the halo of loose hair and wasn't contented till the front locks were twisted & hair-pinned together behind as usual. Miss Florence was asleep. The rest of Sunday Mother & I stayed in the house and Monday morning. Monday was warm & lovely, my cold almost gone. I went to Boston at noon and attended my Conference Board Meeting, with as much pleasure as I usually have nowadays, it isn't what it used to be with Mr Sears & Mr Green. Mr Hall of Cambridge is our new member. I hope he will make it pleasant and feel pretty sure he will. Have you ever heard stories of his dog? I have. The dog came to the meeting! Jenny Worcester came to tea with us. Tuesday I stayed in and Mrs McClure and Anna came to tea. Poor Mrs McClure! she always does the work of the world and she comes confidently to me to tell me her plans for Temperance work in this town to which I listen with delight but when she assigns me my share I refuse. She bears it with the most ready goodnature, but I feel unhappy for I know everyone else will refuse too. Mother liked her and enjoyed hearing her talk almost as much as I did. On Wednesday I visited Charley & Therchi, then Annie, little Ellen was better than she had been yet. When I came home Mother was hoarse; she had caught a cold too, so we pitied each other and I persuaded her to come down and dine with me for the cold west wind made her room a less suitable place for her than the sheltered dining-room. I found no water in her room to mix her powder with; she proposed Vichy, but I reminded her that we didn't know that its chemical composition would accord with that of the powder. "Are you afraid it will Vichyate its effect?" asked she. She exclaimed at dinner the other day "Did ever an old woman have such luxury before? I can go to bed whenever I want to and can be read aloud to when I am there!" John's hens have begun to promenade in the yard and were not slow to discover the jays' feeding-ground. Mother thought the jays must at least rise earlier in the morning than the hens so for two nights more she scattered corn before she went to bed, but the first morning thereafter we suspected the hens did come first and the second morning there

— 1883 —

could be no doubt that they arrived by five o'clock—before light—so Mother firmly resolved to forsake the jays. But when I came up from dinner she was at the window, this was before she caught cold. "I looked out" she said, "and there wasn't a hen in sight so I thought I'd throw out a little for the jays. I hadn't thrown but one handful before as by magic all the hens were there. How could they have known? I said 'There now! I never will throw out any more' But they picked so eagerly, poor things! that I threw them out two good handfuls, and said 'That is all!' But they seemed so delighted with it, it went to my heart, and I opened the window again and threw them out some more." I meant to have told you that Mrs McClure brought us a little story of Father. She said at tea "Do you remember that a year ago my daughter Anna took tea here when your Father was here?" Of course I did. It was the 14th of April, two weeks before he died, and you know I told you how he undertook to omit his supper and she made him eat it. "Anna recorded this, I wonder whether you will remember it" Mrs McClure went on, "you gave him a biscuit, he took it and let it remain on his plate, you urged him to eat it and he said 'Must I break down his little house,—to build up my own?'" I didn't remember it in the least, but doesn't it sound just like him, and isn't it pretty? Well, I had got to Wednesday noon. After dinner I went to Bible Society at Mrs Todd's where there were twenty-eight members and we had a beautiful time. Mrs Wm. Hunt was there and told me about her adopted baby. Its name is Emily, and 'twill be a year old in two weeks. Teachers' Meeting at Mr Bulkeley's followed in the evening; Beth was the object of my delighted contemplation, discipline the subject of discussion. When I came home Mother's cold still made her hoarse, but she put me to bed as the worst of the two, and then brought me your flowers. Thursday Kate Rouse came. Mother & I viewed the flowers with admiration. It was Charley Prescott & Ida Davis's wedding-day, so we sent them the orange-blossoms, the rose, the heliotropes and some acacia. All the rest we kept at home because Mrs Cheney & Caroline & the Bulkeleys were coming to dine. Mother is charmed with the great pink Bouvardia. They came to dine and we had great pleasure all together. Mr Bulkeley never seemed so crazy about his wife before, and I was delighted to see it. She played for Mrs Cheney after Mother had gone upstairs. At seven I went to the wedding. The room was full of new-married people & engaged pairs, and Mr Bulkeley's prayer suited them well. Mr Reynolds married the couple beautifully, according to the King's Chapel service

though the "I, Ida, take thee Charles" was omitted. Today Mother's cold is almost gone. It is mail-time. Affectionately
Ellen.

Concord 2 April 1883

My dear Miss Dabney,

I haven't written to you since I wrote to tell you about Father's death, and you have written to me a great many times meanwhile. I have been trying to answer the kind letters that came to me from everyone after he died and I have not yet answered nearly all. I knew you would let me leave you in silence a long time and would not be displeased nor wonder at me, so I have gone right on with others first, and now I shan't have to let your birthday pass. I can write today. Your letter to me about your room was written April 27th the day Father died. It came to me in May when I was spending with Edith the first weeks of her confinement when Alexander was born. Then in July came your dear letter about Father and about our baby's birth. Alexander is a beautiful baby, not strikingly handsome but without a striking defect and with the most perfect colouring. In your October letter you spoke of reading Dean Stanley. I wonder what book it was. I sometimes in extracts from his speeches, in the papers, have seen things that seemed to me up to his fame, but the books I have read do not delight me, except as recalling him, and I love *him*. I have within a week or two begun to read to Mother his book on "Christian Institutions" and I like its opening very much. You said in that letter too that dear Miss Dabney had sent out to you an account of our Mr Bulkeley's Ordination, tell her I thank her very much for that. It was a very beautiful day in all our lives. This was to more than three-fourths of the Congregation the first Ordination they had ever seen, it was some fifty years since there had been one in Concord. This made it very impressive to them. And the dear boy himself felt all that anyone could. Then the whole concourse went over to the Town Hall to the dinner, and there, after dinner, heard that Mrs Bulkeley had died. It was most affecting to us to have Mr Bulkeley come right to the Hall and speak to us before he went away. He lived with us from Sept. till January when he was married. This was great comfort to Mother & me and we miss him still. We love his wife however and they are good children to us. The enthusiasm of the Parish over a new and young minister is delightful to feel and to witness, the young people of his age and younger, down to quite little girls & boys who were growing up, or had already grown up, in absolute indifference to the church now consider it their church and come with zeal and listen & rejoice. I was fortunate enough to catch a little visit from Roxa as soon as she arrived, it was only coming at night and going in the morning, but I valued it very much. Miss Dabney must have told you how she went to Saratoga last September to the Conference, and I hope she told you we sat together at a meeting which ended in a very interesting and exciting Temperance discussion. I enjoyed being with her that day exceedingly. Saratoga was delightful in a social way and very interesting, but as in 1878 I came away in 1882 with a sense that there was nothing religious in the Conference. We do not seem to me to be a religious people, we have good sense, good moral principles, cheerful views, are a highly civilized set, and likely to be friendly and generous. That is all. Those to whom I complained four years ago said "But you didn't go to morning-meeting. If you had you would have seen the religion and felt it through the day." So this time I went to every morning-meeting, but my impression was only confirmed.

Your dear kind birthday letter came the day after my birthday. Thankyou for writing in season for it to come. And behold! since I began this letter a most unexpected chance to send it to you presents itself! Two of our Concord girls are going out. One is Caroline Wheildon, she goes out now invited, a beloved aunt, by her sick nephew to make his voyage more worthwhile I understand. And with her goes the joy & pride of our town, our "beauty", Beth Hoar. She is Elizabeth Hoar, Aunt Lizzy's niece & namesake, Judge Hoar's youngest daughter, sister of my Clara. Oh! I haven't told you about my Clara's deed of last summer. She went to the Training-School for Nurses at the City Hospital and is being trained there. This gives me such constant delight! I think it is the right thing to do; people who have had every advantage, ladies by birth and breeding, seem to me to be the very ones that ought to throw themselves into the hard places, then they can use their powers for their fellow-men and show that they do care for them, and don't mean to leave the humble to do all the labour & suffering. And if Clara takes the active end of this cross Beth takes the passive end in the same spirit and with entire sympathy. She loses Clara and takes her place at home. Now I want to tell you what I desire they should see. Of course they will see the silver tree, but I suppose nespras [loquats] & camellias will be gone, and probably callas; yet do take them some day to the banana quarry in the Canada garden. If possible let them see the en-

— 1883 —

chanting moon-rise from Bagatelle garden, and if San Lorenzo is what it once was I wish they might see that, the camphor-trees and the box-trees, and get them to go to the top of Monte Carneiro and Espalamarca if they are good pedestrians. I hope the donkeys will seem to them as great a privilege as they did to me, and that everything great and small will be the pleasure to them it was to me. I know they will come home like everyone else rejoicing in Fredonia. Affectionately
E. T. E.

Concord, 6 April 1883

Dear Edith,

Thankyou for sending Violet's letter eagerly read by her ancestors. I tried hard to induce her or her papa or brothers or all to come up to "Ruth" on Wednesday night, but they all refused, and so did five others that I wrote for. I had to give away the tickets. But Mother and I went and enjoyed it. First there was the fun of going into the Town Hall. I never fail to experience a rising of spirits as I enter its dear doors, then to look round and see the people was a pleasure. Mother & I sat the second seat from the front, Mr & Mrs G. H. Conant on my right, the Stow family on Mother's left. In front Lizzy Bartlett, the Langs, Anna Pratt and Helen Blanchard, across the aisle the Chamberlaines & M. Weir, and the Wheildon family, behind us Nine Acre Corner, behind them the Emery family. We spent twenty minutes in affectionate converse with all these neighbors, then Alice Wheildon, bless her! I say, bless her! made her appearance with Amy Houghton & Florence Whiting. Mother, like me, went off the handle at the first sight of Alice. There is hardly a more affecting spectacle to me than she always is. "Look at her!" cried Mother "Splendid creature! How much soul she has!" She mounted her leader's throne and sat down with her back to the audience. I now noticed that there were two pianos one on each side of her. Florence took the one on her right, the left one was exactly in front of us, so that my sweet Amy came straight to me, so gentle and bright and unconscious, a delight to the eyes in a different way entirely from Alice. "I'm sorry" said Amy, "they have told me to make all the noise I can. I'm afraid I shall deafen you with this piano." Alice had a very superior white baton. The curtain went up and the sorrowing Israelites appeared, stood a moment, then Alice raising her hand they all took a breath and the singing began. I picked out all my friends, Martha Derby Smith, Constance Emery, Annie Bartlett, Alice Linder,

— 1883 —

Fanny Norcross, Lizzy Surette, Emma Collier Butters, but where was Anna? At last I found the head of the man in front of me eclipsed her. They were all done up in gray & black shawls and most of them looked their plainest. The next scene was in Moab, Naomi dismissing Orpah & Ruth. Nelly Webster was Naomi, she's young & light & a soprano; Miss H. Clark, Orpah, is thirty & a soprano; Miss L. Richardson, very young, dark, pretty and an alto was Ruth. The words of the Bible were often introduced. The acting was rather omitted and I was sorry. Black dresses & white veils, becoming & graceful. Next we returned to Bethlehem to find thirty or forty of the inhabitants in gorgeous array having a religious festival because there was a good crop. The dresses were so beautiful I didn't tire of examining them all the evening, and they were becoming too. The stage was as full of singers as it could be, and it was a long time before we found out who was there. Naomi returns and there is a very interesting scene between her and her old friends; Ruth is introduced. Lizzy Surette was a most oriental figure in pomegranate satin and white mull, with three broad bands of the satin in her hair. By and by came the harvest scene. A capital foreground of real standing wheat and a load of straw on the ground. They sang all sorts of songs & did all sorts of work, it was lively and very pretty. Now the great Boaz made his first appearance, Charley Brown. You have no idea how big he looked among the rest. He wore a heavy & long black beard and gorgeous embroidered garments, the mightiest turban on the stage crowned the effect. He sang better than he used to, Bible words chiefly, & withdrew, reaping went on. Finally Ruth, left alone in the field, falls asleep & Boaz reappears and serenades her. In the next scene, the wedding which we infer rather than behold is carried on. Each character sings an appropriate Psalm, and the chorus sing their psalms, and there is a rearrangement of position of persons several times. Indeed arrangement was so contrived that we had a different front rank every time. Besides all the delight of the eyes which we experienced, there was that of feeling the control Alice was exercising over them, managing all the time not only with her book & baton but with her eye, and not the least enchanting feature of the evening was her having to push aside the curtain in one of the long waits and call for Dr Titcomb. Imagine how the Wheildon family and Mother and I embraced all round in the wildest enthusiasm the moment the entertainment was over, and how glad I was of a chance to see how the Emery family felt about it! Miss Leavitt dined with us yesterday and I feasted her on photographs. You would have enjoyed her scream when Alexander's came in sight. We had four hours of comfort together. Tonight Cousin Elizabeth comes to tea. Tomorrow we are to dine at the Bulkeleys.

Affectionately
E. T. E.

Concord, 10 April 1883

My dear Annie,

We have begun on the new dispensation, dinner at 2.30. It did not make Mother so happy as she expected yesterday, and it made me very cross & hungry almost all day. We are trying to manage better today, and I hope in a week or two to be peaceful under it. Lizzy Barber & the children are here, came to settle with us last night. They are a real pleasure, Lizzy seems like a sister and the children do not appear uneasy or bored but make themselves a part of the conversation though rather silently. It appears that the distress is not so great as we at first supposed; Alice has taken no interest in the Spaniard, it was all managed by the Irish coachman bribed by the Spaniard, and trusted by Lizzy as Alice's escort when she could not go with her herself. Alice threatened by the coachman, was quiet till he was found out and turned away, then she told the whole story. Mother is sitting by me making out orders for roses from all the various nurserymen. She is very much impressed with the failure of her powers since she did the same work last year, but she is very funny about it. She says it will be sad not to know anything or do anything but she will willingly put up with being a burden for the sake of the pleasure it will give her dear Ellen to carry the burden, and when I laugh she is amazed at the want of sentiment I exhibit. If I could remember as I once could I would record her jokes—they were delightful—but I forget now.

11 April. We have a letter from Edward at last and are delighted to get it. We had a heavenly day yesterday that I don't believe could have been better at Lakewood, but Edward's description of what you are enjoying sounds attractive, and I hope you feel at leisure to suck in all the spring beauty there is. Our minister on Sunday was Mr Russell of Bedford. I got him & Mrs Bulkeley to come and dine with us, and oh! what a good time I had with Mr Russell! He always, like Dr Jones, understands what I say and answers me, so that I know more after talking with him. I brought Mother in a whole handful of snow-drops

this morning, they came out on Sunday. Fred Hosmer came yesterday and photographed the study. Mother sends her love to Edward and says his letter cheers her to the bottom of her heart. We managed better with our meal-times yesterday and Mother thought them delightful.
Affectionately
E. T. E.

Thursday afternoon 26 April 1883

Dear Edith,

I spoiled a letter that I wrote to you yesterday. I'll try to succeed with this before the five o'clock mail goes. From Annie's letter we gather that you are by this time travelling again in search of a fairer clime. It is cold here today but very pleasant; good sun, a West wind not too strong, small pretty white clouds, and the grass a mixture of dead & green. In the garden squills and yellow crocuses & hepaticas do abound; a few purple crocuses appear. Mother since it is the day of the week that Father died feels, like me, that it is the real anniversary more than tomorrow will be, so we went over to Sleepy Hollow this morning. Mother sent me out for flowers and I brought her all that I have named. She took the path across the hills, and had many memories by the way of how Father & Uncle Charles Emerson almost always walked this way, and how Miss Minott sat at the window and watched, and missed Uncle Charles very much when he came no more. Of the three hours' solitary walk which once she took there herself with Father's watch, and lost and found it. Of walks with Miss Searle and Mrs Goodwin. When we came to Father's grave we found someone had just put a plant of budding saxifrage on it. Mother left her flowers, glass and all, just as they were gathered, not arranged. I am anxious about the bad taste of the colours, but she thinks the yellow will harmonize the blue & lilac. I must tell you about our Parish Association meeting last Thursday. Mother went, stayed all through and properly enjoyed it. Do you remember whether a carpet for our vestry was proposed before you were married? I have fought against it with vehemence whenever it has been mentioned, in company, at Teacher's Meetings, in sessions of Committees for many a year in private and in public so that my sentiments are known. Well what do you think! In the midst of our solemn conclave the other afternoon, Mother who sat in the open space in front of the President's table in a central and conspicuous position, suddenly piped up in a moment of absolute silence, "By the way, why don't we have a carpet for this vestry?" There was a pause; my heart went down to my boots; every eye turned on me; everybody's colour rose as they drank in the deliciousness of the situation, and all at once the assembly burst into a roar of laughter and clapping. The innocent Mamma not guessing what caused the universal joy concluded she had made an excellent suggestion, and went on to complete the delight of my friends by using the argument which those of my mind frantically spurn "The Orthodox have a beautiful carpet in their vestry," At this second speech of Mother's the uproar was repeated; Mrs Hoar turned, flushed with pleasure, to cast one more glance of mischievous triumph at me, then discreetly answered Mother that our vestry was larger, and resumed the business of the meeting. And Mother never knew that she had walked into my dearest prejudice till at tea-time as we discussed the meeting she said to Jenny Worcester "*I* was clapped once!" Then I explained the state of things. I had a good walk last night with Mrs Sanborn. Mother sends her love to you.

Your sister.

I have little Alice Arthur with me this week. I've just lost the 5 o'clock mail.

3 May 1883 Thursday morning

My dear sister,

It is nearly or quite a week since I wrote to you. C. Wheildon and Beth are going to Fayal, and I have used my time to get letters etc. ready for them. They sail on Tuesday. Your box of beautiful corydalis & Mayflowers delighted your Mamma's heart as well as your sweet letter. I have been remarking with surprise and joy that age is fast removing Mother's sad mind. She no longer dwells on painful things. The lowing of a cow is quickly forgotten, and any anxiety or little misfortune scarcely disturbs her. The anniversaries we have just passed were interesting, not painful, to her, just as they were to me. How beautiful an experience it all was!

I suppose you will reach home tomorrow. I will come by 6.30 train on Monday, spend the night & go with you to Mary Morse's wedding. Does that please you? I'll bring V.'s ticket & key wh. she left.

E. T. E.

22 May 1883

Dear Edith,

I desired to thank you earlier than this for the flowers you sent to

— 1883 —

Mother and me. They came most opportunely. Mr & Mrs Cabot came on Wednesday afternoon. I understood Education pretty well and had many and perplexing remarks & amendments to offer, so I sat by Mr Cabot and read the manuscript with him word by word. His patience in following me through the labyrinths of my proposed changes was wonderful. He accepted most of them. In one case he refused, but when Edward came in he requested Mr Cabot to yield. I said, no, Mr Cabot was chosen by Father because he knew what should be published and what not, and he ought to have the say in the end. Edward said "Father added 'acting with my children' so that we might have our way too." So it goes in our way. Then Edward followed Mrs Cabot into the study and read to her there Father's poetry, and Mr Cabot & I continued Education till tea-time and most of the next day. At 10 on Thursday dear Mrs Cabot went. Edw. & Mr C. worked in the Study and I alone in the dining-room. Rev. Mr Dutton about to be settled at Clinton came to ask for "We love the venerable house" to be sung at his Installation. He sat & copied it opposite, begged a duplicate of Father's M.S. and departed. I went to Bible Society at Mrs Grout's and was introduced to the new Mrs Prescott Hosmer, who seemed energetic, social & cheerful. Friday Mother was inspired to call on Cousin Elizabeth in the forenoon and come home over the hills to visit Father's grave, and we did. It was an excursion of an hour and a half, all on foot, and very pleasant; 'twas a beautiful day. Cousin Elizabeth had been sick and Cousin Mary was at the Manse, so we saw her too. That afternoon Nina Lowell arrived. She had said she would come if she could, but 'twas improbable. But here she was, and oh what a good time I had with her whenever I had a minute! She delighted in Alexander's big amused photograph, seemed to drink health from it. She visited little Florence and Edward read her some of Father's poetry. At 11 I took Hilda & brought home my dear four friends, Mrs Sanborn, Miss Leavitt, Anna McClure & Mrs Emery who had been invited for the Reminiscences of Eton Life reading. Nina entered cordially into the occasion. Your letter a great treat. I'll finish this tomorrow.   E. T. E.

4 June 1833

Dear Edith,

I'll try to finish that letter. I had got as far as the festivity of 19 May when Nina was here and my four friends, and we read the "Reminiscences of Eton Life". Oh admirable story! Mother meanwhile arranged the flowers you had sent to her and some of mine. Nina departed at

— 1883 —

1.30 in the middle of dinner. After dinner we walked and walked in the garden which was in full glory of tulips; Mother has had a show this year, far surpassing anything heretofore, and the narcissus were just appearing, perhaps 6 in bloom. Lilies of the valley had one or two bells open. At last we all came merrily back to my room and eagerly returned to Eton Life. We had not advanced three pages when Mrs Emery's horse came for her. We all howled with dismay. She invited us to come next Wednesday and spend the day with her to finish together the enchanting tale. Then Miss Leavitt & Anna and I walked out onto the hills while Mrs Sanborn took a nap, and this ended the festivity, for on our return Hilda was harnessed and we all rode up with her. On Monday I went to Boston to my Conference Board meeting, did every imaginable errand and spent the night at Nina's. She said Harry James was coming to dinner and her nephews Algernon Coolidge & Frank Lowell & Frank's wife, Cornelia, were to be the rest of the party. They were a set for an aunt to be proud of. Nina enjoys the marriages of her brother's children exceedingly. Harry was very interesting company, except that his preference for Europe did shine out, which excites a little indignation. He told me Alice was at the nervine asylum, and talked over Wilky and Bob a little. I had also one or two very good talks with Algernon. The old photograph book came out. Harry said "It is pathetic to see all one's friends young. I always feel it when I look at old photographs." "Why," said Frank "the costume in them is such that people look older to me in the photographs than they do now." "I consider that interesting too," said Harry, "one traces the progress of luxury by it." The next day it poured and Nina brought me to the depot in her coupé. Wednesday was the day at Mrs Emery's. Mother & I reached her house at about twelve and found Mrs Sanborn there. Everyone was shining with delight. Something caught Anna in the kitchen, she never reappeared till dinner-time, but we were all perfectly happy over Mrs McClure's photograph-book and the family daguerreotypes. At dinner-time anxiety was expressed lest we shouldn't finish Eton Life today either. At last we got to it, but Mother had to go. She chose to lie down at home and return to tea. Mrs McClure had not heard the beginning of the story, so we read back a little for her, then went on, and finished. Every time we stopped to laugh I was slow to begin to read and oh how much talk we did have over it! Perfect happiness is the only name for that afternoon! After the reading Mrs Sanborn & Anna, Miss Leavitt & I went to walk & Mrs Emery to lie down.

— 1883 —

Miss L. couldn't come back to tea, but Mother and the rest of us did. There was a lively little skirmish on the Golden Rule between Mrs Sanborn and the gentlemen at tea-time. Right after tea Mr McClure & I went to the sing, Mother stayed & read "Transcendental Wild Oats" in the evening, but didn't half finish. At the sing I had a very happy time with Mrs King & Fanny Norcross. The next day came the meeting to consider whether we would establish a coffee-house. Mr Todd presided, and made the evening one long frolic while business proceeded evenly and handsomely. I sat between Mrs Hoar & Mrs King. The executive Committee was made up of two Orthodox, two Unitarians, one Episcopalian and one no-church man to show itself not sectarian, and the Catholic priest sent word that he heartily favoured the plan, would recommend it to his people and subscribe to it himself. On Tuesday Lucy Derby came, and was the brightest loveliest guest imaginable. And on Wednesday Decoration Day

Last part of letter is missing.

June 13th 1883

Dear Edith,

Dr Furness was as lovely as ever, and it was pathetic to have him so sick and so entirely beyond all reach, for being of the homoeopathic persuasion neither he nor Mrs Furness would take advice from Haven or Edward, and he rigidly fasted, yet worked like a well man. To think of his going to church & preaching without a mouthful of breakfast, and then with no dinner but an orange & a banana preaching and reading for us all the afternoon & going supperless to Boston at six! We had a letter from Mrs Wister saying that he was so ill on Monday that her Mother had to telegraph for her. June 23rd. I have since had a beautiful note from Mrs Furness saying that he improved sufficiently to return to Phila. and though weak & rheumatic had no more severe pain. I have pleasures & life sprinkled through every day making my lot 3/4 roses, but of a kind that preclude writing to my sister e.g. a visit from Edward to read us his catalogue of antiquities for the Putnam's Adirondac Shanty, then a Woman's Parish Assn. picnic up at Nine-Acre-Corner, calls of my friends, notably Mrs Storey who came with Annie the other day. Last night Miss Leavitt invited us & the dear Mrs Emery and Anna to tea. I was tired when I went but as we came into the parlour after tea I wondered where the fatigue had gone to. After tea,

Mother though recalcitrant was induced to lie down in Miss Leavitt's room, and returned rested to the evening's discourse. We stayed very late—till 9.30, and walked home through moonlight too beautiful to imagine, more than my capacities could take in. I wish, & Mother wishes daily, you could be here now, the glory of roses was never greater, three great basketfuls daily, no bugs or slugs to speak of. Dear Cameron's letter gave us great comfort. Affectionately,
              Ellen

                 [July 1883]
 Now my dear brother thou shalt have a letter on dust-pans. Start not at the humble theme. It is an undeniable part of life, and curiously came into prominence twice on Sunday morning giving me such delight I thought I must tell you. You know how it poured all Saturday afternoon and night. Well, when Cousin Sarah [Ansley] appeared with shining face to recount the mercies of the Lord at breakfast on Sunday morning one of her first exclamations was "All the dust-pans are washed out!" then she explained, "Why, when sister Hannah went to ride up in our largest Cemetery, which we think is so beautiful, it was a dry time, and all she seemed to think of was the dust. 'Every leaf was a dust-pan!' she said. So since then I always think of it when it is dusty."

 When Mother was dressing for church and looking for her go-to-meeting black silk I told her it was in the Nursery closet. Presently she exclaimed from the closet "It is hanging *close to a* DUST-PAN!" in tones which made me wonder whether it would suffer from the neighbourhood really very seriously, or whether it was the want of respect to the high station of a best silk that so shocked her. But she continued as she returned to the room "If there is a sound in the world that I dread, it is the clang of a dust-pan, it throws me into an agony." I asked whether it had clanged. "No, it gave a slight growl and I fled! If it hollered, I should have had a fit, I shouldn't have gone to church, every nerve would have been unstrung. I am most thankful for my escape." Mamma was serious, yet she smiles. These are simple tales I know, still I think you'll appreciate them. Send it to Edith.
                E. T. E.

              Concord, July 12th 1883
Dear Edith,
 Thankyou for your letter which came last night. The delectable tale

of the journey was almost equal to that of last year. It sounds to me as if you were going to have a very handsome house, I always thought it handsome in its old form.

In 1877 Dean Stanley wrote to Father "I have taken the liberty of placing a few verses from the Problem with a slight alteration to be read with other choice fragments from our own poets by chance visitors to the Abbey." We never knew before what was the slight alteration; I think that part of the information did not attract Father's attention. Dean Stanley spoke of it again when he was here and Father only let it pass like any compliment.

I am very glad Edith dear that you can persuade yourself that I was of much use to you. I wonder you can; and should be very sorry I left you so early, only at the time I didn't think it safe to do otherwise. I have naturally meditated much on our conversation, it has an effect, but probably not so prevailing an effect as you would desire. I cannot set my foot down without a feeling of ground under it, so I must wait for that sense to grow, by which I mean that I must not do anything that seems to me wrong, nor obey unreasoningly another person's wishes in an affair of this kind where I alone am in a position to know its various points and issues. I believe I do wish to do right about it. Then about the dress. I recognize the affection & the care of which I have such constant experience in you, and I know you know a great deal and have good taste, and that gratitude should lead me to accept it. On the other hand I do not, as I told you, like the colour or the material and I know it would last me ten or twenty years. I have a multitude of afternoon and evening dresses on hand which entirely please me and which I think are likely to need no addition to their number for years to come; I shouldn't wonder if they lasted beyond my ability to wear them, so you can see how it is that I ventured to say you had better hold your hand.

Yesterday we had a very gay day. I asked Sarah Richardson to come and spend it with me. Messrs. & Mrs Bulkeley were invited to dine and Mother had summoned the Emerys to a "Transcendental Wild Oats" reading in the evening. Cousin Sarah & Cousin Edwin [Cotton] were invited to dine at Aunt Susan's, so we were only six at dinner. The conversation was general. We had a very cheerful time. They stayed till nearly four. Then something was said of the Aeolian harp and I got it out. 'Twas windy enough for it and it sang like an angel. Sarah was in ecstacies she had heard this one once when a child, never any other. After tea Mother remembered "Silver Pitchers" had been left at Miss

— 1883 —

Leavitt's so Sarah & I took the wagon post-haste, invited Mrs Kimball to go with us and rode up to get it. We found the Leavitt's porch packed with company, it looked most festive & inviting. They brought out the book, and we drove home fast passing the Emerys soon & Mr McClure by Mrs Gregory's. Then began one of the most joyous evenings imaginable. We love them all so much and feel so at home with them, it was a delight all round apparently to get together. Mr McClure has never heard an Aeolian harp, the wind had died & not a whisper could be extorted from ours, but today it sings mightily and I'm going to carry it up there. You ought to have heard him & Anna talk about it. He hunted up the mechanism & touched its strings & said "you see it is tuned between fifths & sixths." We all fell to talking so fast that 'twas almost impossible to begin reading. The reading was interspersed with much general conversation and it seemed too hard to stop & break up at half-past nine, but we did with that active consciousness which distinguishes Mrs McClure's children. After we went upstairs Mother, Cousin Sarah & I devoured your letter with rapture. I enclose Edward's. Dear Edith, your approving & grateful and affectionate sister,

E. T. E.

Concord, 20 July 1883

Dear Edward,

I send you Mr Cabot's reply. How kind and domestic it is! except that he doesn't approve of Essays 3d Series. Alicia I find feels almost as strongly against it as Lizzy and I do. I sent your letter to Mr Cabot yesterday. I perfectly understood about sending Preacher, Va. & Tragic direct to Mr Cabot. I have written to Mr C. today for several hours and have given him a detailed account of everything. So he is answered, yet you are neglected. Few moments now left before mail.

Oh happiness of hearing W. James! Mr Sanborn has sent you & Mother & me season-tickets to the School. W. J. read the first evening. I told Mr S. to send him to us. But Mr S. didn't see him. He came up with wife & sister-in-law, expecting to take tea somewhere. In vain. Found himself as he thought obliged to repair to the Sch. of Ph. without time to come to us for comfort. So fasting they lectured, walked to the train & reached home having no food for ten hours! Naturally he didn't lecture at his best, but it was a pleasure to see & hear him. I asked him to stay here, he refused but promised to come next Thurs. and spend the night. I found Psychology was no more one of my themes than Hegel,

— 1883 —

so doubted whether I w'd go next time, but Thursday noon dear Mr Blake made a beautiful call on me, every moment interesting and delightful, and told me to go to the second lecture. At night W. came to tea, and we did have such a good time! hereditary friendships are a blessed thing! After tea he went to Mr Howison's lecture, and I told him he w'd see us no more till morng. After breakfast he told us his sad experience of hunger on Wed. & retired to finish his lecture. Presently finding he had gone without speaking I followed him down to the school. A lady was hastening along behind me, she caught up. It was his faithful wife who had tended baby all night & taken the 8 A.M. train to hear him. We sat together. This morning he was as Jamesy as could be desired, full of fireworks, How we enjoyed him! I soon found Mrs James was more of my stripe than a metaphysician. We held a sort of intercourse throughout the lecture which made us friends in no time. They would come home with me, have a luncheon & go at 1.30. Miss Peabody hailed me "Are W. J. & his wife going to lunch at your house?" "Yes." "Well I want you to invite me too. I have no other way of seeing him & we want to have an interview."

Give my love to Annie & the Babies.

23 July 1883

Dear Edith,

Your letter came on Friday morning and was most welcome; so were all its enclosures, especially Violet's letter and Mrs Cunningham's note. I send them back, and several of ours, or things about Father. We have just lost the pleasure we were expecting today of having Wm. & Mrs James spend the day. They had promised it, but a snarl of affairs before departing for the summer made it seem impossible. They were here half an hour, both perfectly charming. I gave him our letters from his Father. He appreciated them. Mrs James comforted me on past sorrows; had, I mean, never heard Father but once; that was at Divinity Hall when he read "The Preacher", & she had greatly enjoyed it at the time and valued the remembrance since. You know that Mr Thayer and Dr Hedge told me that night that he must never speak in a hall again, they couldn't bear to have young people who didn't know what he had been see him and hear him so. Mother has been very feeble for a week, but seems to Cousin Sarah and me a little less so since Saturday. We have had a beautiful visit from Lizzy Simmons who made Cousin Sarah her butt and we laughed all the time over their skirmishing. After she

— 1883 —

went Mary Watson came and I had two very pleasant days with her. She brought her zither and charmed Lily K. & Cousin Sarah with it. I haven't time for more tonight, perhaps I never shall pick up exactly at this spot, but I'll try to

28 July 1883

Dear Edward,

It begins to be time for me to answer your letter. Business seems to swallow up both you & me when we attempt to write. Mother tells you & Annie hereby that she misses you both very sadly, and if I had given her the chance she should have sent a great deal of love to you both and to the offspring every time I have written. Florence is often a subject of conversation here. Your news that you are effectively changing your style of painting is very interesting. Do you think I shall like the new as well? Do you know I have to divine "your motto-plan". I don't remember hearing of it before. I highly approve of it, and of what you have done about M[ary]. M[oody]. E[merson].

I suppose Forbearance was principally founded on Mr Thoreau, but not without a look at Mr Cabot. "Amita" was read before Woman's Club in Boston either in 1869, 70 or 74, I should say. I'll try to look up what you wish. Mother & Cousin S. went to Boston yesterday to see Edith and to buy a straw carpet for the Weirs' parlour. Not a min. more. Love to you all

E. T. E.

28 July 1883

Dear Edith,

I was telling you how Mrs James had cared to hear Father. They agreed to stay all day after Wm's next lecture. I meant to make this a great gala and to have tea on the Pond if it was pleasant, so I invited the Emerys & Sanborns who refused and all the Harrises & Mrs Edward Hoar & Florence, Lidian J. & Anna McC. who agreed to come. But no sooner was the lecture over than Mrs James told me they must whisk right home at half past 12. Dismay! They came with us to have a drink of water, and we took the wagon and went to show Mrs James the Minute-Man, had a happy ride, and just as we reached the train remembered endless numbers of things to say to each other. William had read the letters from his Father which I had lent him, and asked to keep the one about Wilky's wound. They departed. In the afternoon the

— 1883 —

clouds increased, at 4 it rained. I abandoned the picnic & Anna & I sat down to write letters industriously. Cousin Sarah who was taking Mrs Weir to ride, came home all wet, and said she had landed Lidian in Walden woods just before the rain came. Poor Lidian! At 5 it looked quite clear; Mr Harris called to say it would rain no more and ask if they should come. I thought of Lidian and my principles generally and said yes! and began rushing round about the supper. It was the cook's afternoon out. No one to help me at all! I asked Anna; she came right down and so did Cousin Sarah and in a wonderfully short time we were ready to start. Just as we passed the front-gate after an elaborate packing-in down came the rain. We drove back into the shed and waited. Another shower came while we were buying cream at Mrs Stow's. The embarcation at the Pond, we had agreed, should occur at 5.45. It was 6.10 before we left Mrs Stow's. As we approached the gate of the woods we descried Lidian who looked neither wayworn nor weather-beaten though she had paced up & down in storm & calm for over two hours. She reported Messrs Harris & Snider as marching undaunted through the shower under big umbrellas. In the course of another half hour we succeeded in getting afloat. I talked much to the man about the leaky boat he gave you and me last month and demanded sound ones that he could warrant. But just when everybody in both boats had a saucer of berries & sugar & cream in one hand and a piece of bread & butter in the other, a mug of milk by his (or her) side, and various pails & baskets wedged in between every two pair of feet, a flood, a fast-rising flood! appeared in the bottom of one boat, and the iron entered my soul. Everything was upset, as when you and I went, dresses soaked, tea a mere snatch amid difficulties, Mr Harris set to bailing diligently. It was almost immediately time for the gentlemen to return, as they had to walk all the way to the School of Philosophy before 7.30, so poor Mr Harris who had kindly braved everything, shower & leaky boat and labour, & had neither pleasure nor supper, rowed the leaker back & left all the ladies in the good boat. After this we who remained had all that I could desire, a warm still evening, the water like glass, the sunset sky beautiful; we finished our supper in peace, rowed into Halcyon Cove, landed & visited the cairn, chased a bull-frog, looked down at the bottom of the pond & saw it disappear in greenness as we rowed out. Anna & Lidian were gay, the Harris ladies though quiet were evidently enjoying themselves. So I wasn't sorry after all. We had a lively ride home too, and Mother and Cousin Edwin and Cousin Sarah were delighted to receive us back; they had begun to think we were drowned. On Tuesday, as usual, I wrote in the morning. Cousin Edwin went at noon. He told us many a tale of his own day and his father's, and sometimes he & Mother would tell quite different versions of a story. You ought to have been here to hear. On Wednesday Mrs McClure & Mrs Emery came to dine and once more we had the happiest day and grudged to see the hours fly. Thursday A.M. Dr Bartol lectured and afterwards came here. Mother saw him in the parlour for awhile then we all took him in the carryall as far as Mr Alcott's and left him there. We went to the Edward Hoar's & Mr Hoar & Florence showed us their garden. This was a great pleasure. Affectionately

           E. T. E.

           31 July 1883

Dear Annie,

Your letter was delight itself from beginning to end. It filled the empty spaces in our mental picture of you all. We begin now to feel as if we could imagine you quite clearly. I promised Edward that I would take up where I left it the tale of the Jameses and Miss Peabody, and now I have a chance to do so. Mrs James when I told her said "Oh I know what the interview is about. Miss Peabody is anxious to get William to interest himself in a Dr Buchanan". So we walked home all together. I promised Mrs James to do what I could and took Miss Peabody for my partner to talk about the Piute princess, but before we reached the Dutch house William came forward and took her with him so I fell back with Mrs James. I got quite well acquainted with her. She seems to be just of the right kind, very real and serious and affectionate, and a New Englander to the back-bone, a quality I sympathize with and value. Of course when they were settled in the house I had to go to attend to the lunch and expected when I returned to see my friends writhing under the torture of Dr Buchanan. By no means! They were talking easily together about Mr James's books, and I saw my wrath & terror had been rather thrown away. At luncheon I told Wm about his father's letters to Father, and brought them down to read him the beauty about Mr Hawthorne. I had just embarked on it when I remembered Miss P., and had to withdraw from the undertaking! Pretty bad! But I left no moment for meditation, I rushed into another letter almost as good and gave them the pleasure of hearing it. Wm begged for the whole file and I gave them on condition of their being returned. I lost my dear Lizzy Simmons the day of Wm's first lecture. That noon Mary Watson came, the second day she was here Alicia came and spent the night. Then Anna McClure came and made me a good long visit of five days. Since then no guests, but Mrs Sears & Edmund came to tea, and Aunt Susan & John's daughter the night before, and one other but I forget who, so that we feel quite gay and in the world.

[Unsigned]

Monday, Aug 6th 1883

Dear Edward,

I have received your letter enclosing Mr Cabot's, also your letter about the tournament and above all! Annie's letter! Thankyou dear Annie for every word. I have sent the letter to Edith. I hope some day Uncle Edward will get up another tournament at Naushon and teach Cameron & Don & Edward to joust. I am delighted with the tales of Florence and wish very much to see her. Edward distresses me by the tone he takes about Ellen's sins. I don't know what they may be, but these philosophic papas who account for all misdemeanours in a way to obliterate the guilt don't promise to be good disciplinarians. As Uncle he was an admirable one, but as Papa he peters out sadly. You on the contrary do rather better as Mamma than you did as Aunt. Have I told you that Mrs George Brooks has asked Sarah Richardson and me to visit her at Pigeon Cove? I propose to stop at Beverley Farms on my way home. I have had Bible Society here this last week, the largest meeting I ever had, fifty. Sarah Richardson came in the morning and stayed. Annie made the cake, Erena washed the windows & cleaned the silver. Kate who was here made Mother a new cap. I didn't suspect that I had an unusually large meeting till I counted at 5. Then I ran out and told Annie who, always equal to emergency, made up a batch of sour milk muffins. She had baked 103 muffins at six, & meanwhile Cousin Sarah & she had cut & buttered the white bread. Mother was lying down so I called out Mrs Emery to cut three more basketfuls of cake. Sarah Richardson ran over & borrowed Mrs Whitcomb's napkins, tumblers & spoons. All went smoothly. I, and apparently everyone else, had a glorious time. Mother exclaimed when she went up stairs "Well! it has been very pleasant!" On Saturday came off the visit to the State's Prison. Mother has received a most cheerful impression of it. The Warden padlocked her & Mrs McClure into a solitary cell with two other ladies. Cousin Sarah was shocked & can't recover from it. "To think of it! When she requires so much air & room always! I should think it would have choked her. How could he!" But Mother doesn't seem to have been at all impressed by the experience. Last night Miss Peabody and the Piute lady to tea. Anna McClure came in the evening, also Miss Ellison. Anna made Mrs Hopkins sing an Indian song. Very interesting. Affectionately

Ellen.

Tuesday, 4 Sept. 1883.

Dear Edith,

You do not mention having received two notes from me at the Bowditches', but I hope this does not mean that they failed to reach you. I mourn very often, dear Edith, that you and I can be so little acquainted; I wonder if we must wait till heaven to see each other more. On Saturday my dear teachers arrived, Lizzy just before tea with the news that Dr Vincent Bowditch had forbidden her to teach before New Years, so she can only stay a week. This is a blow for neither Jenny [Worcester] nor I know whom to ask in her stead. I told Jenny in the beginning that we wanted two, so we both feel quite awkward and upset about it within, though we don't mention the subject. We had been severely exercised by fires in the woods Thursday P.M. & Friday & Saturday all day. No sooner would John & Eddy & Johnny get home all tired & hungry than a new column of smoke would be seen to rise and off they would start again for another fight. One fire menaced our grove, the other all our acres beyond the Pond. So far we have escaped. On Saturday morning Rev. Dr Putnam brought a Hindoo representative of the Brahmo Somaj, Mr Mozoomdar to call on us. Mr Mozoomdar said that the English reading Oriental always loved Father, that they claimed him as their own for he had an Oriental mind and all his Indian lovers felt sure that they had a deeper understanding of him than any European or American reader was likely to be capable of. "When in the midst of his grand pregnant involved sentences he quotes a sentence from our Sacred Books it is to the Hindoo like a flash that illumines & warms his inmost being." Sunday noon Edward brought my junior to call on us. We went down into the garden, the hated column of smoke was in plain sight. I ran to tell John & stopped. I hadn't the heart. This was Sunday. But Edward saw him coming and called out "Well, John, we'll go to the woods. Harness the horse & I'll give the alarm." So away they all went with a load of shovels at their feet. Edw. returned on foot

— 1883 —

just a little while after the wagon-load of men. The fire was stopped. At four we all went to church & found a goodly number of people assembled to hear Mr Mozoomdar on the Brahmo Somaj. I thought we might be in for fatigue. Oh no! for pure delight! A superior mind, a natural orator is Mr Mozoomdar. No one was ready to have him stop. As I came home I detected new fires. I told John if he'd get me the donkey I'd go for Edward. He said he would go himself, met Edward on the way, had the bells rung & away they went; and that fire beyond the Pond occupied them & the Fire Department till 8 P.M. 4 men watched it all night. It broke out Monday morning, John couldn't come home for meals, and though he slept at home was off again this morning. More tomorrow. E. T. E.

Wednesday, 5 Sept. 1883

My dear Sister,

I promised to continue my yarn today. Dr Putnam told me that he took Mr Mozoomdar to the Cemetery and that at Father's grave he cried, so Dr P. thought it better to leave him and walked on, but when he came back he was still crying though ready to go. So in the evening I asked him if he would like to see Father's Hindoo books. He was very much interested in them all but deeply disappointed that we had given away the Bhagavat-Geeta, which he seemed to think the important one. Then Mother got him out several of the journals, and I think he wished to sit right down & read them through, but the expectant guests had come and he had to come in and open his conversation. Edward was detained by the fire in the woods and didn't come at all. Poor Edward who returned on Wednesday from Beverly told me that as he passed by the Walden Ledge in the cars on Monday he saw the whole back of it in flames and no man there. He almost felt like giving up his journey, but concluded that haste with the book was more important than even "My Garden". The Keyeses including Annie were glad that he was away through those three terrible days of fire. They thought him rather too much exhausted by Sunday's work, and were sure he would have blindly killed himself if he had remained at home. Yesterday, Friday, the fire was kept down by only three men, and for the first time wasn't watched by night. Only an acre or two of ours is burned, but almost the whole region from Mr Baker's to the Pond is burned. The reason that anything is saved is that the wind was strong East till Monday and since Monday has been from the West, so that the advance

— 1883 —

toward the Pond has been against the wind. Annie & the baby came home on Monday, the baby has improved in looks somewhat. Mother walked that day first to the cemetery to see our new turf, which looks well, and then up to the Emery's garden. We met Mrs Sanborn and she went in to enjoy it with us, and induced Mother to continue her walk & have some luncheon with her. That was a very pleasant occasion. Edward said Mr & Mrs Cabot had been most kind to him, and his visit had been delightful. Alice Arthur is coming tomorrow with her children to spend Sunday. I have a great deal more to say. Affectionately
          Ellen.

              92 Carver St. Boston
              28 Sept. 1883.
Dear Edith,

 Here I am sitting hopelessly waiting for a chambermaid, as four times before since Erena went. This time no one has offered in Concord. I am usually overwhelmed with applications there. Your letter arrived on Wednesday night and was delightful. Mother and I have read V.'s letter like a novel in three installments. I sent it and little Edward's by the noon mail without a word, for we were hastening to go to Cattleshow. I hear this is the last Cattleshow, but so I heard of last years. If we do have another I mean to send pears and apples again. The show of them was very small, and the tables would look fatter and better for what even poor Bush can produce. We are hobbling along as well as we can in the house. Annie tries to do all the before-breakfast work before I come down, and rushes madly upstairs to do Jenny's room while I am at breakfast, so that my morning is made easy, and all day long she labours to get ahead of me, besides doing her own work better than usual. How can I otherwise than feel continually grateful to her? Jenny also insists on doing a great deal, clearing the table with me, and shutting up the house and endeavouring to get me to bed early. I was delighted the other day to see Alicia leading Mrs Keyes down into the garden to get some marigolds. I had a very pleasant talk with Mrs Keyes. The dentist was a common interest, for I had just come home and she was just going. Yesterday we duly went to Cattleshow. First we looked at the animals. A horse neighed. "What a noise!" cried Mother much distressed. Next a cow began to bellow "Oh dear! poor creature! Where is it? How loud it is! I'm afraid it is suffering!" Then a child blew its whistle. "Is that another creature? What is it? Is it in distress?" I

concluded that Cattleshow was not a favourable ground for Mother's enjoyment, but handsome calves began to attract her attention and she soon became very happy, and thought they looked comfortable and in good condition. Cows and calves were but a small part of the exhibition, pigs were the main body. I think there never were so many pigs, it gave the impression that our farmers now kept pigs instead of cows. What a hopeless-looking animal it is! I haven't seen one before for several years. There was one family of little pigs sucking away. This sight delighted Mother. As soon as we came into the Hall I caught sight of Mr Cummings, who bowed and presently brought Mr Robinson who should be our next governor to introduce to me. They were just going up to dinner. Mother had strayed on to see the giant red coxcombs and so lost seeing them. I don't know whether Effie & Lotta are with you or at the Mansion-House; with you I hope. I was happy in their visit to me.   Affectionately
E. T. E.

Concord 3 Oct. 1883.
Dear Edith,

Today has been a beautiful day and I have hoped you were having an out-door festivity. I have thought over your wedding again, that beautiful day,—perhaps the brightest of my life, though it seems ungrateful to pick out one day and say it was the very best, as it seems to imply there was only one best, and how many dazzling days of glory I have known! Mother and I have talked about the eighteen years. We are afraid we old folks don't do as much in eighteen years as children do, and that Ralph and Violet have climbed many more rounds of the ladder in that time than she & I have. Anna McClure invited me out to dine on the river today, and though it seemed impossible, at least improper, to take the time I did go for the weather was so glorious and the chances of excursions for this year so limited that Mother & Jenny and the kitchen all rather pushed me off, so I have sat for three hours in the boat & seen gorgeous trees and very soft little clouds, and meadows with the sun on them. On my return I found Annie & daughters here and heard about Sally and about Violet. Edward the other night charmed us with a tale of nephews & sheep. How I do rejoice in you all. With love to you & Will and the daughter & six sons.   Farewell.
E. T. E.

— 1883 —

92 Carver St. 29 Oct. 1883

My dear Edith,

We have missed you all very much. The Baby impressed Anna & Mrs Emery delightfully. On Thursday morning Mother & Frances went up in town and came home with the news that Mrs Bulkeley had a little daughter, born the night before. They had proceeded straight to Mr Bulkeley's to see the little creature, and Mr Bulkeley had brought and exhibited her with delight. Annie had carried over her little basket for Miss to live in and it had been a very welcome comfort. That day Jenny Worcester came home from school sick and had the Doctor, and has been sick ever since, poor child. She is dressed and comes down, but feels weak & wretched. The wicked Edward visited me after I had gone to bed, and forbade my going out on Friday. Friday came and was a day of bad weather; but I couldn't let Mrs Emery's dinner fail because of me. Mother wouldn't go without me, so I let her think I was going till the last minute and proposed to stay at home, but she was so aghast, and felt so unable that I did go. I have not regretted it. We had a very happy visit, talked all dinner-time as fast as we could, and then looked at the photograph-book which is my great amusement every time I am there long enough. I am trying to think what could be the third event of the week. I know it seemed to me wonderful that three such events as Beth's engagement, the Bulkeley's baby and one other should come in one week. Uncle George took tea with us Friday night; Charley & Therchi dined with us Saturday and we had a delightful time with them. Cousin Elizabeth is going to New York this week. Mr Bulkeley called on Mother on Saturday night, and it was very pleasant to talk church and baby with him.

Oct. 30. What a heavenly day! It is Waldo's birthday. Yesterday I visited Florence on her first birthday. She had intended to call on her grandmother but weather forbade and we were all disappointed. I rode with Edward in the train this morning. I told him you like slate in gravestones. He denied it and said you liked granite. Do you? He urged me to take Mother at once to Plymouth, he thinks it would be a very happy occasion for her, and do her good. If she wanted to go, or if I had anyone to conspire with against her and carry her off by force as I did to the wedding, I could, but to do it single-handed seems impossible. I asked Mother about Thanksgiving and she has consented to have it. I am going to see Cousin Elizabeth and write to the Thayers to ask if they are willing to come.

[Unsigned]

— 1884 —

Concord, 20 Nov. 1883

Dear Edith,
I have just made her birthday call on Caroline Cheney and have come home a little too late for a letter. Louisa is excellent, if she will only stay! We came home without accomplishing much, Mother is very feeble in reality. In the cars we opened the box of flowers, discovering with joy two passion-flowers, four hibuscus buds and a *Eucharis Amazonica*. I at once looked around for friends. Not a Concord soul except Mr & Mrs E. H. Whitcomb. I carried them to them to exhibit and when I held up the Eucharis two ladies rushed forward from the back of the car to behold *"that white flower!"* One said she was from Minnesota. Their admiration was unstinted, they had never seen one before. We have gained by our visit to you besides enjoying every day. I wish I could have been of more use to you. I met Mrs Sanborn today and she said Miss Fanny Prichard talks of "that Fair that the Unitarians are getting up for the Episcopalians". Mrs Bulkeley drove down here today and Mother spoke to her in the carriage. We called on the Weirs and carried them some of the flowers. They were delighted with the Passion-flower.

Goodnight, dear good child.
Ellen.

Postcard.

Concord, 6 Jan 1884

We came home in triumph and safely in every way. All the trunks with us, and I do believe nothing left behind. Except E. Weir's Arctics. How fortunate to have forestalled this storm! House beautiful, tidy, & blazing hot.

Concord, 22 Jan. 1884

Dearest Edith,
I don't forget you but am trying to work a little way into my involved accounts so for a day or two more you may scarce hear from me. Mary is morally more than anyone can desire, but Dr. T. says she is as feeble as she looks strong & I must let her go at the end of the week, she has however been of great service & a source of constant pleasure. Annette is here & seems sensible and satisfactory, but then she only came this morn.

Mother walked to Edward's yest. & we took tea with C. & T. with great pleasure. She has a little cold today caught by having too much window last ni. I have much more to say but no time. Affec.
E. T. E.

Thursday 24 Jan. 1884
Dear Edith,

It is a shame not to have written. Annette does well, Mary too, and I am sorry to let her go. Dear Mr & Mrs Cabot came this afternoon to stay with Edward but at present they are working in the study so I have the pleasure of beholding them for a while. They don't speak, they are so busy, and I cannot help them. You know I want to see Cousin Mary's letters to you when Father was sick to help write out the account of his last days for Mr Cabot. So have them where they can be found in February. I'll try to write first without them & correct by them, as well as correct them. Mother is well again today. We have been reading some letters of 1834–43 which were uncommonly good. I like all my New Years presents very much and so does Mother hers. I luxuriate in bowl spoon vase butterfly bureau-napkin, and prospectively in cleanser cement & embroideries. Mother tried her champagne-tap yesterday on Apollinaris-water, has her vases on her mantel-piece, her almanac on her table. The lamp & the brackets aren't yet put up.

Monday morning. I haven't been able to write since Mary went. Annette has absorbed my whole attention. She told me yesterday that she was going on Tuesday & this morning that after the insults I gave her the moment she came into the house she could not stay & had only remained to earn her fare & save her pride with her friends by not returning as they had prophesied *instanter*. The insults she said were contained in the talk about the things she mustn't do. She is no loss, for though willing, kind, and morally excellent on the whole she cannot sweep clean, and is slow, feeble, and unable to handle a table-cloth or napkin rightly, or to remember anything. Mother went to church yesterday. I had much to say & on business, but 'tis mail-time. How do you do? I hope 'tis a time of peace with you.   Affectionately
Ellen.

Monday 4 Feb. 1884.
Dear Edith,

I am very sorry you are down, and wish I could help you, but 'tis impossible for me to arrive before Thursday night, indeed 'twill be a close shave to do that. Mr & Mrs Cabot propose to come We. at 3 & stay till Thurs. at 5. I'm just going to telephone them to come if they can do almost without sight of me, if they want me they must wait till I get home. I didn't know till now that Bible Society Annual Meeting came this week. I was working towards my Report but supposed it wouldn't be for ten days. It comes Thursday aft. I shall bring Mother on Wed., return by 5.30 ex., shut myself up Thurs. forenoon to write the Report & go early to the Soc., ask leave to read it at 4 & come Milton-wards by the 5 Lowell train. The Cabots can be here, rejoice me at meal-times & prosecute their work independently if they think best. I rejoice in the prospect of soon seeing you. Oh Edith what a good full treasury of stories you have written! & many many thanks for an allamanda & 2 hibiscus buds.   E. T. E.

Concord, 26 Feb. 1884

Dear Edith,

It was very thoughtful and very energetic to get off my birthday celebration so that I should receive it on Saturday night, tied in bed as you are! It was very festive for me and everything was a pleasure. Of course I opened the beautiful box of flowers first, and found very gorgeous things in it. That dark red carnation and the white one, that mighty hibiscus, those perfect little camellias, a whole settlement of heliotrope and another of *boules de neige*! I got an enormous bunch of azaleas out of that box, and there was beautiful cineraria, which is very bright & healthy yet in a glass bowl with ferns. I wondered to find a Eucharis lily at this late day. I dressed my room up with three or four bouquets and squandered others in other directions. On Sunday I opened the rest and find myself rich and well pleased. Don't give me the other present till next New Years. You have already given me too much. Mother sends her love & says she daily takes a walk in your greenhouse and she feels better as soon as her spirit-hand opens the door of it.   Affectionately,

Ellen.

Concord 10 Mar. 1884

My own dear Kitty,

I can't help it; I do the best I can. I'm very sorry not to write and I don't forget to try, but it seems impossible. Your letter was a jewel which I read four times yesterday to Mother & to myself. Edward also heard some of the stories.

There is no chance whatever of Mother's coming she sorrowfully bids me say. Give her bed & her chair to someone else. She has desired & hoped & planned to come both night & day, but she grows weaker, though not sick. What time does the play* come off? When do you want me? I can't leave Mother long. Some of my flowers are still living and pretty.

Affectionately
Ellen

Concord, 22 March 1884

Dear Edith,

Forgive me, forgive me! I have hoped each day, each mail, to write, but have lost the opportunity. Alas! I may never be good again, for sorrow & resolutions no longer avail. Your beauteous story—about canaries—your kind offer enchanted me, but I know you aren't strong enough to do errands.

Edward's lecture at each word interesting. Too condensed. Three evenings would be better than one. Everyone pleased. Mother went. She rides out again today. Will any dear bairn, will Ralph honour me with a visit? When shall we see you. Perfect day at Pauline's. Cousin Sarah's letter gets on slowly.   Affectionately

Ellen

Concord, 2 April 1884

My dear Miss Clara,

I have thought of you a great deal today. Mary Watson came this noon and we have been counting that it is 15 or 16 years since our dear winter at Fayal already. Sixteen more will bring us to 1900! Miss Harriet Ware told me yesterday that she had just begun to realize that she was very likely to see the next century come in, a prospect that filled her with dismay. So it does me. I, feeling my powers already giving way in several directions, and having watched it in Father & Mother for years, seeing too that most of their relations live to a great age, perceive with fright how my health and strength persist in increasing. Unless I'm blown up or otherwise earlier disposed of I may too easily go on to ninety. Thus did Miss Ware and I discourse, and consoled ourselves

---

*"The play" was a dramatization of Scott's *The Lady of the Lake*, acted by members of the family to celebrate J. M. and S. H. Forbes' Golden Wedding Anniversary.

1884

that doctors said people loved living better & better as they got used to it. I hope your birthday today is a very interesting day to you, and I think it is. Mine was, dear Miss Clara, an interesting day to me. It came on Sunday, which I liked, and your delightful letter came on Monday. Mother and I enjoyed every word of it and I learned a great deal. You little know the depths of my ignorance. I was pleased to carry the letter to Beth. Her engagement has been a great event in Concord. It is a really beautiful engagement. Everyone who knows them is pleased. My dear scholar Clara told me all good and pleasant things about it. Cary Wheildon was here last night. I am continually kept reminded of the joy those girls had in Fayal last summer, and am very grateful to you. I am having a great pleasure this week in a visit from Edith's Edward & Don. They are a continual feast to my eyes and ears. They have Frank Cunningham with them and the three play together very happily day after day without any quarrels at all, and never come to ask "What shall we do?" Time is only too short for them. Our Ralph is 17, and Violet 16, beginning both of them to look rather grown up, and how proud I am of that! Violet & Cameron have gone to make their first visit to Washington with Will & Edith, all delighted to go and to go together. Waldo and the Baby are to come here meanwhile. I am going to enclose two photographs lately given to me to show you. Please return them. You will like to see this of Sarah Malcolm and her sons. I never forget what you said about her when she came to Fayal on the Rambler, and I see as I come to know her, how true it is. She came here one day last autumn, and made everyone happy who saw her. Miss Worcester who boards with us said "I can only say she is almost the loveliest person I ever saw." Pauline Shaw and she seem to me alike, and like no one else. The other photograph is of Edward's little girls, my nieces whom I don't know at all, but I enjoy the hope of becoming acquainted. I haven't said a word about Mr [Matthew] Arnold. I do quite agree with almost all that you say. It seemed to me that if he criticized Father he yet set him very high, and that the object of the lecture was after all to express affection and gratitude, so that it rather tormented me to have the papers scold so much and notice only the fault he found, criticizing the criticism, without acknowledging the main drift and purpose of the lecture. But the number of articles written on the subject for a week or two amused & interested us all. Edith made a collection of them. Mr Arnold gave his lecture on "Numbers" in Concord, and he and Mrs Arnold stayed here. Mr & Mrs Elliot Cabot, and Edith and Ralph were

— 1884 —

here too. We all felt at once well acquainted with the Arnolds, they were like relations, and we hated to have them go away. Mr Arnold said Boston had been a great surprise to him. He had formed his idea of it from American books, so he blamed nothing but Yankee rhetoric. He thought he was to find Boston bay surrounded by a flat & tree-less waste,—bare sand, from which mighty boulders of granite stood up among the scattered houses of Boston. So that when he found a solid regular city built on hills without a rock anywhere visible, above all when he saw the beautiful towns of Brookline & Jamaica Plain his amazement was unbounded. Civilization everywhere! and an old civilization too! and such beautiful trees! They both expressed great pleasure in the warm houses, and especially in the furnace registers in the floor. Goodbye, I am sorry I write so seldom, but I cannot do better and I am glad and grateful that you still remember me and write to me. Please give my love to Mrs Dabney, and Miss Dabney.
>
> Affectionately
> Ellen T. Emerson.

April 24th 1884

You dear Violet, what a good niece you are! All the little tales of papa, mamma & Cameron were sweet words, plums in the cake. It was good that you went to see Mrs Bancroft and Mrs Ward, and saw so much of Ruth & the other cousins. I found it very pleasant to keep having these letters from you, except that I couldn't at the time, or till now write you any answer. I have first found the chance here at Plymouth. How long it is since I have had a visit from you. You are to have one from me first. I am coming with Grandmamma in nine days. I hope your Aunt Annie's baby won't be born till I get home. It was a happy surprise to find your Mother waiting in Boston for us yesterday. Tell her all went well. Grandmamma & I dined each in our own fashion, I like the fox, she like the stork, at the O.C. depot, and got into the train, into the car marked for Plymouth. Before we sat down two ladies, one of them old, exclaimed "Why Mrs Emerson! how do you do? You are really going to Plymouth, aren't you?" Mother just answered them and attacked me to know who they were. I told her they were her girl friends, not mine, she must find out. She was quite sure she had never seen them before. When we came near Plymouth they hunted her up once more, and introduced themselves as Mrs Thomas Hedge & her daughter Mrs Lothrop, and Mother recognized them at once. I was quite right. She is blessed with a N.E. storm today and asks nothing better, she can repose as much as she wishes. She says "How absurd to have brought a best dress! Everyone is dead; there is no one to come to see me, only four or five feeble old ladies for me to go to see, and nobody who would ask me to tea." But perhaps we shall still be glad of the dress. Cousin Mary has been talking about the boys & babies last summer, and we have been telling her about them this winter. I shall write to Cameron and to Mamma today or tomorrow, tell them, and shall soon behold you all.

Your proud aunt.

Plymouth May 9 1884

Dear Edith,

Mother sends much love to you and thanks you for the strawberries. She sat by the register in the O.C. Ladies' Room and ate them and drank egg nog till my dinner was ready in the refreshment room, when she joined me and ate a little bread & butter. Everything goes very prosperously, she is very well. It rained Wednesday night, and all day Thursday, so she has not yet gone out at all, but Mrs Sue Davis called on her last night and said that her mother though confined to her chair wanted us to come to tea some night. Later Mr Wm. G. Russell's daughter Lily, now Mrs Roger Allen, who has a house right across the street came in and called on us. I went to bed at eight and Mother sat up and had the pleasure of a game of whist.

3 p.m. Today it clears up and Mother is about to set forth and take me to walk. Luly showed me round last night a little. We have brought Dr Thacher's History of Plymouth and I am reading it aloud to Mother. Mother desires you to thank Sarah Malcolm for the good little wafers, so do I. They put me to sleep at dead of night. No news yet from Concord. Alas! it is almost 5 o'clock & Mother will not get up. I'm afraid she is going to simply collapse as she often does in Milton & refuse to go out of the house, the pressure of errands & garden which keeps her active at home being withdrawn she takes to her bed. I hope this won't be the case.

E. T. E.

Plymouth, 10 May 1884

My dear Edith,

Mother did, soon after I closed my letter, rise and go forth. The first

— 1884 —

natural sight (if it hadn't been re-painted) was the Samoset. Then Luly pointed out Mrs Isaac Hedge's house. "Oh yes! Mr William Hammett built that house for Aunt Esther's daughter Esther Parsons." She subsequently related that once when she was a child she went to tea there and she thinks it must have been uninvited, since they were making the wedding-cake for Miss Lucia Hammett, Mrs Austin's mother. Next we came in sight of the Thomas Hedge house quite unchanged, and very handsome. Mrs Cox's was then descried. Then Luly pointed to the house ahead & said "There's Mrs Bartlett, Miss Lucia Bartlett's mother, at the window." Accordingly I looked to see if she would recognize Mother. She did and bowed. We met Mrs Davis who turned round and walked with us. Aunt Squire's was the next place of interest on the other side of the street. Mother had boarded there ten months between leaving Uncle Doctor's and going to the Winslow house. Then Mr Andrew Russell's house & Miss Mary Russell's, and Luly's grandfather Watson's, and now Uncle Doctor's house was in full view and the Loud house where Mrs Hedge & Mrs Davis now live is just opposite. The object of the expedition was to call on Mrs Hedge, so Mother & I went in with Mrs Davis, and Luly went on her ways. Here we were introduced first to Mrs Hedge & Priscilla, then to the pictures of five generations. How puzzling it is! Mrs Davis had a miniature tall clock, only 3 or 4 ft. high. "Don't you remember it always in Grandma Cotton's parlour?" she asked. "Oh yes indeed!" cried Mother. After a little call we departed, invited to tea tonight, and Mother said she was not well enough to go down North street but would like to push along to the Town Square. So we did, and came to Uncle Thomas's house, Uncle William & Aunt Esther had lived on the farther side, Uncle Thomas & Aunt Sally on the other. These were the identical steps down which Uncle William handed Aunt Esther by her finger-tips every Sunday morning as we have so often heard. It is now occupied by milliner, photographer etc. Luly opened the door and we marched right in. "This—oh! this was Aunt Esther's parlour, and that was Aunt Sally's" As we mounted the stairs I asked if they were the old ones. "Yes! oh yes! but they have grown narrower & steeper." I asked where the door at the head of the stairs led to. "To the back of the house. In this house Sophia Brown died." "Which room?" "In one of these back rooms" "Whose room was this?" "It was Aunt Lucy's then. She was here when Sophia died. It was Frances Maynard's house then and Aunt Lucy was boarding with her. In old times it was Aunt Esther's room" Highly delighted with so much information and with the appearance of the entry, and seeing a sign "Reception-room" on one chamber door, I tried it, but it was locked. It was 6 o'clock & business was ended.

Saturday 24 May 1884

Dear Edith,

All went smoothly. Mother rather enjoyed the ride into Boston, and showed her usual decision the moment she was face to face with the silver-ware. She brought home pie-knife, macaroni-helper and a bell, and the next day I carried them to show to Clara who presently went to consult Beth. And Beth came down affectionate and sweet and said "May I come and choose my own present?" She showed the same knowledge of her own mind that Mother had. She instantly took the macaroni-helper, and clave unto it. "And this will be marked *E. H.* won't it?" she asked as if she wished it to be considered a present to Aunt Lizzy's namesake. It pleased both her & me very much. To go back to our return home. We found Jenny at the depot with the carryall, and she looked pleased to see us. As we passed Miss Prichard's we saw the Whaleys. They had come across the sea. When we came to the house John hung back till Mother called him and then came with speed. We were received with many smiles in the kitchen, and the whole house had been made clean. Jenny, naughty girl! had gone through alone the perplexing & endless job of putting up Mother's newly done-up bed-curtains, and Mother's carpet had been taken up & put down and her room & closets scoured. Jenny had moreover arranged flowers for the bureau & table.

This is the second sheet of my letter though it is now June 2d. and I have received this morning your letter and am very glad to hear from you. It was a letter of unmitigated good news except Will's poison. I was pleased to have you have a delightful visit in New Bedford; I infer however that Will was poisoned by gathering the Rhodora. What a pity! Do bring all five children & never hesitate to bring them to the wedding, they will be welcome. On Saturday night we had Mrs Sanborn & Miss Leavitt to tea to play whist, Miss Rood who was making me a visit to take the fourth hand. Mother was arranging her flowers as of old, when she ought to have been cutting the cake. The express drove up and brought your garden of trees & plants, now all successfully set out & flourishing in our garden, and your tight packed box of flowers. Mother at once fitted them in with hers with unusual skill, the vases looked far richer & handsomer than usual and called forth great enthusiasm in our guests. We all agree that the new columbine is the prettiest ever seen, a great acquisition. Delightful Decoration Day. Chas. & Therchi spent it with us. Sunday quiet, Miss Rood, Mother & I. Monday Jamaica Plain. This morning Edward drove me over to see Kate Rouse. She is dying, may not live a week. The dear children absolutely devoted & very sad.

28 May 1884

Dear good Edith,

I can't write enough today to go on with my letter begun, but I hate you should hear nothing from me. Our new nephew is perfectly satisfactory. Scarlet as Ralph, round head, not very dark or very long hair, but plenty of it, a smooth beaver head like Ralph's, good ears like little Charles's, a face of a different type, like his eldest brother William, who you know was entirely different from Charles, Ellen & Florence, but not like John. He cries finely, has very fat arms, and collops "like a bull-purp" behind his neck. His nose is pronounced, his chin short but wide. I haven't seen Annie but expect to today, she is as well as usual. Mother sends her delighted thanks for Monday's box of flowers. The hyacinths are an ever-new delight to her.

Affectionately
Ellen.

Concord, 7 June 1884

Dear Edith,

Kate died last night and will be buried Monday. I suppose Edward & I shall go to the funeral. Annie & the baby are delightful. I have just visited them. Don't fail to bring all the three boys to the wedding. Beth would like it & all your friends would afterwards speak of them to their aunt. Yesterday as I passed Mother's door she exclaimed "Gracious me! All my spectacles have married & been blessed with offspring to such a degree that I can't find my way among them!"

No time for more.
Ellen

23 June 1884

My dear Edith

Thankyou very much for the honey. We have eaten one box of it with much pleasure. If you are likely to have time I'll come to Boston on Wed. to choose my best hat with you. If not I don't mind much, for I think with the brown one you gave me, the white chip & the blue one I may properly expect to go safely through the summer. I have a feeling too as if I were likely to have a particularly quiet summer, I am not going anywhere and can't think of anyone who would be willing to come here. Mother & Edward & I hope you are nearly ready to give your consent to the cutting of the fir-balsams, one is dead & red all over, the other two you know have long been moribund. Yesterday Jessy Barrett Dennie's Ruth, Cora Brown's Roger, Amy Houghton's Ruth, & Mary Alice Bulkeley were christened in church, the last-named talking very prettily to the flowers & riding & jumping violently all the time in her mamma's arms. While her papa held the water on her head, she turned round & opened her eyes wide to the congregation. Roger Brown resisted & lifted up his voice for a moment, Ruth H. took it quietly, Ruth D. gazed fixedly in Mr Bulkeley's face and was still. As they filed out she was the last & looking back she cried "Bye!" & shook the prettiest day-day. Unspeakable delight in the pews was the natural result. Goodbye, dear Edith, I hate to neglect you. Mother not very well today, Jenny gone.

Affectionately
Ellen.

Concord 1 July 1884

Dear Edith,

I seize a moment for you. On Thursday I think it paid to stay home though I did hate to lose the party and to fail you at your need. On Friday Mr Harlow sent an invitation to the Frolic Club to go *en Masse* by steamboat to Plymouth the next day. Dear Miss Leavitt sent me word that 'twould make her sick to go so she would come and stay with Mother if I wanted to go. Mother declared that she should be wholly satisfied if I went, so to my own amazement I was sailing down the harbour at ten o'clock on Saturday morning with the Frolic Club. All of course were in the highest spirits at first, but of course this didn't last long, and Annie Bartlett & Miss Buttrick became very sick, but Miss Buttrick toughed it out on deck. I was one of the best sailors and braved the cold & wind better than many and felt quite elated. Before our sorrows began we enjoyed the fine view of jelly-fishes, also of islands, light-houses & fortifications. Later I sat with Cary Perry & Mary Brown

— 1884 —

& Jane Hosmer, also Mary Wood & Anna McClure and we had a very good time. Mrs Wood, Mrs Smith, Mrs Todd, Jane Loring were also of the party. 'Twas a very valuable day in a social way and I had time to see the Burying Hill & Pilgrim Hall, and to show Anna & Constance our three houses, and the largeness of the Winslow house windows, also to bow to Dr Briggs. Miss Peabody came to Bush in my absence and is to stay till July 7th. Edw. dined with us with Ellen & little W[illiam]. F[orbes]. E[merson]., his first entrance into the ancestral halls.
       Affectionately
       Ellen.

           17 July 1884 Concord
Dear Edith,
 A new girl yesterday absorbed and absorbs me. I should have written otherwise. I consulted Edward about going to Naushon. He says if Mother hadn't been twice & always sick there he should advise it, but as she has he hardly thinks it worthwhile to run the risk again, and I believe I agree with him. She is so easily sick, and there is no doctor there nor eagerness to get up & out which cured her in Plymouth. Then even if she isn't sick, if she is as depressed as both other times 'twould be hard all round.
 Thankyou for your beautiful long chronicle. The whole story of the move, all sweet to the ears, the adventures of Cameron & Don amusing & most exciting. I can't think what spite of fate has removed the letters of former years about the move. Some may be in my closet. I have two boxes full waiting for sorting. The Mr & Mrs Bush introduced by Effie are to take tea with us tonight. I can't go to Boston before 1 Aug. I fear. I should enjoy it & like to be of use to you.
       E. T. E.

          Milton, 29 July 1884
Dear Edith,
 I have come to visit Mary for two days, and am having a beautiful time. I seize the first moment to write to you that I have had. You must have begun to feel grieved at my long silence. I didn't "decide not to come to Naushon", I said "Unless Mother felt like it I should let it pass" or something like that. I think it quite worth while to propose it to her and see. Perhaps it would be a success. She is at present always planning for a game of whist. She is pretty well. The School of Philos-

ophy is all about Father so far. We don't go of course. Cousin Sarah is devoted to it, so was Lizzy while she was here. Alice Arthur came up on purpose and all say it is delightful, delightful, and long to have me hear not only the lectures but the talk. I had the pleasure of Lizzy and Alice Barber for a week, and of Alice Arthur for a day, of Miss Powell, now Mrs Bond, and a particularly charming little son Edwin, ten years old for two days. Last week the Bible Society met with us, and was as usual a gay occasion. Sophy [Ripley Thayer] now lives in Concord, has suffered as Will did in the spring with ivy-poison ever since she came, is just recovering. She says Cousin Mary's house is beautiful and full of memories. To her it is principally the house her Mother died in, and that little Lucia lived and died in. Sophy's joy in being at home was beautiful to hear. There is a certain Dr Holland of N. Orleans who comes to the School of Philosophy, in his boyhood a rebel soldier, now an Episcopal minister, a very interesting man. I heard him preach last Sunday, and it was an event, a positive Christian sermon such as we seldom hear. He spent the evening with us, and talked about the South. Julian's lecture on Father "as an American" was very good. It is printed in the August No. of the Manhattan Magazine. Not another min.

Ellen.

11 August 1884

Dear Edith,

I have two weeks of pleasure to tell you of. First the week when I was at Mary Russell's. Mary offered me the chance to ride over with Ellen & Mary who were going to call on Mrs Theodore Lyman and stop at Pauline's. How could I but accept? At Pauline's Ida herself came down to the door to say I might come in. Pauline looking quite sick was lying on the parlour sofa. We sat down to endless comfort & conversation, snugged up together as close as possible, as is our wont, and Mr Shaw who was cleaning his paintings in the room followed our discourse and sometimes joined in it, which was a pleasure to me. Ida told us about her visit to Lily Ward, her looking up all the haunts of her childhood at Freiburg, her conversations with the peasants. Pauline told me about Louis's wedding and his farm. At this point Mary Morse Elliot & her husband came in and the circle had to widen a little. Pauline & I had a little discourse. She had enjoyed Naushon and seeing you so much, and we congratulated one another on it all. Then Ellen & Mary came back for me and we departed. Arriving at Mrs Cunningham's where we were to drink tea a little too early before she had returned from her drive we went into the garden which I had never seen before. It was so long, so large, so old and full of aged & uncommon things that I was enchanted. Next Ellen took me over to her Aunt Rose's garden. Then we went back to Mrs Cunningham's and there I had the joy of seeing Will who told us stories about the children which were just what their aunt desired to hear. Mrs Cunningham was very good to me. Will invited me to take a drive, and each lady in turn, all refused except Ellen Russell, and after tea they drove away together. Mary & young Mary and I had our moonlight ride home, which was very beautiful a little later. In the morning I found Edith Perkins going to Boston in the same train.

Eighteen pages of the letter are omitted here. ETE was invited by Edith Perkins to bring friends from Concord for the night, and they visited various Milton houses and gardens which are described in some detail.

And now I must leave off, omitting my visit to Mrs Brooks at Pigeon Cove, my perfect day with dear Mr & Mrs Cabot, my afternoon & night with Ida Higginson. No more time tonight. Love to you all. You may not hear from me again for two weeks, I've postponed business to write so much. Thanks for pretty letters from you. Affectionately
      Ellen.

                Concord, 2 Sept. 1884
My dear Edith,

 We never wonder or murmur at you when your letter delays a little we think when it comes what a good daughter and sister you are. Uncle George, Cousin Elizabeth [Ripley] and Margaret Ames came to bid us goodbye on Wednesday night before they sailed. Sophy told us that when they rode through the town in the barge going up to the Junction the whole Mill-Dam turned out to wave & to shout goodbye, and all the way up the street people came to their gates to see them off. Miss Bartlett said she never realized till the last minute what a sheet-anchor was gone in Cousin Elizabeth, but then it suddenly came over her. What glorious moonlight they have had for their voyage! Uncle George said he was expecting great delight in the evenings on deck with this harvest-moon. And I have had it on land. Sunday night there was no need of my being at home to tea, Miss Sage, our new boarder hadn't arrived, Cousin Sarah was company enough for Mother, so

— 1884 —

Anna McClure came down & we took a Sunday afternoon walk carrying a basket with us, and sat down on one of your Fairyland hills to see the sunset and eat our supper. The lights were enchanting, the foliage below very rich and of different shades. Then came a beautiful yellow light. It was as warm & dry as noon. When we came out by the sycamore at the corner of the causeway we met the very wind that always brings the words "gales from Eden breathe", and the pines before us were black against a dark red sky. By the time we reached home it was clear moonlight and we walked through the garden which looked romantic as possible. Tuesday night Cousin S. & I through many difficulties did lead Mother forth to see what Anna & I had seen on Sunday. We hoped she would ride almost all the way on the donkey, but she alighted as soon as we reached the Walden road. She was particularly sick & unhappy all the way, but by the time we came to the hill-top of Sunday night she declared she felt better, and I had the pleasure of showing her & Cousin Sarah the various beauties I had noticed then. As we came down the hill there was the loveliest effect of water against the darkness of the hill on the other side seen through leaves lighted by the yellow sunset. Mother at once rejoiced in this pretty sight and said it was the best yet. 'Twas moonlight before we reached home and we admired it together and after tea took another walk to enjoy it. It was most enchanting on the eastward-turned faces of our row of sunflowers which remind Cousin Sarah's teaching mind of a class standing up to recite. The next day Lizzy & Cary came. The weather once more very hot. I proposed Walden & tea in the boat and away we went with Cousin Sarah. Boats alas! all beached. But we took tea in our pasture, ran down afterward to see sunset colours on the pond, then rode home in moonlight. Thursday night I went to the Meeting, but after it Cousin S., Mother & I had a walk. Heavenly! Friday night Anna & I took our supper on the N. Branch and saw the glorious moon again. So for four nights I had it well. No time.

Ellen

Cars F.R.R.
16 Sept. 1884

Dear beloved Edith,

I'm perfectly happy that you & dear good Violet and the babies will ornament our anniversaries. What time will you arrive? How long can you stay? I had meant silently to have **Mr & Mrs Keyes & Prescott** &

— 1884 —

Alice & Charley & Therchi to tea, nothing more. But it appears Aunt Susan & Lizzy heard from you, they told the Bartletts, the B.'s Sophy, and Sophy says they are all coming with presents & poems after tea. Mr & Mrs Keyes are to invite them all to dinner as usual at 12.30. I want to have a great "old Concord" tea-party on Saturday for Mother's birthday. Do you approve? Prichards, Hoars, Brookses, Keyeses, Miss Barrett, Bartletts, Sanborns, Cheneys, Wheildons, Alcotts, Damons, the Fay Barretts, Gourgases, John Browns, for they asked me to their party just now, and if there be any other you desire.

Nov. 10th 1884

Dear Edith,

Thankyou for the pretty notes sent by Annie. I much desired to come to see you but am prevented. I am going to the dentist on Wednesday morning and I want your wool-cards if you can lend them to me. If V. will carry them to school I'll stop there for them but I should like better to find them at Sears Building where I have to carry some money. Ned Bartlett's little Mary has narrowly escaped dying, but they seem to believe she has escaped. Lizzy was telling what a comfort & companion to her Father she is, and how she seems to all of them as if she was all they had in the world. Mother is out walking again and went to church twice yesterday. At dinner she rescued a fly from her tumbler and when I proposed to put him out-of-doors she reproved me. When I saw her carry six carefully on a pudding-plate which they were unsuspiciously feasting on to the window after dinner & put them out, I asked why I couldn't be allowed to put out my victim before. "Why, because he was all wet, & he would be very cold, perhaps take cold."

Affectionately
Ellen.

Concord 14 Nov. 1884

Dear Edith,

I hadn't seen those magnificent chrysanthemums when I wrote. They surpass all I ever saw. We are delighted with them. I am also much obliged for the pinks and the dwarf irises and the wool-cards. Your stories in the last letter were better than ever, a series of joyful surprises to Mother and me, and they "came in handy" to reconcile Mother to taking quite a long ride, and seemed to me to lift her cheerfully through a day of unusual feebleness. Alas! I grow more and more unable to feel any special preference for Cleveland over Blaine. Both seem about as poor candidates as we could desire—or put up with, and both parties unscrupulous.

After three days of weakness Mother seems to me better this morning. We are to dine with the Chamberlaines at two, and tonight the Club meet with us, and Mr Emery has written a paper for the occasion. What do you think of having Minnie make Mother's new velvet basque, trying it on while we are with you?   Affectionately
Ellen T. Emerson

Concord, 20 Nov. 1884

Dear Edith,

We are sorry to hear you are sick. Mother is having a very feeble week, suffering much, enjoying little, and yet, Edward says, not showing any symptom of sickness. She considers herself very sick, because she feels so dreadfully, but I keep her to the habits of health lest she should become sick, and it is a pretty sorrowful time. She does not know that Thanksgiving is near so I don't attribute it to that. I shall try throughout the preparations to keep the care of Mother uppermost, so if the house & dinner are not quite what they should be, I may not have to blame myself about her. Today C. Cheney and her Mother dined here. Therchi was here too and made it pleasanter to us all. She & C. picked all my currants for the mince. Yesterday the Bulkeleys dined here, it is a constant surprise to me to find how much I *love* them. I don't miss them, I don't know that I care for them at all; but let them come, and when they have gone I feel that I have had a feast, as when I have seen my own family. At Edward's the three children look well. My Lord William was exhibited in the cleanest of gowns, looking rather heavy. And now tell us how you do, as soon as you are able to write a word. Oh how we have enjoyed our chrysanthemums! Burglars, my dear, are horribly prevalent & successful here, always enter by upper windows. I send flannel tomorrow if I can.

Ellen.

Concord 2 Dec 1884

Dear Edith,

Mrs Sanborn brought your message that you would rather have us come later & stay over Christmas to New Years and that pleases me very much if it can be managed. I have thought how pleasant it would be to stay and not come home, but till I got your message I thought you would rather we should not be there at Christmas. Your letter has come since I began this. Thankyou we will come on Wednesday and stay till the Saturday after New Years. Almost four weeks, which will be in every way delightful to us if Mother is well enough. Mary Sage thinks she can get friends to stay with her. Edward says we must both remember that it is an experiment to move Mother, & that it may prove best for her not to stay long, but oh! I hope it will do her good and that we may have the whole time. If Minnie will match that flannel I shall be much obliged. Mother was better on Friday, on Saturday walked out, Sunday dined at Edward's, Monday bad day, today she is better again & has ridden out.

Affectionately
Ellen.

Milton, 24 December 1884

Dear Cousin Sarah,

I have been too much hurried or interrupted to write till now, though feeling very sorry to treat you so. Now we have been at Edith's for a fortnight, and are to stay another. Mother has just eaten up her breakfast with unwonted piety and faithfulness, and is reposing after it as I write. I have been reading her a few pages of Dr Holmes's life of Father. A minute ago she sounded the alarm, the flannel she must have was lost. I succeeded in dragging it to light "You good, good girl! You deserve to be patted," she said most affectionately, "for finding it and for springing so spry." So you see she is more amicable than we are used to seeing her. Perhaps because I am writing and not persecuting her. The reason for persecuting is removed this morning, for it snows and we cannot go out. She is well-pleased to see the snow storm. Usually I get her at least to go over to the green-house. There we view the roses in the rose-house, then wander round the hotter room to see the great yellow allamandas & the cactuses & begonias, and there Edith has in a corner a cinnamon plant, an allspice, a pepper and a coffee-plant, which interest me very much. Then we enter the winter-garden, where the acacias, oranges, banana & camellia & abutilons grow, and there are the family birds all loose & flitting about, except Cameron's thrush & mocking-bird which are always found scurrying about the roots of the plants. Here also we usually find Ralph & Cameron watching them. They are the ornithologists of the household. They are very polite to their Grandmamma and do her the honours of the place. Don is apt to be practising songs, and so is Ralph when he is in the house, and these two seem to enjoy Waldo & Alexander most, more even than Violet. Violet is as much as ever shut up in her own room. I wish she were sociable. But she sleeps with me, and when we are dressing and undressing we have beautiful times. Little Edward's eyes are not quite well-made, and he has to put on spectacles to read. It was a bitter sentence to the poor boy, but he has got used to it in two weeks, so that he often forgets to take them off. Waldo is learning to read, to dance and to sing and shows facility in all three directions. For Edith her house is one vast store-room of Christmas presents at this moment all labelled and tied up. I should think they must count up to four or five hundred. I never was so stunned by the possibilities of thought & labour in the Christmas direction. Presents for innumerable people, and one from each of her family of 9 to almost each of the unnumbered. Edward comes twice a week to see Mother and brings good news from home. We rejoice that you went to Cousin Charlotte's & to Cousin Hannah's. All you write is nuts to us. Do write more. I have been too long out of Edith's sight & must run back. Much love from Mother & me & Merry Christmas!

            Affectionately
            Ellen.

            Concord, 3 Feb. 1885

Dear Edith,

I don't think you have even been formally thanked for your goodness in receiving and keeping us for a month. It has certainly been of eminent advantage to us. Mother was made better both by the change to Milton and the change back to Concord, and has been for the last two weeks herself again, and as she was in the autumn. She goes out willingly twice a day, and sometimes appears with her things on to see whether I will go, when I should have thought it too cold to propose it to her. Also we enjoyed our visit. I remember with great pleasure many things that happened and many talks. I thought the present-giving on New Years Eve was more delightful than either last year or the year before. My dress is very much admired by the few who have seen it. Mary Sage declared that something about it, the red, the ruche, or something had been so becoming at dinner-time that she could imagine me under twenty. I wear it on Sundays whenever we have company,

and shall honour the Cabots with it. I love its solidity and its stiffness. The new tea-spoons were welcomed by everyone, and I am growing vain of them and quite attached to their shape. I have them put round to the plates at breakfast, and on the pudding-plates at dinner, but allow only ELT's* in the spoon-holder. Your Canada letter is delightful. How much they did and planned for you! You must come home with me on Friday. Mother says you must because she is your Mother and she wants to see you. I'm delighted with your taking a walk with Don on shoeshoes. Alas for Ralph's health. How does our dear Violet do? I'll come out at one tomorrow. Affectionately
         Ellen

            Wednesday, 11 Feb. 1885
Dear Edith,

Have you read Judge Holmes's speech at the Bar Association dinner? Edward had it in his pocket on Saturday to read to us after dinner and we were delighted with it. As Edward says it gave us the first idea we ever had of the possibility of attractiveness in the legal profession. Read it to Ralph if he means to be a lawyer. On Monday I undertook a tea-party which Mother has said we ought to have and she desired. The elder Holland family, Mr Holland's Father, Mother & sister. First I consulted & invited Edward & Annie as they drove to the train. They approved and Edward said he would come but Annie's cold was too bad. So I went up to the Hollands who live in Cousin Mary Simmons's house. They consented to come very cordially. Then I successfully invited the Bushes and Miss Amelia Prichard. When I went home I was reminded of Anna's sentence "Mrs Forbes always seems very near to me because of the marks of her thoughtful care for your Mother and you which I keep seeing." I thought what shall we have for fruit and there were your beautiful preserved strawberries. I began to get ready the parlour and found your flowers of Friday still fresh and pretty. Lizzy said "Are there saucers enough?" and I gave her those you brought Mother from California. The guests arrived, all cheerful as could be, and what was more, remained so. The Hollands have a parrot which talks beautifully. They feed jays. When they came under Polly's window she called "Where's the cat? Where's the cat?" On Christmas day they forgot her breakfast. In mid-forenoon Mrs Holland passed

---

*Ellen Louisa Tucker's.

through the dining-room and was arrested by the most pathetic voice. "Poor Polly! Poor Polly doesn't get attended to." Then a week or two ago two telegrams came for Mr Holland while he was out and there was a good deal of talk & excitement as to whether to go out to hunt him up and Polly shouted from the other room "What *is* the matter? What *is* the matter?" They told various other stories of her. Then Edward arrived and he looked very handsome and took hold with a master-hand. At tea I put the waiter at the window end of the room and poured out myself, Edward took the other end and Mother commanded the bell, and helped to the strawberry with eminent satisfaction, it seemed to her a proper thing to offer to a tea-party and she has never had such a luxury before, I don't remember any preserved strawberry in our whole career. Miss Amelia Prichard was like an own aunt and laid herself out to see that all went smoothly, which was comfortable and sweet too. The evening went on wheels, and Mother looked handsome and talked all the time so that Edward said the next day "Well, your dangerous and even dire undertaking met with unmerited success."

Feb 16. Annie had Charitable Society meet with her on Wednesday and I went for the first time in my life, and evidently my coming surprised them all. Alas! they told me there of the death of Mrs Damon's baby, the little Helen. Saturday afternoon I had a party for grammar-school-children and George Bartlett knew it was coming off, so he proposed to assist me. I refused, for I had never tried this age before and I wished to measure my own personal strength with it and see whether I could carry it on, for the sake of knowing what I might dare in future. This age proved easier to deal with than younger children, we had a truly delightful time. I had a large staff of friends to help play, and Therchi managed the supper. The tea to which I invited you is to be Wed., I wish you would come.   Affectionately
Ellen.

Concord, 24 Feb. 1885

My dear Edith,

I seem possessed to leave things at your house. I hope I can come soon to pick them up. On Wednesday morning I had just time to get across to the 11 train. When I reached home I found the Bulkeleys who had been asked to dine, already in the parlour. We had a great deal of parish talk and consultation, very interesting to us indeed. That night you know I was to take tea with Miss Bartlett. We sat round the beloved old square table, but you know the house is changed; it is another dining-room. Presently our Edward knocked at the door and wanted me. He told me of the girl's diphtheria, and that he had just left Ellen at our house, and begged me to go straight home to her. So I did, and the occasion was abruptly terminated. Little Ellen certainly is a dear. She has a pert disagreeable way of talking, a failing I have seen in many children of her age, but for obedience, good sense, conscience helpfulness and even temper she is all one can wish. She stayed till Sunday night, and Edward & Annie came to dine with us on Sunday. I was in Cambridge Friday and Saturday and all about that I desire to tell you and will if possible. I had callers steadily all the afternoon yesterday, which was very gay, but did interfere with the letter to my dear sister.

Affectionately
Ellen.

Thursday, 26 February 1885

Dear Edith,

I will come on Monday and remain till Wednesday. I shall have all marking convenience and will try to accomplish something. I think the Florida plan sounds very interesting only Uncle Edward is afraid you'll have bad colds all of you on your return to pay you for having gone to meet the summer. I had a remarkably interesting and delightful birthday. Mother wondered what to give me so she took me up in town and at Mr Whitcomb's and Mr Brown's she bought me whatever I liked, and we mightily enjoyed the occasion and brought home spoil. We had invited Miss Bartlett & Lizzie to dine and just as they came Edward & Annie & daughters came too. I hoped they had come to dine, alas! they hadn't been asked—I didn't know Edward was to be at home. Ellen came with a big white camellia and a bag of white peppermints. Then Annie, with beautiful ruffles with real lace edging which she had made for me herself, and flowers in a basket from her & Edward, and Edward, with a box of candy. Lizzy now rang the dinner bell, and after a few runs through the entry my nieces & their papa & Mamma went home and we put my flowers in water and went in to dinner. Therchi came, and brought me a monstrous new French linen sheet. Wasn't that an original present? and a delightful one too? After dinner Mother was showing her usual solicitude about dumb animals and Therchi, charmed, rose and kissed her hand, and said to me "Oh! that angel! Oh!

I hope all die Posaunen* blow when Aunt Lidian in the Heaven comes!" Just as they rose to go Anna knocked at the door. She made me a little visit and brought me a new tidy for the inside of my dressing-case, very pretty. After Anna went I began to write, but found John needed help in putting down the dancing-cloths, and just as they were tacked down Mrs Bush came to make a party-call. Before she went came Mrs Cheney & Caroline not knowing it was my birthday but just to return a book. I had returned to my room when I saw Mrs Sanborn, Miss Leavitt & Elsie arriving, and I had a great gala with them. No sooner were they gone than the first division of my party arrived and they poured in steadily till about half-past six. Louisa Norcross came very soon and Mary & Miss Brown took right hold with her and me so we got along beautifully. Alice Linder, who is indeed a host, came later, and just as we began to dance Anna & Constance, who had refused, appeared. So at last things went on wheels, and we learned Grand Right & Left, danced the Virginia Reel and All the Way to Boston, and then sat down to cool and Louisa Norcross showed us how to play Lawyer till 8 o'clock when they all very piously bade me goodnight and departed. The boys who roused my admiration were Jimmy Clahane, Jerry Callahan and Edgar Hunt. Oh! I discovered your flowers in the East Entry, and your letter, just before Mrs Sanborn & Miss Leavitt came, and oh how much they were enjoyed and admired. Thankyou dear Edith.

Milton, 4 Mar. 1885

Dear Cousin Sarah,

How barbarous that I have let your letter lie so long! We were very glad, as we always are, to hear from you, and we often look forward to your coming. You don't know how beautifully Mother has got through the winter. She is better and younger now than she was in November, though not quite so well & young as when you left us. I am not sure whether I wrote to you that Edith provided a nurse for her, Miss Brown, who has been with us two months. I have been free and had all my time to myself, and Mother has been taken care of. Edith is just starting for Florida with Ralph, Cameron, Edward, Waldo & Alexander. She thinks R., C. & W. will be better for a change, and perhaps

*Trumpets (German).

— 1885 —

Edward and isn't willing to leave A. behind. Twenty years ago yesterday W. & Edith were engaged. I spent the day here in Milton and enjoyed beholding the results of those twenty years. Ralph is already big enough to be the escort to Florida. Violet is the most excellent of daughters & nieces. The singing school met here yesterday afternoon and I had the delight of hearing Don & Edward sing "My Ain Countree", a hymn which was Aunt Lizzy's delight the last year of her life, and which was sung at her funeral. When I tell you that I have had all my time to myself, it strikes me that I ought to have written to you long ago, but though I no longer stand by Mother as I did, I am driven by other things, and am in short the same old sixpence you are accustomed to. I hope Cousin Hannah will have real comfort from her pension. Thankyou for writing us about it. Mother has just been talking about your coming. She hopes you clearly understand you are engaged to us for next summer, next June. She sends her love to you. I lately spent a day at Sophy Thayer's and heard very happy letters from Cousin Elizabeth from Dresden. Edward & Annie are going to have a dancing-party at the school-house behind their house this Friday. What fun!.

Your loving cousin
Ellen.

16 March 1885

Dear Edith,

I wonder why we don't hear from you—and you wonder equally why you don't hear from me. With me it is hurry, with you I wish and hope it is lazy enjoyment of your dear sons and beautiful out-of-doors. I want to tell you about Edward's ball. He & Annie and a carpenter & Mr Donovon and one of their girls worked valiantly from dawn till dark and converted the school-house into a ball-room hung with white & red; five large looking-glasses, two on each side and a sideways one at the end. Over this last was a lamp between two star-spangled banners displayed on a dark ground. The March Hare was glorious in one corner & the sign Aries in the other. The lobby was a ladies' room, and had a carpet on the floor, a washstand & dressing-table with every imaginable convenience. The coal-closet was a gentlemen's room prepared with equal splendour. Edward & Annie rushed home for tea & to dress with scant time. Dr Titcomb awaited them and carried off Edward to a consultation over Prescott Hosmer who had pneumonia alas! alas! Edward had the key of the school-house and forgot to leave it.

Annie desperate, almost supperless, took all their keys, and had a long fight with the door, but conquered at just quarter of eight. To hear her tell the whole story would melt a stone to compassion. The insuperable difficulties that met her at every step from 7 to 8 must have kept her in a state of hopeless fright. But only four or five people & the music came before she got the lamps lighted. No one else knew there had been a hitch. Handsome dresses, delighted countenances were on every side when our family arrived at 5 m. after 8. They asked both Miss Brown & Miss Sage to my great joy. But Edward didn't come till nine, and Annie wouldn't begin till he came, she said, if he stayed all night. She would let the party be a failure rather. The moment he came the dance began. It was a party principally of young married people, bachelors & buds. The list of dances was just what I like. Three country-dances, two cotillions, Lancers, Caledonians, and some round dances. It was evident from the beginning that people were perfectly happy. Mr King, Sidney Barrett & John Keyes cut pigeon-wings gloriously. Every dance was danced with enthusiasm. Many an astonished youngster said in departing. "I never enjoyed a party so much in my life. I never thought there could be any fun in square dances, but I think they're delightful." So Annie & I hope they'll remember it. Prescott got his Mother to dance with him. Mrs Holland said she hadn't danced for many years. We got her to dance the Caledonian. Edward & Annie have of course been as happy as they could be about it ever since. Next I want to tell you of little Ellen. On the day of the Circuit-Meeting she came trotting along the front entry with a note from her Mamma saying that she might spend the day with me if I liked. There were rooms to be prepared & I no sooner began than Ellen said "I want to help", and help she did, like a grown-up person. Mr Hussey arrived an hour early, and his room wasn't half ready, so he had to be shut up in the parlour. So Lizzy was dusting in the redroom, and I clearing away the many things that everyone loves to tuck into that room and giving Lizzy directions. Finally I said to her (never thinking of Ellen who was bringing in the pincushion to the bureau) "When you've done that you may tell Mr Hussey his room is ready and show him in here." Then I went into the closet to take away some extra pillows and used sheets and was startled by Mr Hussey's saying "How do you do, Miss Emerson? I don't know that I'm right, but your little niece—is it?—asked me in and said you sent her." I was tripped up indeed, but of course it didn't do any great harm. He is an old friend and has stayed here three times. So Ellen took him back

— 1885 —

into the parlour and stayed with him there. When his room was ready and I went for him he said "I have been let into a great deal of family history." What it may have been I don't know, but have some anxiety, for when Mrs Nathan Stow arrived and I exclaimed "Really I have nowhere to ask you to take off your things", and she rejoined "It must be a great care to get so many rooms ready", Ellen piped up "Yes, we've been very busy. We've been changing slop-bowls." I couldn't but fear that Mr H. had been treated to the same information. Mrs Stow had been afraid to come, but she said afterward "It was delightful." I never saw Mr Bulkeley so happy. Mr Hussey and my friend Mr Green were here, and two new men whom I had hardly seen before, Mr Dillingham of Charleston, and Mr Butler of Beverley. They listened, commented, answered, but did not show their colours at all. At the Meeting in the evening they did, and I liked them both very much. The next day these two & Mr Green stayed and talked till ten, and I had a feast in hearing. Saturday we spent at the Emery's. Oh I forgot to tell you that Mother was uncommonly handsome when she came down to see the ministers. I felt they must all think she was a picture worth coming twenty miles to look at. Well at the Emery's Mother took the "Angel in the House" after dinner and read it aloud to the company with such pleasure that when John came for her she sent him away to return three quarters of an hour later. After she went they all said she looked beautifully. It rather plagues me when we read Coventry Patmore to find that not only Mother but really all the ladies are inclined to agree with Felix that women are immeasurably superior to men. I prefer to have men think that & women think the other way. That night we went to the Saturday Club. George Bartlett read a paper on Saving and Giving, a paper, he said, not intended to give the views of the author, but to show both sides of the question. It was very characteristic, the company laughed all the way through. I have omitted the startling occasion of the night before—Friday March 6th. The Concord Artillery had a Military Ball, and Edward invited Annie & me! and we both went with him!! Yea, and dragged Mother at our chariot wheels. She was very shy of appearing at a Ball, but Edward and I both thought it a good thing. The dressing-room was filled with beauties, most of whom had great beds of fresh glorious roses on their dress-fronts. Mother enjoyed these exceedingly and many girls came to show theirs to her. We found her a seat between Anna Pratt & Lizzy Bartlett and then Edward & Annie marched while I pointed out to her who was who. Edward asked me for the first dance, and when it was over Mother was discovered to have left her seat and her friends that she might find a place where she could feast her eyes on the sight of the Precious Lamb dancing with her Ellen. It was half past nine by that time and she & I went home. Edward & Annie enjoyed themselves so much that they danced till two in the morning. The last week I made a visit of two days to Nina Lowell and had a very good time with her. Ida was with her when I arrived, and I saw her for a few minutes. Julia Paine came to tea to read us a club-paper she had written about Michael Angelo which seemed to me very interesting and oh how good!

Your letter to me came on Monday just after I had mailed mine to you. I was delighted to get it and thankful you should say what you did. We are having the coldest weather, 5 above zero this morning. Edward & Mother scold at it well. I send much love to every bairn you have with you, and visions of visits from them always dance in my head, and to you & Will who I rejoice to hear has gone to you.

Your affectionate sister
E. T. E.

Lowell R.R. 26 March 1885

Dear Edith,

I have so much to tell you only it never will be told. I have just been spending Tues. & Wed. with Cousin Abby. Mrs Larkin was there too and you can imagine I have had the utmost rest & comfort. The first day we sat in the little parlour after dinner, and I yarned on to Cousin Abby till I was afraid she would be tired. Then we took a walk, and sat afterwards by the fire where Mary soon joined us and we talked Illustrated London News and the Court Calendar and Princess Beatrice. Dr Faulkner had been at Grafton & came home at night. As a democrat he is exceedingly happy, and I know that Edward is happy too, about the way things go on at present at Washington. Dr F. says "If they only can go on!" He doesn't feel sure they will, but he says, "They really have it in their power now, and if they prove to be strong sensible men and to work together, they can make a real reform! But then—" and he shakes his head, not believing in so great a good. They are all extremely interested in a book called "Ben Hur, a Tale of the Christ". Mary says it is a story for a lover of horses. I thought perhaps you would like to try it on in your family. Yesterday we went to see Dr Faulkner's tenement houses. He has two tenements of five houses each. Each house contains two tenements, one up stairs and one down, three rooms to each with cellar, clothesyard, door and entries quite to itself, very ingeniously contrived and perfectly made. So you see he has twenty families in them. Next Cousin Abby drove me to Mrs Cabot's. She gave me 80 pages of the Life of Father which she had copied for me from Mr Cabot's manuscript. Cousin Abby was delighted and from the moment I got home till ten o'clock we read together those 80 pages. They are very interesting, not dry but lively & sparkling. I came in with Lilian Clarke in the train. She asked for you & sent her love to you.

Concord April 2d 1885

My dear Miss Dabney,

I wonder why I usually have a busy day on your birthday. Today I have thought of you from morning to night, but now it is bed-time. So I'll only send my love to you and best birthday wishes, and write more tomorrow. Thankyou for the beautiful birthday letter you wrote me. I am always delighted when you speak of having heard from Beth. It is so good to have you like each other. I heard yesterday that she expects a baby in July. Clara has just ended her training as a nurse, and is at home, but I have no doubt she means to go to Beth and be with her this summer. She has loved her nursing and would rather go on with it than not, I am told. Edith & Will Forbes have just come home from Florida. They took five sons with them, and all gained by the journey. Ralph is almost nineteen, and proved sociable enough in disposition to get acquainted with many people at the hotel and go to the dances and the singing. Dancing interests me very much, and I have had a dancing party just now, for the people of my own age principally, but for their children too, and we revived Hall's Victory, and Ladies Triumph, and other Contra-dances of our youth. Edward & Annie had a similar but much finer Ball with the same dances, and I mean to have another. Won't it be good if we can make the young people like them enough not to let them die? The other day I went to Milton and spent a day and night with Mary Watson. She is always at some training or self-improvement, none of my other friends—except Lizzy Simmons—seem to do it. In the evening all the married children except Sylvia came with their spouses to see us and we had a very cheerful time. We saw Mr & Mrs Forbes & Sarah Malcolm. I learned from Mr Forbes that he wasn't anxious or disturbed about the new President's having put so many Southerners into office; and that has made me quite comfortable in mind on that subject ever since. Edith and Will came here yesterday to see the stone Edward has brought to stand at Father's grave. Poor Edward has tried very hard to get what he wanted, big beryls in their natural bed of quartz; but all in vain; and at last he has given up and brought a big piece of quartz. The result of last night's family council seemed to be a decision to set it up rough and have a bronze plate sunk in it. Still they may change their minds again. Edward has a good strong little son ten months old, named William Forbes. Little Ellen is a big girl now, very good at dusting and at doing errands. Florence is a mine of joy, lots of natur' in her, and courage and high spirits.

Mr Cabot is working steadily at his "Life" of Father. *We* delight in it, and so do the people who remember his early years. Mother is well again now, almost as well as last summer. She cares for your letters and thanks you for your messages. She sends her love to you, and so do I, and to dear Roxa and Alice. I hope you are coming soon to America and will at last give me my desired visit. Affectionately

Ellen T. Emerson.

Dear Edith,

I have been at Mrs Folsom's lovely domestic funeral. Coming back Alice Wheildon invited me to lunch with her. She took me up to her house which is the top room cor. Beacon & Mt Vernon Sts. with widest view. She pushed aside her sofa & revealed her kitchen in the corner behind it. She heated tomato, then stewed the oysters she had bought on the way home over the kerosene stove, while the bread toasted over the coal grate, and in an incredibly short time the table was set and we had fancy-roast oysters & tomato & bread & butter. It was all uncommonly good too. Meanwhile we had pretty good talk. Then I skipped away to my Board meeting, visited the new Unitarian House on the cor. of Beacon & Bowdoin Sts and wondered that I had never known of its location before, then I went to Carter Rice & Co's and bought paper of our cousin Mr Low. Do you ever go to him? Will you give me a day to do my dress errands with me within a month? Affectionately

Ellen.

Concord 28 Apr. 1885

Faithful & dear Edith, thankyou for letter, plants, promises & admonitions. I have written once to Mrs Cabot & write today again. I send you the pages that Edward & I have already studied, and will bring the

rest on Thurs. Mrs Sanborn and I will meet you at 11.10 at Hovey's. I must come up on 3 o'clock train as Mrs Hemenway comes that night. I am tired & driven dear Edith or I would have written before. I am expecting my dear Violet & 5 brothers, & Ralph thought Jim perhaps tomorrow to my Ball. How I wish you were coming! Edw. has already set out irises. My pinks did live & irises too. Affly
                                    ETE

                                    Concord 16 May 1885
Dear Edith,
I got an accomodator who, I imagine, may prove permanent, and took Effie. So I am set up. Mother seems not to want to have Miss Brown come to Milton, so if you think it not too great a risk to run I will come with her and leave the girls to get along as they can. My opening with Edward & Annie & Mother was the greatest success & joy. Edward said "There's a bonnet now, as *is* a bonnet! Turn round, turn round! and show Mother your eave-tiles! There, Mother, look at them! Aren't they pretty?" By this singular name he designated the gold-lace behind. The hat they all think perfectly beautiful as an *objet d'art*, "with that effect of a light frost over the whole," Edward said; but look on me in it with a doubtful air "Not becoming to you, not quite your style" was the first impression. However they said on the whole it did very well. They studied the silk question with ardour. Annie went strong for the lilac, Edward for the green. So did Mother. Edw. tried the green onto me & approved so strongly that Annie gave way. After they were gone I found a note saying they missed the train to N.Y. & couldn't buy the silk themselves so enclosed the wherewithal!! The dears! The marsaline & pina and above all the yard of purple satin excited both to admiration, and Edward's final speech was "Well, I guess henceforth Semiramis & the Queen of Sheba & the rest will 'have to get under a bushel basket if a half bushel won't cover them' when you're round."
                                    Your grateful Ellen.

                                    Concord, 12 June 1885
Dear Edith,
Mrs Weir died last night and is to be buried on Sunday afternoon. Never was anyone more bitterly afflicted than the girls. They see nothing in it but loss. And Mother and I saw Mrs Weir two days ago and

were much touched by the ways & manners of the children with her. As Therchi says "No queen was ever so treated."
              Ellen

              Concord, 17 June 1885

Dear Edith,

We are hoping you will come soon to us. I have what appear to be competent girls again. They have done well enough in this first week to make me hopeful, and they have both of them a bright and busy air which looks contented. Maria & Lizzy are most thankful for your flowers & letter. They seem still blankly wretched. Their physical condition is such that they cannot begin to rally, poor girls. Almira is staying with them; the best thing that could happen, I suppose. Mother visits them daily. Miss O. Dabney comes today till Friday.
              Ellen.

              Concord, 30 July 1885

Dear Edith,

It seems as if I could never write at all. Either Mother or the house or callers fill the days when I don't have company. Edward has been here and persuaded Mother to go to Coffin's Beach, and we are expecting to arrive there tomorrow afternoon. Mother thrives wondrously on the School of Philosophy, goes twice a day, and sometimes tucks in an extra lecture in the afternoon. Edward's departure yesterday morning filled Mother with fright, so that she at once became sick and wanted him sent for, but last night's lecture from Mr John Fiske operated like a charm and restored her to perfect health. It was a glorious lecture. I believe everyone concedes that he is a wonderful man. Charley came home on Monday noon and visited us with Therchi Monday evening. He is sunburned, and close-cropped & black-bearded as possible, and seems just as usual to me. Edward thinks he looks better. Your room is papered. I found Mother in it the next morning all aglow with admiration of its beauty, she thinks it the handsomest paper and the handsomest border she ever saw. The paper is so nearly the same colour as the old paper that I said to John no one would ever know there had been a change. "Oh the shine of it on the walls would show them it was new," he said. He says he came to us twenty-one years ago last week. Frances Browne spent a week with us. We had a very pleasant time with her and Lizzy Barber and the children. One night we took them and Aunt Susan's family and Therchi out to tea on the pond. It was delightful. I have enjoyed the moon very much. One night there were wonderful effects of brilliant silver boughs against darkest shadows in the front yard, and one morning at three there was a fairy-land of mist & apple-trees behind the house and a moon of light close by not way off in the sky as usual. Your many heliotropes are beginning to bloom & I am rich.   Ellen.

E.R.R. 5 Aug. 1885

Dear Edith,

Mother and I are on the way home from Edward & Annie's, and have had a beautiful time, of course marred on Mother's part by perpetual alarms, and I think it well we did not come to Naushon because they would have been worse away from her doctor, but she has been very well and has enjoyed every day and seen many new and interesting things besides the children. Your letter gives the impression of much happiness & a thorough immersion in the sparkling of young life. We feel the comfort you have in dear Violet's return to you. Annie read us of the Puritan's success in the preliminary race, and I was delighted to think of Will's being on her, & Ralph, Handasyde & Co close by on the Hesper. Indeed Annie had read the day before of the Hesper's arrival at Newport. Good that you went to Gay Head! What a shame that the sky wasn't right. Now to tell you of our visit to Edward's. They live in a place which since it resembles Uncle Adams's beach at Lynn, being the true thing, broad, hard, white, and having surf constantly breaking, with no land between us & the horizon, seems to me the perfection of seaside. How you would have liked to be there this noon and see the infant Florence coming slowly

8 Aug. 1885

Dear Edith,

Seeing no hope of finishing my letter I sent it off yesterday. Edward & Mother & I concocted this beautiful plan. Fifty years ago Father celebrated the 200th ann. of the settlement of Concord and went on the 14th to Plymouth to be married. This year Edward is on the committee to celebrate the 250th ann. on the 12th of September, and on the 14th he & Annie & I & we hope you, and Will & 1 to 5 if they take an interest, will keep the fiftieth wedding-day in Plymouth with Mother. Curiously the days of the week are again Saturday & Monday, as they were in 1835. Write me what you think of it. Have you heard of Beth's baby? Samuel Bowles Jr., born Friday July 31, weighs 10½ in his clothes. We are all very vain of him.

[Unsigned]

Concord, 24 Aug. 1885

Dear Edith,

I have been having talks with Cousin Sarah, and have collected several interesting facts. We have heard before of Grandmother Ripley's sternly reproving her when she was seven years old for climbing a fence, and it seems the school-mistress was just as rigid, the little girls were not allowed to run, and one day, when, at recess-time, some great stone pillars for a Boston Church were carted by, they did run to the fence to look over at them. After recess Miss Wheeler said "You will all lose your certificate this week. I presume you know why." Another tale of the school was that the little girls must curtsey, *and not bow*, when they met anyone they knew, just bend their knees. One day Cousin Sarah met Dr Ripley, and didn't know whether she ought to curtsey since she had just had breakfast with him, so she omitted it. At noon Grandmother or Aunt Sarah, was waiting for her with reproof, Grandfather had been passed by without due reverence. You know it was she who rode to Grandfather Haskins's in Boston with Father, when he was on his way to marry Mother fifty years ago. I have been asking her about that. She was 19, and infinitely enjoyed the Bicentennial. She said there was plenty of enthusiasm, at the Manse at least, over Father and his Oration, and over Uncle Charles who was chief-marshal. "They had refreshments in the Court-House," she said. Then I plied her with questions about the ride to Boston. You remember that the chaise came up to the Manse on the Sunday P.M. with new bright yellow reins, and Cousin Sarah said Father's first care was to stop at the stable to have them changed for green ones "lest people should think he had been weaving them of golden-rod." She does not remember much about the ride except that she asked Father about Swedenborg and his replies settled it in her mind that it would be a waste of time for her to undertake to read his writings. "But you don't mean that he didn't talk about Mother?" I said. "Oh no! he talked of her very beautifully, but the only words I remember are 'The'—I can't remember the word but it means people who didn't know as much as they ought to—'baptized her Ly-

— 1885 —

dia, but her name is Lidian.'" He took her to Grandfather Haskins's, but went himself to a hotel, and continued the ride to Plymouth the next day. I asked her if he looked handsome to her then. "Oh yes always! that is, he was lovely-looking just as he remained, just as you knew him. Charles was the handsomest. It was always a time of rejoicing at the old house when any one of them appeared." She told of one occasion when Uncle Edward came to spend Sunday when he was teaching school somewhere, and there came on a tremendous blocking snowstorm. They made a great effort & drove him back successfully to his school on Sunday afternoon "and the next morning while we were at breakfast he walked in! He said he had come over to see how they got home. So provoking you know! There was great sport. I enjoyed it so much." "Sport?" I said "Who was there to sport?" "Why Aunt Sarah." "Was she a sportive aunt?" "Yes very! She used to love to have fun with those nephews, Hannah is like her. Aunt Ripley used to have the text 'Nevertheless let me run' for her before she applied it to Hannah. I remember she was too much in haste to serve. Once she cut her hand cutting the bread too fast, and once she fell down cellar because she was in such a hurry to bring something." Now all these were new ideas to me. I had always the idea that Aunt Sarah was much such a person as Cousin Charlotte, quiet and gentle and decidedly serious. One other scrap I learned from Cousin Sarah, that Uncle Charles arrived for the Bicentennial after Aunt Lizzy had gone to the Church, and when he found her in the Gallery he kissed her, and they were all talking about it, because he kissed her in public. Cousin Sarah is a mine of treasure.
E. T. E.

In the cars. 3 Sept 1885

Now Edith dear I'll write & write all the daylight I have. Mother & Cousin Sarah & I have had a very happy two weeks. We have read about two hundred pages of Mr Cabot's Life. Cousin S. is delighted with it, and I am. Another of our pleasures with her is her delight in Father's gravestone. We have twice visited it with her, and her "Oh" of admiration and affection says all one could desire. I have had the like pleasure with everyone to whom I have showed it except Dr Hedge & Miss Peabody. They were a little doubtful. I think each said "I don't quite understand the idea. It isn't evident to me *why* you chose such a stone. Oh yes it is agreeable enough—I don't dislike it, only one wonders why anything so singular was chosen. It does not explain itself." But dear

— 1885 —

Roxa *loved* it, and so did Mrs Rackemann. They enjoyed its beauty, which has so grown upon me that I think of it when I am away from it, and when I am there cannot contemplate it enough. Still another treat we and Cousin Sarah had together was reading over all your letters. Do dear Edith describe each child to me. I haven't seen them for a long time. Are they good, are they communicative to you, are they sociable and gay together? Is our V. at home? What does she? Write me a postal card to tell me where you do settle when you come to N.Y. though I suppose I can't see you. Do look at a hat in Hostyn's show-case. It is dark blue straw, braided with gold or I sh'd have bo't it, trimmed with dk blue velv. & a blue wing, price $8.00. It is so handsome that I thought it would be a good present from Mother to Annie at New Years, but the gold spoiled the taste for me. The moment I get to Far Rockaway I'll despatch this. If you write to Mother don't mention Plymouth, she would be sick with apprehension.

[Unsigned]

Far Rockaway 4 Sept. 1885

Dear Mother,

When the cars stopped at this station I looked out and there sat Ruth & Susy waiting for me, both looking very pretty. Susy's complexion is beautiful and she looks well. The moment we reached the house Willy came tearing down to see me, kissed me in the friendliest way and maintained conversation with ease till the others came in. I was disappointed to learn that Helena & Julia had been sent lately to Somers to remain till after I go home. After dinner Ruth read a French story in French aloud to her Mamma & me, and Willy & Haven went out with their boat-club. Susy was going to an afternoon tea at Mrs Curtis's and I was to go with her, but just as she was putting on her dress Haven arrived from New York and said he couldn't spare me in the hours he was at home, I must go with him instead to the beach. So I went with him, and those mighty breakers were tumbling there, and the wind blew furiously. Ever so many gentlemen were in the water, and Haven went in too. They enjoyed themselves without the least care of hair, of course, and it was good fun to see them. Haven said these waves were blown up by the S. wind and were soft & feathery when they broke, very different from the heavy solid ones that come after an Easterly storm. In the evening I got out the minerals Charley sent to Haven & Willy and the interest they took in them surprised me. They said they were

— 1885 —

most beautiful, and were thoroughly pleased with them. Ruth liked her box and admired it very much. The Guinea peas were divided among the children, and Susy was pleased with her embroidery. Goodbye, I shall get home Wednesday night. Ask Miss Brown to carry Mrs Emery some *milk either Monday night or Tuesday morning*, and a basket of pears.

Affectionately
Ellen.

Note attached to letter in Edith E. Forbes's handwriting: "About the visit to Plymouth to keep the fiftieth Anniversary of the Wedding day of our Father & Mother; we three children, son-in-law & daughter-in-law and several grandchildren went to Plymouth & spent 2 nights & the day."

Concord, 21 Sept. 1885

Dear Edith,

Edward & Annie went to Pilgrim Hall after losing you, and Mother and I followed to invite them to visit with us the Grandfather Jackson house, but Mother once inside the Hall was eager to stay. We promised a return tomorrow, and she consented to call on Mrs Hedge for the 5 minutes which Edward & Annie needed to complete their visit to the Hall. So we went to Mrs Hedge's and found her just the same as last year. When Edw & A had come and talked a few minutes we proceeded to the Grandfather's house where Mary Ann & Lydia were most hospitable. They allowed us to see every room, and E & A showed the keenest appreciation of every charm. Mother trotted them out into the garden and showed them all the old places. They were entertained afresh by the account of the bed in the keeping-room with its green damask curtains; the little stair-case in the corner beyond delighted them, and when they found the upstairs door, behind, which leads out to the barn they liked that best of all. Mother repeated to them the story her Aunt Harlow used to tell of grandfather & grandmother Jackson, that one night the grandmother waked at eleven o'clock and found her husband had not yet come home, so she jumped out of the bed with the green damask curtains, dressed herself, and marched up the steps into the yard of our grandfather Jackson's house, then inhabited by her husband's father or brother, Mother forgets which, and tapped at the keeping-room window. "Is Thomas in here?" Sure enough he was in

— 1885 —

there, but at the first sound of her voice he whispered "Keep her there as long as you can!" and whisked out at the back-door, and in at that upstairs back-door of his own house, down into the keeping-room & the bed with green damask curtains. Meanwhile the family in the upper house opened the window and desired to know the circumstances, were full of sympathy, wondered where Thomas *could* be, and had so much to say that it was long before our greatgrandmother returned to her own keeping-room. The moment she came in, her husband, piously in bed, began "Why Sarah, where have you been? Gadding at this time of night?" *Then*, said Aunt Harlow, "she opened her ground-tier upon him." Mother gave this with magnificent effect, and we felt that of all Aunt Harlow's naval & nautical speeches this was the finest. I had often heard it before. I don't know whether Edward had, but with the whole scene of the little drama before us it was much more amusing, and we laughed and laughed over it. After this visit we went to dinner, and planned to go immediately afterwards over to the Salisbury Jackson's house, where Mother's octogenarian cousins Miss Louisa Jackson & Mrs Kapsa live. Their niece Miss Rebecca Jackson had called on us in the morning, and told us her aunts were away, but she would receive us and show us the house. Alas! just as we left the table to put on our things for this expedition down came a shower. That was the great disappointment of the week. Instead, we had a reading of the Life of Father in Mother's room. Then E & A departed. We took tea at Cousin Mary's, Miss Elizabeth Russell being also there. We had a lively time before and at tea. I told Mr Watson how much Mother wished to see her Grandmother Cotton's house, and that she was uncertain which it was. He talked with her about it, made up his mind exactly which it was, and agreed to come the next day and take us to see it. The hours between were so full of questions, decisions & actions on the subject of going home, that I felt as if it had been several days instead of one that had passed. At half past eleven the trunk being packed Mother and I set forth to bid goodbye, and encountered Dr Russell almost immediately. He said he was coming to call on us, and instead accompanied us. We called on Mrs Warren, on Dr Briggs, on Mrs Lord and Miss Kendall. As we came to Deacon Spooner's Alley, Mother desired to go through that once more, so we did. Then she said she must just go over to Aunt Harlow's. Having pointed out her house, and showed me the garden which had not a feature left which looked natural to her, she exclaimed that the front of the house would be

— 1885 —

interesting, I must at least walk past it and look at it. So we did and as we paused at the front door it opened and a very aged woman came out. Mother looked at her, took her hand, and said "Do you know me? This is my daughter." So the old lady said "How do you do?" and looked hard at Mother showing she didn't. "I'm Lydia Jackson," cried Mother. "What, Charles's Lydia?" "I am your Uncle Charles's daughter Lydia." "Oh do come in! Oh! I'm so glad to see you! I felt real bad to think you never came to see me when you were here before." It was Cousin Lucy Marcy, and she showed us Aunt Harlow's room, and presently asked Mother her age, and said she herself was 91. Mother said she wanted to go to Training Green and see the house where Aunt Harlow lived in her husband's life-time. He was Captain of the company and "Aunt H. always knew when there was to be a training, and used to send for us children to come round and see it." By this time seeing how ardent Mother was to see and do, and that she walked as fast as my usual pace and had no trouble with breathing I made up my mind there was no need of going home tonight, and was amused and well pleased when she proposed staying till Saturday. After dinner she lay down, received calls from Miss Sever and Mrs Tolman; Mrs Davis & Mrs R. Morgan had called in the morning. We weren't quite ready at 4.30 and Mr Watson had to wait for us but when we did get started there was no end to Mother's eagerness, she said yes to everything and we visited the burying-hill first, then her Grandmother Cotton's house, then the Pilgrim Spring, down by the brook behind the mills. If darkness hadn't cut off the expedition it would have lasted several hours. On entering the Cotton house, which is now occupied by three families, we were received by Mrs Thomas, a widow, daughter of John Cobb Lanman who was the carpenter Mother delighted in, who mended up all her furniture before she was married, and made the rocking-chair you have just had copied. So Mother was much interested in talking over her father with her. We recalled the stories of the life in that house; in the kitchen we remembered Aunt Harlow doing the washing and telling her Father she would let out the drop of royal blood, if she knew which vein it was in, into the wash-tub. In the parlour we remembered the sisters sitting round the fire, the whiz past the head of one and the unaccountable dropping of blood on her apron; in the chambers we thought of the apparition of Grandfather Cotton; in the study of the sheet of gingerbread he kept in his cupboard for the children. Mr Watson next showed us all the oldest buildings in the neighbourhood. That evening Mother called on Mrs George Tolman, came home soon after nine,

— 1885 —

went right to bed and slept all night like youth and health. If we could give her as happy and active a day every day she would be very well. I thought however that since she really had a cold I would go right away in the morning, and though after breakfast she suggested staying till afternoon, I still think it was best. She remembers her visit with delight, especially the united family part. Her cold goes off quite easily, but she hasn't entirely recovered. She was much set up by your birthday letters and Edward's. Many friends sent her flowers, she went to church, and had a happy day.

Ellen.

Concord 29 Sept. 1885

Dear Edith,

The other day Charley began reproaching me with never having visited their new estate nor interested myself in their project of building and Therchi proposed coming for me in the buggy and taking me to visit which she accordingly did this afternoon. We found C. at work spading up the land as Messrs. Alcott & L[ane]. meant to do at Fruitlands. He has already got a little plot laid down to rye. The day was lovely, they were both happy & I enjoyed them very much. Then Therchi took me to the Chamberlaines to invite them to dine. They agreed to come, and I invited R. James to meet them. They sent a note at night to draw back. So the next morning Mother & I went for the Bartletts, and Miss B. & Mr Watson consented to come. We had a very agreeable dinner-time and a gorgeous centre-piece of yellow flowers which Miss Brown had constructed for her table the night before at the Episcopal fair adorned our table. I have two little stories of Mother. I was telling of Mrs Manning's having broken her leg in just crossing her own kitchen-floor by stumbling over the cat when Mother cried out "Poor Pussy! Was she *much* hurt?" showing that she really & innocently regarded the cat as the point of the story. Last night she said "Weren't you just telling of something that we were out of?" "Yes. Rat-Exterminator." "Oh! don't poison rats! I take an interest in their happiness and all their interests and their little ones." I gave up.

Love to E & A & to all my nieces & nephews.

Ellen.

Concord, 3 Oct. 1885

My dear Edith,

Of course I have been thinking of twenty years ago, how anxiously I

— 1885 —

looked to see whether it was a pleasant day. We were most fortunate in that day and in everything that happened, except my catching your hoop in your back hair. Have you forgiven me? I never get over it, nor forget how good you were about it. And I feel as if I most of all was benefited by your marriage, having had the comfort of so excellent a brother and children and the most interesting place in the world to visit, all free, gratis, for nothing. I am struck also with the shortness of a period of twenty years. I have been interrupted, and now here comes Jimmy for the mail. Mother is very well, enjoyed Jenny Worcester on Wednesday, Edward's beautiful long letter & later Col Russell & Mary on Thursday, and yesterday a dinner at the Chamberlaines with Uncle George and Miss Bartlett, and a tea at the Emery's last night in honour of Anna's birthday, and a game of whist after it. I infinitely rejoiced in Edward's journey down to Naushon with Messrs Lowell & Holmes. Goodbye, goodbye & love to you all from us both.

Ellen.

Friday, 6 Nov. 1885

Dear Edith,

I have not had your scrap-book a second time, I think. I am as sure of it as anyone can be who is never sure. I am sorry it is out of the way. I haven't written for a great while. Edward & Abby Hosmer and I went to South Boston last week to visit the Idiot School. We enjoyed our visit as usual, indeed I liked it and understood it better than formerly, and beheld every idiot with the same interest & curiosity, while I had besides the great pleasure of watching the proceedings of my companions. They both took hold so practically. First we went to the lowest grade school where the children are who can learn to sit still and do something. One girl can sew, many can pick out red buttons & string them on one string & green buttons & string them on another string, one boy can build blocks, and one can look at pictures, several can say a few words, and several can draw & write on slates. Each comes in turn to the teacher and says the words it knows and tries to learn another. Abby went round and sat with the various children and tried to make acquaintance and have them show her what they were doing. Some of them were seven & some twenty and even thirty, and all ages between. From that room we went into the Kindergarten and saw the mistress singing and playing hand & finger games for them to learn. This was a more intelligent grade of idiots. They all looked happy & clean. Edward arrived and immediately began to make remarks to the mistress & ask questions of the doctor-kind, which amazed me at the difference between his eyes & mine. "Has that child paralysis? Her hands don't move alike?" I couldn't see that they didn't. "Yes, she has been paralyzed on the right side." He sniffed round too about the ventilation, which however satisfied him. He, like Abby, took hold with child after child. Then I asked for, what always interests me most, the lowest idiots, and we were all showed down there and found them at dinner. Here Edward became the papa rather than the doctor, the readiness with which he went up to the frightful little creatures & babied them & showed them his watch was surprising to me. Some of them took no notice, some of them were delighted and affectionate in return. Several grown-up idiots who knew something were employed as assistant nurses, and they ran to shake hands with him. The horrors of seeing them eat were unexpected to me, and seemed to shock him still more, but as doctor he minutely inspected the process, made inquiries and criticisms. Next we saw the dinner of all the rest and Edward looked after that carefully, and interviewed the doctor of the establishment, telling him that the attendants fed the most helpless too fast, and enjoining him to look to it that they should do properly. Having finished our inspection we went up to the reception-room to take our shawls & bags up again, and behold! there were great bundles there from a toyshop. Edward proved himself a true son of his mamma, he had bought all sorts of playthings for the idiots. I never admired him more than I did that day.

Last part of letter is missing.

Concord 21 Nov. 1885.

Dear Edith,

Though I am so silent I hope you forgive me. Now it is your birthday which I always think of as Mr Sanborn taught me when I went to his school as the ornament of the month of November. It doesn't look as bright as I wish it did today out of doors but I have learned this year new and lovely things about my sister and I wish I could say I had given her less trouble than usual instead of more. So I send you a birthday kiss with much affection and a desire to improve.

Once you said your travelling sewing-case was used up, and hoping you would like one like mine I send you one which your Mamma has

— 1885 —

stocked as well as she could in Concord, the knife and scissors she chose among all others, they pleased her particularly. She said last night "When I grow older and my selfishness has gone to seed I shall demand that all my three children shall sit always before me, not even taking turns, so that not one of them may be ever out of my sight. I grow babyish and I want them all the time." I forgot before she went to bed to tell her to send you a birthday message, but I think this is better.

Your affectionate sister
Ellen.

February 1886 - December 1889

Raymond Emerson born. Temperance conference. Talks, picnics, and meetings in Concord. Visits to Milton and Naushon. 1888. Forbes family travels in Europe. John Forbes dies. Visit in Milton. 1889. Quiet year at home. Short visits to Naushon and Lenox.

Concord   13 Feb. 1886

Dear Edith,

It was a great disappointment that you could not come. I hoped till tea-time. Your box of flowers was uncommonly beautiful as a spectacle on being opened. Mr Cabot appreciated it. Thankyou for the beef-tea, the eggs, the left handkerchiefs and the chest of tea which comes very opportunely, we are nearly out. Mr & Mrs Cabot came, and Edward & Annie. We read together about 150 sheets of manuscript and talked it over. Very pleasant. Mrs Cabot and I also found time to talk about the various young people in whom we are interested. We are going to Jim Putnam's wedding on Monday. Your Mamma sends her love and thanks to you for all your delightful presents of Thursday. I am glad Alexander is about. Mother sends him & W[aldo]. Valentines tonight.

Concord   2 Mar. 1886

Dear Edith,

Shall you come to Boston next Friday? I am to stand for my picture, and Edward devotes the time to amusing me. You could have great fun there. I shall begin about 12. If I should go to Mrs Nash's should I wear my green silk? It has occurred to me that I might go down at 1.30, have a stand till 4, go to Mrs Hemenway's to spend the night, and do my errands & stand next morning, coming home by 1.30 train on Lowell Road. Does that seem a good plan. If so, please forward this note to Mrs Hemenway. I shall be glad to attend to the genealogy *if* I ever have time. I see by Hovey's bill that you bought my dress. Thankyou. Did you do anything about ruching? Oscar's little daughter was born on Alice's birthday, 25 Feb. Aunt Susan has gone to New York to spend a month. Cousin Edwin Cotton died on Saturday. This long continued gale has done Mother good. She has had better nights since it began. Last night to celebrate Mary Sage's birthday we had Miss French and Miss Stodder to tea, set the table ceremoniously, had four candles, and first dropped eggs, afterwards cream-cakes & icecream and finally sugar-plums. We had a beautiful time and Mary was surprised at each new development. Lidian came today & admired the restored chairs.

Ellen.

In the cars, 4 Mar. 1886

Thankyou dear Edith for advice and service and pretty stories and delightful invitation, which mightily drew me but unluckily the Frolic Club *play* for this year, in which several of my friends are to make their *debut*, Miss A. Ball & Miss Harriet Buttrick among them, comes off this Friday night. Therefore, I beg, ask me for your next dance. I have set forth without the green silk. I had no doubt you were right about the dark, and I don't want to crush the green in a trunk for nothing. It is proper for old ladies from the country to dress plainly. I have looked through the box of M.S.S. in Father's closet, but find no "Duplicate & Miscellany" there. I'll write to Mr Cabot for it. Your Naushon ducks were very good, and Mother has liked them. Last night we dined with Charley & Therchi, and had a delightful dinner. Mother ate a good dinner.

E. T. E.

Concord, Mar. 10th 1886

My dear Sally,

Mother neglected to send any money last year to that Society for the Prevention of Vice which she belongs to. So she sends last year's money and this year's together. She is well & bright. At the same time she is restless and can no longer get sleep except by naps which seldom last half an hour, by day, and often are as short at night. Edward's flock are well and charming.

Mr Cabot has been here this week and I have been reading Father's Life with him with perfect delight. I believe Edward & Edith are almost as pleased as I. I am having my portrait painted! I always like such things. This is a great festivity. I was at Milton on Sat. and saw Alexander's *debut* on the stage as "The second Billy-goat Gruff". Gerrit & Harry [Malcolm and Sarah Forbes' sons] were the eldest & the youngest. A spectacle of smiling innocence that enraptured the ancestral eyes. I wish you could have seen.

Affectionately
Ellen T. Emerson.

— 1886 —

Concord, 13 Mar. 1886

Dear Edith,

At this season I always remember 1865 almost every day. We were fortunate to have such lovely weather that year. Last night we had a W.P.A. entertainment at the Town Hall and I was sorry I hadn't sent for you all, it was so pretty. Mr Chamberlaine had painted a great scene of a garden wall with one broken place, and hosts of sunflowers peeping through that and all along the wall against a blue sky. In almost every one was seen the face of a belle, Grace & Mary Keyes, Louise King, Camille Benson, the Blanchards, Mary Buttrick, Cary Wood, Kitty Lang, Ida Prescott, Annie Hobson & ever so many more, who all sang together—as I thought most sweetly—seven original songs, written by themselves full of local jokes, to all sorts of tunes, Mikado & older. It was capital. Finally a farce, very good & very well done on the subject of the Brothers Grimm. Mother isn't so well, has a cold & coughs again, so didn't go. I took Mary Miller,* who mightily added to my pleasure, a dear innocent intelligent & enthusiastic little girl. On Tuesday the W.P.A. have a meeting to hear Kate Gannett Wells. If she doesn't come I am to have the floor. If I knew I should I would invite you to come, though, I remember! you said you disapproved, so forgive me, I withdraw. Dear Edith, the stand of the work-basket came home yesterday and I refitted it with its furnishings and set it up once more. How handsome it is! Mother delighted the invalid Florence yesterday with some of your grapes. She eats her fruit herself with thankful heart.

Affectionately
Ellen.

Concord, 2 April, 1886

My dear Miss Dabney,

We are having here the loveliest birthday for you that April knows how to get up, and I have remembered that it was your birthday ever since I waked and have only succeeded in getting alone with you at three o'clock now in the afternoon. I send you my love and my best wishes and I thank you for my very interesting birthday letter from you. I heard with joy that you and Beth still correspond. She came to Concord on the 20th of February to celebrate her Father's seventieth birthday the next day. He persists in feeling very old, and said that day,

---

*Mary Miller was the granddaughter of Lidian Emerson's cousin Edwin Cotton.

— 1886 —

"My life is ended. I have lived my seventy years." At the same time he was full of bright sayings, and of joy in the grandson who was the important glory of the day in my eyes, and, I doubt not, in those of his family. It is a fine baby, very strong and stout and lively, and with a decided air of refinement. Beth was rather thin. People didn't think she looked well, but she was as charming as ever. Her brother Sherman is to be married this summer. The Hoar family have made Concord happy by an annual great wedding twice already. Sherman's will be the third. His cousin Florence was married last June and Beth the July before that. I had a great delight in Miss Roxa's visit. She made so many different friends of mine her friends, and she seemed to me more lovely and wonderful than ever. I was fortunate in having her come at a time when Mrs Rackemann (who was my Miss Bessie Sedgwick) was coming. Then Mrs Sanborn and Miss Leavitt, my old friends, were here, and with them my newest friends, Anna McClure and Mrs Emery and Mrs Hofman. Ever since it has satisfied my very heart to hear them talk about her. And she liked them, especially Anna. Mr Cabot's Life of Father is almost finished. We have now reached 1872. We read it aloud together and criticize and enjoy at leisure. When we have finished Mr Cabot means to revise it all by the light of the notes he takes on these occasions, and then it will be ready to publish. It is all bright and readable, and its absolute exactness is a great charm in my eyes, for it is my constant trouble in books and newspapers that a true account of anything is so rare that I have come to regard it as hardly possible to writers. On the first Sunday of March, having been persuaded to stay in Milton and see Alexander & Gerrit & Harry act the three Billy-goats Gruff with Waldo for Troll, I went to church in Boston, King's Chapel, and was so fortunate as to meet Mrs John Dabney and Rose going in, so we made a little family, sat in an empty pew together, and stayed together to the Communion Service. I felt very much a stranger, and they were a great comfort to me. I hope they were glad too. Goodbye with much love. I hope I shall not let the whole year pass in silence this time. Give my love to Mrs Sam and to Alice. Affectionately
Ellen T. Emerson

Concord, 12 April 1886
Dear Edith,
   Your flowers last week gave great pleasure to Miss Leavitt, Mrs Tuttle and Mrs Simon Brown. Mrs Brown asked me to give you her love and tell you she was delighted but at her age a note was such a

bugbear! "Yes," I said, "I know people sometimes dread a note so much that they would rather not have the thing." "Oh I *want* the thing!" she cried, "I want the feeling that she remembers me!" The Prescotts were also happy in the box you sent to Madam P. Norvelle Whaley is engaged to Louis Brown. Great satisfaction on all sides. Mother *walked* from church yesterday up to Miss Prichard's to see the roses people have sent to Norvelle. Uncle George was here yesterday, and read a paper at A. Gourgas's club. Come on the 19th with all your family. Mother, while well, has a hard time with nervous distresses.

Affectionately
Ellen.

Concord, 18 June 1886

Dear Edith,

I could not write before for company and house kept me very busy. Letters & accounts still wait, for besides the garden which in rose-time takes about two hours a day, a meeting to see about an Old Ladies' Home took one afternoon, a lawn-party another and yesterday Anna took me to Groton—a day's drive—which was delightful, as good a place to go to, Groton is, as Bolton, charming old hotel, capital cooking, pretty place. Today Edward came from Wayland to take Dr Titcomb's patients and dined with us. He pictured the children's amusements since they reached their new home. No sooner had they arrived than they were missed, they were found hanging out of the attic window, spitting down. Next William fell into the well, fortunately dry. Afterwards they laboured to carry bricks charged with soot & creosote and drop them into the trough where Roland is watered. Two windows had been sawed down, they were "of the guillotine variety" and Florence & William found it a charming game to creep in & out abreast, always just missing the supporting stick which inclined to crawl out with them and drop the sash upon their necks. They cost their parents almost the whole afternoon's time they discovered so many dangers & mischiefs, and were cross besides. Ellen had too much to do in helping her Mother to be caught by Satan at all. Miss Brown came Monday and we positively enjoy her every day. She is delightful to Mother this time. How do you do? Did you enjoy the Bowditch's Reception? Are you going to Class-Day? I am going to Pigeon Cove Monday 28th and shall stay till Tuesday. Love to all the children,

Affectionately
Ellen.

— 1886 —

June 24th 1886

Dear Edith,

Yesterday the picture came home at noon. Oh what a mighty box was landed in the East Entry! [. . .] I went down town at once for a cord, and we hung it over the piano, John, Mrs Maguire, Miss Brown and I. Miss Brown at once exclaimed "Oh I wish it were pleasanter!" Mother said "Yes, she looks slightly displeased with her Mother, looks very natural to me." Then having contemplated it longer "I don't know whether it does. It isn't quite so severe as I thought. I begin to like it very well." [. . .] The next day Edward & Annie and all three bairns & nurse drove over in the rain to dine. The spirits of the family were high about Wayland. It is all delightful. [. . .] Mother is at present particularly well, has good nights, and eats unurged. She needs some urging to go out into the garden but when there takes an interest in it and often stays out quite long. Once or twice indeed she has asked for the shears and gone out alone as in old times returning with a load of roses, and has then demanded vases and arranged them at the pier-table in the dining-room, and carried the various vaseful to their places without any thought of weakness or difficulty. Usually she doesn't want to cut. If she does not give over almost as soon as she does begin, she at least throws down her flowers the moment she comes in and says "I hope someone else can arrange them, I can't," and drops onto the sofa. The sharpness of her repartees is delightful, and I am always meaning to write down her play but never do.

On Saturday I hastened to Cambridge, and told John to await Cousin Sarah. She came. At Cousin Greene's* I saw Mrs Haskins & Fanny for a few minutes, but when we went into the Study they withdrew. I wonder at it with great amazement. Then began the most delectable reading & talking. We knew a few things in common. I proved to know several that he either dimly remembered or had forgotten or not known. Of course he had much to tell me. He took me to see the grave of Grandfather Haskins's Grandfather Mr Philip Cook in the Cambridge graveyard, and walked with me to Emma Diman's gate. I had a very pleasant peaceful day with her, and we talked over children, property, life, church and house as usual. She conducted me round her grounds, and

---

* David Greene Haskins was the son of RWE's uncle Ralph Haskins. He published in 1886 a small pamphlet entitled "Ralph Waldo Emerson. His Maternal Ancestors. With some reminiscences of him by David Greene Haskins, D.D."

told me the winter had been delightful, everyone had been cordial & hospitable. She took me to the Ep. Theological Seminary and showed it off to me. It is beautiful. Then we parted and I loitered along to Porter's. When I reached Concord the family were at tea, and Cousin Sarah came out to meet me. She looks well & young. Dear Miss Leavitt had already arrived and we had a very gay tea-time. [. . .] Maggie & Katy Rouse came to call on Sunday and seemed well and good. I tried to make it pleasant for them, but they seemed shy. After we came home from evening church I had to pack for Pigeon Cove. I didn't wish Cousin S. should know about it for she always gets up and carries my bag to the train. So I told Miss B. not to say a word, but Mother unfortunately remembered, and I forgot to caution Miss Leavitt, and it leaked out. At 5 the next morning her night-capped head peeped in at my door and she smiled & nodded triumphantly. Yes she was dressed before me & she carried my bag. I am ashamed.

Concord, 3 July 1886

Dear Edith,

Your note seems to cut off all hope of seeing you before you go, as I have every day filled with company except the Fourth & next Sunday. I am very sorry. Write me your summer's programme. Tonight I go to a Frolic Club Picnic at Miss Harriet Buttrick's. C. Walcott praises Edward's dinner-speech at ΦBK Dinner as the one he should have chosen among all that were made as what he should have liked to do himself, and says he never once hesitated—spoke with ease & very well. Edward has been in this morning, pretty happy. I could not get out of him that he received any applause or congratulations, but Mr Lee was there and spoke to him affectionately before dinner, Dr Bowditch too. He says William stalks pompously about the house & talks condescendingly of E. & F. as "the children". Affectionately

Ellen.

16 July 1886

My own dear neglected Edith,

I have company and dress-makers and Philosophy is in full tide. I have neglected you from sheer incapacity to find a moment for writing. I have risen betimes to send this word, enclose these notes, and promise that next week I'll try to put on paper some of the store hived for

— 1886 —

you in my heart these last three weeks. Miss Brown stayed four weeks and was truly enjoyed all the time. Miss Leavitt has returned rested and takes hold beautifully. Cousin Sarah is a daily joy. She and Mother drove to Wayland & spent a happy day. Your unforgetting Sister.

21 July 1886

Dear Edith,

This is the 25th Anniversary of the battle of Bull Run and the Concord Artillery aided by Mr Reynolds and all the gathered veterans of Capt. Prescott's company are going to celebrate it tonight at the Town Hall. I am going to spend today with Ida, and Mrs Agassiz and both Paulines are there. I am looking forward to much delight. Your beautiful letters are devoured with gratitude. Violet's letters were very interesting. Your Tarpaulin Cove quarters are charming we think, and the whole plan seems to me very good. Mr Stone told me this morning that two steamers were ashore at Naushon. That must add a zest to life to the boys. We let our girls go to Boston Sunday & Monday, and had all the work to do. Miss Brown took the brunt of it, but I had no time to write. Then came the Conways & Emma Smith and Lucy Spencer & two babies the next week. Aug 2d. Now I am able to write for a while. Anna McClure came on Saturday and she is going to take me in hand. She began this morning, leading me up to my room right after breakfast and has locked me in and carried away the key at my suggestion so that no one can get in and I can't get out, so that I may have an uninterrupted hour with you. Violet's letters have been sweet morsels, devoured twice by Mother and me in the small hours of the morning, and invaluable both times as arresting Mother's attention when little else could, and filling her with extreme delight, which finally carried the day over physical discomfort, so that she could lie down and sleep when morning came. I have just had a two days visit from Addy Manning. George Bartlett took her and me to a Poor Children's Picnic at Walden, very interesting to us both. On Friday we had Mrs Sanborn, Miss Leavitt, Miss Brackett, Anna & Mrs Joe Emery to spend the day with Addy. The School of Philosophy had closed the day before, and the conversation naturally ran much upon the School, every one was interested to know what every one else had thought. Every one visited my portrait, and we had a gay time over it. All scattered at four and Addy and I took Mother to ride. On Saturday night Addy went and we got Aunt Susan's family to come to tea. After their departure Anna McClure arrived.

— 1886 —

Cousin Sarah had gone to Providence to visit the sons of her brother William. Each evening Anna sang to Mother. She likes to make Mother sing too, she thinks her voice is very sweet and pretty, and Mother thus encouraged sings with great pleasure. Wednesday morning we all frolicked so at breakfast that we could hardly eat and Miss Leavitt laughed till she seemed (like Miss Angelina Ball) to feel as if this was too good fun for sinners. Thursday Cousin Sarah returned and I invited Anna to ride Graciosa to the Cliffs to tea. We had a happy excursion, found beautiful blackberries, enough for our supper and our box full to carry home. We saw the view, took our supper and had a good ride home, enjoying the weather all the way. At home your letter awaited me and the length and the goodness of it alike delighted us. Yesterday we carried your box to the Weirs, who were indeed amazed and pleased. Mother went in with it to their house and they had a delightful time over it. While Mother opened box with them, Cousin S., Anna & I hied away to river and took tea up the N. Branch, sunset, moon, reflections, pleasure. Tell Edward Forbes his dear picnic-box is a treasure.

Affectionately
Ellen.

F.R.R. 7 Sept. 1886

My dear Edith,

How delightful is the remembrance of your visit. I don't flatter myself that you got any rest out of it, but I wish you yet may out of some visit. Miss Leavitt went on Thursday and Mrs Nesbitt stepped in ten minutes after her departure. She is as usual a comfort. Mother is wonderfully well, and though I hear her about in the night, and sometimes singing hymns she has not once called anyone since you were here. Mrs Nesbitt and I both get our sleep. Maries Sage & Miller came on Saturday night, Miss True was to come today. On Saturday night Cousin Sarah's brother Ralph turned up "to make a short call", he said, which he later confided to Mother would be till Tuesday, so we have every room in the house full, and every person under the roof contrived to sit under Mr Bulkeley's preaching in the morning, and to leave the house standing open & vacant, but nothing happened. In the evening the piano was again opened and a delightful hymn-singing filled the evening. Affectionately

Ellen.

— 1886 —

Concord, 15 Sept 1886

Alas! dear Edith, I am again prevented from writing. I enclose a note to Mother from the Woman Suffragettes; read it and judge of my state of mind. It resembled Edward's when asked to contribute towards giving the Putnams a large dog,—but my case was worse, for he could refuse, and I was morally certain Mother would consent to the meeting with its triple offence, Woman Suffrage, a Fair, and a Reverend lady. To my surprise and relief she at once said she was not well enough, and with joyous speed I have communicated this reply to the authorities.

I went last night to take tea at Caroline Cheney's, with her cousin Laura Emerson from Amherst, and found the Norcrosses there too. Louisa N. detailed to us some of her late experiences with her cat Solomon. You would have laughed as the rest of us did. Edward you know has gone to Coffin's Beach. This fact I have concealed from Mother, for fear she should be taken sick. I am trying hard to keep her well till he returns on Tuesday. She is full of answers as usual. When I impatiently said "My one desire is to see you flat, that you may the sooner rise and go out." "Ah!" she said "you think that will lay me out flat." "If it only would!" I exclaimed. "I assure you I'm not flattered by it," she returned. And this kind of talk goes on almost uninterruptedly. She thirsts for whist and I must try to manage a party for her tomorrow night. I have had two teas outdoors since you went away. One on the Pond of such extraordinary glory as to make me think September is the best month for it. We took the 4.23 train to the Pond. There were six of us—one boat-load—afloat soon after five. The most brilliant cloud show began about that time all over the heavens. We had our tea, then sunset, yellow glow, rose glow, fading west, bright moonlight. long row, echoes, and when it was already dark stopped the 7.17 train for Concord. The other was at Fairy-land in the finest part of the oak & birch wood. We stayed till quite dark & the moonlight effects against the impenetrable darkness of woodland distance were unimaginable, most beautiful, and to me quite new. A week ago Alice Wheildon invited me to her cabbage-dinner, an annual festivity, which I have heard of, but never before participated in. There were eleven of us. The cabbage occupied a mighty platter at one end of the table, a vast pile of hot corn another equally large at the other, the corned beef a modest one under its lee. There were four or five other vegetables, this is a point much dwelt upon, that every vegetable shall be represented. The table was elaborately dressed with ferns & flowers all over, and every dish garnished with cut beets & carrots & turnips & parsley, so that the whole made a gay picture. It was a lovely warm day, and almost everyone arrived in a clean linen lawn, and enjoyed their own and other peoples. Mrs Wheildon was well that day and added a charm to the feast, which was long and very gay. Lizzy Simmons has returned to Concord and tonight I am going to take tea at the Manse with her and Cary Brewster. Last week Lotty Brown and I went to tea at Miss Leavitt's. Mrs Sanborn came too, and we had a most beautiful time together studying John III for Sunday-School and having much talk besides. How do *you* do? Love to all of you.

Ellen.

Thursday 23 September 1886

Dear Edith,

I am writing very little this week. I have been impatient however to tell you of the Birthday, and other pleasures. I went to Boston Monday then after a few errands returned and ate my dinner in Mother's room which I found illumined by your and Violet's letters and adorned with many bouquets. Eliza Hosmer had sent gentians, then came Sarah Richardson with a bunch of nasturtiums as round & red & vast as the setting sun. Then came C. Cheney with roses red & rare & a pretty note. While Mother ate her dinner (and Miss Leavitt says she did finely) a box of yellow roses arrived with Josephine's and Mr Hofman's love. So Mother's bed was surrounded with a flower-garden. When I went up in town I passed Mr Wheildon with the handsomest and most gracefully arranged bouquet of asters & goldenrod ever collected, posting down towards our house. I wasn't surprised when I returned to see that bouquet also on Mother's table. She was dressing for her ride, and just as she was ready Mr & Mrs Wm Prichard and Miss Prichard called. They asked to see my picture, and they praised it except that it was "grim". After our ride John went for Susy & little Haven, and we hurried with tea. When Mother came down Miss Leavitt gave her a beautiful basket of grapes & plums & peaches which pleased her very much. Then we opened your biggest box and disclosed the imperial mandarin. We instantly put it on to Mother and admired her in the truly Mikado-like costume. While she was taken up entirely with her own magnificence Edward "gently oped the door" and came round the table and stood before her. She was much amazed and delighted for I had thought he couldn't come till the next day, and had told her so. He produced his

— 1886 —

presents, from himself a brass waiter, from Annie a feather-duster, from Ellen he brought a large white clam-shell. Mary Sage and Miss True came downstairs and surveyed the whole show of gifts with interest. We opened the box of flowers and the basket of fruit and admired. After a very cheerful tea-time at a table covered with vases of flowers, Mr & Mrs Sanborn arrived. Presently the doorbell rang and Mrs William Prichard sent Mother a great handsome vase, into which Josephine's roses were soon plunged to drink their fill. Mother enjoyed everything so much that she has been better ever since, and before she went to bed she wrote her letter to you. I hope you received it. It went to the Crawford House.

5 Oct. 1886. I have sent one page, and add another since I have time. Last Saturday I had an Easterbrook picnic, our whole family. Mrs James, Mrs Sanborn, Mary Miller, Mr & Mrs Emery, Anna & Mr McClure were the grown-up, and Haven, Ellen, Philip and his friend John Nash accompanied. We went through the lime-kiln field and the boulder-field, and in the third enclosure sought & found a spot combining all possible advantages, and there settled our headquarters for the day. The children were all enthusiasm. They raced round and explored, they brought the baskets & blankets and climbed the rocks. Meanwhile Mrs James & I read Elsie Venner. We began to feel very hungry and to consult watches and wonder why Mother didn't arrive. We gave the babes each a sandwich, and soon heard a shout and went forth to meet the rest of the party. I found Mother, on Mr Emery's arm, but utterly despairing, struggling through sweet-fern thickets. She was much cheered by finding me and still more by arriving at the camp & the cot-bed which was prepared for her with great luxury. Mrs Emery sat down by her to amuse her, Anna started her kerosene stove, Mr McClure cut up the cheese. Everyone chose seat & mug & the feast began. The Welsh rarebit was praised and the coffee was found very good. When the children saw that the elders had finished they filled their pockets with pears & crackers & the bottles with water & climbed to the top of the boulder where they made a rowdy tableau. Then Mrs Sanborn, the Emerys, Miss French & Mary Sage went barberrying, Mrs James sat with Mother & Miss Leavitt & I cleared up. In the afternoon we called together on Mrs William Prichard. The next morning Anna McClure appeared to say that she should like to take us out on the river. First we ate our dinner on the foot of Fairhaven Hill, then crossed to Conantum where Lizzy Simmons and Mrs Emery met us. We had the

greatest pleasure imaginable, sitting on a sunny hillside, talking & laughing with a sense of freedom and holiday that one gets by being long out of doors. Mrs Emery & I rode home together and arranged for a day at Easterbrook next week.

Your full and charming chronicle of the White Mt. journey received & highly appreciated.   Affectionately
Ellen

Concord, 22 Nov. 1886

My dear Edith,

I send this morning for it lost the express on Saturday, that having changed the hour of its going from 1 to 12, your Mamma's birthday present of a new portfolio, and the tribute of the Estate, of a barrel of Bellflowers. From me there is a little pincushion as a sort of dummy. Dear Edith we send our love on your birthday and our gratitude is renewed for all your goodnesses and dearnesses of this past year. It was especially a comfort to have you here those two happy weeks this summer. Today as usual I am prevented from coming to see you by Thanksgiving business. I should like to. I wonder whether you have had any ceremonious invitation to Thanksgiving. If not, Mother sends her compliments & desires the pleasure of Mr & Mrs W. H. Forbeses company from Wednesday of this week to Monday of next week with all their promising & promise-fulfulling family, and as much more time before & after above dates as they can give us. We trust Will will not run away. Affectionately
Ellen.

Concord, 8 Dec. 1886

Dear Edith,

I have neglected you that I might when writing was possible send off some of the notes that Thanksgiving had forced to wait. Daily visits to Aladdin [Raymond Emerson] revealed little more than I first saw, for he was evermore asleep, except that I sadly made up my mind that his ears are crumpled by nature not by his blankets, but Monday noon I caught him naked, scarlet & blinking in the wash-bowl and thought he looked like a good sweet sensible baby, but with a larger mouth than I supposed Sunday. I had been so happy as to see Annie very pretty & rosy and all finished off with clean everything and a cap on with a highly refined bow. Mother and I together visited her & baby Monday,

and admired both. I have taken M. Sage, M. Miller, & Anna to see him. Edward & I have consulted endlessly on names. His favourites after Aladdin are Michael, Edmund & Richard, I gather. Mother & I have had a blissful visit from Miss C. Leavitt and one from Mrs Hemenway who left us this morning. Mr & Mrs Bulkeley came to dine and Alicia & Lidian were here, we had a long table. Very good talk on Charities. Oh! the Orthodox Examination was all my fancy painted it. Mother went all day, walking home both times and was seated beside Aunt Susan at the Episcopal church at 7.15 that same evening. She & I were rested by the day, *all* our friends were exhausted. There is no strength in Concord like ours. Your beautiful letter has come, full of sugar-plums for me. I am delighted that you like the plates. Game club amusing. I shall come to you on Friday afternoon. Affectionately
                                        Ellen T. Emerson.

                                        Concord, 5 Jan. 1887
Dear Edith,
    Mother & I came gaily home & Miss Leavitt seemed to enjoy the journey in every particular. Aunt Susan & Lidian stayed till today—through my visit to Mrs Hemenway, which was a great pleasure to Mother.
    I had a happy day & evening with Mrs Hemenway. Pretty Lotty was there. I told them about V.'s dresses & she was quite excited about them, wants to see them. When Mrs Hemenway heard V. was going to the Ball tonight she said she hoped she might take her to a Ball sometime.
    I haven't yet unpacked my trunks but I have invited Annie & Aunt S. & Lidian, Mrs Emery & Anna, Mrs & Miss Leavitt & Mrs Sanborn to dine on Saturday off your pudding, and see the Opening of all our presents. Miss Sage, Miss Leavitt & I are trembling with eagerness for Saturday to come. Mother and I send out love to you & everyone, and thanks for a delightful visit. I hear I have grown fat. Affectionately
                                        Ellen.

                                        Concord, 29 Jan. 1887
Dear Edith,
    I am sorry you should hear from me so seldom. Your Washington letter ought to have been answered on the instant. We hope the Telephone hearing will be most interesting and absolutely successful. The

1887

reason I could not write was that I have been having so much pleasure. I went on Tuesday of last to Cary Hoar's Frolic Club where for fifteen minutes I saw my Clara blooming like a rose, and her dear Mother very handsome and very cordial sitting stately with her knitting in a corner. Then they withdrew as old maids poured in. We played bean-bags and of course enjoyed it. The next day Anna and I visited Mrs Hemenway's Cooking-School all day long, admired, learned much. and saw there Mrs John Dabney and other ladies interested & interesting. Edward came up in the train with us. He had consulted with Jim Putnam about Mother, decided on a new course which he explained, and he gave me two big bottles of medicine. Thursday night I had a party which delighted me. The Jameses all, Edward & Annie with Haven & Ellen, Mary Miller & Mrs Garland with her three young children. We played games. Edward & Robertson took hold most kindly & beautifully. From 5 to 8, full of joy. Mother was as happy as I and often said the next day, "Do let us have another." Saturday I started out to beg for Gen. Armstrong and make my wedding call on Florence Brown. I met Caroline Holden and learned that Florence's baby had been born the day before after a labour of 24 hours, a fine child but Florence was in great danger. They have only homoeopathic doctors, and all the street and Edward & Annie feel that proper care would have saved her. Nelly French my Sunday-Scholar & little Ellen's first teacher spent Sunday with us, and that was a pleasure to us all. Monday rained and we had a quiet day. On Tuesday morning Mrs Sanborn came by appointment to spend the day and help take Mother to Boston. I had tried by myself once before and had failed, and ever since I had been talking up the project, which left no apparent trace. Mrs Sanborn brought with her "Little Lord Fauntleroy" and read it aloud. Miss Leavitt dressed Mother for her journey and prepared her bag. I alternately sat by and ran away to get everything else in train. We had dinner at twelve, but Mother as usual desired to come down late, to lie on the sofa, to sit absently over her plate without once lifting her hand to it, so that our utmost endeavours only brought her half through her helping of soup before the hack arrived. Then we told her our design. She refused to go. I put on her gaiters & rubbers while Miss Leavitt dressed her with jacket & bonnet, and Mrs Sanborn rushed to put on her things. Bella put up a luncheon and at 12.27 we were merrily seated at the depot waiting for the train which was only a minute or two late. For two hours Mother could not be roused to take any interest at all in her shopping. She bought her black silk dress, and her new stockings, only by being continually led anew to the subject and refused all cooperation. She first asked Mrs Sanborn and then me to choose for her, and after it had gone on so till I feared the salesman was exhausted and disgusted, she decided I think rather in desperation than with attention. Flannel was the next subject and this roused her a little more, and by half past three she began to take an interest, and we had after that a really delightful afternoon. Everything almost that Mother wears had to be bought for she has not done a shopping for more than a year. We rigidly made her do the whole herself. On the way home she began to feel quite elated and eager to go another day. I am very grateful to Mrs Sanborn. Without her it could hardly have been accomplished. The next day was the day of the winter Conference. At Walden. The subject was "How can a Temperance Society be wisely conducted?" Some of the Orthodox Temperance ladies consented to go with me, Mrs Cummings and Mrs George F. Wheeler. The Essayist remarked that the Unitarian denomination had always inclined to dodge the Temperance business, and knew every method of stepping over and round it, and that it had amused him to notice the Unitarian flavour of circumspection and non-committal in the form of question which the Conference had chosen in which to bring the subject for discussion for the first time. I was delighted with this for it is true, and my Orthodox friends enjoyed it. I told Mrs Cummings in the cars that I must forewarn her that Unitarians never had a public meeting without making many disagreeable remarks about the Orthodox and she might be sure that the laity hated to have it so. These little slaps began almost immediately, and Mrs Cummings turned round and smiled at me. When I lamented to Mrs Wheeler she very kindly said she considered it not only wholesome but interesting to see ourselves as others see us occasionally, and she thought here was truth enough in one hit at least to justify it. My dear Josephine came from Cambridge to sit with me. She considered all Total Abstinence teaching very wrong, and when the Church Extension contribution came she considered herself as a High Churchwoman not at liberty to give one cent towards Unitarian work, but she said "I enjoy coming to Conferences very much, and Unitarians impress me as an honest earnest set of people. I like them."

It is now the 10th of February. Florence Brown still lingers between life and death. The baby does well, drinks skilfully out of a tumbler. I have told you as far as Jan. 26th. On the 27th came the annual meeting of the Bible Society. It met with dear Miss Angelina Ball who was charming. There were over fifty ladies present. I read the letters about the box we sent at Christmas twice over. After tea I invited my beloved Mrs Damon to go to the Unitarian Thursday evening service with me. There was a good fire in one of the big open fire-places, and I was pleased that she should see the vestry quite full and looking so bright. After Mr Bulkeley's sermon he asked for discussion. A good many spoke, Cary Hoar, Fanny Norcross, Mr Blanchard and I and to my joy and Mr Bulkeley's Mrs Damon did too, so that he asked her questions and made her say more. On Saturday of that week Edward read his paper on McClellan at Miss Leavitt's Saturday Club. I think you know how affectionately Edward feels towards McClellan. Mr Sanborn on the other hand looks on him a very poor sort of general & patriot, and at every pause made his criticism, which drew Bob James out to defend McClellan, and Edward had plenty of answers ready. This made the paper last till quarter of ten, so there was little time for general discussion. On Sunday we invited the whole Emery family to tea that the gentlemen might see the pictures of Mrs Hemenway's Summer-School. This was a very happy night. They took the greatest interest in the show, and after it was over Anna went to the piano, and we all sang hymns for nearly an hour, everyone in the room joined in, even Mother, who enjoyed it extremely. On Monday night Mr George W. Cooke began a course of lectures here. Mother & I went, and found the first one very easy to follow and instructive. On Tuesday night came the Frolic Club, always good. On Wednesday Charles & Therchi dined with us, Therchi & I went to Mr Bulkeley's Class for Religious talks, and in the evening to the Parish Tea-Party where I heard from John Brown his experiences in the 5th Massachusetts which were nectar & ambrosia to me. On Thursday the Cheerful Companions spent the day at Mrs Emery's together, and Mrs Damon with them. We had our usual joy together. Mother & I stayed to tea. The rest went at 5. We talked Edward's paper with the gentlemen, & Grant's life, and war subjects generally and had a very lively tea-time. After tea Anna took her guitar and sang for us. On Friday I invited the School-Committee to tea; all came except Mr & Mrs Hudson & Mr & Mrs Meigs. Mr Lufkin's wife is dead. We sat round the table, conversation was not wanting. I allowed cats & rats & sealing-wax to go on till half-past seven when I called the meeting to order. They went at nine. Mother only sighed to have them again. On Saturday we had a children's party which was easy and joyful. Clara stood by me like another self, and Constance & Margaret Blan-

— 1887 —

chard & Louise King played right in among the children with Miss Sage, and Miss True. When we came to dancing Anna arrived and did the piano-playing. On Sunday we had a circuit-meeting and Mr & Mrs Moors of Greenfield, Mr Hall of Cambridge & Mr Tiffany came to stay with us. We had much delight in them. They left us on Monday morning, and no one can sufficiently praise Mr Hall's beauty. I hear it ever since. I will begin again to write as soon as I can.

          Affectionately
          Ellen.

          Concord, 25 Feb. 1887

My dear Edith,

 I am most grateful for your visit, and appreciate the effort you made for me. It was the greatest pleasure and honour of my day of pleasures. What a pity you did not bring with you the wondrous treasure-houses which the expressman brought at tea-time. How I should have liked to have you open and explain both to my friends as well as me! Never, never did I see such a box of flowers, and the riches of that wonderfully adapted & furnished basket took an hour to examine. Long and deep were the attention and admiration the whole set-out elicited. The beloved Edward was here and enjoyed it all with us, and then reluctantly accepted Annie's share of the flowers and went home. He brought me ice-cream and stayed to tea himself. We were all in clover. I think the knives and the forks are probably for Mother, and very acceptable to us both. We hadn't quite enough of either. Now we abound. Then the Japanese napkins, how pretty and how grand! the rubber bands and waxed paper,—oh marvel of practical affection, and acme of forethought! Mary Sage and I drank in each development with full sense of its worth. The plates handsome, and *strong* and oh fitting so perfectly by being *square*! the platters too! Nothing could exceed the whole. It would have been bliss if you could have showed it yourself. Now I have hidden it till that great occasion comes when I can first use it. Do be here then! and finish the joy & thankfulness of

          Ellen.

          Concord, 12 March 1887

Dear Edith,

 Everyone has inquired for you most zealously since my return, and I have puffed your virtues, and in the domestic circle related also your

trials with me, which I must say you bore nobly. Annie told me last night that Edward had read to her his Life of Father and that it had charmed her more than she expected. She also related what her Father had said, who considers it the most interesting and beautiful piece of work he ever met with. Annie says it is wonderful to see the different effects produced by Mr Cabot and Edward with the same material. Ellen is well, Raymond has grown homely, but has a cunning & winning little smile. Alas! his mouth hangs wide open. John is sledding wood for Edward, and Florence & William "help" him unload, and then ride on the sled for a certain distance, are tumbled off & run home. I brought with me from your house "The Oak Staircase" & "The Lamplighter". I had a most beautiful time. Tell my dear Edward & Don I wouldn't have missed the play for anything. Affectionately
                                    Ellen.

                                        Concord, 6 April 1887
My dear Edith,
I never forgot you with regard to the Agassizs' coming, but waited till I should get their answers to my notes reminding them, which when they came were so unpromising that finally I in despair visited them personally on Monday though on the way to the train I found a note from Ida saying they would come without Pauline, and they did. They took much notice of house & rooms and rejoiced in the sameness of everything now with what it had been in old days. I told them about the paper and they both said "Oh always have it marbled!" with decision. I asked Mother what her choice was and there is no shadow of doubt that it is for the marbled paper. You mustn't forget that Mrs Walsh is coming Apr. 12–15, and that Edward proposes reading his Life of Father on one of those evenings, for the sake of your combining that with the dress-visit. We are thriving. My life is crammed with gaieties, which I do not refuse though they keep me from letter-writing, lest I get no more invitations.
                                    Affectionately
                                    Ellen.

                    Boston, 27 April 1887. At M. Blake's.
                    I left the first sheet at home.
[To Edward]
Mother has remained as well as when you went away. We concealed

your absence on Monday & Tuesday, and expected to go on successfully several days longer, but unhappily I went to Boston on Wednesday, and Mother taking her ride at noon went to see you. The unsuspecting Lizzy, surprised at her ignorance, told her all about it; it made an impression as distinct as it would upon me and has never been forgotten. She has occasional frights about her health but is very well. She walks out into the garden every day after dinner and gladly takes her rides. Your two letters were delightful to us, also the one that Lily read us, the one from Sharpsburg. I rejoiced very much over the sentences about Ellen, and the things you said about seeing the battle-fields, and that you found it as good as you hoped. My love of interiors is much gratified by your descriptions of the hotels. Josephine Hofman spent Sunday with us and took an interest in all these descriptions. I went to see the children on Monday. Raymond was fat & smiling though running at the nose. His hair looked to me a little less wild, some of that on the crown leaned forward & held the top-knot down. William seemed more glad than usual to see his aunt, took my hand and walked about with me, a thing he would not think of doing if his parents had been at home. Miss Brown came on Friday, Miss Leavitt went away after dinner. Mother enjoys Miss Brown, and had enjoyed Miss Leavitt very much. I am very sorry not to have written earlier. Give my love to Haven & Susy & the children.

         Affectionately
         Ellen.

         Concord, 21 May 1887

My dear Cameron,

 I have remembered all day that you were seventeen and wished to write to you so that the letter would arrive on your birthday but in vain. I send my love and Grandmamma's. I have the pleasure of knowing that your robust appearance satisfied your Uncle Edward the other day, and that the preparation for college goes forward hopefully, and I hope you will come soon to Concord that I may behold you for myself. We had a good visit from Mr & Mrs Cabot this week and took tea in the boat on the brimming river—I could not help using that word, it describes the look of the river that night so perfectly, and the fields were so green, the trees had such pretty soft young foliage that with the pink sky and the still soft air the whole scene was Paradise, perhaps we can do it again, this river-picnicking, on Decoration Day. Uncle Edward and Aunt Annie came to see Mr Thayer & Cousin Sophy who were here last night, and told us that while they were at Gettysburg, & hearing stories of slaves all the time, little Ellen who had never heard of slavery before was very much exercised about it, all the time asking "But how old were the children they sold?" They found that she was really afraid since she was in a country where they sold children that she might be sold. She has always been afraid her parents might forget her or lose her in some way. Affectionately

Aunt Ellen.

Concord, 22 June 1887

Dear Edith,

Thankyou for your beautiful letter about our beloved Don. We can't bear to think of his being sick, and I hope you have been teaching him not to be too considerate of others for his own good. Mother sends her love, and assurances of love & anxiety & pride to her dear Don, whom she begs to get well as fast as he can. The words about the Naushon house are full of interest to us both. And oh! what visions of youth & pleasure rise at the mention of Jim's Class-Day! I hope it will be glorious. Mr Ferris is here, putting the walls of the front entry in order for the paper, and on Monday Mr McDonald is to put down the carpet. Gregory & Brown wrote that they had not enough of the ivy-border, so sent only the red & gold striped one which entirely suits Mother & me.

We have had a most blissful time with Mrs Sanborn & Francis, Mr & Mrs Hofman & Lizzy Simmons. Rose-gatherings early, arrangings of roses in Mother's room & reading a story, walks, a day at Walden. Whist in the evening for Mother. Mother went to the Walden picnic & enjoyed it but did not get into the boat, & this morning she has gathered roses herself. Every plant you sent me has lived! Affectionately

Ellen.

July 2d 1887

My Cousin Sarah dear.

Mother and I pine for you in all sorts of ways. No one comes down angry to abuse cold mornings, no one goes to ride with Mother & me, no one watches the garden with me, no one but Mother, Miss Leavitt & I come to meals and we wish you were with us. Our dear Mary Sage has gone home sick, gave up a month before school closed. I always ask you every year whether Mother has changed since your last visit; this time you want to ask me. I am not sure whether I am a good witness, but I think she has not. She is well, goes to church, walks home, enjoys company, replies sharply, refuses food, has days of absolute sleeplessness, and other better days; will absolutely not go into the garden, but after I have gone comes down quite unconsciously, often says she shall never touch a flower again, but occasionally marches out, gathers a quantity and arranges them, just the same as a year ago in all ways. The best story I have to tell of her is that in May Mr & Mrs Cabot came up for the night. It was warm and clear and we went out for a River-tea. Mother of course positively refused to have anything to do with such a plan. About five she sent for me & asked "When are Mr & Mrs Cabot coming?" "They are here." "Are they! Well, what is the programme?" "We are going out to tea on the river." "What time shall you come home?" "Oh, about nine o'clock." A groan. Then, "Why didn't you invite me?" "I did. In the beginning! But you refused. You are now very earnestly invited again." "Well, I think I'll go. I don't want to stay at home alone." And go she did. No one believed she would, and she kept giving up and then going on. At last, when she was to get into the boat, she gave up once more, but John had already got away with the carryall. "Well," she said, "I'll sit on the bank and wait for you." "Why we shan't come home till nine o'clock." Thereupon she embarked. We had a perfect evening, and the river was full—as you never see it, a fine broad stream without weeds. We used for the first time Edith's birthday-present to me, a picnic-outfit. Everyone greatly admired. That night when Mother was going to bed I asked her whether she had had a good time. She said with fervour, yes. "Will you go next time, Mother?" "Why certainly! I always have," she said!!!! I fell on the floor, so to speak.

27 July 1887. I have had another delightful letter from you, and you set the day for your return! May nothing defer it! Mother and I insist on having a month's visit from you. We have missed you very much. Why, what is the School of Philosophy without our Cousin Sarah? Yet, to my surprise Mother does go to the School both morning and evening and enjoys it and thrives upon it. She is as well as can be at this moment and has had many quiet nights, waking only once, sometimes not calling Miss Brown at all, for at present Miss Leavitt is away and Miss B. taking her place. Our dear Mary Sage is dead, and is to be buried tomorrow. The good child has in the most inexplicable and causeless manner faded swiftly away since the first of May or rather earlier. She was

twenty-four in March. She has lived here three years and had become a part of the family. She was a successful teacher, and loved her work. I send you Raymond's photograph taken when he was 5 mos. old. Ralph Forbes was 21 this month. Affectionately

Ellen T. Emerson.

Concord, 2 Sept. 1887

Dear Sally,

On my way home from Naushon I remembered that I was to send you the dollar for the Hindoo book, and when I came home I found the book had already come. I am sorry I forgot it so long. I haven't yet showed the book to Mother, but mean to today. We had a happy visit at Naushon, and Mother not only enjoyed it at the time but looks back on it as a season of unusual health as well as pleasure. She hastened to get up & dress every time so as not to lose the rides with Edith, instead of deferring starting out as she does at home, so that she was out of doors two or three hours more in a day than she has been for a long time, which was beneficial as well as agreeable. Charley & Therchi were here at tea, very bright, though they had refused your invitation. T. wished very much to go I understand, but C. prevented. Affectionately

Ellen.

Concord 7 Sept. 1887

My own dear Edith,

I have felt badly to neglect you so, but could not get round to writing. All was very pleasant at home. Dear Mrs Sanborn had brought flowers from her garden, and Miss C. Leavitt had sent a great bunch of nasturtiums. Therchi had brought a great bouquet of goldenrod. So the house was well lighted up with flowers as well as lamps. Mrs Sanborn was lovely and took the greatest interest in our adventures, and said Miss Caroline Leavitt had staid here during our absence, and they had had a very good time together. While we were still sitting round the table after tea there was a ring at the door-bell and the dear Miss Prichard and Miss Amelia entered. They had come down to talk it [their visit to Naushon] over with us, and we set to the task at once with eagerness. I found that what most had impressed them was the island life, the necessity of crossing the water, the luxury of a steam-launch, the beauty of the drives, and in the house the children's parlour, and the pleasantness of the parlours in general. Miss Leavitt has most to say of the views from the windows, she found them ever-varying in colour & effect and always beautiful.

There was in the East entry a parcel awaiting which I am sure is a present from you, an icepail for picnics! Thankyou dear girl for your endless thoughtfulness. Mother remembers her visit as a sort of vacation of health and happiness, and only desires to repeat it annually. Saturday night Anna McClure came for the month. Miss Legate came on Tuesday the 6th instead of Monday because the first Monday in Sept. is a holiday, set apart by law this year & henceforth. How are you all?

Affectionately
Ellen.

Concord 12 Nov. 1887

Dear Edith,

We are preparing for Thanksgiving and I want to know whether Waldo & Alexander still fit their cribs. I suppose that Alexander has outgrown his. Edward said last night that Will asked whether he was wanted for Thanksgiving. Why of course he is, he knows he is, much wanted, depended on, delighted in. So are all of you. Mother is in some respects better, much less dependent yesterday and today, but has had several times great difficulty with her breath. Edward is going to give her something for that.

Affectionately
Ellen.

Concord, 20 Jan. 1888.

Dear Edith,

Thankyou for three kindnesses, a good long letter which we value very much, a note telling of Sarah's & Ethel's babies, and a three-story bundle of delights which came last night,—notices, flowers & ducks. We have a lecture tonight and Mother is especially glad therefore of the flowers. How sorry we are that you are sick! I wish you would come sometime for a visit in bed. No one should know you were here, we would keep you as a delightful secret, and I should mightily enjoy tending you. Your New Years pudding was even better than last year and highly appreciated by the favoured souls who tasted of it. Mother sends her love and says "We have many things to thank her for. If I could I should write a volume." Affectionately

Ellen.

— 1888 —

March 3, 1888

Dear Edith,

We think of you constantly, and yet we don't know where to think of you for the Boston Post does not tell what vessels sail from New York. Your letter from the Str. gave us great satisfaction. The Japanese stove's performance—its making itself actually useful—electrified us all. So did the size of your staterooms. Why, the two together are almost as long as the dining-room, as we reflected on talking it over. Edward & Annie have had a letter from Susy about you which I have not seen. Annie & her three dined here on Friday. Raymond came after dinner and entered on the nurse's arm, saying, as I thought Bapa, but he soon supplemented it with clucking & saying "Ge'up!" He had seen the rocking-horse in the entry. Vainly we tried to turn his thoughts to other channels. The rocking-horse and nothing else could make him happy. So in came Diamond, and Raymond sat on him smiling & rocking in full content during his whole visit. Annie says he takes after Edward & likes a horse better than anything. On Sunday afternoon Cary Perry died of pneumonia, and was buried on Tuesday. On Tuesday Mrs William Prichard had a cold and Mr P. sent for Haven. Haven came, & said she needed no medicine. He came again the next day, and said it was nothing, but in the afternoon she got worse, and died the next day. The funeral was yesterday, and Mr Reynolds was minister. Everyone is sorry to lose her & remembers her with delight. Yesterday, too, died Mr Alcott, and Story Gerrish. Mrs Sanborn came to see Mother, and said that with the message about Mr Alcott's death came one that Louisa, who is not at home, but at Jamaica Plain, has cerebro-spinal meningitis, and is dangerously ill. To think of so many deaths among our immediate acquaintance in one week! Miss Leavitt says that Mrs Cheney's death was the only one that occurred the first year she was here among our friends, and she often thought to herself "Are there never any deaths in this town?" Mrs James & Mary dined here on Friday with Annie, so did Sarah Richardson & Cousin Sarah. Mother sends love to you. She talks about you every night, and counts the days of your voyage.

Affectionately
Ellen.

Concord, 12 Mar. 1888

Dear Edith,

We are enjoying a snowstorm only equalled by that of Jan. 1866 &

Ellen T. Emerson in 1888.

— 1888 —

the one of March 1861. No train arrived from above after four o'clock yesterday, and by this morning six of them stood blocked between here & So. Acton. When we reached the depot at 8 this morning, the train that should have come at 7.35 was coming along, and for half an hour, assisted by gangs of shovellers kept making feeble efforts to get as far as the R.R. bridge, but when we came away was not out of sight of the depot. The down track as far as you could see was buried under heavy, hard-packed snow, and groups of men were shovelling on it, Hardly anyone was out, only one or two vehicles had broken their way along the roads. The atmosphere was still white and fine flakes were slowly falling, the streets were long beautiful white aisles, and the clapboards & casings of every house frosted an inch deep. Some big boughs have fallen. Our dear Ralph surprised us on Saturday night, and was a most welcome & delightful guest. He talked a great deal with Mother who revived under it. He sang as usual most of the time, and that was a feast to us. He read the Scarlet-Letter, also, and went twice I think to Uncle Edward's. He promised to come again soon, seemed very well and said Don was. I began about the snow, and didn't quite finish. I just called Mother to her bay-window to admire the garden & pines and she exclaimed "Now here is trouble indeed! The cats will get under the piazza and won't be able to get out, and they will suffer!" It seemed to me most characteristic, the far-fetched difficulty relating to the dumb animal is as spontaneous in her thought as it is foreign to everybody else's. In a few minutes I heard Edward entering and ran to ask him his views of the season. His disgust was too deep for speech, he made a face and finally he said he could not forgive himself for being in Massachusetts when a train for California had left the Fitchburg Depot today. (That train took two or three days to get to Greenfield however.) Mar. 16th. Edith Perkins's visit was delightful. Mrs Sanborn, Miss Leavitt & the Weirs were here when she arrived to dine with her, and all were delighted with her every speech. After dinner we sat in the parlour round my new comforter, putting yellow centres into its white daisies, and talked most cheerfully & cosily. At five the company went, and Edith retired to her room "to curl her hair and reflect". She was full of the C.B.Q. [Chicago, Burlington & Quincy Railroad] strike. At 6 Anna came home, Edward & Annie arrived to take tea, Sarah Richardson also & Abby Gourgas. Edw. & Edith told many charming Burlington stories. No more time tonight.

            Ellen.

— 1888 —

F.R.R. 21 Mar. 1888

Dear Edith,

Cameron surprised me on Saturday afternoon. He said he & Ralph & Don had all dined at Edith Perkins's on Thurs. and arranged that he should come this time to us & Don next. He went out into the kitchen with me, for I had just sent Nelly away for not answering Mother's bell, and cleaned the knives. He said he had never practised that industry before. I recited to him Father's youthful verse "Melodious knife"—He was delightful & useful all the time. He went up to see George Keyes & Francis Sanborn & George came the next afternoon and visited him in the study. Edith Perkins's visit was delightful to us, and Mrs Sanborn & Miss Leavitt enjoyed her mightily. I have been at Mrs Hemenway's for two days, and saw there Rose Lamb who stayed an hour or so in the afternoon. This morning Mrs H. & I have been at the Art Museum, and Gen. Loring has showed us round himself. I wish I could now show you the same things. Now let me thank you & Violet for the dear steamer-letters which came the very day I expected them. I enjoyed every word & read them to Mother & Cousin Sarah & Lidian. How lucky you were to have mild weather! I have only a few minutes to write and must speak of the Bartletts. They have a strong sense that deliverance and peace has come to Ripley, and while they don't believe that he went out with fixed plan—but rather that it was an impulse as he was crossing the river on his way home to dinner, for his melancholia as is usual, was worse when he was hungry, they say—& it sounds like them—if he wanted to do it they are glad he should do as he wanted. Mother went to see the family on Monday, and as I was away went to the funeral on Tuesday. Ralph has sent me Violet's letter. How good that she saw beautiful sights of sea & sky! The seasick don't get much chance. I suppose that is why I never did. Sorry to send poor letters. Affectionately

Ellen.

April 2d 1888

My dear Edith,

Mother asked this morning about—oh! let me tell you how she came to, it was so lovely for me. She rang for her tea, and the new cook, a young girl only nine mos. over from Ireland brought it up while I was out of the room. When I came back Mother was drinking it and said "She said when she gave it to me 'There's another stone in the cup, Mrs

Emerson' " and Mother was as much delighted with the novel appellation of the lump of sugar as Father would have been. I said "There you didn't send the hot-water-bottle down by her to be filled." "Why no!" said Mother, "I was so surprised by a new face." So I ran down for the hot-water-bottle and when I brought it up and said "Here it is! Clasp it to your heart!" she answered "Yes, it is a comfort, but I have a better comfort." "What?" I asked quite unsuspicious. "My daughter! My good daughter Ellen", she said. This was a great pleasure. "I have still another good daughter," Mother went on "my Edith! Won't she come to see us today? I hope she will very soon." "Probably not just now," I told her, and she said "Why not? Oh yes! I believe she did go away lately. What did she do?" Having had all explained, and having ascertained that she might expect to see you in June, she was satisfied and fell asleep.

On Saturday Mrs Sanborn, Miss Leavitt & I were asked to lunch with Edith Perkins [in Milton]. As we approached we saw her & Alice [Forbes] Cary watching for us at the window. Alice & I were very glad to meet & talk over your whereabouts & the boys. Were you ever in Edith's house? Very interesting, beautiful, highly finished, crammed with pretty things. When we went in to lunch the table struck me as the most gorgeous, complex and luxurious show I had ever seen. It was round—oh beautiful! and the flowers were everywhere, and all yellow. Edith likes so much to give you presents of that colour that I associate it with her, and it seemed most characteristic. The talk became general, and story after story from different quarters was heard. In the midst of this perfect pleasure I discovered that it was time to go to the 3.05 train and made a rush for home. Mrs Sanborn said this was a great offense, and I have written and apologized.   April 5th. Fast Day. I have been invited to May Furness's wedding and have had the pleasure of seeing her married by her Grandfather. I went on Tuesday afternoon to the College Chapel. Ben Watson was the usher who received me. Dr Furness when he rose looked altered from four years ago, but his entirely original & beautiful service was as perfect & free from mistake or faltering as if he were still young. When he came to the questions he said "Harry, do you take our dear May to be your wedded wife?" The moment there was any danger of Dr Furness's leaving the church I rose & regardless of appearances went to him. No one frowned on my action as far as I could see. He was very affectionate, and said he had even had thoughts of coming to Concord.   April 6th. I went to Cambridge yes-

terday to see Dr Furness and had a few minutes with him. He said Mr Cabot was to be congratulated on the Life, everyone seemed to agree that it was a model biography. "Ah! but you don't say what I want to hear," I said "Do *you* like it?" "It is a little conceit in me," he said "I feel that I knew him better than Mr Cabot did." More I did not succeed in learning, though I burrowed a little, and if time had served should not easily have given over. He said he was fond of declaring that English had never been handled as Father could handle it by anyone but Shakspeare. "Now in the Titmouse 'Hurling defiance at vast death'—that is Shakspearian to the core!" Yesterday afternoon I visited Edward & Annie. Edward has water on the knee. The olive-branches there are quite charming. Raymond works himself round the floor with great speed but doesn't creep. Florence asked to come home with me and spend the night. I am much honoured & expect delight. Your good long letters to Annie & me came on Monday and were a great pleasure. Miss Leavitt is crazy to hear your letter and she is going to. Affectionately
                  Ellen.

                     12 May, 1888
Dear Edith,
 I had just despatched my last letter when your 8 page volume from Venice & Milan arrived. Cousin Mary's visit ended last night with her reading her reminiscences of Concord—or rather of Father—valuable and lovely. Luly read it, as her Mother cannot see in the evening. We got out of Cousin M three little stories, two about Dr Ripley. We rode through the cemetery one afternoon and stopped to read Madam Hoar's grave-stone, Mother made some remark about her activity, and Cousin M. said "Yes, I remember Dr Ripley said he 'should as soon think of kissing a chipping-squirrel',—something had been said about his kissing her." Then she told us that when Mr Goodwin was buried Dr Ripley would not have the stone cemented down all the way round. He saw to it personally that one side was left unfastened "because" he said "it would be easier for him to rise at the judgement-day." She told us also that Waldo used to call our piazza "the spider-house". On Saturday I went with them to Cambridge to Mrs William Goodwin's reception. Dr Briggs was there. He said when he preached once for Dr Ripley, Dr R. stood up while he was reading the text of his sermon, out of respect to the Scriptures. I asked him if that was common, and he said he had never seen such an act except then. Edward came in this

— 1888 —

morning to talk over the summer. He surprised me by saying that he considered Mother decidedly more feeble in the last month. I haven't, but he may be more able to judge. It is true that Mother after beginning to go to church has now for two Sundays stayed at home, and she has a bad cough which of course causes the weakness—the question is whether she is going to get well of the cough directly. Ralph came up on Wednesday to dine & spend the afternoon and very much did we enjoy him. As he departed he said he shouldn't come again till Thanksgiving. He told us he was Captain of something, a crew or a team, and should be utterly occupied. Miss Leavitt desires me to tell you that she has had & mightily enjoyed a weeks vacation. Mother sends her love.

        Affectionately
        Ellen.

        Concord, June 24th 1888

Dear Edith,

This is my last letter to you, I fear 'twill scarce reach you too. Your beautiful long one to Mother was devoured by us both with delight. "Quiet St"—what a wise and charming name! At the last town-meeting our Road-Commissioners were instructed to insult the town by nailing up at every corner boards inscribed in large letters with the ugly & inappropriate names they have chosen to give to the streets, and we are smarting under the recent infliction of this indignity, so that we appreciate the prettiness of Bath's monosyllables. Your experiences of birds known in books, and of wild English flowers was deeply interesting, we felt as if we had been at a Maying. I have been counting that you are likely to arrive in less than three weeks. How delightful it will be! Mother & I are depending on your bringing the whole flock to Concord. I, of course, mean to be on hand when you reach Milton. Our dear Cameron & Don we suppose are hard at their examinations today. Edward & Annie came over yesterday from Wayland in high spirits. They are perfectly happy there. They had enjoyed Will's visit, and said that he appreciated their surroundings. Mother is very well. Sleeps quietly all night every night, eats her meals like other people, has no ailments of any kind, though the old alarms continue unabated—no, not unabated, but quite frequent. She has not tasted one drop of wine, beer or anything stronger than tea for three months, and takes no medicine except the old 16 drops of McMunn & one dose of chloral at night. Her rides are longer than ever before, she goes daily into the garden with less worry than it gave her last year, when she noticed only defects & didn't look at the flowers. The other evening she darned a stocking for me. Sometimes we have lovely times together. We have our dear Cousin Sarah with us now. Goodbye for a few days. Happy voyage to us to you!

Ellen.

Concord 13 Aug. 1888

Dear Edith,

I consider Mother quite well again today in every respect. Edward has not seen her since Sunday. Then he said she was much enfeebled. So she was, for the time; she couldn't understand or talk much better than when you were here, but last night everything seemed to come straight, and she slept nearly twelve hours, and today she seems herself again. Mrs Emery, Anna & I were invited on Sat. to go huckleberrying to the Cliffs by Mrs Damon. We went and had success, the loveliest view and a very happy time. We saw moreover a wonderful bird, as big as a song-sparrow with head & back of light bright robin's-egg colour. It looked tropical. When between us & the sun he seemed as well as we could see to have dk blue wings & tail. Did Cameron ever hear of such a bird? The tea-party at Mrs Sanborn's was also a great pleasure.

Affectionately
Ellen.

Concord, 25 Aug. 1888

Dear Edith,

Your letter after so long a silence was hailed with joy. I find that stories of Regattas are to my taste. Can our Violet sail a boat herself? I am vain indeed of what you tell me of her. I think much of our dear boys too, and picture Ralph at the helm of the Hesper, and Cameron with his banjo, and Don on Plum. Since Mother's illness we have not visited Wayland & Edward is so busy that since she got well he comes very little. He is teaching Annie to ride with all the little tricks he learned of the Haute Ecole, and she and the new horse enjoy it as much as Edward, and he is giving Ellen lessons both in riding and driving. He says she pays attention and doesn't feel afraid, so those are also delightful. Last night I had the Lafayette teaparty, and I wish you could have heard the letters Mrs Bush read. I think I must yet have you hear them. My two girls did very well, and Mother enjoyed the occasion. I haven't told you

— 1888 —

that Edward came the next night to tea, saw the lilies still handsome & was really pleased & impressed. Seeing the big red under the lamp reflected in the looking-glass he said "Why, it looks like the 'light that out of darkness springs!' " Affectionately
Ellen.

Milton, 28 August, 1888

Dear Sally,

I hasten to tell you about Don. I hope the faithful & dear Annie has preceded me, and written you about him. He was taken on Wednesday 22d with inflammation of the worst kind, his nurse told me today, and died on Sunday evening. None of the family suspected that he was seriously ill, and though I did not ask her the question, I think the nurse did not expect him to die. Edith and Will had gone out to ride and the nurse was getting her rest on Sunday afternoon, when Ralph who with Violet was watching him saw that he breathed too fast and ran to call the nurse, who found him in a state of collapse. He had begun to die. In an hour and a half, she says, the others think it was not till quarter of nine he died. His last conscious talk was with his parents in the morning, who took care of him all day long, delighted to be with him, and to witness his delight in their presence, till at noon he slept two hours and waked bewildered, after which there was little communication. You know how gentle and bright-tempered he was, the cushion always of the family, the nurse as much as Violet of the little ones, so each of them seems to be the one who has lost most. Aug. 30th. They spent last night in Milton and return today to Naushon. When I went on hearing of his death I saw the Puritan & Hesper had their flags at half-mast, and again when we returned with him to Woods Hole. The box containing him was covered with the big Forbes plaid, and that gratified me. It looked like the family affection still round him. Mother went to the funeral and bore it as well as anybody. She and Cousin Sarah send love.

Affectionately
Ellen.

Sept. 1, '88

Dear Edith,

Mother came safely home and is most thankful that she went. It was a great thing to her to see you all and to see Don's beauty once more. Oh how beautiful, how beautiful he did look! The sorrow of you all, of each of the dear children is very heavy on Mother's heart. People here are all interested and kind. Unlikely people,—Mr Wm. Hunt, Horace Walcott. I have everything to say, but it is mail-time, and I want to send one word today. With much love to all

Ellen.

Manchester, 14 Sept. 1888

Dear Mother,

This is your wedding-day! I trust Cousin Sarah will be able to find a four-o'clock for you in the garden, though last week's frost did very much injure the plants. It is a lovely morning. Please celebrate the day by hearty meals, long rides & many pleasures with children and grandchildren. I was met at Manchester by Hatty's very handsome son Jim who drove me to the house. Lucy Russell was on the piazza with Mr Harry Lee who was full of stories & presently Mr & Mrs Putnam came up from the beach,—they had been out sailing together. Mr Lee praised Sherman Hoar. He said he had his Father's power of repartee. He began "My son Joe is sitting at the feet of three Gamaliels, one of whom is Moorfield Storey, one is a Thorndike, and one is Sherman Hoar. Well, the Judge came in, he doesn't agree with Sherman in politics, and he said 'Sherman, I wouldn't study the Tariff question. I have tried to study it all my life,—and I don't know *anything* about it.' 'Yes,' said Sherman 'Judge somebody was talking with me the other day and said he "Sherman, you have begun where your Father left off." ' " Effie & Lotta came in the afternoon and talked President in the evening.

Affectionately
Ellen.

Boston, 15 Sept. 1888

Dear Mother,

I have come so far on my way from Manchester to Naushon, and stop in the depot to write morning greetings to you and to beloved Bush, made your home fifty-three years ago this day. I have had many delights at Manchester. Hatty's house is a very happy home, each of her children is handsome and charming, she and Mr Putnam are interesting talkers and very kind hosts. Lucy Russell was there and told us various pretty stories. One was sweet to my malicious ears. One of her friends, she said, sent her little boy to a kindergarten, and being asked

— 1888 —

where he went to school, he answered "I go to a school where they 'tend to learn and never really learn, and 'tend to play and never really play!" Yesterday Hatty went out to her garden and brought me in seeds to sow in yours. Then Lotta & I drove over to Marian Jackson's, and there we found Mrs Charley Jackson, Amy Folsom, Bessy Perkins, Lucy Bowditch, and Annie Hooper's daughters, & Nina Lowell's nieces, Alice Lowell & Mea Coolidge, & Elinor Curtis, and Effie read to us a little lecture on what Charity is, and what are our duties to mankind. Oh how wise, how beautiful, how practical and easy to understand it all was! She promises to come to read it in Concord next summer for I could not let our young people go without hearing it. Then in the afternoon we all went to Mrs Hemenway's and heard about her Arizona expedition. Everyone asks for you and sends love to you. Affectionately
Ellen.

Torn-off last page of a letter to Edith. September 1888.

We are interested in hearing about Cameron's going to College. The story about Waldo is also very good, it shows a capacity to deal with difficulties I think. I am sorry for poor Alice and for Mr Forbes. [Edward Cary died at Naushon in September of heart-disease.] You know I came up in the train with Mr Forbes and he said several things which perhaps he has said also to you, but, if not, you will take an interest in them. He said "Do you believe in presentiments? One ought not to. And yet *sometimes*! Now the very night before Don died,—we had been on the Shearwater to Gay Head, pleasant party, most *lovely* day! and all had been perfect. I came ashore at the Cove, met my horse and galloped home through the woods, and I felt so *happy*, so perfectly happy, that I said 'I am too happy. Something is going to happen.'"

Then he told me of Cameron's coming over to the Mansion House to tell him Don was dying, and his feeling that he wouldn't let him die, and exclaimed "Strange that we feel so about death! when at the same time we believe that it is the best thing that can come to anyone. Where should we be without it? It is frightful to think." Then he said "Dear little Don! he was very happy. He has enjoyed his summer. When he had had his picnic and everyone had had a good time and the day had been beautiful, he said to his Aunt Alice, quoting the song 'Just to look at it, just to think of it, Fills my heart with joy.'" I understood that this was a late occasion, but I do not remember hearing of his having had a

picnic this summer. Beyond this I do not think Mr Forbes talked about him. My time is gone & I had much more to tell.
Ellen.

21 Sept, 1888

Dearest Edith,

Mrs Sanborn was on her way as I drove home. Edward had given leave to Miss Leavitt to have Mother down at tea-time; all her friends had called and brought flowers, so that her room was a garden. We flew round & made a gala. Long table with candles in your brass candelabra, eight great vases of flowers. Mrs Gillan presently produced *her* surprise, a frosted birthday-cake, the first Mother ever had. Now appeared Edward & Annie & Ellen & Florence in state garments. We had a high festival. After tea we spread the red cloth, replaced the candles but not the flowers, and gave Mother her presents. Yours was admired with enthusiasm but better than all the presents, better than all the fun was your note. "Like snow on wool its fallings were." Oh how great a possession is that story of Waldo! Affectionately
Ellen.
Mother sends love & thanks more than the letter can carry.

Concord, 2 Oct. 1888

My dear Caroline [F. Cheney],

I have thought of you, and especially have felt that it was wrong not to write when Don died and tell you about it, for I thought you would care, and in your helplessness would feel very far away and all the more anxious to know, and be brought nearer by a letter; but this is the first chance that I have had to write. On Saturday evening, 25 Aug., we had a letter from Edith which alarmed me, though she didn't say that she felt anxious, and I opened the letter that came on Monday noon expecting no good tidings. But when I read "Don died this evening" it seemed beyond belief, too sudden a breaking of the family circle for us even to contemplate, much less accept as a fact. I went to Naushon that afternoon. The island flags were at half-mast, the family all in tears or just keeping them back, the dear boy, still sunburned and not much thinner from his illness, looking older in death, as often happens. Our dear Sunday-child had died on a Sunday, just one day before his seventeenth birthday. The doctors had examined him and had told Will that it had to be, he would not have lived, the peritonitis of last year had left some

— 1888 —

trouble which was bound to end fatally. On Tuesday morning the brothers helped to carry him out to the wagon, and the Forbes plaid was wrapped round the box that held him. The wagon went down to the boat, we following on foot. Don was placed forward, we sat aft, the flag was at half-mast in the stern, and so we came to the mainland. Will had one of those cars with a baggage-room at the forward end secured to us, and Don was placed in that, and the conductor kept other people from coming into the car, so we were a family party all the way, till Malcolm met us at Quincy with carriages, and we went to the Milton house. I came home and Edward went down and helped about having photograph & cast taken of him. The next day Mother & Annie & Cousin Sarah, Aunt Susan & Lidian, Lizzy Bartlett & Mrs Sanborn & Miss Leavitt & Charley Emerson & I went from Concord to the funeral. The coffin was in the parlour and on it was a wreath of lilies which the *little* boys of the neighborhood had got from the river for it. He was by nature the champion of *little* boys & they all loved him. He was wrapped in white, as we did Father, his Mother's pansies and a rose from his Father lay on his broad chest, and bunches of flowers from two young men, his friends, were at the foot. Dr Morison read Whittier's "Gone" & a part of "Threnody" then one of the hymns Don had enjoyed Edith's saying to him on Sunday, and the verses of the Bible which he cared most for—a service all arranged by Edith—and made a prayer, and then we took him to his grave. Many people had to go straight to the train, but many others stayed to the burial. The next day the family returned to Naushon.

I ask other people about you, dear Caroline, and hear that you are coming home soon. I hope then to see you. Affectionately

Ellen T. Emerson.

Concord, 3 Nov. 1888

Dear Sally,

Your letter was full of information very interesting to me, and ought to have a good long one in return. I went to Milton on Will's birthday last week and saw all but Ralph & Cameron. Will looks very sad, but they consider his health improving (that is from the very serious fatigues of the telephone years), he is better than he was when he first came home from Europe. Alexander in trousers but with his long white hair untouched is a good scholar at school, can row a boat & ride at a gallop, but is considered a mere idiot by his brothers because at six

— 1888 —

& a half he is good for nothing at football. Dan French's bust of Don is good. Edward's children are thriving. Florence is just six & after a year of indifference & apparent stupidity at school has within two weeks blossomed into the most ardent interest in all her studies. Raymond is a big boy. Mother is well but has little comfort by day because she shivers all the time and always thinks she is just attacked with a violent fever. At night she sleeps almost as well as in summer. I hope we shall get a visit at Christmas. Affectionately
Ellen.

Concord, 21 Nov. 1888

Our dear Edith,

Ellen is coming on Friday and going to spend the night & Saturday in helping get ready for Thanksgiving. Mrs James B. Wood today told me that when you come her husband desires to see you, he had a design of giving you something which was our rev^y grandfather's. And tomorrow is your birthday dear child, Mother sends her love and says she is glad you are born and glad you are here, but declares herself incapable of writing. She is happy that in another week she shall see you. Stay as long as you can at Thanksgiving. Lizzy S. will come & Sarah Thayer too. Edith dear, you are a good & dear sister & daughter & friend and our pride, always present to the mind of your mamma & your sister
Ellen.

Concord, 10 Dec. 1888

Dear Edith,

A great many of your flowers are still bright. Mother has been getting over her cough, and gained every day till yesterday when she was uncomfortable & seemed to me to have a little more fever, but Edward & Miss Leavitt think she didn't. I should not be surprised if she made a rapid recovery, but neither should I be surprised if she hereafter kept her bed and grew weaker. She is usually clear, but not always free from illusions. She has grapes & oranges daily from your & Mr Forbes's bounty, and they are not half gone yet. Mother says "I have just observed a quiet conversation among these bedclothes. This one said if he could be pulled out really straight they would be quite comfortable." "Well, what did the other say?" "He said he thought so too."
[Unsigned]

— 1889 —

Concord, Jan 25th 1889

My dear Edith,

It seems to me you are all the time more and more kind to me and as I know that I am rather more trying than less so in every way to get along with I attribute it to real growth of patience and forbearance in you, and I am glad for you and for me. I have been very sorry to let four days go by without thanking you for a whole list of good deeds. I found Mrs James & Jenny Barrett and Mary all at work for me on my return. So it was not till the next day that I opened either the box of fruit to discover the wealth of oranges, Tangerinas and bananas, nor the duck to learn that he had brought an armful of parsley and a trunk of tomatoes. A profound impression was made upstairs, downstairs, in parlour, kitchen and in the Lady's Chamber by the opening up of all this wealth of earth's gayer productions. First let me tell you that Mother by your visit or some other means has improved, comes to dinner willingly and rides out with pleasure each day since. And next I want to talk about precious Violet. Her visit was a breath of summer to our aged hearts. Helen Legate began "Miss Forbes has such a sweet face, such a lovely way. I think she is one of the most attractive girls." Two weeks ago when Anna was at work in Mother's room, Mother suddenly sat up straight in bed and said "I want to praise our Violet, so attend, all of you! If there ever was a good dutiful piece of good sense & sweet temper it is she." Applause & great encouragement to go on were lavished but Mother's eloquence failed. After this visit Helen said "What will all your family do when your niece is married? Of course she will be married." I said "I hope so, but one cannot be sure", and Helen went on "I think she must be—she ought to be, she seems as if she had an affectionate nature, and I can't imagine how a man could look at her and not fall in love with her. If I had been a man I should have offered myself to her before I went to school this morning. I should be so afraid I should lose her." Chance to send to tonight's mail.

Ellen.

Concord 1 Feb. 1889

My dear Edith,

Your great profusion of gifts came to your family day before yesterday and we are very much obliged. Miss Leavitt is delighted with the duck and everyone with the parlour rug. The dividend from Parnassus with Father's pretty speech and your brilliant adaptation thereof we

— 1889 —

also enjoy. The wax lights Mother contemplates with reverence, the shade is a size too small for the lamp. Can I change it do you suppose? Tues. 5 Feb. How ill I am treating you! One day I went to Boston and talked instead of writing. I have almost left off writing on the train. I find some townswoman always to sit with. The other day I did write and the elder Mr Holland who sat near me said when I got out that 'twas the first time he ever saw a lady write in the cars. Have you heard that William has pneumonia? Edward says he has been very sick as far as discomfort goes. But he also says that he considers it a slight case, and thinks it will do the child no harm. William is touchingly good and patient. Mother is perhaps a little better, and never fails to come down to tea. Affectionately

Ellen.

Concord, 19 Feb. 1889

Dear Edith,

I shall be very glad to stay on Saturday after the "Sports" at the Academy are over. You know I bought two tickets, and I invited Anna to go with me to see them which she is much interested to do. After them I will come and stay till 3.51 as hitherto. Anna will go right back to Boston of course. I'm glad you aren't going till Monday and that you feel a little better, poor dear. I hope I can be of some use to you on Saturday. Affectionately

Ellen.

Shall I see Will on Saturday? I wish to ask him what he thinks about my having the house painted this year. I listened to all said about it when painted last time, and fixed it in mind that in 1889 it should be done again. I have enough money of this quarter's income left to do it, and to carry me through otherwise till April, besides having laid up three hundred for the taxes, so that I feel strong and able to do it. If I shan't see Will, will you read him this & tell me what he says?

Concord, 25 Feb. 1889

Dear Edith,

I have had a very happy birthday and you have sent me beautiful things. Thankyou for the pitcher, it is very handsome. I admire it and it is admired. The ruche is a beauty, is it for the green silk? Dear Violet's poem was a precious piece of indulgence. Mother & I like it equally. How could a cake have more rich & romantic appearance and character than mine. The flowers gave great delight. I arranged them in five vases. Everyone has been pleased with the long sprays of spirea, and has spoken of spring. Dear little William is again very sick, with pneumonia on the other lung. He was taken last Thursday. Every day he has been worse, yet Edward & Annie are less despairing than I have seen them for slighter cause. Edward says if William can ride out the next forty-eight hours he should get well, by the natural history of the disease. Of course both Edward & Annie stay by him a great deal, but William sleeps a good deal at night, and they do. Raymond has had a bad bronchitis but is better, Florence well again, Ellen in fine health. Mother is dressing at this moment to ride out. On Sat. she says she "had a very curious dream". The upper sheet spoke to the under-sheet. She could not remember distinctly about it, but catechizing drew from her these sentences. "It was about the hem of the counterpane." We asked to whom it spoke. "To the general existence of which it was the ornament. It was the broad hem, you know, this hem." Well, and what did it say? "I cannot remember exactly. It was the tone of dignified calm consideration that I noticed." I am sorry to say that I cannot remember another equally charming and unexpected statement on the subject.

[Unsigned]

Edward's. 6.50 A.M. 1 Mar. 1889

Dear Edith,

I am happy to say that William is better. They have now a good nurse to help them and all smiles on them once more, except that William has a hard recovery before him in the way of cough. Lily says William when the nurse exhorted him to eat on, calling him "dear baby", produced a fist at once, and afterwards whispered to Lily "I hate her—she called me a baby. Show her my trowsers!" Delightful letter from you last night.

Ellen.

Concord, 4 Mar 1889 7 A.M.

Dear Edith,

On Saturday Tom Sanborn killed himself. He was at home. I think Mrs Sanborn found him, but naturally she is silent on details. It seems as if it was the hardest form of loss. The funeral will be private on Tuesday. William, Edward thinks, is no better. He seemed hopeful yesterday. This morning he is discouraged. Cousin Mary & Mr Watson

came to read about Herbert to the Club on Saturday. Because of Tom we stopped the Club but that enchanting paper gave us great domestic delight & we had a happy day with them yesterday. Affectionately
Ellen.

Concord, Mar. 12, 1889

Dear Edith,

Your box of flowers came this morning and came in good order, the violet & butterwort perfectly fresh and the jessamine picking up amazingly before dinner. Your box of fruit for William came last night. John carried it right to him. It contained enormous & scarlet tangerinas. He is pleased and especially with the grapes. He was lying in broader light than hitherto, looking as white as could be, with slender white hands, and playing with pasteboard horses. Poor Edward says he is not yet out of danger. Mother and I visited Mrs Sanborn yesterday. She said you had written her a lovely letter, and that they had many and the effect of receiving so many was very sweet and helpful, it showed so much kindness in the world. Amy Folsom has forwarded me her letter from Violet, and I have devoured it with much appreciation. I am glad it seems pleasant at Magnolia [Florida] and that you are all lazy and like to be. Lidian sent me your jars of preserves and tumblers of jelly. We have enjoyed strawberry already & begun upon a quince tumbler, and we all send thanks for your bounty.

[Unsigned]

Concord, 15 Mar. 1889

Dear Edith,

Till today Edward has disapproved of my sending any postal-card about William, because he was more feverish and Edward was cast down about him. Today he is better than yesterday and yesterday better than the day before. Edward & Annie spend almost every minute over him, and make interesting, yea delightful amusements for him. He looks handsomer & brighter, and his face very little thinner than when he was well. He has no fever today and has had an egg and milk-toast. Miss Helen Sanborn has come to stay with Mrs Sanborn. They are looking over and putting away Tom's clothes. Yesterday a great many people called and she saw them. Today she is not so well. The Bartletts are lovely. Miss Martha I think is a comfort to Mrs Sanborn. Mother is

very well. She goes every day to see William. It is mail-time. Affectionately
Ellen.

Concord, 1 April 1889
Dear Edith,

I forgot alas! my orange, and perhaps in the unpacking of my bag I left a pair of brown kids I had just bought at the Centimeri Glove Co.'s. I very much enjoyed staying to breakfast yesterday. Thankyou for making me. And I felt ashamed at making the scurry and hope I am sufficiently ashamed to do better in future. Miss C. Leavitt was here eager for tidings of you all. I caught the ten o'clock horse-car, and was in tolerable season for church at Mr Winkley's. Affectionately
Ellen.

Concord, April 1889
Dear Edith,

It was hard for me to refuse to come to the launching of the Merlin, yet when I wrote in haste at the P.O. I forgot to say so, and have had ever since that added regret. To have been with my beloved family on such an occasion, to have had for once such an experience was a great temptation, & I mourn that I could not. Edward brought William here on Sun. for the first time.
Ellen.

Concord, 21 May 1889
Dear Edith,

I write on my beloved Cameron's birthday to congratulate you and all of us on him and say that I feel very happy about him today. Then you know I told you how I had asked young Mrs Hemenway & Augustus with their companions Mr & Mrs Gray to spend a night here on their river journey and you approved. It appears that they are likely to be here the night before Decoration Day. I can manage as to sleeping by sending our boys to Edw.'s for that night, and I think you won't be sorry to see them there, shall you? We regular dwellers will all move into Den, give Jessy & A. the Blue Room, V. & Miss Fiske the nursery, Mr & Mrs H. my room & Gray the Redroom, you of course yours. I had a loveliest visit at Nina's and got home in good season for everything

— 1889 —

Sunday. Fatigue is almost gone now. Shall I come & go to Susy Lowell's wedding with you?

Ellen.

Milton, 5 June '89

Dear Mother,

Beauteous time at the wedding of Cousin Lucy Lowell's daughter, a very lovely-looking girl, and there besides her Father and Mother we saw the Cabot's, Mrs Augustus Hemenway and Mr & Mrs Gray. We wept on each other's sleeves. There too shone upon my sight my dear Mrs Rackemann. And Mr Brown of Brookline and his wife and daughter. I came home to find Edward playing on his banjo, Violet sitting at her window, Edith and Will very cheerful. W. hates weddings and wouldn't go. Edith, V. & I enjoyed it all. Alexander is at this moment showing me his "record", about 18 in., for "running high jump, but for running broad jump his record is 6 ft. 6". Now he is laying the tape on the hall-floor to show me everyone's record on the standing & the running broad.

The first part of this letter is missing.

June '89

Mrs Sanborn is to come next week to board with us, taking charge of her own room, and Mr Sanborn will make us his headquarters, going & coming as his work leads him. His desk is to arrive Saturday, Mrs Sanborn sometime next week, and he later. The arrangement to continue while their house is let, till Sept. 15th. We are very much pleased, for Helen Legate goes on Sat. and Anna two weeks later, and Cousin Sarah does not promise to come for some time yet. We really were in danger of being left only three for the month of July. Every one is content over it. On Tuesday morning came Mary Faulkner with her very pleasant friend Mrs Sedgwick, and we had good times with them. Again the weather interfered, with constant showers, to prevent our proposed excursions, but we finally spent three quarters of an hour yesterday afternoon on the river. The river is very beautiful. Tonight we are going to have our first Pond tea. Edward & Annie alas! will not go because he will not accept a boat at the hand of the Fitchburg Railroad. Lizzy Simmons is to be of the party & to stay with us one blessed week. And now let me speak of dear young Mary Russell's engagement. I think it must excite the family at large & I hope you are all pleased.

— 1889 —

Mary sr.'s account of Mr Amory sounds pleasant. Can he be such a charmer as he ought to be? Tell me about Class Day. If it is the hottest day of all the year I'll wear my white muslin, purple bonnet & purple belt, or would the pina be better? I prefer to dress & figure as the aged Aunt who finds a place behind the stove. How are you all? Our roses are in glory.

Affectionately
Ellen.

Concord, 5 July 1889

Dear Edith,

Edward came yesterday to talk barn with me, and said he had just telephoned to Will and had been answered by Cameron that the Merlin still sailed the northern seas. He desires to talk with Will when you do get back. When he visited Mother he told her he had promised Ellen to keep the Fourth with her by going out on the river for lilies, so she had waked him at six. While he was dressing he "heard William from his room, waking up and hustling out of bed like the fussy old gentleman he is, with 'Why! Why! My gracious!' as if he felt he was running the risk of being late at the fireworks in the evening by having slept so late in the morning." The fireworks however did not come off last night. They are postponed to tonight as it rained in the afternoon. We had a good old-fashioned town occasion at the Town Hall in the afternoon, got up by Lizzy Bartlett for the Old Peoples' Home. Games & dancing for children from 3 to 5, and at 5 George Bartlett showed children in scenes on the stage. I came home for Mother and she saw the scenes with great interest and pleasure, it seemed to make her well. One of them was "Concord's Light Infantry", little girls under 7, dressed in long clothes & caps, & looking as if they were only 8 to 10 mos. sitting & singing "Thankyou pretty cow that made", while they industriously used spoon & bowl, "Rockabye Baby upon the Tree-top", and waving their dolls in the air meanwhile, also three or four other Mother Goose and Nursery Rhymes, winding up with "Hush my babe" tune to "By-bye, baby", and all falling fast asleep on each others shoulders. Concord was utterly ecstatified by this show. People applauded and screamed for joy, each one called on all his neighbours to see how sweet! how innocent! how pretty! The parents nearly split with pride.

Aug 5th. This letter has been lost for a long time. I have had two tea-parties, and we have done a great deal of blackberrying which takes

— 1889 —

time. Our course of life has been quite regular, errands, housekeeping etc. till eleven, at which hour Mrs Sanborn & I repair to Mother's room to stay till dinner-time. We read four chapters of the Prophet Ezekiel first, and then the day's letters or a book. After dinner we go out in the Brown's Carryall which I call the Town Hall and Mother & I are very proud of. But in the eyes of the modern and fashionable Mrs Sanborn and Miss Brown it is a scandalous object. Mother, Mrs S. & I always go, and occasionally we take Miss Brown. When we see glorious blackberries on the roadside we look round for a house for the law appropriates to a householder all berries which grow along the road close to him, and *the house is there* as sure as fate. We may not have seen a house for half a mile, and usually we haven't seen a berry either, but where the berries hang thick & black, a chimney is sure to poke its nose above the thicket or a kitchen window, or corner of a barn to peep out just ahead of you. We are amused & disgusted. Mrs Sanborn is convinced that farmers always build where they see a blackberry bush. Well we gradually acquire such a thirst for berries that we ride on & on in quest of one hermit bush, and when we find it Mother willingly alights & gathers the berries with us. We often don't get home till Miss Andrews has sat patiently for two hours and there is no time to write to you. On Sundays we always read Pilgrim's Progress. Oh dear Edith, how excited I was over your letter about the Merlin and the "three Forbes sailors" and I thankyou for telling me about my beloved Edward's birthday.

        Affectionately
        Ellen.

        Prov. R.R. 19 July 1889
Dear Edith,
 I have just made my visit to Emma Diman and have had a good time. Her little Emily now sixteen and very sweet & fair came down to meet me at the train. I have seen some of her friends and heard them talk over the book "Looking Backward" which they seem to respect and to some degree believe in. Yesterday as I was going down I stopped at 30 Sears B[uilding]. to have some conversation on property with Mr Stone, and asked him whether any of the family had been seen since the Merlin's race. He said he had met Cameron who was happy about the race and said it had been fun, though his hands were almost raw, and he was so stiff all over he could scarcely move, from pulling ropes. We all at home take great interest. Mrs Sanborn says "Why here am I reading

all this boating-talk which I always thought was stupid and which I don't understand. It shows the demoralizing influence of having Ellen going to races." Mother waked up one morning last week and related that she had had a dream—the sheet had smiled. "How it could smile without a mouth I can't imagine, but somehow what with the hem & the corner it did make a very real smile." "What did it smile at?" I asked. "It smiled to the curtain." "Yes, but what did it smile about?" "Why, I don't know, I thought it seemed pleased with its broad hem." I am wearing this summer all the time my lilac calico, which is so handsome it is a pleasure to wear it, and everyone makes fine speeches about it. I haven't properly thanked you for my day on the bay. It seems to have done me a great deal of good and especially to have raised my spirits very much. We approach Boston. Goodbye. Affectionately

              Ellen T. Emerson.

            Concord, 27 July 1889

Dear Haven,

Please let Cameron bring Helena and Julia home with him and I will meet him in Boston and steal them away for a week in Concord before they go to Naushon. I am glad it is to be in berry season which always seems to me a festive time. If you come this way yourself I hope you are sure to turn in at the accustomed gate, even if Edward gets a part of your visit. Today John and I are going forth to view our burnt wood-lot. There was a fire this spring on the other side of Walden where all our woodland is, that is the wood we depend on for fuel, and Edward says it is very thoroughly burnt up, and we are to see today whether the summer has charmed life back into any part of it. Fires in the woods are very sad. Our old wood-paths where we used to walk are growing up with young trees. Father, Mr Channing and Mr Thoreau seem to have no successors to keep them open. Father used to talk about the School of Walkers, said he was a Professor of Walking, and used to watch to see whether anyone else valued it, and said he found but one man who might be said to belong to the school—perhaps merit a degree—and that was an elderly Mr Pulsifer. All are thriving here, Mother very well. She gathered blackberries herself in Lincoln yesterday, though it was after all rather a put-up thing. She was willing to do it, and we led her to the bushes and held them to her & pointed out the berries; there was no spontaneity in it. It seemed to give her pleasure, and she liked the rest of the ride better than she had the first part. She goes occasionally into

— 1889 —

the garden but nothing seems to her half so good as her own room and her bed. Edward is on the board of Health and busy about it,—making other people busy too. They must think him very troublesome. Happily he troubled us last year, and now he can find no fault with us. The children are dear and promising and interesting, their Aunt Ellen says so, and their perfect Mother is meeting her deafness like the heroine she is. Affectionately

Ellen.

ETE's letters to her mother August 22–30 describe in detail the activities of the Forbes children at Naushon and are thus omitted here as not being of general interest.

Concord, 2 Sept. 1889

My dearest kindest Edith,

I have only ten minutes to say that I came most safely and smoothly to Boston and found Josephine Hofman just returned from Dakota was going to Concord to spend the day with Miss Selmes. So we came up together very happily, and when I went round the depot to look for our wagon it was on hand, driven by Anna McClure! I hadn't expected her till night. Mrs Sanborn met me at the door, looking very pretty in a white dress, as Anna did in a blue muslin, and dear Cousin Sarah came trotting down in a black & white cambric that I never saw before, so all delighted my eyes and taste. I ran right up stairs and found Mother dressed and seated in her rocking-chair waiting for me and naturally Miss Brown in front of her contemplating and attending. After all the how do you dos & rejoicings we all went into my room which Minnie had polished & Miss Brown had adorned with flowers. Then came dinner & then the opening of the Naushon Garden. Everyone appreciated the various beauties. I'm in too distracted haste to say anything right. I'll write again.

Fri. P.M. Sept 6th 1889

Dear Edith,

I desire to thank you more at length for my visit and all your dear kindness to me. I never once got a good talk with you but all else I did have, a constant sense of your goodness & thought, and the pleasure of seeing you and all your works and haunts and friends. William & Haven came Monday night, and I am happy over them all the time. I

— 1889 —

haven't tried to give them one minute of attention, and yet feel quite acquainted with them. They are dear domestic talking fellows, very willing to be useful, and I am very proud of them as relations. Edward has hired a steam-launch which will carry fourteen and is going to take his family, W. Buttrick, Philip W. and from our house W. & Haven, Cousin S., Anna & me to Billerica on the river tomorrow. After the journey Wm. & Haven go home with him. Every day since they have been here has been full of plans and engagements of their own with the Concord boys,—tennis, canoeing, photography. We had all the James family here at tea on Tuesday and Edward & Mary were as charming as ever, while Robertson & his wife both seemed brighter and younger, we were all very happy together. I read them all Mr James's letters to Father, and they appreciated them. Robertson read us a little Essay of his Father's on the relation of the sinner to the Heavenly Father which brought on a very eager discussion. Haven & William followed me afterwards into the entry & said "Wasn't the talk very interesting! We enjoyed it ever so much." Goodbye my dear sister. Affectionately
           Ellen.

           Concord, 12 Sept. 1889.
My dear Edith,
 I have been having a very pleasant visit from William and Haven. They are so well brought up, so gentle and ready to help, so full of life and interest. I never felt them on my hands. On Friday night I gave them a tea-party. Haven selected as guests W. Buttrick, Geo. King, Walter Vialle, Edward James & Ralph Putnam. I added Roy Whitcomb and Walter Bush. My dear! it was as pleasant and lively a tea-party as I ever had, those boys felt at ease and full of talk as they could hold, and took me in. After tea Haven had thought he should like games, but there was no need of anything when tongues ran so fast. Talk went smoothly on till half past eight when all bade goodnight & Haven & Wm. gave thanks very prettily and went up stairs. Then the next day Edward took us all to Billerica in the steam launch, a very pleasant and interesting journey. The river large & deep and quite imposing, scenery often prettier than in Concord, distant view striking. Among ourselves great fun. Edward told many a funny story, so did every elder present. It was like a Monadnoc dinner time, the sense of fun & leisure. We found at Billerica the pier of an old bridge jutting out into the river, its stones inhabited by spiders, and its top grassed over. There we dined

very happily. On our homeward way, we drew & guessed Historical Scenes.

Lenox, 3 Oct. 1889

My dear Edith & Will,

This twenty-fourth anniversary is just as beautiful a day as the original wedding-day and finds me here at Mrs Rackemann's house, preparing to go with her and the children to Louise Thoron's wedding on Mr & Mrs Ward's forty-ninth wedding-day. When I arrived last night Mrs Rackemann and Bessy had just come home from a reception given by Mrs Secretary Whitney to Mrs Cleveland and Mrs Endicott. They were pleased with Mrs Cleveland, Mrs Rackemann said all the praise she has heard of her seems not too much. They tell me that Bessy and her husband are here, and Tom and all his family. So I shall get one peep at them, alas! no more. Mrs Rackemann says ever so many people stayed in bed yesterday as a preparation for the wedding today—that a lady said to her lately "It is true I have no time to breathe, or eat, or sleep, but I like it",—so hard does society push its pleasures here in the summer. We are all to go over to the wedding in a three-seated open wagon. Loulou has had two hundred presents and written her two hundred notes, and already many a trunk has been packed and sent to Salem. Tom's Bessy is to be the only bridesmaid. Wilfrid Rackemann drove me over from the depot to the house. He has just landed from a voyage to New Zealand. He stopped at St. Helena and Ceylon and had a voyage home of 134 days. Time for mail. Best love to you both and to our dear children, from a most proud Sister & Aunt,

Ellen.

Concord, 25 Oct. 1889

There now my dear Edith, my neglected sister, I'll begin while Mother is reading the newspaper after dinner on the dining-room sofa and tell you some of the things I've been saving, though I shall see you on Monday. First I wish to preserve Mother's latest remark. (I believe I told you that she said "Miss Leavitt has a way of catching me, very much as you catch a chicken, and taking me whither she will.") *This* one was made on Wednesday when a Unitarian minister from Liverpool, introduced by Mr Ireland called. His name was T. Lloyd Jones and I couldn't forbear asking him whether he was related to Mr J. Ll. Jones,—you know, my beloved Buffalo of the West. He replied that he was his cousin and he had just been visiting him. He had no sooner said that than I asked him in to dinner, out of joy at hearing again from Mr Jones. He told us in answer to our questions that *my* friend now preaches in Chicago, and described his church. Mother meanwhile was enjoying her dinner in an unusually passive state of mind, but after Mr Jones went she presently said "Americans have nothing like that delight, hurry & confusion which seems to be the natural state of the Englishman." It seemed to me to be pretty true, not of him particularly, but of English manners when they are cordial. It was somewhat so with Sir Edwin Arnold. Only think! that I should never have written you about that visit. It was a very happy day for us. I must tell you some of the stories with which he & Mr Sanborn treated us, and how Mr & Mrs Cabot stayed all night, and how I laid all sorts of perplexities before Mr Cabot and got my answer in every case, short, amusing, enlightening. Then came my journey to Lenox to the wedding. After my Lenox visit I had scarcely time to turn round, before I was again gadding. This time I stayed 26 hours with Mr & Mrs Cabot and 25 with Pauline. Mr Cabot was so polite to me, it almost frightened me. He stayed in the parlour after lunch till walk-time when I knew he wanted to be at his work, he also stayed by after dinner, and he had to take me the walk all by himself, for a caller kept Mrs C. at home. But I had a most beautiful time with him and learned all I could. When I came to Pauline's her family was at dinner. My visit here was much like my visit to the Cabots, to the heads of the family only, and to both of them. Mr Shaw stayed by all the time almost, and how I did enjoy him! He is most lovely to Pauline, and he is a particularly charming man to talk *to*, also he enlightens you, understands you & answers you when he talks. As for Pauline she is the gentlest most considerate, conscientious, affectionate being, it does me good to be in her society. She drove with me all the way to Fitchburg Depot & saw me into the cars herself with a box of flowers for Mother. Yesterday Edward, Abby Hosmer & I went to see the Idiots, & I invited Anna to go too. I want you to go some day. It is worth a great deal to see Edward with them. To see how much he sees, how much he has to say and to ask about them & their training is edifying, but oh! when he leaves the teachers and goes to them it is wonderful. One of the least intelligent of them, lying on his back playing with his foot, held out one hand to him, then both. "Want to come?" said Edward and took him on his knee. The child instantly hugged him tight, laid its cheek to his. I expected to see Edward draw back. I should. Far from it. Edward held him & patted him & bent his head to him, so that he could have the full comfort of "loving" him. "Oh Mumma *dear*!" the child said, again & again. Edward asked about his parents. "Never had any. He was picked up in a basket," was the answer. "Singular," said Edward to me "that phrase for a child that never had a mother." The most frightful ones he took right up on his knee, and thought of ways to make them all happy. He jumped the poor things that couldn't move their own feet, and made them shout with delight, he showed them his watch, drew pictures for them, did just what he would do for Raymond. Everyone ran after him, a big boy kissed his hand. Edw. & all of us considered everything in that asylum wise & wonderfully thought out & carried out. It seems that this is mainly due to Dr Geo. Tarbell. Edw. marvelled at the improvement in many of the children. When we came away Anna said of Edward "I admire & love that man more every time I see him!" No time for another word tonight. Much love.

Ellen.

Nov. 2 1889.

My dear Edith,

I have never told you that we like Mother's birthday lamp very much, it illuminates the parlour most effectively. Mother and I are at this moment sitting together by the dining-room fire after dinner, and she has just surprised me by laying down her newspaper and asking me whether I remembered that song "Fear not"? I certainly didn't, and after some meditation she said it was in a play to which she took us children, and Father went with her to see it too. Then after reading the paper for a while she looks up and says "Oh! it was in 'The Sleeping Beauty'. 'Ethelinde in sleep awaits her lover, Fear not, Angels round her hover, Fear not' ". There isn't that a piece of memory? Do you remember anything about it yourself? I cannot in the least recall it. Mother is always bringing up, for the first time that I know of, some scrap of the past. I'm today writing the invitations to Thanksgiving. I'm sorry W. Thayer is away.

[Unsigned]

December 1889

Dear Will and Edith,

Of course Mother and I accept with gratitude so great a present, so great a source of pleasure, so dearly associated as it is with your first

— 1889 —

housekeeping, your Opera and all the singing of those beloved early days, and with the New Years songs for twenty years or more and oh how much more delight. Then all our children have played on it and played with it. I thought Mother would surely say 'twould interfere with the windows. By no means, she "looks out for the main chance" unfalteringly, and says "Certainly we want it" Annie & Edward, everyone, is thankful. As to place you will, when

Last page is missing. Note by EEF: "W.H.F. offered to give them his piano, his wedding-present from his mother."

Concord, 23 Dec. 1889

Dear Edith,

The piano has come! I stirred round Saturday morning and found that several people would like my old one, among them Aunt Susan & Lidian. I had not been at home more than an hour or two before I saw yours standing in a wagon at the front gate! I raised the alarm, the household began to take action, John was quickly on hand and exclaimed to me that 'twas lucky the painters were here so we could have plenty of help. We were at dinner, and I thought I would sit still till it was set up after I had once showed what was to be done. Not so. Mother couldn't lose the scene and came into the parlour and took the rocking-chair. The painter, Wm. Craig, & John were as much interested. When it stood in place it added certainly a more palatial air to the parlour than the old one with its polish and grandeur. Mother surveyed it with pride and admiration. It doesn't seem at all too large. [. . .] At dinner Mother told how Will had given it and sent it up and desired special messages from her of appreciation & thanks. At tea-time she was all anticipation of what it would be to hear it in the evening, and Anna played till nine o'clock to her lying on the sofa. Anna's pleasure is all our fancy hoped & painted "I *love* its tone" she has said several times, and she runs to have a few minutes music when she can. [. . .] Edith dear, I have many letters to you unwritten which I hope sometime to write, and I think you must have been hurt by my not coming to see you as I intended when I was at Sarah's last week.

Letter left unfinished.

January 1890 – December 1892

*1890–91. Short visits. Lidian Emerson losing strength. 1892.
Quiet year. Ellen and household take care of LE, who has her 90th birthday
in September. LE dies in November.*

Jan 6 1890

My own dear Edith,

Do I again see a chance to write to you? Let me improve it, quick! How do you do? Here we drag through days of slowest convalescence. Margaret & Sadie have happily got well, I am now almost well, Edward is rather displeased with me that I won't say quite. Mother is decidedly better, yet the same conditions obtain as when you saw her, except that she is a little stronger and understands a little better. Miss Leavitt is right in the depths of weakness, pain, sleeplessness & nervousness, also without appetite. Helen [Legate] is just beginning to emerge but finding life up-hill work. Still as the majority of the household are pretty well again, we feel as if we were beginning our new year of work, three of us very cheerful about it. Edward considered Mother's illness as likely to be serious till Saturday, when he changed his tone and thinks now she is doing beautifully. Can you go with me on my black-jacket-hunt? I suppose Mother will be well enough to leave any time after Saturday. I have been reasoning with myself about your oft-expressed and oft-pushed wish that we shouldn't throw things into the fire-place. I know you are right though I love (in this one instance) untidiness so much, and I propose to bring myself round and try to be neat and to wish to be clean. Affectionately

Ellen.

Concord, 21 January 1890

My dear Edith,

I went to Springer's, tried on my jacket, liked it, and sent it to the depot. It is looked on with approval at home and I am much pleased with it and again thankful to you for buying it. I had a good journey to Boston with Violet. Anna went marketing with me and we found Katy Bowditch in Faneuil Hall market, and had a word with her. I gave Anna the flowers and she enjoyed them as of old. When I got into the cars to come home behold! Edward was with Alicia on the other side of the

aisle. And Lily told me she had spent last evening with Mother who seemed bright and very comfortable with Miss Ball beside her. When I reached the house Miss Leavitt said she had got along beautifully, and not missed me very much. So I am more easy about going to Bessy Tudor's on Friday. Goodnight now. I enjoyed you last night and was much flattered by my invitations from Mary and Alice. Your grateful
Ellen.

Concord, 31 Jan. 1890

My dear Haven,

These letters are a perfect delight to me, please send some more. What a happy life Bryn Maur seems to offer and how ready Ruth always is to find and taste to the full the happiness there is in life! Susy wrote to Annie a very interesting expression of disapproval of Christmas presents, which found sympathetic feelings here. Edward had just been making very earnest proposals to the family to give up New Years presents entirely and instead to give to each other the solid time they now absorbed, which he thought must be from two to three days. If that part of the plan were faithfully carried out, it would be well worth while, and I hoped that Will and Edith would listen. They did, but in silence. We don't know how it struck them. If they would all consent and all come and stay here for three days without an engagement, or letter or schemes, and be idle together & walk & read & dance & sing and talk endlessly 'twould be glorious. Perhaps you would come too, and we and the young generation should be happier for it all the year through. I have not heard from Edith since she came to Uncle George's funeral. I enclose you the accounts of him which we all like. Mother mourns him very much, he was the last dear old companion left to her, and she continually looked forward to his Sunday visits, and asked all winter how soon he was coming back. He was always a delightful visitor. Mother asks to whom I write, and says "Give my love to him and his Wife." Charley & Therchi have just stopped at the door in very good spirits. They are coming to dinner tomorrow. Love to you & Susy. Affectionately
Ellen.

Concord, 31 Jan. 1890

Dear Edith,

Your coming was a great pleasure. Mother is still just the same as when you were here, sick and frightened all day, and feeling bright and

— 1890 —

comfortable in the evening. Yesterday Miss Ball came to spend the day. Mother kept expressing pleasure in her visit, and in the evening played whist with her and Helen. Monday 3 Feby. I am sorry it should be so long since you have had a letter. Yesterday Mr Chamberlaine came down and invited Mother and me to dinner. Always before I have thought "Mother will think she cannot leave her bed, but she can & shall and 'twill be a great pleasure to her." But yesterday I said "She hardly leaves her bed at all now except at tea-time" with a very clear and sudden conviction that there was as much of a change as Mr Chamberlaine evidently understood from my words. Then it happened as it always has before when I came to that state of mind. She came down to dinner, and after a nap on the sofa, sat up in her place and ate her own dinner. Before it was finished William and Florence entered all cold and rosy and smiling to say that Papa & Mamma had gone to Mrs Chamberlaine's to dinner and they were to stay here meanwhile. Whether the children's presence, always very inspiring to Mother, was the reason or not I don't know, but Mother was well and comfortable all the afternoon, stayed downstairs nearly an hour before proposing to go up, and then lay down and rested very peacefully. Presently Mr Sanborn was announced and Mother decided to dress and go down, and was comfortable for four hours in the dining-room, never speaking of her bed. She talked with Mr Sanborn, quite herself. When he rose to go, Edward & Annie came in. They of course were a great pleasure to Mother, and when they had carried off their bairns, Helen came down and tea-time had come. In the evening Helen went to church, I read Mother a sermon, then she sang "Guide me O thou great Jehovah" to the tune of Tamworth, all three verses. Then we took a walk to see the entry and the study and see in what pleasant places our lines had fallen, and about nine o'clock first Helen came in and then Miss Leavitt, Mother testifying great content each time. No more today. Affectionately

Ellen.

Concord, 18 Feb. 1890

Dearest Edith,

I'm trying to write you a letter, but haven't finished a page. I'm trying to have my ball on Thursday. If I succeed could you come up and bring a son & daughter. This is only the trial ball. A better one may come later. Last night we had the Jameses to tea. Mary was most useful

— 1890 —

& watchful to bring the shawl, to find the spectacles, to set the cricket, and seemed to fully appreciate the fun of her dear grandfather's letters which we read aloud together. Bob does idolize his Father. Mother is now riding out again, and very bright in her bright moments. There is no time now to write more. Affectionately
Ellen.

Concord, 25 Feb. 1890

Dear Edith,

Thankyou for your dear note, oh how good it felt to me when I read it. And for the glorious show of flowers which delighted all my birthday tea-party, Aunt Susan & Lidian, Charley & Therchi, as well as the dwellers in the house. And for the magnificent birthday-cake which impressed me greatly, its mammoth size, its interesting quality of frosting, its lovely festal adornment of pink and white almonds. Thankyou also for the most delicate dress apron I've ever had yet. I like it very much. Mother grows more and more dependent, really objects to my going into my room or anywhere out of her sight very seriously, and sends for me in a few minutes if I stay so long. So I shall try not to go away oftener than once in three or four weeks. I had a letter from Roxa this morning saying what seems to intimate that a Friday night party came off at your Milton house in your absence under Violet's successful superintendence. I imagine that R. & C. were there. Affectionately
Ellen.

Concord March 3d 1890

Almost as much snow this morning as there was rain quarter of a century ago into which you bravely went out, darling girl, and returned so happy! I hope you will have another quarter of a century with Will, and shine upon your home and your kind with the same ingenuity of beneficence that you and he do now dispense. I had great pleasure in seeing something of you all and hearing Will's letters. And didn't we enjoy the theatre! How I wish we could have sat together! Please, dear child, fix a day when you can come to Concord and my Ball shall be that day. Mother sends her dear love to you. I brought home the cocoa-nut-cake from the lunch and to my surprise Mother ate it with pleasure. Sorry to have to go to dinner & despatch this unfinished. Affectionately
Ellen.

1890

Concord, 18 March 1890

Dear Miss Dabney,

Thankyou for writing me a birthday letter and sending me a perfectly beautiful present. What a good time I was having that day! It was lovely and warm and the first willow-pussies were brought in. Mother took her first ride since November too. Spring really seemed to begin that day and the struggles of winter to keep his hold prove ineffectual this year. Everything is pushing up in the garden. I had a glorious celebration of my birthday. The family declared it began with my ball on the 20th, and ended with going with Edward & Annie to the theatre, with Edith too, after a birthday lunch at her Mount Vernon St. house, on the 28th to see Rosina Vokes. Nine days of various celebrations. Thankyou for telling me that you enjoyed Edward's book. You ask whether I had any hand in it. No, that is Edward's alone. I didn't hear it till 'twas done. I have not seen the article by Geo. S. Merriam about Father which you speak of. I will look it up. I must tell Edward of it. He cares for what people say about Father, very much. I saw Roxa yesterday. Mrs Jones was so kind as to send me a ticket to the Antigone, and when I went and was wedged securely into my place, I saw one after another of my friends come in and sit down too far off for me to reach them. I saw Roxa come in, and afterwards she waited for me and walked to the depot, nearly, with me. She has promised to come up and see our little Concord Operetta. Last month I spent a day with her and Alice, young Edward Forbes was staying there too and Roxa was very good to him and played the guitar with him every day. It was to me a most blissful occasion when they gave a concert for my benefit. Give my love to Mrs Oliver. How sorry I am you are all so far away. I am glad you have beautiful mountains near you. Affectionately

Ellen T. Emerson.

Concord, 15 April 1890

Dear Edith,

I have a note from Mary Russell asking me to come Friday and spend the night, that I cannot do, but I have promised to come by 9.3 on Sat. and mark five or six hours. Lizzy Brown & Frances are coming on Friday to make a little visit. I think they will excuse my absence for that time. Now let me acknowledge your present to Mother of primroses and violets which came by the morning's mail, they are fresh & Mother has had them all day. She is getting well, she took up her books and

1890

began to read to herself again yesterday, and has been much brighter. Mrs Richardson & Sarah have spent the day with us and we have all been happy together.

Ellen.

Concord, 28 April, 1890

Beloved Edith,

Many little outs & ins, plans, counter-engagements, changes, letters, have gradually made my scheme out thus. I shall come out to you in the train nearest to ten on 1 May, go home with Mary Blake and spend the night with her, call on Mrs Perkinson at 10.30 Fri. morn., take the 11.30 home, have the children's party & go to the Wheildon's ball that afternoon & evening, go down Sat. morning and bring up Mr & Mrs Perkinson at noon to spend Sunday. Poor Mother is asleep and wakes every ten minutes to say "Ellen, I'm *very* sick", and a minute after "How can I get Edward." This is always the way in the forenoon. Usually in the afternoon she is awake a little more, and is less alarmed about her health. For the last five days she has been quite herself in the evening, and I'm going to have Mr Channing to tea, at last, if I can get him. William again has his foot in a splint and sometimes cries with pain. This is Ellen's birthday, she is not to have a party, but a family tea-party, ten guests, ten candles, ten viands, ten vases, here at Bush. Her guests are C & T, Edw. & A, Fl. herself and our four here. The first tulips of your last Nov.'s present have just bloomed.

Affectionately
Ellen T. Emerson.

There is an unexplained shortage of letters between April and July. There are no letters for May, and only a few short notes in June, with one long journal letter describing ETE's visit with friends at Naushon. Probably there was telephone communication; during this decade there is a marked change in the number and type of letters written, probably because of the telephone having come into general use.

Concord, 2 July 1890

Dear Edith,

Your letter thankfully received. Ruth is coming today. Edward & Annie & tribe migrate to Coffin's Beach this morning. Those white poppy-seed you gave me did little last year but their seed self-sown have brought forth a show equal to what you saw in the old lady's garden. Mother, Edward, everyone admires. Wm Emerson is to stay here overnight and see Ruth. Tomorrow I'm to have the Manse children to tea. I'm delighted with your good times. My love to Will and the children.

Affectionately
Ellen.

19 July 1890

My dear Alexander,

I have just had a great surprise; what do you think it was? Why John was hoeing the thick tall weeds down and he called to me to see what some little plants were. I ran and they were so beautiful, with dark green shining leaves, prettier than any that ever came up in our garden before, indeed they looked to me like young orange trees. Then I saw your white stake and knew they must have come from what you carried out that day in June, that it must have been seeds from the oranges which your Mother had put into that very good mixture of fruits which she made for her last tea with us.

That same day our barn was finished, the 18th of July, and today the vane, regilt and mended, is swinging in its old place again for the first time for many weeks. The moment it was put in its place it hastened to tell me which way the wind was. Edward Clahane put it up. Tell Violet Aunt Ellen blesses her for her letters and will answer as soon as she can. How glad I am the Merlin won the race! I hope the little orange trees which are now less than two inches high will be thriving finely when you come to see them.

Aunt Ellen.

Far Rockaway 31 July 1890

Dear Mother,

I enclose an invitation for Mr Channing which I beg you will leave at his house when you drive out on Saturday. Ask Miss Leavitt if she has not already done it to find out about Bible Soc. and if I am to have it, to help Margaret with the cake, if she pleases. I am having a beautiful time. Happily it is warm, and we could sit out & see the moonlight from the piazza and hear the surf roar last evening. This morning I slept till quarter of 8 and had to have a breakfast at 9 all by myself. It won't happen again though. Then all the children (except Ruth) and I

went over to the shore and bathed. The temperature of the water was 73° so I could stay in and enjoy the great waves twice as long as usual. It is delightful to see these amphibious children kicking and rolling about in the water & rising on the swell or springing through the crest of a great wave just about to break. They don't mind wet bathing-dresses or fear to catch cold. They play a long time on the beach after they come out, and presently go in again and stay in as long as at first. I never before saw people get the joy of water to the very full with *no* drawbacks before. I mean to come home on Tues. by 12.9 train and have asked Mr Channing to tea that night. Ask Sadie if she has remembered the milk-bills. My love to all. Affectionately
Ellen.

Far Rockaway, 4 Aug. 1890

Dear Mother,

Yesterday I had a very good Sunday. Ruth went to church with me to a little Presbyterian Church, absolutely new and very charming, built in what was lately a wood, so that through the back windows you looked into the wood and every window and door was open which seemed romantic and delightful. The service was unusually good. Then Ruth & I had a good walk home together to find the surprise of Mr Prichard and Miss Amelia just arrived to spend the day. How much we all enjoyed them! I read Miss Prichard my letters from Anna and then brought forth the photograph of you on your 82nd birthday, which was received with acclamation. Mr Prichard said "Let me see, Ellen, weren't you building a most ambitious barn when I came away?" Ruth has just been telling me of her ride on horseback with Cameron at Naushon, how she cantered! and the joys of tearing up a hillside in apparently an inland region and finding the sea at your feet when you reached the top. Her hair came down, she lost her hat, but C. picked it up without dismounting, and pulled out horsehairs with which she tied up her hair again and came home quite tidy. Affectionately
Ellen.

[Concord some time in July 1890]

Dear Edith,

I have had to give my writing hours to the garden while John was working there,—and it has been unusually full of pretty poppies, and hollyhocks have been in their prime, and besides the great tropical features, your pineapples & Alexander's orange-trees, both monuments of those famous Decoration Day compôtes) it has several new glories, carnations and H. Putnam's coreopses. Cousin Sarah helps me very much, trimming every day.   Aug. 7th.   This is the first I have written to you for six weeks and you meanwhile have sent me four. I went to Far Rockaway on July 29. Cousin Hannah arrived with me, by Cousin Sarah's swift-sent orders. We had a day there together. I stayed till Monday 4 Aug. when I went to Wmsburgh to dine with Cousins Hannah & Charlotte, and Miss Amelia Prichard. I came safely back by Monday night's boat—Mr Dodge was on board and very kind. And having done my errands and had an hour & a half with Dr Hopkins I came home at noon to a rousing welcome. It is now Friday and I have naturally many arrears of business after a week's absence. At Far Rockaway I was very happy, delighted with them all, made much of, and favoured with health and hot weather so that I went in to water daily. I am growing old. I succumbed to the temptation I have smiled at in others, I brought home a bag of stones. And Susy took me on Saturday to see people play Polo, which was a new sight to me. While I was gone Miss Ball was here, and at the depot in Concord I found the carryall, Miss B. & Mother behind and John in front, John explaining that he wouldn't trust Mrs Emerson without him at the Lowell depot where Selim was not so well-acquainted as at the Fitchburg. Mother evidently thought it a special providence, a good not to be expected, that I had come home safe.

Aug. 16th.   More than a week has passed. The first event was the arrival of Mary Miller. Fresh from Vassar, charmed to return to Concord, full of enthusiasm & affection and very ready to help, she has been a most agreeable addition to the family. She is a dear valiant child, earning her own way through life. She earned not only a scholarship of $200 for her next year at Vassar, but some money at sewing and is promised tutoring for next year to the amount of 150 & sewing to the amount of 50, so that she won't have to borrow at all. When she came home in June she immediately took a place at service for two months. Now she is having vacation and makes herself useful to me besides.

Aug. 25th.   Last week's events were first my going to Manchester. Cousin Sarah returned from the Manse to take care of Mother in my absence, assisted by Mary Miller. Lotta met me at the station and we took a little drive for eggs before going to the house. Effie senior & Will Putnam helped me & bag out and the sight of Effie and the sound of her

— 1890 —

voice was beyond expectation welcome. How attractive and worthwhile she is! Hatty always makes me at home and is perfectly lovely to me. She had me up stairs to see the baby who with his curly wig and double chin looks already like a judge of the Supreme Court and closes his mouth with decision. We had a good ride, a good sitting and sewing time, and finally a sunset walk which showed me all the beauties & advantages of their situation. They talked planets and found them. After tea we sat on their high piazza, and they talked not only planets but constellations, zodiac, ecliptic. Mr Putnam brought out a telescope, and sitting peacefully in a chair I saw the moon & its craters, then Jupiter & 3 moons, then red Mars, finally little Effie found and showed me a double star in Sagittarius. My first experience of a united family of zealous astronomers. Eight of them, men and women, boys and girls, all looking, all knowing, all caring. Wasn't it beautiful? and the warm still night and general ease and comfort too!. The next morning Hatty said that Effie Lowell had calmly proposed that the united family should read the Greek Testament daily for an hour. Though they had never touched Greek and were amazed at the thought, Hatty herself, her daughter Elsie and her daughter-in-law Bessie set to work and learned the alphabet, Mr Putnam provided half a dozen Greek Testaments, and at it they all went. They had been reading for a fortnight and they already got along very respectably. I was admitted to the hour, read my share, warmed up mightily at the sweet touch of a forgotten tongue, and longed to keep at it three hours more. Ida arrived just as we finished. I came home by noon train and had a young tea-party for Mary Miller. The young people all looked well to my aged eyes, they seemed intelligent polite children, capable of amusing themselves and each other. They were sociable at tea time and after tea. I asked them to sing and Belle Wheeler played and they all sang. Then they danced. Mother enjoyed the whole and stayed in the parlour all the time, remembering it the next day with pleasure. Goodbye for this time. Affectionately

            Ellen.

           Concord, 29 Sept. 1890

My beloved Edith,

 Since you left us I have been meaning every day to write. I want to tell you of Ralph's visit which gave us much comfort. Especially the fact that he spent one evening amusing us with discourse and song, amusing us most efficiently. I have felt better ever since, for my part. His visit has made me feel a little acquainted again and as if we were relations. Mother talked for some days after of "her dear boy". Lizzy & Maria Weir have called to see Mother. One day they met a baby in her wagon, a baby "with beautiful blue eyes, with a light in them." Those eyes she fixed on Maria at a distance and never looked away from her as she approached. So both she and Lizzy stopped and spoke to her and the nurse and asked her name "Amelia", said the nurse "this is little Amelia Forbes." "Forbes! oh!" cried Lizzy, "I know Mr William Forbes's children." "This is Mr Malcolm Forbes's baby," said the nurse, "we are up here. We came for the children's health." So ever after Lizzy & Maria watched, but saw neither baby nor anyone else, except once they saw a gentleman in a fine vehicle who must have been Malcolm, he looked so like Will, and that was a satisfaction.

I am enjoying the daily spectacle of Mother surrounded by her attendant ladies. There are now so many of them that it makes a fine show. Cousins Sarah & Charlotte, Caroline Cheney, Miss Leavitt, Helen & I. Every one of the six considers it her own special business to look out for Mother, and Mother seldom leaves her chair or asks for water, a blanket or a handkerchief, that at least four don't jump. If she proposes to go to the sofa, one offers an arm, the next puts on her falling shawl, a third flies to arrange the cushions, a fourth removes the obstacles from her path. They follow her round in procession sometimes, but usually Mother easily affords a task apiece, and so naturally wears a lofty indifference of aspect that I see in her that native Empress that Aunt Lizzy considered her. She has not yet got over her cold enough to go out. The fine fruits you brought have been delightful and freely used and Mother has yet enough for another day before descending again to the fruits of our own soil. Frost struck us on the 23d. But we still have tomatoes and some good melons. You were a good girl to come in on Monday. Affectionately

Ellen.

Concord, 24 Oct. 1890

Dear Edith,

The venison is very tender and very good. We all like it and renew our thanks. Mother's knee is well again and gives her no trouble in walking about her room, but that she never voluntarily undertakes. Her cold is nearly over, and she is brighter—for instance when Edward

came yesterday she was able, unprompted, to tell where I was and when I might be expected back. But on the whole she sleeps more, wanders more and is much less herself still, in spite of Edward's pronouncing her well enough to go downstairs; and it is hard to induce her to rise and sit by the fire once or twice in the day. I have lost Edward's visits for several days, so cannot give you the latest news of that family. Florence's eighth birthday comes next Wednesday. I am going to give her a party. Edward went to hear Carl Schurz the other night and heard him with great pleasure. I can write no more tonight. Affectionately
Ellen.

Thurs. 6 Nov. 1890

Dear Edith,

It seems impossible for either of us to find time to write though I save many things to tell you. I can't wait another moment however to say that Edward is going to lecture before the Concord Lyceum, Nov. 19th, and the subject is Mr Thoreau. I hope you and some children will come. Edward cautions me not to have Will told of it, even, he would so hate to come or to be expected to come. Effie arrives Friday noon to stay till Sunday noon. I thought about you all a great many times on Will's birthday and hoped he was having as happy and special a time as I did in beginning my second half-century. Here I am with four objects, to either of which I could devote all my time, your family, Edward's family, Mother & the house, to say nothing of the claims of society in general, and whatever I attend to I mourn at turning my back on the rest. Affectionately
Ellen.

Concord, 9 Dec. 1890

Dear Edith,

Thankyou for your long interesting letter. The story of Alexander's pacing achievement electrified me, and I wished I could show it to Anna. Mother and I prepared for her funeral service at eleven this morning, and I kept wishing for Mrs Sanborn, for I had not seen her since Anna died. There was a ring at the door. It was! It was Mrs Sanborn, Miss Leavitt & Elsie. I asked them if they would stay to our service, and dear Mrs Sanborn cried "Heaven sent us." So we read the Episcopal Service together, and I liked some of it very much. Then we read Anna's letter to Mother and talked of her a while, and then kissed each other and they went home. And now all is over, except the memories and, I hope, her influence for good. Thankyou for letter about Mother's room & enclosed check, received this morning. I will attend to all as soon as I can.

Affectionately
Ellen.

Concord, Jan 4th 1891

My dear Sally,

We were very much disappointed that you could not come, and I wished to write immediately, but New Years makes writing impossible. 'Twas hard that your vacation, short as it was, should be shortened by sickness. Charley & Therchi were sick that day so they couldn't come, and Waldo Forbes too had to be left at home with a cold, so we missed four from the celebration. Mother, Edward had arranged, was to lie down after dinner and the family was to take a walk meanwhile, and give the presents when she came down from her nap. But no! Mother firmly refused to go up stairs, lest she should lose some of the pleasure, and ordered that the present-giving should begin at once. She sat in her chair three hours at a stretch, giving and receiving, enjoyed everything and was not too tired the next day. Oh! would you could have been here in the evening to behold my favourite show of Alexander singing to Edward's guitar and falling off into reveries meanwhile, so that Edward keeps him going by perpetual digs of the elbow, playing away uninterruptedly just the same, varied this year by Cameron's assistance, C. having his hand in Alexander's hair. May you only come next year!

Affectionately
Ellen.

Concord, 17 Feb. 1891

Dear Edith,

What a pleasure to get a letter again! I hadn't heard before that you belonged to a Gymnasium Class. Perhaps you only matronize. I belong to one here. I thank you for the punctual box of flowers, beautiful and sufficient, which came on Saturday night, and greatly adorned my party, a fine bouquet on every place big enough to hold one, in parlour & study, also one on Gentlemen's and one on ladies' dressing-table and three on the tea-table. The party was charming till it came to the dancing which did not go well—but there was only an hour of it.

I wish you could hear Mother on the subject of your Edward. "Who was it? Were you here? Did you know about that lovely new cousin that came? A beautiful boy, *so* tall" (showing) "oh so dear. I felt as if an angel had come. Who was he? What! am I his Grandma? Think! I never saw him before. I mean since he grew & changed so." "Is his Mother in town? Do call on her, do ask them here. What? Our dear Edith? Our sweet Edith. That makes him doubly dear." I can't remember the prettiest things she said.

Ellen.

Concord, 26 Feb. 1891

Dear Cousin Sarah,

I rejoice to say here is an afternoon of great domestic peace, Mother feeling quite comfortable, Miss Andrews on hand, no engagement for me, so I shall at last write to you. I have just had a birthday and the family celebrated it very much. Edith came, and Edward & Annie and all the children, even the smiling Raymond. Each one brought a present. The children and Annie all gave paper presents, tags, labels, waxed paper etc, and Edward gave me a fork to fish for olives in the bottom of a bottle. Edith brought me this paper, and quantities of flowers, and a marvellous hardware-cabinet for the house, made of the wood of the ash we cut down two years ago. After dinner, and reading of letters and some family conversation we all walked out to doom certain beloved trees to be cut down. Edward wishes to secure a certain view for the dining-room and nursery, and I am quite willing. It always pays to thin out your trees, and now that I have learned to save them for boards and planks, it seems less destructive than to burn them. Then Edith and I went to Boston and met Will and Miss Fiske at Parkers where we had supper, and then we four went to the theatre together. I enjoyed the play itself, and enjoyed perhaps as much seeing Will and Edith laugh. Then I went home with them to spend the night, and Edith showed me her various devices and improvements. Miss Leavitt and her nieces dressed my place at the breakfast-table with green and flowers. That was their present, and it was very pretty. I saw Edward and Waldo just while they breakfasted, but it amounted to very little. After breakfast Miss Fiske and I packed Edith's trunks. She & Cousin Mary are setting

— 1891 —

forth for a month at N.C. Hot Springs. Then I came back to my mourning Mother at four. You will have heard from Cousin Hannah and the others about Edward's new plan of lecturing. He is going to Chicago, St. Louis and other places to read his two lectures, one on Mr Thoreau and the other on the Revolutionary Grandfather, I believe. I suppose too you may have heard that he has bought the house he now lives in, as well as Mr Fuller's Walden wood-lot which adjoins our own. So he says he thinks himself now settled for life. I suppose you have come home again by this time, and hope you are happy with your children and grandchildren. How is little Freddy? Is he to recover entirely? We think it is wonderful that your

End of letter is cut off.

The third of March 1891

Beloved Edith,

I rejoice anew as usual over this bright anniversary. It rains today almost as it rained on the original day. I always remember that as the rainiest day that ever was. I have had a very quiet celebration this time, studying S.S. lesson in the morning, reading old letters to Mother through the middle of the day—one of hers to Aunt Lucy in July '65 saying that you were planning to have your silver and linen handsome that you might leave it to be your descendants' pride, but you intended economizing on your furniture. I had not remembered these plans, and was much interested to hear them. Mother has been enjoying Miss Leavitt particularly lately. She said to Edward "Did you know I had a Mother?" "Whom do you call your Mother?" I asked. "Why, this tall, careful lady," said she. Miss Palfrey and her sister Mrs Leavitt came up on Thursday to spend the day, and Miss Palfrey was to me a very interesting guest. She talked a little about Waldo and Alexander and said she felt as if Alexander was continually intently employed upon his own life-work and it might possibly be that when he was put into the habits and made to follow the plans of the rest of the world he was in fact hindered. But that doesn't seem to me sound. Until he learns to live in strictest bonds of time and rule and finds that they are not bonds but wings, he is not thoroughly equipped for any work, common or peculiar. March 6th. Your letter has come and is full of good meat. How good that you are having so many pleasures! I hope the drawbacks will

— 1891 —

soon pass away. I well remember the scarlet gravel and clay of Virginia. Give my love to Cousin Mary. Affectionately
Ellen.

9 Mar. 1891

Dear Haven,

Edward and I rejoice to hear of the California plan and hope all will favour it, and that you will have innumerable side-benefits and unthought-of pleasures in it besides all that now promise. You certainly have stayed at your post with immense fidelity and deserve the holiday. Ralph came up to spend Sunday. He is a dear grandson who comes of his own accord to see us, and brings his sister's letters in his pocket that we may have the good of them with him. He has just seen his Grandfather, his Aunt Mary, and her youngest, off to Bermuda. Last week Edith & Cousin M. Simmons went to N.C. and Violet departed with Uncle Malcolm's family the week before, and his talk made us feel as if his family covered a large part of this hemisphere at this moment especially when we added your prospective journey. Edward and Annie and little Ellen & William came to tea and Edward who has just discovered the Moody family book gave us beautiful Moody stories. Little William who has always been the most virtuous of the family is "becoming bumptious" his father complains, and there is no doubt a certain swagger about him that didn't use to be. Mother is very well and bright and enjoys this family company—indeed all company, but she is perpetually relapsing into the belief that Edith's boys are the Plymouth cousins of her youth. It is pleasant news to her every few hours that this beautiful, this charming young fellow is her own grandson. Edward is to start for the West on the 21st and Aunt Susan Jackson starts with him going to see Alice in Dakota. Affectionately,
Ellen.

21 Mar. 1891

Dear Edith,

You have sent us a beautiful letter which we have fully enjoyed reading, both when it came and again today. It does sound as if you were having sweet and varied pleasures. Good that you ride on horseback! Do peep into Tennessee sometime. It seems to me as remote as Alabama. Is Round Top a mountain famous in our war? Edward has just

— 1891 —

taken leave and started on his lecture journey in the most gloomy sloppy drizzling day you can imagine. Mother sent for me as soon as he had gone "to see a broken-hearted woman". So I went and promised her her heart should be mended next month. Yesterday I came home from spending a day and night with Addy Manning. She took me at 5 to Miss Allen's Gymnasium where I saw the exercising with joy and envy. We came home to a dinner-party. One of the guests was Mr Huntington—proved to be Will's fellow-prisoner, great sensation. I told him tales of his prison-days, and he told me more. After dinner came Frank Cobb & Kate and Miss Mary Dewey and I had good talk with them all. I had such a delightful evening I could hardly sleep after it. I haven't told you that Mr Huntington said "Will Forbes saved a great many lives in the rebel prisons by his generous use of the money and things his Father sent him." When I came home Aunt Susan and Lidian came to dine and at tea Helen had company. I don't think I have thanked you for two or three boxes of flowers which have pleased Mother on Saturday nights. Now for your dear little boys. They came in time for tea to the joy of all, and described to us the beautiful fort with a wide doorway and a turret! which Edward & Cameron had built them of hard snow bricks, and how its building lasted till dark and then rain fell so it was never used. In the evening we played Buckle, buckle beanstalk, and Alexander showed us "I've seen a Ghost", and did it as brightly & firmly as Cameron could. Waldo didn't feel as if he could remember & left it to him. Waldo's manners were very good. How we did enjoy their talk about Venice at noon. They played out of doors principally on Saturday. No more time. Goodnight.

Ellen.

Concord. 28 Mar. 1891

My dear Miss Clara,

I trust I am not too late to wish you joy on your birthday. I meant certainly to write yesterday, but it was a day of interruptions, and of packing the Freedmen's box at this house full of clothing, dishes, and all sorts of things not further useful here to be prized at a much higher rate—so much higher that we are continually surprised—in Virginia. Miss Holley receives them and distributes them as wages for various jobs done by her black scholars and their parents, and to celebrate Christmas etc., and on the Fourth of July and other patriotic occasions she makes presents of the playthings and pretty things that go in the box. She always observes the 19th of April, our day of the Concord Fight in 1775, and we time the departure of our spring box that it may reach her in time for that celebration. This week I have had my dear Anna McClure's niece with me and have had the great pleasure of hearing of her last days and words and the good she did people, and today we have been reading her letters together. Good news today from dear Sarah Malcolm, which relieves many hearts here and in many places. I love to hear of your walks on the piazza enjoying the mountains, the sky and the stars, and I am sure you also take pleasure in the garden and the house. Every now and then I hear what good you and Mr and Mrs Oliver do to all about you as of old, sometimes things are said that make me feel as if I had seen you all myself. I wish I could. Affectionately,

Ellen T. Emerson.

31 Mar 1891

Dear Edith,

I send along these two letters, since I cannot write myself. Alas! I hardly dare open today's news from Sarah, yesterday's was so alarming. I thought yesterday of our dear little baby's death, and of Sarah's little Ellen's birthday. Mother is well and sends her love. Mrs Nesbitt is here. When shall you come home? Give my love to our Violet, our Edward & Will if he is with you—I fear he is not.

Affectionately
Ellen.

Concord, 2 April 1891

Dearest Edith,

I see with you the greatness of your loss and the unutterable darkness of the future for Malcolm and the children. I know Sarah was truly as you say the heart and soul of the family, for whom each one was thankful every day of her dear life. She has done us all serious good all the time. I shall come tomorrow night.

Ellen.

We. April 8th 1891

My dear Edith,

I have abandoned and destroyed the letter I have already written to you, it was not just what it ought to be because I am not able to make it so, but I wish to say at least that it was a privilege to be with you all last Friday and Saturday and you were all very good to me. I send my thanks and my love to every one of you. Mother wishes also to send her love to her dear child. I have just been up garret to look for something and have seen on my green dress the lace Sarah Malcolm gave me. How good and how pretty that was of her! And her taking interest in my party last year and sending me all those flowers was another act of the same kind. I have twice read with Mother the selections for her funeral. I have had a letter from Clara Holmes about Edward's visit to Davenport which I'll send you when Annie has seen it. Annie & William still have the "grip" and Mr & Mrs Keyes and Philip are all having it so that they have a nurse there. Ida has invited me for the night of the 23d and the 24th. Mother every day asks me to look at the beauty of her lookingglass and then desires me to see that Will is thanked for it and told that she appreciates it. Affectionately

Ellen T. Emerson.

Concord 19 May 1891

Dear Edith,

Happy days with Charley & Therchi & Lidian since I saw you. Mother only pretty well. She enjoyed your beautiful pansies. William & Florence walked down to breakfast with us this morning, William with his hand in a sling, the sickle having dropped upon it and cut it. Florence invites me to breakfast at their house and see how her bird loves her and flies to her and follows her. Is my Cameron still sick? How do you do yourself? Oh how good it was to see you & Violet! Edw. & I have just returned from Mrs Minot Pratt's funeral, 85 yrs. Yesterday we went to Mr Nathan Hosmer's. Last Friday we were at Jane Loring's. She died of Bright's disease. On the principle that death was near and could not be much delayed by carefulness, she has gone out more than usual this winter, especially to Frolic Club, she loved all "the girls". Col. Russell & Mary are coming up Friday night & Edward & Mr Dennison too, I hope, tell him.

Ellen.

Concord, 29 May 1891

My dear Edith,

I am very sorry that you are sick and that I cannot come. Miss Legate

— 1891 —

goes away tonight, and Miss Leavitt who is sick and cannot come to meals or do more than is necessary, is the only one besides me to man the wall. If you don't go on Monday I'll try to come for an hour or so Tues. But Robert Perkins's wedding takes Wednesday, and Monday is full of engagements, so that it really means leaving Mother for three successive days. Cameron has been delightful to us. I lost part of his visit by being at Bible Society. I rejoice that Waldo has begun with the violin. We mourn that Decoration Day is no family festival this year. We think here in the house that Mother loses strength. I haven't asked Edward. Therchi is very much struck by it, and cries over it sometimes. Affectionately

Ellen.

Concord, 16 June 1891

Dear Edith,

We had last week a visit from Mr & Mrs Cabot which was full of pleasures. Mr Cabot told me of the many acquaintances he had made in reading Col. Perkins's business letter-books, all Mr Forbes's relations, his father, uncles & brother, yea even his grandfather. He has learned the character, adventures & business of these and innumerable others. It is a mine of history. I showed him all the corners of the yard and asked his advice about every tree & bush and learned something worthwhile. John & I have now carried out some of his suggestions. Mrs Cabot & I read a book together, and we all three borrowed the lame William as guide and drove to Wayland that Mr & Mrs C. might see the summer abode. Mr Cabot told me what bird was singing—the bay-winged sparrow—and discovered him later and showed him to me. Edward came for one short hour to Bush and we all read "Boston" together. Happy time! I love that lecture. Mrs Cabot after dinner on Friday read "The Revolt of Mother" to Mother & me, & Mr Cabot sat & listened. When Mr C. & Edw. took a few minutes' ride together Mrs C. rejoiced, and said Mr Cabot always had a good time with Edward and that he admired his performance, the perfection of finish which he always put to his work. She also praised Edward as a social treasure "*everyone* considers him a most agreeable companion". So you see we had much joy out of them. This week we have had Mary Faulkner & E. Denny for a day, and Alicia & her friend Miss M. Lang took tea with us & them. We got Miss Lang—a musical genius—to hear Mother sing "Friendship to every generous mind", and write it on the score, that it may not be lost. Dearest girl I am grateful that you are better. I'll write soon.

Ellen

Concord 8 July 1891

My dear Edith,

Will's letter telling of your sickness on Monday came after tea last night. Oh! dear child, I am sorry enough. I shall come out on Friday morning and spend half an hour with you before going to Mary's. It seems monstrous not to come to you but I see no chance but Friday. Nina comes today for a week, and next Wed. my new girls come & Sadie & Margaret leave, so I must stay to teach. I haven't told you how glad Mother was of your note to her. It touched the very spot where it was wanted. She kept it on her bed and read it *herself*—which is an unusual thing—once or twice a day, and I was often asked to read it to her, till Edward carried it to Wayland to read with Annie. Cousin Sarah has just walked in upon us, to our great joy. Thank Will for his goodness in writing to us, we *do* want to know, and wish we could help.

Your loving & sorry
Ellen.

Concord 29 July 1891

My dear Edith,

It is delightful to hear good news of you. I have hated not to write but new girls naturally absorbed all my time and just as they were getting wonted enough for me to leave them a little to themselves, Emma Diman's truly pleasant visit to us began, and as it was short I wouldn't take time for writing. Mother enjoyed her very much, we all did, and the two girls flattered their elders by often joining us in readings and discourse & sewing. How much the friendliness of the young charms the old! They sang and played, and Mother was delighted. We have had the kitchen painted and have had endless satisfaction in gazing at its clean shiny walls, just as we did at Mother's room last winter. Cousin Sarah is a mine of memories and when she happens to bring them out they are so interesting that I wish to record them. If I could only remember them! But here are two or three. She told me one day which Psalms and chapters of the Bible she knew by heart. I told her how Grandma gave me a quarter of a dollar to learn the XII of Romans and she said "Grandma Ripley had me learn the XIV John and then I recited it to her every afternoon or evening while we were waiting for the lamps." Then another time she said "Brother Samuel says when he was going away to the Seminary when he was young, Mother said to him 'Your Wife is probably already living now and you ought to be praying for her.' " Every reminiscence of her childhood at the Manse interests me. One day I was bent on killing the ant that coursed over the tea-table and Mother was eagerly forbidding me, and Cousin Sarah said "Your Father wouldn't let me kill ants; if he saw me step on them on the marble walk he would stop me and say 'Lidian wishes them to live' " Mother has taken great pleasure in your letter to her. I hope you are having a good time every day and gaining. Give my love to Will and each of my dear nephews and tell precious Violet her letter was sweet as honey and shall be answered.

Your loving sister.

Concord 21 Aug. 1891

My dear Sally,

It is a shame not to have sent a little note immediately on receipt of your last month's letter to tell you that Mother's cold was passing away and Edith was getting along beautifully. She seems to have no arsenic in the Naushon house, and is gradually getting over the effects of what she has had. She goes on the steam-yacht with Mr Forbes and Violet to accompany the N.Y. yacht-club cruise and simply enjoys it. She has come to the table at dinner and tea, and sat in the parlour in the evening, and has had a daily ride in the wagon. They fuss over her a good deal and keep questions and duties from her as much as possible, and Violet says she looks rather pale and weak, and feels numb still. Edward has gone to Naushon and has taken Ellen and Florence to stay a few days. Indeed I think they have the house full of company all the time just as usual, but young Edith is the housekeeper. Here Cousin Sarah and young Alice Arthur and Mary Miller are staying with us, and Miss Leavitt is having a vacation, so that we have a new nurse meanwhile, a Miss Buncher. Mother has ceased coughing, comes to dinner and tea and rides every day. Yesterday we had the Bible Society, a sewing-circle. She came down for the last hour of it, and said afterwards it had been very pleasant to her to have an opportunity to talk with so many friends whom she seldom saw, which shows that she was bright at the time. Often she is passive and seems incapable of understanding, refuses to know who anybody is. A caller interrupts. Farewell. Affectionately

Ellen.

— 1891 —

Concord 26 August 1891

My dear Edith,

I have just come from Sherman's wife's funeral. One cannot but think of Aunt Lizzy and of Kate and feel as if they must have hastened to receive Carrie into the other world. Sam & his wife are in Europe, but oh! how many near and nearest relatives this dear girl had and leaves to grieve! There was much crying at the funeral. Edward took tea with us last night, and told us about you all, at your house, the Mansion-house, and Uncatena. Very eagerly we listened and much comfort did he give us. He was flattered to see his little girls so happy and at home with their cousins, big and little, and grateful to Violet for her goodness to them. He told of your lending Ellen a banjo and of the boys' all showing her how to manage it. I know well what day it is today. I have allowed myself the pleasure of telling Alice Arthur stories of Don, and she liked them so much that it was a great pleasure. I wish I were at Naushon with you today. I shall always wish it when the day comes round. Tell me stories of each child. I see so little of them now I want them brought before me. Mother sends her love to you. She has come down early for tea and is lying on the dining-room sofa. She says "Tell her I want her to come for a visit." She often says "How long it is since I have seen my child Edith."

Ellen.

Concord 3 Oct. 1891

My dear Mary [Miller],

I take this scrap to send the love of the family who were very glad to hear from you and all about the Baby and tell you that Alice has gone to Albany, and Edward's family have moved away from us today and begun housekeeping again. That Edward F. has begun his college career, and Cameron is again at work at football and Edward James & William Emerson of N.Y. are to be chums. Such is the family news. Alice & Lidian, Cousin Sarah and I went to Coffin's Beach with the Weirs, Miss Ball and Lotty Brown and had a happy time cooking, eating and praising our three meals a day, wandering among the hills of sand, appreciating the glorious weather which lasted throughout, and the moon and stars at night, but, most of all, the bathing,—all eight going in in line every day. You have now all our Concord news except that Mr Garland has seventeen scholars, and that C. Cheney's house where Dr Braley now lives caught fire and burned from the back up as

far as the kitchen where it was stopped. As I have indicated I'm glad you have tasted the joys of auntship. It is good news too that your place for the winter is so pleasant. Affectionately
Ellen T. Emerson.

Oct. 3. 1891

My dear Edith and Will,
I rejoice that another anniversary finds you after all the sickness of the spring well again, together and happy, and with only increasing reason for pride and pleasure in the dear children. I have just been telling Alice Arthur the history of twenty-six years ago. If you had only looked far enough into the future in 1865 I think you would have been married in September that all your college-boys might not be ruthlessly torn from you just before the wedding-day came round. I care very much about Edward's beginning at Cambridge. Cameron rejoiced us by coming last Saturday, and Uncle Edward's joy in him was a constant delight to me. How proudly I gazed on his crew-ribbon! Affectionately
Ellen.

12 Oct. 1891

My dear Edith,
We send our thanks for a quarter of venison on which we mean to subsist for several days this week, also to call in our friends to feast with us. I sent my thanks for a former one by Annie; I hope she duly delivered them. Cousin Sarah has gone away, and cold weather has set in. We are getting into winter trim. I went this morning to the funeral of Florence Richardson's mother. Chilton Cabot was there with Louise, and they are soon to be married I hear, and are thinking of taking Cousin Mary's house. Mr Channing has sold his house to Charley Emerson. Poor Mrs Witherbee, thereby turned out of her nest, is coming to live where Mrs Phebe Foster used to, and be across the entry from Miss Andrews. Cousins Elizabeth, Mary and Sarah invited me up to have breakfast with them on Saturday [at the Manse]. They had a good fire in the open fire-place in the dining-room, and Cousin Sarah showed me the little brass knobs over it which pulled out to let warm air from the chimney-back into the room, and said they were there when she was a child. Just as we were finishing breakfast Edward & Annie came in. They began to talk over the fire-place, as Edward's new building makes him curious in such matters, and I was interested too,

but the liveliness of the conversation between Annie & Cousin Mary soon drew all my attention. They were discussing Naushon. Cousin Mary was considering how it could be that your family living in such a beautiful and finished palace could enjoy visiting 5 Phillips Place [Cambridge], as if it wasn't the people and not the house that made one's pleasure. Mother often asks how long it will be before her dear Edith comes. I suppose you will move up this month. Affectionately
            Ellen T. Emerson.

                 Concord, 17 Oct. 1891

My dear Edith,

What good news your letter brought. We are in a state of joyful expectation of the 26th ever since it was opened. I hope you will all give us all the time you can. Mother and I have just been at Edward's for the first time since they moved in, and have been much pleased with their new windows and carpets and papers. Now I am sitting with Mother while Miss Leavitt has gone out. Oh what a month of beauty this has been! And last night the moonlight was the most glorious we have had I don't know for how long. I wish I could be out of doors all the time. You sent me lovely notes from Ida and Mr Minot. I send you two pretty ones from Alice Arthur, and one from Cousin Sarah. I hope you will have quiet times here and find it does you good to be at home as it certainly does us to have you. Affectionately
                 Ellen.

                     3 Nov. 1891

My dear Cousin Sarah,

I remember you on the first opportunity of writing. I am in the cars going to see Cameron play a football match, Senior eleven against Junior eleven. Edith, Violet & Alexander have settled at Bush for the month of November, the rest of the family is scattered but last Sunday all but Ralph were with us, and all Edward's family came to tea Saturday night, except Edw. himself who dined in Boston at the Saturday Club. Sunday was Will's birthday. Five children went to church with me, & Florence appeared at church also. In the afternoon Edward and Annie came and brought Florence, William and Raymond, and Miss Leavitt agreeing to stay with Mother we all went to walk together, except Cameron—thirteen of us—to Fairyland and to Walden. Even Raymond cheerfully accomplished the whole distance. In the evening

— 1891 —

Cameron whistled and played on the piano while Edward accompanied with the guitar. This gave Mother great pleasure. She has ever since spoken of Sunday as "The Party". She is confused by the large family as before, and sometimes asks when we are going home. But she enjoys every one. Edith is pretty well, but tired after moving. Alexander is as Miss Legate has long wished in the Emerson School for the month, and does pretty well. Cameron didn't play football today and the game went against his class, but I enjoyed seeing it with Will, Malcolm and Violet & Margaret. I came home to find with joy your letter. Goodbye with much love to my cousins from Mother & me. Affectionately
                                                    Ellen.

                                            Concord 20 Nov. 1891
My dear Edith,
   I hope we shall get your address, which I forgot to ask, in season for me to get this to you on your birthday. Mother and I send much love, and rejoice that you are still spared to us, and that we at last have had a little visit from you, and that it is not over, and desire to see you back again. I slept in Mother's room last night, and she thus addressed me. "Are you willing to buy me another watch as good as my other?" I consented, but suggested that the bathing-room watch would do. "Oh no! I want to put it in my will, that the baby may have his rights." "Which one do want to leave it to?" "The youngest, I suppose." But after a while she said "Do you think that beautiful boy that I fell so much in love with would like it for his share?" I thought well of the proposal. "I think Edith would be pleased, I think his Father & Mother would like to see him have it," she said several times. "If I never mention it again, you'll buy the watch, won't you? And put it in my will?" Then she began to wander and before she fell asleep she said "Do you think Mr & Mrs Sanborn will be pleased that the wonderful child has his rights?" This in a tone not of anxiety, but of happy anticipation. You will find Susy Arthur here on your return. She is to arrive on Monday. Alexander came for the night on Thursday, and made himself cheerfully useful. He carried letters to the P.O. and tacked the address-cards onto the Freedmen's box. Lucy came & was a most agreeable and useful visitor. She made all the mince & apple pies & the Portsmouth gingerbread, and we parted with her last night with regret. We send our love to Will & Violet and long to see you all here. Your grateful & affectionate sister.

— 1892 —

Concord, 28 Dec. 1891.

My dear Edith,

How can I tell you how much delight I have had in your two boxes without encouraging you to do the like another year? I will begin by forbidding your ever noticing Mother and me at Christmas, and then relate that those flowers were a most dear and touching remembrance of you to Mother & Miss Leavitt and me. The roses were remarkable. Did you ever raise such before? The dear hibiscus bud behaved like an angel, blossomed gradually & perfectly and adorned first the dining-room and then Mother's room. The paper narcissus is glorious to this moment. And that big box of candy was delectable, I have growled over it up in your closet half a dozen times already. I must stop

F.R.R. Dec. 30th 1891.

My dear Edith,

To think I haven't yet thanked you! That box of candy so kindly sent, those gloves, those amusing pins, are very dear, all of them to my heart. There never were prettier calicoes than you sent the girls, and I am grateful for them, as well as for Miss Leavitt's handsome dress, and for the fruit and for the guava jelly, and Mother's cup. She sends her love and thanks for all. I want to know what Mother shall give Will. I rather imagine you have no Chaucer in the house. Would you like that for him? Or would a Dante be better? I have not chanced on any reading friend lately to ask what is desirable. Can you tell me whether Waldo would like a music-roll? If you can conveniently, I should like my receipt for white gems back again. I have, I think, presents for all but for Will and perhaps Ralph. Sally is coming to dine & spend the night I am glad to say. As Miss Andrews is reading I can't think what else I want to ask & tell. Probably this will reach you when you are too busy even to read it. I don't know why I am so behindhand with everything. Affectionately

Ellen.

Concord 11 Jan. 1892

My dear Edith,

We are of course electrified by your West India plans, and especially by the long and lengthening train of sons & daughters you propose taking along. Mother has been well up to this time—I feel thankful for every day of Edward's absence that passes and leaves her still well, for

— 1892 —

now she is so old and especially now that someone dies in Concord every week, I should almost feel it a duty to write quick to Edward and on the other hand I should hate to destroy his tour for a simple cold such as Mother often has. Now, Wednesday, she is better than she was yesterday. I have invited Mr Sanborn to read to Mother, Susy and me the lecture about Father which he has read in the West this winter. He has chosen this evening. I fear that I shall not come to Boston this week, and thus miss meeting you at studio. On Friday last, Florence's great journey to Newburyport with Helen to see little Grace Legate finally came off. Helen says she won everybody's heart by her discreet and lovely behaviour & thoughtfulness. The same might be said of Susy Arthur here. She is wisely and sweetly useful all the time. I enclose Edward's note. I should like some day to write you a letter again & will if I can. Mother sends her "love to both Ediths". So do I.
               Ellen.

              Concord. 20 Jan. 1892.

My dear Sally,

 Mother sends her ten dollars to the Society for the Prevention of Vice. I don't think it is quite time, but as she has the money today I send it along at once for fear I should spend it. We have good news from Edward every day. He is having a good time. Mother is very well and all goes on as usual at this house. Edith & Will are preparing to start for the West Indies. Florence & William dined here today, Florence quite lovely, W. a little inclined to show what a big & rude boy he knew how to be. What a pity charming children love to affect the non-charming! Charley & Therchi are again pretty well and go out every day. William of N.Y. came to spend Sunday, bright & handsome, friendly and happy. The Jameses gave a dance and he came up to go to it. He said he wished his Mother could have seen how much he danced. He studied his German, he visited all his relations and wrote his letter home besides being a most agreeable visitor. Edward writes joyful letters, Annie has just read me a very funny one. I hope you are well and I wish you had been here at New Years. Affectionately
               Ellen T. Emerson.

              F.R.R. 10 Feb. 1892

My dear Edith,

 There has been no day when I have not wished to write you, to tell

1892

you that Mother enjoys her oranges, that the candy you gave me still holds out, that the barrel of sweet apples has to this day supplied a favourite luxury to us. Mother has changed her habits a little. She no longer likes to remain in bed, she is up & sitting by the fire in the forenoon for an hour or two, quite as often as three times a week, and though she is as eager as ever to lie down after dinner, she asks to get up every day before four, and stays dressed till bed-time. For this reason she is tired earlier in the evening, which gives me the impression that she is much more feeble, but perhaps she is not. I am on my way home from Milton, Alice invited me to lunch with the Dabneys, all were there except Alice who was sick at Malcolm's. Rose Dabney was at Sears Building this morning when I went there to see about the C.B.& Q. bonds, she & Bert [Dabney] were at work in the inner office. At lunch we found her returned & installed. I had a pleasant time seeing Mr & Mrs Dabney at lunch. After lunch Alice Cary took me up to her dressing-room to get a chance to read our Violet's letter. She said none of them had yet heard from your party, but they presumed you were already embarked & headed for St. Thomas.

Concord. Now how wrong that I have said nothing about Edward. I found when I came home from Milton that he had reached home at noon, and visited Mother at five o'clock. The next night I saw him myself, and every night since I have seen him. Everyone remarks on his good spirits and improved appearance. He says he read twenty-two times. Twice he gave readings of Fathers poems, and he says he likes to do that. He found cousins of every degree and kind, among them one of Gov. Kent's daughters—or nieces—her maiden-name was Ellen Emerson Kent. Annie says the moment he hears the word cousin at home he puts on a perplexed expression as if he shouldn't be able to fathom the intricacies of relationship; she always keeps the matter clear in her mind for him as far as she knows his kin; but how he looked when these cousins presented themselves is a question interesting to her.

11 Feb. This morning has come your missive from Brunswick. I'm pleased that you have found warm weather already, amused at the will difficulty, I know how labyrinthine wills always prove; should fully enjoy Alexander's hair-cutting if only his Papa and Grandpa had superintended it as well as the others. Aunt Susan & Lidian & Caroline Cheney dined here today, on the Naushon turkey, for which and its attendant ducks & chickens & eggs my profoundest bow & best thanks. Last

— 1892 —

night Edward & Annie with Ellen & William came to tea, and Charley & Therchi. We had a very pleasant time. Edward after tea began telling Charley of the people he had visited to learn about Col. Lowell's last day, and the stories they had told him about Cedar Creek. It appears Charley was at that time in the Shenandoah Valley and had seen all the ground and heard the day's doings talked over at the time, and he told Edward all he knew. This made a very interesting conversation, and William seated on Mother's cricket on the rug was an absorbed listener. Charley has a letter from Lizzy Browne saying they are anxious about Frances & taking her to Plym. for a change. Affectionately
Ellen.

22 Feb. 1892

Dear Edith,

Mother said she was cold. I put the fur rug on her, which she meanwhile admired and, with gratitude to you, called "a great present". Just now she has found it too warm, and the sun is resting on its whole length on the floor. Happy Mother! Happy Sun! Skillful Edith! I have finished reading your letter for the second time to Mother. It is full of sugar-plums for the mind. The Georgia Hotel, the green hot bath— was it warmed by subterranean fires?—my beloved Cameron's arrival, and studies, the little boys good time together, the seas on which you sail, the Nassau harbour, every mention of precious Violet. Yesterday morning Mother kept saying, "I don't know what I can do." By and bye she added "The only thing I *can* do is to keep saying that, as they keep saying 'Cuckoo' ". They, no doubt, meaning cuckoos. In the afternoon we drove up to Edward's as it was mild and pleasant, and Mother was anxious lest he was very sick. William of N.Y. was there spending his holiday. He said he often visits Edward F. now that he is left alone. He envies him his music, which admits him to three musical clubs. He told me that the Glee Club are to give a concert here on the 29th and that Edward James wanted to know whether we could entertain any of the boys. I said I'd take four and forthwith wrote to Ralph to ask him to come play host for me on the occasion. I shall feel well fortified if he will. While we were at Edward's Florence came in and brought her canary to exhibit, let him out of his cage and let him hop about and come onto her finger. When we took leave Mother had much difficulty in getting into the carryall with her great weight of wrappings and Edward, William and Annie came to help. When we reached the Red

— 1892 —

Bridge she said "Write a note and put it into the Post Office to ask whether Edward caught cold and whether the bird is lost." "Why no" I said, "there bird was *there*." "Yes, but it was out of the cage, and while they were helping me perhaps it got away." Tomorrow is my birthday. Susy is coming home and Edward's family is coming to tea. I hope you'll see & eat breadfruit, mangoes, nespras & all tropical things.
          Affectionately
          Ellen.

                Mar. 3d 1892

My dear Will and Edith with whom I always remember this day, I received this morning from Mr Stone the news that you had reached Trinidad, and I picture you to myself in the most tropical scenery, arranging some walk or ride or other cheerful celebration of the happy occasion. The telegraph is a great comfort; I love to know you are in Trinidad while you are there, instead of first finding it out when you are already somewhere else. You know it is almost as amazing, as romantic, to me as it would be to hear that you were in the moon. And how do you all like it? How does my dear Violet enjoy her travels? I am sure Cameron thoroughly appreciates the pleasure of seeing foreign places; it is, so to speak, his first chance, I don't believe he remembers his early European experiences. Now I must tell you of my birthday. Florence and William came right after school. They told Annie they wished to hear me read Marmion to my class. But arrived, they changed their minds, crept into the parlour and solaced themselves, F. with the piano, Wm with the stereoscope. Meanwhile Mary Bartlett, Milly Linder, Bernice and the others came with congratulations in their mouths. I read them "Edinburgh after Flodden", and they were enthusiastic. My cake came from Lucy before they went. I opened the bundle in their presence and behold! besides the beautiful cake, two doz. lemon patties, so I could give each one. All the family came to tea. The table was adorned by a dish of beautiful azaleas from you, also many fine viands. After tea Ellen played a march, I headed the long procession to the parlour, where a birthday table of gifts & candles & candy glittered on the S. side of the room, and poems were read: Then we all sang Fair Harvard & one or two more songs, and ended up with games. No time for more yarn. Mother & I send love to you all.
                Ellen.

— 1892 —

Oh! what a feast came by Saturday morning's mail, Edith dear! Two from you, two more, one from blessed Violet, and one from my beloved Cameron. Frances Browne had come that morning—evidently much better, this last illness was the clearing-up shower,—and she and I repaired to Mother's room with the mail and the atlas. I could now stand an examination on the geography of the West Indies, a region of knowledge hitherto dreaded as dim and involved. The domestic life on board is the sweetest thing to the mind of all the news your letters tell. Thankyou for remarks on my birthday and my Valentine.

F.R.R. Mar 24. Just after I left this letter Cousin Mary Watson & Luly came, and I didn't write because when I had any time I wished to give it to them. And since! Our good John! On Thursday 17th Annie had asked us to dine there, and I went to the window to order the horse. Jimmy was sawing at the wood-pile, and I asked him where his Father was. "He has pneumonia" said Jim and told me that he came home yesterday noon with a headache, that he had such an aching night & so much difficulty in breathing that he sent for the doctor early in the morning. On Monday afternoon, 21st at 3.15 he died. I see at every turn his shovel which he expected to use Wednesday night, his basket in which he meant to bring Mother her wood before tea, his potatoes he had just sorted, the wood-pile he had just framed, the carryall, the washing of which in the fierce windy Tuesday of last week, I fear, cost him his life. Everything speaks of his care and faithfulness. Edward C. came last night to talk with me. No man ever left his children with a better elder brother I think. I listened almost with surprise to the wisdom and kindness evinced in all he said. And our dear brother has been so kind too and watchful, both at our house and John's, and takes up so readily the duties probably more distasteful to him than any else that ever come, of finding a new man and attending to all the awkward points that rise, and the necessary bargainings, that I am grateful every moment, and pity and admire. I quail at the very thought of it all and know he must.

[Unsigned]

Bush. 11 Apr. 1892

Dear Edith,

I cannot remember whether I have acknowledged your last letters, but I think I haven't, and I wish to express my interest in your Carib-

— 1892 —

bean sea voyage, your sojourn in Jamaica, where I felt great sympathy in the satisfaction of being on land again, and among mountains. The wild Gulf-Stream day was thrilling. All of Washington too was especially interesting to me. On Fast-Day there was a great fire in Mr Chamberlaine's woods across the river from Edward's. When he & Annie came at night I learned that various men were working for Edward and in the neighborhood, and Edw. had got his boat from the barn with their help, onto a cart and carried it down to the river, and then as each man had a shovel, but no oars they had rowed across, 7 in a boat, with shovels, and run to the fire which was tearing towards them before a high S. wind. And after a long fight they had mastered it. Yesterday was another windy day & just after dinner Jim came in and said there was a fire in Walden woods. He took Selim & the wagon and his shovel and departed. He came back at 4 saying that Mr Stow's & Miss Prichard's woods were burned, but ours not, and the fire had been put out. Last night Edw. & Annie had a tea-party, and Ellen was in her element setting & adorning the table. All the children worked hard. We do hope you'll get here soon. Mother sends much love to her dear Edith. So do I.

Ellen.

Concord 27 Apr 1892

Dear Edith,

It is ten years today since Father died. I have been thinking over what you said, and I am glad if that is the reason you have for supposing that I don't care for him. I didn't know before what it was. The reason I don't read those books is not because they are his, it is because they are books. I am no reader as you well know. Have I ever looked at one of the great authors of this age or any other, except for special purposes? and how little, even then. With you & Una & Uncle George I have read Tasso & Manzoni, with Aunt Lizzy Dante & Homer; for the High School Class I have read some hundred pages of Carlyle, and once to Mother a part of Sartor at her request. My Milton & Shakespeare I got at school & from Father, and so on. In my early days on R.R. journeys I read the French memoirs that my school lessons started me on, Coventry Patmore at Father's desire; and I am acquainted with a dozen devotional books. There is the history of my life's reading. I have yet to open my first book of real *reading* & I expect to die without doing it. Stories & poems I have heard read or have read to Mother. There is no disrespect to Father in my attitude. I know him & his works as well as any other author, and take as much pleasure in him as you could desire. So don't feel quite as you have heretofore. Why do you call your dear boys & yourself trying? I consider you all most exciting & delightful.

Ellen.

7 May 1892

Dear Edith,

Mother, just looking out on her round bed and quarter-circle exclaimed "There! See all the beauty!" Your tulips, the Chrysolora, the Wappen v. Leyden, the red Van Thols, are in full bloom along both beds' edges, and do look beautifully. Jim is giving the garden such a thorough working over as it hasn't had for several years, and the innumerable tulips, hyacinths & daffodils look brilliant against the smoothly raked brown ground. I think these innumerable tulips one of the finest things you have given us. I have been at Cousin Abby's for one day, or rather for four hours, and read her your letters, which she cared for, as much as I hoped. I send her note and many another. Mrs McClure and her grandson are to spend Sunday here, before she goes back to Hoosac Falls. Dear Edith, you asked me to your sewing-circle, and I considered it, but to my shame, forgot to say no. Someday I will come, but 'twill be best to come to see my family principally, since I can leave home so little. Affectionately

Ellen.

21 May 1892

Dear Edith,

You are a dear sister to write me all you have and enable me to fully enjoy this great mercy to Malcolm, and to Rose [Dabney] too, I think. It made me cry, but I do like it. I think each of them is so good and charming and though Rose is young, it is not as if she were only twenty. Thankyou for telling me about Margaret & Mrs Jones and Amelia. Alice Cary was so kind as to write. Your letter & hers came in the same mail. I opened hers first, and yours was a great blessing to answer all the questions which hers raised in my mind. I congratulate you today also on my dear Cameron's 22d birthday. I hope he will spend it at home, or at least come to spend the night. It seems as if this last year had been a good deal less bright than the former ones, with all the sickness he has had in it, and the exclusion from games. I hope the

— 1892 —

choice of a business which I suppose is the duty of the coming year, will not be too perplexing.

Thankyou for your yesterday's letter about plans for Dec. day. Edward came to say that the Supt. of Schools has told him he will have to give his "Lesson of the Soldier" to the schools on Thurs. 26th in the afternoon. Can you come? It is William's birthday, and I hope to have all the family to tea. Affectionately

Ellen T. Emerson.

Concord, 31 May 1892

My dear Sally,

Thankyou for your letter, full of things we were glad to hear. Charley & Therchi have moved back to their farm again, and it is no longer easy to go to see them. They took tea here the other night, and both seem to me well and cheerful. They belong to a French class which meets every Monday. This is one of the best fortunes that ever came to them, for they enjoy and are enjoyed. Many people who before regarded T. as a dangerous person have become attached to her, and she in her turn to them, and Charley's powers as a teacher are recognized and valued, and he enjoys the occasion so much that he willingly dresses himself and goes, and is no longer such an utter solitary as he desired to make himself. Edith with numbers 5, 6 & 8, that is Edward, Waldo & Alexander came up to hear Edward's lecture on Col. Lowell which he read at the Town Hall to all the older school-children. So we had a little visit from them. Edward studied principally, but came into the parlour in the evening and gave us concerts with the little boys. Cameron and he have laboured with them, and they sing in parts with much spirit various absurd songs and some pretty ones. Florence & William are both especially fond of Alexander and Ellen & Waldo are great friends, so that I get something more of Edward's children when Edith's are here. I am glad your vacation time is near, and hope you will have a good summer. Mother sometimes says "Dear Sally! *dear* Sally!" when looking at your shawl. Affectionately

Ellen T. Emerson.

Concord Aug 9–16 1892

Dear Edith,

Your Yacht-Cruise & Goelet Cup letter was read with the greatest interest & joy. First the story of Waldo's hindrances & final deliverance

to be on the Merlin on her great day! Next precious Violet's coming. Then your seeing Ida & all the Agassiz guests. Then Malcolm's return with Rose and the family dinner! Edward exclaims "This piracy on the high seas should be stopped! They've got another Goelet cup!" Aunt Susan has been spending a week with us. We have at every available moment read together the old family letters, equally interesting to her & to us. We have burned many and kept as many more. One day she went out into the kitchen & taught Margaret to make a huckleberry hollow. On Monday came the lovely couple Helena & Julia. We enjoyed every minute of their society. One morning we all went blackberrying along the Flint's Pond road, and very successfully. Then on Wednesday afternoon I had a dance in the barn. Otherwise no events marked their stay. They sang to us in the evenings. Alice Arthur also is here much of the time, and Cousins Charlotte & Sarah, so we have a family of cousins. On Friday the children went away. On Saturday Mrs Hoar and the Misses Prichard dined with us, and we had a talk about Mars and what people and the newspapers have said about flashing to it. Your letters lately have gone unacknowledged for want of time to touch the pen, but not unappreciated. They have been read by ourselves and to our friends and at Edward's and have given immense delight. Affectionately
            Ellen.

           Concord, 26 Aug. 1892

My dear Edith,

 I think towards this day and tomorrow always as they approach, and I know that each of you does. We talk often of Don, and I am learning that the other children of those days are as much lost to me as he is, they have grown into other and older people, dear and interesting as ever, yet different. Nevertheless I remember and enjoy them as they were and him with them. How good every kind and happy word is to remember! How it still lives and still fills one with joy every time it recurs! I think you will dress his room tomorrow and that Cameron, who I suppose is gone, will remember him where he is. Yesterday I spent with Edward & Annie. The moment I arrived Ellen told me she was invited to Nonquitt and was going at noon, and I took much interest in seeing the preparations and the start, the first one independent of the family that she has ever made. Edward took me down to the river through his garden and field and told me 'twas the very field that Father bought and owned for a year when we were young. Did you know

— 1892 —

that? I didn't. I read them your letters and we enjoyed them together. Thankyou for telling me the sweet stories of Malcolm's children and of Rose and of Margaret's & the boys' darning-lesson. Especially for giving me a glimpse of Ralph & Violet rowing together. Today I have a dear letter from her. Give my love to Will and to each child. Mother is still in the same state, gets no better but is well enough to come down in the evening. Dearest Edith, may tomorrow be as sweet as sad! Affectionately
          Ellen.

          Concord 2 Sept. 1892
Dear Edith,
 Mother is much better today, awake all the time and looking very well, and having apparently no further disease, but anxious, trying every minute to arrange for going home, planning for a man to drive, for packing the things etc, leaving her bed the moment we are out of sight, so that this noon Miss Leavitt being a little delayed in coming to her when Cousin S. & I went down to dinner, she got half way down the front stairs in her nightgown. This Miss Leavitt says is very dangerous, as she is sure to fall, so we have taken extra pains to be present all the time. Edward's letter came last night, and was a feast to us all except Mother, who was too anxious about the projected move to listen to it then, but today she really seemed to attend and to care about hearing it. I am beginning to wonder whether you will come to Mother's ninetieth birthday. If she should be pretty bright I am sure you will, and I hope you will whether or no. Tell Edward the Doctor has been here today and is much impressed by Mother's fine pulse, good tongue and generally healthy appearance. The single dahlias you were so kind as to give me are in bloom, scarlet and maroon, I like them very much, thankyou! Rose wrote me a lovely note, thank her for me.
          Affectionately
          Ellen.

          Tuesday, 6 Sept 1892
My dear Edith,
 Mother looks and seems so much better that I am ashamed & grieved to have called Edward home. Really she is better today than when he went away. But how delightful last night to hear his voice at midnight! And what a happy day I have spent in his company! For he simply sat

— 1892 —

by in Mother's room all the morning. Thankyou for your kind letter received last night. Edward brings best of news of you all. Mrs Sanborn & Miss Leavitt hastened last night to see Mother, & the Misses Prichard this morning, dear guests! Also Therchi, most tender & affectionate. Love to Annie & you & all.

Ellen.

Concord, Sept. 20th 1892

My dear Alice [Arthur],

Thankyou for remembering Mother's ninetieth birthday and thankyou also for writing me twice and giving me a share of Aunt Susan's letter about your return. I was delighted to hear that your house looked so pretty. Now let me tell you a little about Mother's birthday. Many people brought her flowers and her room looked very much dressed with them. In the morning Aunt Susan came, also Edward & Annie, and in the afternoon came Therchi and then Edith, and presently Judge Hoar. He made a little call on Mother in her room and said to her "You are now giving proof of your wisdom. Long life indeed is mentioned by scripture as of more value than some things that a good many of us value a good deal more. 'Length of days is in her *right* hand, and in her *left* hand riches and honour!' " Edith & I were much delighted with this speech, and Mother, who was hardly strong enough to take it in, felt his kindness very much. Then came Will, and Ralph, and presently Edward brought Ellen to tea, and we did have a lovely time. Aunt Susan gave Mother one of the loveliest blue vases ever seen, and Lidian one of the prettiest of blue baskets. How pretty & appropriate your blue forget-me-nots were! At tea-time Mother came down stairs all dressed in new gown and prettiest things, and when we came in to tea behold! a new surprise, a beautiful cake from Alice Wheildon & Fanny Willis! So from beginning to end we had a happy day, and since Mother has gained wonderfully and is almost as well as when you first came. Goodbye. Love to you & Alice & Susy. Affectionately

Ellen.

Oct. 18 to 21 1892

My dear Edith,

Thankyou for your long and beautiful letter, which gives me the knowledge of your doings as a family which I sigh for. I'm glad Ralph asked Charley Cabot to Naushon. I hope my dear Edward's lameness

— 1892 —

was well again before he went back. I greatly enjoy and sympathize with your readings with your boys. Glorious! Thankyou for telling of Margaret's send-off and welcome home. Anything about Malcolm's children is eagerly received. Mother is apparently in perfect health, sits up longer & longer, but dares not walk alone and will hardly stand at all. On Tuesday night we had a family Columbus festival. I invited Edward's family, Charley & Therchi and Mrs Sanborn. To my joy every soul came. At tea we finished Mother's birthday cake. You know the Town Columbus celebration is coming off this week. The children who have been learning songs at school for it are to march with banners behind the Company (which has a handsome new uniform) to the music of a brass band from the school-house to the square, and Florence & William are full of enthusiasm & anticipation, delightful bairns! Everyone was lovely at my celebration and Charley read his Columbus ballad & Edward Mr Charles Ware's "The game of Chess" about Ferdinand & Isabella, both of which were very good and were appreciated. Then we offered the incense of a bowl of marigolds before the photograph of the statue of young Columbus sitting on the dock, and each lighted a candle-end to burn before it in a ring around the bowl, and I thought it a pretty little spectacle. With much demur our children consented to stand up, as a choir, and sing their school songs, or rather a verse or two from each. Even Raymond joined in softly.

Oct. 21. I have just got home from the Columbus celebration. Each school had a banner. The Emerson school had the Stars & Stripes, with a white streamer with EMERSON SCHOOL on it in gold letters. The High School had a square white banner with Concord High School emblazoned in gold on it. The Ripley School in which Raymond, dear soul!, was marching had a purple one with its name in gold, and the West Concord School a glorious cardinal red one with its name and a gold ship. Oh! my dear, the joy of this affectionate little Town Celebration was immense. Crowds of relatives drew up at Stow St. and smiled to see the banner at each school-house door, and the front rank of four files of our youth motionless behind it. At last the brass band is heard; out step the columns. "Oh there come the infants! Oh how cunning! Little dears!" cried a voice, as the Ripley School begins to pour forth, all the babes taking hold of hands. Why, we had over five hundred children there on Stow St. sidewalk. The military advance, solemnly led by Ashley How. One gun of the battery follows. Then the G.A.R Post; now the

— 1892 —

schools fall in. The town rushes after, lines of wagons accompany, both sidewalks are full. The Town being at last arranged round the Soldiers Monument, as on Decoration Day, Prescott Keyes addressed them and said we would first raise the flag. The gun fired; every horse & every creature started, then commanded itself. The flag was raised, and suddenly Dong Dong! cried the Orthodox bell, and the Unitarian swung wildly to & fro trying to get ahead with the Ding. A moment of great delight. "Now Three Cheers for the Flag!" cried Prescott. Given well. Then *William* and the Schools *sang with the brass band*. Then Mr Reynolds addressed us; and it rained, but stopped very soon. Then the Town sang America with the brass band; and with much gratulation on all hands the celebration ended. Affectionately
Ellen.

Concord, 26 Oct. 1892

Dear Cousin Sarah,

Your letter last night gave Mother and me great pleasure and today I have a chance to write which I will not lose. I have been breakfasting with Edward who is quite happy about the board of Health business. He thinks something is to be done. (28th) And this morning he and I, with Mr Mackintosh who is to design the gravestones, have been visiting the hill burying-ground to see what stones have pretty proportions & designs. I incline very much to adorn Aunt Mary's with the regulation death's head & cross-bones & hour-glass, and Memento Mori. But Edward inclines to have instead the Egyptian symbol of the sun with wings. He is to have his say about everything, and no doubt 'twill be that. Grandma's is to have a scallop-shell. Waldo's is to have a flower. I trust next summer you will see them all completed. Thankyou for three good letters to me and one to Mother. I have read them all to her several times and she likes to hear them. I think she is in the same state still that she was when you left. She eats more willingly perhaps and endures the evening about ten minutes longer, and her cheeks perhaps are a little rounder. I imagine she is gaining as slowly as possible, but certainly not losing. Mother has just waked. She wants me to thank you for your kindness, and her speech continues but it is unintelligible except the one word "church". Please give my love to all the cousins. I hope you are restored to your own family now. Affectionately
Ellen.

— 1892 —

8 Nov. 1892.

Dear Edith,

We were all much grieved at your non-appearance today, I most, I think. Oh do come tomorrow! It looked such a prospect of joy. Your three baskets have been thankfully received, not yet emptied. We had the ducks for dinner today. Thank dear Ralph for the venison from his big buck. Mother was borne in Edward's arms to the dinner-table today but only sat there during soup-time. She has lost all the time for the past week. Edward said yesterday that he thought she failed steadily. I don't think so. I think she gained for some weeks. She still occasionally leaves her bed, crosses the room and opens a drawer without assistance, without a word to anyone. But commonly is lifted and helped in every movement, seeming hardly able to stand even with support. Your letter last night telling your plans was sucked in with avidity. I'm sorry not to have you longer at Thanksgiving but see clearly that your business must press so at that time that it is generous of you to come at all. I trust Will and the travelling boys will come. Give my love to dear Violet. I'm glad Will means to return for your birthday. And glad to all our ears was the announcement that Cameron had come home. I think over the lives of all our children a great deal.

[Unsigned]

Concord, Sunday, 13 Nov. 1892

Dear Edith,

Mother has seemed to gain a little in the middle of the week. I don't think she has been down stairs since you were here, but yesterday I was thinking she was going to rally when I went out after dinner, but when I came back she breathed as if she had a heavy cold, and before we went to bed Miss Leavitt was seriously alarmed. So that in spite of Edward's seeming today to apprehend nothing I felt as if there was no doubt the end was near. In the afternoon I took charge of her. Mary Miller came in and asked me to lie down and let her take care of Mother for two hours. So I did. Then Edward came and she went. I asked his opinion which seemed not to agree with mine. He went. I asked Mother if I should read to her. She asked what. I said Father's letters to Mr Carlyle, and she said "By all means." I read and she slept. At about seven I tried to give her some hot milk from the spout-cup. She said "I can't." I asked if it tasted bad. She said "Proper good." But still she would only take one swallow and say "I can't". Suddenly she struggled to a sitting posture helping herself by pulling on the counterpane. I put a shawl round her and held the cup to her again. The rattling in her throat stopped, she opened her eyes, I saw she was dying for they were dead. Miss Leavitt was trying to sleep, Helen away. I rang and told Sadie & Margaret to bring their books and sit in the room. At 7.35 I think she breathed her last, but from the moment the rattling stopped she breathed so easily that one could hardly tell when she ceased. Then I sent for Miss Leavitt and for Edward.

And now she lies all mute & pale but with the sweet expression Heaven has granted her to retain whenever she has been at rest through all these years of failing. Dear Edward came and has been a wise and skillful hand and a great comfort. He says the funeral will be on Wednesday at 3 o'clock. My love to you and Will and all the dear children.

Ellen.

Concord. 19 Nov. 1892.

Dear Mrs Forbes,

I am most grateful to you for your note and for thinking of coming to the funeral. I love to think that Alice and Malcolm and Sarah and Mr Hughes and Colonel Russell came. It was very good in them when the journey was so long and the day so rainy. And I saw also Jeanie Perkins and Annie Ladd with great pleasure and gratitude. I wish I could have spoken with them, I wanted to thank them. I hope they all saw Mother for she looked young and to our eyes lovely. Don't suppose I am sad. I begin to think I do not know how to be sad. I am grateful that my dear Mother did not have to lose still further. She had few very comfortable moments, but always thought the present moment's ills were new and exceptional, saying "I have been perfectly well before, but now I am sick", and "Oh! I always sleep beautifully, but tonight I'm afraid I shan't", so that she was content with the past though anxious about the immediate future, and it was a much happier state of mind than if she had settled on the thought that she was always uncomfortable. All has been well and right and merciful.

Affectionately
Ellen T. Emerson.

— 1892 —

Concord, 7 Dec. 1892.

My dear Mary [Blake],

How good of you to remember me and picture to yourself my state! But you draw the picture too dark. I am very well and busy as a bee. My affairs and papers, letters, accounts, house, have had to be neglected so long that it will take me some time to catch up. It was not hard to take care of Mother this last year, at least all the hardness came on Miss Leavitt, not on me, and I am not in the least tired. A season of comparative sleeplessness must always follow on a death which comes near to one, but now that is passing away. I get better rest at night and am not too much hurried by day. I shall not leave the house, but Miss Legate and I, and I hope eventually another boarder or two, shall live on as hitherto. I am glad you do not yet ask me to visit you for if you did I'm afraid I couldn't say no. I would rather stay quiet for awhile and order my belongings before I leave the house at all. My cousin Sally Emerson advised me long ago to stay still and get quite used to any loss or break before going abroad, and I believe it is the best advice. I enjoy every word you say about Mother in your letter. It was very good of you when you had just come home to come out to the funeral, and I thank you. Give my love to the girls and thank them and Mr Blake for their kind message. I hope you have had a good time and are all well. Affectionately

Ellen T. Emerson.

Concord. 7 Dec. 1892

Dear Miss Clara [Dabney],

I have three lovely letters to thank you for, and I have hoped all along to be able to send at least a note of acknowledgment, which at last today is possible. I thought of you when Mother died. I knew you would care, but I thought it was too much to expect when I was already in your debt that you would write. Yet the letter came! All the last fifteen or sixteen months Mother has been less able to read, quite unable to sew, or clear up a drawer or do anything, and has forgotten all Edith's children except Ralph & Edith, also many friends and people whom she had till then recognized. Then in August she failed for a month constantly, and in September, perhaps she fainted, I don't know what it was; her nurse, Miss Leavitt, thought she was dying, and certainly she changed very much in colour and appearance, but she began to recover and for about six weeks she grew stronger, yet oh! how evident it was that life was over! She came down to meals and sat in the parlour but she no longer took part in anything. There was something very gentle and dignified and affecting in her manner of letting go; a beautiful being, all she did or rather ceased to do had its own beauty. This struck me as a great mercy. She always looked venerable and lovely in her naps on the sofa too. It seemed to me that death was so near that I asked Edward once or twice if he didn't think so. He said he didn't know but he thought Mother might live another year. About two weeks before she died she had some little trouble for several days, but threw it off and seemed to gain, but on Saturday afternoon 12 Nov. there was a rattling in her breathing and that must have been the beginning of the end. Edward however thought it might pass off. At bed-time Miss Leavitt said she was alarmed, and thought Mother though she said nothing looked at her and looked round as though she was questioning whether this was death. So Miss Leavitt and a friend who had come to spend Sunday with her watched by turns that night all the time till I came home from Sunday-school the next day at noon when I took her. As I came home I had no strength at all and it interested me to see that I could feel the blow in that way. If it had not been for that I should have said it had not affected me. When I came to her Mother rejoiced very much. I sat with her a good while, she could not talk intelligibly, but I think she was only talking about the arrangement of the bed-clothes, the windows, the fire and such little details as make much of the conversation in a sick-room. Edward came at five and again I asked him how long he thought she could live, but he said probably not through the winter, yet she might. He thought she was not now very ill. I returned to her. She talked constantly. I thought it must tire her to try so long and so vainly to make herself understood so I asked if I should read to her and proposed a letter from Father to Mr Carlyle, and in wonderful contrast to all she had said before "Oh! by all means!" was her answer perfectly clear and very hearty. I read and she fell asleep. When some hot milk came up I waked her and tried to make her drink some brandy punch. She would take one swallow and say I can't, and the rattling in her throat was dreadful to me but she said nothing about it. Suddenly she pulled herself up and sat up quite straight and the rattling as suddenly ceased. Much pleased I offered the milk again but she did not drink and then I looked her in the face and saw her eyes were dead. She was breathing very quietly and seemed to have fallen asleep. I thought she was dying, but I remembered what Edward had just said, and thought I might be

— 1892 —

mistaken. I remembered that Anna McClure had hoped when she died that she might be able when the rest of us died to come to help us through; and Mother, while she could remember, had several times in speaking of death thought with great relief of that, and said "Anna will come to me! I feel as if all the rest were farther off, but it seems as if she would help me." I tried to think that Anna was perhaps here and helping Mother with the same gentle skill and strength that used to be such a comfort to her. But then I thought perhaps Mother was not dying. I am sorry that I had no fit sense of the event, I was thinking like a very Martha what I ought to do. Edward had just gone home tired; Miss Leavitt certainly needed rest; there was no apparent need of anybody's assistance, Mother was more comfortable than she had been all day. But I had never seen anyone die, and there might be something about it that demanded experienced care. At last I rang for the two girls in the kitchen and told them to bring their books up and sit in the room—'twas Sunday evening, you know. So they did. They kept coming to look at Mother, and I watched expecting to know when she ceased to breathe but I couldn't tell, only at last I thought she had died and we brought a cold glass, and there was no breath on it. I remembered that when my Grandmother Emerson died it was in the night and Aunt Elizabeth Hoar sat and held her hand without moving her till morning and I thought I would let Mother sit propped up as she was till Miss Leavitt should wake, but the girls said that wouldn't do and went and called her. She felt very sorry she had not been called earlier. I sent for Edward then and he came by eight o'clock. Mother had died just after half-past seven. And when he and Miss Leavitt had laid her down and Miss L. smoothed her hair she became perfectly beautiful. Edith came at noon the next day and stayed till Thursday and Edward & Annie were here a great deal. The grandchildren came Tuesday night & Wednesday, and it gratified me to see how it made Edith Forbes & Ellen & Florence cry. Everyone of the children will remember Mother. I enjoy thoughts of all her life, but I feel no wish that she should return or that her death might have been delayed. The house does not seem to me so different as people think it must. Life looks as full and as interesting as it did before. I see that I am not made exactly like other people and death does not grieve me no matter how near it comes. Yet I am not wholly insensible, I feel that I have had a most interesting and affecting week that I love to look back on, and so do Miss Leavitt & Miss Legate, and we like to talk it all over.

— 1892 —

And now to come to your other two letters. I was delighted that you wrote to me about Rose's marriage in which I am interested on both sides, hers and Malcolm's, and every word you said was delightful to me. I am sorry you didn't go to the wedding, tears do no harm at all, and the feeling of having all one's relations round does much good. I heard of Amelia Jones's sensible but lovely speech "This is *Rose*'s wedding and it ought to be in every way festive." Edith wrote to me from Newport of the reception of Rose and the family dinner on the yacht. I am glad she wrote to you too. I have not yet made my wedding-call on Rose, but I shall when I go to Milton at Christmas. Edith's letters to me sometimes mention her as looking very pretty, and describe her dress etc., and she says Margaret seems to defer to her just as she ought. You were also so good as to write me about Cameron's coming to see you which interested me very much. It has been very pleasant to hear directly from you through Cameron and the Keyeses.   Affectionately
Ellen T. Emerson.

Epilogue

One era of Ellen's life had ended with the death of her father, and she had devoted herself almost entirely to the care of her mother, whose death ended another era for her. Ellen was tired, and was easily persuaded to go abroad with her sister Edith and her younger nephews. The Concord house was let, and the party sailed for Europe in April on the *Teutonic*. They spent the summer in England and Scotland, the winter at Moret and Antibes in France, where Edward and his family joined them. They returned to England for the summer, coming home in October on the *Buffalo*. During this time abroad Edith's older children had visited them from time to time.

In the fall of 1894 Ellen went to housekeeping again, with Helen Legate and Grace Heard, Concord schoolteachers, as boarders. For Thanksgiving she visited her cousin Samuel Haskins and his three widowed sisters, Sarah Ainslee, Hannah Parsons, and Charlotte Cleveland, and she spent Christmas and New Years in Milton as usual. The following year she made a great many visits to friends and relatives, and spent some time at Naushon, a pattern which continued for most of the rest of her life. Thanksgiving at Bush continued to be the tradition, with the Forbes family coming to help in the preparations. Her friend Sarah Richardson had become a regular boarder, and other friends made long stays in the summer. A young cousin, Mary Miller, often came to stay and to do the housekeeping when Ellen was away. In 1897, as she continued to have trouble with a lame knee, Ellen spent a month at Hot Springs, Virginia, with Edith and William, the latter not well and troubled with a persistent cough. He was sent to Dublin, New Hampshire, for his health for the summer, but returned to Naushon in September, and died there on October 11, of tuberculosis of the throat. Ellen spent a quiet Christmas and New Years in Milton. Cousin Sarah Ainslee had become a regular boarder in Concord. Ellen continued making visits to her friends, somewhat troubled by her knee and a bad bout of grippe in 1900. Cousin Hannah joined her sister Sarah as a permanent boarder, with Cousin Charlotte visiting frequently. Ellen's letters during this whole period are almost entirely short notes, and a few long descriptive ones about her travels or about Naushon. She followed with great interest the activities of her nephews and nieces in Milton,

Epilogue

Concord, and New York. There were funerals also. Mr. and Mrs. John M. Forbes and J. Malcolm Forbes died, and others of her older friends. But there were engagements, marriages, and the first great-nephews and great-nieces to be enjoyed. Ralph and Edith Forbes, and Ruth, Haven, and Florence Emerson were married. In 1904 the family group at Thanksgiving amounted to twenty-nine people.

The families became widely scattered; Cameron was in the Philippines, Edward in Europe a good deal, Waldo and Alexander traveled and stayed at the ranch in Wyoming, Edith and Kenneth Webster were in Cambridge. The family continued to gather together whenever possible. In Concord in 1907, Cousin Hannah and then Cousin Sarah died, after illnesses and mental difficulties. Ellen gave them devoted attention and had nurses available for them. Edward Forbes was married, living in Milton, as was Ralph with three children. Florence Emerson Forbes had died. Ellen did rather less visiting, becoming more and more handicapped by lameness.

In 1908 Ellen was persuaded to close the Concord house, spend a month at Hot Springs for treatment, and return for the spring in Milton and the summer at Naushon. In October she made a few short visits. The last one seems to have been to the Bulkeleys in Beverly, and in a letter written from there to her sister Edith on October 23 she described what her schedule was to be—a visit to her brother Edward till November 5, then one at Edith's and Kenneth's in Cambridge, till she should return to Concord for Thanksgiving. She had planned to visit Pauline Agassiz Shaw in December, and go to Milton for Christmas as usual. This seems to be the last letter of hers that can be found. As a letter from her sister Edith about her to Cameron in early January refers to "two months of descent" it seems that her health must have failed by early November, and she must have been moved to Milton. A long letter from her niece Edith to Cameron describes New Years in Milton, where at Ellen's request, the entire family, twenty of them, gathered round her bed, Rosamond and David being the little babies. Ellen wished each one of them "Happy New Year" in turn. Two more letters to Cameron from his mother describe Ellen's last weeks, with all the family standing by. She still recognized her sister and niece Edith and her sister-in-law Annie on the 11th, then slept and was unconscious until her death early on the 14th. Edith and Waldo had spent part of that last night choosing selections for her funeral service, and Edward Emerson helped put them together.

Epilogue

In the morning the bells of the Concord church pealed to announce Ellen Emerson's death. The funeral was held there Saturday, January 17th, a cold stormy day, with Mr. MacDonald and Mr. Bulkeley reading the service. Eight nephews, Edith wrote, "carried her shoulder-high—how much her bearers would have pleased her!" Then Edith added, "Uncle Edward and I could not mourn, we rejoice for her, and tried to make that the keynote of the day. The town may truly mourn—she was an influence and presence such as will never be there again."

Appendix

This letter from ETE to James Elliot Cabot concerns RWE's speech at the University of Virginia in 1876. The tactful Cabot used very little of this in his A Memoir of Ralph Waldo Emerson, *and a comparison between this letter and ETE's letter written to her mother at the time of the oration is most interesting (see Vol. II, p. 210).*

Concord 26 Sept. 1882
but begun 12 Sept. and
written on whenever I could
since.

Dear Mr Cabot,

You have not put down all the books you have read over. I was so sure of it when I read your list that I sat down and looked through CD, CL, KL, SO, VO, & NY [RWE's notebooks], and have found your marks in each. I feel equally sure that you have had several others and found nothing in them to mark, and I think I remember correcting copy from RO & DO, which books I haven't yet had time to look over. I have never seen any I or M or Q. You have looked over S which is the same as "Salvage", and you will find you have some copy from it. I believe I have sent you W & XO by Edward. I have not found any FO nor KO. I think there may be a few that I supposed by mistake you had read. As AC & TV, but it is quite possible that these are those you found nothing in.

I told Uncle George to tell you that the Ripleys do not know of any letters from Father to their Mother. I do not believe that she exercised a strong influence over him, and Uncle George says he should not say she did. Of course she was always a loved and honoured friend, but I believe Aunt Mary alone can be said to have powerfully influenced Father. I have never yet written to Haven Emerson for his Father's letters from mine. I shall some day. I will write about Virginia now. Have you found the letters to Father from the young men, McKenna & two others? They asked him to deliver the oration before the Washington and the Jefferson Societies, on the 29th of June [1876]—I think it was. He was of course very much interested and pleased, and had no hesitation in saying he should go—as I remember. (Of course I may

Appendix

have urged it, I don't know.) He wrote them a very pretty letter which I think said that he had given up speaking, but could not refuse an invitation from Virginia, and would come, charging them only his expenses, and I think I remember "my daughter who always travels with my age will accompany me." We went first to Philadelphia, and stayed from Friday till Monday with Mr Sam Bradford, going as I think to tea at Dr Furness's once. It was at the time of the Centennial Exhibition, and we spent Friday and Saturday there, accompanied by Dr Furness, Mr Bradford & the Bradford young ladies. Dr F. showed Father everything, and he was able to enjoy it enough to be willing to go again. I don't remember what pleased him best. He looked often at the crowd of people and said "Here people ought to wear the name of the State each comes from, where we could all read it." Both days he often asked to go to the Massachusetts house, so the second day we did go there, Father saying what a capital plan it was to have a house where the people of each State could rendezvous. When he had looked through the parlours and entries once he was in haste to leave the house. He had expected to see superior & handsome people in the Massachusetts House, and it was a bitter disappointment to find that all there looked ordinary. He spoke of it several times. On Sunday I think he did not go to church but tried to work on the Oration. Every time he read it to me he found the same weak places in it, but never would improve or even mark them, so they always remained troublesome. I had therefore taken a list of them and began before we left home to make him patch up one at a time. But this work was already difficult, he could not do it unless I left him alone and if I left him alone he began to read the place, read on, and forgot it. So it seemed as if he never could do the little jobs. I should think however that one or two were finished that day in Philadelphia. The water was beginning to make us both sick, and after a pretty sick Sunday night we started early on Monday morning for Washington. We went to the Riggs House, and Father was received and treated with the greatest kindness and respect by the proprietors. Again he worked on the oration. We never left it till late in the evening, but much remained to be attended to. We started for Charlottesville (on Tuesday) the next morning. The heat was extreme and we both felt sick and were consumed with thirst. Father seldom remembered water and was more delighted than I ever saw him before with any comfort every time I brought him ice-water. I didn't know that it was the water which made us sick till after I came home. Our miserable journey from Washington

Appendix

to Charlottesville was solaced by ice-cream brought in at one station and left us to eat on our way to the next. It was hot and very dusty and there were very disagreeable things in this ride, and much delay, but when this ice-cream came Father made all sorts of speeches complimentary to the civilization of the South. We reached Charlottesville before we knew it, for we stopped outside of the depot and were kept waiting quarter of an hour, supposing we were still a station or two off. Professor Holmes and three students, Mr Thom, Mr McKinney and Mr Page, presently appeared. I thought at once that they were looking for us. I caught Prof. Holmes's eye and turned round significantly to Father, but Professor Holmes seemed to take no notice, went on, and returned much later to ask if we were we. Then to our joy we were informed that we had arrived, and left the cars for a carriage in which Prof. Holmes and Mr McKinney I should say rode with us. On the way Father asked whether this was the place from which could be seen the houses of five Presidents of the United States, and I believe Mr Holmes said it was, and pointed them out. I remember Jefferson, Madison, Munroe, I can't imagine who were the other two. Were they Van Buren & Polk? When we arrived at the University we found a large family at Mr Holmes's, his wife, two daughters, a son, Mr Southall a Professor of Laws, who makes his home with them, and several guests. The introductions over, Mr Holmes led Father to a portrait of Gen. Robert E. Lee and said "This is the man whom we delight to honour,—General Lee." Under this portrait was a very handsome picture of a very handsome flag. In the course of my visit I learned that this was the flag of the Confederacy. It was like the Russian flag, only that the blue X cross was starred. Till then I had never heard of any other flag than the original stars-and-bars. I feel now as if I saw that picture in other houses of the University but I am not sure. It was already dinner-time, and I saw when we came to dinner that Father was all confused, unable to understand, unable to remember, as he often was in later years, but he seldom had been so much so up to this time. And he was so all the time we were there, at the table, and at parties. Sometimes he could talk pretty well with Mr Holmes about the few names that both knew, and since he seemed to remember the smoking hours with some pleasure I hoped that the gentlemen at such times saw him more himself, but I early feared they were blaming me for letting him come, he seemed so much older and feebler than usual, and as he had to stay in his room most of the time working on the faults of the oration, and I couldn't leave him

Appendix

to himself safely more than 20 m. at a time I feared they might think I had a hand in the oration myself. Mrs Holmes was a lovely, sincere, and social person. Every minute that I could get I sat with her and felt at home. We had happy talk together on every subject that came up. The girls were young and had company, and besides were afraid of me. I saw very little of them. Mr Holmes talked altogether of the war, of the chivalrous character and exploits of the Confederate Generals, and the brutal conduct of the Union Army. It seemed to me an awkward subject best met by silence, and Father was as silent as I, but I could not tell whether it was of choice or because he felt unable to remember what was best to say or do. No, Mr Holmes did not talk altogether of the War, he talked much of Jefferson, and of the University—Father questioned him—and about the students and the relations between them and the Professors; and then of the old School-System of Va. and its superiority to the Northern system now thrust upon the State, which he said could never take root and prosper there. In the evening we went to the Exhibition or Anniversary of the Washington and Jefferson Societies. I remember now little about it except that it seemed to be like Class Day at Cambridge, all the young ladies out in glory and all the students feeling that it was their occasion. I wrote about the speeches in the letter to Mother which I sent to you. There was one young man, the son of the bursar or treasurer of the university, who spoke in a tone which delighted our northern minds. Father spoke to him afterwards, and several times spoke of him, asking questions about him of the Professors, who seemed to me to take care not to praise him, and assured Father that his father's views were so different from those the boy expressed that his hair must have stood on end when he listened to his son. I think it was this night, but it may have been the next, after Father's oration, that many officers of the University made speeches, not so much patriotic as college-domestic, personal and funny. The next day after breakfast we were shown the library and buildings, people came to call on us, many professors and their wives, and Mrs Holmes took me to return one or two calls; but the oration was not finished and every moment that he was not wanted in the parlour Father was labouring away at it in his room, I visiting him every 15 minutes or so to tell him again what was to be done, or to find the next unfinished place. Mrs Holmes meanwhile was telling me of her youth and her visits to Saratoga or Sharon Springs. She said she cared most for Boston people there and hoped she should live in Boston when she

Appendix

grew up, and that the men she enjoyed most were Col. Perkins, and Mr Gray, who were old gentlemen that brought their families there. She asked me whether there were any pictures of them, if there were she would give a great deal to see them. I remember that among the people who called Prof. Gildersleeve, the Greek Professor, was the person with whom I felt most comfortable, the only one except Mrs Holmes who did not keep me reminded that we were in an oppressed and abused country. This may be unfair, but it is the way I remember it. There was to be a great evening party, and tea was sent to everybody's room. We were told to dress for a ball before going to the Hall for the oration. That was finally in shape just in time for Father to dress, and we all went over to the Hall. I went before with Mr Holmes and the University carpenter and had the desk raised and lamps placed right so that no difficulty of reading might be in Father's way, and that was right, but Mr Holmes asked anxiously about his voice and told me that it was a Hall very hard to speak in. In my letter to Mother which I sent you I told exactly what happened, and can add nothing except that I thought there was a little less body to Father's voice than it often had, and remembered with dismay that he had only had tea in his room and had eaten no supper. I ought to have attended to that. Of course I suffered agonies all the time seeing that he could make no headway against the noise, but I saw that he was himself as in old times, he was reading beautifully, and not at all giving up to the chatterers but expecting to win the day. At the end of half an hour however he saw that he should not, and began to turn over leaves and choose sentences to draw to a close. This looked to me very hazardous, and all sorts of tragic conclusions seemed possible, but to my wonder and joy he chose exactly right and made a swift but handsome winding-up. I felt that to those who did hear him he had shown that he was able to speak from the platform still, if he was too old to talk in the parlour, and that he had justified his coming down to Virginia, but I suppose hardly a hundred people heard him. Mrs Holmes, who sat by me, often said she was very sorry for the noise. I asked her whether she had heard Father, and she said "Yes, partly, but I often could not catch the whole sentence." Now on this picture [drawing of floor plan of hall] I have marked where she and I sat, and you can guess by that how many people could hear. I was very humble then, and really felt what I said (when Mr Holmes, walking home with me apologized for the conduct of the audience) that it was the orator's business to conquer his audience, and that Father's

Appendix

voice was not so strong as usual. But Father was indignant, and when he spoke to me on the subject in the cars the next day and I told him I supposed it was his voice that was to blame because he was hungry, he said "Not at all! I was delighted that my voice was so loud. If they would have given me the *least* chance I should have made them hear. They had no manners." We were very unhappy. And long afterwards I remembered that the night before, I, sitting far back in the middle of the hall, heard every word, and so did everyone else when the boys and the Professors were speaking, and that made me begin to think that this was intentional hostility to a Northern man. But to return to that evening after the oration—when we went home to Mr Holmes's the great company began to arrive and we had no time to remember our mortification. There were many many people there who had read Father's books and really cared about him, and he was made much of by them to a degree not surpassed anywhere, people from many different states, and I had a delightful time myself with a host of agreeable strangers. He got along with his friends as best he could; of course he could not enjoy it very much, but when the company went down to supper, with the connivance of Mrs Holmes he was shut up in the library with one or two gentlemen whom he seemed to like, and I carried him his icecream which he thankfully ate up there. No, I think this was after supper, seeing that he wouldn't eat downstairs. The next morning he went over to the Commencement Exercises while I packed and at noon we came away escorted by Mr Holmes and I think the same boys. We found in the depot and on the train many of the friendly people to whom we had been introduced the night before, and I had a very pleasant time with them. They were going to Philadelphia for the Centennial Fourth of July. It was a long train, and all the way to Washington people came in succession to ask me if this was Mr Emerson, some asked to be introduced, some only walked to and fro in the aisle and watched him, one said "We are from Arkansas", and some were from Louisiana, others from Alabama. I never took a R.R. journey with him when he was so much visited. He soon asked me to save him from being talked to because he was an old man and could not answer. Two days after, when our trunks separated us in Washington, and I discovered that there was a probability of my not finding him again easily, as I travelled alone towards Philadelphia I remembered that one young man had asked me soon after I got into the cars whether he was on the train, and I hoped he might have as many lovers here as on that Southern train. So I asked everyone within my reach whether they had ever

Appendix

heard his name; no one had. Neither had anyone that I asked in West Philadelphia.

Perhaps in all this long story I have not given what you wanted to hear. I hope I have. I wouldn't send anything till I finished the tale. You asked me what our hopes and expectations were in going. I think that Father was delighted to be asked, and felt that Virginia was offering amity to Massachusetts. He accepted the invitation partly with that patriotic feeling, and partly because he desired to see the famous State. When I wrote the letter to Mother I remember that I thought it best to make the pleasantest statement I could, but I wonder still how they came to invite Father at all. The young men who wrote to him did not seem to care about him. My consolation then was, and since has been, the thought of the knot of students in each aisle who had come forward to listen and stood all the time, and the two clusters who hung over the galleries overhead. Those twenty or thirty boys meant to hear him and did, and perhaps they belonged to the Societies and invited him. They did their duty, I mean the boys who wrote, and the authorities did their duty by us in receiving, entertaining, paying and despatching us, and Mrs Holmes and many people were affectionate and kind yet the visit on the whole left a most painful impression, and two years later a lady, I think it was Mrs William Rogers, said she had lately come from the University of Virginia where she had been asked whether the speech of the young Peyton if that was his name had misled Father into thinking that he was hearing the usual sentiments of young Virginia when that was only got up out of compliment to him. I felt no happier after that talk with her. Mr Mayo last winter said to me he had been at Charlottesville. "They still keep your memory green there," he said, "I heard all about your Father's visit." And I forbore to ask what he had heard. I wish now that I had asked. I have a delightful remembrance of dear Mrs Holmes and wish I could see her again.

You ask when the notice of Mr Cheney was written. Probably in 1870. I can I think find the exact date.   Later. I enclose it.

I am glad Mrs Cabot is so soon to come home and that she has had a good summer. Do come and bring her as soon as you can make up your minds to leave home. I have been very thankful for all the news of her that you have given me when you wrote and have wished to send this answer to your questions earlier, but I could not finish it.

Yours truly
Ellen T. Emerson.

I don't return your list, shall I?

Appendix

Endorsed, presumably by J. E. Cabot, "Miss E. T. Emerson about U Virginia speech." The following comments are included in the letter to Mr. Cabot describing RWE's death (see following letter, Appendix), on a page inserted into that letter.

In his VIRGINIA.
He saw many very friendly people, and was most hospitably entertained. Yet (with one exception) the speeches made by the young gentlemen of the Societies which invited him at their public meeting, and the tone in conversation of most of those whom he saw in private was such as to show that war rather than reconciliation was still in their feeling, and he was surprised that he should have been sent for. He thought that inviting him must have been the work of a comparatively small number of students who during this oration sat very near him or hung over the edge of the galleries just above him, and seemed to follow it with close attention.

ETE wrote the following account of her father's death for James Elliot Cabot, who wanted the information for use in his biography of Emerson; he used little of it in the Memoir, *however. This letter includes many details ETE omitted from her letter to Miss Clara Dabney in May, 1882 (see Vol. II, p. 463).*

Concord, 16 Aug. 1882

Dear Mr Cabot,

I send you Father's letters to John Sterling, found in a box of old letters belonging to Mother which she opened this morning for the first time in a year or two. I am most thankful.

I will begin today the account of Father's illness which I promised you.

On the 16th of April which was Sunday he went to church as usual both in the morning and in the evening. Young Mr Theodore Williams preached, a classmate of Mr Bulkeley's, he preached very well and I was sorry that Father did not seem to recognize it. In the last months he often fell asleep in church-time, but I should say that till January he had usually listened, and had a clear opinion of each sermon, which he usually expressed and I enjoyed hearing how true an idea he could convey of it though his language was confused. Mr Bulkeley says that on the evening of Sunday 23^d Oct. when he had preached for us all day

Appendix

Father told him the evening sermon was better than the morning sermon.

Well, on this last Sunday, we walked along the Boston road, past the Hawthornes' I think. John's wife tells me that every Sunday afternoon when we passed by her house she told the children to watch and let her know when we came in sight returning, so that she might look out and see him pass. But I don't know whether she could see us on the upper road. On Monday we had company to tea. They stayed till nine. After their departure I looked for Father. He wasn't in the house. I attended to several little jobs and looked for him again. He was not to be found. It was getting to be half past nine. I had never known him to go out in the evening of late months so I was rather disturbed and decided to go and tell Edward. But when I had put on my things & reached the door I heard steps and waited to see who was coming. I waited a long time he came so slowly but it proved to be Father, and he said he had walked far down the turnpike. I do not remember whether he had been already hoarse. Oh yes I do. He had been very hoarse all day Monday and I told Edward so, and Edward meant to come to see what was the matter before he went off on Tuesday but couldn't manage it.* Father however absolutely insisted that he had no cold, and even that he wasn't hoarse. On Tuesday he was quite as hoarse and took many walks. Annie & the baby came to dinner and told how Edward was making all his visits against his absence, so couldn't come with her, for he wanted to get off by the 4 o'clock train so as to spend the night before the oration at the Putnam's, and if he stopped for dinner at our house he wouldn't get through his visits in time. She had a great deal to tell us about him. We were perfectly happy and said it was better to have her come without him than with him. Father of course was sucking in every word she said, he liked to hear Edward talked about and everything today was connected with the oration which was a department of the subject of Edward he cared particularly about. On Wednesday morning he became anxious about money. We always pay John on the 20th & this was the 19th. He was afraid all the time that he might let the day pass, and

---

*Note in EWE's writing clipped to this letter: "All that Tuesday until 3 P.M. I was kept at Maynard by a serious accident to one of the mill-hands. Then I saw two very sick patients in Concord and could not reach Father's until about 6 P.M. I went in and he was at his place at the tea-table & there were several guests, so as he seemed merely to have a hoarse cold and did not care to leave the table, I rushed to take my train for Boston to finish my Oration free from interruptions.   E. W. E."

Appendix

usually began by the 25th to ask how soon John's day was coming again, and seldom forgot to inquire every day or two. I assured him there was money enough. But when I was up in town I accidentally heard that he had just gone into the Bank so I ran in and found him there. He wondered how I came. I wrote him a check for a hundred dollars, but didn't stay till he left the Bank, and learned two or three weeks later that when he saw the money he said he didn't want so much, half would do. Of course I supposed meanwhile that he had lost 50, for I could only find 50. That day it began to rain in the afternoon, and he was caught in the rain and told Mother so as he came in, but it did not cross her mind that he had got wet. She thought the next day that perhaps he did. I met Edward just returned from giving his oration and he asked eagerly how Father did. I told him the hoarseness continued but he declared himself perfectly well. Edward said he had been on thorns all the time since he went because he did not attend to the cold before he went to Boston, and he was now on the way to see what sort of a cold it was. At tea-time it rained very hard, but my Aunt Susan Jackson and the Miss Bartletts came to tea and to play whist with Mother. Father told us he had walked round the two-mile-square, had taken longer walks today than for a great while. Afterward in the entry he said "I have walked far today, because I didn't feel well in my chair." There was a Ball that night at the Hall and when I was dressed and came to Father for an umbrella he was shocked at the idea of my walking to it in the rain, and tried to dissuade me. Finally he said "You may go if you will promise to take a carriage to come home if it rains. How much will it cost you?" I told him half a dollar. He looked over his purse for some time and gave me a five-dollar-bill, and evidently thought that was half a dollar. He was very glad to see me when I came home. It didn't rain, so I walked both ways. In the morning, Thursday 20th, Mother called me and said Father was sick. Edward had left medicine for him the night before and he had taken it, but he didn't feel well and was very drowsy so I mustn't wake him. I waited till nearly nine. Then I went up stairs and he was awake. When I went to help him finish dressing he didn't speak of being sick and I thought he did not feel sick. But he stopped and sat down. This he had never done before. Yet he did not seem to notice it, or any unusual feeling, and I said nothing and went on doing for him as he sat. When I held his coat for him he rose and we picked up his things and put them away as usual. As we went down to breakfast he walked slowly along the entry till just after we had passed the store-closet door

Appendix

under the front stairs, he stopped, looked very sick and cried "Oh *dear!*" as if he felt a mortal stroke. I was frightened, and took hold of him. He said nothing. I did all the talking, he stood a minute, then rather staggering and with his feet far apart he went on into the dining-room. I led him to the window and opened it. He couldn't give any idea of what he felt. I ran for a bowl thinking it might be nausea, but when I came back he was sitting by the window and after I had looked at him a while I was sure it wasn't nausea and put the bowl away, having shut the window. Then when he had sat still some time I proposed breakfast and he came to the table but said as he came "I hoped it would not come in this way. I would rather—fall—down cellar!" This he said with great feeling. He ate little breakfast but showed no objection to eating. The Study was very warm and after breakfast we went there. We counted out John's money, and then I called him in and Father paid him. Presently I went for Edward, who came and told me to keep him warm and in one room. He sat in the green roundabout chair, and talked to me about something, but he had many words I had never heard, and the familiar words were not put in the right place. At last I was pretty sure of what he meant, so I asked him "Do you think you are going to die, and do you want me to draw near and receive your last instructions?" I was rather jeering because I knew he always thought sickness meant death, and I didn't believe this was going to be serious now that he felt better and had eaten his breakfast. But he said "Yes" very seriously, so I sat down before him and he said "You will be the head,—you and Edward—and"—he tried to think but couldn't think and shook his head in despair then began "You must all be good". I think he said more but it had no meaning, was only a confusion of words. He soon found the sofa and slept there most of the day, though he came to both his meals. Edward sat with him in the afternoon and tried reading to him. Father tried to listen but didn't understand. That evening came Miss Adams's letter telling what her brother had said about Edward's oration. Oh how it did delight Father! And Edward himself told us his adventures. That Father enjoyed hearing. The next morning Edward came by seven o'clock I think and said Father mustn't get up. He did have his breakfast in bed, but by ten he was dressed and in the study, nobody could prevent it. He was not inclined to leave the study so he was pretty safe there. Mother said to me that Friday evening that Edward had found Father better tonight than he had expected to find him. So we supposed he was nearly well. At dinner that day he had sat in his

Appendix

place and eaten something and yet seemed to feel very heavy and unwell. He had me recite every word of the history of Edward's oration three times, and smiled at himself for wanting me to begin again. Before tea he came up to Mother's room. She was lying down and he asked to lie down too. He expressed the greatest consolation on laying himself on the bed, and Mother covered him very warm with downs. When tea-time came he begged hard to stay where he was, but Mother advised his coming down because tea would refresh him and going to bed would be more comfort after having been up. So he came down. I remember the fidelity with which he ate what was given him to eat though it was evident it had no taste at all to him. He gladly went right to bed after tea. On Saturday morning Edward again came very early. Mother had told me Father had had a quiet night, so I confidently expected that Edw. would say yes when I said is Father better when he came out from examining him. But he said with an alarming tone in his voice "No, he is worse, and going to be worse. Come down into the dining-room." So down we went and he said "It is pneumonia", and said he should send at once for a nurse and Charley Putnam and Cousin Mary Simmons, and write to Edith, and Father must by no means leave his bed. So we tried hard to induce him to stay still, and from minute to minute did succeed till after dinner, but in the afternoon he could dress himself & insisted on doing so and going down. On Saturday afternoon he sat in his study for the last time, took tea there and feeling very weak and ill consented to go upstairs early, but would not accept any help in preparing to leave the room for the night. He took his fire apart as he had done all his life, set the sticks on end on each side, and separated all the brands, and took his lamp in his hand to carry out with him. One of the family desired to take it for him, which he objected to, and ran upstairs all the way, indignant at being supposed to be unable to do for himself. He never came down again. But each day more than once he rose and tried to dress, not so much with the desire to return to the study, as because he had the illusion most of the time that he was making a visit and was with his family detained by his illness to the inconvenience of some hospitable friend, so that he ought to see at least whether he could bear the journey home. Yet he had no real delirium, and the moments when he did not fully recognize everyone about him, and understand all that was said to him were rare. On Sunday Monday & Tuesday he wished often to say things himself, but language was no longer at his command, while occasionally successful in making

Appendix

himself understood he tried much of the time in vain. One of these days he had talked at intervals till afternoon looking all the time very earnest & patiently keeping up his endeavour to express what was in his mind, while those about him listened and guessed in vain, before the word "bills" suggested that he wished to speak about money affairs. Everything in that connection was at once gone over to him, he listened with eager attention, questioning when? where? how much? as it went on, saying at the end of each piece of information, "Oh, very well!" and when the recital ended with the assurance that there was money enough in the Concord Bank to carry the quarter through comfortably, he said joyfully "I am glad!" ceased to talk and slept or was quiet the rest of the afternoon. Another day he tried all day long to make himself understood, and quite in vain, which seemed sad. On Wednesday & Thursday he had nothing more on his mind than the desire to take the journey home if possible, and again & again we succeeded in convincing him that he was at home which consoled him till he forgot it. On Thursday morning came his friends to say goodbye to him, at least Edward and they so understood it. [Pencil note: "It was certainly so. E. W. E."] I didn't at all, for Edward had led me to suppose that Father was likely to get well, [Pencil note: "Ellen misunderstood me. E. W. E."] and knowing that Father had seemed pleased not only with the coming of Edith and the grandchildren (for two of them came Tuesday & two Wednesday, and while Ralph & Cameron felt so badly that they hastened away, Violet on Tues. and Don on Wed. liked to stay by and remained over night going in every once in a while to delight his eyes) but of each friend who had been admitted, and when he heard that this person or that person had been in the house, complained "And he didn't come in to see me", I concluded that Edward thought it would gratify him and help to pass time to have visits made to him. Judge Hoar came, Mr Staples, Mr Channing, in the morning. What Father said to them indicated that he regarded it as farewell. His mind was clear enough as to who it was in each case, and to Judge Hoar & Mr Staples he tried to sum up the relation he had held with each through life, this was plain though he couldn't say two words of a sentence right. Mr Channing came when he was more tired I remember, but I have no recollection of what he said either to him or to Mr Sanborn. I feel as if they each were rather discomfited. Father had tried to speak but they could not understand, and he showed no pleasure. Mr Channing had gone some time before you came. When I ran

Appendix

up to tell Father you were below he smiled and exclaimed "Elliot Cabot! Praise!" and when he saw you he tried to say that you had done for him more than one man can be expected to do for another and that his gratitude was beyond saying, but as always throughout his illness the words were wrong, and while the intention was clearly to be caught when he began it soon was lost in meaningless syllables, and the next time he spoke he no longer seemed so bright, it was as if he were drowsing somewhat, and you went down-stairs. As you drove out of the yard in the afternoon Dr Putnam & Mr Sanborn drove in, coming from Boston. Mr Sanborn's visit was least satisfactory of all, and Mr S. presently went to speak to Cousin Mary who was in the room, then he returned & shook hands & said goodbye. Father looked at me to desire me to take things in hand. It was the last time, the last real communication, for Mr Sanborn immediately took his leave, and was hardly down stairs before Father was seized with the sharp pain which brought the doctors in haste, and for which they gave him ether, telling us that he would never wake after it. I wrote to Charley Emerson and to Judge Hoar and sent John at once to let them know that it was so, and they came and sat below. Edward stayed by also, and Mr Keyes came to go when all was over and have the bell rung. It had been arranged that when Father died it should be announced by the tolling of our church bell. Mother sat by Father most of the time, but I think she and I were neither of us there, only Cousin Mary and Edward when the last moment approached. For Edward came for us, and we went back, and stood round the bed till Edward said "This is the last breath, probably, but he may breathe once more". It was quite a long time after—a minute or two I should think—that he did breathe once more, and Edward said it was the end. Then he went down for Judge Hoar and Charley who came up to see him. But Father at that moment did not look right, he had a heavy and helpless expression. After I had been out of the room some time Edward came for me again and said he looked beautifully. I think he and Mr Farrar (the undertaker) had been straightening his face. And he did look right, all but that his mouth was not quite happily closed, if it had been he would have been a beautiful sight. It was a little too set-looking. So it remained, and all the rest was so right and that so little wrong, that everyone that saw him thought he looked just as he ought to look, they all expressed great pleasure that he was so beautiful, and we kept going every little while to see him. John brought his children, and his wife came, indeed all our neighbours. And the

Appendix

Sanborns and other friends. Edith wished that all her children should look at him, though one or two were unwilling, and some of them when they once seen him kept desiring to see him again.

On Sunday morning (the day of the funeral) a change from lifelikeness to deathlikliness had already occurred, there was less freshness of skin and less expression, yet people spoke of his appearance then as beautiful and what they should have wished.

End of letter written in pencil. Unsigned.

Index

Note: This index is only to "well-known" persons outside the Emerson family, and, obviously, the definition of "well-known" is difficult and somewhat arbitrary; emphasis has been placed on those persons in whom there is some scholarly interest outside Emerson. Four very important names have not been indexed because the frequency with which the entries would appear would make them useless. The first two concern the schools run by the Sedgwick and Agassiz families, and they play a major role in the early letters. The school run by Franklin Benjamin Sanborn in Concord is also very important, and, in addition, Sanborn himself plays a significant part throughout the letters from 1859 on. Later in the correspondence, about 1874, James Elliot Cabot appears, and continues to appear frequently to the end of the volume.

Finally, family members themselves are not indexed because they appear on virtually every page of this edition.

Alcott, Amos Bronson, I: 7, 137, 141, 210, 227, 239, 251, 309, 329, 364, 417, 451, 454, 504, 572, 607, 618, 619, 651, 664, 691. II: 175, 183, 254, 262, 307, 348, 389, 427, 445–46, 448, 464, 467, 512, 557, 585
Alcott, Louisa May, I: 82, 181, 258, 260, 261, 309, 393, 402, 522, 681. II: 93, 255, 305, 340, 427, 466, 488, 585
Arnold, Sir Edwin, II: 611
Arnold, Matthew, II: 89, 523–24

Bacon, Delia, II: 86
Bancroft, George, II: 32, 34, 36, 37
Beecher, Henry Ward, I: 33, 51, 68, 71–72, 73, 80, 81, 93–94, 225, 241, 305–6, 475–76, 478, 673–75
Bradford, Gamaliel, II: 254
Brown, John, I: 211
Browning, Robert, II: 34, 82, 83

Carlyle, Thomas, I: 670, 691, 696. II: 13, 15, 16–17, 75, 78, 80, 83, 187–88, 408, 409, 418, 419, 458, 473, 484, 489, 654, 657

Channing, William Ellery (1817–1901), I: 89, 146, 196, 201, 208, 210, 258, 259, 274, 305, 356, 361, 364, 380, 381, 382, 384–85, 403, 429, 452, 565, 585, 603, 608, 612, 614, 617, 619, 623, 628, 640, 672, 675, 691. II: 17, 109, 110, 137, 235, 266, 272, 273, 274, 285, 328, 363, 375, 379, 389, 390, 391, 464, 479, 607, 619, 620, 621, 637
Channing, William Henry, I: 259. II: 75, 83, 254, 259, 262, 476
Child, Lydia Maria, II: 207
Clarke, James Freeman, I: 101. II: 254, 323
Clemens, Samuel L. *See* Twain, Mark
Conway, Moncure, I: 91, 216, 264–65, 266, 454, 636, 690. II: 15, 74, 77, 78, 80, 81, 84, 193, 394, 493
Cooke, Rose Terry, II: 368
Cranch, Christopher Pearse, I: 286
Curtis, George William, I: 34, 537, 619

Dickens, Charles, I: 206, 453–54. II: 39

Eliot, Charles William, I: 208. II: 104

Index

Eliot, George, I: 537. II: 82, 83

Fechter, Charles Albert, I: 548–50, 551
Field, Cyrus W., II: 82–83
Fields, James T. I: 322, 438, 452, 632–33, 642, 648, 657, 659, 699, 700, 701
French, Daniel C., II: 170, 313, 340, 344, 345–47, 352, 363, 367, 378, 598
Froude, James Anthony, II: 74, 75, 77, 78, 83, 89, 473
Fuller, Margaret (Ossoli), I: 37, 86, 206. II: 4

Gladstone, William, II: 83
Grant, Ulysses S., I: 476–77
Greenough, Horatio, I: 123, 125
Grimm, Herman, I: 636. II: 65, 66–67, 478

Hale, Edward Everett, I: 560. II: 163, 254, 323–24, 386
Harte, Bret, I: 611, 613, 617, 618–20. II: 213, 274
Hawthorne, Nathaniel, I: 256, 259. II: 512
Hayes, Rutherford B., II: 257
Higginson, Thomas Wentworth, I: 206, 207, 263
Holmes, Oliver Wendell (1809–1894), I: 172, 355, 659. II: 96, 103, 128, 183, 254, 257, 278
Holmes, Oliver Wendell (1841–1935), I: 166, 262, 642. II: 538
Howe, Julia Ward, I: 292. II: 407
Hughes, Thomas, I: 562, 570, 571. II: 14–15, 16, 77, 78, 81, 83, 141
Huxley, Thomas Henry, I: 670. II: 83

James, Henry, I: 229, 284, 291, 295, 297, 537, 560–61, 654. II: 21, 26, 47, 60, 62, 64, 504
James, William, I: 229, 262, 291, 292, 295, 297, 655, 699. II: 47, 66, 128, 424, 508, 509, 510, 512–13

Kemble, Frances Anne (Fanny), I: 166

Landor, Walter Savage, II: 80
Lazarus, Emma, II: 291, 352
Leland, Charles Godfrey, I: 34
Lewes, George Henry, II: 82
Longfellow, Henry Wadsworth, I: 400, 452, 642, 659. II: 457
Lowell, James Russell, I: 85, 122, 172, 255, 322, 329, 406, 586, 642. II: 14, 19, 20, 21, 34, 58, 65, 67, 69, 70–71, 72, 73, 139, 140, 155, 183, 197, 262, 371, 432

McDonald, George, I: 700, 701
Mann, Horace, I: 256, 267–68
Miller, Joaquin, I: 618–19
Müller, Max, II: 74, 76, 77, 79, 81, 84, 85

Osgood, James R., II: 148, 157, 189, 193, 254, 305, 476
Ossoli, Margaret Fuller, Marchese d'. *See* Fuller, Margaret (Ossoli)

Parker, Theodore, I: 87, 146, 178. II: 254
Peabody, Elizabeth, I: 138, 258, 356, 357, 377, 426, 669. II: 335, 352, 360, 509, 512, 514, 530
Phillips, Wendell, I: 125, 329

Renan, Ernest, II: 72
Roosevelt, Theodore, II: 56–57
Ruskin, John, II: 34, 84, 88–89

Schurz, Carl, II: 414, 625
Sedgwick, Catherine Maria, I: 59, 62
Sherman, William Tecumseh, I: 558
Stedman, Edmund Clarence, II: 256, 257
Stoddard, Charles Warren, I: 618, 619
Stowe, Harriet Beecher, I: 73, 106
Sumner, Charles, I: 108, 125, 264, 336, 400, 406, 646–47. II: 126, 158, 213

Index

Taine, Hippolyte, II: 72
Taylor, Bayard, II: 65
Tennyson, Alfred Lord, I: 691. II: 34, 86
Thoreau, Henry David, I: 6, 85, 86, 125, 127–28, 133, 142, 144, 146, 154, 174, 178, 184, 196, 215, 216–17, 270, 274, 311, 330. II: 274, 285, 376, 448, 452, 473, 510, 607, 625, 628
Turgenev, Ivan, II: 72

Twain, Mark, II: 25, 39, 250
Tyndall, John, I: 670. II: 39, 71, 83

Very, Jones, II: 355

Warner, Charles Dudley, II: 349
Whittier, John Greenleaf, I: 165, 623, 689. II: 107, 108, 127, 597
Wright, William B., II: 107, 109

EDITH EMERSON WEBSTER GREGG is the great-granddaughter of Ralph Waldo Emerson and the grand-niece of Ellen Emerson. She is the editor of *One First Love*, the letters written to Emerson by his first wife, Ellen Louisa Tucker. Mrs. Gregg is also author of several books and articles of family memoirs, and on gardening.